BLUE GUIDE CONCISE

ITALY

Somerset Books • London

First edition 2009

Published by Blue Guides Limited, a Somerset Books Company
Winchester House, Deane Gate Avenue, Taunton, Somerset TA1 2UH
www.blueguides.com
'Blue Guide' is a registered trademark

ISBN 978–1–905131–28–0

A CIP catalogue record of this book is available from the British Library

Distributed in the United States of America by
WW Norton and Company, Inc.
500 Fifth Avenue, New York, NY 10110

The editor and publisher have made reasonable efforts to ensure the accuracy of all the information in *Blue Guide Concise Italy*; however, they can accept no responsibility for any loss, injury or inconvenience sustained by any traveller as a result of information or advice contained in the guide.

Statement of editorial independence: Blue Guides, their authors and editors, are prohibited from accepting any payment from any restaurant, hotel, gallery or other establishment for its inclusion in this guide or on www.blueguides.com, or for a more favourable mention than would otherwise have been made.

Every effort has been made to contact the copyright owners of material reproduced in this guide. We would be pleased to hear from any copyright owners we have been unable to reach.

All other acknowledgements, photo credits and copyright information are given on p. 424, which forms part of this copyright page.

Your views on this book would be much appreciated. We welcome not only specific comments, suggestions or corrections, but any more general views you may have: how this book enhanced your visit, how it could have been more helpful. Blue Guides authors and editorial and production team work hard to bring you what we hope are the best-researched and best-presented cultural, historical and academic guide books in the English language. Please write to us by email (editorial@blueguides.com), via the comments page on our website (www.blueguides.com) or at the address given above. We will be happy to acknowledge useful contributions in the next edition, and to offer a free copy of one of our titles.

INTRODUCTION

Italy is a vast subject. The history of ancient Rome or the art of Florence alone, for example, could fill several volumes, and—as the Italian tourist board is proud to point out—UNESCO estimates that 40 percent of the world's artistic heritage is here. Not surprisingly, Italy is one of the most popular tourist destinations in Europe, a place where people flock in search of great buildings and great art, fine food and wine, lovely landscapes, sunshine, relaxation and *la dolce vita*.

Any attempt to sum up such a country in a little over 400 pages is audacious in the extreme, and some might say impossible. Nevertheless, 400 pages is about as much as a person can reasonably be expected to carry around with them, contains as much information as anyone can reasonably be expected to absorb, and covers as many sights as he or she will reasonably have time to see.

The problem, of course, is this: when confronted with great art and great buildings, will we know what we are supposed to think? Why is there such a crowd in front of this painting and no one at all in front of that one? Where did these things spring from in the first place, and what do they all mean? And will we recognise the source of inspiration when we see something similar back home—Royce Hall at UCLA, for example, or Chiswick House in London?

This aim of this book is to empower the visitor to answer all these questions with knowledge and confidence. This is not just a checklist of must-see cities, museums and monuments: it tries to get fully to grips with its subject. Italy has only been a single, united nation for 140 years, but men have always been striving to bring it under a single control, from the Romans to the popes to Napoleon. Soldiers, kings, pilgrims and prelates travelled the length and breadth of the land, and their legacy is scattered everywhere. So too did artists: Tuscan painters were active in Lombardy; Lombard architects in Rome; Roman artists worked in Naples; Sicilian painters in Venice. Italy is intensely regional, but it is essentially one. Instead of presenting a catalogue of beautiful but unconnected places, this guide gives a sense of the country's overarching coherence, showing how the constituent parts fit together.

This book is explicitly selective. Italy here is pared down to its essence—so do not be disappointed to see things left out. In a country where almost every village has its priceless masterpiece, many are inevitably passed by. Many artists of unique and original talent are not mentioned. There are so many claims on a visitor's attention, and a short guide cannot hope to do justice to any but the most characteristic and important. Each aspect of Italian history and artistic development, from the Etruscans and the Romans down to modern times, is covered in the place where it can be seen and understood best and most enjoyably. Inevitably the selection has been personal; we will be only too happy to consider suggestions for the next edition.

Annabel Barber

CONTENTS

NORTHERN ITALY

Northern Italy today is home to some of the most visited places in the country, including Venice, Florence and the incomparable lakes. And it is no accident that visitors are drawn here. The Italian nation, one might say, owes its very existence to the north, whose prosperous and cultivated regions have contributed as much to the country's identity as they now contribute to its GDP. Culturally the northern cities have always been pre-eminent. Name any world-famous Italian painter or sculptor and the likelihood is that he was born and worked in the north. Titian and Tintoretto were from Venice, Michelangelo and Leonardo da Vinci were Tuscan. The great architecture of the Renaissance had its roots here too, in the work and ideas of Brunelleschi and Alberti. The Italian language as it is spoken today is a northern invention, derived from the Tuscan vernacular of Dante. Even Italian clichés have their roots here: fashion in Milan, the Vespa from near Pisa, Ferrari from outside Modena, Chianti from the rolling hills south of Florence, pesto from Genoa.

Wealth and success has led neither to homogeneity nor to a bruising modernity. The great towns and cities all preserve noticeably separate identities, and their centres are historic and immaculately kept. Styles of art and architecture are as distinct as styles of cooking. These differences are due in part to local pride and in part to historic antipathies. North Italy in the Middle Ages was a land of city states, first ruled by a government of the people and later, as these assemblies proved unable to maintain stability, by a dominant local clan. Though these clans fought incessantly with each other and were also at intermittent loggerheads with the two founts of power and patronage in the peninsula, the pope and the Holy Roman Emperor (*see p. 234*), they also proved great patrons of art, literature and science, and the flowering of Italy dates from this time.

The hegemony of the local lords came to an end in the mid-16th century. For many years before that, France and Spain had been fighting over Italy, and now, at the Treaty of Cateau-Cambrésis in 1559, control of much of the northern part of the peninsula was assigned to Habsburg Spain, in the person of Philip II. He did not rule directly, but the leading families (the Florentine Medici are a good example) ruled with his interests at heart, ushering in the era of the Counter-Reformation and of extended papal control.

The regions of the far north joined Italy comparatively recently. Parts of the Alto Adige and Friuli came as a result of the dismemberment of Austria-Hungary after the First World War. Italy had long been feuding with Austria, which gained control of Lombardy and the Veneto. In his bid to recreate Charlemagne's Frankish empire, Napoleon reshuffled great swathes of Italian and Austrian territory, but after his fall in 1815, Venice and Milan were both restored to the Austrian emperor. Which brings us to the Risorgimento, the name given to the great surge of nationalist feeling which swept across all Italy from the mid-19th century, but which was, at root, a northern phenomenon, led on an intellectual level by a Genoese, Giuseppe Mazzini, founder of the Young Italy movement, while popular support was won by the charismatic Piedmontese Giuseppe Garibaldi. The political reality of a united Italy was made possible by the great statesman Camillo Cavour, who was Prime Minister to the king of Piedmont, Vittorio Emanuele, the same Vittorio Emanuele who was eventually to become king of the new Italian nation.

VALLE D'AOSTA

The mountainous Valle d'Aosta (*map p. 422*) lies on the borders of alpine France and Switzerland. It is the smallest and least populated region in Italy, and also one of the most independently minded, with a strong tradition of home rule. The region's principal attractions are its magnificent mountain scenery, its Roman remains and its castles.

The Valle d'Aosta in history

Historically the Valle d'Aosta is a poor area, its steep terrain and extreme climate hostile to agriculture, its isolation inimical to trade. Nevertheless, people have lived here without interruption for at least 5,000 years.

By the 5th century BC the region was inhabited by the Salassi, a Celtic-Ligurian people. Pliny the Elder describes them as proud farmers, but they may also have engaged in mining and—given their proximity to the Alpine passes—in trade. They conducted a long and bitter struggle against Rome, finally capitulating in 25 BC. The Romans celebrated their conquest by founding *Augusta Praetoria Salassorum*, the present-day Aosta, and then settled throughout the region, bringing with them their systems of land management and town planning and, above all, their roads.

Aosta became an episcopal city in the 5th century, but was overwhelmed as waves of invading tribes, among them Goths and Lombards, swept through the region. The bishops of Aosta re-established their sovereignty in the 10th century, reviving earlier ties with the kings of Burgundy. It was the French royal house that gave the title of Count of Aosta to Umberto Biancamano, the first of the Savoy dynasty, in the 11th century. Control of the region was shared between the Savoy overlord and local barons, who in the 16th century obtained considerable political autonomy, based on a parliament and on a code of laws, the *Coutumier*. The balance between the Savoy rulers and the local lords—among them the powerful Challant family—remained substantially stable until the establishment of the Italian Republic in 1946.

Geography of the Valle d'Aosta

The Valle d'Aosta lies at the meeting point of the western and central ranges of the Alpine arc. Towering above the landscape are the **Gran Paradiso** (4061m), **Mont Blanc** (4807m), the **Matterhorn** (Monte Cervino, 4478m) and **Monte Rosa** (4634m). These are the highest peaks in Europe. The most important Alpine passes are the Piccolo San Bernardo (which leads to France) and the Gran San Bernardo (which leads to Switzerland). Both are named after Bernard of Menthon (d. 1081), who built guest houses for mountain travellers here. The specially trained dogs that bear his name helped track down wayfarers lost in the snow.

All the principal towns are clustered in the valley of the Dora Baltea river, one of the principal affluents of the Po. The region has an alpine climate, with severe winters and mild summers. Broadleaf forests grow on the lower slopes; chestnuts are particularly

The most distinctive architectural trait of the Valle d'Aosta is its high number of fortified feudal residences, military garrisons and royal retreats.

abundant, and for many centuries were an important food source. Higher up are magnificent conifer forests and above this, to the limit of the perennial snows, the ground is covered with high-altitude grasses and shrubs, including stunning rhododendron.

Agrarian activities would have vanished years ago were they not subsidised by the regional government. Cattle raising and dairy farming are the main activities. The wealth formerly generated by the lignite mines at La Thuile and the iron mines at Cogne, both now exhausted, has been replaced by revenue from hydroelectric power. The real driving force behind the economy, however, is tourism. The region's population increases six times during the peak winter and summer seasons.

Food and wine of the Valle d'Aosta

Cooking in the Valle d'Aosta is simple but tasty. The region is noted for its *fontina* cheese, some of which is still made in the old slate-roofed farm buildings raised on wooden stilts. Other specialities include *mocetta*, a salami made from goat or chamois meat; and the highly prized *lardo d'Arnad*, made from the fat of pigs fed on chestnuts. Polenta is an important staple here, and veal is also popular.

Vineyards in the Valle d'Aosta are small, stolen from the mountainside. But winemaking is heavily subsidised and some of the wine is of genuinely high quality. A single DOC (Valle d'Aosta/Vallée d'Aoste) covers the whole region. The indigenous Blanc de Morgex grape is used in the delicious Valle d'Aosta Blanc de Morgex and La Salle.

Caffè valdostano is the traditional way to end a meal: strong, hot coffee, flavoured with lemon and lots of grappa, and served in a communal wooden cup with multiple spouts.

WHAT TO SEE IN THE VALLE D'AOSTA

The majority of the inhabitants of the Valle d'Aosta live along the valley floor and on the nearby hills: these areas are consequently packed with residential, commercial and industrial building, with an alarming number of infrastructures—roads, railways, and high-tension electricity lines. The impression is of a continuous city where nature has been brought firmly under human control, and it can be quite difficult to believe that the region possesses some of the most beautiful landscape in Italy. Away from the Dora Baltea, in the verdant side valleys, however, things are quite different—in fact, here one finds the closest thing to wilderness that Italy has to offer. Much of this area is now protected. The Parco Nazionale del Gran Paradiso, originally the royal hunting reserve of the Savoy kings of Piedmont-Sardinia, is the only place in the Alps in which the ibex (*stambecco*) has survived in its natural state.

Aosta and its environs

Aosta (*map p. 422, A2*), the regional capital, is a pleasant miniature city surrounded by snow-capped mountains, where the prevailing atmosphere is more French than Italian. The old centre, less than 2km square, is still enclosed by well-preserved Roman walls and contains many Roman monuments including the **Porta Praetoria**, a large double gateway; a cryptoporticus of the forum; the theatre; and the **Arch of Augustus** (24 BC), erected to celebrate the Roman victory over the Salassi. The church of **Sant'Orso** was founded by St Anselm (d. 1109), a Benedictine theologian whose *Proslogion* is famous for its ontological proof of the existence of God: God must exist, because the very existence of the concept of God shows that such a thing must be. In 1093 Anselm was elected Archbishop of Canterbury. Five years later he went to the Council of Bari to defend a clause in the Nicaean Creed (*see p. 355*). Both this church and the **cathedral** retain fragments of remarkable 11th-century frescoes. Those in the cathedral, under the roof, illustrate the story of St Eustace. The Sant'Orso cycle includes expressive depictions of Christ and his disciples on Lake Gennesareth and the Wedding at Cana.

The most distinctive buildings of the region, however, are its castles, which have been used both for defence and leisure. Among the men who have left their footprint here are members of the Challant family, feudal overlords of the region from the 11th–18th centuries; military troops from the days of ancient Rome to those of Napoleon; and the first king of united Italy, Vittorio Emanuele II, who hunted ibex in the Gran Paradiso (his base camp was the castle of Sarre). On seeing how many trophies, victims of his marksmanship, are displayed there, it occurs to one to wonder how the species survived.

The Val di Cogne

The side valleys of the region are renowned for their immaculate farms, stony little villages and majestic alpine vistas. One of the four main such valleys is the Val di Cogne, west of Aosta. At the valley entrance the road passes the 14th-century castle of **Aymavilles** (*map p. 422, A2*), an extraordinary sight on a mound, dominating the sur-

Scene showing a butcher's shop (16th century) from the castle courtyard of Issogne.

rounding landscape of mountain and vineyard. The four stout, chesspiece towers at the corners seem to crowd oppressively around what is in effect an elegant villa (the castle was converted to residential use in the early 18th century), with a steep, shingled roof, wide loggias and *oeil de boeuf* windows. Below the village, a byroad (signposted) descends right to the hamlet of Pondel (Pont d'Aël), with a remarkable **Roman aqueduct-bridge** across a ravine. As the inscription states, its construction was funded in 3 BC by Caius Avilius, son of Aimus Patavinus, from the Roman colony of what is now Padua (the name Aymavilles is thought to derive from these Roman names). A single round arch supports the thick stone construction, the middle section of which contains a narrow walkway (you can still walk across) with arched entrances at either end, and lit by small, conventionally spaced windows. The open water channel runs above. Originally it had waterproofed walls and was fed by a spring. Information boards at the site, in French and Italian, explain the structure and provide diagrams. They also suggest that the aqueduct was used to supply water to a private estate on the site of the present-day village.

Castles of the Valle d'Aosta

The most famous medieval fortress of the region is **Fénis**, east of Aosta (*map p. 422, A2*). The castle (*open for tours Oct–Feb Mon–Sat 10–12 & 1.30–4.30, Sun and holidays 10–12 & 1.30–5.30, closed Tues; March–June and Sept daily 9–6.30; July–Aug 9–7.30*), with numerous towers and a single dovecote, enclosed by double walls with swallowtail battlements, is the former seat of the branch of the Challant family who styled themselves lords of Fénis, Ussel and St-Marcel. It was built c. 1340 by Aimone de Challant, one of the most prominent members of the dynasty, over an older fortress dating from Roman times (*Castrum Fenitii*)—though much of what you see today is a 19th-century restoration. Visits are by tour only, and the guide will show you the residential apartments (and explain that the beds are short because the habit in those days was to sleep in a sitting posture) as well as the tax-collector's office on the ground floor: it is here that the Challant lords received their tithes and tribute. The main courtyard, with its wooden balconies, is very fine, and has frescoes in the International Gothic style by Giacomo Jaquerio and his school. Jaquerio was the foremost Savoy artist of the early 15th century.

The castle of **Issogne** (*open July–Aug daily 9–7.30; March–June and Sept daily 9–6.30; Oct–Feb daily except Thur 12–12 & 1.30–4.30, Sun and holidays 12–12 & 1.30–5.30*) was rebuilt by Georges de Challant, prior of Sant'Orso in Aosta, in 1497–98. This is an excellent example of a late medieval residence, still with some of its original furnishings. Particularly memorable are the 16th-century frescoes in the courtyard, with scenes of everyday life including some vividly rendered shops. The wrought-iron fountain in the shape of a pomegranate tree (the Challant family emblem) dates from the same time. Next to the dining room is the kitchen, divided into two distinct halves, one for the use of the family, and one for the retainers.

The imposing fortress of **Bard** (*map p. 422, A2–B2*), an 11th-century foundation, was largely reconstructed in the 19th century and today has a distinctly barrack-like appearance. Count Amedeo IV of Savoy, aided by the Viscount of Aosta, who was a member of the Challant family, seized the castle and its lands from Ugo di Bard in the 13th century for territorial and strategic reasons (the castle controlled a narrow pass along which all travellers in the Valle d'Aosta had to go to avoid the river). In the 17th century the Savoy made it the principal fortress of the region. After crossing the Alps in his bid to regain Italy in 1800, Napoleon was held up here for several days, finally managing to slip away by night, after muffling the wheels of his gun carriages with straw. The fortress is now home to the Museum of the Alps (*open Tues–Fri 10–6, Sat–Sun 10–8*).

At nearby **Donnas** (a few kilometres further south), just before the village, you can see a stretch of the Roman road to Aosta (above the modern road on the left). Impressive survivals are the arch hewn out of the rock, the carriage ruts in the large stones, and the milestone, just beyond the arch, which shows 36 Roman miles to *Praetoria Augusta* (53km to Aosta).

Pont-St-Martin (*map p. 422, B2*) has a Roman hump-backed bridge (1st century BC) over the Lys. In popular legend, it is one of the many 'devil's bridges' in Italy (the devil is said to have claimed the soul of the first creature to cross, which usually turned out to be a dog). The village was a staging-post on the Via Francigena, the medieval pilgrim route from Canterbury to Rome. Another staging point on the route was the pretty village of **Arnad**, north of Bard, where there is a lovely old church and another fine hump-backed bridge with three arches.

VISITING THE VALLE D'AOSTA

GETTING AROUND

• **By car:** The best way to explore the region is to hire a car, as public transport is sparse and infrequent. The quickest route to Aosta from Turin is the A5 *autostrada*, though it can be very busy on Fri and Sun evenings. The main road (SS26) between

Pont-St-Martin and Aosta is more convenient for visiting the castles. Car parking (free) in Aosta in Piazza Plouves, within the old walls; paid parking at numerous points around town. Parking is available at or near most castles, and in the centre of most villages.

• **By bus:** There are bus services (www.savda.it) from Turin to Aosta (journey time 2hrs), but only twice a day on weekdays and once on Sun. The same company runs buses between Aosta and Milan (2½ hrs), but again, services are few and far between.

• **By rail:** Slow local services connect Turin and Milan to Aosta via Chivasso, where a change is sometimes necessary. Journey time from Turin is just over 2hrs; from Milan it is 3–4hrs.

WHERE TO STAY IN THE VALLE D'AOSTA

Many of the hotels on the valley floor are welcoming but somewhat charmless and over-modernised, with functional furniture and wipe-clean floors. If you are staying in the area for some time, it is worth seeking out the places higher up in the side valleys, which have more atmosphere. **Résidence Lo Péyo** at Antagnod in the Val d'Ayas is a good example (*T: 0125 306412, www.residencelopeyo.it*). Another charming place is the **Hotel La Barme** just outside Cogne in the Valnontey, 20km from Aymavilles (*T: 0165 749177, www.hotellabarme.com*).

Aosta
€€ **Milleluci.** ■ Comfortable, rustic-style family-run establishment on a sunny hillside just 1km north of the centre (from the Arch of Augustus, cross the Buthier, and take the road to Porossan). With swimming pool. A good base. *Località Porossan Roppoz, T: 0165 235278, www.hotelmilleluci.com.*

€ **Albergo Mancuso**. There is no shortage of places like this in Aosta: modern, central, clean, functional. The Mancuso has exceptionally good rates. *Via Voison 32 (just south of the railway line), T: 0165 34526, www.albergomancuso.com.*

Donnas
€ **La Maison des Vignerons**. Old stone-built B&B charmingly restored, to the right of the river and road as you come from Aosta. Six rooms with wooden floors and traditional furnishings, all with modern bathrooms. Pretty breakfast room and garden. Dinner on request. A lovely spot. *Grand Vert 100, T: 0125 807637, www.lamaisondesvignerons.it.*

Fénis
€ **La Chatelaine**. Small inn with four rooms, just at the foot of the castle. Home cooking. Slightly annoying 'medieval' décor. Restaurant closed Tues. *Frazione Chez Sapin 105, T: 0165 764264.*

Issogne
€ **Brenve**. Simple hotel and bar near the castle. *Via Colombiera 20, T: 0125 921611.*

WHERE TO EAT IN THE VALLE D'AOSTA

Aosta
Two restaurants stand out: the €€€ **Vecchio Ristoro** (*Via Tourneuve 4, T: 0165 33238; closed Sun and lunch Mon, 1–10 Nov and all June*) and €€ **Le Foyer**, considered one of the best in town (*Corso Ivrea 146, T: 0165 32136; closed Mon evening, Tues, Jan and July*). Another nice little place is € **Degli Artisti**, with a good atmosphere and very reasonable prices (*Via Maillet 5–7, T: 0165 40960; closed Sun, midday Mon and two weeks in July*).

Arnad
€ **L'Arcaden**. Simple, stone-built bar and *osteria* serving typical regional dishes, including plenty of *fontina* cheese, and of course the famous *lardo d'Arnad*. *Fraz. Champagnolaz 1, T: 0125 966928.*

PIEDMONT

The region of Piedmont (*map p. 422*), an ancient principality, stands proudly *al pie' dei monti*, 'at the foot of the mountains' that form an arc around it. Turin's natural backdrop of snow-clad peaks is glorious on a sunny day.

Piedmont is a highly industrialised region, and even today its wealth is based on heavy industry. Fiat, the largest Italian industrial corporation, has its base here. But the region offers much in terms of history and art. It also produces some of the finest wines in Italy, and its deeply rooted tradition of fine cuisine makes gourmet destinations of even the humblest villages.

Piedmont in history

The history of Piedmont is complicated but important. Struggles for control of the heart and mind of Italy have either taken place here or took their impetus from here. To understand Piedmont is to get to grips with Italian political identity.

The territory of Turin first came into the hands of the House of Savoy by marriage in 1046, though the capital remained on the transalpine (French) side of the mountains. In the 16th century France and Spain invaded Italy, and Piedmont was occupied by the French in 1506. In 1557 the Savoy duke Emanuele Filiberto 'the Iron-Headed' led a Spanish counter-invasion and defeated the French in battle. Rewarded at the Treaty of Cateau-Cambrésis with the city of Turin, he moved the seat of his duchy there in 1563. Further territory was gained in the early 18th century when Duke Vittorio Amedeo II was appointed king of Sicily. Sicily was transferred to Austria in 1713, but Vittorio Amedeo received Sardinia in exchange, and his kingdom became known as Piedmont-Sardinia. Although its existence was blotted out by the Napoleonic conquests, the Congress of Vienna reinstated the Savoy kings at Turin and also gave them suzerainty over Liguria.

The decades that followed witnessed the emergence of Piedmont as the principal agent of Italian nationhood. The Savoy king Vittorio Emanuele II was blessed with a particularly astute prime minister, Camillo Cavour, who secured the aid of Napoleon III in Italy's war of independence against Austria (which occupied northern Italy from Milan to Trieste). The Austrian army was crushed in a succession of defeats, most notably at Solferino in 1859. Lombardy was annexed to Piedmont, and the Piedmontese dominions west of the Alps (Savoy and Nice) were claimed by France. After this, Italian provinces began to be added one by one to Vittorio Emanuele's new Kingdom of Italy. In 1865 he transferred his capital from Turin to Florence, and the history of Piedmont became merged in the history of the fledgling nation.

Food and wine of Piedmont

The cuisine of Piedmont is considered by many to be the best in Italy. Indeed, most visitors to the region come here to eat rather than to look at monuments and museums. Piedmont's traditions have been influential, but they also remain local and self-contained. Each valley and each village has its own, peculiar culinary repertoire. But Piedmont is also home to many items of food and drink that have become household names. The native arborio rice used for Italian risotto is mainly grown in the wetlands of the Po valley around Vercelli and Novara. Cinzano, Martini and Campari all have their roots in Piedmont (the first two in Turin, the last in Novara); *grissini* were invented here to aid the delicate digestion of King Vittorio Emanuele II, who found ordinary bread too hard on his stomach. Piedmont is a land of butter, not of olive oil. The cooking is not Mediterranean. Pork, veal and game birds feature prominently. The wines of the region are extremely important. Barolo and Barbaresco, both from the hillsides of the Langhe, are the most aristocratic of all Italian wines.

TURIN

Turin (*map p. 422, A2*), the first capital of the Kingdom of Italy (from 1861–65), has a superb historic centre, the supreme masterpiece of the architect and set designer Filippo Juvarra. In 1714 he was appointed architect to the king of Sicily, Vittorio Amedeo (later king of Piedmont-Sardinia; *see above*) and given the commission to rebuild and enlarge Turin. His style, highly decorative, light and gracious, typifies the transition between the Baroque and the Rococo. Turin is one of the few 'ideal cities' of Europe to have withstood the test of time. The old centre has a regular street plan that dates from ancient Roman days, when Turin was the colony of *Julia Augusta Taurinorum*. The grid plan was deliberately retained, and the buildings which line the long, straight streets are elegantly classical in their lineaments.

Turin was badly damaged during the Second World War, after which new suburbs were built to accommodate the growing number of migrant workers from the south of Italy. Post-industrial Turin can be a bit scruffy, but substantial efforts are being made to restore it to its past splendour.

Piazza Castello

The huge, rectangular Piazza Castello (*map p. 17, 6–7*) is the centre of historic Turin. The *castello* of the square's name, seat of the dukes of Savoy, is now called **Palazzo Madama** after two regents: Maria Cristina, widow of Vittorio Amedeo I, and Giovanna Battista, widow of Carlo Emanuele II. Both were entitled Madama Reale, and both lived here. The palace is noble and imposing, still at heart a four-square castle of the 15th century, though one side has been replaced by a graceful, statue-topped wing and façade of 1718–21, by Juvarra. The palace was the seat of the Italian Senate in 1861–65, the period when Turin was capital of Italy. It is now home to the Museo Civico di Arte Antica (*open Tues–Fri and Sun 10–6, Sat 10–8; last entry 1hr before closing*), with exhibits on the palace's history (including the Roman foundations, visible through a vertiginous glass floor, and a seemingly unending suite of sumptuous rooms) and a collection of works of art. Among the exhibits are a number of valuable codices, including the illuminated 14th-century statutes of the city of Turin and the celebrated *Book of Hours of Milan* (1422), attributed to a number of hands, largely anonymous and referred to simply as 'Hands A–K'. The most interesting is Hand G, who may have been Jan van Eyck.

Palazzo Reale (*map p. 17, 7*), begun in the mid-17th century, was the centre of governance of the Savoy state, occupied in succession by the dukes of Savoy, the kings of Piedmont-Sardinia, and Vittorio Emanuele II at the start of his reign as king of Italy. The simple, austere façade masks a lavish interior created from the mid-17th–mid-19th centuries. The state apartments (*open Tues–Sun 8.30–7.30*) have splendid ceilings and floors, finely crafted furniture, porcelain, tapestries, and allegorical paintings celebrating the virtues of the Savoy sovereigns. The **royal gardens**, approached through the palace (*and normally open May–Oct daily 9–dusk*), were laid out by André Le Nôtre, architect of the gardens of Versailles (though there is little to be seen of his original design).

The former royal chapel of **San Lorenzo**, adjoining the palace on the northeast corner of Piazza Castello, is a superb Baroque edifice by the architect and mathematician Guarino Guarini. Its beautiful, luminous interior of 1667 is filled with the curvilinear forms that are Guarini's hallmark. The colour scheme is all pinks, whites, creams and powder blues, and the use of natural light, which floods in from the handsome lantern, is unsurpassed.

Also by Guarini is the **Palazzo Carignano** (*map p. 17, 6*), a remarkable brick building with an undulating Baroque façade of 1679, whose ingenious interplay of concave and convex lines is strongly reminiscent of the work of Borromini in Rome (though we think of him as a Roman architect, Borromini was in fact born near Como). The palace was the birthplace of Vittorio Emanuele II in 1820. On the first floor is the **Museo Nazionale del Risorgimento**, the most important museum in the country devoted to this formative period in Italian history (*the palace and museum were closed for restoration at the time of writing, but reopening was scheduled; T: 011 562 1147*).

The duomo and Holy Shroud

Turin's cathedral (*map p. 17, 7*), built in the late 15th century by the little-known Tuscan architect Meo del Caprino, is less splendid or obtrusive than one might expect, considering the palatial nature of the adjacent piazza. The façade is pleasantly simple and regular, and quite unsuited to its hulking Baroque campanile, redesigned in the 18th century by Juvarra. The simple grey-and-white interior contains a superb polyptych (second south altar) in a fine Gothic frame, attributed to Giovanni Martino Spanzotti and his pupil Defendente Ferrari. It was painted c. 1498–1504 for the guild of shoemakers, and shows their patron saints Crispin and Crispinian, as well as Sts Ursus (Orso) of Aosta and scenes of mercantile life.

The duomo's chief draw, however, is the Chapel of the Holy Shroud (**Cappella della Sacra Sindone**; *open daily 9–12 & 3–7*). It was built by Guarino Guarini in the late 17th century and restored after a fire of 1997. Situated at the extreme east end, beyond the apse, and directly accessible from Palazzo Reale, this masterpiece of Baroque theatricality contrasts black marble on the lower walls with bright white stucco above, to create an allegory of man's fallen state and the redemptive power of the sacrifice of Christ.

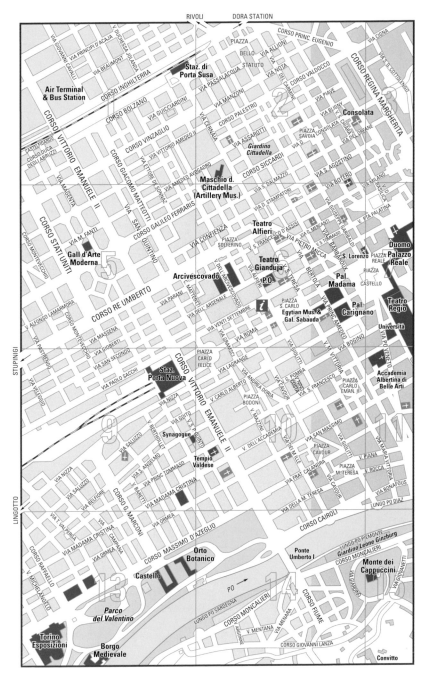

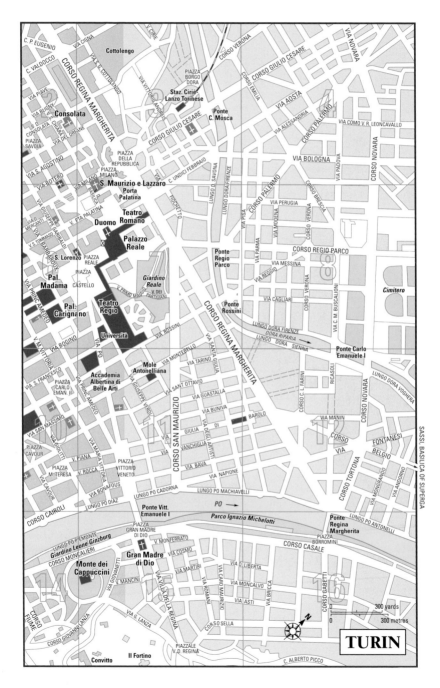

TURIN

The eye is drawn irresistibly upward by the light from the lantern, which rushes impetuously over the elaborate basketwork geometry of the tall, tapering cupola.

The greatly revered sacred relic for which this chapel was built—the shroud in which the body of Christ is believed to have been wrapped after His descent from the Cross—is said to have been taken from Jerusalem to Cyprus, and from there to France in the 15th century, from where it was brought to Turin by Emanuele Filiberto in 1578. In 1988 carbon dating seemed to point to a date between 1260 and 1390, but discussion still continues, particularly as another, still fainter image was detected on the reverse side of the shroud in 2002. The relic is closely guarded and is rarely on display: public outings for this century to date are/were 2000 and 2010.

Piazza San Carlo

The western gateway to the Baroque city centre is the arcaded Piazza San Carlo (*map p. 16, 6*), a handsome monumental square begun in 1640. The equestrian monument to Duke Emanuele Filiberto (*El caval d'brôns*; 1838) shows him sheathing his sword after his victory over the French (*see p. 13*). Beneath the porticoes of the two long yellow and grey *palazzi* are several cafés, including, on the corner of Via San Teresa, the well-known **Caffè San Carlo**. This and the **Caval d'Brôns** (at no. 155) have excellent chocolate and *gianduja*. At the east end of the piazza, on the south side of busy Via Roma, is Guarino Guarini's Palazzo dell'Accademia delle Scienze, now home to two outstanding museums. The **Egyptian Museum** (*open Tues–Sun: June–Sept 9.30–8.30, Sept–June 8.30–7.30*) is the finest Egyptian museum in Italy. The **Galleria Sabauda** (*open Tues, Fri, Sat, Sun 8.30–2, Wed and Thur 2–7.30*) presents the paintings collected by the royal house of Piedmont from the 16th century onwards. Rich in Flemish and Dutch works, it is interesting also for its paintings by Piedmontese masters, some of them hardly represented elsewhere. There are good works by Gaudenzio Ferrari, who worked extensively in Piedmont and Lombardy.

The paintings on the second floor reflect the artistic taste of the Savoy dynasty. The first section (from Emanuele Filiberto to Carlo Emanuele I; 1550–1630) has some splendid works from 16th-century Venice (Bassano, Veronese and Tintoretto), by the Florentine Agnolo Bronzino and the Bolognese Guercino, and by Caravaggio's Lombard followers. The second part (from Vittorio Amedeo I to Vittorio Amedeo II; 1630–1730) has 17th- and 18th-century paintings including Guido Reni's particularly gruesome *Apollo Flaying Marsyas*, as well as works acquired for the royal residences under the guidance of Filippo Juvarra. The third section (from Carlo Emanuele III to Carlo Felice; 1730–1831) focuses on 18th-century academic painting and the early 19th-century taste for *veduti* and landscapes.

Via Po and the Mole Antonelliana

It is difficult to say if Via Po or Via Roma is Turin's most striking street. Via Roma, connecting Piazza San Carlo with Piazza Castello, is certainly the more elegant, lined with the city's best shops; but Via Po, leading from Piazza Castello towards the river, provides a splendid architectural frame for the wooded hills on the Po's south bank. This neigh-

Close-up view of Guarini's extraordinary cupola of the Chapel of the Holy Shroud. Though taken before restoration, this image clearly shows the intricate woven effect of the stonework, which clambers upwards tier on tier to the golden symbol of the Trinity at the summit.

bourhood is also home to the building that has become the symbol of Turin, the **Mole Antonelliana** (*map p. 17, 11*). It was begun as a synagogue in 1863, just months after Vittorio Emanuele II granted freedom of worship to Jews in the new kingdom of Italy. The architect, Alessandro Antonelli, was commissioned to build something 47m tall, but changed the plans to something over twice that height. The delays and additional cost sparked a dispute which led to the City of Turin giving the Jewish congregation a new site, and providing Antonelli with the funds to complete his building, which rose to a final height of 167m. Recast by the municipality as a monument to Italian unity, it was the first seat of the Risorgimento Museum now in Palazzo Carignano. In the 1990s the building was fitted with a glass lift (*open Tues–Fri 10–4, Sat–Sun and holidays 9–7;*

closed Mon), which whisks you to the rooftop terrace in just under a minute. Mario Merz's *Flight of Numbers* was installed on the roof in 1998. Merz was an important exponent of the Arte Povera movement (*see opposite*). The Mole now houses the **Cinema Museum** (*open Tues–Sun 9am–8pm, Sat 9am–11pm; last entry 45mins before closing*).

Lingotto and the old Fiat factory

Fiat (Fabbrica Italiana Automobili di Torino) was founded in 1899 by the industrialist Giovanni Agnelli (1866–1945), who in effect introduced one of Italy's greatest passions to the country—the car. By 1915 the workforce of 10,000 was producing over 4,000 cars a year. This cutting-edge factory, admired by Le Corbusier, was built in the suburb of Lingotto (*beyond map p. 16, 9*) and opened in 1923, drawing thousands of immigrant workers to the area, for whom housing and other amenities were specially built by the company; it was the largest car factory in the world. The production line ran from the bottom of the five-storey building to the top; raw materials entered the building on the ground floor and completed vehicles emerged onto the test track on the roof (made famous in the 1969 film *The Italian Job*). By the 1970s, global competition and advances in technology rendered the building redundant and it was closed in 1982. The question of what to do with the factory was tackled by Renzo Piano, who redesigned it as a multi-purpose complex, which includes the Le Méridien Lingotto hotel. The rooftop test track is now a jogging rink for hotel guests (*Via Nizza 262; T: 011 664 2000, www.starwoodhotels.com*).

Superga

From the suburb of Sassi (*beyond map p. 17, 12; follow Corso Belgio, cross the Ponte di Sassi and then head north along Via Agudio to Piazza Modena*) a cog railway (*Mon–Thur 8–12 & 1–5, Fri 8–12 & 1–4*) takes you to the magnificent **basilica of Superga** (*open daily 9–12 & 3–4 or 6*), splendidly situated on a wooded hilltop. It was built by Vittorio Amedeo II in gratitude for the deliverance of Turin from French assault in 1706. It was the Treaty of Utrecht, at the final conclusion of the conflict with France, that awarded him the kingdom of Sicily. This basilica is considered Filippo Juvarra's finest single work. The main body of the church is circular in form, surmounted by a huge dome, with a projecting columned portico at the front and two lateral wings with bell-towers. The interior is very sumptuous, and in the crypt are the tombs of the kings of Piedmont-Sardinia, from Vittorio Amedeo II (d. 1732) to Carlo Alberto (d. 1849).

AROUND TURIN: THE SAVOY ROYAL RESIDENCES

When Emanuele Filiberto, Duke of Savoy, moved his capital from France to Turin in the mid-16th century, he began a vast series of building projects. Construction was continued by his successors, and today these royal residences are among the finest examples of European monumental architecture of the 17th and 18th centuries.

At **Stupinigi** (10km southwest of the city centre; *map p. 422, A3*) is the magnificent Palazzina di Caccia, a hunting lodge built for Vittorio Amedeo II in 1729–30 by Filippo

Juvarra. It has an ingenious plan featuring four diagonal wings, which the architect intended to recall hunting trails, meeting in an elliptical central hall. Benedetto Alfieri, who succeeded Juvarra as court architect, built more wings, and raised the height of the central pavilion. Now the property of the Mauritian Order (*at the time of writing scheduled to reopen after restoration*), it presents a marvellous sequence of period rooms. The original 18th-century bronze stag that used to crown the roof is displayed inside.

The **Castello di Rivoli** (*map p. 422, A2*), a huge, square castle, left unfinished by Filippo Juvarra in the early 18th century and once a favourite residence of the counts of Savoy, now houses the Museo d'Arte Contemporanea (*open Tues–Thur 10–5, Fri–Sun 10–9*). Highlights include works by the masters of Arte Povera, a term coined by the art critic Germano Celant to describe the work of a number of young Italian artists in the late 1960s and early '70s who explored the relationship between life and art using natural, inexpensive materials. The term 'poor' refers not only to the materials but also to the anti-elitist idea behind the movement, which sought to fight the commercialisation of art. Well known Arte Povera artists include Mario Merz, Jannis Kounellis, Michelangelo Pistoletto and Giulio Paolini. The museum restaurant combal.zero offers 'conceptual' cooking that is at least as taboo-breaking as the art—and not by any means *povera* in its use of raw material (*T: 011 956 5225 to reserve*).

VISITING TURIN

GETTING AROUND

• **By air:** Turin's Caselle airport is 16km north of the city. Buses run by SADEM (www.sadem.it) go from outside the arrivals hall to the bus station at Corso Inghilterra (*map p. 16, 1*) every 30–45mins. Journey time c. 40mins. Tickets from the Turismo Torino office, Ricevitoria or the ticket machine, all in the arrivals hall. Tickets can also be bought on the bus but are slightly more expensive.

Buses from the city centre to the airport also stop at Porta Nuova and Porta Susa railway stations. Tickets can be bought at the bus station and bars or on board.

Trains link the airport to the Dora railway station at Piazza Baldissera (*beyond map p. 16, 2*). Departures every 30mins until 9.15pm. Journey time c. 20mins. From there bus no. 11 (c. every 10mins) takes you to the centre. Trains from Dora to the airport run until 7.30pm. For details see www.gtt.to.it.

• **By car:** The centre of Turin is closed to traffic and the surrounding areas are restricted zones. There are convenient central car parks at Piazza Vittorio Veneto and Piazza San Carlo.

• **By rail:** Porta Nuova (*map p. 16, 9*) and Porta Susa (*map p. 16, 1*) stations have services to/from Rome, Milan, Florence, Bologna and Venice. Porta Nuova also serves Genoa.

• **Public transport in Turin:** Public transport (metro, trams and buses run by GTT, www.comune.torino.it/gtt) is the quickest way to get around, though you can walk across central Turin in about 40mins. Bus 55 links Piazza San Carlo (stop on the corner of Via XX Settembre and Via Bertola), Piazza Castello and Piazza Vittorio Veneto.

For **Stupinigi** take bus 35 from stop no. 39 (Porta Nuova station) on Piazza Carlo Felice (*map p. 16, 10*) to stop no. 892 (Vittorio Veneto) in the suburb of Nichelino; the palace is 3mins away on foot. Total journey time 40mins. The **Castello di Rivoli** is 13km west

of the city centre. Take the metro from Porta Susa to Fermi (Collegno) station, then the shuttle bus to the castle; journey time 40mins.
• **By taxi:** T: 011 5737, 011 5730, 011 3399.

SPECIAL TICKETS

The **Torino Piemonte Card**, valid for 1, 2, 3, 5 or 7 days, gives free access on all urban public transport and free entrance to museums, monuments and royal residences in Turin and Piedmont. It is also valid for free rides in the Mole Antonelliana lift, boats on the Po, or the Sassi-Superga cog railway, as well as reductions of up to 50 percent on theatre and concerts. The card is available online at www.turismotorino.org/ torinopiemonte_card, at Turismo Torino information points, hotels, and participating museums and monuments.

WHERE TO STAY IN TURIN

€€€ **Grand Hotel Sitea**. Luxurious hotel in the centre of town. Typical four-star décor and every comfort. *Via Carlo Alberto 35, T: 011 517 0171, www.thi.it. Map p. 16, 10.*
€€ **Boston**. Art hotel in the heart of a residential area west of Porta Nuova station. Rooms have works by contemporary artists, often from Turin. *Via Massena 70, T: 011 500359, www.hotelbostontorino.it. Beyond map p. 16, 9.*
€€ **Victoria**. ■ An elegant, family-run boutique hotel in an unassuming building in the heart of town. Lovely, individually decorated rooms, an indoor pool, and private parking. Guests borrow bicycles to get around, and the breakfast buffet is second to none. *Via Nino Costa 4, T: 011 561 1909, www.hotelvictoria-torino.com. Map p. 16, 10.*

WHERE TO EAT IN TURIN

€€€ **Del Cambio**. This is indisputably the restaurant of Turin's high society: the décor was the same when Cavour dined here a century and a half ago, and the cuisine has maintained the same high standard. Closed Sun and in Aug. *Piazza Carignano 2, T: 011 546690. Map p. 16, 6.*
€€ **Neuv Caval'd Brôns**. A well-known traditional restaurant on Turin's most theatrical square. Closed midday Sat and Sun, and in Aug. *Piazza San Carlo 151, T: 011 565354. Map p. 16, 6.*
€ **Porto di Savona**. This popular restaurant boasts a warm friendly setting as well as honest, wholesome Piedmontese cuisine, including ratatouille. Not far from the Mole Antonelliana. Crowded in the evening. *Piazza Vittorio Veneto 2, T: 011 817 3500. Map p. 17, 11.*

LOCAL SPECIALITIES

It was Duke Emanuele Filiberto who introduced drinking chocolate to Turin in 1560, and Turin is renowned for chocolate to this day. As well as the mass producers such as Ferrero and Caffarel, there are small, specialist chocolatiers producing exquisite confections. The gold-wrapped *giandujotti* are chocolate mixed with roasted chopped hazelnuts. The best places to buy chocolate are **Baratti & Milano**, Piazza Castello 29; **Confetteria Giordano**, Piazza Carlo Felice 69; **Laboratorio Artigianale del Giandujotto**, Via Cagliari 19/b; and **Avvignanno** on Piazza San Carlo. The Chocopass gives you 23 tastings over three days of chocolate products in selected shops and historic cafés in the city. It is available from the tourist information office or online on www.turismotorino.org. One of the best places for coffee is **Al Bicerin** opposite the Consolata (*map p. 17, 2*), which gave its name to a drink of cream, chocolate and coffee.

THE LANGHE

The **Langhe** (*map p. 422, B3*) is a historic area of Piedmont famous for its wine. The *bassa langa*, with Alba at the centre, is known also for its truffles. The *alta langa* is the higher and more wooded area bounded on the west and south by France and Liguria. The Langhe are not dependent upon tourism for their livelihood, and the countryside is not postcard-perfect. Nevertheless, on sunny days it can be very striking—especially in spring, when the meadows come alive with wild flowers, or in autumn, when the leaves begin to turn. Almost every village has its castle (there is a complete listing at www.castelliaperti.it), and armies of vines stand in neat formation on the hills.

Asti and Alba

Strung out about 25km apart along the banks of the Tanaro are the wine towns of Asti and Alba. **Asti** (*map p. 422, B3*), of Roman foundation, occupies a picturesque position among gentle, undulating hills and cultivated fields and vineyards, with the snow-capped Alps rising dramatic as a backdrop. It is chiefly famed for its wine (Barbera d'Asti). It was also the birthplace of Italy's great tragic poet, Vittorio Alfieri (1749–1803). His main theme was the overthrow of tyranny, and his works helped fan the flames of nationalist ardour, which culminated in the Risorgimento movement. In fact Alfieri's tomb (by Canova, in the south aisle of Santa Croce in Florence) is the first monument to show a personification of a united 'Italy'.

Small hilltop towns among fields and vineyards: typical landscape of the Langhe.

Grinzane Cavour, just south of Alba, gave Italy its greatest Risorgimento name of all. Camillo Benso, Count of Cavour and the architect of Italian unification, spent part of his childhood here and was mayor of Grinzane for more than a decade. He devoted much time and labour to the care of the vineyards, which continue to produce excellent wines and grappas. The castle (*open daily except Tues 9–12 & 2–6; closed Jan*), one of the most famous landmarks of the Langhe, houses a small museum with Cavour memorabilia as well as an *enoteca* where wines are offered for tasting.

The atmosphere of the red-brick market town of **Alba** (*map p. 422, B3*) is relaxed and comfortable, and the main Via Vittorio Emanuele, lined with medieval, Renaissance and Liberty town houses, is a pretty place to stroll. It is the home of Barbera d'Alba wine and is also the white truffle capital of Italy. Truffle vendors abound in season (Oct and Nov), when there is also a truffle market held on Saturday mornings in the deconsecrated church of the Maddalena. To the east is the wine-growing area of **Barbaresco**, which fills the triangle formed by the three villages of Barbaresco, Neive and Treiso.

Cherasco

Cherasco (*map p. 422, A3–B3*) is an attractive small town founded in 1243, with a neat, regular street plan concentrated in an area once encompassed by fine defensive ramparts. It was here, in 1796, that Napoleon signed the armistice with Vittorio Amedeo III that ceded Nice and Savoy to France. But Cherasco's most distinctive monument is its 18th-century **synagogue** (*Via Marconi 4; open for guided visits April–Oct Sun 2.30–6.30; www.debenedetti1547.org, T: 347 489 1662*). Piedmont was the nearest realm where Jews fleeing eastward from persecution in France or Spain could settle in relative freedom and the region still has one of Italy's largest Jewish populations. The synagogue at Cherasco is typical of many synagogues in town ghettoes in Europe, being situated on the upper floor of a house and bearing no outward mark of its existence. Stil to be seen are the characteristic long balconies that connected one house to another and made it possible to reach the synagogue without leaving the ghetto.

Barolo

The castle of Barolo (*map p. 422, B3*), first built as a fortification against Saracen incursions, houses the Enoteca Regionale del Barolo (*open daily except Thur 10–12.30 & 3–6.30; closed Jan*) and a museum on the history of winemaking in the Langhe.

VISITING THE LANGHE

GETTING AROUND

• **By train:** Reasonably good rail services serve the Langhe from Turin. The journey to Asti takes about 40mins. From Turin to Cherasco you change at either Carmagnola or Bra (journey time just over 1hr). Trains to Alba (change at Bra or Asti) in c. 90mins and there is also a station at Neive (near Barbaresco, change at Asti or Bra; journey time c. 90mins).

• **By bus:** Local buses run by SAC serve the towns and villages of the Langhe, and also link Turin with Cherasco. For timetables, see www.viaggisac.com.

WHERE TO STAY IN THE LANGHE

By far the best places to stay are in the countryside. The €€–€€€ **Castello di Sinio**, in Sinio, south of Alba, is a truly splendid place in a 12th-century castle in the midst of rolling countryside. Restaurant, swimming pool and garden. (*Vicolo del Castello 1, Sinio, T: 0173 263889, www.castellodisinio.com*). Fifteen kilometres north of Alba, forming the tip of a triangle with Alba and Bra as the base, is Canale with the €€ **Villa Tiboldi**, a beautiful old farmhouse converted into a stylish hotel. Swimming pool and restaurant. (*T: 0173 970388, www.villatiboldi.it*). Just east of Sinio, south of Alba, € **Cascina Sant'Eufemia** is a friendly and comfortable B&B on a working farm of vines and hazel groves (*T: 0173 263986, www.cascinasanteufemia.it*).

WHERE TO EAT IN THE LANGHE

There are many fine restaurants in the Langhe: gastronomy is very important here.

Alba
€€ **Il Vicoletto**. Good local cooking has earned this place a strong local following. Closed Mon and July–Aug. *Via Bertero 6, T: 0173 363196.*
€ **Osteria dell'Arco**. Simple, friendly place serving good regional dishes. It was born as an *enoteca* and has an excellent wine list. Closed Sun, midday Mon, and Dec–Jan. *Piazza Savona 5, T: 0173 363974.*
€€€ **Locanda del Pilone**. Just 5km outside Alba in the heart of the Barolo wine district, this is an elegant brick-vaulted restaurant with stunning views and a Michelin rosette (rooms to rent also). *Località Madonna di Como 34, T: 0173 366616, www.locandadelpilone.com.*
€€–€€€ **La Piola & Piazza Duomo**. Right in the centre of Alba, this is two restaurants

under one roof. La Piola is a relaxed *trattoria* offering traditional food of the region, with the menu written up on a chalk board. Upstairs at Piazza Duomo, chef Enrico Crippa offers modern dishes between candy pink walls. Closed Mon. *Piazza Risorgimento 4, La Piola T: 0173 442800; Piazza Duomo T: 0173 366167.*

Asti
€€ **Gener Neuv**. ■ Popular, elegant family-run restaurant where cooking is strictly seasonal; Sept–Dec is the best time for white truffles. Closed Sun and Mon Jan–July, Sun evening and Mon Sept–Dec, all Aug, Christmas–6 Jan. *Lungo Tanaro dei Pescatori 4. T: 0141 557270.*

Barbaresco
€€ **Antinè**. One of the finest restaurants in the Langhe. Country ingredients such as pheasant, rabbit, quail and tongue are prominent on the menu. Superb wines. Closed Wed, most of Jan and mid-Aug. *Via Torino 34/a, T: 0173 635294, www.antine.it.*

Barolo
€€ **Locanda nel Borgo Antico**. Well-loved *osteria* serving excellent local fare. Closed Tues and midday Wed, and a few days in Aug. *Località Boschetti 4, T: 0173 560935.*

Cherasco
€€ **Operti 1772**. Cherasco is the Italian capital of *elicicoltura*, the breeding of edible snails, which (like everything on the menu— there are other choices) are prepared with great skill here, in the frescoed opulence of Palazzo Burotti di Scagnello. Closed Tues. *Via Vittorio Emanuele 103, T: 0172 487048.*

Treiso
€€€ **La Ciau del Tornavento**. Another of the famed restaurants of the Langhe, La Ciau has received encomia in all the gastronomy guides: *Michelin, Wine Spectator, Gambero Rosso*. Outdoor summer seating overlooking the vineyards. Closed Wed, midday Thur and Jan. *Piazza Baracco 7, T: 0173 638333, www.laciaudeltornavento.it.*

LAGO D'ORTA

This small Alpine lake just west of Lake Maggiore (*map p. 422, B2*) is one of Italy's lesser known beauty spots. Balzac and Nietzsche were among its first modern admirers. The most attractive place on the lake is **Orta San Giulio**, a charming village with elegant old town houses and some grand villas on the outskirts. It is an atmospheric place even in winter, when the lake is shrouded in fog or the chill of the north wind brings flurries of snow from the Alpine peaks just a few kilometres away.

To the right of the parish church, a lane (Via Gemelli) leads uphill past the cemetery to the monumental gateway of the **Sacro Monte** (also reached by car from the Via Panoramica). From the gate (*usually open 9.30–4; otherwise enquire at the Capuchin monastery at the top of the hill*) a path offering good views over the lake continues uphill and through the woods to 20 pretty little chapels dedicated to St Francis of Assisi. The *sacro monti* of Piedmont, a characteristic feature of the Alpine foothills, were built during the Counter-Reformation as a 'bastion of faith' against the Calvinist north: most, like this one, contain remarkable groups of life-size terracotta figures.

Isola San Giulio

Close to the eastern shore of the lake is the peaceful, car-free Isola San Giulio, largely occupied by a huge former seminary, now home to a closed order of Benedictine

View over Lago d'Orta, with the islet of San Giulio.

nuns. Boats from Orta San Giulio dock in front of the basilica of San Giulio, dedicated to its founder St Julius, who supposedly banished all snakes from the island. The interior of the church is mainly Baroque, but the frescoes are earlier, and include one attributed to Gaudenzio Ferrari, the greatest artist of the Piedmontese school (d. 1546), whose work is charmingly old-fashioned, betraying no inkling that the Renaissance had ever happened. More works by his hand can be seen in the Galleria Sabauda in Turin (*see p. 18*).

VISITING LAGO D'ORTA

GETTING AROUND

• **By train:** Lago d'Orta can be reached in c. 2hrs from Milan or Turin, with a change at Novara. The station for Orta San Giulio is Orta-Miasino.
• **By boat:** Regular motor boats (c. every 20mins) run from Piazza Motta in Orta San Giulio to the Isola San Giulio. Private motor boats are available for hire. See www.moto-scafisti.com for details.

WHERE TO STAY & EAT ON LAGO D'ORTA

The lake has a number of hotels whose restaurants are also Michelin-starred destinations in themselves. At Orta San Giulio there are two: €€€ **Villa Crespi**, an extraordinary late 19th-century folly, a cross between a Moorish kasbah and a Tuscan town hall: the garish drapes and arabesques may well make you feel you've landed in a silent movie set. Extensive gardens. (*Via Fava 18, T: 0322 911902, www.villacrespi.it; open Feb–Dec*). The other is the €€€ **San Rocco**, less amusing as a hotel (it's a bit 'corporate'-feeling, though it does have a pretty lakeside pool), but with an equally acclaimed restaurant (*Via Gippini 11, T: 0322 911977, www.hotelsanrocco.it*). The third grand hotel and restaurant is the €€€ **Al Sorriso**, part

of the Relais & Châteaux group, in the small village of Soriso, not on the lake itself, but slightly to the south of it (*Via Roma 18, Soriso, T: 0322 983228, www.alsorriso.com. Restaurant closed Mon and Tues*).

For a simpler hotel in Orta San Giulio, there is the lovely €€ **La Contrada dei Monti** ▪, an old town house where an atmosphere of graceful living is successfully recreated. Rooms are spacious, furniture is tasteful and unfussy, good breakfasts are served in the pretty walled courtyard in summer, and dinner is served by arrangement at a restaurant on the water (*Via Contrada dei Monti 10, T: 0322 905114, www.lacontradadeimonti.it; closed Jan*).

For a taste of ordinary local cuisine rather than lucullan extravagance, there is the €€ **Taverna Antico Agnello**, an *osteria* in the heart of Orta San Giulio serving wholesome traditional fare (*Via Olina 18, T: 0322 90259; closed Tues except in Aug and Dec–Feb*).

There is only one place to eat on **Isola San Giulio**: the Ristorante San Giulio, which serves ordinary food in an extraordinary setting (*T: 3939 502080; open from Easter onwards*).

LOMBARDY

Landlocked Lombardy (*map p. 422–23*) is a prosperous region. Shakespeare, in *The Taming of the Shrew*, speaks of 'fruitful Lombardy, the pleasant garden of great Italy'. This fruitfulness has been pecuniary as well as agricultural, and the lack of a coastline was no impediment to trade. Lombardy is criss-crossed with waterways, which in the Middle Ages were fully navigable, and many of the main towns acted as port cities. Lombard bankers were famously astute (they invented double-entry book keeping), and the Lombards were also keen moneylenders. Any city with a Lombard Street owes the origin of that name to a pawn shop that once stood there.

Lombardy in history

The name Lombardy derives from the Lombards, a Germanic people who invaded Italy in the 6th century. They rapidly spread through the peninsula, establishing duchies around Spoleto and Benevento and driving the Byzantines out of Ravenna (*see p. 152*). When they were forced back by the Franks under Pepin and his son Charlemagne, they consolidated their power here until 774, when Charlemagne defeated them absolutely, and had himself crowned with their famous iron crown (*see p. 45*). Lombardy remained nominally a part of the Holy Roman Empire until the 12th century, when its chief cities formed the Lombard League, to resist the increasingly assertive power of the emperor, Frederick Barbarossa. The League defeated Barbarossa at Legnano, between Milan and Lake Maggiore, in 1176. In the following two centuries, power was in the hands of local dynasties. The most prominent of these, whose names echo down the centuries of Italian history, both as warriors and as patrons of the arts, were the Visconti and the Sforza at Milan, Pavia and Bergamo; the della Scala on the borders of the Veneto; and the Gonzaga at Mantua.

After the fall of the Visconti in the mid-15th century, the expanding Venetian Republic took territory from the eastern part of the region. During the 16th century, when Spain and France were battling for control of Italy, the Lombard lands were invaded first by the French, and then, in 1535, the Duchy of Milan passed to the Spanish Habsburgs. When the Spanish royal line died out in 1700, Lombardy was transferred to the Habsburgs of Austria and—with the brief intervention of Napoleon's short-lived, shifting kingdoms (1797–1814)—it remained an Austrian subject province. In 1859, following the allied French and Piedmontese defeat of Austria at Magenta, Lombardy was brought beneath the Italian flag.

Italian unity is not as sanctified a concept as the idealists of the mid-19th century might have hoped, however. Affluent Lombardy has become the centre of a federalist movement which claims the right to spend Lombard taxes solely on Lombardy, a repudiation, in other words, of the current policy of redistributing funds to regions with a greater need. It is hard to imagine Italy going the way of the former Yugoslavia, but these are uncertain times, and the seed of unrest is firmly planted—in rich Lombard soil.

The geography of Lombardy

Lombardy extends from the summits of the central Alps to the fertile plain of the Po. Within those borders are contained areas of remarkable diversity. The higher plain in the north, ill-suited to agriculture, is traditionally a place of industry. The lower plain, by contrast, is verdant, fertile and intensely cultivated.

Lombard winters are foggy and severe, and its summers hot and humid. The great lakes, however, because of the enormous mass of water they hold, enjoy a particularly mild microclimate that permits the growth of Mediterranean trees such as olives and lemons, as well as splendid camellias, oleanders and holm oaks. The scenery around the lakes is some of the loveliest in Italy.

Lombard food and wine

Lombard cuisine is characterised by abundant meat and cheese, and by the use of butter rather than olive oil. The tastiest appetiser is *bresaola*: salted, air-dried beef. Good first courses are *risotto alla milanese* (rice cooked in meat broth with saffron), and the Mantuan *tortelli di zucca* (large tortellini filled with pumpkin and spiced apple, usually served in a butter and cheese sauce). Main courses include *costoletta alla milanese* (the famous breaded veal cutlet known to most English speakers as *Wiener Schnitzel*: the Austrians, it seems, learned the recipe during their occupation of Milan), and *osso buco* (sliced veal shin cooked in tomato sauce and *gremolada*, a mixture of lemon zest, rosemary, sage and parsley). An interesting condiment served with boiled meats is *mostarda di Cremona* (a fruit chutney made with honey and white wine).

Good Lombard desserts include the Milanese Christmas cake *panettone*; Bergamasque *polenta dolce* (flavoured with almonds, butter and cinnamon); and Mantuan *torta sbrisolona* (a dry almond cake that is crumbled rather than sliced).

The DOCG Franciacorta is the finest Lombard wine. Franciacorta red is made from Cabernet Franc and Cabernet Sauvignon grapes blended with Barbera, Nebbiolo and Merlot. Franciacorta white is Chardonnay and Pinot Bianco. Other interesting wines are the Valtellina reds, made from Nebbiolo grapes (here called *Chiavennasca*) by small 'boutique' growers. Late-pressed grapes make the rich, strong and very special Sfurzat.

MILAN

Milan (*map p. 422, C2*) is the second largest city in Italy and the commercial and industrial centre of the country. Both these facts make it busy and hectic, and a visit needs to be planned with care. Nevertheless, it rewards time spent on it, being full of historic and artistic interest, with magnificent art collections, the renowned La Scala opera house, the famous duomo, and Leonardo da Vinci's fresco of the *Last Supper*.

Milan in history

Commerce has always been central to Milan's existence: the ancient city occupied a key position on trade routes between Rome and northern Europe; by the 4th century AD it had a population of nearly 100,000 and rivalled Rome in importance—a rivalry that is still going strong today.

During the latter days of the Roman Empire, Milan was its administrative centre. It was by an edict pronounced here in 313 that the emperor Constantine officially recognised Christianity, and the city went on to become a major centre of the new faith. One of its early bishops was St Ambrose (340–97), who baptised St Augustine.

In the Middle Ages Milan evolved as a typical Italian city-state, at first governed by an assembly of citizens. This free '*comune*' gave way to rule by a succession of powerful families, including the Visconti, who held power from 1277–1447. The city enjoyed a period of particular splendour under Gian Galeazzo Visconti (1385–1402), who founded what is still the city's most impressive monument, the duomo. A disputed succession was brought to an end by the mercenary general Francesco Sforza, defender of Milan against encroaching Venice, who had married Bianca, daughter of the last Visconti. He founded a dynasty that lasted until 1499, when Milan was taken by Charles VIII of France. From then on the city followed the fortunes of Lombardy, passing from France to Spain, and then, in 1713, to Austria. In 1796 it was seized by Napoleon, who named it capital of the Kingdom of Italy in 1805 (with himself as king). After Napoleon's fall, the Austrians returned, remaining in power until the revolt of March 1848 (known as the *Cinque Giornate* in Milan), when Venice and Milan rose up against them. The Austrians were temporarily driven from Milan, but their troops defeated Carlo Alberto of Savoy at Custoza later that year. It was only following Austria's defeat at the Battle of Magenta in 1859, by Carlo Alberto's son Vittorio Emanuele and his ally Napoleon III, that Milan finally joined the nascent Kingdom of Italy.

Milanese art and architecture

In the early Middle Ages Milanese architecture followed the style known as the Lombard Romanesque, the earliest expression of a type of building which blended elements from the Western Roman tradition with Early Christian elements from the East. A good example of the style is the basilica of Sant'Ambrogio (*see p. 40*).

The court of the Sforza attracted many great artists during the Renaissance. Some of the names are well known (Michelozzo, Bramante); others did not move outside Lombardy (the sculptor Amadeo, and the painters Foppa and Bergognone). Bergognone is an important exponent of the native Milanese style, a style he clung to despite the artistic revolution that took place around him. For Milanese art was completely transformed by the arrival from Tuscany in 1483 of Leonardo da Vinci. While he was here, Milan became the centre of an artistic and humanistic flowering that continued until the fall of the Sforza in 1499. Important pupils of Leonardo were Bernardino Luini and Boltraffio. The sculptors Bambaia and Cristoforo Solari also felt his influence.

Towards the end of the 16th century Camillo and Giulio Procaccini introduced a new, Baroque style of painting from Bologna, and Galeazzo Alessi imported Baroque ideas from Rome into architecture. But it is not until the early 20th century that a style emerges that can once more be termed distinctly Milanese. This was Futurism, a product of the new industrial age. The Futurist movement was launched with a manifesto,

'We sing the glory of great crowds fired up by work, by pleasure or by riot. We shall sing the multi-coloured and polyphonic tides of revolution in our modern capitals…' This work by Umberto Boccioni (*Brawl in the Gallery*, 1911) could almost be seen as an illustration to the *Futurist Manifesto*, which hailed the new mechanical age and gloried in the ideas of violence and turmoil.

published in 1909 in the Paris newspaper *Le Figaro*, and written by the Italian poet and playwright Filippo Tommaso Marinetti, in the form of 11 bullet points. In ringing tones Marinetti hails the new world of mechanical forces and denounces all attachment to the past. He promises to destroy museums and libraries as reliquaries of fossilised culture.

'We sing the love of danger,' he thunders, 'an appetite for energy and for daring. Courage, bravery and rebellion shall be the essential elements of our song.'

In the 1920s Milan saw the birth of the movement known as the Novecento. Its leading figure, the former Futurist painter Carlo Carrà, called for a return to a quieter, figurative style based on traditional values. In other words, the Novecento artists sought to return to the forms of the past, and rejected the avant garde '–isms' that lay sprawled across the century to date. The leading Novecento architect was Marcello Piacentini. The movement was embraced by the Fascists because of its emphasis on tradition and national identity. The rise of a functionalist trend in architecture, known as Rationalism, was also a 1920s phenomenon. Though initially apolitical, the movement later won the support of the Fascist regime. The protagonists of the movement were Giuseppe Terragni and Giuseppe Pagano. Later, as elsewhere in Europe and in North America, the dominant architectural trend in Milan became the International Style, which advocated the adoption of common standards in all buildings, regardless of location. Giò Ponti and Pier Luigi Nervi's Pirelli Building (*map p. 36, 4*) is a good example.

The 1950s marked the beginning of Italy's economic miracle: the standard of living grew, creating demand for high-quality consumer goods. Industry responded by increasing production and by involving some great creative talents in product design, giving rise to that distinctive look for which Italian products are so famous.

WHAT TO SEE IN MILAN

The duomo

Milan's cathedral (*map p. 37, 11; open daily 8.30–6.45*) is a strange palimpsest, the product of many centuries of development, of patrons changing their minds, and of shifting styles of architecture. It is Gothic in name, but quite unlike any other Gothic building in Italy or anywhere else. Oscar Wilde described it as an 'awful failure'; John Ruskin as some enchanted product of fairyland, a delicate, brittle thing such as Jack Frost might have left on one's window pane. But then he thought twice, and called it 'a lie from beginning to end'. So what should we conclude? It is helpful, at least, to know some dates. Building work began in 1386 under Gian Galeazzo Visconti, to a design attributed to Lombard masters. In the 15th century Giovanni Solari was employed as master mason, and Giovanni Antonio Amadeo, the most gifted sculptor of the Lombard renaissance, also worked on it. In 1567 St Charles Borromeo, Archbishop of Milan, appointed Pellegrino Tibaldi as architect, and under Borromeo the church was dedicated. Tibaldi's plans for a classical façade were abandoned, and the new 'Gothic' design was completed in 1805, just in time for Napoleon to crown himself king of Italy here (the façade was in fact completed to Napoleon's orders). It is on its façade that the duomo is first judged, and it is this curious fusion of classical and Gothic that lies at the heart of this building's paradox: for all its intended integrity, it comes across as a pastiche. If you stand back to analyse the west front, you see at once that it is not Gothic at all, but a curious amalgam of Gothic verticality, Gothic pinnacles and Gothic pointed arches with classical entablatures, pediments and plinths.

Gothic and classical elements combine in the eclectic façade of Milan's duomo.

The interior

The interior of the duomo is lofty and magnificent, the double-aisled nave a forest of tall columns, each of which rises to a circlet of sculpted figures in canopied niches, before soaring higher into the vault. The splendid effect is heightened by the stained glass of the windows, which is one of the glories of the cathedral.

It is easy to feel overwhelmed by the sheer volume of things to see. Some of the monuments are of exceptional quality, and many are the work of local Lombard masters. The best and most interesting are described below, and numbered on the plan overleaf.

(1) Tomb of Ottone Visconti: Here lies the founder of Visconti power in Milan (d. 1295). After defeating his rivals in battle in 1277, he did much to enrich and beautify the city during his tenure as overlord and archbishop.

(2) Edict of Milan plaque: This historic decree, passed by the emperor Constantine in AD 313, allowed freedom of worship to all Christians within the Roman Empire.

(3) Tomb of Gian Giacomo de' Medici: This splendid monument commemorates a *condottiere* of the Milanese forces and brother of Pope Pius IV. It is said that the Florentine Medici acknowledged no kinship with their humble Milanese namesakes until one of them was named pope: the familiar Medici coat of arms of six balls certainly appears on this tomb. The bronze statues of Gian Giacomo (d. 1555) flanked by *War* and *Peace* are rem-

MILAN DUOMO

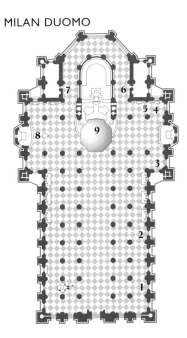

iniscent of Michelangelo's works for the New Sacristy of San Lorenzo in Florence (*see p. 185*). They are the work of a Lombard sculptor and medallist, Leone Leoni, a man of violent and even criminal temperament (he served a year as a galley slave) but conspicuous talent.

(4) **Altar of the Presentation:** The marble altarpiece is a bold exercise in architectural perspective, with a central group of the *Presentation of the Virgin* by Bambaia (1543), vividly conveying a sense of eagerness as the figures at the top of the steps crowd together to watch the child's approach.

(5) **St Bartholomew:** This statue (1562) is one of the most extraordinary works in the cathedral. It shows the saint with the attribute of his martyrdom, his own flayed skin, draped over his shoulder like a cloak. His body is a masterpiece

of anatomical sculpture, with every vein and sinew exposed. It is the work of Marco d'Agrate, one of the sculptors who worked on the cathedral façade (where this statue originally stood).

(6) **South sacristy door:** This exuberant and glorious manifestation of the Gothic sculptor's art should on no account be missed. Above a very simple doorway rises a hood of extreme delicacy, soaring upward with slender, crocketed pinnacles. The group of the *Lamentation over the Dead Christ* is particularly beautiful. The work is dated 1389–91 and is ascribed to the German sculptor Hans von Fernach.

(7) **North sacristy door:** Carved in 1389, at the same time as the south sacristy door, this is much more restrained. The lunette over the doorway shows Christ flanked by the Virgin and St John the Baptist, each with a symbolic offering. The Virgin offers the milk of motherly love while the Baptist offers his own head, a token of his devotion. It is the work of a Campionese master (*see p. 48*).

(8) **Altar of the Virgin of the Tree:** The wide entrance arch is decorated with bas-reliefs by Lombard sculptors. Particularly good is the charming *Nativity* on the left, by Cristoforo Solari (1520). At the foot of the altar is the tomb slab of Federico Borromeo (*see p. 42*).

(9) **Presbytery:** It is in this sacred space that the Counter-Reformation principles of St Charles Borromeo are most clearly seen. Borromeo was present at the concluding session of the Council of Trent (*see p. 65*), and when he returned to Milan he wanted to create a church that was fit for purpose: suited, in other words, to the task of repudiating Lutheran heresy, and providing a theatre where the mystery of the Eucharist could

be powerfully witnessed and understood by the people. The space was organised to the designs of Pellegrino Tibaldi, with two enormous hooded pulpits facing the congregation. The theme of their gilded copper reliefs is the gift to mankind of the Word of God, illustrated by the Old Testament prophets on the right and by the Evangelists on the left. In the centre of the sanctuary is the ciborium, housed in a gorgeous *tempietto*, the gift of Pope Pius IV to his nephew, Charles Borromeo.

The crypt and roof

The **crypt** (1606), the work of Milan's foremost Baroque architect, Francesco Maria Richini, is the last resting place of St Charles Borromeo. His body is enshrined in a casket of rock crystal. Since 1961 his face has been covered by a silver mask (taken from his death mask): it is said that the features had become so decayed that ladies were prone to fainting at the sight. The excavations beneath the church are entered from the west end. Here you can see the 4th-century octagonal baptistery where St Ambrose baptised St Augustine in 387.

The entrance to the **roof** is in the corner of the south transept, near the Medici tomb. The climb (up 158 steps) allows you to inspect the sculptural detail from close to. There are superb views from the base of the central spire.

Museo Poldi-Pezzoli

The north side of Piazza del Duomo is connected with Piazza della Scala by the **Galleria Vittorio Emanuele II** (*map p. 37, 11*), a huge glass-roofed shopping arcade with cafés and restaurants, opened in 1878. Beyond it lies Piazza della Scala, which takes its name from the church of Santa Maria della Scala, founded by Regina della Scala, niece of the great Cangrande of Verona (*see p. 115*) and wife of the same Bernabò Visconti of Milan whose equestrian monument is one of the chief exhibits in the Castello Sforzesco (*see p. 40*). On the site of that church now rises the most famous opera house in the world, the **Teatro alla Scala**, built for Empress Maria Theresa of Austria in 1776.

Beyond all this again, at Via Manzoni 12, is the Museo Poldi-Pezzoli (*map p. 37, 11; open Tues–Sun 10–6*), once the home of Gian Giacomo Poldi-Pezzoli, a wealthy Milanese collector. It has interesting works by the Lombard school. Three *Madonnas* by Boltraffio, Foppa and Bergognone powerfully demonstrate the effect on Milanese art that Leonardo da Vinci was to have after his arrival in the city in 1483. The works by Foppa and Bergognone are restricted in their colour range and notably medieval in atmosphere. The *Madonna* by Boltraffio (*illustrated on p. 39*) is in marked contrast, with the Virgin dressed in a rich blue gown, her face clearly showing the influence of Leonardo, and the chubby, wriggling child reaching out to grasp a rose, an allusion to the crown of thorns which He will later wear. Other masterpieces of the collection include works by Mantegna, Giovanni Bellini and Piero della Francesca.

Pinacoteca di Brera

The Pinacoteca di Brera (*map p. 36, 7; Via Brera 28; open Tues–Sun 8.30–7.15; last entry 45mins before closing*) is the best place to acquaint yourself with the great figures of

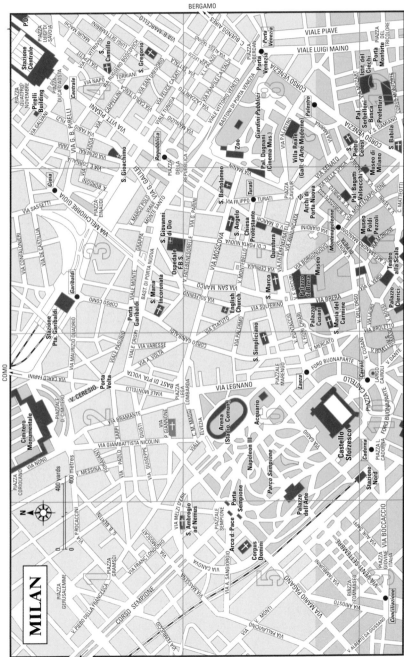

MILAN

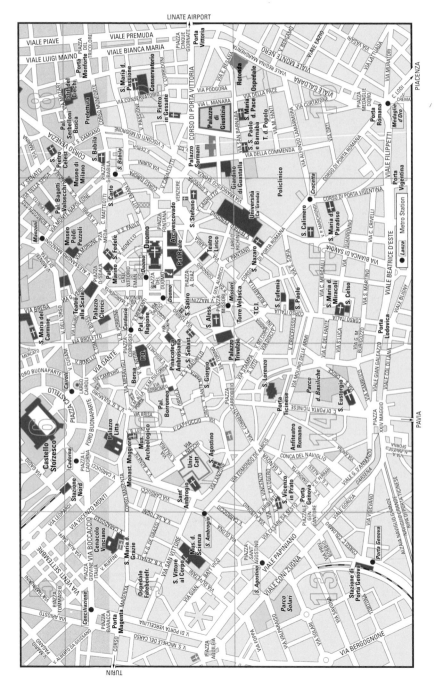

northern Italian painting. The gallery, as is the case with so many fine collections of art in Europe, owes its existence in large part to Napoleon, whose frenzy of ecclesiastical suppressions and his conqueror's lust for portable booty created vast troves of art to be housed across his ever-expanding empire. In the monumental courtyard is a heroic bronze statue of him by Canova (1809). Napoleon is said to have disliked it, objecting that the winged image of Victory appeared to be about to fly away. The Duke of Wellington enjoyed this idea, and the marble version of the statue stands in his former residence, Apsley House, in London.

The collection includes some superb works by Venetian artists, including **Mantegna's Dead Christ** (Room VI). The body is drawn with remarkable foreshortening and the open wounds are treated with the greatest naturalism. Works by Mantegna's brother-in-law **Giovanni Bellini** (in the same room) show how he broke away from Mantegna's severe aesthetic to develop his own softer, more naturalistic style. The splendid *St Mark Preaching in Alexandria* (Room VIII) by Gentile and Giovanni Bellini shows Alexandria as it existed in the artists' imagination (the three bays of the church façade are remarkably similar to St Mark's in Venice). The giraffe is a delightful detail.

The long gallery (Room X) displays early 20th-century works (particularly the **Futurists**). The best Lombard works are in Rooms XIII–XIX. The attachment to the Lombard tradition represented by **Vincenzo Foppa** and **Bergognone** can be seen in Foppa's *Grazie* polyptych (Room XV). The **Pala Sforzesca** by an anonymous Lombard painter (c. 1490–1520), known from this painting as the Maestro della Pala Sforzesca, shows the new, more naturalistic style. Here we have a Virgin with the characteristic modest, downcast eyes that artists learned from Leonardo da Vinci. Her throne is decorated with *grottesche* (see p. 395) and on either side of it kneel the last great Sforza ruler, Lodovico il Moro, his wife Beatrice d'Este and their two children. Bernardino Luini's celebrated *Madonna del Roseto* is displayed in Room XIX, and once again the Leonardesque artist is shown side by side with a contemporary whose art clings to the habits of the past: in this case Bergognone, with his haunting *Madonna and Child with St Catherine of Siena and a Carthusian Monk*. It is thought that the panel was painted for one of the cells of the Certosa di Pavia (see p. 46), and would have been used for solitary devotion.

The most famous works in the collection are in Room XXIV: **Raphael's Marriage of the Virgin** (the *Sposalizio*; 1504), with a remarkable, idealised circular temple in the background; and **Piero della Francesca's Montefeltro Altarpiece**, with the Madonna surrounded by angels and saints in the presence of Federico, Duke of Montefeltro (see p. 306). This is Piero's last known work and has a highly refined architectural setting.

Caravaggio brought about a revolution in painting in the late 16th and early 17th centuries, introducing a classical naturalism that is completely divorced from classical idealism. The 'warts and all' approach earned him as many detractors as it did supporters. In his later works his use of intense darkness suddenly illuminated by patches of visibility are an instantly recognisable feature. The most striking piece in this room is his *Supper at Emmaus* (c. 1600; Room XXIX), where the painter's controversial realism and powerful use of chiaroscuro are in full evidence. Room XXX holds a very different rendering of a mealtime scene: **Daniele Crespi's Last Supper**, a superbly

Giovanni Antonio Boltraffio: *Madonna and Child* (after 1483). Boltraffio was a pupil of Leonardo da Vinci, and this work in the Poldi-Pezzoli museum clearly shows the influence of the master and the way his tutelage brought Lombard painting out of the Middle Ages and into the Renaissance.

detailed, colourful and crowded work, profoundly melancholy despite the frolicsome angels at the top. One of the disciples brandishes a knife; but he is not Judas. The Judas figure is the bearded man closest to the front, who looks out at the viewer in sudden anguish, his guilty green bag of blood money concealed under his cloak. Crespi, who

Leonardo's famous and influential *Last Supper* (1494–97), vividly showing the disciples' consternation as Christ calmly announces that one of their number will betray Him. For more on Last Suppers in art, see the caption on p. 216.

died tragically young of the plague, was the exponent *par excellence* of the devotional world of Counter-Reformation Lombardy. He makes no use of the stagey sensuality of the Baroque, but has recourse instead to a sincere and sympathetic naturalism.

Castello Sforzesco

Gloomy, down at heel and lacking in atmosphere though it may be, the Castello Sforzesco (*map p. 36, 6; open Tues–Sun 9–5.30; last entry 30mins before closing*) is nevertheless one of the major sights of Milan, and as the former citadel of a famous ruling dynasty, deserves a visit. It was built for Francesco Sforza in 1451–66 on the site of the castle of his predecessors the Visconti. In the old residential part of the castle, the **Museo d'Arte Antica** displays Italian sculpture from early Christianity to the late Renaissance. One of the finest Lombard Romanesque pieces is the tomb of Bernabò Visconti by Bonino da Campione (1363) and assistants. The sarcophagus, carved with figures in relief, is mounted on numerous columns. Surmounting the whole is an equestrian statue of the deceased, showing him stiff and erect in the saddle. Bernabò was by all accounts a cruel ruler, not averse to tearing men's tongues out. He died the alleged victim of poison at the hands of his nephew Gian Galeazzo. The masterpiece of Bambaia is in a later room: the monument to Gaston de Foix, the flower of French chivalry who died in battle at Ravenna in 1512 (*see p. 152*). Also here is Michelangelo's unfinished *Rondanini Pietà*.

The **Pinacoteca** displays Italian painting of the 13th–18th centuries, with special emphasis on Lombard and Venetian masters.

The church of Sant'Ambrogio

Alumni of UCLA will recognise this building: it is the model for Royce Hall on

Westwood campus (1929). This Milan version (*map p. 37, 10; open 8–12 & 2.30–6*) was founded by St Ambrose and originally built in 379–86, though much enlarged and restored since. Austere in aspect, this is the prototype of the Lombard basilica. Preceding the church is a fine atrium of the late 11th century, reconstructed in 1150. The façade is very plain, of brick with stone dressings, and has a double-tiered narthex with five arches below and five above, gradated in size to fit the gable.

The interior contains some celebrated monuments and relics. The Romanesque **pulpit** on the left is an extraordinary structure, reconstituted from fragments saved after the vault collapsed in 1196. Beneath it is a **palaeochristian sarcophagus** (4th century) with a rim of swastikas and intricately carved scenes. It is known as the Tomb of Stilicho, though it is probably unrelated to the Roman military commander (d. 408) of that name.

At the end of the south aisle is the **Sacello di San Vittore in Ciel d'Oro**, a 4th-century sepulchral chapel dedicated to the soldier-martyr St Victor. The second part of the name refers to the splendid 5th-century mosaics, with a golden dome containing an idealised representation of St Victor in the centre, the Evangelists in the pendentives, and six panels of named saints (including St Ambrose) on the walls.

The **crypt** contains the bodies of St Ambrose, with the two protomartyrs of Milan, Sts Gervase and Protase, in a shrine of 1897. St Augustine claims, in his *City of God*, that St Ambrose found the bodies of the two martyrs, and that, in the presence of many witnesses, the relics restored the sight of a blind man.

Santa Maria delle Grazie and the Cenacolo

The brick and terracotta church of Santa Maria delle Grazie (*map p. 37, 9; tram 16–18 along Corso Magenta*) was erected in 1466–90 to the design of Guiniforte Solari, engineer to the Duchy of Milan in the days of Francesco Sforza. In 1492 the last great Sforza ruler, Lodovico il Moro, ordered the striking new choir and unusual lantern (known as the *tribuna*), which are both usually attributed (though perhaps wrongly) to Bramante. The church contains some interesting works of art, including frescoes by Gaudenzio Ferrari in the fourth south chapel (1542), but the chief claim to visitors' attention is unquestionably the famous ***Last Supper*** (1494–97), in the refectory (*cenacolo*) of the adjoining convent, commissioned from Leonardo da Vinci by Lodovico il Moro (*open Tues–Sun 8.15–6.45; reservations required, no tickets on the spot. You should arrive at least 20mins before the given time with your booking number. Visits are limited to 15mins. Book online on www.cenacolovinciano.org or on T: 02 8942 1146. Visitors go through a series of glass 'cubicles' installed with air-filtering systems*). This remarkable painting was to have a lasting influence on generations of artists. The room in which the supper takes place is shown in perfect perspective, with all lines converging on a central focal point: the figure of Christ. Light enters from the real windows on the left and radiates around Christ's head from the painted windows behind Him, which give onto a serene landscape. The room appears as an extension of the actual refectory, and the fact that no one is seated at the near side of the table draws us in as if we ourselves were guests at the feast.

When Napoleon saw this work, he instantly looked on it with covetous eyes and ordered its transportation to Paris. When this proved technically impossible, he had a copy made instead. We should be thankful that Leonardo's failed experiment with a new painting technique (this is not a fresco, and has deteriorated badly) ultimately preserved his work *in situ*.

Museo Nazionale della Scienza e della Tecnologia Leonardo da Vinci

Italy's leading science museum (*map p. 37, 9; Via San Vittore 21; open Tues–Fri 9.30–5, Sat–Sun and holidays 9.30–6.30; last entry 30mins before closing*), housed in a former monastery which still contains frescoes by Bernardino Luini, has a section devoted to Leonardo da Vinci, exploring his activities—artistic and scientific—during the 20 years he spent in Milan. The exhibit consists of explanatory panels and reconstructions of his inventions; there are no original works.

Pinacoteca Ambrosiana

Palazzo dell'Ambrosiana (*map p. 37, 10–11; Piazza Pio XI 2; open Tues–Sun 10–5.30; last entry 1hr before closing*) contains the library and art gallery founded at the beginning of the 17th century by Cardinal Federico Borromeo, younger cousin of St Charles Borromeo. Federico, like St Charles, was a supporter of Counter-Reformation reforms in the Catholic church; he was also a humane and merciful man, a great patron of the arts and letters, and he rose to become archbishop of Milan like his cousin before him. His statue stands behind the railings outside the library building. The library is famed as the first public library in Europe after the Bodleian in Oxford. The gallery was created as a teaching aid (hence the many copies of famous works), not only to help artists with their technique, but also to inculcate in them an aesthetic sense that conformed to the principles set forth at the Council of Trent (*see p. 65*). The collection is arranged chronologically, with works from Borromeo's original bequest in the first rooms (1 and 4–7).

In his *Musaeum* (1625), a collection of views and critiques of works of art, Cardinal Borromeo reveals why he chose certain paintings for his collection. We know, for example, that he regarded Bernardino Luini's *Holy Family with St Anne and the Young St John* (Room 1; from a cartoon by Leonardo) as the very height of artistic perfection, and that he considered Titian's *Adoration of the Magi* (Room 1; 1560) a rich source of material for students of drawing to copy and learn from. Also in Room 1 is a celebrated portrait of a lady, attributed to Giovanni Ambrogio de Predis, but which was for long believed to be by Leonardo, and to represent Beatrice d'Este, the beautiful and accomplished young wife of Lodovico il Moro (*see pp. 46–47*). In Jacopo Bassano's *Rest on the Flight into Egypt* (Room 4) Cardinal Borromeo admired the tenderness shown to the Child by Joseph. The Raphael Room (Room 5) contains the cartoon for the *School of Athens* from the fresco cycle in the Vatican, purchased by Cardinal Borromeo in 1626. The figure of Heraclitus is missing from the cartoon: he was an addition that Raphael made to the final fresco (sitting writing on the steps in the centre; *illustrated on p. 274*), using Michelangelo's features. Room 6 displays Caravaggio's exquisite *Basket of Fruit*. Cardinal Borromeo notes that he tried to find a work to hang beside this extraordinary still life but that he could find none worthy. The concluding room of this section contains works by two Flemish painters whom Borromeo knew personally and whose skill at rendering works of nature (both landscapes and still lifes) he greatly admired. These are Jan Brueghel and Paul Brill. Brueghel's small painting on copper of a mouse with roses, a caterpillar and a butterfly was sent to Borromeo by the artist.

The remaining rooms contain a fine collection of paintings (mainly Italian, with some Flemish, and some excellent examples of Lombard art) from the 14th–19th centuries. Extremely famous is the reliquary containing a lock of Lucrezia Borgia's hair. Byron wrote enthusiastically to his friend and fellow poet Thomas Moore, 'I have been to the Ambrosian library … For me, in my simple way, I have been most delighted with a correspondence of letters, all original and amatory, between Lucretia Borgia and Cardinal Bembo … I have pored over them and a lock of her hair, the prettiest and fairest imaginable—I never saw fairer … If I can obtain some by fair means, I shall try.' Byron did obtain a few strands of the hair—if by fair means who can say—and sent them to his sister Augusta Leigh.

Galleria d'Arte Moderna

Milan's gallery of modern art (*map p. 36, 8; Via Palestro 16; open Tues–Sun 9–5.30*) occupies the Villa Reale, once home to the regent Eugène Beauharnais and to Field Marshal Radetzky, who died here in 1858. Highlights include works by Canova, the large *Quarto Stato* by Giuseppe Pellizza da Volpedo, and portraits by the Romantic painter Francesco Hayez. The Futurists are also well represented.

VISITING MILAN

GETTING AROUND

• **By air:** To and from Malpensa airport: **Malpensa Shuttle** from Terminal 1 every 20mins. Journey time c. 50mins. Tickets from Airport 2000 on the arrivals floor or on the bus. It also stops at Terminal 2. From the city to the airport, tickets can be bought on the bus or from the air terminal at Stazione Centrale. **Malpensa Bus Express** also from Terminal 1 between 6am–12.30am. Journey time c. 1hr 10mins. Tickets from Agenzia Autostradale on the arrivals floor or on the bus. The bus also stops at Terminal 2. Both buses drop you at Piazza Luigi di Savoia outside the Stazione Centrale railway station (*map p. 36, 4*). Buses to the airport leave from here.

To and from Linate airport: **Starfly** runs services to Stazione Centrale every 30mins from the arrivals floor. Tickets from Agenzia Autostradale Linate or on the bus. Tickets in the other direction from the air terminal in Stazione Centrale or on the bus. **ATM** operates a service (no. 73) to Piazza San Babila (*map p. 37, 12*) every 10mins. Tickets from bars and newsstands in the airport. ATM tickets to the airport are available from bars and newspaper kiosks in Piazza San Babila.

• **By car:** Traffic is always heavy in the centre of Milan and parking is restricted and expensive. The most central car parks are Meravigli (near the Castello) at Via Camperio 4; Velasca (near the duomo) at Via Pantano 4; Rinascente (duomo) at Via Agnello; Augusto (duomo) at Corso Europa 2; and Diaz (duomo) at Piazza Diaz.

• **Public transport in Milan:** The system, run by ATM (www.atm-mi.it), is very efficient. There are information offices, with a map of routes, in the underground station of

Piazza Duomo and at the central railway station. Tickets, which can be used on buses, the underground or the famous trams, are valid for 75mins (flat rate fare). They are sold at ATM offices, automatic machines at bus stops, and at newsstands and tobacconists, and must be stamped or swiped on board. Tickets valid for 24 or 48hrs can also be purchased at ATM offices or newsstands.

Milan has three **underground** lines: Line 1 (red) links San Babila to the centre, stopping at Duomo and Cairoli (for Castello Sforzesco). Line 3 (yellow) links the central station with the duomo.

• **By taxi:** T: 02 4040; 02 6969; 02 8585.

WHERE TO STAY IN MILAN

There are hotels to suit all moods and budgets in Milan. At the top end of the scale are the €€€€ **Manzoni**, quiet, comfortable and popular, and a good all-around choice in the heart of the Via Montenapoleone shopping district (*Via Santo Spirito 20, T: 02 7600 5700, www.hotelmanzoni.com; map p. 36, 7*) and the €€€€ **Grand Hotel et de Milan**, the city's finest for over 130 years, occupying a patrician palace within easy walking distance of the duomo (*Via Manzoni 29, T: 02 723141, www.grandhoteletdemilan.it; map p. 36, 7*).

Two charming and more modest places are €€ **Alle Meraviglie** ▪, which has just six individually decorated rooms in an 18th-century town house between the duomo and the Castello Sforzesco (*Via San Tomaso 8, T: 02 805 1023, www.allemeraviglie.it; map p. 37, 10, S.Tom.*), and €€ **Antica Locanda Leonardo**, a pleasant, quiet, family-managed boutique hotel in a 19th-century town house, a stone's throw from Leonardo's *Last Supper.* (*Corso Magenta 78, T: 02 4801 4197, www.anticalocandaleonardo.com; open all year except for a few days in Aug and Dec–Jan; map p. 37, 9*).

WHERE TO EAT IN MILAN

Milan is famous for its Michelin-starred restaurants, constantly contriving ever more outlandish and original dishes, as much designed to startle the eye as to jolt the palate into newness of life. Most of the fêted establishments are some way out of the centre: they work well for dinner, and it is best to go by taxi. They include **Sadler**, west of Parco Sempione (*Via Ascanio Sforza 77, T: 02 5810 4451, www.sadler.it, open evenings only, closed Sun, Aug and Jan*), and **Aimo e Nadia**, beyond the Darsena (*Via Montecuccoli 6, T: 02 416886. Closed midday Sat and all day Sun, Aug and Jan*). An *haute cuisine* restaurant in the heart of town is **Cracco** (formerly Cracco-Peck), where the 'coffee contact lenses' are famous (*Via Victor Hugo 4, T: 02 876774; closed Sun; map p. 37, 11*). €€€ **Il Sambuco**, in the Hermitage hotel, is Milan's most acclaimed fish restaurant (*Via Messina 10, T: 02 3361 0333, www.ilsambuco.it; closed Sat lunch and all Sun; map p. 36, 2*).

Places to enjoy a simpler meal or a good lunch, within easy distance of the main sights, include €€ **La Brisa**, close to the Ambrosiana and the Cenacolo, in the same street as the ruins of the Roman emperor Maximian's palace (*Via Brisa 15, T: 02 8645 0521; closed Sat, midday Sun, Aug and Dec–Jan; map p. 37, 10*) and the famous €€ **Trattoria Milanese**, loved by many, though some say it is now too much on the tourist circuit (*Via Santa Marta 11, T: 02 8645 1991; closed Tues, mid-July–end Aug; map p. 37, 10*).

The Milanese tend to head out of the city at weekends, and Sunday can be a trying time for hungry visitors (most places are closed). One good place that doesn't close is €€ **Mauro**, which specialises in fish (*Via Colonnetta 5, T: 02 546 1380; closed Mon, Sat lunch, Aug; map p. 37, 12, V.Col.*).

MILANESE SPECIALITIES

Shopping is one of the delights of Milan. Prada and Armani are local names, Versace opened his first shop here, and Missoni is based here. The smart boutiques are all on and around Via Montenapoleone (*map p. 37, 7–11*). Milan fashion houses present autumn/winter collections in Feb; spring/summer collections in Oct (*www.milanovendemoda.it*).

Milan is also home to the *aperitivo*: Campari and Fernet Branca are local labels. The most famous delicatessen is Peck (*Via Spadari 9, corner of V. Hugo; map p. 37, 11; closed Mon morning*).

La Scala's opera season begins 7 Dec; ballet and concerts run Sept–Nov (*www.teatroallascala.org*).

MONZA & PAVIA

The prosperous industrial town of Monza (*map p. 422, C2*), 15km north of Milan, is famous for two things: its Formula One racetrack, and the iron crown of Lombardy. The crown is housed in the cathedral, a splendid 14th-century building with a façade by Matteo da Campione (*see p. 48*), who died here in 1396 and is buried inside, in the Chapel of the Rosary. The cathedral (*open Tues–Sun 9–1 & 2–6 except when services are in progress*) stands on the site of an oratory founded c. 595 by the Bavarian princess Theodolinda, wife of Agilulf, king of the Lombards. It was with Theodolinda's help that Gregory the Great had concluded a peace treaty with the Lombards; on Gregory's instigation Theodolinda had also converted her husband to Christianity. The crown, which is enclosed within the altar of the Chapel of Theodolinda, is not iron at all, but is made of gold and enamel and cabochon gems. Within it, however, at the centre, is a thin iron strip said to have been hammered from one of the nails used at the Crucifixion. The crown became an important symbol of the Lombard kingdom, and following that, of the Italian territories within the Holy Roman Empire. The first Holy Roman Emperor certainly to be crowned with this diadem was Henry VII in 1312. Tradition also makes earlier claims for Charlemagne and Frederick Barbarossa. Fully aware of the symbolic significance of the crown, Napoleon crowned himself king of Italy with it in Milan in 1805.

PAVIA

Pavia (*map p. 422, C2*) stands on the River Ticino, a waterway that flows into the Po, and which was once linked by canal to Milan. The Lombards made the town their capital. Their kings were crowned here, with the iron crown of Theodolinda (*see above*), and in 774, when Charlemagne defeated the Lombards, he had himself crowned (probably with the same crown) as king of the Lombards and Franks. Another important victory was that won at the Battle of Pavia by Charles V, Holy Roman Emperor and king of Spain, over Francis I of France in 1525, an important step towards Spanish dominion in Italy.

The **Castello Visconteo** lies at the northern edge of the old town, surrounded by public gardens. The great fortress was built in 1360–65 by Galeazzo II Visconti, after his family took possession of the town in 1359. A huge park, famed for its game, extended north from the ducal residence as far as the Certosa di Pavia. The famous Battle of Pavia took place in this park. Via Liutprando leads northwest from Piazza Castello to the Lombard church of **San Pietro in Ciel d'Oro**, whose name comes from its former gilded vault. The high altarpiece is the Arca di Sant'Agostino, a masterpiece of Italian sculpture executed c. 1362 by Campionese masters, with statuettes and bas-reliefs illustrating the story of St Augustine (d. 430), whose relics it is said to contain. The large crypt contains the remains of Boethius (476–524), the poet and statesman clubbed to death in Pavia by order of Theodoric (*see p. 152*), on charges of allying himself with the Byzantines. He wrote *The Consolation of Philosophy* while in prison awaiting execution.

The Certosa di Pavia

A few kilometres north of town stands the beautiful 15th–16th-century Certosa di Pavia, a Carthusian monastery now classed as a national monument (*open Tues–Sun 9–11.30 & 2.30–4.30, 5, 5.30 or 6*). It was founded by Gian Galeazzo Visconti in 1396 'in viridario suo', in the park of his estate. His intention was that the church would serve as a family mausoleum. It was built by the same Lombard masons who worked on Milan cathedral for the same patron. Gian Galeazzo died in 1402, and work continued under Giovanni and Guiniforte Solari, father and son. The monastery was finished in 1452 and the church (except for the façade) in 1472, under the Sforza, for whom Guiniforte Solari acted as chief engineer. The long delay explains the interesting combination in the exterior of Romanesque (e.g. the round arches and arcaded galleries) and Gothic (e.g. the pinnacled buttresses).

The rich decoration of the west front of the church, begun in 1473, is one of the finest achievements of 15th-century Lombard sculpture. It is the work of Cristoforo and Antonio Mantegazza (whose style is characterised by an angularity of line, and a tense quality in the rendering of drapery, which almost looks more like folded paper than cloth) and Giovanni Antonio Amadeo, who modified the original Solari design, incorporating Renaissance elements. The design of the main doorway is probably his. The incomplete and simpler upper part dates from the 16th century.

The interior

The interior is purely Gothic in plan, with the painted decoration of the vaults completed at the end of the 15th century to an overall design by Bergognone. In the south transept is the elaborate tomb of Gian Galeazzo Visconti, whose remains were brought here in 1474. Contrary to his hopes, no other members of his family were buried in the church. The adjacent altarpiece is by Il Cerano, and shows the Virgin with Sts Charles Borromeo and Hugh of Grenoble. St Charles Borromeo was Il Cerano's greatest patron. The latter saint is represented here because it was he who gave to St Bruno the charter for the land on which he founded the Grande Chartreuse, or Carthusian mother-house. In the conch over the altar is a fresco by Bergognone of Gian Galeazzo Visconti (*see illustration*). In the centre of the north transept are the tomb effigies of Lodovico il Moro and Beatrice d'Este by Cristoforo Solari (1497), brought from Santa Maria delle Grazie in Milan in 1564 (the tomb is empty). Beatrice, daughter of the

Gian Galeazzo Visconti in the company of his three sons, presenting a model of this church to the Virgin and Child. Fresco by Bergognone (1488–94).

Duke of Ferrara and his Neapolitan wife, and younger sister of Isabella d'Este (*see p. 59*), was clever, pretty, extravagant and musical. Twenty years her senior, Lodovico was initially an unenthusiastic husband, but found himself captivated by his young bride in the end, and was left desolate after her death in childbirth at the age of only 22. The fresco in the conch here is also by Bergognone, and shows the *Coronation of the Virgin* with Lodovico il Moro and his son Francesco as the donors.

The monastery

From the south transept a doorway by the Mantegazza leads into the small cloister, the work of Guiniforte Solari. A passage leads from here into the great cloister, also the work of Guiniforte, and which is impressive in its dimensions (125m by 100m). Quarters for 24 monks open off three sides of it, each with two ground-floor rooms (*studium* and *dormitorium*) and a balconied upper room and small garden.

VISITING PAVIA

GETTING AROUND

• **By bus:** Bus 3 runs from the railway station to the centre. Buses to the Certosa (8km north) run every 30mins from the bus station (Via Trieste); from the bus stop it is a walk of c. 20mins along a busy road. The Certosa can also be reached by bus from Milan (Famagosta metro stop) in c. 30mins.
• **By train:** Fast trains run from Milan in c. 30mins. Trains also go to the Certosa; it is c. 10mins walk from the station.

WHERE TO STAY IN PAVIA

€€ **Italia**. Converted farmhouse between Pavia and the Certosa. Comfortable rooms, restaurant attached, good value. *Corso Partigiani 48, T: 0382 925656, www.italiacertosa.pavia.it.*

WHERE TO EAT IN PAVIA & THE CERTOSA

A good traditional *trattoria* in Pavia is the €€ **Antica Osteria del Previ** on the picturesque right bank of the Ticino, with good views over the town (*Via Milazzo 65, T: 0382 26203; closed Sun, early Jan and Aug*). Choices near the Certosa include €€€ **Locanda Vecchia Pavia/Al Mulino**, a restaurant whose garden commands a view of the Certosa (*Via al Monumento 5, T: 0382 925894; closed Mon, midday Wed, Jan and Aug*) and the € **Bar Certosa**, a simple café in the picnic area outside the Certosa.

THE LOMBARD LAKES

There is nowhere in Italy where nature and human intervention come together so perfectly as in the Lombard lakes. High rainfall and a mild climate account for the exotic vegetation on their banks. The snow-capped peaks of the Alps form their backdrop, while the villas and gardens of the Milanese aristocracy, built since the early 19th century along their shores, tame the wild beauty of water and wood, creating an environment as far from wilderness as the landscape background of a Renaissance painting, yet filled with the power and awe the Romantics held so dear.

The lakes were home to two important groups of master masons and sculptors in the Middle Ages: the *maestri comacini* from Como (*see p. 54*), and the Campionese masters from Lake Lugano (partly in Switzerland). The best known of the Campionese masters, from the late 14th century, are Matteo, Giovanni and Bonino da Campione, whose works can be seen in Verona, Milan and Bergamo.

LAKE MAGGIORE

Magnificent Lake Maggiore (*map p. 422, B2*) sits in a circlet of snow-capped mountains, forming a natural divide between Piedmont to the west, Lombardy to the east and Switzerland to the north. The Romans called it *Lacus Verbanus*, from the verbena (vervain) that grows profusely here. In the Middle Ages fishing communities grew up around its shores, along with a scattering of castles of the local lords, who included the Milanese Visconti and Borromeo families. Centuries of quietude came to an end in the early 19th century, when the lake was discovered by tourists from northern Europe, whose ecstatic reports home made a celebrity of the place, a status it has enjoyed ever since. Tourism today is the mainstay of the economy.

The finest scenery is to be found in the northern reach of the lake. The central part, around Stresa on the Piedmont bank, is the most interesting historically. The lake is also home—swimmers take note—to *Hirudo verbana*, the Lake Maggiore leech.

The Piedmont side of the lake

The Simplon road from Geneva to Milan, constructed by Napoleon in 1800–05, skirts the lake's southwestern shore. Close to the southern tip is **Arona**, birthplace of St Charles Borromeo, Archbishop of Milan and noted figure of the Counter-Reformation, whose family took possession of the town in the 15th century. The saint was born in the castle, whose ruins are now incorporated into a public park. Further north is the small town of **Stresa**, once a fief of the Visconti, which like Arona came under the control of the Borromeo in the 15th century. Since the 19th century it has been a popular resort; its many hotels also make it a favourite place for international conferences. The grandest of the hotels is the monumental Hotel des Iles Borromées, which opened in 1863, and features in Hemingway's A *Farewell to Arms*. Stresa is a good starting point for trips around the lake. Regular boats leave from here (*see p. 50*). Pretty little **Baveno**, northwest of Stresa, is a quieter resort. You can also reach the islands by boat from here.

The Borromean Islands

Isola Bella is the most famous of the Lake Maggiore islands. It is completely dominated by the vast grey palace (*open late March–late Oct daily 9–5.30*) built in 1631–71 for Count Carlo III Borromeo, in honour of his wife Isabella, from whom the island takes its name. The building is still used as a family home, but some of the rooms can be visited, as well as the chapel in the entrance courtyard where, behind a grille, you can see three family tombs with elaborate carvings by Giovanni Antonio Amadeo and Bambaia, brought from demolished churches in Milan. The greater draw, perhaps, are the famous terraced gardens with their colony of white peacocks, their extraordinary shell-encrusted grottoes, and their exotic vegetation, which includes bamboo, breadfruit, sugar cane, tapioca and tea and coffee plants. By the pier outside the garden gates are a few restaurants and cafés.

Near Isola Bella is the **Isola dei Pescatori** (Isola Superiore) with a pretty little fishing village, a hotel and restaurant. **Isola Madre** is entirely occupied by a Borromeo villa and its botanical park (*open late March–end Oct daily 9–5.30*). Though famed from the writings of Flaubert, who called the island an earthly paradise, the gardens today are not the same as he described, but are a replanting from the 1950s (by the English botanist Henry Cocker). Nevertheless, they are paradise enow, and are home to a wonderful variety of exotic and tropical species, including the taxodium tree, or swamp cypress, whose roots send curious knobbly shoots known as 'knees' up above the soil. The famous ancient Kashmir cypress was uprooted in a storm in 2006, and though replanted, may only have partially survived. There is a single restaurant on the island (but note that you cannot go to it without paying entry to the gardens).

Verbania

Verbania was created in 1939, an amalgamation of the towns of Pallanza and Intra, which lie on either side of the Punta della Castagnola promontory. Its name recalls the ancient Roman name for the lake, *Verbanus*. On the promontory itself is the 19th-century **Villa Taranto**, with famous and much-visited botanical gardens (*open late*

March–early Nov 8.30–6.30, Oct until 5; the villa has a landing stage served by regular boat services). The estate was bought by a Scottish army officer in 1930, and together with the botanist Henry Cocker he created a garden with an outstanding variety of exotic plants, which he himself had collected on his travels around the world. The species include the astonishing Victoria Regia (*Victoria amazonica*), the largest water lily in the world. A fully grown plant can grow to a diameter of 15m and the larger leaves can support the weight of a baby. The scented flowers are night blooming—sadly, because of the opening hours of the gardens, only the park keepers can enjoy their full magnificence.

The Lombard side of the lake

Luino is the most important centre on the eastern shore. Bernardino Luini, the great Lombard follower of Leonardo da Vinci, takes his name from the town, though he was probably actually born at Runo or Dumenza, higher up above the lake. A Wednesday market has been held in Luino since 1541. Reputedly the largest street market in Europe, its 300 or so stalls stretch all over the centre of town and down the waterfront (driving along the lake here is impossible on market day).

Ranco, further south, is noted for its Michelin-starred restaurant (*see opposite*). Beyond it lies **Angera**, probable birthplace of the sculptor Cristoforo Solari. Its castle, the Rocca Borromeo (*open end March–mid-Oct 9–5.30*), was formerly held by the Visconti, and passed to the Borromeo in 1449 (it is still owned by them). The Sala di Giustizia has 14th-century frescoes commissioned by Giovanni Visconti, Bishop of Milan, with episodes from the battles of Archbishop Ottone Visconti, founder of the family fortunes.

VISITING LAKE MAGGIORE

GETTING AROUND

• **By air:** Milan's Malpensa airport is 16km from Lake Maggiore. Buses run by SAF depart from Terminal 1, exit 4, stop 22 for Arona (30mins), Stresa (50mins), Baveno (1hr), Pallanza (1hr 15mins), Intra (90mins) and Verbania (1hr 45mins), leaving at 7.30, 10.30, 2.30, 5.30 and 8.30. Buy your tickets on board.

• **By car:** Roads are good between Milan and the lake, but on Fri and Sun evenings traffic is very heavy on the A8 and it is better to take the SS33.

• **By train:** The main railway from Milan runs along the west shore. Fast trains stop at Arona and/or Stresa (both c. 50mins from Milan). The east shore is served from Milan Porta Garibaldi (to Luino c. 90mins), with a change of trains sometimes necessary at Gallarate.

• **By boat:** Frequent services cross the lake between three major points: Arona to Angera, Cannobio to Luino, and Intra to Laveno (car ferries). Frequent boats leave Stresa for Baveno and Pallanza or Intra, calling at Isola Bella (5mins), Isola dei Pescatori (Isola Superiore) and Isola Madre (though Isola Madre is more quickly reached from Pallanza). In summer the Arona–Locarno route, which calls at the main ports, is served once a day by hydrofoil. Timetables change every season (see www.navigazionelaghi.it). Water taxis are also available.

WHERE TO STAY ON LAKE MAGGIORE

The most civilised stretch of the lake is the

west shore. Below are three suggestions from the multiplicity of choices.

Baveno

€ **Villa Ruscello**. Elegant boarding house in a 19th-century villa with garden and private beach. *Via Sempione 64, T: 0323 923006, www.villaruscello.it.*

Cannobio

€€ **Villa Belvedere**. Colourful, comfortable folksy décor in a pretty yellow villa, set back from the water in a quiet position against a backdrop of green hills. Gardens and pool. *Via Casali Cuserina 2, T: 0323 70159, www.villabelvederehotel.it.*

Stresa

€€€€ **Villa e Palazzo Aminta**. One of the Leading Small Hotels of the World. Glittering old villa, now a five-star luxury spa hotel. Open mid-Feb–mid-Dec. *Via Sempione Nord 123, T: 0323 933818, www.villa-aminta.it.*

WHERE TO EAT ON LAKE MAGGIORE

Arona

€€€ **Taverna del Pittore**. Pleasant fish restau-

rant with an open veranda on the lake. Closed Mon. *Piazza del Popolo 39, T: 0322 243366.*

Ranco

€€€ **Il Sole di Ranco**. Michelin-starred restaurant famous for its lake fish and seafood. It merits a side-trip to Ranco, on the eastern shore. Closed Mon evening (except May–Sept), Tues and Dec–Jan. *Piazza Venezia 5, T: 0331 976507.*

Stresa

€€ **Il Piemontese**. Restaurant in a 17th-century town house with private garden, known for its fine regional cuisine— Piedmontese, as the name suggests. There is a lovely little courtyard with a pergola for summer dining. Closed Mon and Dec–Jan. *Via Mazzini 25, T: 0323 30235.*

Verbania

€ **Caffè Delle Rose**. Reliable old-fashioned place on the main pedestrian street of Pallanza. Good for lunch after visiting Villa Taranto. *Via Ruga 36, T: 0323 558101.*

There are simple places to eat on all the islands.

CASTIGLIONE OLONA

In the heavily built-up area between Lake Maggiore and Lake Como, to the right off the road from Varese to Saronno, is the charming little town of Castiglione Olona (*map p. 422, B2*), the so-called 'Tuscan isle in Lombardy'. The description derives from the fact that the town is home to some remarkable Florentine Renaissance frescoes, commissioned by Cardinal Branda Castiglione, who practically rebuilt the town in the early 15th century. Among the artists who worked for him was Masolino da Panicale, whom the cardinal had met on a papal mission to Florence. **Palazzo Branda Castiglione** (*open Tues–Sat 9–12 & 3–6, Sun and holidays 10.30–12.30 & 3–6*), where the cardinal was born and died, has frescoes attributed to Masolino in the study; the rocky landscapes are those of the Hungarian city of Veszprém, where Castiglione was bishop from 1412–24. Masolino also knew Veszprém (at that time seat of the Hungarian court), having been called there in 1425, probably by Sigismund, Holy Roman Emperor and king of Hungary. The **Collegiata** (*open Tues–Sun April–Sept 10–1 & 3–6; Oct–March 9.30–12.30 & 2.30–5.30*) at the top of the hill was rebuilt in 1422–25, and it is here that the cardinal lies buried. Above the portal is a lunette of the *Madonna with Saints and the Cardinal*,

The Banquet of Herod by the Florentine artist Masolino (1435), a superb transitional work between the Gothic and the Renaissance. The architecture betrays acquaintance with Classical Rome, and there has been a bold attempt to render perspective. Yet Masolino still makes use of the medieval device of showing several stages of a story unfolding in a single frame.

(1428). On the vault are six frescoed scenes from the life of the Virgin signed by Masolino. Across the garden is the entrance to the little **baptistery**, dating from 1435. It is decorated with frescoes of the life of St John the Baptist, seen by many as Masolino's masterpiece. On the right wall is *The Banquet of Herod*, with the king shown feasting on the left, while on the right, sitting composedly with her ladies at the head of a long loggia, is Salome, nursing the head of the Baptist on her lap, calmly waiting to choose her moment. In the sanctuary is the *Baptism of Christ*, with the pale green river disappearing into the distance and the Holy Spirit hovering over the hilltops. The nude figures on the right are themselves awaiting baptism (one is shown peeling off his hose).

VISITING CASTIGLIONE OLONA

If you are coming by car along the A8 *autostrada*, take the Varese Est/Gazzada exit, from where it is 5km on local roads to the village. It is possible to get here by train, to Venegono Superiore station (direct from Milan's Nord Cadorna station in under an hour), from where the village is 10mins away by taxi. A lovely place to eat is La Cantina del Borgo-Osteria degli Artisti, an old-fashioned place serving old-fashioned food, with a warm, comfy atmosphere, tucked away in a pretty courtyard (*Via Roma 40, T: 0331 859021*).

LAKE COMO

Everyone has their favourite among the Italian lakes. Some consider Lago d'Orta to be the most beautiful. Most would agree that Lake Como (*map p. 422, C1–C2*) is the most historically and artistically interesting. Both the Plinys had villas here; the English Romantic poets were enraptured by its sublimity; Franz Liszt called it a place for passionate love (he was enjoying a heady affair at the time). The development of the shoreline is similar to that of Lake Maggiore: many of the small towns began their lives as fishing villages, only to surrender to tourism in the 19th century.

Bellagio and the Centro Lago

The town of Bellagio occupies a promontory on the most beautiful part of the lake, from where its three reaches radiate out: southwest to Como, southeast to Lecco, and north past Varenna. Despite two centuries as a holiday resort, Bellagio retains its integrity as an old Lombard town, and the local industries of silk-weaving and olive-wood carving still thrive (Lake Como is the northernmost place in Europe where olives can ripen).

A well-known attraction of Bellagio is the park of the **Villa Serbelloni**, now a study centre belonging to the Rockefeller Foundation (*ticket office behind the church of San Giacomo in the arcaded piazza left of the car ferry station; park shown by guided tour April–Oct at 11 and 3.30 to a max. of 30 people, daily except Mon or when raining; tours last c. 90mins*). The younger Pliny's villa 'Tragedia' is thought to have occupied this site (his other villa, called 'Comedia', was at Lenno). The park you see today, a mixture of formal terraces and groves of trees, was laid out at the end of the 18th century.

To reach Bellagio's other famous garden, at **Villa Melzi**, it is a 5–10-min walk south from the car ferry station along Lungolario Marconi (all the lakeside roads around Como are called Lungolario, in reference to the Latin name for the lake, *Larius*). The villa is a handsome, well-proportioned building, built in 1808–10 as a summer residence for Francesco Melzi d'Eril, who had been vice president of Napoleon's Italian Republic from 1802–05. Franz Liszt stayed here in 1837, with his mistress, the Comtesse d'Agoult. Their daughter Cosima was born here on Christmas Day. The gardens (*open April–Oct 9.30–6.30*), for the most part laid out *all'inglese*, stretch along the lake for almost a kilometre, and contain beautiful trees and shrubs, including rhododendrons and azaleas. Liszt and his countess are popularly remembered as having read Dante to each other in the little Moorish pavilion here, which in turn inspired the composer's famous 'Dante' sonata. At the southern end of the gardens is the Melzi family chapel, with fine Neoclassical tombs.

Como

The town of Como, still discernibly Roman in its plan, has a very attractive old centre. The cathedral is a splendid Gothic building with remarkable sculptures inside and out. The silk-weaving industry still survives here, and silk products can be purchased all over town. In fact, Como is responsible for almost 80 percent of Europe's total silk output. The **silk museum** has interesting displays (*Museo Didattico della Seta; open*

Tues–Fri 9–12 & 3–6; Via Castelnuovo 9; a few mins' walk from Como Borghi station; turn down Via Aldo Moro and then left into Via Castelnuovo).

The centre of life in Como is **Piazza Cavour**, a broad square created in 1887 by filling in the old harbour. To the right you can see the funicular to Brunate, a hilltop village from where there are fine walks. To the left along the waterfront is the Tempio Voltiano, a memorial to the physicist Alessandro Volta (1745–1827), who developed the 'voltaic pile', the precursor of the electric battery. The volt is named after him.

Via Plinio leads away from the lake to Piazza del Duomo. The **cathedral** (Santa Maria Maggiore), built entirely of marble, has a tripartite west front, adorned with vertical flights of 15th-century statues. It is late Gothic in conception, with the addition, on either side of the main portal, of Renaissance images of two famous natives of Como, Pliny the Elder (right) and Pliny the Younger (left). The statues are from the workshop of Tommaso and Jacopo Rodari (local sculptors from Lake Lugano), whose work is also seen in the carving around the two side doorways. Work on the cathedral ended with the completion of the dome in 1770 by Filippo Juvarra. In the interior is the Altar of St Abundius (fourth south chapel), a bishop of Como (1514). It is a masterpiece by Bernardino Luini, a native of Lake Maggiore and follower of Leonardo da Vinci.

Via Vittorio Emanuele leads south from the cathedral to the church of **San Fedele** with its five-sided apse The angular northeast doorway has remarkable bas-reliefs. The Como area in fact gives its name to a school of artists, the *maestri comacini* (Como masters), masons and stone-carvers of the early Middle Ages who organised themselves as an itinerant guild, working first around the lake and later spreading across all Lombardy. Their art is characterised by stylised representations, in low relief, of human forms, animals and interlaced foliage, often seeming to be of Eastern inspiration. The best examples in Como are at San Fedele (particularly in the choir) and the external choir windows of the **Basilica of St Abundius** (on Via Sant'Abbondio on the western outskirts).

On a bay on the east bank, beyond Torno, is the **Villa Pliniana** (1577), with a loggia on the lake. At the back of the loggia is the famous intermittent spring described by both the Elder and the Younger Pliny, and also studied by Leonardo da Vinci. The abundant flow of water increases and decreases in intensity at intervals throughout the day.

The western shore

Beyond Como to the west is **Cernobbio**, a pleasant resort with a small sloping waterfront where boats lie pulled up. To the left is the huge Villa d'Este hotel, with its floating swimming pool, which occupies a villa built in 1568 by a local cardinal. It was here, in 1816–17, that Caroline of Brunswick, Princess of Wales, lived in exile after her estrangement from the Prince Regent. She had the park landscaped in the English style and turned the villa into a house of pleasure.

From Sala Comacina, boats leave to Lake Como's only island, the **Isola Comacina**, a pretty wooded islet with a single restaurant (*see p. 57*). It was a place of alternate raid and refuge during the Middle Ages. In the 20th century it found peace when it was presented to the Accademia delle Belle Arti of Milan. Walking trails lead around it, passing the remains of several medieval churches.

View of the wooded Isola Comacina.

Boats also leave from Sala for the **Villa del Balbianello**, with some of the loveliest gardens on the lake (*open mid-March–mid-Nov daily except Mon and Wed 10–6*). They are a popular destination today because of their appearance in a spate of recent films including *Star Wars II*, *Casino Royale* and *Ocean's Twelve* (with George Clooney, whose own villa is nearby at Laglio). **Lenno** was the site of Pliny the Younger's villa 'Comedia': it was in the waters around Lenno that he famously claimed the fish to be so abundant that he could simply toss a line out of the window from his bed and catch something.

The shore between Lenno and Cadenabbia is known as the Tremezzina. At Tremezzo (Cadenabbia) is the prominent **Villa Carlotta** (*open April–Sept 9–6, March and Oct 9–5, 1–15 Nov 9–4.30*), built at the beginning of the 18th century though altered since. It has had a number of owners; its present name comes from Charlotte, Princess of Prussia, whose mother bought the villa in 1843 on the occasion of her daughter's marriage to the Crown Prince of Saxe-Meiningen. The opening scenes of Stendhal's *La Chartreuse de Parme* (1839) take place here; Stendhal was guest at the villa in 1818, at a time when it was the residence of Giovanni Battista Sommariva, a lawyer-turned-marquis who had been a supporter of Napoleon and had hoped for the vice presidency of the Italian Republic. He was turned down in favour of Francesco Melzi d'Eril, hence the local legend that the two men vied with each other to create the grandest lakeside villa (the Villa Melzi stands opposite at Bellagio; *see p. 53 above*). The interior of the villa preserves Neoclassical works including (in the main salon) Thorvaldsen's frieze of the *Triumphal Entry of Alexander into Babylon*, made for

Napoleon in 1811–12 and intended for the throne-room at the Quirinal (the plaster cast is still there). Also here are works by Canova and a copy of his famous *Cupid and Psyche* by his assistant Adamo Tadolini. In the gardens, two styles prevail: the formal Italian and the English Romantic. The formal gardens tumble down the front of the house, on either side of stepped terraces. The magnificent wooded park was laid out by Princess Charlotte. It has beautiful camellias, rhododendrons and azaleas in spring.

The upper lake

Varenna, on the lower eastern shore of the upper reach of the lake, is a delightful place, its port only accessible on foot, by narrow stepped streets. The spring of Fiumelatte, active from May to Oct, can be reached from the piazza by a pretty path (c. 1km south) via the cemetery. Like the spring at the Villa Pliniana (*see p. 54*), its flow is intermittent.

VISITING LAKE COMO

GETTING AROUND

• **By air:** Buses (no. C250) go from Milan Malpensa to Como (journey time c. 1hr).
• **By car:** There is plenty of pay parking in Como, and some spaces on the waterfront.
• **By bus:** There are bus services between all the main centres around the lake. Como to Bellagio takes c. 70mins; to Cernobbio c. 30mins; to Sala Comacina c. 50mins. See www.trasporti.regione.lombardia.it.
• **By train:** Como is reached by frequent train services from Milan. Fast trains depart from Stazione Centrale and the journey takes 45–60mins; slower trains depart from Porta Garibaldi station. Como has two train stations. San Giovanni serves the state railway with trains from Milan, Lecco, and on to Lugano. Como-Lago (on the lakeside; the most convenient station for visitors) serves trains from Milan via Saronno. The journey from Milan to Varenna takes 1hr 15mins; Milan to Colico takes 1hr 40mins. A railway line also skirts the eastern shore of the lake from Lecco to Colico.
• **By boat:** Boats and hydrofoils operate throughout the year between Como and Colico, calling at Bellaggio, Menaggio and Bellano on the way (www.navigazionelaghi.it). Tickets valid for 24hrs or several days can be purchased. The timetable changes according to season. Most of the boats run between Como and Bellano (boats in c. 2$^{1}/_{2}$ hrs, hydrofoils in c. 1hr), while most of the hydrofoils continue to Colico (Como to Colico in c. 90mins). There is a less frequent service between Bellagio and Lecco in summer (only on holidays for the rest of the year). In the central part of the lake a service runs between Bellano (or Varenna) and Lenno. A car ferry runs frequently between Bellagio and Varenna (in 15mins), Bellagio and Cadenabbia (in 10mins) and Cadenabbia and Varenna (in 30mins). Boats for Villa del Balbianello leave from Lenno and Como.

WHERE TO STAY ON LAKE COMO

As one would expect, the offering is vast and varied. In Bellagio, for example, visitors can choose between the €€€ **Grand Hotel Villa Serbelloni**, the luxurious winner of many plaudits, in a former Serbelloni family villa on the headland, with stunning views, a lakeside pool and excellent restaurant (*Via Roma 1, T: 031 950216, www.villaserbelloni.it; open April–Nov*) or the simple € **Silvio**, with basic, comfortable rooms and a fine restaurant, close to Villa Melzi, within walking distance of central Bellagio (*Via Carcano 12, T: 031 950322, www.bellagiosilvio.com; open Feb–Nov*). The most luxurious hotel of all is the renowned €€€€ **Villa d'Este** in Cernobbio (*see p. 54*), now one of the Leading Hotels of the World (*Via Regina 40, T: 031 3481, www.villadeste.it; open March–Nov*). Above Varenna is the €€ **Eremo Gaudio**, a simple place, plainly, even austerely furnished, with a huge terrace commanding magnificent views (*Via Roma 11, T: 0341 815301, www.eremogaudio.it*). In Como itself, the €–€€ **Albergo del Duca** is more than adequate as a base (*Piazza Mazzini 12, T: 031 264859, www.albergodelduca.it*).

WHERE TO EAT ON LAKE COMO

Bellagio

The best-known place is € **La Barchetta**, an old-established place (with rooms) with tradi-tional cuisine (*Salita Mella 13, T: 031 951389; closed Tues, Wed, dinner only mid-June–mid-Sept*). Also good is € **Bilacus** (*Salita Serbelloni 30/32, T: 031 950480; closed Mon and Nov–March*).

Cernobbio

€€ **Terzo Crotto**. Set back from the inland side of the main street, a vine-clad house with cool, lush gardens. Good food. Closed Mon in winter. *Via Volta 21 T: 031 512304.*

Como

Como has two acclaimed restaurants, but both are some way out: €€€ **Navedano** (*Via Pannilani-Velzi, T: 031 308080; closed Tues, Jan and Aug*) and €€ **Sant'Anna 1907** (*Via Turati 3, at Camerlata, a suburb to the southeast, T: 031 505266; closed Fri, midday Sat and all Sun*). For a simple, honest meal in town, there is € **Le Colonne**, attached to the Albergo del Duca hotel (*Piazza Mazzini 12, T: 031 266166*).

Isola Comacina

€€ **Locanda dell'Isola Comacina**. Simple set menu and a beautiful setting. *T: 0344 55083.*

BERGAMO

There is plenty of reason to linger for a while in Bergamo (*map p. 422, C2*). Its division into two parts dates from Roman times, when the city grew up on the hill with its suburbs on the plain below. The lower town now contains most of the hotels and shops. The Città Alta, the lovely old town, is connected to the lower town by funicular.

Two of the great feudal and feuding families of the Middle Ages enjoyed overlordship of Bergamo: the Visconti and the Malatesta. Their rule ended in 1428, when Venice took the town, and Bergamo remained a Venetian possession until the fall of the Serene Republic to Napoleon in 1797. From 1815–59 it was part of the Austrian empire. Its most famous citizens were Bartolomeo Colleoni (*see below*) and the composer Gaetano Donizetti.

The upper town

West of Bergamo's cathedral stands the church of Santa Maria Maggiore, against the south wall of which is the famous **Colleoni Chapel**, commissioned from Giovanni Antonio Amadeo in 1472 by the mercenary general Bartolomeo Colleoni as his funerary chapel. It is one of the most important High Renaissance works in Lombardy, and Amadeo's undisputed masterpiece.

The chapel stands on the site of the church sacristy, which was demolished to make way for it. It was even said that Colleoni supervised the demolition himself, defying the wishes of the church council and pushing his plans through willy-nilly. There is unlikely to be any truth in this: but nevertheless, the story of Colleoni obtruding himself onto perpetual public notice is a familiar one from the tale of his equestrian statue in Venice (*see p. 91*). The highly elaborate façade is decorated with coloured marbles arranged in a lozenge pattern. The rose window is flanked by busts of two great empire-builders, Julius Caesar and Trajan, and the reliefs on the lower level use the Labours of Hercules to allude to the physical prowess of Colleoni himself. The interior contains the tomb of Colleoni (d. 1476) and the tomb of his young daughter Medea (d. 1470), both by Giovanni Antonio Amadeo (though the gilt wood equestrian statue of Colleoni is a later addition of c. 1493). The tombs contrast rather strangely with the later decoration, which is Rococo in feel and includes ceiling frescoes by Tiepolo.

Right beside the Colleoni chapel is the extraordinary entrance porch to the church of **Santa Maria Maggiore**. It is the work of Giovanni da Campione (*see p. 48*) and dates from 1353. The south porch, less elaborate but with a similar exotic flavour, is also by Giovanni (1360), and above it is a narrow crocketed tabernacle with statues by Hans von Fernach (1401), who also worked on the duomo of Milan.

VISITING BERGAMO

GETTING AROUND

- **By air:** An airport bus runs from Bergamo airport to the railway station and back every 30mins. Journey time 10mins.
- **By car:** There are numerous paid parking spaces in the lower town.
- **City transport:** Bus no. 1 runs from the railway station through the centre of the lower town to the funicular station for the upper town (same ticket). The funicular runs from c. 7–midnight every 10–15mins.
- **By train:** Trains run from Milan Centrale or Porta Garibaldi in c. 1hr via Treviglio Ovest; or 1hr 15mins via Monza and Carnate-Usmate, where a change is usually necessary. Branch lines to Lecco in 40mins.

WHERE TO STAY IN BERGAMO

€€ **La Valletta Relais**. A lovely converted villa in the hills 1km northeast of the old town, ideal if you have your own transport. Good walks can be taken in the adjacent Parco dei Colli. Open Feb–Nov. *Via Castagneta 19, T: 035 242746, www.lavallettabergamo.it*

€–€€ **Alba Chiara**. B&B in the historic centre very close to the Colleoni Chapel. Large rooms and some even larger bathrooms. Charming and friendly. *Via Salvecchio 2, T: 035 231771, www.bbalbachiara.info.*

WHERE TO EAT IN BERGAMO

Haute cuisine is alive and well in Bergamo, and you can get it in two well-known establishments in the upper town: €€ **Taverna del Colleoni dell'Angelo**, on the lovely main square (*Piazza Vecchia 7, T: 035 232596; closed Mon and in Aug*), and €€ **L'Osteria di Via Solata**, a rather rustic-looking place, but don't be fooled: there is nothing simple about the menu (*closed Sun evening and Tues, and in Feb and Aug; Via Solata 8, T: 035 271993*). For good plain cooking try € **Al Donizetti**, also in the upper town (*Via Gombito 17/a, T: 035 242661; closed Dec–Jan*) or € **La Colombina**, where you can sample *polenta taragna* (with cheese) or the pasta dishes *foiade* and *casoncelli* (*Via Borgo Canale 12, T: 035 261402*).

MANTUA

Mantua (*map p. 422, D2*) sits on marshy ground on the banks of the River Mincio, which widens at this point to form an elongated lake. The city's fame dates partly from very early times (Virgil was born in this region c. 70 BC), and from the Middle Ages, particularly after 1328, when it became the seat of the Gonzaga dukes. The duchy owed its prosperity to agriculture and wool; the boggy land which we might view as an inconvenience today was a boon in the early Middle Ages, when this area and indeed the whole of Lombardy was criss-crossed with navigable waterways, making effective trading ports of many of the leading towns. The Gonzaga used their wealth in part to turn Mantua into a centre of art and learning. The greatest patrons were Lodovico II (1444–78), Francesco II (1484–1519) and his cultivated wife Isabella d'Este, and their son Federico II (1519–40).

The city was sacked by Spanish troops in 1630, and at the Treaty of Cherasco (*see p. 24*) Mantua was impelled to bow to Spanish authority. The duchy was finally extinguished in 1708 by the Austrians. Mantua joined the Kingdom of Italy in 1866.

Notable among the artists and architects who flourished under the Gonzaga are Pisanello, Leon Battista Alberti and Luca Fancelli. Andrea Mantegna was court artist from 1460 until his death in 1506. Giulio Romano, architect and painter, was called to Mantua in 1524 by Federico II, and worked there until his death in 1546, leaving numerous monuments in the city (most important of all is Palazzo Te; *see overleaf*).

Palazzo Ducale

Open Tues–Sun 8.30–7; last admission 6.20. Admission is usually by guided tour only, unless there is an exhibition in progress. Booking for exhibitions is optional, but since everyone must book to see the Camera degli Sposi, it makes sense to reserve; T: 041 241 1897.

The vast, rambling fortress-palace of the Gonzaga, on Piazza Sordello, is the product of many centuries and many architects. Since most of the great Gonzaga art collections have been dispersed (many paintings were bought by Charles I of England), the palace is now mainly interesting for its decorations, including the famous Camera degli Sposi and Giulio Romano's Cortile della Cavallerizza, where the columns are teased into outlandish corkscrew forms, an affectation which appears quite often in the paintings of Veronese (*see example on p. 125*). The Camera degli Sposi is in the part of the palace known as Castello di San Giorgio. It was decorated in 1465–74 for Lodovico II by his court painter Andrea Mantegna. On the north wall, above the fireplace, the marquis and his wife are shown surrounded by their family, courtiers and messengers. The vaulted ceiling has a *trompe l'oeil* oculus in the centre, a superb example of aerial perspective in painting, a technique that was not to be seen again until Correggio made it his special-

The basilica of Sant'Andrea at Mantua is the most complete architectural work by the great Renaissance theorist Leon Battista Alberti. Here we see the use of the giant order, rising through three storeys, which was later to become a feature of Michelangelo's architecture. The tripartite façade is also drawn from Classical models, being a sort of fusion in foreshortened dimension of a porticoed temple-front and a triple triumphal arch, with the entrance under the central barrel vault.

ity half a century later (*see p. 145*). The scene shows a balustrade, open to the sky, on which putti are playing; visible over the top of it are four women, a Saracen and a peacock.

The city centre

Opposite the Palazzo Ducale are two battlemented palaces of the Bonacolsi, the family who ruled Mantua before the Gonzaga. Above the first rises the **Torre della Gabbia**, from which an iron cage, the *gabbia*, protrudes (seen from Via Cavour). In this cage condemned prisoners were exposed, both to the elements and to the jeers and insults of the populace below. At the end of the piazza is the duomo, with an unattractive façade of 1756 and a light interior by Giulio Romano. It is eclipsed in fame and architectural importance by the **Basilica of Sant'Andrea**, flanking the charming market square, Piazza delle Erbe. This church was commissioned from Leon Battista Alberti by Lodovico II in 1470, to house the relic of the Holy Blood (an important symbol for Mantua, which appeared on its early coinage). Built by Luca Fancelli in 1472–94, after Alberti's death, then enlarged in 1530 under the direction of Giulio Romano, and with a dome added by Filippo Juvarra in 1732, Sant'Andrea is nevertheless wholly Alberti's in conception. The huge interior has a spacious barrel-vaulted nave without columns or aisles. The rectangular side chapels are also barrel vaulted. Mantegna lies buried here, his tomb adorned by a bronze bust. The Holy Blood is still housed here, in the crypt.

Palazzo Te

On the southern edge of the old town, about 1.5km from Piazza Sordello, is Palazzo Te (*open Mon 1–6, Tues–Sun 9–6, last entry 30mins before closing*). It was built in 1525, on the site of the family stables, by Federico Gonzaga, son of Isabella d'Este and the first duke of Mantua, as a summer villa. It is Giulio Romano's most famous work, and an important example of Mannerist architecture: inside the courtyard he subverts the rules of Classical architecture by designing sections of the entablature (every third triglyph) to look as though they are slipping out of place. The interior of the palace is famous for its painted decoration. The **Sala dei Cavalli** has frescoed portraits of horses from the Gonzaga stables. The Gonzaga were famous connoisseurs of horseflesh: Henry VIII of England, it is said, insisted on a Mantuan horse for ceremonial occasions. The **Sala dei Giganti**, in which painting and architecture are united in a theatrical *trompe l'oeil*, was designed by Giulio Romano and executed by his pupil Rinaldo Mantovano and others. It represents the *Fall of the Giants*, crushed by the thunderbolts of Jupiter hurled from Mount Olympus. Standing here and looking at these extraordinary scenes, it is difficult to believe that they sprang from the brain of a pupil of Raphael: just as Giulio plays with the canons of Classical architecture, so he here goes completely beyond the dignified bounds of Classical art. The debt he owes to Michelangelo (the Sistine ceiling had been unveiled in 1512) is clear. The notorious **Sala di Psiche** is covered with scenes from the story of Eros and Psyche, unabashedly erotic in content.

Detail from Giulio Romano's *Fall of the Giants* in Palazzo Te (1528).

VISITING MANTUA

GETTING AROUND

• **By bus:** APAM (www.apam.it) operates a handful of daily bus services from Mantua to Sabbioneta (c. 1hr) and to Sirmione on Lake Garda (c. 90mins). The bus station is close to Piazza Mondadori, just southwest of the railway station.

• **By train:** The railway station in Mantua is at Piazza Don Leoni, by the bank of the upper Mincio (Lago Superiore). The journey from/to Milan Centrale takes between 2 and 2¹/₂ hrs via Codogno, where a change is sometimes necessary; Verona is 35mins away; Modena 1hr 15mins.

WHERE TO STAY IN MANTUA

The venerable €€ **San Lorenzo**, across the street from the church from which it takes its name, is elegant and refined, with genuine antiques and a rooftop terrace with magnificent views over the city (*Piazza Concordia 14, T: 0376 220500*). €€ **Rechigi** is a medium-sized hotel in the town centre. Some of the rooms are quite large, all are furnished in a modern style (*Via Calvi 30, T: 0376 320781, www.rechigi.com*).

WHERE TO EAT IN MANTUA

Again, there are two clear places to recommend: €€ **Aquila Nigra**, a small but refined restaurant across the square from the Palazzo Ducale, offering good regional dishes (*Vicolo Bonacolsi 4, T: 0376 327180; closed Mon, Sun evening in April–May and Sept–Oct, all day Sun at other times, and Jan*) and €€ **Grifone Bianco**, which offers excellent Mantuan cuisine (especially first courses) and a pleasant atmosphere (*Piazza Erbe 6, T: 0376 365423; closed Tues, midday Wed, and in Feb and July*).

SABBIONETA

Sabbioneta, 34km southwest of Mantua (*map p. 423, D3*), was planned in 1556 by Vespasiano Gonzaga (1531–91), son of a *condottiere* from the cadet branch of the family, as an ideal fortified city. Lying within the compass of hexagonal walls, it contains some beautiful buildings, including two palaces, a gallery and a theatre, all of which reflect Vespasiano's admiration for Classical Rome. The **Teatro all'Antica**, for example, built by Palladio's pupil Vincenzo Scamozzi (who had just finished work on the great Teatro Olimpico in Vicenza; *see p. 123*), has an inscription on the exterior taken from the famous *Seven Books of Architecture* by Serlio: 'Her very ruins show how great was Rome'. The church of the **Incoronata** is the duke's burial place. His monument, adorned with rare marbles, incorporates his bronze statue by Leone Leoni. Once again Leoni seems to have been influenced by Michelangelo's sculptures in the Medici Chapel in Florence (*see pp. 34 and 185*). The simple little **Synagogue** was built in 1824, on the top floor of a house, on the site of a much older temple (a Jewish community is recorded here since 1436). Just to the east of Sabbioneta, at Borgofreddo, is a Jewish cemetery.

To visit the monuments you need to book a guided tour at the information office in Palazzo Giardino (*Piazza d'Armi 1; T: 0375 52039*).

TRENTINO-ALTO ADIGE

The territory of the upper Adige Valley and South Tyrol (*map p. 423*) is a semi-autonomous, multicultural region with a typical mountain climate of cold winters and cool summers. In many ways, this region has more in common with Austria and Germany than it does with Italy. Although the province of Trento (Trentino) is almost entirely Italian-speaking, in Bolzano (the Alto Adige) the language is German. The two provinces represent respectively the old ecclesiastical principalities of Trento and Brixen (Bressanone), both of which in the Middle Ages paid nominal allegiance to the Holy Roman Empire. In the 14th and 15th centuries, prince-bishops held the balance between the rising power of Venice to the south and the Counts of Tyrol to the north, and in the 16th century the valleys were practically independent. In 1545 Trento was chosen for the famous ecumenical congress known as the Council of Trent (*see overleaf*).

In the 17th and 18th centuries, here as elsewhere, local powers began to decay. During Napoleon's campaigns the region was transferred first to Austria, then (in 1803) to Bavaria, returning to Austria in 1814. Dissatisfaction with Austrian rule in the 19th century led to a movement for absorption into the Veneto. The collapse of the Austro-Hungarian empire after the First World War brought the Trentino under Italian control, and the frontier was extended northward to the strategic line of the Brenner Pass, the main channel of communication between Italy and Germany.

Trentino-Alto Adige, as it became, was a poor region until the later 20th century, when it underwent an economic boom. Nevertheless, it remains free of many of the

Detail of *June* from the Cycle of the Months (c. 1400) in the Castello del Buonconsiglio in Trento. In these far northern regions of Italy, the art is more Gothic and the architecture more central European (note the onion-domed church on the previous page).

problems that usually accompany burgeoning wealth. The population density is low. A third of the inhabitants live in villages or on farmsteads. Traditions are carefully kept alive, and each valley has its own distinct character.

Food and wine of Trentino-Alto Adige

The main ingredients of Trentine cooking are polenta and cheese. The most typical polenta is made from potatoes; dressed with cream and baked with lard and sausage, it is known as *smacafam*. Not every *malga* (chalet) had its own cheese these days, but interesting local varieties are still to be found: *spressa* is a low-fat cheese (the fat was traditionally skimmed off to make butter) typical of the Val Rendena west of Trento; the famous *puzzone di Moena* is from the Val di Fassa southeast of Bolzano (its memorable name, 'stinker', doesn't do it justice).

In Bolzano, Bressanone and the Dolomites a marked Germanic bias prevails: here you will find dumplings (*Knödel*; Italian *canederli*), *Gertensuppe* (barley soup), *Rindgulasch* (beef goulash), *Speck* (smoked and cured pork) and strudel.

The Alto Adige produces some exceptional wines. Among the reds are the full-bodied Lagrein Dunkel and Blauburgunder (Pinot Noir), and the lighter Vernatsch (Schiava). Among the whites, there is the aromatic Gewürztraminer, less pungent here than the famed wine of Alsace.

TRENTO

Trento (*map p. 423, D2*) is an appealing place, encircled by spectacular mountains and filled with fine palaces and churches. Its greatness dates back to the Middle Ages, when its bishops acquired the temporal power that they held almost without interruption until Napoleon's reorganisation of the region's affairs in 1802–03. The citizens were not always pleased with the rule of their prince-bishops, but conquest by Venice was a fate they feared more. Aided by the Count of Tyrol, the Tridentines won an important victory over the Venetians in 1487, and in 1511 Austria established a protectorate over the Trentino. In the 16th century the city rose to prominence under two great bishops: Bernardo Clesio and Cristoforo Madruzzo. It was during the episcopate of the latter that the famous Council of Trent met here (*see box below*). The last prince-bishop escaped from the French in 1796. In 1813 the Austrians took possession of the town, holding it until 1918. Despite this long heritage as part of the Habsburg empire, Trento has the feel of an Italian city, and is completely Italian-speaking.

THE COUNCIL OF TRENT

The 19th ecumenical council of the Roman Catholic Church (1545–63) was convoked under Holy Roman Emperor Charles V to redefine the spiritual and pastoral strategy of the Roman Catholic Church in the face of the rise of Protestantism. The results of its deliberations, through which the voice of the Counter-Reformation speaks, included a repudiation of Luther, Calvin and Zwingli and the establishment of the Nicene Creed as the basis of faith. The Catholic Church also defined its stance on Original Sin, Transubstantiation, purgatory, indulgences, the veneration of relics and the role of the saints. The Protestant question was not settled, but the Council's decrees formed a manual for Roman Catholicism that remained unchanged up to 1967.

Castello del Buonconsiglio

This great castle, once the stronghold of the prince-bishops of Trento, is the best and most famous monument in the town. It can be pleasantly reached from the central, monumental Piazza del Duomo by following Via Belenzani, which leads north out of the square. This is the city's most elegant street, and is flanked by Renaissance palaces showing a strong Venetian influence. The 16th-century Palazzo Geremia (no. 19) has exterior frescoes showing the Holy Roman Emperor Maximilian I, who stayed here in 1508–09.

At the end of the street, turn right into Via Manci and on to the end of Via San Marco. The Castello is in two parts. The crenellated Castelvecchio was built in the 13th century (altered in 1475). The Magno Palazzo to the south is a Renaissance edifice built in 1528–36 by Bishop Clesio, then imperial chancellor, who intended it to express the power his position had brought him. The castle museum is housed here (*open Tues–Sun: Jun–Oct 10–6, Nov–May 9.30–5*). The state apartments include a suite of magnificent rooms decorated by Dosso Dossi (1531–32), a great lover of allegorical and mythological scenes. His father was from Trento, but Dosso worked principally in

Ferrara, and it is to the Ferrarese school that his work is stylistically assigned (though his works also have a marked Venetian flavour to them, reminiscent in the best instances of Giorgione). On the second floor is the Sala Grande, where state ceremonies were held. The frieze, painted by Dosso Dossi and his brother Battista in 1532, incorporates Clesio's first name, 'Berenardt', and elements of the Clesio arms mixed with symbols of spiritual and temporal power. The private apartments include Clesio's bedchamber and large, luminous library. In the coffers of the original wood ceiling are depictions by Dosso Dossi of pagan and Christian sages, orators, poets and philosophers, reflecting the bishop's Humanist tastes.

The towers are the highlight of the visit. The **Torre del Falco** was decorated after 1530 by an anonymous German painter with a delightful series of hunting scenes (including falconry and angling). In the **Torre dell'Aquila** are the castle's most famous frescoes, commissioned from a Bohemian artist c. 1400. Known as the 'Cycle of the Months' (March, unfortunately, has been destroyed), they display the agricultural year in the South Tyrol in the most charming detail.

VISITING TRENTINO-ALTO ADIGE

GETTING AROUND

• **By train:** Trento is on the main line from Verona, Florence and Rome. Journey time from Verona to Trento is c. 1hr.

WHERE TO STAY IN TRENTINO-ALTO ADIGE

There is no shortage of places to stay in the region. The town centres are home to many venerable old inns, mostly completely renovated and restructured inside, attractively enough, although on the whole in a rather impersonal style. Right in the heart of Trento is the €€ **Aquila d'Oro** (*Via Belenzani 76, T: 0461 986282, www.aquiladoro.it; closed late Dec–early Jan*). Grand establishments on the outskirts of the towns include the €€ **Villa Madruzzo**, a fine hotel and restaurant in a

19th-century villa above Trento (*Località Ponte Alto 26, T: 0461 986220, www.villa-madruzzo.it*). East of Trento at Pergine Valsugana is the atmospheric € **Castel Pergine**, a medieval castle once owned by the prince-bishops. Breakfast is served in the throne room; candlelit dinner in the baronial hall (*Via al Castello 10, T: 0461 531158, http://195.186.62.252; open April–early Nov*).

WHERE TO EAT IN TRENTINO-ALTO ADIGE

A good traditional restaurant in Trento is €€ **Chiesa** (*Parco San Marco, T: 0461 238766; closed Sun, Wed evening and Aug*). €€ **Le Due Spade** was established in 1545 and has been in business ever since (*Via Don Rizzi 11, T: 0461 234343; closed Sun and midday Mon*).

THE VENETO

The Veneto (*map p. 423*) is a rich region, not only materially, but in terms of its artistic heritage. The city of Venice is its greatest draw. But here also are Verona, Vicenza and Padua, all of them towns warranting a full day or more of exploration; and Lake Garda, with its sublime scenery and its wine.

Venice has informed much of the history of the region. When her maritime expansion in the east was checked by the rising power of the Ottoman Turks, she turned her interests to the *terraferma*, and numerous cities chose to join the Serene Republic. By 1420 the whole territory, including Verona, Udine and Padua, was under the banner of St Mark. Further extensions to Bergamo in the west, Rimini in the south and Fiume in the east (now Rijeka, Croatia) provoked the jealousy of the powers beyond the Alps, and the League of Cambrai (1508) put an end to Venice's ambitions. But the Venetian holdings in Italy remained united for 300 years.

The Napoleonic invasion saw the dismemberment of the Veneto. After the Treaty of Campo Formio in 1797 Venice and the area east of the Adige was ceded to Austria in return for parts of the Low Countries. Austria also took control of areas in the west after the Congress of Vienna. She lost many of those in bloody battles against the united armies of Napoleon III and Vittorio Emanuele II. When Austria was defeated by Prussia in 1866, the Veneto voted to join the Kingdom of Italy.

The Veneto today is the centre of the 'Miracle of the Northeast'. It is one of the wealthiest regions of the country, productive and industrialised and yet still relatively unspoilt.

Geography of the Veneto

Well over half the territory of the Veneto is flat, but though the land is fertile, it is often waterlogged and thus unsuitable for agriculture. The Venetian lowlands require continuous maintenance and occasional reclamation from flooding. Even more delicate is the system of lagoons that line the coast, whose low, sandy beaches extend for almost 200km. The most important of these is the lagoon of Venice, whose waters now threaten to submerge the great city; the severe floods of 2008 were the latest reminder of the catastrophe that threatens. North of Venice, the Alpine foothills reach northward from Venice to Lake Garda and the Venetian Dolomites.

A salient characteristic of the Veneto is what Italians call the *città diffusa*. This term describes urbanised countryside—not exactly urban sprawl, which implies a sort of ripple effect around a central point—but continuous linear development along the main transport routes. This particular aspect of the landscape will have quite a bearing on your progress if you plan to drive through the region. Due to intense local traffic, travel times may be longer than you expect, particularly in fog or rain.

Food and wine of the Veneto

In the area around Venice rice is a basic ingredient of the cuisine. Classic specialities are *risi e bisi* (risotto with peas) and *risotto nero* (coloured and flavoured with the ink of cuttlefish). Thick soups are also popular. The best of these is *pasta e fasioi* (pasta and beans), which is eaten lukewarm.

Fish and seafood form the basis of Venice's best main courses. Local specialities include *granseola* (lagoon crabs), *sarde in saor* (marinated sardines) and *seppioline nere* (cuttlefish cooked in their own ink). An outstanding seafood dish is the *brodetto di pesce*—rigorously *in bianco* (without tomatoes), which testifies to its origins in an age before the discovery of America. Polenta is another staple, often served with the famous *fegato alla veneziana* (calves' liver and onions). *Tiramisù* is the favourite dessert, though you'll also find rich cakes and pastries of Austrian inspiration.

In Vicenza you'll find a wide range of *risotti*—with pumpkin, asparagus, hops and quail. Nevertheless, the best-known of local specialities is *baccalà alla vicentina* (salt cod stewed with milk and onions and served with grilled polenta). Snails (*bovoloni*, *bovoletti* or *bogoni*) are also popular, and a leading role is played by the famous radicchio from Treviso, which is eaten in salads, grilled, fried or in risotto.

Veronese specialities include *zuppa scaligera*, a rich dish made with chicken, pigeon and white wine, and *gnocchi* topped with the famous *pastizzada de caval* (horsemeat ragout). The most delectable sweet is the great fluffy cake known as *pandoro*.

The Veneto makes some good wines. From Lake Garda comes Bardolino. Soave makes an excellent dry white, while the Valpolicella region makes a well-known red. In the hills between Venice and Vicenza lies the Valdobbiadene, home of sparkling white *prosecco*. A favourite drink is Aperol spritz: *prosecco* and a dash of soda water mixed with a light, orange-based aperitif.

ART & ARCHITECTURE OF THE VENETO

Of all the arts of Venice, painting is the one for which she is most renowned. By the mid-15th century, the Bellini family (Jacopo and his sons, Gentile and Giovanni) were capturing the luminous atmosphere of the city in their beautifully rendered altarpieces. In fact Giovanni Bellini (c. 1433–1516) is the artist who may be credited with launching the Venetian Renaissance. A highly original painter, he also learned much from others, including his brother-in-law Mantegna and Antonello da Messina (*see p. 371*). Acknowledged as the greatest Venetian master during his own lifetime, and appointed official painter to the Republic, he launched many younger artists on their careers, including Giorgione and Titian. Later artists of profound importance are Paolo Veronese, who mixed illusionistic perspectives with sacred and profane themes, and Tintoretto, who worked quickly and impressionistically, sharply focusing his dramatic light effects, and left hundreds of paintings in his native city. The era of the great Venetian painters closes in the age of the Grand Tour, when the *vedutisti* such as Canaletto painted lyrical images of the city which capture most poetically its unique atmosphere.

After Venice, the richest artistic centre in northeast Italy is Verona, most famous of whose artists are the early masters Stefano da Zevio (Stefano da Verona) and the medallist and painter Pisanello.

The frescoes in the Scrovegni Chapel in Padua by the great Florentine artist Giotto gave rise to a flourishing local school of 'Giottesque' painters (including Guariento and Giusto de' Menabuoi). The Verona-born Altichiero, active in Padua in the 1380s, was one of the most creative interpreters of Giotto's achievements before Masaccio, filling the gap between the two. The Renaissance came to Padua with the arrival of another Florentine, Donatello, in 1443, to work on his equestrian statue of the mercenary general Gattamelata and on the high altar of the Santo. He was to have a profound influence on Andrea Mantegna (1431–1506).

The architecture of the Veneto is varied, in its earlier manifestations owing much to Byzantium and the East (the shape of the domes and archways and the chromatic interest of the façades), thanks to Venice's links with Constantinople. The greatest name of all, however, is Andrea Palladio. The villas, palaces and churches that he designed throughout the Veneto would add a new aesthetic to the region and inspire a host of imitations. For Palladio everything was about proportion, harmony among the different elements, careful siting, and homage to the forms of Classical antiquity.

VENICE

It was fugitives from the barbarian invaders swarming across northern Italy in the mid-5th century who first settled in the reedy islets in this area between the rivers Brenta and Piave. Their numbers were swelled during the Lombard invasion in 568–69, and by the 9th century a centre of habitation and commerce was firmly established in the area around today's Rialto. This growing though still fragmented city was ruled first by *tribuni* nominated by the Byzantine governor of Ravenna. To strengthen the western edge of the Byzantine empire, Emperor Leo III united the islands under a single ruler, the doge. With little or no land to cultivate, the Venetians had to turn to the sea for their livelihoods and they cultivated their skills as sailors, boat-builders and merchants. Venetian ships brought back a wealth of luxury goods: ivory, silk, gold and most precious of all, spices. Hand in hand with this mercantile success came a lucrative banking insurance industry. With their trading links radiating out across the Mediterranean and far into the East, the Venetians became great political strategists, regularly shifting alliances with governments to improve their trading position.

But Venice's heyday wasn't to last. By the 16th century, with Turkish expansion, the strengthening of other European powers and the discovery of alternative trading routes, Venice had begun a slow and steady decline. In 1797 Napoleon conquered the city and dissolved the Republic. In 1866, after half a century of Austrian rule, Venice joined the Kingdom of Italy.

Topography of Venice

Venice is divided into six districts called *sestieri*: San Marco, Dorsoduro, Castello, San Polo, Santa Croce and Cannaregio. Each has its own particular character and atmosphere. Highlights of the *sestieri* are given below, as well as a general description of the Grand Canal, one of the best single sights in all Venice.

THE GRAND CANAL

The Grand Canal, just over three kilometres in length, six metres deep and between 40–130m wide, has been the city's main thoroughfare since the earliest days of the Republic. It follows the course of the ancient river bed of the Brenta, and trading vessels laden with exotic produce would have sailed up it to the markets of the Rialto and to the warehouses of the wealthy merchants who lived along it. Travelling the length of the canal today, watching the procession of buildings glide by, is an excellent way to get to know the city and is a fascinating journey through its architectural history. Vaporetto no. 1 stops at every landing stage. The slightly faster 82 makes fewer stops.

Palaces on the Grand Canal

The Grand Canal was once the most sought-after address in Venice, and it is lined with magnificent dwellings, mostly dating from the 14th–18th centuries. A *palazzo* on the canal was not only a family home, it was also a place of business. The ground floor, with a water gate on the canal, would be used as storerooms and offices; the *piano nobile* (first floor) was used to entertain visitors and would be lavishly decorated. The upper parts of the *palazzo* were used by the family, while the servants lived in the attic rooms. A famous example of such a *palazzo* is the **Ca' Dario** (*map p. 72, 14*), built in 1487, its façade inlaid with marble and porphyry. The most celebrated of all is the **Ca' d'Oro**, the so-called 'Golden House' (*map p. 72, 6*), built in 1420–34, an outstanding example of the Venetian Gothic. The lustrous gold leaf which gave the house its name has long since worn away, but that does not diminish its beauty. Its façade, with delicately carved ogee windows, open loggias, oriental pinnacles and coloured marble inlay, has a truly exotic appearance.

Bridges across the Grand Canal

The bridges that span the Grand Canal are just four in number. People wishing to cross where there is no bridge must use the *traghetti*, gondola ferries that ply back and forth for a token fee of a euro or two. The most famous of the bridges is the **Rialto Bridge** (*map p. 72, 6*), built in 1588–91 to a design by Antonio da Ponte, who beat off competition from many more famous names in an open tender. It is remarkable for its single span, which stretches 48m and was high enough (7.5m) to allow galleys laden with merchandise to pass underneath. It is lined on both sides with shops, mainly selling jewellery and leather goods at a premium. This area has always been

The Fondaco dei Turchi on the Grand Canal. The Eastern character of medieval Venetian architecture contributes to what W.D. Howells called the city's 'peerless strangeness'.

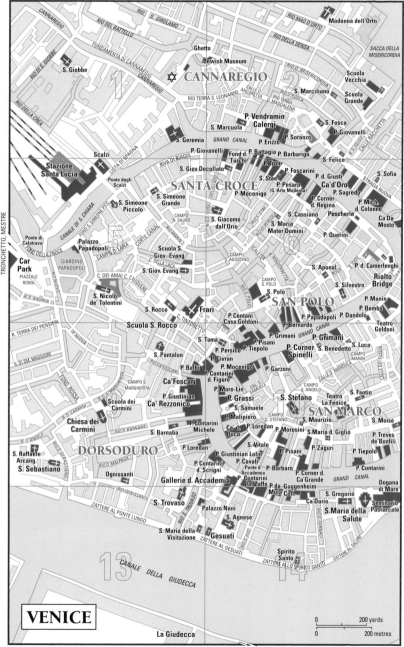

CANNAREGIO
RIO DEL BATTELLO
RIO S. GIROLAMO
RIO MAD D'ORTO
Madonna dell'Orto
RIO DELLA SENSA
FONDAMENTA DI CANNAREGIO
SACCA DELLA MISERICORDIA
Ghetto
RIO DI S. GIOBBE
Jewish Museum
S. Giobbe
CANNAREGIO
RIO D'MISERICORDIA
Scuola Vecchia
CALLE D. ANCORETTA
RIO TERRA S. LEONARDO
RIO TERRA S. MADDALENA
RIO S'FOSCA
S. Marciliano
Scuola Grande
RIO DELLA CREA
S. Marcuola
P. Vendramin Calergi
S. Fosca
P. Soranzo
S. Giovanelli
RIO S. FELICE
CALLE RACCHETTA
S. Geremia
GRAND CANAL
P. Erizzo
P. Giovanelli
Fond d. Turchi
P. Battagia
P. Barbarigo
S. Felice
Scalzi
LISTA DI SPAGNA
RIVA DI BIAGIO
P. Giovanelli
P. Tron
S. Giov Decollato
S. Foscarini
Stazione Santa Lucia
Ponte degli Scalzi
SANTA CROCE
S. Stae
P. Pesaro (G. Arte Moderna)
P. d. Giusti
S. Sofia
STRADA NUOVA
CANALE DI S. CHIARA
FOND. S. SIMEONE PIC.
S. Simeone Piccolo
S. Simeone Grande
CAMPO N. SAURO
P. Mocenigo
Ca'd'Oro
P. Sagredo
S. Mich. d. Colonne
Ponte di Calatrava
FOND. DELLA CROCE
Palazzo Papadopoli
CORTE CANAL
RIO MARIN
S. Giacomo dall'Orio
S. Maria Mater Domini
P. Corner d. Regina
Pescheria
Ca'Da Mosto
Car Park
PIAZZALE ROMA
GIARDINO PAPADOPOLI
CAMPO D. LANA
Scuola S. Giov. Evang.
C. DELLA LACA
CAMPO S. AGOSTINO
S. Cassiano
RIO NUOVO
C. DEI AMAI C. CHIOVERE
S. Giov. Evang.
RIO DI S. STAE
S. Aponal
P. Querini
P. d. Camerlenghi
R'S. ANDREA
S. Nicolo de' Tolentini
RIO MARIN
CAMPO S. POLO
RUGA
Rialto Bridge
R. TERRA DEI PENSIERI
C. TINTORETTO
S. Rocco
Frari
P. Centani Casa Goldoni
S. Polo
SAN POLO
S. Silvestro
P. Manin
P. Bembo
RIO NUOVA
Scuola S. Rocco
P. Bernardo
P. Papadopoli
P. Dandolo
Teatro Goldoni
R. DI SM. MAGGIORE
S. Toma
P'Grimani
GRAND CANAL
P. Grimani
P. Pisani
RIO TOSCANA
S. Pantalon
P. Tiepolo
P. Corner Spinelli
S. Benedetto
S. Luca
FOND. ROSSA
RIO S. PANTALON
P. Persico
P. Givran
P. Balbi
P. Mocenigo
CAMPO MANIN
CALLE DEI FUSERI
CAMPO S. MARGHERITA
Ca'Foscari
P. Contarini d. Figure
P. Garzoni
Scuola dei Carmini
Ca' Rezzonico
P. Giustinian
P. Moro-Lin
SAL S. SAMUELE
CAMPO S. ANGELO
Teatro La Fenice
S. Fantin
R. D. CARMINI
P. Grassi
S. Stefano
SAN MARCO
Chiesa dei Carmini
RIO S. BARNABA
S. Malipiero
S. Samuele
CAMPO S. STEFANO
S. Maurizio
S. Moise
R. D'ANGELO
RIO S. SEBASTIANO
DORSODURO
S. Barnaba
Ca'd. Duca
P. Loredan
P. Morosini
S. Maria d. Giglio
P. Treves de'Bonfili
S. Raffaele Arcang.
RIO D. MALPAGA
P. Loredan
S. Vitale
P. Pisani
P. Zaguri
P. Tiepolo
S. Sebastiano
Ognissanti
P. Contarini d. Scrigni
P. Cavali
P. Barbaro
P. Corner d. Ca'Grande
P. Contarini
RIO OGNISSANTI
Gallerie d. Accademia
P. Giustinian Lolin
Ponte di Accademia
P. Contarini dal Zaffo
P. da. Guggenheim
GRAND CANAL
Dogana di Mare
S. Trovaso
RIO D. S. TROVASO
Palazzo Nani
Mula Coll
Ca'Dario
S. Gregorio
S. Maria della Salute
Seminario Patriarcale
ZATTERE AL PONTE LUNGO
S. Agnese
RIO D. FORNACI
ZATTERE AL SALUTI
S. Maria della Visitazione
Gesuati
ZATTERE AL GESUATI
Spirito Santo
ZATTERE ALLO SPIRITO SANTO
CANALE DELLA GIUDECCA
VENICE
La Giudecca
REDENTORE
TRONCHETTO, MESTRE

0   200 yards
0   200 metres

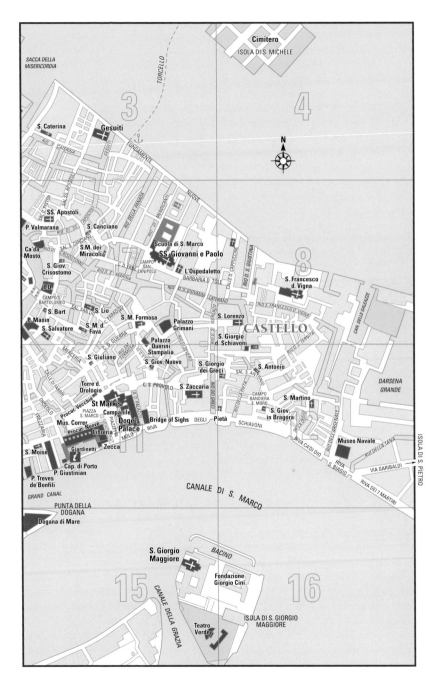

the commercial heart of the city and remains so today, though the commerce largely revolves around tourism. More rewarding in the Rialto area is the **Pescheria**, the fish market. The best time to visit this is very first thing in the morning. It is a wonderfully lively place and the array of fish and other wares on sale are a work of art in themselves. Bright red awnings protect the merchandise from the sun; be sure to look at the carvings of the capitals, decorated with fish, shellfish and an octopus.

The wooden Ponte dell'Accademia dates from the 1930s. The newest bridge over the canal (opened 2008) is the controversial **Ponte di Calatrava** (*map p. 72, 5*), a sleek construction in glass, steel and Istrian stone named after its designer, the Spanish architect Santiago Calatrava. When it first opened there were reports of people falling and suffering from twisted ankles because of the irregularly spaced steps and the somewhat disorientating effect of the sectioned stone and glass flooring. Others have hailed it as a striking and welcome addition to the Venetian skyline.

Warehouses along the Grand Canal

Just beyond the Rialto Bridge is the huge **Fondaco dei Tedeschi**, now Venice's main post office (*map p. 73, 7; marked P.O.*) but once the most important of the trading houses on the canal. It was used by merchants mainly from Germany and central Europe (hence its name; *tedesco* means German). On the higher reaches of the canal is another warehouse, the Veneto-Byzantine **Fondaco dei Turchi** (*map p. 72, 2–6*). Dating from the 13th century, it was originally a home of the Pesaro family, and is in fact a perfect example of a two-storey Venetian *palazzo*, with the ground floor opening directly onto the canal and used as warehousing, and the living quarters above, built around a central courtyard. In the 17th century it became the headquarters of Turkish merchants and was extensively remodelled to accommodate a bath house and mosque. Today it is a natural history museum, with a collection concentrating on the flora and fauna of the lagoon. Next to it is the rather grim-looking crenellated **Deposito del Megio**, the city's grain store, with a 15th-century façade. The Republic owned several such granaries around the city, built to ensure that the population could always be supplied with food at a reasonable price. The largest were near San Marco (and were knocked down by Napoleon to be replaced by the gardens just behind the San Marco landing stage).

THE SESTIERE OF SAN MARCO

San Marco is the most crowded and touristic of the *sestieri*—not surprisingly, because it contains the most famous landmarks in all Venice: St Mark's Square, the Basilica of St Mark, and the Doge's Palace. For centuries **St Mark's Square** (Piazza San Marco; *map p. 73, 11*) was the political, judicial and social heart of Venice, as much a symbol of the city as the winged lion of St Mark. Almost every adjective and superlative has been used to describe it, but one thing is seldom mentioned—you won't be alone. Every day, thousands of people converge on this space to admire the architecture, to queue to enter the basilica, to see the Moors on top of the Torre dell'Orologio strike the hour, to browse the shops in the arcades of the Procuratie Vecchie and Procuratie Nuove and sit in the cafés or simply to perch like the pigeons on the duckboards stacked up in readiness for *acqua alta*. Don't let this detract too much from your enjoyment, but do be prepared to share the Piazza with people from all over the world.

That is, after all, the way it was meant to be. Towards the end of the 12th century Doge Sebastiano Ziani decided to enlarge the space outside the basilica by having the Rio Batario filled in (the canal still runs beneath the paving) and the church of San Gemignano, which stood opposite the basilica, moved further west (it was ultimately demolished altogether by Napoleon). The size of the Piazza was doubled and this was the stage on which all the grand processions, spectacles and public ceremonies that were such an integral part of Venetian life were played out. They were as much for the benefit of native Venetians as they were to welcome and impress visiting dignitaries, as they reaffirmed the Venetians' feelings of pride and self-importance.

On the left side of the square as you face the basilica are the **Procuratie Vecchie**, the first of the two wings built to provide accommodation and offices for the Procurators of St Mark's, the only officials of the Republic (apart from the doge) who were elected for life, and who were in charge of the administration and upkeep of the basilica. Building began some time after 1512, and the top storey was added by Jacopo Sansovino in 1532. Under the arcades is one of the square's most famous institutions, the elegant **Caffè Quadri**. It opened in 1775, 55 years after its rival across the square, Florian's (*see below*), and was the favoured haunt of the Austrians during their occupation of the city.

At the farthest end of the Procuratie Vecchie stands the beautiful Renaissance **Torre dell'Orologio** (1496), designed by Mauro Codussi (an architect best known for his distinctive church façades). It stands at the entrance to the Mercería, the main thoroughfare towards the Rialto. The clock shows not only the time but also the phases of the sun and moon and the signs of the zodiac, all beautifully picked out in gold. Above the clock face is a niche with a statue of the Madonna. Originally figures of the Magi and a trumpeting angel would emerge on the hour from the doors on either side and glide in front of the Virgin and bow before her, but in 1858 they were removed and the mechanism modified to make it easier to read the time (at night the numerals are lit from behind). During Ascension Week, though, the figures are returned. At the top of the tower two Moors strike the hours on the huge bell.

The **Procuratie Nuove**, on the south side of the square, were also used as apartments for the procurators. Planned by Sansovino, work was started by Palladio's pupil Vincenzo Scamozzi between 1582 and 1586, and continued by Baldassare Longhena (1640). Under the arcades, **Florian's** café exudes the same old-world charm as its rival. This was the meeting place of Italian patriots during the Austrian occupation, and during the confrontation between the two sides in the Piazza in 1848, wounded Italians were carried here to safety. Both cafés have been a stop-off point for writers, artists, musicians and Grand Tourists over the centuries. Whichever café you favour, you can enjoy a coffee or *prosecco* sitting in the square, listening to their orchestras as you watch the world go by; it won't be cheap, and the service might be offhand, but it is as much a part of visiting the city as a visit to any museum or gallery.

The west end of the Piazza, facing the basilica, is closed by the **Ala Napoleonica**, built on the orders of Napoleon to create a wing of grand reception rooms and a ballroom. The façade of the two lower floors reflects the pattern of the Procuratie Nuove; above is a decorative frieze and a row of statues of Roman emperors. The gap in the middle was intended for a statue of Napoleon which was never erected. Napoleon's grand double staircase now leads up to the Museo Correr (*see p. 83*).

The Piazzetta

The two pink and grey granite columns framing the waterfront were brought from Constantinople in the 12th century. It is still considered bad luck to walk between them for it is there that executions once took place. On the top of one column is the lion of St Mark. On the other is a statue of St Theodore, the original patron saint of Venice.

The west side of the Piazzetta is flanked by the graceful Istrian stone façade of the Libreria Marciana, the library of St Mark's, also known as the Libreria Sansoviniana after its architect, Jacopo Sansovino. It was greatly admired by Andrea Palladio as the most beautiful and richest building since Antiquity. Sansovino, a Tuscan by origin, came to Venice from Rome after the Imperial troops sacked the city (*see p. 238*), and in so doing introduced a classical style of architecture as yet unseen here. Work began in 1537 at the corner nearest the Campanile. In 1545 disaster struck and part of the building fell down, for which Sansovino was thrown into prison. Two years later and with the help of influential friends he was back at work, and paid for the reconstruction himself. After his death, the work was completed by Vincenzo Scamozzi.

The red brick **Campanile** (*open daily 9 or 9.30–dusk*), nearly 100m tall, is one of the first landmarks of Venice to be seen from the sea. There has been a tower (probably a lighthouse) on this site since the 9th century but the Campanile as we see it today follows a design of 1511–14 by Bartolomeo Bon. Galileo demonstrated his telescope from the top in 1609. In 1902, with very little warning, the tower collapsed completely. No one was injured and it was rebuilt exactly as it had been.

Basilica of St Mark

Map p. 73, 11; Vaporetto 1 to Vallaresso; 1, 51, 52 to San Zaccaria. Entry is free but fees are payable to see the Pala d'Oro, museum and Treasury. Basilica, Pala d'Oro and Treasury open 9.45–4 or 5, Sun and holidays 2–4 or 5; museum 9.45–4.45.

Visits follow a designated route and the sheer number of people can be overwhelming. If you prefer simply to sit in silent contemplation of the very special atmosphere of this holy place, it is useful to know that the north transept is often set aside for prayer. A memorable way to see the basilica is to visit it for the reason it was intended: worship. Services of 30mins are frequently held at 9am, entrance by the north door (details on the board outside).

One of the paws of the winged lion of St Mark is always shown resting on a book. Normally the book is shown open (in times of war, the book was closed, and the lion held a sword), and on its pages can be read the following Latin legend: 'Pax tibi Marce, evangelista meus'. These, according to tradition, were the words spoken by an angel to St Mark in a dream. The saint had been on his way to Rome when he was blown ashore on one of the Venetian islands. An angel appeared to him and told him that Venice would be his final resting place. In 828 the angelic prediction came true, when two Venetian sailors stole the relics of St Mark from Alexandria and smuggled them home. St Mark immediately became the principal patron of the city, and a new basilica was begun in his honour.

The design of the church was based on the Church of the Twelve Apostles in Constantinople (destroyed in the 15th century). Throughout the ages it has been adorned and embellished by the doges, particularly after Venice's conquest of Constantinople in the Fourth Crusade of 1204, when many treasures were brought back as booty. The basilica became the cathedral of Venice in 1807. Before that it had been the doge's private chapel, with its own entrance from the palace.

The façade of St Mark's

Impatience to see the lovely interior coupled with reluctance to lose one's place in the queue leads most people to overlook the exterior of the building. This is a pity, for it is magnificent and rewards close study. Five doors lead into the basilica, each topped by mosaics. The one on the far left, above the **Porta di Sant'Alipio**, is the only original mosaic (1260–70) to survive and shows with typical Byzantine austerity the *Translation of the Body of St Mark to the Basilica*. What makes this particularly fascinating is that it is the earliest depiction of the basilica as it was in the 13th century, with the four horses (*see below*) already installed on the loggia The central door (used as the main entrance) is richly decorated with Romanesque carvings, some of the best in Italy. They represent traditional themes (prophets, the Months and Virtues) and, more interestingly, on the underside of the outer arch, the trades of Venice such as fishing and boat-building. Notice the figure of a man on crutches at the bottom of the frieze on the left. Apocryphal legend says this is the unknown architect of the basilica, lame because such genius comes at a price.

The interior of St Mark's

Inside the basilica, allow your eyes to adjust to the subdued light, and gradually the scale of the building and the exquisite softly glimmering gold decoration on the upper walls and vaults will emerge—a rich combination of Eastern and Western influences.

(1) Dome of Pentecost: The decoration is from the 12th century and represents the descent of the Holy Spirit at Pentecost. Red tongues of flame are clearly visible on the heads of the Apostles.

(2) South transept: On the right-hand wall is a mosaic depicting the miraculous rediscovery of the body of St Mark, dating from the same period as that of the Porta di Sant'Alipio.

(3) Treasury: This is the basilica's storehouse of gold and silverware of the highest quality, much of it plundered from Constantinople during the Fourth Crusade (1204). The incense burner in the shape of a Byzantine five-domed church is a remarkable piece of craftsmanship dating from the 12th–13th centuries. The icon of the archangel Michael, his robe encrusted with jewels and enamelwork, is a beautiful example of 11th-century goldsmith's art.

(4) Dome of the Ascension: The central dome over the crossing depicts the Ascension. Made by Venetian masters in the 13th century, it nonetheless shows strong Byzantine influence.

(5) Sanctuary: The dome (12th century) shows the prophets. Christ Pantocrator is represented in the apse. The relics of St Mark lie in the high altar, above which rises a magnificent baldacchino, richly carved with scenes from the lives of Christ and the Virgin.

One of the basilica's greatest treasures is the **Pala d'Oro**, behind the high altar. Commissioned in 975, it was made in Constantinople for Doge Pietro Orseolo, with further decoration added in 1105, 1209 and 1342. This astonishing altarpiece, encrusted with gems, is a piece of outstanding craftsmanship. The Virgin, Christ Pantocrator, the Archangel Michael, saints, the Empress Irene and Emperor John Comnenus are all depicted in exquisite cloisonné enamel.

(6) Madonna Nicopoea: In a chapel in the north transept, is the precious icon of the Virgin as bringer of victory, stolen from Constantinople in 1204, part of the considerable haul taken after the

BASILICA OF ST MARK

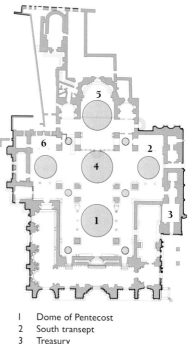

1   Dome of Pentecost
2   South transept
3   Treasury
4   Dome of the Ascension
5   Sanctuary and Pala d'Oro
6   Madonna Nicopoea

Fourth Crusade, when Venice subdued Constantinople and increased her holdings in the Mediterranean as a result. It was thought to have been carried into battle by the emperor.

Museo di San Marco

The museum is reached from a staircase in the narthex, to the right of the main entrance. Its chief exhibit is the magnificent quartet of gilded copper horses, which once stood on the loggia on the façade. It is thought that these proud beasts were made in the 2nd century AD, perhaps commissioned by the emperor Septimius Severus, who was known to mark his conquests with triumphal arches crowned by *quadrigae* (Roman chariots pulled by four horses). They were brought to Venice as plunder from the Fourth Crusade. Only slightly larger than life, they are beautifully cast, each in a slightly different pose but all alert and powerful. Muscles, sinews and veins are all accurately executed, as is part of their tack.

Always a potent symbol of Venetian supremacy, their removal to Paris by Napoleon in 1797 must have been a bitter sight for Venetians to witness; they were returned by the Austrians in 1815 after the Battle of Waterloo.

From the museum you can go out onto the loggia to see the replica horses which stand there now. You will also get a grandstand view of the Piazza.

The Doge's Palace

Map p. 73, 11. Open Easter–31 Oct 9–6 (last admission); 1 Nov–Easter 9–4 (last admission). The palace is usually very crowded; there is much to be said for waiting until the end of the day and entering at the last admission.

The Doge's Palace was not just the residence of the leader of the Most Supreme Republic of Venice; it was also the engine-room of its government and the palace of justice. It came to be the symbol of Venice's power, wealth and dominion.

The entire history of the building is one of fires, reconstructions, expansion and remodelling. The Gothic exterior façade you see today dates from 1340–1422. The courtyard façade was begun in 1483. Many of the finest paintings and decorations of the interior date from after the two fires of the 1570s.

The palace is made up of three wings arranged around an inner courtyard. The meeting room of the Grand Council overlooked the waterfront, the offices of the judiciary

The famous four horses in gilded copper, perhaps made for Septimius Severus (2nd century AD).

and legislature overlooked the Piazzetta and the doge's private apartments overlooked the Rio di Palazzo, the canal that is spanned by the Bridge of Sighs.

The matchless Gothic façades overlooking the Piazzetta and waterfront, of pastel pink and white Verona marble, are light and delicate—the very essence of the Venetian Gothic style. The scheme of trefoil ogee arches of the colonnade supporting quatrefoil roundels gives the façades a sense of movement and fluidity. The capitals of the colonnade facing the Piazzetta are beautifully decorated with medieval carvings (some are 19th-century replacements) of the Virtues, signs of the zodiac, trades and crafts and sacred subjects—*Adam and Eve* on the corner and the *Judgement of Solomon* beside the Porta della Carta next to the basilica are particularly fine examples. The Porta della Carta (1438–43) is a magnificent gateway opening onto the Piazzetta. It was designed by Bartolomeo Bon and his workshop, which produced so much work in the city. Above the door Doge Francesco Foscari kneels before the winged lion of St Mark. Both sculptures are reproductions; the originals were destroyed by Napeoleon's men in 1797.

Interior of the Doge's Palace

Beyond a series of rooms displaying original sculpture from the exterior, you enter the magnificent **courtyard**, its façades a lace-work of loggias and windows. The broad staircase at the far end, the Scala dei Giganti, was designed as a backdrop for the coronation of the doge. The *giganti*, Neptune and Mars, designed by Jacopo Sansovino, represent the Republic's domain over land and sea. You reach the **Doge's Apartments** on the first floor (*primo piano nobile*) by the Scala d'Oro (1558–59), designed by Jacopo Sansovino and enriched with gilded decoration by one of Venice's greatest sculptors, Alessandro Vittoria. The **state rooms** on the second floor are more impressive still, spacious chambers for the various councils, each more imposing than the next, with ranks of wooden seats and rostra, and heavy ceilings filled with paintings, many of them mythological allegories celebrating the power and dominion of the Venetian state, which is the function that Venetian secular art chiefly fulfilled. There are information boards in each room. The numbering given here is the same as that currently *in situ* (*see plan overleaf*).

State rooms on the second floor

(16) Sala delle Quattro Porte: This room, designed by Palladio, was where visiting dignitaries would wait for an audience with the Republic's officials or with the doge. The fresco in the centre of the ceiling, by Tintoretto, shows Venice receiving territories on the Adriatic from Jupiter. Titian's *Doge Antonio Grimani Kneeling Before the Faith* is on the long entrance wall. It was completed after Titian's death by his nephew Marco.

(17) Anticollegio: Four works by Tintoretto hang here: *Venus, Bacchus and Ariadne, Vulcan's Forge, Minerva Dismissing Mars* and *Mercury and the Graces*. The themes are political allegories of the Venetian state: the dismissal of Mars, for example, represents wisdom chasing away strife. Opposite the windows are Paolo Veronese's *Rape of Europa* and *Jacob's Return to Canaan* by Jacopo Bassano.

DOGES & THEIR COUNCILS

The doge of Venice, the personification of the grandeur of the Republic, was the focus of every major ritual. His election was an intricate procedure conducted by the nobility, and though his office was a grand and a symbolic one, his power was also severely restricted. On assuming office, he had to make a *promissione ducale*, a solemn vow that he would obey certain rules which constrained his authority. He could not leave Venice without authorisation, nor could he open state letters in private or meet foreign ambassadors unless councillors were present. Much of the government was conducted by the Great Council (Maggior Consiglio), whose membership was restricted after 1297 to those families who had already sat on the council. These included both nobles and merchants, and they inherited the right to sit on the council for life on reaching the age of 25. This signified the introduction of an oligarchic form of government. The size of the council varied over the years; the greatest number it reached was 1,700. Clearly such a large body was too cumbersome to conduct power on a day-to-day basis; increasingly its power was delegated to the Senate, which met three or four times a week, and whose scope included jurisdiction in commerce and navigation as well as international affairs, diplomacy and defence. Eventually it had 230 members. The Senate in its turn appointed a smaller committee, the Collegio, a group of 26 counsellors presided over by the doge, which met almost every day to deal with everyday affairs. Major executive decisions were taken by a still smaller council, the Signoria of ten members, all of whom were also members of the Collegio. Separate from all these organs was the Council of Ten, first set up in 1310, which was given the task of supervising internal security. It soon became the dreaded 'Ten', notorious for its secret operations and its readiness to intrude into all matters of business. All these councils met in the Doge's Palace.

It is just this proliferation of councils that helps explain the power the doge might exercise. A doge remained in power until death—unless forced to abdicate—while most other posts lasted only a year. Behind the façade of oligarchical rule, a shrewd doge could manipulate his smaller councils with their changing membership to his advantage.

The government of Venice proved impressively stable in comparison to the faction-ridden cities of the rest of northern Italy. Yet by the 18th century the system appeared increasingly archaic. The Council of Ten was seen as repressive, and it was this image of decay from the centre that Napoleon was able to exploit when he forced the Republic to dissolve itself in 1797.

(18) Sala del Collegio: This chamber, designed by Antonio Palladio, must have been one of the most sumptuous in the palace. Foreign ambassadors were officially greeted here, while Venetian ambassadors returning home would sub-

DOGE'S PALACE: SECOND PIANO NOBILE

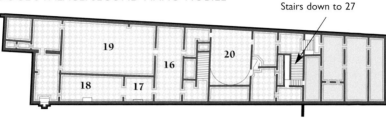

Stairs down to 27

16 Sala delle Quattro Porte
17 Anticollegio
18 Sala del Collegio

19 Sala del Senato
20 Sala del Consiglio dei Dieci

mit their reports. It is decorated with paintings of doges kneeling before saints. The most impressive work, by Veronese, is behind the doge's throne and depicts Doge Sebastiano Venier offering thanks for the Venetian victory over the Turks at Lepanto (1571). On the ceiling is a further beautiful work by Veronese: *Venus Ruling with Justice and Peace*.

(19) Sala del Senato: This room was designed by Antonio da Ponte, architect of the Rialto Bridge, who also worked on the Bridge of Sighs. The ceiling, *Venice Exalted Among the Gods*, showing Venice's maritime supremacy, is by Tintoretto.

(20) Sala del Consiglio dei Dieci: The Council of Ten, set up after a rebellion in 1310, kept a watch on the Senate, the Collegio and the doge. In 1355 the Ten ordered the execution for treason of Doge Marin Falier (*see below*). The ceiling paintings are by Veronese (the one in the centre was taken to France by Napoleon).

Sala del Maggior Consiglio

The Scala dei Censori leads back down to the first floor, and to this vast apartment **(27)**, which runs along almost the entire waterfront side of the palace. This was where the laws of Venice were ratified and the most important officials were elected. The enormous *Paradise* (1588–92), which takes up the whole entrance wall, is the work of Jacopo Tintoretto's son Domenico. It shows the Virgin, Christ and the Holy Spirit, with all the saints gathered around. The beautiful ceiling is divided into 35 painted panels, each with images glorifying the Republic. The finest of these are the central panels: Veronese's *Apotheosis of Venice* (1583) nearest the throne, and Tintoretto's *Niccolò da Ponte Receives a Laurel Wreath from Venice* (1584), which shows enemies of the Republic laying down their flags and arms at the feet of the doge in submission. You can just see the façade of St Mark's in the background. On the wall opposite the *Paradise*, look up at the frieze of doges' portraits around the cornice: a black cloth hides the face of the doge Marin Falier, executed for treason.

The prisons

The palace had two prisons: some criminals were held in cells just below the leaded roof, known as the *piombi*: this is where Casanova was held and he famously escaped by breaking through the roof. The more dangerous criminals were imprisoned on the ground floor. New prisons were built on the other side of the Rio di Palazzo, overlooking the Riva degli Schiavoni, reached by the Bridge of Sighs, built in 1600.

Museo Correr

Map p. 73, 11. Open Easter–Nov 9–6; Nov–Easter 9–4. Vaporetto: 1 to Vallaresso.
The Museo Correr is an exceptionally enjoyable museum. It tends not to suffer from the overcrowding of many Venetian museums and is full of fascinating items relating to the history and art of the Republic.

The first-floor displays cover the history of Venice and the office of the doge. The picture gallery on the second floor displays works by Paduan, Ferrarese, German and Flemish artists, but it is also, in a quiet way, a good place to get to grips with the art of the Venetian school, from its earliest master, Paolo Veneziano, to Giovanni and Gentile Bellini, Carpaccio, Alvise Vivarini and Lorenzo Lotto. Cosmè Tura's *Pietà* (c. 1460) is an important work by this artist from Ferrara showing his distinctive hard-edged style. Antonello da Messina's *Dead Christ* (1475/76), though badly damaged, shows masterly skill in depicting the effects of colour and light. Although he only stayed in the city for a year he was hugely influential on Venetian art; Giovanni Bellini in particular learned a great deal from him (*see p. 371*). Bellini's *Transfiguration* (c. 1460) was painted before he met Antonello and shows instead the influence of his brother-in-law, Andrea Mantegna. The foreshortening of the disciples' bodies, the way one holds his arm over his head and the crossed feet of another, are particularly accomplished.

Vittore Carpaccio's *Two Venetian Ladies* (c. 1490) is open to several interpretations: are they courtesans or just wealthy women whiling away a hot afternoon with their pets? The beautifully embroidered sleeves of their dresses are slashed in the latest fashion, their blonde hair carefully curled and dressed. Venetian ladies would spend hours on their *altana* (roof terrace) bleaching their hair with a combination of sunlight and mare's urine. The particular ruddy gold colour that resulted is captured well in the paintings of Veronese.

THE SESTIERE OF DORSODURO

Dorsoduro is perhaps the pleasantest of all the *sestieri*. Not because of its major sights (though they are important), but for its peaceful residential canals and *calli*, and the lovely waterfront promenade of the Zattere, where on a fine day people sit on the steps of the Gesuati church to catch the last of the sun.

Gallerie dell'Accademia

Map p. 72, 10. Open 8.15–7.15 (last admission 6.30), Mon 8.15–2 (last admission 1.15). Call centre 041 520 0345 for advance bookings and information. Vaporetto: 1, 82 to Accademia. The gallery is usually very busy, so try to visit early or towards the end of the day.
Venice's foremost art gallery, the Gallerie dell'Accademia, is home to the largest collection of Venetian art in the world. The collection is displayed in roughly chronological

order and the paintings are well labelled. Though the art of Venice can certainly be said to possess a recognisable style, notably in its use of colour and in its keenness to celebrate Venice's own glory, it was never formulaic. Indeed the writer Pietro Aretino, a friend of Titian, attributed the lack of a dominant taste to the absence of a court.

Paolo Veneziano's polyptychs of the *Coronation of the Virgin* (1325) and the *Virgin and Child with Donors* are among the earliest works in the collection. The *Coronation* combines two artistic traditions. The central Gothic panel depicts Christ crowning the Virgin, while the 20 smaller outer panels are Byzantine in style.

The greatest Venetian artist of the 15th century was undoubtedly **Giovanni Bellini** and the gallery holds several of his masterpieces. Some, such as the *Pietà* (c. 1505), are surprisingly small, yet the detail they contain and the intensity of their colour and content are extraordinary. The San Giobbe altarpiece (c. 1478) is a particularly beautiful work. It shows the sublime mastery of perspective and the use of light and realistic colours which influenced so many of Bellini's contemporaries.

The meaning of **Giorgione**'s *La Tempesta* (c. 1506) has been debated for centuries. The heavy green colouring and the build-up of thunder-clouds create a feeling of oppression and humidity. The landscape is threatening and the subjects peculiarly melancholy. Giorgione, a pupil of Bellini, was a pioneer of the Venetian Renaissance.

Paolo Veronese's massive *Christ in the House of Levi* (1573) is a magnificent work. Teeming with life and activity, it represents a grand banquet held in what appears to be a Venetian *palazzo*; all the guests are magnificently dressed, attendants bring food on sliver platters, while clowns wait their turn to entertain. Because of its secular atmosphere, the Inquisition objected to its original title, 'The Last Supper'. Veronese changed the name before the painting was installed in the refectory of Santi Giovanni e Paolo.

Also here is a series of paintings by **Jacopo Tintoretto**: the *Theft of the Body of St Mark*, the *Miracle of St Mark*, *St Mark Rescues the Saracen* and the *Dream of St Mark*. They date from 1562–66 and were intended for the Scuola Grande di San Marco (*for the definition of a scuola, see p. 398*). They show Tintoretto's characteristic imaginative flair; the camel in the theft scene adds an exotic touch, while the breaking storm adds a feeling of menace. They also display his vigorous way of working, using only a few, sweeping brushstrokes.

Another series of narrative paintings produced for one of the *scuole* is **Vittore Carpaccio**'s set of nine scenes depicting the **Legend of St Ursula** (1490–96). They were painted for the Scuola di Sant'Orsola between 1475 and 1495, and contain the same sort of delightful detail as his work for the Schiavoni (*see p. 88*).

The Accademia also displays many fine portraits. The standard Italian court portrait of the 15th century showed the sitter in profile. Portraiture in turn-of-the-16th-century Venice changed fundamentally as artists acquainted with Flemish painting substituted the more naturalistic northern vision, almost always characterised by the

A favourite theme of Venetian art is Venice itself. Tintoretto's *Dream of St Mark* (1562–66) illustrates the famous story of the Evangelist shipwrecked in the Venetian lagoon, dreaming of an angel who foretells that Venice shall be his eternal resting place.

three-quarters view. One of the great masters of portraiture was **Lorenzo Lotto**, whom Vasari says trained with Giorgione and Titian in the workshop of Giovanni Bellini. He is one of the most individual painters of the Renaissance, though during his lifetime he enjoyed little material success.

Eastern Dorsoduro

The **Peggy Guggenheim Collection** in Palazzo Venier dei Leoni (*map p. 72, 14; open Wed–Mon 10–6*) consists of over 200 works of art from the 20th century. Guggenheim had a good eye for talent, and befriended and encouraged many artists just starting out on their careers; Jackson Pollock was one of her 'discoveries'; Max Ernst was one of her husbands.

Further towards the far eastern tip of the *sestiere* is the great church of **Santa Maria della Salute**, which presents a unique silhouette at the mouth of the Grand Canal (*map p. 72, 14; open 9–12 & 3–6.30; sacristy open 3–5.30, sometimes 10.30–12. Vaporetto: 1 to Salute*). Dedicated to the Virgin Mary, it was built in thanksgiving for deliverance from an outbreak of plague. It was designed by Baldassare Longhena and is the most important building of the 17th century in Venice. The 32-year-old architect started work in 1631 and spent the rest of his life working on it; it was completed in 1687, five years after his death.

Longhena's intention was to build the church 'in the form of a crown', which he achieved with a design of 12 spiral volutes, topped by statues of the Apostles around a beautifully proportioned dome. A statue of the Virgin wearing a coronet of 12 stars stands on top of the lantern.

The church's most important works of art are kept in the sacristy to the left of the high altar. *St Mark with Sts Cosmas, Damian, Roch and Sebastian* is an early work by Titian (c. 1510). The use of colour and the masterly rendering of the folds in the saints' cloaks show the influence of Giovanni Bellini. The composition of the painting is interesting: St Mark, patron of Venice, sits in an elevated position in the centre, where we would expect to see the Virgin and Child. On the left are Sts Cosmas and Damian, the twin doctor saints. On the right are St Roch and St Sebastian, both of whom were traditionally appealed to for deliverance from the plague.

The **Dogana di Mare**, the former customs house, stands at the entrance to the Grand Canal. At the time of writing it was being restored as an arts centre.

Ca' Rezzonico

Map p. 72, 9. Open Easter–Nov 10–5 (last admission); Nov–Easter 10–4 (last admission). Vaporetto: 1 to Ca' Rezzonico.

This beautiful museum of 18th-century Venice is housed in one of the few *palazzi* open to the public. The building was commissioned by the Bon family from Baldassare Longhena in 1667 and was later bought by the Rezzonico family, who spent a huge proportion of their fortune on building and decorating it with works by Tiepolo, among others. Their extravagant parties entertaining prelates (Carlo Rezzonico was Pope Clement XIII), kings and dignitaries finally lead to financial ruin, and towards the end of the 19th century the palace was bought by the poet Robert Browning. This is a superb place to get a feel for life in a Grand Canal *palazzo*. It contains furniture, statues and other items from the period, fine works by Tiepolo and his son Giandomenico, and others by Guardi, Canaletto and Pietro Longhi, whose faithful renderings of everyday life in Venice are particularly engaging. One shows a noblewoman, wearing an expensive ermine gown, having her hair done; notice all the accoutrements on her dressing table—a mirror, a porcelain powder case, combs and powder puffs. By contrast, the woman's wet-nurse, holding her child, stands to one side, her face ruddy and her hair undressed.

Western Dorsoduro

Western Dorsoduro is a pretty district of narrow *fondamente* snaking alongside quiet canals, lively *campi* and beautiful churches. Of the latter, two are particularly worth seeking out. The church of **San Trovaso** (*map p. 72, 13*), with large thermal windows, stands next to an old *squero*, or gondola workshop, still in use today. The church contains a fine *Last Supper* by Tintoretto. In a remote district further west, prettily situated across a little bridge, is the church of **San Sebastiano** (*map p. 72, 9; open Mon–Sat 10–5. Chorus Pass. Vaporetto: 61, 62, 82 to San Basilio*), a place of pilgrimage for all lovers of Paolo Veronese. In 1555 the artist started work on the decoration which was to occupy him for the following ten years, making this not just a glorious showcase of his work but also one of the most harmonious church interiors in Venice.

Veronese chose to depict a variety of themes in his local church (he lived nearby). Frescoes on the upper walls show the martyrdom of St Sebastian. The foreshortening of figures and treatment of the awkward body positions are particularly skilfully executed. These scenes are almost theatrical in effect, with architectural features such as columns, staircases and niches giving the impression of the building extending further upwards and outwards, an imaginative way of creating the impression of space in this small church. Another ingenious image is that of an archer on the left-hand wall who shoots arrows right across the nave at St Sebastian on the right-hand wall.

The central panels of the ceiling tell stories from the life of Esther, the Jewish wife of the Persian king Ahasuerus, who interceded with him to prevent the destruction of her people. The *Coronation of Esther* demonstrates the artist's mastery at painting sumptuous clothing, jewels and fine fabrics. The panel depicting the *Triumph of Mordecai* is a superb example of his accomplished use of perspective. It is fitting that Veronese, who left so much of his work here, should also be buried in the church.

THE SESTIERE OF CASTELLO

San Zaccaria

Map p. 73, 11. Open 10–12 & 4–6, Sun and holidays only 4–6. Vaporetto: 1, 51, 52, 82 to San Zaccaria.

In a quiet campo close to Piazza San Marco is the church of San Zaccaria. Adjoining it was a convent where daughters of patrician families were sequestered, but which was famous for its laxity. The convents of Venice were numerous: typically only an eldest daughter would command a dowry. The others lived behind cloister walls. The same San Zaccaria convent today is the headquarters of the Carabinieri.

The church was begun in 1458 and completed in 1515 by Mauro Codussi: the triple curved crowning (echoed in the three-aisled interior) and roundel windows are characteristic of his work. The interior is richly decorated with paintings of the 17th and 18th centuries; the undoubted highlight, however, is an earlier work: Giovanni Bellini's *Madonna and Saints* (second north chapel). This is one of Bellini's last works, painted in 1505, the year before his death. The Madonna and Child are shown sitting in an apse-like niche with Sts Peter and Catherine on the left, Sts Lucy and Jerome on the right, with an angel sitting at the foot of the Madonna's throne, playing a stringed instrument. The folds and creases on the painted piece of paper, or *cartellino*, next to the angel are incredibly lifelike; on it you can see Bellini's signature.

San Giovanni in Bragora

Map p. 73, 12. Open 9–11 & 3.30–7, Sun 9–12. Vaporetto: 1, 42 to Arsenale.

Campo Bandiera e Moro, a very domestic square, and a favourite spot with local children for a game of football, is home to the church of San Giovanni in Bragora, which is home in turn to some masterpieces of Venetian art. Chief of these is the high altarpiece of the *Baptism of Christ* by Cima da Conegliano (1494). The scene is set against mountains and hill villages, a typical landscape of the northern Veneto of the artist's birth, bathed in golden sunshine, while red, blue and golden cherubim emerge from the clouds, along with the dove of the Holy Spirit. This painting had great influence on painters of the later Renaissance.

The church also contains work by Alvise Vivarini, Cima's master. Another member of the Vivarini family is also represented here, Bartolomeo, Alvise's nephew, who painted the *Madonna Enthroned Between St John the Baptist and St Andrew*.

Antonio Vivaldi was baptised in this church (there is a copy of his certificate of baptism near the font).

Scuola di San Giovanni degli Schiavoni

Map p. 73, 8–12. Open Mon 2.45–6, Tues–Sat 9.15–1 & 2.45–6, Sun 9.30–12.30. Vaporetto: 1, 51, 52, 82 to San Zaccaria.

The Schiavoni (Slavs) were merchants from Dalmatia (the modern Croatian coast), which had historic trading links with Venice and came under permanent Venetian rule in 1420. The merchants supplied the hard-wearing white limestone which formed the foundations of countless churches and palaces, as well as the pine trunks which were driven into the lagoon bed as supports for the city's buildings. In 1451 they estab-

Giovanni Bellini: *Madonna and Saints* (1505) in the church of San Zaccaria. This was one of the earliest Venetian works to be painted in oil, a technique which Bellini may have learned from Antonello da Messina (see p. 371). The luminous, enamel-like effect of the colours is instantly striking, and the way light is shown playing against different surfaces and textures is masterly.

lished their own confraternity, which they dedicated to St George, St Tryphon and St Jerome. They commissioned Vittore Carpaccio, perhaps the greatest narrative painter of the period, to produce a series of paintings to decorate their small, square meeting house. The result is one of the most fascinating cycles of paintings in Venice, and unusually, still in the place for which it was commissioned, this being one of the few religious institutions not to be suppressed by Napoleon.

Pulling back the heavy curtain you enter a room lined with works by the man whom Jan Morris described as the only Venetian artist with a sense of humour. The *Duel of St George and the Dragon*, on the left, is perhaps the most famous of the cycle. It shows the golden-haired knight plunging his lance into the dragon's neck, while the princess, who would have been devoured if the dragon had lived, looks on with obvious gratitude. But it is the detail that makes Carpaccio's paintings so fascinating: here the ground is littered with half-eaten bodies and old bones, lizards and serpents wriggle and spit. In the next painting, the *Triumph of St George*, the scene has shifted to the king's court. St George holds the dragon by the princess's girdle and is about to deliver the *coup de grace*. The final scene is *St George Baptising the People of Silene*. The king, queen and princess agreed to be baptised if St George killed the dragon and here they are shown kneeling before the saint, the scene witnessed by a rather imperious looking hound.

The St Jerome cycle on the left wall begins with the *Lion Led by St Jerome into the Monastery*, a particularly delightful panel, full of incident and detail. The monks flee

The Lion led by St Jerome into the Monastery (1502–08), by the greatest Venetian master of narrative painting, Vittore Carpaccio, in the Scuola di San Giorgio degli Schiavoni.

in terror, their habits billowing out behind them; there is a particularly comical scene in the background as the monks stream up the stairs to safety, while another monk hobbles away on crutches. The *Funeral of St Jerome* is calm and touching, as the monks kneel in prayer before the saint's body. You can just pick out the lion, its head thrown back in a roar of grief. The final part of the cycle is the *Vision of St Augustine* showing an episode from the story of St Augustine: as the saint was writing a letter to St Jerome to ask his advice on the book he was writing about the saints in Paradise, St Jerome died. The moment is caught by the study being filled with light and St Augustine looking out of the window as he hears Jerome's voice, warning him against describing Paradise before his own death. But most of all the work is fascinating

Verrocchio's bronze monument to Bartolomeo Colleoni (1488), with the horse's front left hoof lifted clear off the ground, like the 2nd-century Horses of St Mark's (see p. 79) and the statue of Marcus Aurelius in Rome (see p. 242), but unlike Donatello's *Gattamelata* (see p. 106).

for the detail it gives of a monk's study. The purity of the light reveals the tiniest details of the room—the gold book binding, the notes in the music books, the studs which secure the green fabric of the table and the rich red upholstery of the chair and *prie-dieu*. Best loved is the tiny white dog which sits alert, listening to his master's voice.

Santi Giovanni e Paolo

Map p. 73, 7. Open 9.15–6.30, Sun and holidays 3–6.30. Vaporetto: 1, 82 to Rialto; 41, 42, 51, 52 to Ospedale.

This huge church stands in the impressive campo of the same name, over which the powerful equestrian statue of Bartolomeo Colleoni stands sentinel. This was the last work of the Florentine Andrea del Verrocchio, though the actual casting took place after his death in 1488. Verrocchio here abandons the rigid formality of other equestrian monuments such as Donatello's Gattamelata in Padua (*see p. 106*) and the great prototype, the statue of Marcus Aurelius in Rome (*see p. 242*). This work has movement, the horse mettlesome, the rider twisted in the saddle as if to rein in his mount. Verrocchio was also a goldsmith, and his skills at portraying the finest detail were fully exploited. Notice the veins on the horse's body, the folds of its skin and the power in its muscles.

Colleoni's face is a perfect picture of a man in command. Originally from Bergamo (*see p. 58*), he was a successful soldier of fortune, fighting for both the Venetians and the Milanese Visconti. He amassed a huge fortune and when he died he pledged it to the Republic on condition that they erect a statue to him in front of St Mark's. However, as statues to individuals were forbidden in the Piazza, the wily Venetians reinterpreted the conditions of his will and erected his statue here, outside the *scuola* of St Mark.

The church

This is the Dominican church of Venice. The transept and apses were completed in 1368 and the church was consecrated in 1430. It is remarkable for being the burial place of some 25 doges and is an exceptional showcase of funerary art, particularly the work of the Lombardo family.

(1) Monument to Doge Pietro Mocenigo: Pietro Lombardo's monument to Doge Pietro Mocenigo (d. 1476) is his undisputed masterpiece. The Lombardo family (Pietro and his sons Tullio and Antonio) introduced Renaissance sculpture to Venice. This monument takes the form of a triumphal arch and any reference to physical mortality is deliberately resisted. Instead, Mocenigo is shown standing on his sarcophagus, dressed in his armour, a *miles Christianus* or soldier of Christ. The inscription on the central panel, 'Ex hostium manibus' (from the hands of my enemies), is a triumphant reminder that the spoils of war paid for this monument. The only Christian reference is a relief showing the women at the Sepulchre at the very top.

(2) Polyptych of St Vincent Ferrer: This altarpiece was commissioned from Giovanni Bellini in 1465 and is one of his early works. St Vincent Ferrer, a Spanish Dominican friar, is flanked by St Christopher and St Sebastian.

(3) *Charity of St Antoninus:* This painting by Lorenzo Lotto (1542) shows the Archbishop of Florence, Antoninus Pieruzzi, considering the petitions of the poor. St Antoninus was the founder of the friary of San Marco (*see p. 186*).

(4) Choir: There are some interesting tomb monuments on the wall of the choir. The tomb of Michele Morosini (d. 1382; **a**) was condemned by Ruskin in *The Stones of Venice* as 'voluptuous and over-wrought', an example of how 'Renaissance errors' crept into the stonemason's art and led to a style which he

SANTI GIOVANNI E PAOLO

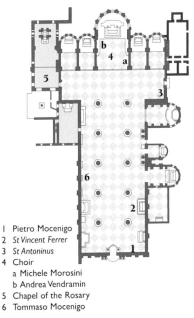

1 Pietro Mocenigo
2 St Vincent Ferrer
3 St Antoninus
4 Choir
  a Michele Morosini
  b Andrea Vendramin
5 Chapel of the Rosary
6 Tommaso Mocenigo

termed 'degraded Gothic'. He had mixed feelings about the tomb, however; later in the same work he praises it for its richness.

The tomb of Doge Andrea Vendramin (d. 1478; **b**), the work of Tullio Lombardo and his brother Antonio, is fully Renaissance in style. Like their father Pietro's tomb of Pietro Mocenigo, it takes the form of a Classical triumphal arch, and the quality of the carving is admired as a masterpiece today. Ruskin, predictably, detested it, and reserved particular vitriol for its description: 'The whole monument is one wearisome aggregation of that species of ornamental flourish, which, when it is done with a pen, is called penmanship, and when done with a chisel, should be called chiselmanship; the subject of it being chiefly fat-limbed boys sprawling on dolphins...'.

(**5**) **Chapel of the Rosary:** This chapel was built to commemorate the Battle of Lepanto (7th October 1571, the feast day of the Madonna of the Rosary), a pivotal naval victory over the Turks. Paolo Veronese's ceiling paintings were installed here in the 19th century, following restoration after a fire. They include the *Annunciation*, the *Assumption* and the *Adoration of the Shepherds*. Painted with a beautiful use of colour, they also show compositional inventiveness—in the *Adoration*, for example, the infant Jesus is shown with his back to us.

(**6**) **Tomb of Doge Tommaso Mocenigo:** This is one of the most attractive tombs in the basilica and it shows the transition from Gothic to Renaissance. The doge (d. 1423) lies beneath a canopy which two angels close around his body. The design of the tomb was Venetian but the sculptures were the work of two Tuscan craftsmen, who were probably influenced by the work of Donatello. The sculptures of the saints and Virtues in the niches are Gothic in style while the angels, and particularly the soldier on the right-hand corner, show a softer, more naturalistic Renaissance pose.

SESTIERE OF SAN POLO

Santa Maria Gloriosa dei Frari

Map p. 72, 5. Open Mon–Sat 10–6, Sun 1–6. Chorus Pass. Vaporetto: 1, 82 to San Tomà. The Franciscan church of Venice was built between 1330–1442. Titian is buried here, and the church is home to some superb works by his hand.

(**1**) **Monument to Titian:** Designed by a father and son team, Luigi and Pietro Zandomeneghi, in 1843, and commissioned by the Austrian emperor Ferdinand I, it stands where the painter is thought to have been buried in 1576. Canova also designed a monument for Titian, but it was rejected and used instead as his own monument (*see below*). Titian's monument shows the artist seated beneath a grand triumphal arch in front of a relief of his own *Assumption*, surmounted by the proud lion of St Mark.

(**2**) **Sacristy:** The apse painting is one of Bellini's most exquisite works, a triptych of the *Madonna Enthroned with Saints* (1488). The Madonna, dressed in a flowing blue robe, sits beneath a golden dome with the Christ Child standing on her knee, while two angels play musical

SANTA MARIA GLORIOSA DEI FRARI

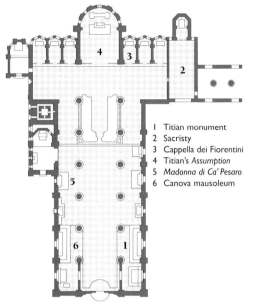

1 Titian monument
2 Sacristy
3 Cappella dei Fiorentini
4 Titian's *Assumption*
5 *Madonna di Ca' Pesaro*
6 Canova mausoleum

Venice. Unveiled in 1588, it was an astonishing painting for its time. Titian's use of the colour red for the robes of the Apostles, the Virgin and the Almighty creates a subliminal triangle and gives a very physical impression of Mary's ascent. The Virgin is physical rather than ethereal. Carried aloft by tumbling cherubim, she is depicted as a beautiful, flesh-and-blood woman.

(5) *Madonna di Ca' Pesaro*: This is another of Titian's great altarpieces, and again he creates the unexpected. The positioning of the Madonna to the right of the picture, rather than in the centre, was an unusual departure. The donor, Jacopo Pesaro, kneels to the left, the banner above his head representing his naval victory over the Turks in 1502.

(6) Mausoleum of Canova: This Neoclassical monument was originally designed by Canova to commemorate Titian, but the Zandomeneghi design was chosen instead. Canova's pupils (including Luigi Zandomeneghi) erected this to his memory. In the form of a pyramid, an ancient funerary convention (*see p. 264; Chigi Chapel*), it shows the winged figure of Genius and the lion of St Mark protecting the tomb, while the Arts are represented as female mourners. Canova's portrait is held by angels above the tomb's open door. The snake devouring its tail is a symbol of immortality.

instruments at her feet. On the left stand Sts Nicholas of Bari and Peter, and on the right stand St Mark and St Benedict.

(3) Cappella dei Fiorentini: Dedicated to St John the Baptist, their patron saint, this chapel was sponsored by the Florentines, and the statue of the saint is by Donatello. Signed and dated 1438, it is his first work in the Veneto, and his first statue to be made of wood. The startling, emaciated appearance of the saint has direct references to his other (later) St John the Baptist in Siena.

(4) Apse: Titian's magnificent *Assumption* hangs here, a masterpiece of the High Renaissance. It was painted for this space and is the largest altarpiece in

Titian: *Madonna di Ca' Pesaro* (1519–26), a new interpretation of the 'Madonna and Saints' type of altarpiece, with the Virgin placed off-centre yet still the focal point of the composition. Many later artists, including Annibale Carracci, were to use this idea in their work.

Scuola Grande di San Rocco

Map p. 72, 5. Open 9 or 10–5.30; Nov–Easter 10–5.30. Vaporetto: 1, 82 to San Tomà.
San Rocco (St Roch) is the patron saint of contagious diseases, and in a city often rav-aged by plague, he was frequently resorted to. In 1564 Tintoretto won the commis-sion to decorate the *scuola* by ignoring the brief to produce a preliminary sketch and instead installing the completed *St Roch in Glory* in the Sala dell'Albergo. He spent the next 23 years producing a most remarkable cycle of paintings.

The paintings on the ground floor tell the story of the life of the Virgin. Tintoretto was a painter of great vigour, and the *Annunciation* on the left wall nearest the entrance is a good example. The angel, accompanied by a swarm of cherubim, forcefully appears through the open door and almost literally bowls the Virgin over, as the dove of the Holy Spirit dazzles her with its power and light.

On the staircase is Antonio Zanchi's *Virgin Appearing to the Plague-Striken*, which depicts the horrors of the plague in Venice in 1630. It was deliverance from this out-break for which Santa Maria della Salute was built (*see p. 86*). The main room on the upper floor, the chapter house, contains Old and New Testament scenes. The Old Testament scenes are on the ceiling. The three main ones—*The Miracle of the Brazen Serpent*, *Moses Striking Water From the Rock* and *The Gathering of Manna*—reflect the charitable work of the *scuola*: healing the sick, alleviating thirst and feeding the hungry.

The Sala dell'Albergo, with *St Roch in Glory* on the ceiling, is dominated by the panoramic *Crucifixion*, 12m wide. Tintoretto always endeavoured to reinterpret con-ventional themes: here he catches the moment when, as the Cross is raised, the weight of Christ's body is thrown forward. This painting is full of activity: the crowd swirls around the Cross; the turbulent sky gives the scene a sense of foreboding.

THE SESTIERE OF CANNAREGIO

Ca' d'Oro

Map p. 72, 6. Open 8.15–7.15, Mon 8.15–2; entrance in Calle della Ca' d'Oro. Vaporetto: 1 to Ca' d'Oro.
The magnificent Ca' d'Oro (*for the exterior, see p. 70*) contains an interesting collection of works of art and a good example of a Venetian courtyard. The finest of the paint-ings is Andrea Mantegna's *St Sebastian* (1504–06), the artist's last work. Sculpture includes Tullio Lombardo's exquisite double portrait bust of a young couple (c. 1493). Vittore Carpaccio's *Annunciation* is a scene of calm serenity. Distracted while at prayer, the Madonna half turns towards the Archangel Gabriel to hear the news he brings.

On the second floor is all that remains of Titian's fresco of *Judith* (or *Justice*) which originally adorned the Fondaco dei Tedeschi (*see p. 74*); also here are fresco fragments by Giorgione for the same building.

Madonna dell'Orto

Map p. 72, 2. Open 10–5. Chorus Pass. Vaporetto: 41, 42, 51, 52 to Orto.
Tucked away from the crowds in the tranquil north of Cannaregio is the church of the

Madonna dell'Orto ('Our Lady of the Garden'), built between 1399–1473 and named after a miraculous statue of the Virgin found in a garden nearby and now in a chapel at the end of the south aisle.

This was the parish church of Tintoretto (he lived on Fondamenta dei Mori close by), and it is where he lies buried, to the right of the choir. The church contains several of his works. On the wall to the left of the high altar is the *Worship of the Golden Calf*, while on the right is the *Last Judgement*; but the loveliest of his paintings here is the tender *Presentation of the Virgin* (1552) in the south aisle. It shows the tiny child Mary, climbing the golden steps of the temple, where a rather forbidding high priest awaits her. Here Tintoretto's exceptionally skilful treatment of light is seen at its most accomplished.

Another great masterpiece is Cima da Conegliano's *St John the Baptist and Four Saints* (c. 1493; first south altar). The castle in the background is that of his home town, Conegliano, in the foothills of the Dolomites.

From this church there are lovely walks into the quieter areas of Venice, including the **Ghetto** (*map p. 72, 1–2*). The Jewish community generally enjoyed a harmonious relationship with the Venetians until the Council of Ten decreed in 1516 that they should be confined to this area of the city. Around 500 Jews live in Venice today. The old ghetto area (the word 'ghetto' is of Venetian origin) is home to three synagogues and a museum (*visits and guided tours 10–4.30 or 5.30, Fri 10–sunset; closed Sat and Jewish holidays*).

TWO PALLADIAN CHURCHES

San Giorgio Maggiore

Map p. 73, 15. Open 9.30–12.30 & 2–5.30 or dusk. Vaporetto: 82 to San Giorgio.

The church of San Giorgio Maggiore is perhaps Andrea Palladio's masterpiece. It was commissioned in 1565 to replace an earlier building, and was completed after his death in 1580. Palladio's genius in building country villas, designed to make an impact when seen from a distance, clearly informed his design for this church. The façade is of crisp white Istrian stone, which perfectly reflects the changing moods of the lagoon and is equally beautiful in bright sunshine, at sunset or on a misty day.

Palladio was a master of proportion, and the front of this church is a superb demonstration of his geometric sleight of hand. It is made up of two temple-fronts, one apparently behind the other, though in fact the whole ensemble is two-dimensional.

The spacious interior is refreshingly cool and plain. Two works by Tintoretto hang on the chancel walls: the *Last Supper* (1592–94) on the right and the *Shower of Manna* (c. 1590) on the left. The story of the Last Supper was one of the artist's favourite subjects and this was his last rendering of it. The table is placed at an angle; this is a relaxed, informal gathering—the disciples talk among themselves as servants unpack the food and set the table, and dogs sniff around looking for scraps. Despite all this activity, the brightly lit figure of Christ stands out above all others, but it is also a portentous scene as wraith-like angels, apparently unnoticed by everyone else, materialise from above and hover overhead. The painting of the *Shower of Manna* is far less dramatic; the Israelites are depicted enjoying a country idyll.

Some people argue that the view from the top of the campanile of San Giorgio is better than that from the campanile of St Mark's. Whatever the relative merits of either, San Giorgio has the great advantage of far fewer people waiting to get to the top.

Il Redentore

Beyond map p. 72, 14. Open Mon–Sat 10–5. Chorus pass. Vaporetto: 41, 42, 82 to Redentore.
Work started on the votive church of Il Redentore (the Redeemer) in 1577. It was built as an act of thanksgiving for deliverance from the plague of 1575–77, in which between 40,000 and 50,000 people died. Palladio was the architect chosen, and once again he selected a spectacular site, on the Giudecca canal, from which the church would make the greatest impression from across the water. The feast of the Redeemer on the third Sun in July is still enthusiastically celebrated today.

The main façade is a series of superimposed porticoes, as at San Giorgio Maggiore. The classical interior is, like San Giorgio Maggiore, light and spacious, using the same clean architectural lines, and also lit by thermal windows.

TORCELLO

Beyond map p. 73, 3. Ferry from Fondamente Nuove. There are no shops on Torcello but there are a few restaurants, including the Locanda Cipriani (T: 041 730150). There is a combined ticket to the cathedral, Santa Fosca and museum but opening times, given below, vary.
If you only have time to visit one of the islands of the lagoon, then head for Torcello. Settled long before Venice, in the 5th–6th centuries, it became a thriving community numbering 20,000. By the 13th century, with the rise of Venice, the silting up of the canals and the incidence of malaria, it had fallen into decline. Today it is a place of peace and tranquillity; only 30 or so people live here.

From the landing stage, follow the canal path past gardens and orchards. You soon come to the little clutch of famous buildings: the cathedral, Santa Fosca and the museum, arranged around a grassy 'piazza'.

Cathedral of Santa Maria Assunta

Open March–Oct 10.30–5.30, campanile 10.30–5; Oct–March 10–4.30.
The Byzantine cathedral was founded in 639 but the present building dates from the 9th century. Even so, it is one of the oldest churches in the lagoon. The curve of the apse is filled with a glorious Byzantine mosaic of the Virgin, probably by a Greek mosaicist. It adheres to the Byzantine iconographic scheme whereby the 'womb' of the apse would hold an image of the Virgin as 'Theotokos', Mother of God. Against a rich golden background, she holds the Christ Child on her left arm while gesturing towards him with her right hand, indicating her son as the Way. In St Mark's, following the cenvention for basilicas, Christ Pantocrator is shown in the apse, as He is also at Monreale (*see p. 372*). The west wall is entirely covered by a superbly vivid 11th-century mosaic of the *Last Judgement*.

The museum and Santa Fosca

The interesting little **museum** (*open summer 10.30–5, winter 10–4*) contains mosaic fragments from the cathedral and pieces collected from the suppressed churches of Venice. The most precious item is the Pala d'Oro. Originally consisting of 42 small plaques, only 13 now remain but they do give a hint at the superb craftsmanship of the whole altarpiece. To the right of the cathedral is the 11th–12th-century church of **Santa Fosca**. The beautifully proportioned interior is unadorned except for the narrow double columns and brickwork patterning. It was built to house the relics of St Fosca, brought here from Ravenna.

VISITING VENICE

GETTING AROUND

• **By air:** Venice airport is 13km north of the city. Airport buses, operated by ATVO, run between the terminal and the car park at Piazzale Roma at roughly 30-min intervals at 20 past and 10 to the hour; buy your tickets from the ticket office in the arrivals hall or from automatic machines; if you're going to the airport, tickets can be bought at the ATVO office on Piazzale Roma (*map p. 72, 5*). The journey takes c. 20mins. City bus no. 5, run by ACTV, also operates services between the airport and Piazzale Roma at roughly 15-min intervals throughout the day; journey time is c. 30mins.

By far the best way to arrive in Venice is by water. Alilaguna (www.alilaguna.com) operates a number of regular boat connections between the airport and Venice: the quickest is the gold line which makes just two stops, at San Zaccaria and San Marco Giardinetti. It runs every hour on the half hour; the journey takes about 1hr. The blue line stops at Murano, Fondamente Nuove, Lido, San Zaccaria and San Marco Giardinetti; the orange line stops at Madonna dell'Orto, Guglie, Rialto and Sant'Angelo; and the red line stops at Murano, Lido, Arsenale, San Marco Giardinetti and Zattere. It is worth checking where your hotel is in relation to these stops as it could save having to struggle with luggage.

Water taxis can also be hired from the airport. They are very convenient, but not cheap.

• **By car:** All roads from the mainland terminate at Piazzale Roma (*map p. 72, 5*), where you have to leave your car in a multi-storey garage or an open-air car park (charges according to the size of the vehicle; rates are per day, and space is limited, especially in summer). The most convenient multi-storey garages are at Piazzale Roma; garages and huge open-air car parks also at Isola del Tronchetto. Frequent vaporetto services serve all of these. In summer, at Easter, and Carnival time open air car parking is usually also available at San Giuliano and Fusina (with vaporetto services). The bus station is at Piazzale Roma.

• **By train:** Venice Santa Lucia Station is at the west end of the Grand Canal (*map p. 72, 5*). Trains connect with Trieste (journey time c. 2–3hrs), Verona (c. 1hr 10mins), Milan (c. 2½ hrs), Turin (c. 4½ hrs) and Genoa (c. 4¾ hrs); Bologna (c. 1hr 25mins), Florence (c. 2½ hrs) and Rome (c. 4½ hrs); and Trento (c. 2½ hrs). There are frequent trains to and from Padua (50mins) and other places in the Veneto.

• **Public transport in Venice:** There are only two ways to get around Venice—on foot or by water. Walking is quick and efficient if you have a good map. For longer distances, you will need to get to grips with the network of *vaporetti* (water buses) and *motoscafi* (motor boats), which are efficient but very often extremely crowded. Vaporetto numbers are given in the text. All ACTV (Venice transport company) ticket offices will supply a free map of the network. Note that *vaporetti* with the same first digit (41, 42) ply the same route but in different directions. Tickets can be bought at most landing stages and from shops displaying the ACTV logo, or on board after hours. Validate your ticket before you board. The Travel Card (*Biglietto turistico*), valid for 12, 24, 36, 48 or 72 hours, is the cheapest way to get around. Time-stamp it before you start. The *Carta Venezia* (not to be confused with the Venice Card; *see below*) entitles you to discounts on all lines; enquire at Hellovenezia information points or visit www.actv.it.

• **By water taxi:** Service in town is metred, and there are fixed rates (published in the monthly booklet *Un Ospite di Venezia*, online at www.unospitedivenezia.it) for the most common destinations, including the airport. Taxi-stands can be found on the quays in front of the station, at Piazzale Roma, Rialto, San Marco and other major points. Water taxis are also available by request: hotels and restaurants will make the call for you.

• **By gondola:** Gondolas can be hired for a leisurely tour of the city, at standard rates or on a custom basis. Be sure to agree upon the duration and price of your ride before setting out.

• **By traghetto:** *Traghetti* (gondola ferries) offer a handy way of getting across the Grand Canal. They are marked by yellow signs. They are extremely cheap (leave a few euros in the boat) and easy; in all but the roughest weather you ride standing up. Most operate from early morning until late afternoon.

SPECIAL TICKETS

The **Venice Card** offers free admission to municipal museums and other participating institutions, including the Jewish Museum; free admission to 16 churches; reduced entrance to exhibitions; discounts at the main car parks; free use of public transport, including the airport shuttle. It comes in 3- and 7-day versions, is available at museums and Hellovenezia info points, or online (at a slight discount) at www.hellovenezia.com. The **Chorus Pass** allows you free entry to 16 churches in the city. The pass can be bought at any of the participating churches including the Frari, Madonna dell'Orto and San Sebastiano.

WHERE TO STAY IN VENICE

Three of the finest luxury hotels in Venice are the €€€€ **Gritti Palace** ■, on the waterfront south of Santa Maria del Giglio (*T: 041 794611, www.gritti.hotelinvenice.com; map p. 73, 10*), the €€€€ **Londra Palace** ■ right on the waterfront, with nicely-sized rooms (*Riva degli Schiavoni; T. 041 520 0533, www.hotellondra.it; map p. 73, 11*), and €€€€ **Cipriani** on the Giudecca (*T: 041 520 7744, www.hotelcipriani.com; beyond map p. 73, 15*). Smaller places of great charm include €€ **Colombina** ■ in Castello, very close to San Marco though secluded in feel (*Calle del Remedio, parallel to Rio S.M. Formosa, T: 041 277 0525, www.hotelcolombina.com; map p. 73, 11*), and three places in Dorsoduro: €€ **La Calcina** ■ overlooking the Giudecca, is the hotel where Ruskin stayed. Rooms are comfortable and pleasantly decorated. There's also a good restaurant (*Zattere, by Rio S. Vio, T: 041 520 6466, www.lacalcina.com; map p. 72, 14*); €€ **Accademia Villa Maravege** is a much-sought after small hotel with lovely rooms, though like many in Venice, quite small (*Fondamenta Bollani, off Rio San Trovaso, T: 041 521 0188, www.pensioneaccademia.it; map p. 72, 13*); €€ **Locanda San Barnaba** ■ in a 16th-century *palazzo* (*Calle del Traghetto, near*

S. Barnaba church, T: 041 241 1233, www.locanda-sanbarnaba.com; map p. 72, 9).

WHERE TO EAT IN VENICE

€€€€ **Da Fiore**. ■ Venice's premier restaurant for fish. If there are just two of you, try to get the tiny terrace on the canal. *Calle del Scaleter (San Polo), T: 041 721308. Map p. 72, 5.*

€€€ **Harry's Bar**. As much a landmark of Venice as the Doge's Palace. Renowned for its jet-setting clientèle and as the place where the Bellini cocktail was born. *Calle Vallaresso, T: 041 528 5777. Map p. 73, 11.*

€€€ **Ai Gondolieri**. Delicious cooking with a focus on meat. On the same canal as the Guggenheim. Closed Tues. *Fondamenta Ospedaletto, T: 041 528 6396. Map p. 72, 14.*

€€ **La Piscina**. Very pleasant restaurant attached to La Calcina (*see above*), good value in an expensive city. *Zattere, T: 041 241 3889. Map p. 72, 14.*

€€ **Riviera**. ■ Superb, refined home cooking at the end of the Zattere. Perfect for a leisurely lunch. Closed Mon, midday Wed. Also rooms to rent. *Zattere, T: 041 522 7621. Map p. 72, 13.*

€€ **Pane e Vino e San Daniele**. ■ Tiny, secluded place serving light snacks and simple, tasty full lunches. Closed Wed. *Campo Angelo Raffaele, T: 041 523 7456. Map p. 72, 9.*

FESTIVALS & EVENTS

Teatro La Fenice (*map p. 72, 10*) is Venice's famous opera house. The Biennale draws international crowds between June and Sept. Carnival does likewise in Feb. Traditional festivals include the *Festa della Sensa* (Ascension Day), recalling the symbolic marriage between the doge and the sea; the *Festa del Redentore* (third week in Sept), with boat processions and fireworks; and the feast of the Salute (21 Nov), when people go to the Salute to light a votive candle.

THE BRENTA & ITS VILLAS

Snaking inland from Venice and running westwards to Padua, through an increasingly rural and attractive landscape, is the Brenta canal (*map p. 423, E2*), a waterway built by the Venetians to facilitate navigation between their city and Padua. In the summer the patrician families of Venice would pack their movables into a barge known as a *burchiello* and have themselves rowed or towed upstream to their summer villa. Today a motorised *burchiello* lazily winds its way from Venice to Padua or vice-versa, stopping to visit some of the villas along the way.

Boats depart March–Oct from the Pietà landing stage in Venice (Riva degli Schiavoni; map p. 73, 12) on Tues, Thur and Sat; or Piazzale Boschetti bus station in Padua on Wed, Fri and Sun. Trips of a whole day, including lunch and three villas, or half a day, can be arranged. Refreshments can be bought on board. The trip includes swing bridges and a number of locks, supposedly built to a design by Leonardo da Vinci. For more information, see www.ilburchiello.it. You can book online, or ask a travel agent or your hotel reception to make the booking.

The Brenta villas

The beautiful summer villas which are such a feature of this area first appeared in the 16th century when, in the face of Ottoman naval expansion, Venice began to look

Villa Foscari (La Malcontenta), built in 1555–60, and a superb illustration of the architecture of Palladio, with its preoccupation with symmetry, proportion and geometry, and its obvious references to Classical antiquity.

inland, and to expand on *terra firma*. On a willow-shaded bend of the canal stands the Villa Foscari (also known as **La Malcontenta**; *open Tues and Sat 9–12*), constructed c. 1555–60 to a design by Palladio. Facing the water is a high, six-columned Ionic porch, designed to catch the breeze and to convey it through the building. Delightful window nooks on the garden side would have been splendid spots to sit and read on a hot day. At the centre of the *piano nobile* is a *salone* in the shape of a Greek cross. Frescoes cover all the walls. In one of the rooms is the frescoed figure of a woman, said to be La Malcontenta herself, Elisabetta Foscari, exiled here when her licentious lifestyle became an embarrassment to her family and an irritant to her husband.

The largest villa on the Riviera is the 18th-century Villa Pisani at **Stra**, named after its original owner, the Venetian doge Alvise Pisani. The lavish aspect of this villa is entirely appropriate, for Pisani was one of the most free-spending of all the 18th-century doges, famous for his feasts and for his prodigality at Carnival time. Despots have subsequently been drawn to the villa: it was purchased by Napoleon in 1807, and in 1934 was the site of the first meeting between Mussolini and Hitler. The interior (*open April–Sept 9–7, Oct–March 9–4*) has fine 18th-century decorations. The *Triumph of the Pisani Family* on the ballroom ceiling is by Tiepolo.

PADUA

Padua (*map p. 423, E2*) is a busy, lively place, with a famous university and a large student population. Its three large central squares float like rafts on the water on which the city is built. Padua is famous for the art of Giotto, and for being the burial place of the popular Franciscan saint Anthony of Padua.

The history of Padua is not dissimilar to that of many other north Italian cities. It was a Roman town; following that came a period of Byzantine and then Lombard rule; it became an independent commune in the 12th century, and evolved within a hundred years into a seigniory. Its university was founded in 1222, and many learned men have been associated with the town, including Dante and Petrarch. The greatest of the noble families were the Carraresi (or da Carrara), who ruled Padua until its conquest by Venice in 1405. It remained staunchly Venetian until Napoleon dissolved the Republic in 1797.

The old town centre

Between the two market squares of Piazza delle Erbe and Piazza della Frutta stands the **Palazzo della Ragione** (*map p. 105, 6; entrance from Piazza delle Erbe; open Tues–Sun 9–6 or 7*) built to house the law courts. Its double tier of arcades and huge ship's keel roof are reminiscent of Palladio's Basilica in Vicenza (*see p. 121*), though this building is much older: the outer arcades date from 1309, and the roof from a year before. The interior is astonishing: a single, enormous hall covered with frescoes and overarched by the remarkable roof, unsupported by columns of any kind. The original cycle of frescoes by Giotto was destroyed by fire in 1420. The current decoration was completed in 1440. It takes the form of an astrological cycle, showing human life as it is influenced and ordered by the heavens. Each month is shown with a zodiacal sign, an allegorical representation of the governing planet and an appropriate scene (threshing in July, for example; gathering fruit in September). The allegorical figure of the Justice of Solomon is a reference to the room's function as a judicial chamber.

To the east of Palazzo della Ragione is the famous **Caffè Pedrocchi** (*see p. 108*). In the other direction is the duomo and its splendid **baptistery** (*map p. 105, 5; open daily 10–6*). The interior is completely covered with frescoes of 1378 commissioned by Fina, wife of Francesco il Vecchio da Carrara, from Giusto de' Menabuoi, a Florentine artist who died in Padua. These are his undisputed masterpiece, and though his Florentine training is apparent, a more orientalising element is also present. The dome is filled by a teeming scene of Paradise, with Christ Pantocrator in the centre surrounded by angels and the blessed. Scenes from the lives of Christ and St John the Baptist adorn the walls, and the Apocalypse fills the apse, where an immense spotted beast steps out of the sea, its seven heads crowned with bishops' mitres.

The Scrovegni Chapel and Museo Civico

Padua's most celebrated attraction (*map p. 105, 4*) stands north of the town centre, on the site of the old Roman amphitheatre, hence its popular name, the 'Arena chapel'.

It was commissioned by the merchant Enrico degli Scrovegni and was used as his family chapel (the rest of his palace has been demolished).

Open daily 9–7. Booking is necessary for the chapel, and visiting it is something of an ordeal. You can book by phone (T: 049 201 0020) or online (www.capelladegliscrovegni.it) and pay by credit card. Bookings must be made at least a day before you visit. In low season, it might be worth going to the ticket office to see if they can let you in sooner. Pre-booked tickets must be collected at least an hour before the time of your visit. You are instructed to arrive at the entrance to the waiting room 5mins before the time printed on your ticket. If you are late, you will be denied entry and will not be reimbursed. The visit (max. 25 people) lasts half an hour, 15mins of which consists of standing in the waiting room while the 'interior microclimate' stabilises. After that you are permitted 15mins in the chapel itself.

Very plain on the outside, the tall, barrel-vaulted interior is covered with important and influential frescoes executed c. 1305 by Giotto and his pupils. Scrovegni's father had been a usurer, a calling that was frowned on by the medieval Church. Like the Medici (also involved in usury) he worried about the salvation of his family's souls, and commissioned these frescoes, whose theme is redemption. This is the only cycle by Giotto to survive intact, and its economy of expression and vivid rendering of drama and emotion were revolutionary in their day. Giotto makes no use, for example, of the conventions of scrolls bearing mottoes, either naming his characters or proclaiming what they stand for. Instead he communicates through physical gesture and physiognomy.

The chapel vault is painted blue and is spangled with stars—a conventional design, as the vaults and domes of churches were held to be symbolic of Heaven. The ceiling of the Sistine Chapel, before it was painted by Michelangelo, had just such a scheme. The scenes on the walls begin with the top band on the right as you face the altar. Both top bands should be read first, followed by the middle bands, and lastly by the lowest. The subjects are as follows:

Top right band: Lives of Joachim and Anne, parents of the Virgin;

Top left band: Life of the Virgin up to the Annunciation;

Middle right band: Visitation; infancy of Christ;

Middle left band: Adulthood of Christ;

Top right band: Passion of Christ;

Bottom left band: Crucifixion and Resurrection of Christ.

On the **entrance wall** is the Last Judgement. **Behind the altar** is the tomb of Enrico degli Scrovegni (d. 1336).

The **Museo Civico**, occupying the former monastery between the Scrovegni Chapel and the church of the Eremitani, contains some good works by painters of the Veneto, including Guariento, a native Paduan artist of the mid-14th century, who was court painter to Francesco da Carrara and his wife Fina. Almost the entire roster of Venetian names is represented here—Bellini, Giorgione, Titian, Veronese, Tintoretto and Tiepolo. Works by Guariento still *in situ* (though much ruined) can be seen in the

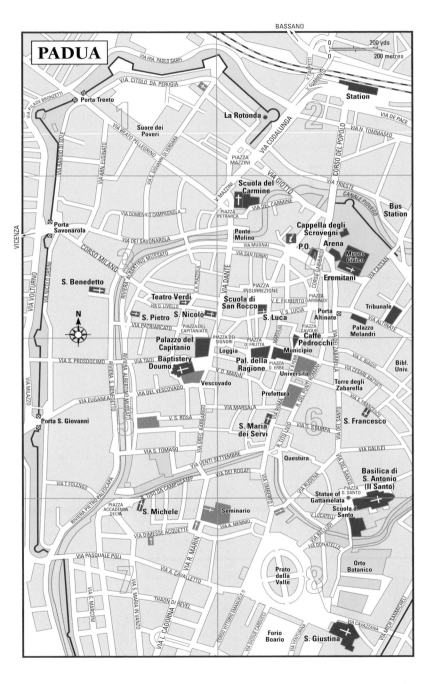

PADUA

BASSANO

VICENZA

0   200 yds
0   200 metres

VIA FRA. PAOLO SARPI

VIA CITOLO DA PERUGIA

Porta Trento

VIA PILADE BRONZETTI

VIA BEATO PELLEGRINO

VIA BAGNO DI STILE

VIA ARN. LUSINATO

VIA S. GIOVANNI DI VERDARA

VIA DOMENICO CAMPAGNOLA

Suore dei Poveri

La Rotonda

VIA CODALUNGA

Station

VIA DE PACE

VIA N. TOMMASEO

CORSO DEL POPOLO

PIAZZA MAZZINI

VIA GIOTTO

VIA TRIESTE

CANALE PIOVEGO

Bus Station

Scuola del Carmine

VIA MAZZINI

PIAZZA PETRARCA

VIA DEL CARMINE

Cappella degli Scrovegni

Arena

P.O.

Museo Civico

Porta Savonarola

VIA DEI SAVONAROLA

Ponte Molino

VIA MUGNAI

VIA SAN FERMO

CORSO GARIBALDI

Eremitani

VIA CASSAN

CORSO MILANO

RIVIERA ALBERTINO MUSSATO

VIA NICOLÒ ORSINI

VIA VOLTURNO

S. Benedetto

R. PIAZZOLA

VIA DANTE

PIAZZA INSURREZIONE

V.E. FILIBERTO GARIBALDI

PIAZZA GARIBALDI

Tribunale

Teatro Verdi

VIA D. LIVELLO

Scuola di San Rocco

V. S. LUCIA

S. Luca

Porta Altinate

VIA ALTINATE

Palazzo Melandri

S. Pietro

S. Nicolò

VIA PATRIARCATO

PIAZZA DEL CAPITANIATO

PIAZZA DEI SIGNORI

MARSILIO

PIAZZA CAVOUR

Caffè Pedrocchi

VIA ZABARELLA

VIA S. BIAGIO

Bibl. Univ.

Palazzo del Capitanio

Baptistery

Duomo

RIVIERA S. BENEDETTO

VIA TADI

PIAZZA D. FRUTTA

Loggia

Pal. della Ragione

Municipio

Università

PIAZZA D. ERBE

VIA CESARE BATTISTI

VIA VESCOVADO

VIA S. PROSDOCIMO

V. D. MANIN

Vescovado

Prefettura

R. DEI PONTI ROMANI

Torre degli Zabarella

VIA S. FRANCESCO

VIA MILAZZO

Porta S. Giovanni

VIA EUGANEA

V. S. ROSA

VIA GREG. BARBARIGO

VIA MARSALA

VIA ROMA

R. TITO LIVIO

VIA C. STAMPA

S. Francesco

VIA GALILEI

S. Maria dei Servi

VIA S. TOMASO

VIA VENTI SETTEMBRE

VIA DEI ROGATI

Questura

VIA T. FOLENGO

RIVIERA PIETRO PALEOCAPA

PIAZZA ACCADEMIA DELIA

S. Michele

TISO DA CAMPOSAMP.

VIA IMBERTO

VIA RUDENA

VAL DEL SANTO

Basilica di S. Antonio (Il Santo)

PIAZZA D. SANTO

Statue of Gattamelata

Seminario

VIA A. MEMMO

Scuola d. Santo

V. LOCATELLI

VIA DEL LUIDI

VIA DIMESSE ACQUETTE

VIA R. MARIN

VIA DONATELLO

Orto Botanico

VIA PASQUALE POLI

VIA A. CAVALLETTO

VIA S. MARIA IN VANZO

Prato della Valle

VIA L. CADORNA

THAON DI REVEL

CORSO VITTORIO EMANUELE II

VIA G. MARCONI

Forio Boario

VIA GIUSEPPE CARDUCCI

VIA CAVAZZANA

S. Giustina

VIA MICH. SANMICHELI

VIA VENTURINA

adjacent church of the **Eremitani**, dedicated to St Philip and St James. In the sanctuary are fragmentary stories of the titular duo and a cycle of St Augustine (the church and monastery were built for the Augustinian Order). *The Vision of St Augustine* is one of the better preserved: the saint is shown sitting in the corner of a walled garden, where an angel appears to him out of the night sky.

The Santo

At the south end of the old centre (*map p. 105, 6–8*) is the city's most important religious monument, the Franciscan basilica of St Anthony, familiarly known as the 'Santo'. The square on which the church stands contains the bronze **equestrian statue of Gattamelata**, the Venetian mercenary general Erasmo da Narni. He was born in Padua around 1370, and his monument, executed ten years after his death in 1443, is a masterpiece by Donatello, inspired by the statue of Marcus Aurelius in Rome (*see p. 242*). Thirty-five years later Verrocchio succeeded in producing a similar bronze where, as with the Marcus Aurelius, one of the horse's hooves is poised off the ground unsupported (Gattamelata's horse places his raised hoof on a convenient bronze ball).

The basilica (*open 6.20–7.45*) was begun in 1232, just two years after St Anthony's death. This much-loved saint, commonly represented as a friar in brown Franciscan robes holding the infant Jesus, was born in Lisbon in 1195. He was on a missionary journey to Africa when a storm forced him off course to Italy. He settled at Padua, where he preached and performed miracles. This church is now an important pilgrim shrine. The exterior, with its distinctive eight-domed roof, has a strongly Eastern appearance.

Gattamelata is buried here, in the first south chapel. In the south transept, the Chapel of St James has frescoes of 1372–79 by the Veronese painter Altichiero, notably a superb Crucifixion scene (*illustrated opposite*). His style is an interesting fusion of the solidity of Giotto with the love of detail and ornament of the International Gothic.

The **Cappella dell'Arca del Santo** in the north transept houses St Anthony's tomb, designed in 1499 by the great Venetian sculptor Tullio Lombardo. The adjacent chapel with the tomb of the Blessed Luca Belludi, St Anthony's companion and follower, was frescoed in 1382 by Giusto de' Menabuoi.

Behind the bronze doors of the choir (*ask a custodian to unlock them*) is the **high altar** (1443–50), Donatello's second major commission in Padua after the Gattamelata statue. It is decorated with splendid bronze works by the master and his pupils. These include four superb large reliefs of the miracles of St Anthony (two on the front and two on the back) and an enthroned *Madonna* between life-size statues of the six patron saints of Padua, two of whom are St Francis and St Anthony.

On the west wall is a fresco of 1985 by Pietro Annigoni of *St Anthony Preaching from the Walnut Tree*. This alludes to a real episode from his life (the tree in question was at Camposampiero, north of Padua).

The Oratory of St George, botanic garden and Prato della Valle

Adjoining the Santo on the southwest are the **Scuola di Sant'Antonio** and the **Oratory of St George** (*map p. 105, 8; open April–Oct 9–12.30 & 2.30–7, Nov–March 9–12.30 &*

Altichiero's *Crucifixion* in the Santo of Padua shows a Giottesque naturalism in the human figures coupled with an interest in detail and a tendency toward crowded composition that clings more to the world of the International Gothic. Though he lacks the robust individuality of Giotto, and though he is less daring with colour, Altichiero is nevertheless the most important northern Italian mural painter of the late 14th century.

2.30–5; combined ticket). The *scuola* contains three early works by Titian (1511) of miracles of St Anthony (the *Healing of the Wrathful Son*, *Miracle of the Newborn Child* and *Miracle of the Jealous Husband*). The oratory is entirely covered with superb frescoes by Altichiero and his assistants (1379–84) showing scenes from the lives of Christ and Sts George, Catherine and Lucy. Their arrangement in horizontal bands clearly owes a debt to Giotto's design for the Scrovegni Chapel, but the obsession with detail, once again, is quite unlike the Florentine master, and owes more to Pisanello.

The quiet Via Orto Botanico leads away from the Santo and across a canal to the **Botanic Garden** (*open April–Oct daily 9–1 & 3–7, winter daily except Sun and holidays 9–1*). Established in the 16th century, this is the oldest botanic garden in Europe.

Via Beato Luca Belludi leads to **Prato della Valle**, a vast and elegantly conceived urban space consisting of an elliptical 'island' surrounded by a canal bordered with a double row of statues of famous *padovani*.

VISITING PADUA

GETTING AROUND

• **By air:** SITA (www.sitabus.it) operates a bus service from Venice airport to Padua and vice versa (buses every hour, journey time c. 1hr). Buses every 20mins from Padua station to the centre.
• **By car:** The car parks in Padua at Prato della Valle and the station have a minibus service to the central Piazza dei Signori.
• **By train:** There are frequent services to and from Venice (journey time c. 50mins). Fast trains go to Verona (c. 50mins), Milan (2–3hrs), Turin (c. 4½ hrs) and Genoa (c. 4½ hrs); and to Bologna (c. 1–1½ hrs), Florence (c. 2¼ hrs) and Rome (c. 4hrs).

SPECIAL TICKETS

The **Padova Card** gives free entrance to the main museums and monuments of Padua, plus free travel on city buses. It can be purchased from tourist information offices, museums and monuments throughout the area.

WHERE TO STAY IN PADUA

The well-liked €€ **Belludi 37**, close to the Santo, offers plain, unfussy, uncluttered accommodation (*Via Luca Belludi 37, T: 049 665633, www.belludi37.it; map p. 105, 8*). A few kilometres south of Padua, at Albignasego (frequent buses from the bus station in 20mins), is the €€€ **Villa Mandriola**, a gracious villa in a huge park, still the family home of the counts of San Bonifacio (*Via S. Caboto 10, T: 049 681246, www.villamandriola.com*).

WHERE TO EAT IN PADUA

The most famous and finest restaurant in Padua is the one at €€€ **Caffè Pedrocchi**. A glass of *prosecco* and a few snacks at the bar are as good a way of experiencing the place as a full meal (*T: 049 878 1231; map p. 105, 6*). € **Isola di Caprera**, just off Piazza della Frutta, serves seasonal Paduan food and good wine (*Via Marsilio da Padova 11/15, T: 049 876 0244; closed Sun; map p. 105, 4*).

THE EUGANEAN HILLS

The Euganean Hills (Colli Euganei; *map p. 423, E2*) are a volcanic feature rising in the Po river basin southwest of Padua. Technically they are laccoliths, domed-shaped formations that occur when molten magma thrusts its way between two layers of underlying rock, forcing the upper layers to form a hump. The hills are famed for their mineral-rich springs (70–87°C) and the landscape is a lovely mixture of cultivated terraces and rich chestnut woods. A good white wine is produced here, and wild mushrooms grow in abundance. Shelley's *Lines Written Among the Euganean Hills* were composed here in 1818, when he was at a particularly low ebb following the death at Este of his one-year-old daughter Clara ('Ay, many flowering islands lie In the waters of wide Agony'). The hills are considerably more beautiful and uplifting than the poet's wretched doggerel.

There are four spa towns, of which **Abano Terme** is by far the most famous. **Arquà Petrarca**, further south, is a very pretty medieval *borgo*, known for its honey, its olive oil and its jujube trees. A festival of the fruit (also known as the red date) is held in October. It was here, in the place he called his 'second Helicon', that the poet Petrarch lived from 1370 until his death in 1374. His tomb, a simple sarcophagus of red Verona marble, is preserved here, and his house (*open as a museum*) is at the top of the village.

Este is an ancient city at the southern edge of the Euganean Hills. It is the ancestral home of the great ruling family of Ferrara, who moved their seat to that city in 1259. After that, Este was squabbled over between the Scaligeri of Verona, the Visconti of Milan and the Carraresi of Padua. It came under Venetian control in 1405. The old, battlemented Carraresi castle still broods over the town. North of its park entrance (*Via Guido Negri 9/c*), in a former home of the Venetian Mocenigo family, is the **Museo Nazionale Atestino** (*open Tues–Sun 9–8*), with an exceptional collection of material relating to the ancient Veneti. The **cathedral of St Tecla** contains a large *St Tecla Freeing Este from the Plague* by Giovanni Battista Tiepolo (1759).

Sixteen kilometres west of Este is **Montagnana**, a perfectly preserved medieval walled town with a broad main street leading between towery gates, and a grassy moat between the walls and the encircling modern road. The walls were in part the work of the Carraresi. The duomo, set at an angle to the main square, contains a high altarpiece of the *Transfiguration* by Veronese.

VISITING THE EUGANEAN HILLS

GETTING AROUND

• **By bus:** Country buses run by SITA (www.sitabus.it) depart from Padua's main bus station (*map p. 105, 4*) to Arquà Petrarca (infrequent service) and Este and Montagnana (services roughly every hour; approx. 1hr to Este, 1hr 20mins to Montagnana).
• **By rail:** Frequent trains link Padua with Abano in c. 7mins. Change at Monselice for Este (c. 40mins) and Montagnana (c. 1hr).

WHERE TO STAY IN THE EUGANEAN HILLS

Abano Terme
€€ **Trieste e Victoria**. Well-established, elegant place with lovely gardens and indoor and outdoor thermal pools. Open March–Dec. *Via Pietro d'Abano 1, T: 049 866 5800, www.gbhotels.it.*

€ **Casa Ciriani**. Warm hospitality, calm and quiet distinguish this family-run B&B, in a small villa in its own green park. *Via Guazzi 1, T: 049 715272, www.casaciriani.com*
Arquà Petrarca
€ **Villa del Poeta**. Basic rooms, restaurant, bicycle hire. An adequate base for exploring the region. *Via Zane 5, T: 0429 777361, www.villadelpoeta.com.*
Montagnana
€ **Aldo Moro**. Comfortable accommodation in a fine old town house. With restaurant. *Via Marconi 27, T: 0429 81351, www.hotelaldomoro.it.*

WHERE TO EAT IN THE EUGANEAN HILLS

All the towns of the Euganean Hills offer standard, simple places to eat. €€€ **La Montanella**, just outside Arquà Petrarca, is a lovely place to come on a sunny day for lunch in the garden (*Via dei Carraresi 9, T: 0429 718200*). The cuisine is experimental and somewhat nouvelle, but has won the approval of many locals.

LAKE GARDA

The largest of the Italian lakes, **Lake Garda** (*map p. 423, D2*; sometimes called Lago di Benaco), partly in Lombardy and partly in the Veneto, is one of the most romantic spots in Italy, and even in the height of summer, when car- and bus-loads of northern Europeans descend via the Brenner Pass to bask on its sun-baked shores, it amply repays a day or two of leisurely exploration.

Tourists have always been coming to Garda. The poet Catullus (?84–54 BC) had a villa near Sirmione. Goethe was entranced by the place, writing that '[my guide book] informs me that the lake was formerly called Benacus and quotes a line from Virgil where it is mentioned: *Fluctibus et fremitu assurgens Benace marino*. This is the first line of Latin verse the subject of which I have seen with my own eyes' (*Italian Journey*, 1786, Tr. W.H. Auden and Elizabeth Mayer). The thrill of seeing with one's own eyes the things one has read about or seen on film is no less intense today than it was then.

The vast mass of water creates a distinctly Mediterranean microclimate. The vegetation is highly varied, sometimes quite wild and always very beautiful. Here you will find olives, cypresses, citrus groves and vineyards; gentle moraines and a harsh, narrow fjord.

The south and west shores

The most interesting town on the southern shore is **Sirmione**, near the end of a long, narrow peninsula. It is a well-known spa town, with a warm sulphur spring (La Boiola) that bubbles up just offshore. It has a very special atmosphere, a combination of the spectacular medieval walls of the Rocca Scaligera (*open Tues–Sun 8.30–7*; originally a stronghold of Verona's ruling family), the narrow lanes of the old town, and the striking views of the lake. Romantically set among olive groves at the northern end of the peninsula are the extensive remains of a Roman villa of the early imperial period, commonly called the **Grotte di Catullo** (*open Tues–Sat 8.30–7, Sun and holidays 8.30–5*) but in fact unrelated to the poet. The view alone justifies the walk out.

More Roman remains have been excavated at **Desenzano del Garda**, the largest town on the lake and a busy transport hub—you will come here to catch a boat at least, though there are things to linger for as well. The small harbour used by fishing boats is very picturesque, and the parish church, just off the main arcaded piazza, has a *Last Supper* by Tiepolo. The Roman remains are of a villa complex of the 1st–4th centuries AD (*open Tues–Sun 9–dusk*) and include a fine mosaic floor with hunting and fishing scenes. An antiquarium has finds from the site.

Salò, the Roman *Salodium*, lies huddled amidst green hills on a little bay. The beauty of the site explains its fame, today somewhat marred by the town's association with

View of Lake Garda, one of the most famous beauty spots in Italy, and one where schoolbook geography is vividly illustrated.

Mussolini's Repubblica Sociale Italiana (or Repubblica di Salò), established under Nazi protection after the armistice of 1943. This agreement brought an end to hostilities between Italy and the Allies and led to the immediate occupation of the northern part of the country by the Germans. Mussolini took up residence with his mistress at near-by Gargnano. The republic lasted until the war's end, 25th April 1945; three days later Mussolini was captured and summarily executed while trying to escape to Switzerland.

Beyond **Gardone Riviera**, with the villa and mausoleum of the eccentric and self-pro-moting poet Gabriele d'Annunzio (Vittoriale degli Italiani; *open daily summer 8.30–8, winter 9–5; house closed Mon, museum closed Tues*), is **Gargnano**, an attractive town of 19th-century villas with a square opening onto the little harbour. An inland road from here to **Limone** passes the hill sanctuary of Madonna di Monte Castello, with the finest view of the whole lake. Mussolini lived here at Villa Feltrinelli from 1943 until three days before his death. The characteristic *limonaie*, arranged in terraces on the hillsides and traditionally used for the cultivation of lemons, are much in evidence here. Slats of wood and glass panels were stretched between the stone posts in winter, to protect the trees. Citrus fruits have been grown around Lake Garda since the 16th century.

The north and east shores

Riva del Garda, the Roman *Ripa*, is a lively little town, popular with windsurfers in the summer. The Museo Civico (*open daily in summer 10–12.30 & 1.30–6; Tues–Sun in winter*) has displays on the early Bronze Age pile dwellings of Lago di Ledro; another museum devoted to these is at **Molina di Ledro**, on the banks of the lovely little Lago di Ledro itself, just west of Riva (*open Tues–Sun 9–5 or 10–6*). **Torbole** is a summer resort famed for the part it played in the war between Venice and the Visconti of Milan. In April 1440 the Venetian general Stefano Contarini used 2,000 oxen and a few hundred men to haul six galleys and 25 smaller boats over the mountains from the River Adige to take the town from Filippo Maria Visconti.

Malcesine was the seat of the Veronese Captains of the Lake in the 16th–17th centuries; their palace is the town hall. The towering 13th–14th century castle of the Scaligeri (*open daily in summer 9.30–7, Sat–Sun in winter 9.30–6*) was restored by Venice in the 17th century. Goethe sketched it in his album and was suspected of being an Austrian spy; there is now a museum dedicated to him here. A cableway runs to the top of Monte Baldo (1748m).

Torri del Benaco has another Scaligeri castle and fine old houses around a pretty harbour. A splendid *limonaia* of 1760 protects a plantation of huge old citrus trees.

The headland of **Punta di San Vigilio** is a lovely romantic spot, secluded in a way, though many motorcades have found their way here, including those conveying Winston Churchill, Sir Laurence Olivier and King Juan Carlos of Spain to the famed hotel and tavern (*see opposite*). A cypress avenue ends at the 16th-century Villa Guarienti, from where a path continues downhill past a walled lemon garden to the hotel and its picturesque little port.

Bardolino is well known for its wine; the tourist office has a list of *cantine* that offer tastings and tours (Strada del Vino Bardolino; *www.stradadelbardolino.com*).

Peschiera del Garda, an ancient fortress and one of the four corners of the Austrian 'quadrilateral' (the other three are Verona, Mantua and Legnago), stands at the outflow of the Mincio. The quadrilateral was part of an essentially defensive rather than offensive strategy, aimed at protecting key crossings over the Po and rendering invasion routes inaccessible. Austria clung onto it until defeated by Prussia in 1866.

VISITING LAKE GARDA

GETTING AROUND

• **By bus:** Bus services run several times daily by the roads on the west and east shores from Peschiera and Desenzano to Riva. Service is frequent between Desenzano, Salò and Riva, and from Riva to Verona.

• **By train:** The Venice–Milan line serves Peschiera del Garda and Desenzano del Garda-Sirmione. Regional trains connect the lake stations to Verona in less than 30mins. Intercity trains stop at Desenzano-Sirmione only, saving just a minute or two.

• **By boat:** Boat services (including two paddle-steamers built in 1902 and 1903) are run by Gestione Navigazione Laghi (www.navigazionelaghi.it), from around mid-March–early Nov (the timetable changes three times a year). A year-round car ferry operates between Maderno and Torri del Benaco in 30mins (every 30mins, but less frequently in winter) and there is a summer ferry from Limone to Malcesine in 20mins (hourly). All-inclusive daily tickets are available, allowing unrestricted travel on all lake services. Tours of the lake in the afternoons in summer are also organised. The main boat service runs between Desenzano and Riva (total journey time 2¼ hrs), calling at all the main towns.

WHERE TO STAY ON LAKE GARDA

Punta di San Vigilio
€€€ **Locanda San Vigilio**. Small establishment on the lakefront with a good restaurant and garden and a distinguished guest list. Open March–Oct. *Località San Vigilio, T: 045 725 6688, www.locanda-sanvigilio.it.*

Gargnano
There are a number of fine places here. Finest of all is the €€€ **Villa Feltrinelli**, a magnificent villa with frescoed rooms set in a waterfront park (*Via Rimembranza 38–40, T: 0365 798 000, www.villafeltrinelli.com; open April–Oct*). €€ **Villa Giulia** is another, less grand, lakeside villa with a lovely garden (*Viale Rimembranza 20, T: 0365 71022, www.villagiulia.it; open April–Dec*).

Sirmione
€€€ **Palace Hotel Villa Cortine**. An Austrian nobleman built this Neoclassical villa as his country house in 1870, and an aristocratic air still prevails in its frescoed rooms and expansive, lakeside park. Open April–Oct. *Via Grotte 6, T: 030 990 5890, www.hotelvillacortine.com.*

WHERE TO EAT ON LAKE GARDA

Fresh fish is usually good on Lake Garda: eel, tench and perch are plentiful. Indigenous to the lake is the *Salmo carpio*, a kind of trout. On menus it appears as *Trota del Garda*—though it is now an endangered species, so do not be disappointed if you do not find it.

Desenzano del Garda
€€€ **Esplanade** is a refined sort of place serving fresh seasonal cuisine and excellent

wines. There is also garden seating overlooking the lake in summer (*Via Lario 10, T: 030 914 3361; closed Wed*). € **Cavallino** is a simple, straightforward establishment serving easy cuisine (*Via Gherla 30, T: 030 912 0217; closed Mon, Jan and mid-Aug*).

Gardone Riviera
€€ **Villa Fiordaliso** (with rooms). This place has been in business since 1890. The food is delicious, and the setting, in an old villa in a small park with summer seating overlooking the lake, is unbeatable. Closed Mon, midday Tues and Jan–Feb. *Corso Zanardelli 150, T: 0365 20158.*

Gargnano
€€€ **La Tortuga**. Very small and very famous, known for fine food and excellent wine. Closed Mon evening (except June–Sept), Tues and Jan. *Via XXIV Maggio, T: 0365 71251.*

Riva del Garda
€€ **Villa Negri**. A fine restaurant offering good traditional cuisine and an exceptional location on high ground overlooking the entire lake. *Via Bastioni 31/35, T: 0464 555061.*

Salò
€€ **Gallo Rosso** is an excellent small restaurant in the historic centre (*Vicolo Tomacelli 4, T: 0365 520757; closed Weds and one week in Jan and June*). € **Osteria dell'Orologio** serves snacks and light meals downstairs and full meals upstairs. A good place to go for a quick lunch (*Via Butturini 26, T: 0365 290 158; closed Wed and June–July*).

Torri del Benaco
€€€ **Gardesana** (also a hotel) is a fine restaurant famous for its lake-fish soup—but the home-made pasta is also delicious, and the wine list is only slightly shorter than *War and Peace*. Closed Tues (except in summer) and Nov–Feb. *Piazza Calderini 20, T: 045 722 5411, www.hotel-gardesana.com.*

VERONA

Verona (*map 423, D2*) is a lively, bustling and attractive town sitting on an S-bend of the River Adige. It was the birthplace of the poet Catullus, whose summer villa was at nearby Sirmione (*see p. 110*), and possibly of the 1st-century BC architect and engineer Vitruvius. It has some impressive Roman remains, the most outstanding of which is the amphitheatre. Verona became a Roman colony in 89 BC. In medieval times it was ruled in turn by the Ostrogoths, Lombards and Franks and became a *comune* in 1100. In 1260 Mastino della Scala (or Scaliger), the elected governor (*podestà*), established himself as overlord of the city and secured a century of power and political influence for his family, as can be seen from the Ponte Scaligero with its characteristic swallowtail battlements, from the dynasty's fortress of Castelvecchio (now the city museum) and from the magnificent family tombs in the Piazzaletto delle Arche. Della Scala rule ended in 1387, when Gian Galeazzo Visconti of Milan (*see p. 30*) overran the city.

Verona allied itself with Venice in 1405 and remained part of the Venetian Republic until it was taken by the French in 1796. The city tried to resist Napoleon's occupation, but resistance was crushed and much of the city destroyed. The city passed between the French and the Austrians, finally ending up in Austrian hands in 1814. It was the strongest corner of the Austrian 'quadrilateral' (*see p. 112*), but with the Prussian defeat of Austria in 1866 it became part of the Italian Republic.

Perhaps Verona's most famous son was the artist Paolo Caliari, better known as Veronese. Born in 1528, he was apprenticed to a local painter before leaving briefly for Mantua, from where he continued to Venice, establishing himself, along with Titian and Tintoretto, as one of the greatest Venetian painters of the late Renaissance.

Central Verona

Dominating Piazza Brà is the massive elliptical amphitheatre or **Arena** (*map p. 117, 7–11; open Tues–Sun 8.30–7.30; during the opera season, July–Aug, 8.30–3.30*). Built in the 1st century AD, it is the third largest Roman amphitheatre in Italy (after the Colosseum and the amphitheatre in Capua) and can accommodate an audience of 22,000. It is the famous setting of Verona's opera season (www.arena.it) where it provides a perfect backdrop for spectacular productions.

Verona's finest shopping street, Via Mazzini (known also as Via Nuova), leads out of the piazza to another famous site, the '**House of Juliet**' (*map p. 117, 7*). Although Shakespeare chose 'fair Verona' as the setting for *Romeo and Juliet*, there is no evidence to suggest that any such tragedy took place here. This is, in fact, a 13th-century Gothic town house, once owned by the da Cappelletti family—a name similar enough to Capulet to have the crowds flocking here to stand on the balcony and re-enact the famous scene. A short way to the north is Piazza delle Erbe (*map p. 117, 7 and inset*), once the Roman forum and which still has a daily market. The column bearing the Lion of St Mark is a common feature of all cities that owed allegiance to Venice.

Passing under the 15th-century Arco della Costa—which takes its name from a whale's rib (*costa*) hung beneath it—you enter **Piazza dei Signori** (*map p. 117, 7 and*

Pisanello's *St George* (1433–38) in the church of Sant'Anastasia. Although in poor condition, traces of the elaborate silvering and gilding are still visible.

inset), seat of city government in the Middle Ages. It was here, in 1277, that Mastino I della Scala, founder of Scaligeri power in Verona, was assassinated by a rebel faction. In the north corner of the square is the Palazzo della Prefettura, with a doorway of 1533 by the local-born architect Michele Sanmicheli. The passage on the right of the palace leads into the little **Piazzaletto delle Arche**, which takes its name from the monumental tombs (*arche*) of the Scaligeri executed in the 14th century by Bonino da Campione and his followers, all master sculptors from Campione on Lake Lugano. A stone-and-iron enclosure bears the family emblem of a ladder (in Italian, *scala*). Inside the enclosure, above the church doorway is the tomb of Cangrande I (d. 1329), the 'great dog', who became sole ruler of Verona in 1311. This formidable warrior makes an improbable bookworm, but Dante dedicated his *Paradiso* to him, in gratitude for being given safe haven in Verona following his exile from Florence. The equestrian statue on the tomb is a copy of the original now in the Museo del Castelvecchio (*see p. 118*).

Sant'Anastasia, the cathedral and the Roman theatre

The Dominican church of Sant'Anastasia (*map p. 117, 4*) is the largest in Verona. It was built between 1291 and 1323 and remodelled in the 15th century. The façade was never finished. Inside, you are greeted by the two famous hunchbacked water stoups, which date from the 16th century. The one with his hands on his knees is attributed to Gabriele Caliari, father of Veronese. The first south altar (1565) is by Sanmicheli. Four chapels radiate off the apse. The first chapel on the south side has a large fresco

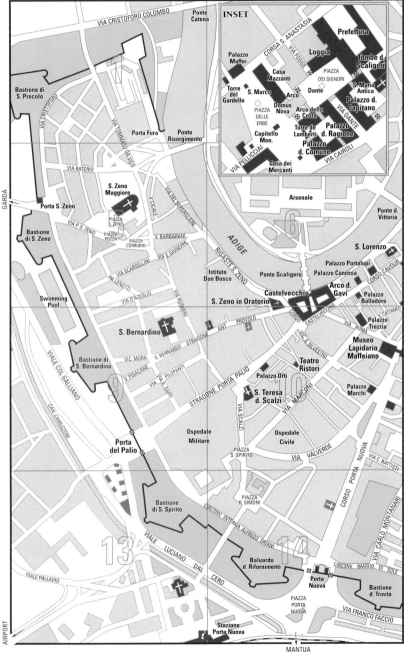

INSET

CORSO S. ANASTASIA
VIA FOGGE

Prefettura

Palazzo Maffei

Loggia

Tombe d. Scaligeri

Casa Mazzanti

PIAZZA DEI SIGNORI

Dante

Torre del Gardello

S. Marco

Arco

S. Maria Antica

PIAZZA DELLE ERBE

Domus Nova

Arco della Costa

Palazzo d. Capitano

VIA DANTE

Capitello Mon.

Torre de Lamberti

Palazzo d. Ragione

Palazzo d. Comune

VIA PELLICCIAI

VIA CAIROLI

Casa dei Mercanti

VIA CRISTOFORO COLOMBO

Ponte Catena

VIA CRISTOFORO

Bastione di S. Procolo

VIA TOMMASO DA VICO

Porta Fura

Ponte Risorgimento

VIA RATERIO

GARDA

S. Zeno Maggiore

V. CICALE

VIA DEL BERSAGLIERE

Porta S. Zeno

PIAZZA S. ZENO

VIA P. S. ZENO

PIAZZA POZZA

PIAZZA CORRUBIO

V. BARBARANI

VIA S. GIUSEPPE

Bastione di S. Zeno

ADIGE

Arsenale

Ponte d. Vittoria

6

RIGASTE S. ZENO

VIA SCARSELLINI

VIA LENOTTI

Istituto Don Bosco

Ponte Scaligero

Palazzo Canossa

S. Lorenzo

Palazzo Portalupi

CORSO CAVOUR

Swimming Pool

VIA D'AZEGLIO

VIA RISMINI

Castelvecchio

Arco d. Gavi

Palazzo Balladoro

VIALE COL GALLIANO

S. Zeno in Oratorio

CORSO CASTELVECCHIO

VIC. S. SILVESTRO

VIA ROMA

Palazzo Trezzia

S. Bernardino

STRADONE ANT. PROVOLO

Museo Lapidario Maffeiano

VIC. MURA

S. BERNARDO

STRADONE

V. PISACANE

VIA A. SAFFI

9

CAN. CAMUZZONI

Bastione di S. Bernardino

V. A. FILOPANTI

STRADONE PORTA PALIO

Teatro Ristori

Palazzo Orti

VIA MARCONI

Palazzo Marchi

10

Porta del Palio

S. Teresa d. Scalzi

VIA SCALZI

Ospedale Militare

Ospedale Civile

VIA VALVERDE

CORSO PORTA NUOVA

VIA C. BATTISTI

PIAZZA S. SPIRITO

Bastione di S. Spirito

PIAZZA R. SIMONI

CIRCONV. INTERNA ALFREDO ORIANI

VIA CARLO MONTANARI

13

VIALE LUCIANO DAL CERO

14

Baluardo d. Rifornimenti

CIRCONV. RAGGIO DI SOLE

Porta Nuova

Bastione d. Trinità

VIALE PALLADIO

PIAZZA PORTA NUOVA

VIA FRANCO FACCIO

AIRPORT

Stazione Porta Nuova

MANTUA

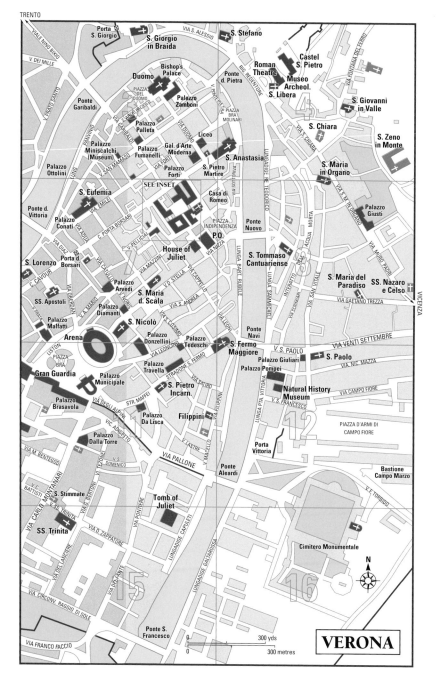

TRENTO

VERONA

by Altichiero depicting the Cavalli family presented to the Virgin (1390–95). Altichiero was born in Verona, though his best known works are in Padua (*see p. 107*). The second is the Pellegrini Chapel: here, above the doorway, is the most famous work of art in the church. It is a fresco of *St George and the Dragon* by Pisanello (1433–38), a masterpiece of the International Gothic style, showing the golden-haired saint and the princess and some superb horses and dogs, with a fairytale towery city in the background. Above the two hanged men on the gibbet rises a rainbow, symbol of redemption.

Northwest of Sant'Anastasia, along Via Duomo, is the **Duomo di Santa Maria Matricolare** (*map p. 117, 3*), mainly Romanesque in its outward appearance. The unfinished bell-tower was begun by Sanmicheli. Broad arches of red Verona marble dominate the interior. Of the many paintings, the best are an *Assumption* by Titian (1430s) and an *Adoration of the Magi* by Liberale da Verona, one of the most interesting of the city's Renaissance artists. He was an exceptionally fine miniaturist and spent many years in Siena (Vasari mentions him in his *Lives of the Artists*), where his style was influential.

Across Ponte di Pietra is the **Roman Theatre** (*map p. 117, 4; open Tues–Sun 8.30–7.30, Mon 1.30–7.30; last admission 45mins before closing*), its semicircle of seats superbly positioned overlooking the river (it is used for performances in summer). Above the theatre, the Renaissance cloister of the former convent of San Girolamo houses a **Museo Archeologico** (*closed Mon*) with artefacts from Roman Verona. The views from the windows and terraces over the theatre, the river and the city are themselves worth the climb.

The Castelvecchio

This stout fortress (*map p. 116, 6*) was built as a fortified residence in 1354–57 by Cangrande II della Scala, popularly known as 'Can rabbioso', the Mad Dog (all the Scaligeri adopted canine epithets). It is connected to the north side of the Adige by the Ponte Scaligero, a bridge used exclusively by the family, and intended as an escape route from the city if required. In those turbulent days in Italy, the della Scala fiefdom was as turbulent as any. Cangrande was murdered by his brother Cansignorio in 1359. On the latter's death, the Visconti claimed Verona, for Bernabò Visconti (*see p. 40*) had married Cansignorio's sister. The della Scala held onto their city, but not for very much longer: the last of the family, Antonio della Scala, having ordered his own brother's murder to make his position more secure, was chased from his castle by the Visconti and their allies in 1387. He died the following year. The task of adapting the fortress as a museum was entrusted to Carlo Scarpa, one of the most prominent Italian architects of the mid-20th century. The resulting **Civico Museo d'Arte** (*open Tues–Sun 8.30–7.30; Mon 1.45–7.30, last admission 45mins before closing*) is famous for its holdings of Veronese painting, sculpture and decorative art.

The highlight of the sculpture collection is the statue of Cangrande I on his caparisoned horse, from the Scaligeri tombs (*see p. 115*). In the **painting collection** are two famous works from the 1420s: the *Madonna del Roseto*, attributed to Stefano da Verona, and the *Madonna of the Quail*, attributed to Pisanello. Both the attributions have been questioned; nevertheless both paintings are exquisite early examples of the International Gothic style. Vasari noted that Pisanello was fond of depicting animals.

Mantegna's San Zeno altarpiece is a superb example of the *Sacra Conversazione*. Unlike the Gothic polyptych, where the figures are isolated in separate compartments, the Virgin and Child are here surrounded in the same space by angel musicians and saints, identified by their attributes (St Peter holds his keys, St Lawrence holds the griddle on which he was roasted alive). The frame is the original, and is ingeniously incorporated into the Classically-inspired architectural setting.

Here we see a beautiful, tender Madonna and her plump, healthy baby in a paradise bower with goldfinches (symbol of Christ's Passion) and a superb quail (symbol of eternal love). There are also works by Liberale da Verona, together with his favourite pupil, Giovanni Francesco Caroto, whose charming *Boy with a Drawing of a Puppet* (c. 1520) shows a young child proudly holding up a stick-man sketch. The Venetian masters who most influenced Liberale da Verona, Jacopo Bellini and his son-in-law Mantegna, are also represented here, as is Verona's most famous son, Paolo Veronese.

San Zeno Maggiore

The basilica of San Zeno Maggiore (*map p. 116, 5; open Mon–Sat 8.30–6, Sun and holidays 1–6; tickets, required for admission, are sold on the left as you enter the square*) stands in the western 'horn' of the old walled city. This beautiful and dignified Romanesque structure was built in 1120–38 on the site of a 5th-century church said to have been built by Theodoric the Great (*see p. 152*) over the site of St Zeno's tomb. St Zeno, eighth bishop of Verona, is the patron saint of fishermen (he is shown indulging in this activity on one of the panels of the lovely 12th-century bronze entrance doors). His remains now lie in the church crypt. The façade gives a marked feeling of verticality, produced by the long, slim pilaster strips which descend to the ground from every fourth dwarf arcade. The reliefs on either side of the main door date from 1135. Those on the right are by Maestro Niccolò (his signature also appears on the porch), and show mainly Old Testament scenes. At the bottom Theodoric is shown on horseback. The scenes on the left (New Testament) are by his pupil, Maestro Guglielmo. The finest work of art in the noble interior is the high altarpiece, the *Madonna and Child with Saints* by Mantegna (1456; *illustrated above; at the time of writing due to return from restoration*). This is one of the artists' masterpieces, and his only panel painting still *in situ*. It is arranged as a triptych, though the scene in fact takes place in a single idealised classical loggia, and the garland of fruit, nuts, vegetables and foliage spans the entire space. Above the Virgin's head hangs a beautifully rendered lamp. St Zeno appears on the left, with a long black beard and bishop's crozier. The predella scenes are copies of the originals by Paolino Caliari, a descendant of Veronese. The originals are still in France, where the painting was taken after Napoleon looted Verona in 1797. In the little north apse is a medieval polychrome and red marble statue known as the 'Laughing St Zeno'. He is shown enthroned, his right hand raised in blessing, with a beatific smile on his face.

San Fermo Maggiore

In the very east of the right-hand 'horn' of the old city, close to Ponte Navi, is San Fermo Maggiore (*map p. 117, 8–12; open 10–6, Sun 1–6*), a complex of two superimposed churches, Romanesque below and Gothic above. The most famous work of art in the church is the Brenzoni monument (1426) on the north side. The sculptural elements are by the Florentine Nanni di Bartolo, with the familiar motif of a baldachin-curtain pulled back to reveal a tomb, though in this case what you see is not the sarcophagus of the defunct but a Resurrection scene. Above are illusionistic turreted niches with trellising painted by Pisanello (his earliest surviving work). In the central niche is a real statue of a prophet. In the side niches are painted statues of archangels. A third archangel, Gabriel, is seen in the Annunciation scene below. He bows low before the Virgin, who is shown in her bedroom, a tiny white dog at her feet. Above we see God the Father sending his Son down to earth in a blaze of cherubim.

VISITING VERONA

GETTING AROUND

• **By air:** Verona airport is 12km southwest of the centre. The Aerobus runs every 20mins between the airport and the railway station.

• **By car:** There are pay car parks in Verona at the Arena (*map p. 117, 7–11*). There is free parking at Piazza San Zeno (*map p. 116, 5*) and Piazza Bra Molinari (*map p. 117, 4*).

• **By bus:** Town buses connect Porta Nuova railway station with the Arena (nos 11, 12, 13, 72 and 73), with Castelvecchio (nos 21, 22, 23 and 24) and with Piazza Erbe (nos. 72, 73). From Castelvecchio to San Zeno take nos

31, 32 or 33. From the station to the Roman theatre, take nos 72 or 73. See www.amt.it.

• **By taxi:** T: 045 532666. Taxi ranks at the railway station, Piazza Brà, Piazza delle Erbe.

• **By train:** Verona stands at the junction of two of Italy's most important rail lines. Trains connect with Venice, Trieste, Milan, Turin and Genoa; Bologna, Florence and Rome; and Trento. Frequent trains also run to Desenzano del Garda in c. 30mins.

SPECIAL TICKETS

The **Verona Card** (1- and 3-day versions) gives

free travel on AMT buses and free admission to museums, churches and monuments. It can be purchased at museums, churches and tobacconists in the city and on Lake Garda.

WHERE TO STAY IN VERONA

€€ **Gabbia d'Oro.** ■ This small hotel (27 rooms), the 'gilded cage', is known for its genteel, cosy atmosphere. Right in the centre. *Corso Porta Borsari 4/a, T: 045 800 3060, www.hotelgabbiadoro.it. Map p. 117, 7.*

WHERE TO EAT IN VERONA

Verona is full of good restaurants. Top of the range are the Michelin-starred €€€ **La Fontanina**, close to the church of S. Stefano (*Via Portichetti Fontanelle 3, T: 045 913305, www.ristorantelafontanina.com; just beyond map*

p. 117, 4) and the splendid €€€ **Il Desco** ■, which bases its reputation on innovative cuisine with strong local roots and a formidable wine list (*Via Dietro San Sebastiano 7, T: 045 595358; closed Sun and Mon and in Jan and June; map p. 117, 7, off Via Nizza*). Other favourites include €€€ **Dodici Apostoli**, in a historic building in the heart of the city centre, which has been serving traditional Veronese dishes since 1750 (*Vicolo San Marco 3, T: 045 596999; closed Sun evening, Mon, Jan and June; map p. 117, 7, off Via Pellicciai*) and € **Al Pompiere**, an elegant little *osteria* run by the owners of Il Desco, just down the street from Juliet's house (*Vicolo Regina d'Ungheria 5, T: 045 803 0537; closed Sun, midday Mon and in Jan and June; map p. 117, 7*). Six kilometres north of Verona is the Relais & Châteaux hotel €€€ **Villa del Quar**, whose restaurant is justly famous (*Via Quar 12, T: 045 680 0681, www.hotelvilladelquar.it*).

VICENZA

Vicenza (*map p. 423, D2–E2*) is an ancient place. It was a palaeo-Venetic settlement, relics of which culture can be seen in the archaeological museum at Santa Corona. It was a Roman *municipium* and its street plan from those days is still clearly recognisable. It owed suzerainty to the Scaligeri of Verona and the Visconti of Milan, before bowing to Venetian rule in 1404, after which time it flourished. But it is for none of those reasons that people visit Vicenza today. They come instead to see the city's 16th-century incarnation, at the hands of a gifted architect called Andrea Palladio.

On and around Corso Palladio

The main street of Vicenza is the stately Corso Andrea Palladio, lined with monumental palaces and churches of the 14th–18th centuries. Running away from it to the north is **Contrà Porti**, a street with a number of Palladian palaces, notably no. 11, which houses a centre for Palladian studies where temporary exhibitions are held. The **Palazzo del Comune** (*map p. 122, 3*), more or less at the halfway mark of Corso Palladio (no. 98), is the masterpiece of Palladio's pupil Vincenzo Scamozzi (designed 1592, completed 1662). Southeast of here is Piazza dei Signori, with Vicenza's most important monument, the famous **Basilica**. Created after 1549, this is one of the best buildings of the Venetian Renaissance and was the commission that made Palladio's name. The task was to create a new exterior for an existing Gothic-style building.

VILLA VALMARANA & VILLA ROTONDA

Palladio's solution was to wrap it in a sort of Renaissance bandage: the original diaper pattern of the old façade can still be seen below the roofline. Palladio's double tier of arcades seems to mirror itself, except that the columns on the ground floor are Tuscan Doric and those above Ionic, an idea derived from the Colosseum (*see p. 250*).

Beyond one end of the basilica rises the slender Torre di Piazza (82m), completed in the 14th century. Below it are two columns, surmounted by the Lion of St Mark and Christ the Redeemer, respectively dating from 1520 and 1640. Across the square stands the **Loggia del Capitaniato**, designed by Palladio in 1571. Once the residence of the military commander, it has immense, engaged Corinthian columns rising from the pavement to the attic level.

Near the end of Corso Palladio is the Dominican monastic church of **Santa Corona** (*map above, 2*), which contains two genuine masterpieces among its many works of art: Paolo Veronese's *Adoration of the Magi* (1573; third south altar) and Giovanni Bellini's *Baptism of Christ* (c. 1502; fifth north altar).

Piazza Matteotti

Corso Palladio ends in Piazza Matteoti (*map opposite, 2*), a broad, open expanse at the north end of which stands the **Teatro Olimpico**, Palladio's last work, completed in 1584 by Scamozzi (*open Tues–Sun 9–5, July–Aug 9–18; last admission 30mins before closing*). It was built for the Accademia Olimpica, founded in 1555, of which Palladio was a member and which produced numerous plays. The opening performance (Sophocles' *Oedipus Rex*) was given in 1585. The theatre, made of wood and stucco, imitates the theatres of Classical antiquity as described by Vitruvius. It has a cavea of 13 semi-elliptical tiers ending in a Corinthian colonnade. The Classical stage set, its architecture derived from ancient Roman buildings, has niches with statues of academicians and reliefs of the Labours of Hercules. Scamozzi designed the magnificent, two-storey fixed backdrop, populated by 95 statues and presenting spectacular architectural vistas of seven streets, supposedly of the ancient Greek city of Thebes, designed for Sophocles' tragedy.

On the west side of the square stands Palladio's **Palazzo Chiericati** (1550–57), a truly extraordinary building. As with the Basilica, we have a double portico of Doric columns below and Ionic above. But here there are no arches to relieve the rectangularity. The central section of the upper level is closed in, the rest is open loggia. If the frieze, pediments and statues were removed, we would here have Socialist Realist architecture of the finest kind. The ground-floor rooms are decorated with frescoes by Domenico Brusasorci, a pupil of Giovanni Francesco Caroto, and Giovanni Battista Zelotti (who also frescoed the Villa Emo, *see p. 125*) and with stuccoes by Bartolomeo Ridolfi, who frequently collaborated with Palladio. The building is home to the **Pinacoteca** (*open Tues–Sun 10–5, July–Aug 9–6*), with a collection of mainly Venetian painting of the 16th–18th centuries.

Villa Valmarana and La Rotonda

Via Massimo d'Azeglio and after that Viale San Bastiano (*beyond map opposite, 4*) wind southeast from the centre (possible on foot) to two spectacular villas. The **Villa Valmarana ai Nani** (*Via dei Nani 8; open March–Nov Tues–Sun 10–12, Wed, Thur, Sat, Sun also 3–6; T: 0444 321803*) is a 17th-century building enlarged and remodelled by Francesco Muttoni, a follower of Palladio. It has a panoramic terrace overlooking the sanctuary of Monte Berico, also by Muttoni and a popular pilgrimage site (the refectory contains a large painting by Veronese, *The Supper of Gregory the Great*; 1572). Five rooms of the villa are decorated with frescoes by Tiepolo (1757), inspired by the *Iliad*, *Aeneid*, *Orlando Furioso* and *Gerusalemme Liberata*. The guesthouse is frescoed with scenes of country life by Giandomenico Tiepolo, Giovanni Battista's son.

A path (Stradella Valmarana) on the right beyond the villa continues downhill to the Villa Capra Valmarana, or **La Rotonda** (*open March–Nov: garden open Tues–Sun 10–12 & 3–6; other days usually on request; interior Wed only 10–12 & 3–6*), one of the most famous of all the Palladian villas of Italy, begun c. 1551 by Palladio and continued after his death by his pupil Scamozzi. Its ground plan takes the form of a circle within a cube, with a portico on each side. The circular core is crowned by a low dome: the combination of portico and dome is reminiscent of the Pantheon in

Rome—and like the Pantheon before it, the Villa Rotonda had a profound influence on later architecture and was copied in numerous buildings, including Chiswick House, London.

VISITING VICENZA

GETTING AROUND

• **By car:** Vicenza has two exits (Vicenza Est and Vicenza Ovest) on Italy's main east–west *autostrada*, the A4, from Venice to Milan. Vicenza Ovest will get you to the city centre more quickly, even if you come from the east. Vicenza has large car parks (with a minibus service for the centre) in several outlying areas; the easiest to reach are near the wholesale fruit market (north of the Verona road) and by the stadium. Limited paid parking is available in the centre of the town.

• **By bus:** The Villa Valmarana is reached in c. 15mins by bus no. 8 from Viale Roma near the station (direction Noventa Vicentina) to Borgo Berga (request stop at Via Tiepolo, 500m below the villa); it continues along the Viale Riviera Berica to another request stop at the foot of Via della Rotonda, 200m below Villa Rotonda. If you plan to visit both villas it is best to take the bus to Villa Rotonda, and from there walk back to Villa Valmarana.

• **By train:** Most trains on the main Venice–Milan line stop at Vicenza. Journey time is 35mins from Verona, c. 2hrs from Milan, c. 1hr from Venice.

• **By taxi:** T: 0444 920600; taxi stand outside the station.

SPECIAL TICKETS

The **Vicenza Card**, available at most museums, gives reduced admission to museums and palaces in Vicenza and to the villas.

WHERE TO STAY IN VICENZA

€ **Due Mori**. Small hotel nicely renovated and simply and tastefully furnished. A great find in the heart of town. *Contrà Do Rode 24, T: 0444 321886, www.hotelduemori.com. Map p. 122, 3.*

WHERE TO EAT IN VICENZA

€€ **Scudo di Francia**. The classic place to go for traditional Vicentine cuisine. Closed Sun evening, Mon, Dec–Jan and Aug. *Contrà Piancoli 4, T: 0444 323322. Map p. 122, 4 (Pianc.).*

ENVIRONS OF VICENZA

Castelfranco, Villa Emo and Bassano del Grappa

East of Vicenza, an easy journey by train, is **Castelfranco Veneto** (*map p. 423, E2*), the birthplace of Giorgione. His altarpiece of the *Madonna and Child with Sts Francis and Liberale* (c. 1505) is still preserved in the Palladian-style cathedral. The 15th-century Casa di Giorgione is the house where Giorgione lived and worked (he painted the chiaroscuro band with symbols of the Liberal and Mechanical Arts in one room).

Fanzolo, a small farm town 8km northeast, is known for the splendid **Villa Emo** (*open April–Oct daily 3–6.30, Sun and holidays also 10–12.30; in other months Mon–Fri 2–4, Sat and Sun 2–5.30*), one of Palladio's masterpieces (c. 1564). The handsome, plain cen-

Giustina Barbaro and her children's nurse: detail of one of the *trompe l'oeil* frescoes by Veronese in the villa at Maser. The twisted columns occur often in Veronese's art, and bear a striking resemblance to those by Guilio Romano in the Cortile della Cavallerizza in Mantua's ducal palace.

tral building, devoid of excess ornament, is entered up a wide stepped ramp and through a deep porch with Corinthian columns. At either side stretch long, low, symmetrical *barchesse* (service wings) terminating in square dovecote towers. The interior is frescoed with mythological scenes by Giovanni Battista Zelotti, possibly with the help of Paolo Veronese. The stuccoes are by the great Venetian sculptor Alessandro Vittoria.

Northwest of Castelfranco is **Bassano del Grappa** (*map p. 423, E2*), the home town of the da Ponte family of painters (Jacopo Bassano, a pioneer of the genre scene, and his four sons, of whom the best known are Leandro and Francesco, both of whom worked in Venice). The picture gallery of the Museo Civico (*closed all day Mon and Sun mornings*) has examples of their work. The most famous feature of the town is its covered wooden bridge over the Brenta river. The design is Palladio's, though the bridge has been replaced many times since the 16th century: the Brenta is prone to flooding and the bridge has been damaged or destroyed more than once. Nevertheless, a wooden structure is more adapted than stone to withstand the force of a flash flood, and the bridge has never been rebuilt in a more durable material.

Asolo and Maser

Picturesquely situated among the alpine foothills, the old town of **Asolo** (*map p. 423, E2*) draws visitors as much for its associations with famous names as for its architecture or its art. The town was offered by Venice to Caterina Cornaro in exchange for the island of Cyprus, of which she was the dowager queen. She accepted the offer, and lived in the castle here from 1489 to 1509, gathering about her men of talent and learning such as the painter Gentile Bellini and the scholar-cardinal Pietro Bembo. In later centuries the poet Robert Browning came here and the actress Eleonora Duse kept a house here, as did the traveller and writer Dame Freya Stark.

At Maser (*map p. 423, E2*), in a lovely setting among vines, is the **Villa Barbaro**, built by Palladio between 1550 and 1560 for Daniele Barbaro, patriarch of Aquileia, and his brother Marcantonio. This villa is one of the architect's finest achievements, in the form of a central manor house with porticoed service wings stretching out on either side. Today it is still a private home, and though open to visitors, hours are not regular (*T: 0423 923004, www.villadimaser.it*). The interior contains beautiful frescoes by Veronese (1560–62), cleverly incorporating the real architectural elements of the building into witty, *trompe l'oeil* scenes. Palladio is said not to have approved of what Veronese had done to the purity of his building. The cross-shaped hall is decorated with idealised rural landscapes with Classical ruins. A manservant and a chubby blonde girl famously appear from behind *trompe l'oeil* doors. This hall leads into an enfilade of frescoed rooms. In the central room we see Giustina Barbaro, wife of Marcantonio, on a balcony with her three children and their nurse (*illustrated above*).

VISITING THE ENVIRONS OF VICENZA

GETTING AROUND

Country buses run by FTV (www.ftv.vi.it) go from Vicenza bus station to Bassano del Grappa (2 buses every morning, journey time 1hr). There are direct trains on the Treviso line from Vicenza to Castelfranco (journey time c. 40mins); change at Castelfranco for Fanzolo (Villa Emo; a further 10mins on the train).

WHERE TO STAY IN THE ENVIRONS OF VICENZA

Asolo
€€€ **Villa Cipriani** is the area's oldest and finest hotel, occupying a 16th-century villa with quiet gardens and incomparable views (*Via Canova 298, T: 0423 523 411, www.villaciprianiasolo.com*) €€ **Al Sole** is a charming place in the centre of town (*Via Collegio 33, T: 0423 528 111, www.albergoalsoleasolo.com*).

Bassano del Grappa
€€ **Ca' Sette**. ■ One of the nicest places to stay in the area, a hotel and restaurant in an 18th-century villa north of town. *Via Cunizza da Romano 4, T: 0424 383350, www.ca-sette.it.*

WHERE TO EAT IN THE ENVIRONS OF VICENZA

Asolo
€€ **Ca' Derton**. Fine restaurant in the heart of the village serving traditional cuisine. Closed Sun evening, Mon and late July–early Aug. *Piazza d'Annunzio 11, T: 0423 529648.*
€€ **Ai Due Archi**. Good, straightforward regional cuisine amidst the warmth of wood panelling. Closed Wed evening and Thur, and in Jan and Feb. *Via Roma 55, T: 0423 952201.*
Maser
There is a snack bar at the Villa Barbaro, and a shop where you can buy wine produced on the estate.

FRIULI-VENEZIA GIULIA

Friuli-Venezia Giulia (*map p. 423*) lies at the point where Austria and Italy meet the southern Slav countries of Slovenia and Croatia. Not surprisingly, there is a distinct atmosphere in the region. The numerous hilltop villages, each with its own castle, preserve their own customs and, in certain cases, their own dialect.

Friuli-Venezia Giulia in history

The history of the region is characterised by the struggle for control between Austria and Venice. Friuli (the former county of Udine) was under the patriarchate of Aquileia until 1420, when it was absorbed into the Venetian Republic. Trieste, as an independent commune, was a rival of Venice for Adriatic trade. After the fall of Napoleon (who had incorporated the region into his Kingdom of Illyria), the whole area came under Austro-Hungarian control and remained part of that empire until its collapse in 1918. The years that preceded the collapse were particularly bitter ones in Friuli: this border region was the scene of some of the bloodiest conflicts of the First World War.

The new region of Friuli-Venezia Giulia came into being after the Second World War. Trieste was returned to Italian rule in 1954.

Food and wine of Friuli

The best-known dishes are a blend of Austro-Hungarian, Slav and Italian traditions. Triestine favourites, for example, include *gulasch*, a Hungarian derivation; *sardoni in savor* (marinated sardines, also popular in Venice); and *cevapcici*, the grilled meatballs that are familiar all over the southern Slav world.

Rice is a major ingredient of the cuisine of Udine. Square-shaped homemade pasta (*blecs*) is served with various meat or game sauces. Polenta is ubiquitous. The lightly salted prosciutto di San Daniele is considered the best in Italy.

The best wines of the Trieste area include Malvasia del Carso (the wine once known in English as Malmsey), made from a white grape of ancient Greek origin. The Grave del Friuli area produces the famous Refosco dal Peduncolo Rosso, and the Colli Orientali del Friuli the equally renowned Picolit. Trieste is also famous for its coffee: Illy, the connoisseur's blend, has been a Trieste name since 1933, when the company was founded by a Hungarian chocolatier.

UDINE & THE WEST

Prosperous Udine (*map p. 423, F2*) is the most picturesque town of Friuli-Venezia Giulia. In the central Piazza della Libertà, set at the foot of the castle hill, is a column with the Lion of St Mark, denoting Udine's status as a town within the Venetian Republic. The most famous landmark is the Torre dell'Orologio (1527), by Giovanni

Tiepolo: *Judgement of Solomon* (1726), a typical example of his fresco style, where clustered figures appear against a light, airy expanse of sky and scudding cloud. The Solomon theme was very popular in buildings which also served as law courts. It tells the story of the Old Testament king discovering by a clever ruse which of two women is the mother of a newborn child.

da Udine. Though born here, he carried out most of his best work in Rome, where he fell under the spell of Raphael. He was also one of the first people to see the newly discovered Domus Aurea of Nero, and his signature is preserved inside (*see p. 256*).

In 452 Attila the Hun sacked Aquileia, and he is said to have stood on the top of Udine's castle mound to watch the city burn. Today's castle was begun in 1517, to a design by Giovanni da Udine. It is home to a **museum and art gallery** (*open Tues–Sat 9.30–12.30 & 3–6, Sun and holidays 9.30–12.30*), with works by the Friulan primitives, a Caravaggio (*St Francis Receiving the Stigmata*) and some good paintings by Tiepolo.

Perhaps the best single sight in Udine is the **Palazzo Patriarcale** (*Piazza Patriarcato 1; open Wed–Sun 10–12.30 & 3.30–6.30*), decorated in 1726 by Tiepolo—indeed it has been suggested that the clear, airy brightness which is so much a hallmark of all his work was inspired by the fresh mountain air of Friuli. The red room contains the *Judgement of Solomon* and four prophets in the lunettes. The blue room has ceiling frescoes by Giovanni da Udine. Tiepolo's famous *Fall of the Rebel Angels* is on the stairs.

Around Udine

Southwest of Udine is **Campoformido**, site of the signing of the historic Treaty of Campo Formio (Oct 1797) by which Austria ceded its holdings in the Netherlands (modern Belgium) to Napoleonic France, and Venice and her territories were given to Austria in return. After signing the treaty, Napoleon occupied the **Villa Manin at Codroipo**, former home of the last doge of Venice, who had surrendered the Serene Republic to France in May of the same year. The villa is now a contemporary arts centre. The building and its large park can be visited (*open 9–6, closed Mon*).

CIVIDALE DEL FRIULI

Cividale (*map p. 423, F1–F2*) was founded as *Forum Julii*, probably by Julius Caesar; a corruption of the Latin gives the name Friuli. It was an important fortress under the Lombards; their historian Paul the Deacon was born here in 723. From the late 8th century until 1031 the town was the seat of the patriarch of Aquileia (*see below*).

Later works of art in the town (from the 15th–18th centuries) are all Venetian. Some are very fine (for example the design of the **cathedral interior**, by Pietro and Tullio Lombardo). But Cividale is visited more importantly for its early monuments. The **Museo Cristiano** (*entered from inside the cathedral or from behind the bell-tower on Sun; open daily 9.30–12 & 3–6 or 7*) contains a beautiful 8th-century altar carved for Ratchis, at that time duke of Cividale (he later became king of the Lombards). On the front is depicted Christ the Victor, borne by four angels. On the sides are the *Visitation* and *Adoration of the Magi*. The museum also displays fragments of a ciborium from the **Tempietto Longobardo**. This temple (*entrance in Piazzetta San Biagio; open April–Sept Mon–Sat 9.30–12.30 & 3–6.30, Sun 9.30–1 & 3–7.30; Oct–March 9.30–12.30 & 3–5, Sun 9.30–12.30 & 2.30–6*), dating from c. 760, is one of the most evocative early medieval buildings in Italy. The nave preserves remarkable stucco decoration on the end wall, with the graceful figures of six female saints, three on either side of a narrow window aperture. On each side the saint nearest the window is veiled and holds her hands in an attitude of supplication. The other two saints are crowned and hold royal regalia. Below the saints is an exquisitely carved door hood, bearing Eucharistic motifs of bunches of grapes.

The Palazzo dei Provveditori Veneti on the cathedral square (built to a design by Palladio in 1581–96) houses the **Museo Archeologico Nazionale** (*open Tues–Sun 8.30–7 or 7.30, Mon 8.30–2 or 9–1.30*). Highlights are the items found in a Lombard knight's tomb (early 7th century), including a gold disc showing a mounted warrior, his shield and lance beautifully rendered, surrounded by a fretwork pattern.

Crowned female saint, part of an 8th-century stucco frieze in the Tempietto Longobardo.

AQUILEIA

Established by the Romans in 181 BC, Aquileia (*map p. 423, F2*) grew to be the fourth largest city in Italy, an affluent market town situated at the departure point for the roads over the Alps to the Danube basin. In 10 BC the emperor Augustus received Herod the Great here. In the following centuries its importance declined because of malaria. Today a sleepy village, Aquileia preserves considerable traces of its former magnificence, offering remarkable vestiges of Roman and early Christian art.

At the centre of the old town stands the **basilica** (*open summer 8.30–7, winter 8.30–12.30 & 2.30–5.30*), built when the patriarchate (bishopric) was founded, not long after Constantine granted freedom of worship to Christians in 313. Aquileia was sacked by the Lombards in 568, and the see was transferred to nearby Grado, returning only 500 years later, when the basilica was rebuilt in Romanesque style (1021–31). After this, Aquileia had a second flowering that lasted until the 14th century.

A short portico abuts the west front, joining it to the Chiesa dei Pagani (now used as a shop), a 9th-century hall for catechumens (Christian converts under instruction), with remains of 13th-century frescoes. The interior of the basilica is famed for its huge polychrome mosaic pavement (700m square), the largest antique mosaic pavement known. It dates from the original 4th-century basilica and its iconographic scheme is fascinating in its combination of pagan and Christian symbols, showing how the two became conflated. The winged figure of Victory holding a crown and palm branch, for example, is a motif that Christianity would adopt as the angel triumphant over death.

North of the basilica, on the other side of Via Vescovo Teodoro (named after the first patriarch of Aquileia), are the remains of **Roman houses and Christian oratories** with superb mosaic pavements. A path, clearly marked by an avenue of cypresses, follows the Natissa stream, once a navigable river as far as Grado. The little **Roman harbour** has a finely constructed quay that still skirts its shrunken waters. The café amidst the ruins, with outside seating in summer, has a variety of good sandwiches.

Across Via Gemina a road leads to the quiet Piazza Pirano (with a fragment of Roman road). Here is the **Museo Paleocristiano** (*open Tues–Sun 8.30–1.45*), in an early Christian basilica (5th century AD) with another remarkable mosaic floor. The display is designed to show the transition of art from Classical Rome to the Christian era.

The **Museo Archeologico** (*open Mon 8.30–2, Tues–Sat 8.30–7.30; last admission 30mins before closing*) is reached from the basilica in the other direction (*turn left down Via Giulia Augusta and then right down Via Roma*). A remarkably well-preserved Roman ship is displayed here, dating from the 2nd century AD.

VISITING UDINE & THE WEST

GETTING AROUND

• **By air:** Frequent coach services (no. 51) connect Friuli-Venezia Giulia regional airport with Udine in c. 40mins and with Aquileia/Grado in 50mins.

• **By car:** Metred parking in Udine is in Piazza I Maggio, in Piazza XX Settembre, and in streets around the historic centre. Metred parking is available on many streets in Cividale; the most convenient place is Piazza Duomo. In Aquileia, there are car parks off the main road and by the basilica.

• **By bus:** Bus no. 1 runs from Udine railway station to the town centre. Country buses go from the bus station at Viale Europa Unita 31 (next to the railway station) to destinations throughout the province.

• **By train:** Fast trains connect Venice to Udine in c. 90mins. Branch lines run from Udine to Cividale (approx. every hour; journey time 20mins). Aquileia is served by Cervignano-Aquileia-Grado station, on the main line from Venice to Udine and Trieste. Buses meet trains at Cervignano for Aquileia itself; total journey time is c. 2hrs from Venice.

SPECIAL TICKETS

The **FVG Card**, valid for 2, 3 or 7 days, gives free admission to most museums in the region, free travel on public transport in Udine, and discounts at selected hotels and shops. It is available from tourist information offices and hotels.

WHERE TO STAY IN UDINE

If you prefer a more traditional place, with massed drapes at the windows and carpets underfoot, stay at the €€ **Clocchiatti**, a warm, snug little hotel in a Belle Epoque villa at the northeast corner of the city centre (*Via Cividale 29, T: 0432 505047, www.hotel-clocchiatti.it*). Minimalist furnishing, cool colours and a whiff of feng shui can be yours at the €–€€ **Suite Inn** in the northwest corner of the old centre (*Via di Toppo 25, T: 0432 501683, www.suiteinn.it*).

WHERE TO EAT IN UDINE & ENVIRONS

Cividale del Friuli
Two restaurants specialising in local Friulan food and wines, both very central, are €€ **Trattoria alla Frasca** (*Stretta de Rubeis, T: 0432 731270; closed Mon and Feb*) and € **Al Fortino**, where the food is served in a setting featuring 14th-century frescoes and a lovely big fireplace (*Via Carlo Alberto 46, T: 0432 731217; closed Mon evening, Tues, Jan and Aug*).

Udine
€€ **Alla Tavernetta** ■ offers excellent regional cuisine and an outstanding selection of wines, very close to the duomo (*Via di Prampero 2, T: 0432 501066; closed Sun and Mon*). €€ **Vitello d'Oro** is a popular *trattoria*, particularly strong on fish (*Via Valvason 4, T: 0432 508982; closed Wed and July*). The historic € **Caffè Contarena**, with décor from 1925, is good for a light lunch (*Via Cavour 1, T: 0432 512741*).

TRIESTE

The port city of Trieste (*map p. 423, F2*) was for many centuries part of the Austrian empire, and retains something of the old-fashioned atmosphere of Central Europe.

Along the waterfront north of the castle hill (San Giusto) stretches the **Borgo Teresiano**, an area of regular, spacious streets developed in the 18th century under the Habsburg empress Maria Theresa. In the main Piazza dell'Unità is the historic Caffè degli Specchi, a good place for a coffee, which is particularly delicious in Trieste (*see p. 127*). A short way northwards along the waterfront is the Canal Grande, constructed in 1750–56 as a safe harbour where merchant vessels could unload directly into the warehouses. At its far end is the Neoclassical church of Sant'Antonio Nuovo.

A little way to the east, on the site of the former Polish Ashkenazi synagogue, is the **Museo della Comunità Ebraica** (*Via del Monte 5; open Sun 5–8, Tues 4–7, Thur 10–1*). The Jewish community of Trieste dates back to c. 1200. Originally moneylenders, they later made their fortunes as merchants, bankers and manufacturers.

Some way south of Piazza dell'Unità is the **Civico Museo Sartorio** (*Largo Papa Giovanni XXIII 1; open Tues–Sun 9–1*), the former home of an affluent merchant family, which gives a superb flavour of what life was like in bourgeois Trieste in its 18th-century heyday. The museum's greatest treasure is a collection of drawings by Tiepolo and his son Giandomenico.

James Joyce lived in Trieste in 1904–15 and 1919–20, at Via Donato Bramante 4 (near Piazza Vico, on the far side of the San Giusto hill). It is here that he wrote part of *Ulysses*.

Eight kilometres northwest along the SS14, in a splendid position on a promontory, is the **Castello di Miramare** (*open daily 9–7; park closes at dusk*), built in 1855–60 for Archduke Maximilian of Austria, younger brother of the emperor Franz Joseph. He lived here until 1864, the year in which he accepted the imperial crown of Mexico (he was executed by firing squad three years later).

VISITING TRIESTE

GETTING AROUND

• **By air:** Coaches connect Friuli-Venezia Giulia airport with the railway station in 50mins. Airport buses take 20mins.
• **By car:** The best places to park are on the waterfront or San Giusto hill. There is a multi-storey car park ('Sì silos') beside the station.
• **By bus:** Bus no. 36 runs to Miramare every 30mins from Piazza Oberdan and the station.
• **By train:** There are direct trains from Venice to Trieste (c. 2hrs). Local trains run from Trieste to Udine (c. 1hr 20mins).

WHERE TO STAY IN TRIESTE

Trieste has many personalities, and hotels to go with each. Austro-Hungarian imperial grandeur can be found at the €€€ **Grand Hotel Duchi d'Aosta ■**, whose restaurant (Harry's Grill) is well regarded (*Piazza Unità d'Italia 2, T: 040 760 0011, www.grandhotel-duchidaosta.com*). Charm and 18th-century well-porportioned design combine in the lovely €€ **James Joyce** (*Via dei Cavazzeni 7, T: 040 311023, www.hoteljamesjoyce.com*), and self-conscious modern style is the tenor of the €€ **Colombia**, between the station and the Grand Canal (*Via della Geppa 18, T: 040 369333, www.hotelcolombia.it*).

WHERE TO EAT IN TRIESTE

€€ **Antica Trattoria Suban** is a Triestine institution, established in 1865 and serving traditional regional cuisine (*Via Comici 2/d, T: 040 54368; closed Mon, Tues, Jan, Aug*). The small €€ **Bagatto ■** is known for its fish (*Via F. Venezian 2, T: 040 301771; closed Sun, one week for Christmas and Easter, and Aug 15*), and the €€ **Elefante Bianco**, in a historic building with a seafront terrace, specialises in regional dishes (*Riva III Novembre 3, T: 040 362603; closed Sat and midday Sun*).

EMILIA-ROMAGNA

Emilia-Romagna (*map pp. 422–43*) extends from the Adriatic Sea to Italy's Apennine spine. The name dates only from c. 1860, though its derivation is much older, from the Via Aemilia, the ancient Roman road that was used as a military thoroughfare to the lands of Cisalpine Gaul. All the principal towns, except Ferrara and Ravenna, lie along the line of this road. Ostensibly one region, in reality Emilia-Romagna is two entities with very different characters. The inland part is Emilia, with Bologna, Modena, Parma and Piacenza. Romagna denotes the Adriatic seaboard, with Ferrara, Ravenna and Rimini. From the River Po southeast to Ravenna stretches a great plain, whose highest point is no more than 60m above sea level: there are important wetlands in the Po delta.

Emilia-Romagna is one of Italy's main agricultural regions, home to vast fields of wheat and corn. It also has a strong industrial base. Ferrari, Lamborghini and Maserati all have their headquarters in the area around Modena.

Food and wine of Emilia-Romagna

Emilia-Romagna is the home of egg pasta (as opposed to the flour-and-water pasta of Naples). The delicious fresh tagliatelle with *ragù* is the original 'spaghetti Bolognaise' (tomato is much less prominent in the true version than in its international namesake).

Emilia is especially renowned for Parmesan cheese, Parma ham and balsamic vinegar. The cheese, Parmigiano-Reggiano, is made only from milk produced in the provinces of Parma, Reggio Emilia, Modena and Mantua, and all authentic cheeses carry ID markings on the rind. Parma ham (*prosciutto di Parma*) is dry-cured in the dark for over a year. The best ham comes on the bone, which prevents it from drying out. True balsamic vinegar is made only in the province of Modena. Grape-must is reduced over an open flame, naturally fermented, then aged in wooden casks.

Emilia-Romagna is the land of sparkling wines, of which the most famous is Lambrusco. The only DOCG is the white Albana di Romagna, allegedly much appreciated by Galla Placidia and her court at Ravenna.

BOLOGNA

Brick-built Bologna (*map p. 423, D3*), the capital of the region, is an easy city to like, famous for its porticoes and for its two tall medieval towers, the roofscape dominated by the huge bulk of the church of San Petronio. The old centre is ringed around by wide *viali*, in the shape of a rough hexagon: these follow the course of the old defensive walls.

Bologna is an ancient place. There was an Etruscan and then a Gaulish town here, before the Romans conquered the plain of the Po in the late 3rd and early 2nd centuries BC. After the fall of the Western Empire, Bologna became subject to the exarchs

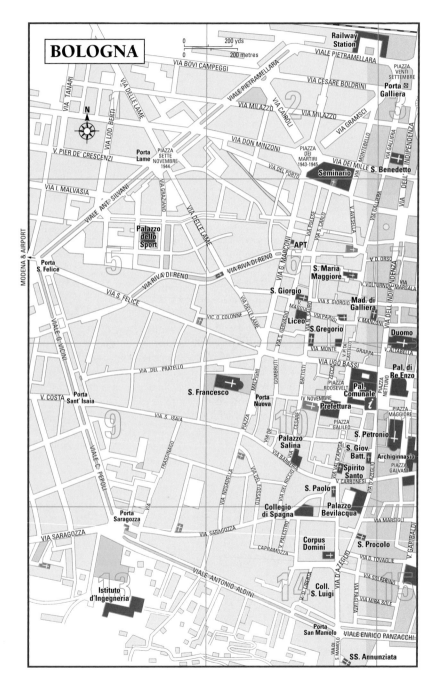

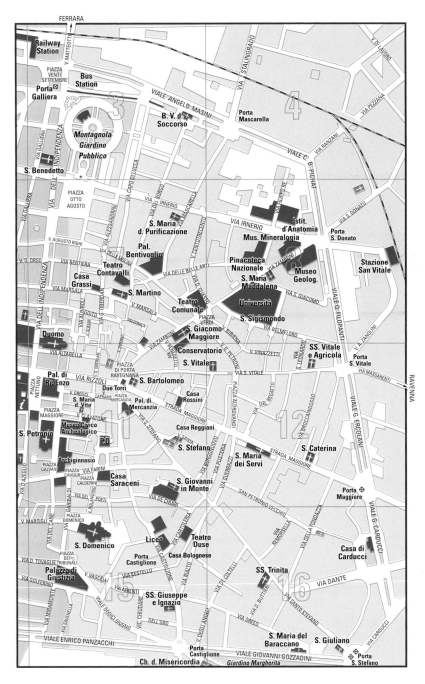

Detail of the Neptune fountain by the Flemish-born Mannerist sculptor Giambologna, who settled in Italy after his reputation was secured by this work. He worked extensively for the Medici, and sculptures by his hand can be found all over Florence.

of Ravenna (*see p. 152*) and later formed part of the Lombard and Frankish dominions. It was one of the foremost cities of the Lombard League, formed in 1167 (*see p. 28*). Bologna became a seigniory in the early 14th century, and was held by a succession of ruling families (among them, for a time, the Visconti). Pope Julius II conquered it for the Papal States in 1506, where it remained for three centuries, except for a brief Napoleonic interlude. From 1849 until the formation of the Kingdom of Italy in 1860, Bologna was subject to the Austrians.

Bologna is the seat of a famous university, renowned since the early 12th century. It is also home to an important school of painting, of which Guido Reni and Guercino are two of the best-known exponents.

Piazza Nettuno

The large Piazza Maggiore, centre of the old city, and the adjoining Piazza Nettuno (*map p. 134, 11*), are both surrounded by fine public buildings. Piazza Nettuno takes its name from its fountain, with a bronze *Neptune* by Giambologna (1566). Behind it rises the **Palazzo di Re Enzo**, with its tall swallowtail battlements. It served as the prison of Enzo (Enzio), illegitimate son of the Holy Roman Emperor Frederick II, taken prisoner in a battle between Ghibelline Modena and Guelph Bologna. He died in captivity in 1272. Opposite is the long façade of Palazzo Comunale, made up of several buildings of different dates, with a bronze statue of Pope Gregory XIII (the reformer of the calendar and a native of Bologna) above the entrance. On the second floor is the **Collezioni Comunali d'Arte** (*open Tues–Fri 9–6.30; Sat, Sun and holidays 10–6.30*), with paintings mainly by Bolognese masters including a *Crucifixion* by Francesco Francia. Also housed here is the **Museo Giorgio Morandi** (*open Tues–Fri 9–3; Sat, Sun and holidays 10–6.30*), with a superb collection of works by the great still-life artist, born in Bologna in 1890.

BOLOGNESE PAINTING

Giovanni da Modena is the most important artist of early 15th-century Bologna. Later in the same century, the ruling Bentivoglio family became patrons of the Ferrarese painter Lorenzo Costa. The partnership that Costa formed with Francesco Francia was the first step toward the formation of a Bolognese school of painting. Francia's most prominent pupil was Amico Aspertini (c. 1474–1552), described by Vasari as eccentric and unsociable and ultimately insane (*see also p. 199*). His frescoes and altarpieces certainly depart from the gentle restraint of Francia, and display a quick-witted, extemporised style that foreshadows Mannerism. At the end of the 16th century the Bolognese school had a second flowering with the Carracci (Ludovico and his cousins Annibale and Agostino) and Bartolomeo Passarotti, master of the genre scene, who probably trained under Annibale. The Carracci abandoned Mannerism for a return to the High Renaissance, and were to have a great influence on a whole generation of artists. One artist to feel this influence was Guercino, who dominated Bolognese painting for a quarter of a century with his exuberant brushwork and dramatic colour and light effects. His near-contemporary Guido Reni also trained under the Carracci, though his style is more softly classical, a legacy of his time in Rome and the influence of Raphael. Another pupil of the Carracci, Domenichino, was to abandon Classicism for the Baroque, when he went to make his name in Naples (*see p. 321*). Ruskin detested both Domenichino and the Carracci, citing their work as 'examples of evil' where 'everything you see is bad' (*The Elements of Drawing*). His far-reaching influence has coloured the reactions of many generations, and the reputations of these Bolognese artists have still not fully recuperated.

San Petronio

The immense church of **San Petronio** stands on Piazza Maggiore (*map p. 135, 11*). The Holy Roman Emperor Charles V received his crown at the high altar here in 1530, from the hands of Pope Clement VII (*see picture caption on p. 178*). The church was begun in the late 14th century and its façade has never been completed, though designs were still being submitted up until the 1930s (including one by Palladio). The central doorway has ten important marble reliefs of scenes from the book of Genesis by the Sienese sculptor Jacopo della Quercia, begun in 1425 and left unfinished at his death in 1438. Note particularly the *Creation of Adam*, at the top on the left. The Almighty is shown stretching out his right hand towards a naked, reclining Adam, whose own right hand is also extended. The similarity of gesture between this and the famous image by Michelangelo on the Sistine ceiling is perhaps too great to be coincidental. Michelangelo was in Bologna after 1492, working on the tomb of St Dominic, and he would certainly have known these reliefs.

Inside the church there are many fine paintings. It is an excellent place to appreciate Bolognese art *in situ*.

Jacopo della Quercia's *Creation of Adam*, possibly the inspiration for Michelangelo's famous fresco of the same subject in the Sistine Chapel (*pictured on p. 276*).

There are 22 chapels in all, eleven on each side. In the fifth right-hand (south) chapel is a *Pietà* by Amico Aspertini, and in the sixth is Lorenzo Costa's *St Jerome*. The tenth has an altarpiece by Passarotti.

The eighth chapel in the north aisle has a painting of *St Roch* by Parmigianino, depicting the saint as a long-legged youth in a yellow tunic, a superb example of the Mannerist style against which the Carracci rebelled. The altarpiece in the seventh chapel is by Lorenzo Costa; in the fifth chapel there are paintings by Lorenzo Costa and Francesco Francia. The fourth chapel, the Cappella Bolognini, has frescoes (c. 1415) by Giovanni da Modena, including a striking *Last Judgement*. In 2006 San Petronio was the target for a planned attack by Islamic extremists, it is said because of this fresco, which shows the prophet Mohammed lashed to a rock, with a demon tearing at his turban.

The Archiginnasio and Santa Maria della Vita

The **Archiginnasio** (*map p. 135, 11*), under the famous marble-paved Portico del Pavaglione, was built in 1562–65 for Bologna university. The monument in front of the building commemorates Luigi Galvani, an 18th-century pioneer of neuroscience. He gave his name to the term galvanism. The upper floor (*open Mon–Fri 9–6.30, Sat 9–1.45; though not always open weekday afternoons*) has a wooden anatomical theatre of 1637. The university was famed as the first school where human dissection was practised.

The domed church of **Santa Maria della Vita** contains a dramatic terracotta *Lamentation* group (c. 1463) by Niccolò dell'Arca (*see below*). The raging, incontinent grief of the women, shown by their billowing garments, twisted hands and open, wailing mouths, contrasts strangely with the solidity of St John and St Joseph of Arimathea, and the stillness of the recumbent Dead Christ.

San Domenico

San Domenico (*map p. 135, 15*) is dedicated to St Dominic, Spanish-born founder of the Dominican Order, who died here in 1221. A chapel in the south aisle preserves his tomb (1267), with scenes in high relief designed by the great proto-Renaissance sculptor Nicola Pisano (*see p. 203*) and carved mostly by his pupils, including Arnolfo di Cambio (who is credited with the design of Palazzo Vecchio in Florence). The decoration of the lid is by Niccolò dell'Arca, who took his name from this work (*arca* = tomb). After Niccolò's death in 1492, a very young Michelangelo carved three figures: St Petronius holding a model of Bologna, St Proculus (with a cloak over his shoulder), and the right-hand angel bearing a candlestick. The other—probably finer—angel is by Niccolò dell'Arca. In the apse is Guido Reni's *Glory of St Dominic*.

In the south transept is a painting by Guercino of *St Thomas Aquinas*, who began his career as a Dominican friar. In the north transept an 18th-century inscription marks the tomb of King Enzo (*see p. 136*). The chapel opposite that of St Dominic has an altarpiece incorporating small paintings of the Mysteries of the Rosary by Ludovico Carracci, his pupil Guido Reni, and others. There is a legend that the Virgin gave a rosary to St Dominic as protection against the Albigenses (neo-Manichaean heretics who—among other things—did not believe in the resurrection of the body). For much of the Middle Ages confraternities of the Rosary were under Dominican control.

The Due Torri area

Looming above Piazza di Porta Ravegnana (*map p. 135, 11*) are the famous Due Torri, two tall 12th-century towers. At one time some 180 towers existed in the city. Bologna was not alone in this: wealthy families all over northern and central Italy built turret-dwellings of this type, both as somewhere to take refuge against insurrection and as a signal of their power (*see p. 218*). The taller tower, the **Torre degli Asinelli** (97.5m), can be climbed (*open daily 9–5 or 6; 500 steps*).

North of here the narrow Via dei Giudei and Via dell'Inferno stand on the site of the **ghetto** of Bologna (the synagogue was at Via dell'Inferno 16). The **Jewish Museum**, at Via Valdonica 1 (*map p. 135, 7; open Sun–Thur 10–6, Fri 10–4*) documents the history of Judaism as a whole and of Jews in Emilia-Romagna.

The Pinacoteca Nazionale

Bologna's Pinacoteca Nazionale (*open Tues–Sun 9–7; map p. 135, 8*) houses an extremely rich collection, particularly of artists of the Bolognese school. Many fine works by the Carracci can be seen here. Ludovico's *Bargellini Madonna* (1588) is strikingly similar in composition to Titian's *Pala Pesaro* in Venice (*illustrated on p. 95*).

VISITING BOLOGNA

GETTING AROUND

• **By air:** Bologna airport is 7km northwest of the city. The Aerobus runs every 20–30mins, 6am–11.40pm (journey time 20mins), stopping in Via Ugo Bassi, Via dell'Indipendenza and at the station.

• **By car and bus:** Traffic is restricted in the city centre; access to hotels by arrangement. Pay parking is available outside the limited traffic zone. The large free car park in Via Tanari (*map p. 134, 1*) has a minibus service every 15mins to the station. Town buses are run by ATC (www.atc.bo.it). The most useful are nos 25, 30, 37 or 90 from the station (*map p. 134, 2*) to Via Ugo Bassi (*map p. 134, 10*).

• **By train:** Main north–south trains run to Milan in 1hr 40mins. Frequent Intercity trains connect Bologna to Piacenza, Parma, Modena and Rimini, making this a good base for exploring the region. Commuter trains (slower service) serve Ravenna.

• **By taxi:** T: 051 372727, 051 534141.

WHERE TO STAY IN BOLOGNA

Bologna hosts a large number of trade fairs. Peak times are Jan–May and Sept–Nov, and at these times it can be difficult to find accom-modation at short notice. Book ahead if you are planning to stay. The €€–€€€ **Corona d'Oro** is a good choice, central and restful in a historic building (*Via Oberdan 12, T: 051 745 7611, http://coronaoro.hotelsbologna.it; closed July–Aug; map p. 135, 7*). Another good place is the €€ **Orologio**, a comfortable hotel in an ancient building with views over Piazza Maggiore (*Via IV Novembre 10, T: 051 745 7411, www.art-hotel-orologio.it; map p. 134, 10*).

WHERE TO EAT IN BOLOGNA

€€€ **Rodrigo**, a short way west of Piazza Maggiore, is a famous fish restaurant (*Via della Zecca 2/h, T: 051 220445; closed Sun; map p. 134, 10*). €€ **Al Pappagallo** is a Bolognese classic in the heart of the old city, where the locals go for a special meal (*Piazza della Mercanzia 3, T: 051 232807; map p. 135, 11*). Another traditional place is €€ **Diana**, reas-suringly the same for 30 years (*Via Indipendenza 24, T: 051 231302; closed Mon, and in Jan and Aug; map p. 135, 7*). The popular € **Trattoria Meloncello** doesn't look much from the outside, but this is the place to come for *tagliatelle alla bolognese* or tortellini soup (*Via Saragozza 240/a, T: 051 614 3947; closed Mon evening and all Tues; map p. 134, 13*).

MODENA

The Via Emilia runs northwest from Bologna through Modena, Reggio, Parma and Piacenza. To the left of the road before Modena is **Vignola** (*map p. 423, D3*), birth-place of the architect Jacopo Barozzi, the most important successor to Michelangelo in Rome, and always known as 'Il Vignola', after his birthplace. On the other side of Modena is **Correggio** (*map p. 423, D3*), birthplace of another artist, the painter Antonio Allegri, known as Correggio, who worked mainly in Parma (*see p. 143*).

Modena itself is a prosperous place, home to a beautiful cathedral and a fine col-lection of paintings. In the Middle Ages its sympathies tended to be Ghibelline, which

God creates Eve from the rib of the sleeping Adam. Relief by Wiligelmus (c. 1110) on the west façade of the duomo of Modena.

brought it into conflict with Guelph Bologna. The Este family of Ferrara became lords of Modena in 1288, and in 1452 it was turned into a duchy. Mary of Modena, who married James II of England, was an Este princess. The duchy survived until extinguished by Napoleon. Modena joined the Kingdom of Italy in 1859.

The duomo

The splendid Romanesque duomo was begun in 1099, the work of northern Italian masters. The architect Lanfranco, from Lake Como, worked together with the sculptor Wiligelmus (Guglielmo da Modena). The work was continued by Campionese masters (*see p. 48*). Works by the hand of Wiligelmus include the west portal and the four bas-reliefs with stories from *Genesis* and the first door on the south side, with six very fine bas-reliefs of the life of St Jeminianus, to whom the church is dedicated.

Embedded in the west façade is a plaque born by figures of Enoch and Elijah with a dedicatory inscription. At the bottom the name of Wiligelmus is mentioned, making him one of the first named sculptors in Italy. The bell-tower of the duomo was undergoing restoration at the time of writing, and had been wrapped for the purpose in a screen decorated by Mimmo Paladino, an artist of the Italian 'Transavantgarde'.

The interior is of red brick with a red and white striped marble floor. The pulpit is by Enrico da Campione (1322). Also Campionese, but from a century earlier, are the sculptures of the rood screen (Anselmo da Campione). The funeral of the great tenor Luciano Pavarotti, who was born in Modena in 1935, was held in the duomo in 2007.

Galleria Estense

In the west of the old town is the huge Palazzo dei Musei, built in 1771 as a poorhouse and now home to the **Galleria Estense** (*open Tues–Sun 9.30–7.30*). The Bolognese school (Guido Reni, Guercino, Ludovico Carracci) is well represented. Fine portraits include two likenesses of Francesco I d'Este, one by Velázquez, the other a bust by Bernini. The two give completely different impressions of the sitter: the former is sober and restrained, the latter presents a flamboyant popinjay. It was for Francesco I that Modena's huge Palazzo Ducale (now the Italian Military Academy) was begun in 1634.

VISITING MODENA

GETTING AROUND

• **By car:** Free parking can be found outside the historic centre. Pay parking is available elsewhere in town. Tram no. 7 runs from the station (Piazza Dante) to the museums and Via Emilia (for the duomo). Details from ATCM (www.atcm.mo.it).

• **By train:** Trains on the Milan line stop at Modena; journey time from Bologna is 30mins. Non-stop services also connect Modena to Rome. Commuter trains run to Mantua (just over 1hr) and Verona (just over 2hrs).

WHERE TO STAY IN MODENA

The finest place in town is the sumptuous €€€ **Real Fini San Francesco**, with a famous restaurant attached (*Rua Frati Minore 48, T: 059 205 1530, www.hotelsfrancesco.it*). €€€–€€ **Canalgrande** is an elegant hotel in an 18th-century palace. Fine garden and restaurant (*Corso Canal Grande 6, T: 059 217160, www.canalgrandehotel.it*). Functional comfort and a central location are offered by the Best Western € **Libertà** hotel (*Via Blasia 10, T: 059 222365, www.hotelliberta.it*).

WHERE TO EAT IN MODENA

€€€ **Fini.** ■ Famed, old-style Michelin-starred restaurant. Fini is a household name in Italy because of its retail fresh pasta products, which used to be made in-house here. Closed Mon–Tues, Dec and Aug. *Rua Frati Minori 54, T: 059 223314.*

€€ **La Francescana.** ■ Another Michelin-starred restaurant purveying an elegant, old-world environment and out-of-this world food. The foie gras encrusted in caramelised almonds and served on a stick like a Magnum ice cream caused quite a stir. Closed Sat, midday Sun, Aug and two weeks in Dec. *Via Stella 22, T: 059 210118.*

PARMA

Parma (*map p. 423, D3*) is a rewarding place to visit, famous for its architecture, its paintings by Correggio, its cheese and its ham.

Two events in history have shaped Parma's present identity. The first occurred in 1531, when this former fief of the Sforza became a papal dominion, which Pope Paul III later presented as a dukedom to his illegitimate son Pier Luigi Farnese. The house of Farnese and their heirs, the Spanish house of Bourbon-Parma, held on to the duchy until 1801. The second event came after the Congress of Vienna in 1815, when Parma was assigned to Marie-Louise of Austria, the daughter of the last Holy Roman Emperor, whom Napoleon had married in 1810. She held the duchy for life, and on her death in 1847 it reverted to the house of Bourbon-Parma, becoming part of the Kingdom of Italy in 1859. Marie-Louise, perhaps alone among Austrians in Italy, was popular with her subjects. It was she who introduced the habit of distilling wild violets for their perfume. In her day it was the Franciscan monks of the Annunziata who made the scent for the duchess's own use. Today Violetta di Parma is commercially distilled.

The duomo, San Giovanni Evangelista and the baptistery

In the centre of the old town is the cathedral square, on which stands the famous **baptistery** (*open 9–12.30 & 3–6.30*), a tall octagonal building in red Verona marble, the most famous work of Benedetto Antelami, begun in 1196. Its extremely interesting design incorporates four storeys of rectangular galleries, with blind arcades above. It was completed after 1216 by Campionese masters. Carvings by Antelami decorate the three doorways. The interior is divided into 16 niched arcades containing painted scenes. The umbrella vault contains paintings of the 13th century.

The **duomo** (*open 9–12.30 & 3–7*) is celebrated above all for its dome fresco of the *Assumption* by Correggio (1526–30; *illustrated overleaf*), showing the Virgin ascending into celestial light through a dizzying tunnel of Apostles, saints and angels. The south transept preserves a relief of the *Descent from the Cross* by Benedetto Antelami. This is his earliest known work (signed and dated 1178). The scene on the right, of the soldiers throwing dice for Christ's garments, is particularly vivid.

Behind the duomo is the church of San Giovanni Evangelista, attached to a Benedictine monastery. The dome contains another, earlier fresco by Correggio (1521), depicting the *Vision of St John the Evangelist at Patmos*. Christ is shown in the company of the other eleven apostles appearing to St John. Over the sacristy door in the north transept is a lunette fresco of the *Young St John Writing*, also by Correggio. The entrance arches of the first, second and fourth north chapels have frescoes (1522–23) by Parma's other great artist, Francesco Mazzola, better known as Parmigianino, painted when he was still a very young man and much under the influence of Correggio.

The Camera di San Paolo

Between the cathedral square and the Parma river is the wide Strada Garibaldi, running north–south. To the east of it is the **Camera di San Paolo** (*open Tues–Sun 8.30–1.30*), part of a former Benedictine convent. This small room was the private apartment of Abbess Giovanna Piacenza, who commissioned the frescoes by Correggio in 1518 or 1519. The Gothic umbrella vault is decorated with a dome of thick foliage supported by a wicker-work arbour, through which you can see groups of putti against the open sky. Over the fireplace is the virgin goddess Diana returning from the hunt. Abbess Giovanna was an enlightened woman but she was powerless to prevent her convent being turned into a closed community. These frescoes remained unseen by the world until the 18th century.

Palazzo della Pilotta

West of Strada Garibaldi, close to the river, is **Palazzo della Pilotta**, built for the Farnese family c. 1583–1622. It now contains the city's principal museums, including the Teatro Farnese, a theatre built in 1617–18 in wood and stucco and modelled in part on Palladio's theatre at Vicenza (*see p. 123*). The most important of the museums is the **Galleria Nazionale** (*open Tues–Sun 8.30–2*), with a collection of mainly Tuscan and Emilian works and an exquisite unfinished painting of the head of a girl ('*La Scapigliata*') by Leonardo da Vinci (c. 1508). There is also a selection of master-pieces by Correggio and Parmigianino. The long-drawn-out languor of the latter artist's style perhaps reflects an aspect of his personality: when he failed to complete a cycle of frescoes for the church of **Santa Maria della Steccata**, he was imprisoned for breach of contract. The ordeal does not seem to have broken his spirit or his style. A refined and sophisticated artist, he perfected the stretched and elongated lineaments of the human form that were to become such a hallmark of Mannerism.

Piacenza

Further up the Via Emilia, on the border of Lombardy, stands Piacenza (*map p. 422, C3*), formerly part of the duchy of Parma created by Pope Paul III for his much detested (and ultimately assassinated) bastard son. The large, rather gloomy Palazzo Farnese, built in part by Vignola, now contains the city's museums. In the archaeological section is the famous 'Piacenza Liver' (*Fegato di Piacenza*), an Etruscan bronze object in the shape of a sheep's liver, thought to have been a training piece for augurers.

VISITING PARMA & PIACENZA

GETTING AROUND

• **By air:** Bus 6 connects Parma airport to the railway station hourly, 6am–8pm.

• **By car:** Free parking in Viale Mentana, the boulevard that encircles the old centre to the east. Pay parking in the underground car park on Viale Toschi just north of Palazzo Pilotta.

Correggio: *Assumption of the Virgin* (1526–30). Scholars believe that the artist may have studied Mantegna's ceiling of the Camera degli Sposi in Mantua: certainly there are similarities of style, notably the use of the *sotto in sù* (literally 'upwards from under') technique, which Mantegna developed in his earlier work. Correggio became a master of the technique, creating an illusion of movement and suspension in space by a daring use of foreshortening.

• **By train:** Parma is 50mins from Milan, 1hr 20mins from Bologna, 30mins from Modena and 40mins from Piacenza. Change at Bologna for Ferrara and Ravenna.

• **By taxi:** T: 0521 252562.

WHERE TO STAY IN PARMA

€€ **Torino**. Friendly and central, on a street leading east off the main Strada Garibaldi. Closed Jan and Aug. *Borgo Mazza 7, T: 0521 281046, www.hotel-torino.it.*

WHERE TO EAT IN PARMA & PIACENZA

For a place so famed for its food, it can be oddly hard to find easy, simple meal in Parma. With the beloved Sorelle Picchi closing down and sushi bars replacing age-old *osterie*, Parma would seem to be going through troubling and changing times. But there is hope:

€€€ **Parizzi**. The personality of owner-chef Marco Parizzi is stamped large on this restaurant. Some rate this the best *cucina parmense* in the city centre. Closed Mon and Sun evenings June–Aug. *Strada della Repubblica 71, T: 0521 285952, www.ristoranteparizzi.it.*

€€ **La Greppia**. Acclaimed restaurant specialising in local cuisine. Closed Mon–Tues and in July. *Strada Garibaldi 39/a, T: 0521 233686.*

Piacenza

€€€ **Antica Osteria del Teatro**. ■ Lovely old restaurant in the heart of Piacenza. Closed Sun and Mon, first week Jan and Aug. *Via Verdi 16, T: 0523 323777.*

FERRARA

Foggy, fabled Ferrara (*map p. 423, E3*) was once the seat of the Este dukes, whose court was one of the most brilliant in Italy. The huge Este castle survives right in the centre of the town. The Este, like so many ruling families of the Italian Renaissance, were a strange mixture of brutality and cultivation: cruel and vengeful, indifferent to suffering, yet possessing great taste and aesthetic sensitivity and a keen appreciation of beauty. They were great patrons of art and literature: the Ferrarese school of painting produced many masters; the poets Ariosto and Tasso were invited to the court (Ariosto died in Ferrara in 1533). The city also has a tradition of harbouring religious difference. The fanatical friar Savonarola was born here; John Calvin lived here for a time under an assumed name; there was a prominent Jewish community from the 15th century until the Second World War. Last but not least, the food of Ferrara is said to be some of the finest in Emilia-Romagna.

The Castello Estense

The most famous landmark in Ferrara is the massive, four-square castle of the Este dukes (*map p. 149, 7; open Tues–Sun 9.30–5.30*), surrounded by a moat and approached by drawbridges. This is where Isabella d'Este and her sister Beatrice spent their girlhood, where Lucrezia Borgia wrote her love letters to Pietro Bembo, and where Pisanello came to take his famous likeness of Lionello d'Este. It is famed most of all, however, for its dungeons. In one of them, visitors are unfailingly informed, Niccolò III d'Este had his lovely young wife Parisina immured and then murdered, after catching her in the arms of his illegitimate son Ugo, by means of a mirror, angled to reflect what was going on in her bedchamber. Ugo was likewise put to death. The atmosphere of the place is well evoked in Browning's *My Last Duchess*, though the duke in the poem is not Niccolò but Alfonso II, who was suspected of poisoning his first wife, a daughter of Cosimo I de' Medici.

THE ESTE AT FERRARA

The Guelph family of Este ruled Ferrara from 1259 until the end of the 16th century, during which time the city flourished, both commercially and artistically. The marquis Niccolò II (1361–88) gave hospitality to Petrarch; Alberto (1388–93) founded the university; Niccolò III (1393–1441) was the patron of Pisanello. His illegitimate son Lionello (1441–50), brother of the hapless Ugo (*see above*), inaugurated the age of artistic pre-eminence that was continued by Borso, another illegitimate son, created Duke of Ferrara in 1471. Ercole I (1471–1505), a legitimate son of Niccolò by his third wife, laid out the district known as the 'Herculean Addition', a grid of broad streets which Jacob Burckhardt called the first modern city in Europe. His daughters Isabella and Beatrice married into the ruling houses of Mantua and Milan. His son, Alfonso I (1505–34), third husband of Lucrezia Borgia, was the patron of Ariosto and Titian (Lucrezia is buried in the church of Corpus Domini; *map p. 149, 11*). Renée, the daughter of Louis XII of France and wife of Ercole II (1534–59), was the protectress of John Calvin; her chapel, which still survives in the Castello Estense, is one of the few Calvinist chapels in Italy to survive the Counter-Reformation. Alfonso II (1559–97) was the patron of Tasso.

In 1598 the city was annexed to the Papal States. Without the Este, Ferrara soon lost its lustre. Indeed, the Grand Tourists of the 18th and 19th centuries describe it as a ghost town.

The old ghetto

The synagogue of Ferrara is in Via Mazzini (*map p. 149, 11*), in the area which was the ghetto of Ferrara from 1627 to 1848, although a large Sephardic community had lived freely in the town during the period of the Este dukes. The **Museo Ebraico di Ferrara**, at Via Mazzini 95, is open for guided tours (*Sun–Thur 10, 11, 12*). The itinerary includes three synagogues.

Palazzo Schifanoia

The pleasure palace of Duke Borso d'Este (*map p. 149, 12; open Tues–Sun 9–6*) betrays little of its frivolous intent from the outside. In the interior, however, is the **Salone dei Mesi**, decorated in 1469–70 with frescoes of the months by Francesco del Cossa assisted by Ercole de' Roberti and others. Each of the 12 months is represented by its zodiacal sign flanked by allegorical figures. Above this is a god in triumph, normally the planetary god associated with that month or sign. Below are courtly scenes. The

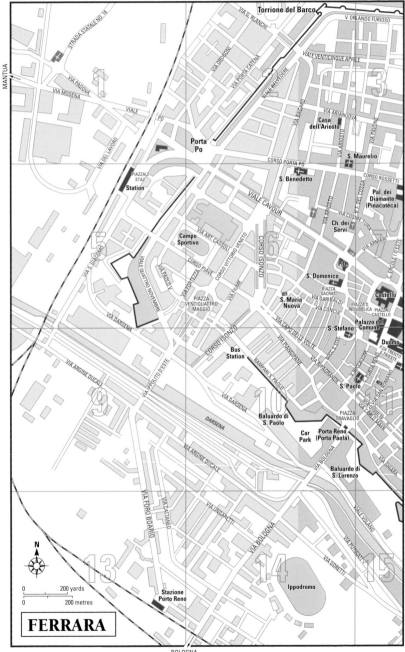

FERRARA

Torrione del Barco
V. ORLANDO FURIOSO
VIA G. BLANCHI
MANTUA
STRADA STATALE NO. 16
VIA PADOVA
VIA MODENA
VIALE
PO
VIA ORLANDO
VIA PORTA CATENA
VIALE BELVEDERE
VIA BAGARO
VIALE VENTICINQUE APRILE
VIA ARIANUOVA
Casa
dell'Ariosto
VIA PAVONE
VIA ARIOSTO
S. Maurelio
Porta
Po
CORSO PORTA PO
S. Benedetto
CORSO ROSSETTI
PIAZZALE
STAZ
Station
VIALE CAVOUR
Pal. dei
Diamante
(Pinacoteca)
VIA DEL COSSA
VIA ARIOSTO
VIA COSME TURA
Ch. dei
Servi
Campo
Sportivo
VIA ARY CASSOU
VIA ARMARI
VIALE QUATTRO NOVEMBRE
VIA S. GIACOMO
CORSO PIAVE
VIA FORTEZZA
VIA PADIGLIO
CORSO VITTORIO VENETO
CORSO ISONZO
P.O.
C. ERCOLE I D'ESTE
S. Domenico
Castello
PIAZZA
SACRATI
VIA DARSENA
PIAZZA
VENTIQUATTRO
MAGGIO
S. Maria
Nuova
VIA FIUME
VIA GARIBALDI
PIAZZA D.
REPUBBLICA
PIAZZA
CASTELLO
VIA CONCIA
Palazzo del
Comune
S. Stefano
VIA CAPO DELLE VOLTE
Duomo
PZA TRENTO
E TRIESTE
VIA PIANGIPANE
Bus
Station
CORSO ISONZO
VIA RIPAGRANDE
VIA SARACENO
VIA PIOPPA
S. Romano
VIA PIPOLITO D'ESTE
RAMPARI S. PAOLO
VIA DARSENA
DARSENA
VIA ARGINE DUCALE
VIA CARLO MAYR
S. Paolo
Baluardo di
S. Paolo
PIAZZA
TRAVAGLIO
VIA CARLO MAYR
Car
Park
Porta Reno
(Porta Paola)
VIA ARGINE DUCALE
Baluardo di
S. Lorenzo
VIA BOLOGNA
VIA GHIARA
VIA FORO BOARIO
VIA CATTANEO
VIA UNGARETTI
VIA BOLOGNA
VIALE VOLANO
VIA PUTINATI
N
VIA GORETTI
Ippodromo
0   200 yards
0   200 metres

Stazione
Porto Reno

FERRARA

BOLOGNA

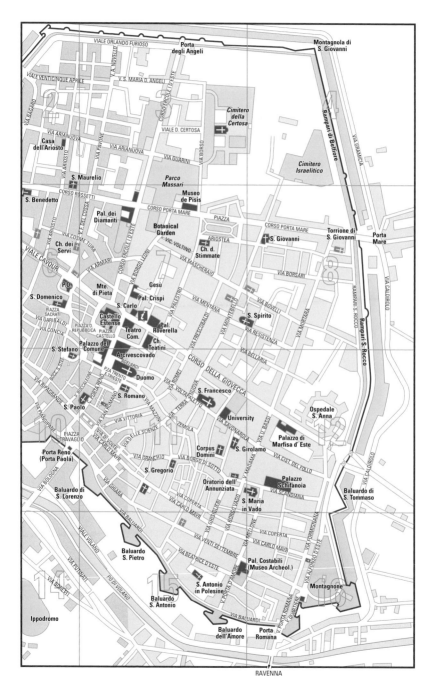

best-preserved section, certainly by Francesco del Cossa, has the month of April with Taurus the bull, the triumph of Venus above, and Duke Borso returning from the hunt below, together with the Palio of St George, a horse race still held at the end of May.

ART & ARCHITECTURE OF FERRARA

One of the finest Ferrarese masters was Cosmè Tura, whose hard outlines and sculptural modelling make his work difficult to forget. The Museo della Cattedrale in the church of San Romano (*map p. 149, 11*) has an *Annunciation* by his hand. Ercole de' Roberti was active in Ferrara and Bologna. He worked with another great Ferrarese artist, Francesco del Cossa, on the zodiac frescoes in the Palazzo Schifanoia (*see above*), and was appointed court painter by the Este. The deceptive naivety of his art masks great sophistication. Other important names associated with Ferrara include Dosso Dossi and his brother Battista, and Il Garofalo, a follower of Raphael.

Ferrara was the birthplace of a great sculptor, Alfonso Lombardi, and of a great architect, Biagio Rossetti, both roughly contemporary (late 15th–early 16th century). Two terracotta busts of Apostles by Lombardi can be seen in the duomo. Rossetti's greatest achievement is the 'Addizione', the northern extension of the city, and a supreme feat of town planning. The extraordinary Palazzo dei Diamanti is also his (*see opposite*).

Cosmè Tura: *Annunciation* (1469), in the cathedral museum.

The north of town: Palazzo dei Diamanti and the Pinacoteca

The area of the city north of Corso della Giovecca and Viale Cavour constitutes the so-called Herculean Addition or *Addizione*, developed for Ercole I d'Este in the early 15th century. It was planned by Biagio Rossetti, who also began the **Palazzo dei Diamanti** on Corso Ercole I d'Este c. 1492 (*map p. 149, 7*). The palace takes its name from the diamond emblem of the Este, repeated 12,600 times in the rustication of its façade. It is home to the **Pinacoteca Nazionale** (*open Tues–Sat 9–2, Sun and holidays 9–1, Thur 9–7*), especially notable for its paintings of the Ferrarese school. Here you will find two tondi by Cosmè Tura (*Judgement and Martyrdom of St Maurelius*) and a beautiful *Pietà* by Ercole de' Roberti. The brothers Dosso and Battista Dossi are also represented, as is Garofalo.

Also in the northern part of town, on Corso Porta Mare 9 (*map p. 149, 7*), is the **Museo d'Arte Moderna e Contemporanea Filippo de Pisis**, named after the artist who was born here in 1896 and to whose works a section of the museum is dedicated. The Museo Boldini on the same site is devoted to the portraitist Giovanni Boldini, also from Ferrara, though he made his name in Paris.

VISITING FERRARA

GETTING AROUND

• **By car:** There is pay parking on streets and squares throughout the city (and bicycles can be hired on Corso Giovecca, next to the information office; *map p. 149, 7*).
• **By bus:** City buses 1 and 9 connect the train station with the Castello Estense. Country buses to Bologna, Modena and points throughout the province leave from the bus stations at Rampari di San Paolo (*map p. 148, 10*) and Piazzale Stazione (*map p. 148, 5*).
• **By train:** Ferrara is on the main line to Bologna (25mins) and to Padua (50mins). From most other places to the south, east and west the quickest way to get there is via Bologna. Commuter trains connect to Ravenna (c. 75mins).

WHERE TO STAY IN FERRARA

€€€ **Duchessa Isabella**. ■ A beautiful, luxurious old town house with coffered ceilings, Ferrara-school frescoes and a good restaurant. Part of the Relais & Châteaux chain. A

gracious place to stay. Closed Aug (*Via Palestro 70, T: 0532 202121, www.duchessaisabella.it; map p. 149, 7*). Two other hotels under the same management are the lovely €€ **Principessa Leonora** (*Via Mascheraio 39, T: 0532 206020*), and the €€ **Locanda della Duchessina** (*Vicolo del Voltino 11, T: 0532 206981*). Both are close to the Isabella.
€€ **Locanda Corte Arcangeli** A former farm on the outskirts of town to the east. Lovely rooms with beamed ceilings. Free bicycle rental. *Via Pontegraella 503, T: 0532 705052, www.cortearcangeli.it. Beyond map p. 149, 12.*

WHERE TO EAT IN FERRARA

€€ **Don Giovanni**. Fine restaurant in the former stock exchange. Open evenings only, closed Sun evening and Mon, and in Jan and Aug. *Corso Ercole I d'Este 1, T: 0532 243363. Map p. 149, 7.*
€€ **Al Brindisi**. Old-established *enoteca* dating back to the 15th century. Wonderful atmosphere. Past customers have included Copernicus. *Via degli Adelardi 11, T: 0532*

209142. Map p. 149, 11.
€€ **L'Oca Giuliva**. A well-stocked wine bar offering good hot and cold meals. Good for a light lunch. Closed Mon, midday Tues and in Jan. *Via Boccacanale di Santo Stefano 38, T: 0532 207628. Map p. 148, 10 (Boc.S.Stef.)*

RAVENNA

Ravenna (*map p. 423, E3*) is a small place today. But for 200 years in the middle of the first millennium AD it aspired to greatness. It remains the best place in Europe to see Byzantine mosaics, brilliant and beautiful and rather poignant.

Ravenna in history

In 401, some years before the fall of Rome to the Goths, the emperor Honorius moved his capital to a marshy lagoon on the Adriatic coast, where the port of Classis had been constructed by Augustus. This was Ravenna, which remained the imperial capital until 476, when the last Roman emperor, Romulus Augustulus, was deposed by Odoacer. Odoacer and his successor Theodoric also used Ravenna as their capital, until it was captured by the Byzantines in 540, after which Ravenna was the capital of a tiny outpost of Byzantium on Italian soil, ruled by the exarchs of the Eastern Empire. The Lombards captured it in 751, as part of their drive into the Italian peninsula. When the Franks drove the Lombards out three years later, they did not restore the territory to Byzantium but gave it to the pope. The papacy retained a nominal suzerainty until 1861, though in the Middle Ages, like any other city in northern or central Italy, Ravenna was first a *comune* and then a seignory. The ruling family of Ravenna was the da Polenta, and its most famous member is Francesca, married to Gianciotto Malatesta of Rimini but lover of Paolo, his handsome brother (*see p. 308*). Dante, who was a guest of the da Polenta after his exile from Florence, and who died here in 1321 (his tomb is near the church of San Francesco), tells the story of the star-crossed lovers in his *Divine Comedy*.

In the 15th century Ravenna belonged to the Venetian Republic, but Venice lost control to the French in 1509. It was at the Battle of Ravenna in 1512, fought between French and Spanish forces for control of the Romagna, that the 22-year-old commander Gaston de Foix was killed. His tomb is in Milan (*see p. 40*).

Sant'Apollinare Nuovo and the Arian baptistery

Sant'Apollinare Nuovo (*map opposite, 4; open daily, summer 9–7, winter 9.30–5.30*) is one of the most beautiful basilicas in Ravenna. It was built by Theodoric in the early 6th century as the chapel of his palace. Theodoric was, like all the Goths, an Arian Christian; in other words he believed that Christ was a later creation of God the Father, a view which had been declared heretical in the 380s. After Theodoric's death, the church passed from the Arians to the orthodox Christians, and was for a time dedicated to St Martin, famous for his detestation of Arians, until the relics of St Apollinaris were transferred here from the basilica on the coast, to protect them from pirate raids.

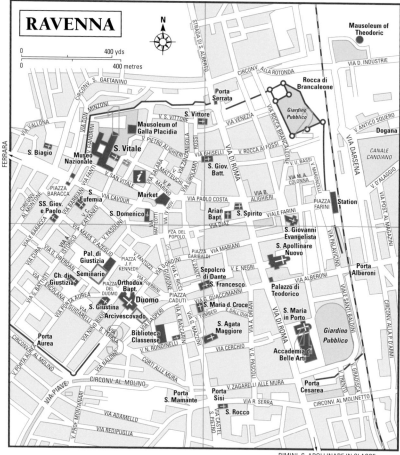

RIMINI, S. APOLLINARE IN CLASSE

In the interior, two magnificent bands of mosaics adorn the nave walls. The mosaics of the upper bands date from the time of Theodoric (Arian), while those on the lower are from the time of Justinian (orthodox). Scholars find personality and idiosyncrasy in the former, while the latter are more ritualised. The two lower bands, which can be best seen and appreciated, show the port of Classis on the left, with a procession of 22 virgin martyrs preceded by the Magi, who offer gifts to the Infant Jesus. On the right is Ravenna, showing a procession of 26 martyrs led by St Martin approaching Christ enthroned. The façade of Theodoric's palace has been much altered. Originally figures of Theodoric and his court appeared under the archways. These have now been obliterated by curtains, added by the agents of Justinian after his conquest, though a number of hands can still be seen peeping out from behind them.

ART & ARCHITECTURE IN RAVENNA

Because so many of the early mosaics of Constantinople were destroyed by the iconoclasts of the 8th century, those of Ravenna have special importance. They are not the earliest in Italy, but their Christian imagery is more developed—and the earliest known narrative cycle of the life of Christ is in fact that in Sant'Apollinare Nuovo. The pre-eminence of Christ the Good Shepherd in the oratory of Galla Placidia is another good example. In contrast with contemporary mosaics in Rome (such as those in the church of Santa Maria Maggiore, built by a bishop with no particular allegiance to an emperor), the mosaics of Ravenna show a close link to royal or imperial power. Thus it was that Theodoric was originally represented beside his palace in Sant'Apollinare Nuovo (*see above*). The Byzantine emperor Justinian, whose army conquered Ravenna in 540, never visited the city in person, but he and his empress Theodora are shown bringing symbols of the Eucharist to the church in the mosaics of San Vitale, as if to underline the powerful relationship between emperor and orthodox Christianity.

Ravenna is often described as a showcase of Byzantine art, because this link between ruler and religion prefigures the theocratic world view of the Byzantine empire. Western Christianity increasingly stressed the need for redemption through the portrayal of the sufferings of Christ. Byzantine art concentrates on the salvation offered by Christ and He, or God the Father, is invariably represented as a protective figure looking down from above, not as a man crucified. The atmosphere of a Byzantine church is deliberately other-worldly. The chanting, the incense and the shimmering light on the gold of the mosaics are all designed to conjure up a vision of heaven.

North of Sant'Apollinare Nuovo is the tiny **Arian baptistery** (*open daily 8.30–7.30*), built by Theodoric in the early 6th century. It contains splendidly preserved mosaics of the Baptism of Christ and of the Apostles in the dome. The other baptistery in Ravenna, attached to the duomo (*map p. 153, 3*), is known as the **orthodox baptistery** or Battistero Neoniano. It was converted from a Roman bath house and still preserves marble inlay from that time. The dome mosaic of the Baptism of Christ is very fine.

San Vitale

San Vitale (*map p. 153, 1; open daily 9.30–5; last tickets 4.45*) is the most famous monumental complex in Ravenna. Building began in 521, using the church of Sts Sergius and Bacchus in Constantinople as a model: it would have been a dramatic contrast to the Roman basilica model. Before the building was finished, Justinian's troops conquered Ravenna, and San Vitale was adorned with magnificent mosaics of Justinian and his empress Theodora, the finest examples of Byzantine art in Western Europe.

The Good Shepherd, arrayed in purple and gold like a secular emperor, a 5th-century lunette mosaic from the mausoleum of Galla Placidia, showing how Classical models were adopted for use in early Christian art.

On the triumphal arch are mosaics of Christ and the Apostles with St Gervasius and St Protasius, the sons of St Vitalis, the 3rd-century martyr to whom the church is dedicated. The semi-dome of the apse shows a beardless Christ welcoming St Vitalis and Bishop Ecclesius (who built the church and chose its design) into paradise. On the side walls are two fine processional friezes: on the left is Justinian with his retinue, showing the ruler as the elect of Christ (Justinian carries a paten for the Eucharistic bread, and note the *chi-rho* sign on the shield of one of his attendants). On the right is Theodora with her court, a stunning portrait of the actress and prostitute who captured the emperor's heart and rose to become the most powerful woman in the Eastern empire.

The mausoleum of Galla Placidia

Galla Placidia was Honorius' half-sister and wife of the emperor Constantius II. After her husband's death in 421, she acted as regent to their son, Valentinian III. The small oratory, once believed to be her mausoleum (*map p. 153, 1; open as San Vitale*), in the form of a Greek cross, is famous for its magnificent mosaics, especially interesting for the classical character of the figures. Over the entrance is the *Good Shepherd* (*illustrated above*); in the opposite lunette is St Lawrence with his gridiron and, on the left, an open tabernacle containing copies of the Gospels; in the side lunettes, below the ceiling, figures of Apostles clad in white flank alabaster windows, with mosaics of doves at drinking fountains below them, clearly derived from Classical models. In the centre of the cupola rises the Cross in a star-strewn sky. Symbols of the Evangelists are in the four corners.

The mausoleum of Theodoric

Lying outside the old town centre, beyond the railway line, is a remarkable tomb composed of two superimposed ten-sided rotundas (*map p. 153, 2; open daily 8.30–4.30*), completely unique in the history of architecture, though it bears certain similarities to the (11th-century) Armenian Church of the Redeemer at Ani (present-day Turkey). It was begun by Theodoric c. 520, and is built of blocks of Istrian stone fitted together without mortar and crowned by an unusual monolithic cupola of Istrian limestone from Pula. It is not known how the monolith was transported here (it weighs about 300 tons). Inside the tomb is a porphyry bath that was used as the royal sarcophagus.

Sant'Apollinare in Classe

About 5km south of Ravenna, on the site of the Roman port of Classis, is the basilica of Sant'Apollinare in Classe (*open Mon–Sat 8.30–7.30, Sun and holidays from 1pm; last tickets 30mins before closing*). It was built in 535–38 and consecrated in 549, after the Byzantine conquest, and dedicated to Apollinaris, a disciple of St Peter, who gave him the bishopric of Ravenna. The church is visited for its apse mosaics, which are extremely interesting, though much altered. On the outside arch are five rows of symbolic mosaics, with figures of saints, palm trees, sheep, and Christ in a roundel with the symbols of the Evangelists. In the apse itself is a Cross on a blue ground with the symbol of the Transfiguration; below is a field of lilies (representing light and life) and trees with birds and sheep (the blessed in Paradise).

RIMINI

Fifty-two kilometres southwards down the coast from Ravenna is the large, sprawling resort of Rimini (*map p. 423, E4*), ancient fiefdom of the Malatesta and home to an important Giottesque school of painting. Its most important monument is the **Tempio Malatestiano** by Leon Battista Alberti (a short walk from both rail and bus station), whose exterior niches were inspired by those on the mausoleum of Theodoric in Ravenna, and whose motif of the triple triumphal arch Alberti took up again for his church of Sant'Andrea in Mantua (*see p. 60*). Like the mausoleum, the Tempio is built of Istrian stone. It was commissioned by Sigismondo Malatesta in 1447–48, and is the burial place of his mistress and later wife Isotta degli Atti (Sigismondo's previous two wives, the first of whom was an illegitimate daughter of Niccolò III d'Este of Ferrara, both died in mysterious circumstances). Fate caught up with Sigismondo in the end: he was a brave soldier and a daring *condottiere*, but excommunication by Pope Pius II destroyed his reputation, and his mausoleum was never completed. Nevertheless its design made a noticeable impact on Italian ecclesiastical architecture in succeeding centuries, and Sigismondo's life and exploits have inspired a number of works of literature, including Ezra Pound's *Malatesta Cantos*.

VISITING RAVENNA & RIMINI

GETTING AROUND

• **By car:** There is pay parking in and around the centre of Ravenna.

• **By bus:** Buses 4 and 44 (run by ATM) run on weekdays from the station (Piazza Farini) to the basilica of Sant'Apollinare in Classe.

• **By train:** Trains from Ravenna go to Ferrara (1hr), Bologna (1hr 10mins) and Rimini (c. 1hr). Hourly trains go to Classe, journey time 5mins.

WHERE TO STAY IN RAVENNA

€€ **Albergo Cappello**. Quietly elegant rooms, some with frescoes, in a centrally-located Renaissance town house. Good restaurant. *Via IV Novembre 41, T: 0544 219813, www.albergocappello.it. Map p. 153, 1 (Via IV Nov.).*

WHERE TO EAT IN RAVENNA & RIMINI

Ravenna

€ **Ca' de' Ven**. *Osteria* in a beautiful old palace offering good regional food. Closed Mon and in Dec–Jan. *Via Corrado Ricci 24, T: 0544 30163. Map p. 153, 3 (Via C. Ricci).*

€€ **La Gardela**. The *gardela*, or grill, is a symbol of the cuisine of Romagna, and this restaurant specialises in regional grilled dishes. Closed Thur, and in Feb and Aug. *Via Ponte Marino 3, T: 0544 217147. Map p. 153, 1 (V. P. Marino).*

Rimini

€€ **La Puraza**. If you make the detour to Rimini, it is worth making another to this fine fish restaurant, which has built up quite a following for its fresh, unpretentious cooking and its skill with shellfish. Located southeast of town, just off the SS72 to San Marino. *Via Sant'Aquilina 2, T: 0541 751046.*

View of Vernazza, one of the Cinque Terre.

LIGURIA

The region of Liguria (*map p. 422*), a narrow arc of littoral backed by the Apennines, with the great port city of Genoa at its centre, stretches between the French frontier and the northern reaches of Tuscany. Its coastline is rugged and grand, its climate exceptionally gentle. Against a backdrop of blue sea and green-brown cliff, the huddled clutches of buildings are painted in rich colours, ranging from deep sky blues to russet reds and dark ochres, posing a vivid chromatic contrast. Add to this primitive wildness the Babylonian luxuriance of Liguria's gardens, and you begin to understand why so many 19th- and 20th-century artists and writers were enraptured by the place.

Liguria in history

Liguria takes its name from the Ligures, a loose grouping of Neolithic peoples who lived in village settlements on the Mediterranean coast from Spain to Tuscany in the 1st millennium BC. They established early contact with the first known navigators of the Mediterranean, the Phoenicians and Greeks. In the 2nd century BC the region came under the dominance of Rome, whose fortunes it followed until the fall of the Empire.

Though Liguria is blessed with a kind climate, it lacks cultivable land, and such prosperity as it has had has come from the water. In the 11th century the city of Genoa emerged as a self-governing republic, ridding the coast of Saracen pirates and building a great colonial empire that extended to the Crimea, Syria and North Africa.

Despite numerous conflicts with maritime competitors (firstly Pisa and subsequently Venice) the Republic of Genoa remained independent until the 17th century, when its sailors first wore the robust cotton trousers dyed with indigo—in French *bleus de Gênes*—that two centuries later, anglicised as 'blue jeans', were chosen by San Francisco merchant Levi Strauss to clothe American gold miners.

Genoa's decline was due partly to the growing might of the Ottoman Empire and largely to the shifting of world trade to the Atlantic. In 1684 Genoa surrendered to France after heavy bombardment, and in 1768 the Genoese sold the rights to their last remaining colony, Corsica, to the French. Napoleon seized Genoa in 1796, and formed the Ligurian Republic in 1802. In 1815, after Napoleon's fall, Genoa was joined to Piedmont. It went on to become a stronghold of the Risorgimento under Giuseppe Mazzini, a native.

Food and wine of Liguria

Tuscans and Ligurians can come to blows when talking about olive oil. What the former consider great virtues in a freshly pressed oil—a spicy tang and a rich flavour— the latter consider coarse and unrefined, arguing that the more delicate Ligurian oil brings out the subtler flavours of fresh fish and vegetables. The two oils are certainly very different, and Ligurian oil does go very well with fish. Ligurian wines are also distinctive, particularly the strong, sweet Sciacchetrà of the Cinque Terre—though it is produced in such limited quantities that an authentic bottle can cost an arm and a leg (beware of imitations). The finest Ligurian wine is Rossese di Dolceacqua, made throughout Imperia province and around Ventimiglia.

Ligurian contributions to Italian cuisine are *focaccia* (the cheese-filled *focaccia di Recco* is even protected by a *Comitato di Autenticità*) and *farinata*, a type of pizza made with chick-pea flour. It is sold in modest snack bars called *farinotti*. Perhaps the greatest Ligurian culinary invention of all is *pesto*, the famous sauce made from fresh basil.

GENOA

The busy port city of Genoa (*map p. 422, B3*) tumbles downhill towards the sea. Inland to the east rises a medieval city gate, the Porta Sant'Andrea, flanked by slim cylindrical towers. A scattering of grand palaces bears witness to the wealth of the maritime families who once controlled the destiny of an entire seaboard. On the whole, however, survival in Genoa has been patchy and haphazard. Like so many naval centres, the city has been sacked and burned, has expanded many times beyond its limits, was bombed mercilessly in the Second World War, and was hastily and shoddily patched up thereafter. All of this makes Genoa a real city. There is nothing of the museum piece about it. It is a place where life is lived in the present, a necessary mixture of energy, hurry, careful plans misfired and accidental beauty. Those who like that sort of thing will enjoy their visit.

The city's most famous native is Christopher Columbus. Paganini was also born here, as was Giuseppe Mazzini, the liberal nationalist thinker who was the brains behind the Risorgimento. A project to revitalise the old harbour has been entrusted to another eminent native, the architect Renzo Piano.

The old centre

From the 10th–13th centuries, Genoa was a dense warren of extremely narrow streets, and survivals from this time give the innermost core of the city its distinctive atmosphere. Not far from the waterfront is **Piazza dei Banchi** (*map p. 162, 6*), where the money-changers had their stalls until the end of the 18th century. The late 16th-century Loggia dei Mercanti became an exchange—the first of its kind in Italy—in the 19th century. Running north of here is Via San Luca, the main street of Genoa in the Middle Ages. Vico Pellicceria leads off it to **Galleria Spinola** (*map p. 162, 6*), one of the best surviving examples of a patrician Genoese residence of the 17th–18th centuries, and home to a representative collection of art (*Piazza Pellicceria 1; open Tues–Sat 8.30–7.30, Sun 1.30–7.30; combined ticket available with Palazzo Reale*). Further away from the waterfront, the vistas broaden. Flanking the broad Piazza Matteotti is the old doge's palace (**Palazzo Ducale**; *map p. 163, 11*), now a cultural centre. The Neoclassical façade conceals a much older building, open to visitors (*Tues–Sun 9–6.30*) and containing the former meeting chamber of the Great Council and the doge's private chapel. Close by is the dignified cathedral of **San Lorenzo**, where one can still see an Allied shell which fell into the building in 1941 but did not detonate.

GENOESE ART & ARCHITECTURE

The monumental architecture of medieval Genoa is characterised by its black-and-white striped church façades, a design said to have been brought back by travellers to the Holy Land. The earliest sculpture comes from the workshops of the Pisano family and the *maestri comacini*, master sculptors from the Lombard lakes (*see p. 54*). Galeazzo Alessi, the Perugian architect, worked here during the Renaissance, and the Gaggini family of sculptors were active in the 16th–17th centuries. The greatest name of the 16th century is Luca Cambiaso (1527–85), a precocious talent who uses geometric forms that almost foreshadow Cubism. Genoa, like any port city, has always been receptive to foreign ideas, and it was influence from outside Italy that inspired the art of its most fruitful time, the 17th century. Through its close commercial links with the Netherlands, the city acquired many Dutch and Flemish paintings. Rubens and van Dyck were in Genoa in the early part of the century; other influences came from Caravaggio, who fled from the law here briefly in 1605. The greatest native artist is Giovanni Benedetto Castiglione (c. 1610–65, known as Grechetto), who was much influenced by the Netherlandish painters and was in turn much admired by Tiepolo.

Some patrician palaces

In the mid-16th century, at the height of their commercial and financial influence, the wealthy aristocratic families of the Genoese republic decided to construct a new quarter in the upper part of the city. The resulting *Strada Nuova*, the 'new street', built in 1551–83 (today Via Garibaldi; *map p. 163, 7*) was 250m long and 7m wide (more than twice the width of some of the medieval streets); it immediately became the city's most exclusive address, the setting for splendid palaces and the theatre of lavish entertainments. A decree of 1576 placed the palaces on the Strada Nuova on an official list, the *Lista dei Rolli*, obliging the owners to give hospitality to distinguished guests of the Republic during state visits.

Due to the slope of the site, each palace was adjusted to fit its particular location. A few characteristics are generally shared, however: most are three or four storeys high and combine an elaborate entrance hall with spectacular courtyards, open staircases and loggias overlooking luxurious gardens arranged on different levels. Nearly all have illusionistic façades with painted and/or stone elements, and interiors adorned with stuccoes and frescoes. The model of the Genoese palaces was exported to other states in Italy and the north, thanks to the work of artists such as Rubens (who published drawings of them). It profoundly influenced Baroque town planning in Germany, Britain and the Netherlands. Three of the palaces are now open as museums. The street was declared a UNESCO World Heritage site in 2006. The museums are **Palazzo Bianco** (*Via Garibaldi 11; open Tues–Fri 9–7, Sat–Sun 10–7*) with some some lovely Flemish and Dutch paintings, works by Luca Cambiaso, and Caravaggio's

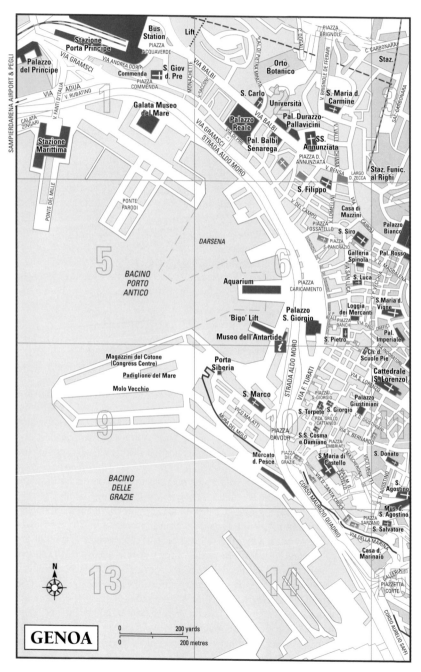

SAMPIERDARENA AIRPORT & PEGLI

GENOA

| 0 | 200 yards |
| 0 | 200 metres |

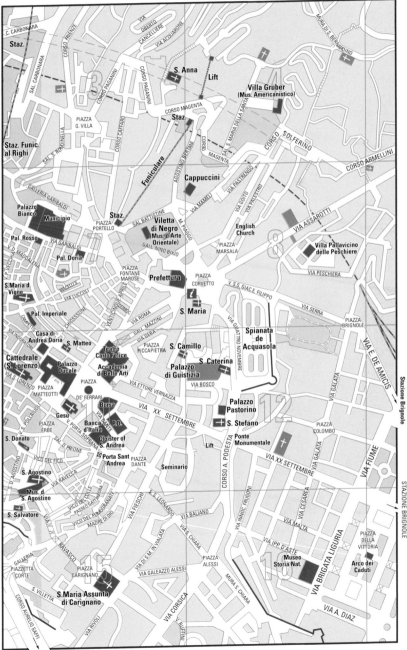

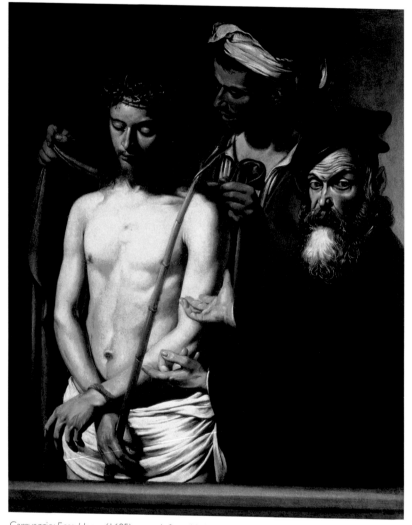

Caravaggio: *Ecce Homo* (1605), a work from his later period, when he abandoned bacchic characters and baskets of fruit for dark-toned sacred subjects intended for devotion.

splendid *Ecce Homo* (*illustrated below*); **Palazzo Rosso** (*Via Garibaldi 18; open Tues–Fri 9–7, Sat–Sun 10–7*) with family portraits by van Dyck and works by the Genoese School (including Giovanni Benedetto Castiglione); and **Palazzo Doria Tursi** (*Via Garibaldi 9; open Tues–Fri 9–7, Sat–Sun 10–7*), which displays the Guarneri violin (1742), which belonged to Paganini, as well as three letters from Columbus.

The northwest waterfront and Pegli

The wide Via Balbi (*map p. 162, 2*) leads northwest towards the bus station, railway station and an area of docks. At no. 10 you will see the red and white **Palazzo Reale** (*open Tues and Wed 9–1.30, Thur–Sun 9–7*), a former palace of the wealthy Balbi family, purchased by the House of Savoy in 1822, fitted with a throne room and used briefly as a royal residence. The Hall of Mirrors on the upper *piano nobile* (c. 1730) is the masterpiece of Genoa-born painter, sculptor and architect Antonio Domenico Parodi.

Just beyond the railway station is the **Palazzo del Principe** (*map p. 162, 1*), a grand residence built for one of Genoa's greatest sea captains, Andrea Doria. In 1528 he became virtual ruler of the republic, though he was careful not to dissolve the senate. A famous portrait by Bronzino (in the Brera, Milan) shows him in the guise of Neptune. His palace (much enlarged and redecorated by his successors) is now open as a museum (*open Tues–Sun 10–5*). A combined ticket is available with the aquarium, and visitors can travel between the two in the so-called Doria Frigate, a small craft based on 16th–17th-century designs. The **aquarium**, on the central waterfront (*map p. 162, 6*), is the largest in Europe and was designed by Renzo Piano. The shark and dolphin tanks, designed to be viewed as though you were underwater, are very popular.

On the point of one of the outer, commercial harbour quays is the slender brick **Lanterna**, famed as the oldest working lighthouse in the world. It was first built in the early 12th century, but dates in its present form from 1543. Its signal was originally a fire of juniper wood; it was later fuelled by olive oil.

In the suburb of Pegli (*beyond map p. 162, 1*) is another former residence of the Doria, now the **Museo Navale** (*close to Pegli station; open Tues–Fri 9–1, Sat and Sun 10–7*), with collections spanning the 11th–19th centuries displayed beneath frescoed ceilings. A less traditional maritime museum, the **Galata Museo del Mare** (*map p. 162, 1; joint ticket with Palazzo del Principe*), is built over the remains of the old arsenal—though you would never guess it to look at the great glass box that now dominates the Darsena waterfront. Traditional displays on the port of Genoa, Christopher Columbus and Andrea Doria mingle with virtual experiences such as a simulated sail round Cape Horn in a storm.

VISITING GENOA

GETTING AROUND

• **By air:** Genoa airport is at Sestri Ponente, 6km west of the city. An hourly bus service (Volabus) leaves the airport on the hour for Principe Station (Piazza Acquaverde; *map p. 162, 1*); journey time is 20mins. Departures from the station to the airport leave on the half hour. Regular buses also connect Principe Station with the airport at Milan (Malpensa).

• **By car:** The best place to park in the cen-

tre is the pay car park in Piazza de' Ferrari (*map p. 163, 11*).

• **By train:** Trains to Pegli leave from Brignole station in the east of town (*beyond map p. 163, 16*). Journey time c. 30mins. Genoa's Porta Principe station (*map p. 162, 1*) has frequent connections to Turin (90mins), Milan (90mins) and Pisa (1hr 40mins).

• **By public transport:** City transport is run by AMT (www.amt.genova.it). Tickets come in various types: timed tickets of 90mins, daily passes, single-journey tickets or books of tickets. They can be purchased at tobacconists and newsstands displaying the AMT logo, or at vending machines around town. 90-min tickets can also be bought on board for a higher price. The Metro has useful stops at Principe station (*map p. 162, 1*), Darsena (*map p. 162, 6*), Palazzo San Giorgio (*map p. 162, 6*) and Piazza de' Ferrari (*map p. 163, 11*).

• **By taxi:** T: 010 5966.

• **By sea:** The ferry to Pegli (NaveBus; regular bus ticket valid) leaves from the southern end of the Porto Antico, once an hour on weekdays, much less frequently at weekends. Journey time c. 30mins. At the time of writing floods had damaged the port; check on www.amt.genova.it.

SPECIAL TICKETS

The **Genoa Museum Card** gives free or reduced admission to selected museums and cultural venues. Cards are on sale at participating museums, the bookshop of the Musei di Strada Nuova, main railway stations, and main AMT ticket offices.

WHERE TO STAY IN GENOA

€€€ **Bristol Palace**. This small but elegant hotel offers 19th-century ambience right in the centre of the city, very close to Piazza de' Ferrari. *Via XX Settembre 35, T: 010 592541, www.hotelbristolpalace.com. Map p. 163, 11.*

€€ **Agnello d'Oro**. A simple, family-run place with basic but comfortable rooms close to the railway station. There is a small terrace overlooking the old harbour. *Via Monachette 6, T: 010 246 2084, www.hotelagnellodoro.it. Map p. 162, 1.*

€€ **Locanda di Palazzo Cicala**. Contemporary design in a venerable old palace in front of the duomo. Very central, with an original kind of charm. *Piazza San Lorenzo 16, T: 010 251 8824, www.palazzocicala.it. Map p. 162, 10.*

WHERE TO EAT IN GENOA

€€ **La Berlocca**. This very simple establishment serves up good regional dishes, with a special focus on pastas, vegetables and seafood. Closed Mon, Sat, Sun midday and July–Aug. *Via dei Macelli di Soziglia 45/r, T: 010 247 4162. Map p. 163, 7 (Macelli S.).*

€€ **Da Rina**. This family-run *trattoria* is famous for its seafood dishes, in the warren of streets below Piazza San Giorgio. Closed Mon and Aug. *Via Mura delle Grazie 3/r, T: 010 246 6475. Map p. 162, 10.*

€€ **Le Rune**. Simple but refined restaurant in the centre of the city, known for its delicious Ligurian dishes, good wines and cheeses. Closed Sat and midday Sun. *Vicolo Domoculta 14/r, T: 010 594951. Map p. 163, 7 (Domoc.).*

THE ITALIAN RIVIERA

The resident population of Liguria is extremely dense and is increased by some three million annual visitors. Most habitation is concentrated along the coast, which appears, especially at night when the city lights sparkle in the terse air, as a single, ribbon-shaped metropolis with Genoa at its centre. The rough, picturesque littoral, the Italian Riviera, is known to the west and east of Genoa as the Riviera di Ponente and the Riviera di Levante respectively, the shores of the setting and rising sun.

The Riviera di Ponente

Most of the resorts on the Riviera di Ponente follow a common plan: an old town on the hillside with steep, narrow streets, and a new town on the coast with attractive villas and hotels, gardens and scenic promenades, and a small seaport, occasionally overlooked by a Genoese fort. Savona and **Albissola** (*map p. 422, B3*) are known for their ceramics. Albissola Marina was a base for the ceramicist Lucio Fontana, founder of the movement known as *Spazialismo*. **Albenga** has a particularly fine historic centre, with a Byzantine mosaic in its cathedral baptistery and a museum (*closed Mon*) displaying the contents of an ancient Roman shipwreck (mainly amphorae of wine, bound from Campania for France). Further west is the lovely little village of **Cervo** (*map p. 422, B4*), host to an international chamber music festival in July and August, but also a place to get a feeling for old Liguria. Clustered on a headland directly above the sea, its weathered beauty— a mix of pastel-coloured walls adorned with brilliant flowers and verdant creepers, and cobbled streets too narrow for cars—make it one of the most charming places on the coast. Its origins date back to Roman times, when it was a *mansio*, or official stopping place, along the Via Augusta. Until quite recently the economy was based on fishing and farming, and though tourism is the mainstay of the economy now, there is still a strong scent of tradition in the air. The usual entrance to the town is from its highest point by one of two gates in the old walls. In the little piazza stands the castle, originally built to defend the population against Saracen pirates. From it the three main streets, Via Salineri and the parallel Via Cavour and Via Volta, all descend to the parish church of San Giovanni Battista, known as the Chiesa dei Corallini because it was financed from the sale of coral gathered by local fishermen off the coasts of Corsica and Sardinia.

Closer to France the coastline is known as the Riviera dei Fiori. **Ventimiglia** (*map p. 422, A4*) has a famous botanic garden established by two Englishmen (Giardini Botanici Hanbury; *open Nov–March 10–4, April–14 June 10–5, 15 June–Sept and Oct 9–6; closed Wed; T: 0184 229507*).

VISITING THE RIVIERA DI PONENTE

GETTING AROUND

• **By car:** The SS1 is the Roman Via Julia Augusta—the road built by the emperor Augustus to carry traffic to and from Gaul two millennia ago. It makes a good alternative to the *autostrada*, which can be very busy in summer or on sunny weekends. Traffic can come to a complete standstill on Fri and Sun evenings, as well as Sat mornings when towns have their outdoor markets.

• **By train:** Trains on the Genoa–Ventimiglia line stop at Cervo-San Bartolomeo or (more frequent service) Diano Marina: the 3km from Diano Marina station to Cervo can be solved by taxi (*T: 0183 495210*), or by the Riviera Trasporti bus, which runs along Diano Marina's main street (the line starts at San Remo and ends in Andora; buses roughly every 30mins).

• **By boat:** A boat leaving from Diano Marina offers daily mini-cruises along the coast.

HOTELS ON THE RIVIERA DI PONENTE

Cervo
€ **Le Notti Mediterranee**. Delightful little

B&B in the centre of the village. You have to walk with your bags (the streets are too narrow for cars). Rooms are cosy, and breakfast is served in the café in the square. *Via Cavour 9, T: 348 333 6899, www.lenottimediterranee.com.*

Garlenda

€€€ **La Meridiana.** ■ In a small village in the hills above medieval Albenga, enjoying splendid views of both sea and mountains, this hotel is a luxurious country house surrounded by gardens, with an excellent restaurant. Now part of the Relais & Châteaux group. A truly lovely place to base oneself. *Via ai Castelli, T: 0182 580271, www.lameridianaresort.com.*

Cervo

€€ **Serafino** is an unpretentious place opening onto a vaulted lane of the old town, with a panoramic terrace for summer. There are also a few simple rooms. *Via Matteotti 8, T: 0183 408185, www.daserafino.com; closed Tues).*

€ **Bellavista** is a simple place famous for its homemade pasta—and for its astonishing collection of ships in bottles, a passion of the late founder. The restaurant is right across the square from the town's upper gate (*Piazza Castello 2, T: 0183 408094; closed Wed).*

THE RIVIERA DI LEVANTE & CINQUE TERRE

Genoa's eastern suburbs, from Nervi to Camogli, abound in beautiful old villas. This part of the Riviera di Levante, in fact, is known as the Bay of Paradise. Property here is owned by seasonal visitors from Milan, Turin and elsewhere in Italy and Europe, and by wealthy residents who feel that the snail-paced commute to and from Genoa is an acceptable price to pay for life in such a 'heavenly' spot.

At the southern end of this broad bay is the famous and beautiful **Portofino peninsula** (*map p. 422, C3*). A scenic road skirts its east shore from the colourful and lively town of Santa Margherita Ligure to Portofino itself, once a humble fishing village and now an exclusive resort. Its position is lovely, partly on a small wooded headland and partly in a little bay that has offered a safe anchorage to boats since Roman times. The little church of San Giorgio, overlooking the harbour, is said to hold the relics of its namesake—patron saint of Portofino, of Genoa, and of England, among other places—brought from the Holy Land by returning Crusaders. The saint's heraldic symbol, a red cross on a white field, was taken as the emblem of the Genoese Republic, of armed pilgrims to the Holy Land and, after the 12th century, by England, initially as a sign to Mediterranean pirates that its ships sailed under the protection of the Genoese fleet.

Beyond Sestri Levante, a quiet and beautiful place huddled between two bays, the coast becomes higher and more dramatic. Here, between Sestri and La Spezia, is the most famous stretch of coast in northern Italy.

THE CINQUE TERRE

'A rocky, austere landscape, similar to Calabria's harshest, the refuge of fishermen and farmers living meagrely on an ever-smaller shred of beach, the naked and solemn frame of one of the most primitive lifestyles in Italy.' This is how the poet Eugenio Montale described the coast of the Cinque Terre (*map p. 422, C3*), the steepest and roughest in all Liguria. From Montale's words one might expect to find a wilderness here, a place where the imprint of human endeavour is unnoticeable. Yet the sheer, vertical landscape of the Cinque Terre is anything but wild. It is deeply marked by centuries of human toil, which have transformed its precipitous cliffs into an immense hanging garden.

The area takes its name from the five little villages—Riomaggiore, Manarola, Corniglia, Vernazza and Monterosso al Mare—that were accessible only by sea before the advent of the railway in 1874. By car they can be reached only along winding, steep inland roads. Tens of thousands of walkers are now drawn every year by the Cinque Terre's perpendicular vineyards, whose terraces—called *cian* in dialect—are the most distinctive physical feature of this 'shred' of earth. How, why and when a project of such vast proportions was conceived remains a mystery. Also unanswered is the question of why grapes, and grapes alone, are grown on the terraced mountainsides. Historical examples of specialised farming like this are rare, and the few there are are all situated in places that are easier to exploit. What is certain is that the terraces, having been created, must be maintained. If they are not, the risk of landslide is immense.

Most of the walking trails in the Cinque Terre are former mule tracks over the great green spurs that separate one village from the next: if you decide to walk from village to village you will have to climb from sea level to an elevation of 200 or 300m, then descend again. Exceptions are the seaside paths from Corniglia to Manarola and from Manarola to Riomaggiore, both of which are without significant elevation gains. The latter, called the 'Lovers' Trail', even has benches. The most scenic walks are those leading from Monterosso and Corniglia to Vernazza, and the magnificent, lofty trail from Corniglia to Manarola.

Villages of the Cinque Terre

Monterosso al Mare, the westernmost village, is clustered around an inlet enclosed by hills terraced with olive and lemon trees and, above all, vines. It, like the other four villages, was taken over and fortified by the Republic of Genoa. A stepped walkway climbs to the Convento dei Cappuccini with its church of St Francis; inside are some works by lesser Ligurian masters, and a *Crucifixion* attributed to van Dyck.

For centuries **Vernazza** was the only harbour of any importance along this stretch of the coast, and as a result it has always been the richest of the Cinque Terre. It is interesting for its architecture: the cylindrical tower is one of Italy's oldest lighthouses, and the harbour square is flanked by colourful medieval houses, some with shady porticoes.

The ancient Roman village of **Corniglia**, perched on a high bluff, is the only one of the Cinque Terre without access from the sea. Pliny the Elder mentions its excellent wine in his *Natural History*, and excavations in Pompeii have turned up amphorae with the trademark 'Corenelia' stamped in the clay. That Corniglia's economy has always been tied to the land rather than the sea is suggested by the fact that its narrow, cobbled lanes and humble houses have more in common with the villages of the mountainous interior than with the towns along the coast. To reach the village from the station you have to climb a long brick staircase (377 stairs, forming 33 tree-shaded flights). The picturesque main street ends at a scenic overlook with breathtaking views on three sides.

Manarola enjoys a spectacular position on a rocky headland around the Torrente Volastra, which flows beneath the main street. The little Sciacchetrà museum (*open March–Nov daily 10.30–5.30*), halfway up the hill on the right, has interesting displays and a beautifully photographed video presentation of winemaking in the Cinque Terre. The steep little alleys are exceptionally picturesque, and there is a fine square at the top of the town offering fabulous views over the cascading rooftops to the sea.

Riomaggiore, the most easterly of the Cinque Terre, seems to tumble down the cliffside into the sea. Its layout is so precipitous that the fishermen have to pull their boats up into the streets in rough weather. The main street is squeezed tightly into the narrow valley of the (covered) Rio Major, and back lanes are so steep that most houses have two entrances—a front door at street level on the bottom floor, and a back door at street level on the top floor. The Italian landscape painter Telemaco Signorini, a member of the Macchiaioli School, often stayed in this village, and Riomaggiore figures in several of his paintings. As a gateway to the Cinque Terre National Park, however, it, like Monterosso at the other end, has lost much of its traditional character as a fishing and farming town.

VISITING THE RIVIERA DI LEVANTE

GETTING AROUND

• **By train:** Trains from Genoa on the Pisa line run to all the villages of the Cinque Terre (journey time c. 90mins), and trains on the La Spezia–Levanto line run frequently from village to village. Trains also run to and from Nervi.

• **By boat:** In fair weather (June–Sept) villages are connected by a boat service.

SPECIAL TICKETS

Visitors' centres at the Monterosso and Riomaggiore train stations sell the **Cinque Terre Card**, which gives access to the main hiking trails as well as discounts on maps, free entry to some museums, and free use of some trains and boats, depending on the type of card you buy. The price of the card goes towards maintenance of the paths. To walk from one village to the next takes 1–2hrs. Trail 2 touches upon all five villages. Going at a good pace, you can 'do' the Cinque Terre in about 5hrs, not counting village visits. See www.cinqueterre.com.

WHERE TO STAY ON THE RIVIERA DI LEVANTE

Cinque Terre

By far the best place to stay in the Cinque Terre is € **La Torretta** at Manarola, small and romantic at the top of the town with stunning views over sea, houses and vineyards. Closed Jan and Feb (*Piazza della Chiesa, Vico Volto 20, T: 0187 920327, www.torrettas.com*).

Nervi

€€ **Villa Pagoda**. Great comfort in an eccentric villa with gardens, just a short walk from the sea and with sea views. Built for a rich merchant in the early 19th century, this offers the best of suburban Genoa as it once was. *Via Capolungo 15, T: 010 372 6161, www.villapagoda.it.*

Levanto

Levanto is the last village before the Cinque Terre, on a train line which links all the villages. The €€ **Stella Maris** is a small hotel near the waterfront with eight charming rooms with painted ceilings and period furniture (*Via Marconi 4, T: 0187 808258, www.hotelstellamarislevanto.com; closed Nov*).

Portofino peninsula

The nice thing about staying in Portofino is that the crowds evaporate at dusk leaving you to enjoy a solitary evening stroll by the harbour, or up to the little church of San Giorgio. The small €€ **San Giorgio** ▮ hotel is a beautifully renovated town house by the water, with simple but elegant rooms (*Via del Fondaco 11, T: 0185 26991, www.portofinohsg.it*). The €€€ **Splendido & Splendido Mare**, also in Portofino, form one of the top luxury hotels in Europe. The Splendido is surrounded by gardens above the town, with magnificent views in all directions; the Splendido Mare, down by the harbour, offers a more informal atmosphere (*Salita Baratta 16, T: 0185 269551, www.hotelsplendido.com; closed Jan–March*).

The fishing village of Santa Margherita Ligure, between Portofino and Rapallo, became a seaside resort at the turn of the century and is still one of the most popular and pleasant resorts of the Riviera. The €€€ **Imperial Palace** seems left over from the Belle Epoque, with its old-fashioned elegance and park and pool by the sea (*Via Pagana 19, T: 0185 288991, www.hotelimperiale.com/ home.htm; closed Dec–Feb*).

WHERE TO EAT ON THE RIVIERA DI LEVANTE

Cinque Terre

The number of hikers in the Cinque Terre is sometimes beyond belief, and the impact of the throngs on the quality of services is noticeable. €€ **Gianni Franzi** in Vernazza is swimming against the current, and his restaurant is very popular. Be sure to book (*Piazza Marconi 5, T: 0187 812228, with rooms; closed Wed except in summer and Jan–March*).

Levanto

€€ **Tumelin**. A typical meal might consist of seafood risotto, fresh turbot and *crostata Tumelin*, a chocolate pie with lemon curd. Reliable, unpretentious *osteria* in business for over 30 years in this busy little resort just before the Cinque Terre. *Via Grillo 32, T: 0187 808379.*

TUSCANY

For many people Tuscany (*map p. 420*) is the quintessential Italy. Its landscape, climate and architecture inform our ideas of the entire peninsula; its painting is where our understanding of European art begins; its food and wine represent the *ne plus ultra* of culinary virtue. And these views are in great part justified. There are other Italies, of course: the prosperous, stylish Italy of Milan and the north; Venice and the formerly Byzantine east; Naples and the chaotic, still-exotic south. But it is to Tuscany that people return, both as visitors and in imagination, over and over again.

The cities of Tuscany as we know them today first sprang to prominence as medieval *comuni*, commonwealths established by an ambitious and outspoken middle class keen to bring about a transition from rule by birthright to rule by law. One by one, however, the popular governments were taken over by the heads of noble families, who carried on intermittent feuds: with each other, with the pope (who at that time wielded both spiritual and temporal power) and with the Holy Roman Emperor. Though the fledgling democracies did not survive, their legacy lived on in the sustained influence of the middle classes. Great riches were made through banking and the cloth industry, and this was used to fund the magnificent churches and altarpieces, the artfully designed town centres, the palaces, villas and gardens, for whose sake we chiefly visit Tuscany today.

The development of art was accompanied by a development of learning. Rediscovery of ancient texts, not only in Latin but also in Greek, led to an exaltation of the political ideals of democratic Athens and republican Rome. Late 14th-century Florence became a centre of the movement known as Humanism, which outlined a course of study based on Classical texts and including grammar, rhetoric, music, history, poetry and philosophy—the subjects we call the Humanities today. Contrary to what is sometimes assumed, Humanism was not a movement against Christianity. What the Humanist scholars did believe, however, was that man could interpret and come at an understanding of God's world through philosophy.

The Renaissance in art is traditionally taken to have begun in Florence, with Giotto, who was the first painter fully to abandon the Byzantine tradition for something more solid, earthy and 'natural'. Many of the newly wealthy families contributed financially and intellectually to the Renaissance through their patronage. One name in particular stands out: the Medici, who ruled first Florence and then all of Tuscany from the 15th–18th centuries, except for two brief republican interludes in 1494–1512 and 1527–1530. The period of their greatest brilliance coincides with Florentine art's most important century, the 15th. Cosimo il Vecchio and his grandson Lorenzo the Magnificent were particularly important patrons, and the artists they supported led a revolution not only in the visual arts, but in the way man conceived and interpreted the world around him.

View of Florence, with the Uffizi in the foreground, Palazzo Vecchio behind, and the duomo behind that, crowned by Brunelleschi's great dome.

Food and wine in Tuscany

Tuscany is one of Italy's richest agricultural regions, and offers some of the country's finest food and wine. Most of the best dishes are tied to rural traditions, offering a wonderful combination of simple ingredients and straightforward preparation. The Tuscan staple is bread. One finds it in *pappa al pomodoro*, a soup made with bread cooked with tomatoes, garlic, basil and pepper, and in *ribollita*, the soup of beans, black cabbage and bread that is prepared a day in advance and then reheated the next day—whence the name, 'reboiled'. The best Tuscan *antipasti* make use of bread, too: *bruschette, crostini toscani, fettunta* (toasted bread with tomatoes or chicken liver or simply oil and garlic) and *panzanella*, a salad of crumbled bread and fresh vegetables.

Distinctive main courses are the *bistecca alla fiorentina*, a T-bone steak grilled on hot coals and served medium rare; *stracotto*, a rich beef stew; and *fritto misto*, a medley of fried chicken, rabbit and vegetables.

The most aristocratic of Tuscan wines is Brunello di Montalcino. The so-called 'Supertuscans' include Sassicaia and Ornellaia, made on the Tyrrhenian coast at Bolgheri, and Tignanello, which is made in the Chianti region. The Chianti Classico district stretches between Florence and Siena, and is known for its easy-drinking reds (*see p. 207*). The most distinctive Tuscan white wine is the dry Vernaccia di San Gimignano, the favourite of Michelangelo. Vin Santo is the famed Tuscan dessert wine.

FLORENCE

Situated on the banks of the River Arno and set among low hills covered with olive groves and vineyards, Florence (*map p. 420, B1*) is the repository of some of the most important works of art and architecture in the world. Naturally enough, this makes it somewhat overwhelming, and the city is as busy and hectic today as it must have been in the Middle Ages, with the addition now of sprawling suburbs, streets filled with choking traffic, expensive hotels and restaurants, and millions of visitors all heading in the same direction as yourself. Do not be daunted. It is eminently possible to enjoy Florence, for it remains at heart a small town, and away from the very obvious tourist sites it is still surprisingly peaceful.

Florence in history

Florence was not an important settlement to the Etruscans; their city was at Fiesole, in the hills to the north. Roman *Florentia* was founded in 59 BC by Julius Caesar. Even then it remained a colony of relative unimportance. It was only in the Middle Ages that Florence came into its own, as a centre of the woollen cloth industry, of banking and of finance. The government of Florence supported the Guelph party, the papal faction in medieval politics, whose members tended to be drawn from the merchant classes. After an important victory over Ghibelline Arezzo in 1289, Florence soon took command of the Guelph coalition in Tuscany and intensified its policy of expansion, which led in 1406 to the conquest of Pisa, by which Florence gained an outlet to the sea.

The 15th century was Florence's apogee. It was then that the Medici rose to power, bringing stability to the faction-riven city and steering it on a course towards commercial, artistic and political pre-eminence. Their rule lasted for almost the whole century, with an important hiatus between 1494 and 1512, when they were chased from power and Florence governed itself as a republic. Medici rule resumed in the 16th century, but this was a time of increasing turmoil in Italy, with French and Spanish troops fighting for territory in the peninsula, and the Medici were unable to restore stability to the city—far from it, in fact: these years were filled with feuding and assassinations. Eventually, in 1570, having annexed the republic of Siena 15 years previously, a minor member of the family rose to supreme power as Cosimo I, Grand Duke of Tuscany. Medici rule now became explicitly monarchical, and important dynastic marriages were contracted with the ruling houses of France and Spain.

The last of the Medici died childless in 1737 and the Grand Duchy passed to the house of Lorraine, which at that time was a holding of the Austrian Habsburgs and Holy Roman Emperors. The representative of the new house who most benefited Tuscany was Peter Leopold (1765–90), who pushed through important economic, civil and cultural reforms. The last grand duke, Leopold II, was forced to abdicate after a bloodless revolution in 1859, when Tuscany joined the new Kingdom of Italy. The capital of that kingdom was transferred to Florence from Turin in 1865. (In 1871, after Rome's fall to the Italian national army, the capital was moved to Rome.)

MAJOR SIGHTS OF FLORENCE

Palazzo Vecchio

To understand Florence and its art, it is necessary to understand the fundamental difference between the form of government under the early Medici and that of Cosimo I and the subsequent grand dukes. The finest place to get a sense of these two periods is Palazzo della Signoria, where the medieval ruling councils had their chambers. Now known as **Palazzo Vecchio** (*map p. 177, 11; open 9–7, Thur 9–2*), it is still the town hall, and its architectural form became the model for town halls all over Tuscany. Its history illustrates the trajectory of Florence from self-governing *comune* to capital of a duchy. The palace was built in 1299–1302 and was used by the governing magistrates, who still controlled the city's affairs in the days of the first Medici. Although Cosimo il Vecchio rose to be *de facto* leader of Florence, he was careful to respect its republican ideals. It is said that his father, Giovanni di Bicci, the founder of the family fortunes, had advised his son never to enter the palace of the magistrates unless summoned there. When the Medici were temporarily ousted in 1494, a statue of *Judith and Holofernes* by Donatello, which had been in the courtyard of the Medici family palace, was set up outside Palazzo della Signoria, as it was called, with an admonitory inscription warning of the fate that befalls a tyrant (a copy of the statue stands there now; the original is inside). Michelangelo's *David* was also commissioned for the position its copy occupies today, and its message was the very same: right will outwit might. The fiery-tongued friar Savonarola, who had already been openly critical of the Medici and disapproved of their

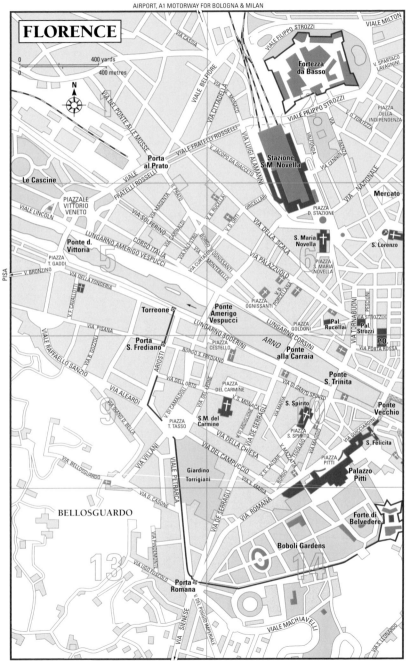

AIRPORT, A1 MOTORWAY FOR BOLOGNA & MILAN

FLORENCE

0 ____ 400 yards
0 ____ 400 metres

N

VIALE MILTON

VIALE FILIPPO STROZZI

VIA CASSIA

VIALE BELFIORE

VIA CITTADELLA

VIA MONACO

Fortezza da Basso

V. SPARTACO LAVAGNINI

PIAZZA DELLA INDIPENDENZA

VIALE FILIPPO STROZZI

L.O. FORTEZZA

VIA DEL PONTE ALLE MOSSE

VIALE FRATELLI ROSSELLI

VIA LUIGI ALAMANNI

V. JACOPO DA DIACCETO

Porta al Prato

VALFONDA

Stazione S.M. Novella

VIA GENNAIO

VIA FAENZA

Le Cascine

VIALE FRATELLI ROSSELLI

VIA IL PRATO

VIA NAZIONALE

Mercato

PIAZZALE VITTORIO VENETO

VIALE LINCOLN

VIA DELLA SCALA

ORICELLARI

PIAZZA D. STAZIONE

S. Maria Novella

S. Lorenzo

VIA SOLFERINO

VIA GARIBALDI

VIA B. RUCELLAI

VIA ORTI

VIA MAGENTA

Ponte d. Vittoria

CORSO ITALIA

LUNGARNO AMERIGO VESPUCCI

VIA PALESTRO

BORGO OGNISSANTI

VIA PALAZZUOLO

PIAZZA S. MARIA NOVELLA

PISA

PIAZZA T. GADDI

V. BRONZINO

VIA DELLA FONDERIA

VIA CURTATONE MONTEBELLO

V.D. PORCELLANA

PIAZZA OGNISSANTI

VIA TORNABUONI

PESCIONI

VIALE STROZZI

Torreone

VIA PISANA

LUNGARNO SODERINI

Ponte Amerigo Vespucci

LUNGARNO CORSINI

PIAZZA GOLDONI

Pal. Rucellai

Pal. Strozzi

Porta S. Frediano

V.E. CAVALLOTTI

VIA B. BUOZZI

ARIOSTO

PIAZZA CESTELLO

BORGO S. FREDIANO

ARNO

Ponte alla Carraia

VIA PORTA ROSSA

P.O.

VIALE RAFFAELLO SANZIO

VIA DELL'ORTO

VIA DEL LEONE

VIA DI CAMALDOLI

PIAZZA DEL CARMINE

V.S. MONACA

VIA DI SANTO SPIRITO

Ponte S. Trinita

VIA ALEARDI

VIA ORLANDO Z. BELLA

PIAZZA T. TASSO

S.M. del Carmine

VIA DE' SERRAGLI

V.D. CAMPORA

S. Spirito

PIAZZA S. SPIRITO

VIA MAGGIO

Ponte Vecchio

VIA GUICCIARDINI

S. Felicita

VIA BELLOSGUARDO

VIA VILLANI

VIA DELLA CHIESA

VIA DEL CAMPUCCIO

V.D. CALDAIE

VIA MAZZETTA

PIAZZA PITTI

Palazzo Pitti

VIA DELLA FONDERIA

Giardino Torrigiani

VIA S. MARIA

BORGO TEGOLAIO

BELLOSGUARDO

VIA D. CASONE

VIA PETRARCA

VIA DE' SERRAGLI

VIA ROMANA

Forte di Belvedere

VIA PINDEMONTE

Boboli Gardens

VIA UGO FOSCOLO

Porta Romana

VIA SIENESE

VIA DEL POGGIO IMPERIALE

VIALE MACHIAVELLI

V.A S. LEONARDO

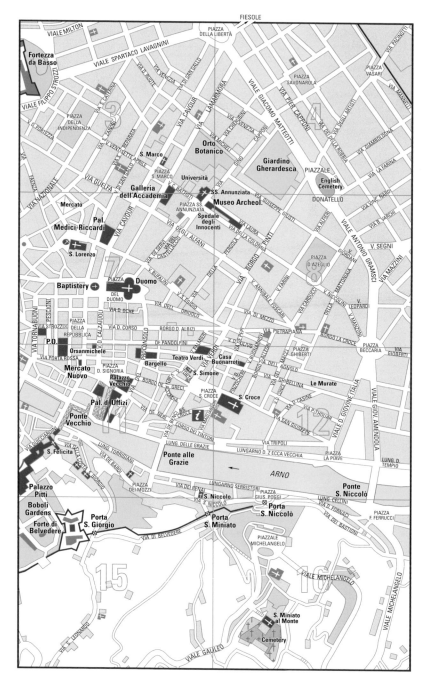

Palazzo Vecchio was redecorated by Vasari for Cosimo I. The decorative scheme includes allegories of Florentine victories and Medici virtues. Historical scenes featuring and glorifying the Medici family are also numerous. This (c. 1560), by Vasari, is one of the finest (notice the interplay of the hands): it shows Pope Clement VII (Giulio de' Medici) in conversation with the Holy Roman Emperor Charles V. Charles' armies had sacked Rome in 1527 during Clement's pontificate, but the two leaders reached an agreement and Pope Clement symbolically crowned Charles emperor in Bologna in 1530.

Humanist leanings, now seized his chance to proclaim a popular republic that would also be a city of God. His puritanical streak was his downfall: in 1498 his political party was accused of treason to the state, he was attainted for heresy and burnt at the stake. A disc in the pavement, beside Ammannati's colossal Neptune fountain, marks the spot.

In 1540, after the Medici's definitive return to power, Cosimo I did something none of his predecessors had ever done or dared to do: he took up residence in Palazzo della Signoria, which accordingly became known as Palazzo Ducale. In the interior today it is still possible to trace vestiges of the old republican seat of government overlaid with the trappings of princely rule. The Salone dei Cinquecento on the first floor, for example, is an immense hall built in 1495 to house the Great Council of the republic. Leonardo da Vinci and Michelangelo were commissioned to decorate the walls with murals representing Florentine victories over Milan and Pisa respectively. No trace of these remains. The decorative scheme you now see is that carried out by Vasari in 1563–65 to celebrate the triumph not of a city, but of one man, Cosimo I. The tiny, exquisite Studiolo was also created by Vasari as a study for Cosimo's son

Francesco I. On the second floor are the apartments of Cosimo's wife, Eleanor of Toledo, decorated for her by Vasari and Bronzino. Relics from republican days include the Sala dei Gigli, with a fresco by Ghirlandaio in celebration of the Florentine republic (the two lions hold the banners of the *popolo* and of the *comune*), and the study that was used by Machiavelli between 1511 and 1512, when he was secretary of the republic. He was removed from office with the restoration of the Medici in 1512.

The **Loggia della Signoria** outside the palace was built in the late 14th century for the use of government officials during public ceremonies. When Cosimo I came to power, he stationed his personal bodyguard here. Since the 18th century it has been used to display public sculpture. The two most famous pieces are Benvenuto Cellini's *Perseus*, commissioned by Cosimo I in 1545; and Giambologna's *Rape of the Sabine*, made for Cosimo's son Francesco I in 1583.

Palazzo Pitti

In 1549 Eleanor of Toledo, daughter of the Spanish viceroy of Naples and wife of Cosimo I, purchased a large palace on the south bank of the Arno. While Cosimo il Vecchio is said to have rejected the earliest plans for his new family palace (now the Palazzo Medici-Riccardi; *see p. 184*) because they were too ostentatious and self-aggrandising, Eleanor had, in modern parlance, 'no problem' with ostentation or self-aggrandisement. She was elegant and ceremonious by nature, had been brought up at the elegant and ceremonious court of Naples, and was fully sensible of her role as 'first lady' of Tuscany. When she and her family took possession of Palazzo Pitti, which they initially used for official guests, state functions and entertainments, the quaint old medieval fortress-palace on Piazza della Signoria was renamed Palazzo Vecchio. A new era in Florentine history had begun.

Palazzo Pitti (*map p. 176, 10; either buy a combined ticket for one of two groups of museums, or a ticket which covers the entire palace collections and its gardens*) was connected to Palazzo Vecchio by a raised walkway almost a kilometre long, known as the Corridoio Vasariano after Vasari, the architect who built it. One cannot use it to approach Palazzo Pitti today—but perhaps that is just as well. For by the way one does approach it, across the cramped Ponte Vecchio and up narrow Via Guicciardini, one is forced to confront its sheer size and extraordinary lack of discretion. Its present dimensions are the result of centuries of rebuilding and extension. Most important of these was the rebuilding carried out by Bartolomeo Ammannati, who created the Mannerist inner courtyard for Cosimo I in 1558–70. Chief of the museums is the **Galleria Palatina** (*open Tues–Sun 8.15–6.50; ticket also valid for the royal apartments; see below*), a gallery of magnificent paintings acquired or inherited as dowry by the Tuscan grand dukes. Many of the rooms have splendid allegorical ceiling frescoes by the Baroque artist Pietro da Cortona, painted in the 1640s for Ferdinando II and his wife Vittoria della Rovere of Urbino. Works in the collection include important masterpieces by Raphael and Titian.

Other museums in Palazzo Pitti are the **Appartamenti Reali**, the apartments of the rulers of Tuscany; the **Gallery of Modern Art** (*closed Jan; combined ticket with the Costume Gallery*), with Neoclassical and 19th-century works, notably by the

Macchiaioli School, a group of *plein-air* painters also known as the 'Tuscan Impressionists'; the **Costume Gallery**, which has gowns from Eleanor of Toledo's time up to the present; the **Galleria degli Argenti**, with *objets d'art* and jewellery from the Medici collections; and the **Boboli Gardens** (*open Nov–Feb 8.15–4.30, March until 5.30, April–May and Sept–Oct until 6.30, slightly later in June–Aug*), laid out for Cosimo I and his successors. They are a good example of a Renaissance formal garden.

The Uffizi

Palazzo degli Uffizi (*map p. 177, 11; open Tues–Sat 8.15–6.35, sometimes later in summer*) was commissioned from Vasari by Cosimo I to serve as government offices. Seeing the size of the building, one quails to imagine what kind of bureaucracy the grand duke had conjured up. Today, however, the place seems small: it can comfortably accommodate neither the wealth of artworks entrusted to it, nor the many visitors who come to marvel at them. The display is arranged chronologically by schools; the first rooms (up to Room 15) include the major works of the Florentine Renaissance.

Automatic signals provide information about the expected waiting time to get in (a maximum of 660 people are admitted at once). To avoid waiting in line, the booking service (see p. 195) is highly recommended. The gallery tends to be less crowded in the early morning, over lunchtime, and in the late afternoon.

13th century: Three important works give context to this collection. All take the same theme: the Madonna Enthroned (*Maestà*), and all treat the theme slightly differently. The earliest example is by a Florentine, Cimabue (c. 1285), and it is still noticeably Byzantine in spirit. The second, the *Rucellai Madonna* (also 1285), is by Duccio, the greatest artist of medieval Siena. Here, even though the work is not naturalistic—the angels float in mid-air like heavenly helium balloons—there is more attention paid to making human forms obey the laws of nature. In Cimabue's painting the Christ Child is not sitting securely on his mother's knee; the position of her legs could not support his weight. In Duccio's work, however, he is clearly seated on her left knee, her hand firmly clasps his middle, and his crooked leg is balanced on something solid under her drapery. The third

work, by Giotto, was painted a quarter of a century later, and conveys noticeably more sense of natural volume.

International Gothic: One of the most famous examples of this elegant, courtly style is Gentile da Fabriano's *Adoration of the Magi*. There are also some splendid works by Lorenzo Monaco, who is perhaps the least 'Florentine' of the early painters. His use of colour and the world of his imagination have more in common with the art of Siena.

15th century: Two of the most famous paintings in the world hang in this section: Botticelli's *Birth of Venus* and *Primavera*. It is said that Botticelli was prompted to burn many of his secular works by the fire-and-brimstone sermons of Savonarola. He could not burn these, for they were in the possession of the Medici. What was new and exciting about them was not so much their tech-

Botticelli: *Birth of Venus* (1485). This work says much about the Florence of the 1480s. It was at this time that the writings of Greek and Roman authors were being rediscovered and enthusiastically imitated, and this work may be based on an ode by the ancient Greek poet Hesiod, which had been rendered in Tuscan by the Humanist scholar Politian. Venus, the pagan goddess, posed like a Cnidian Aphrodite (*see p. 244*) is shown being blown ashore by two winds. She comes to earth to bring springtime and fertility. The nymph Hora flits forward to clothe her with the mantle of the seasons.

nical skill (though that is considerable) but the way in which a subject from Classical mythology is given the kind of treatment previously reserved for a Virgin and saints.

The Tribuna: This opulent octagonal chamber, dating from 1584, was used by Francesco I to display his most precious works. The centrepiece is the *Medici Venus*, of the Cnidian type (*see p. 244*), thought to be a 1st-century BC copy of the famous original by Praxiteles. It was much admired in the 18th century. Images of nudity are so familiar today that it is less easy to understand the spell she once cast: the historian Edward Gibbon used her to illustrate his belief

that sculpture is a superior art to painting. **Sixteenth century:** Masterpieces by Raphael include *Leo X with Giulio de' Medici and Luigi de' Rossi*, showing the first Medici pope (son of Lorenzo the Magnificent) with his two cousins, whom he created cardinals. One of them, Giulio (on the left), later became Pope Clement VII. Raphael's self-portrait also hangs here: Michelangelo jealously attributed Raphael's fame and success to his good looks (Raphael renders Michelangelo's saturnine features and broken nose as Heraclitus in his *School of Athens* (*see p. 274*). The *Venus of Urbino*, commissioned by Guidubaldo della Rovere in 1538, is a famous female nude by Titian.

Medieval Florence

There has been a market on the site of the **Mercato Nuovo** (*map p. 177, 11*) since the 11th century. Florentines call it 'Il Porcellino' ('the piglet') after a statue of a wild boar, a copy (1612) of an antique original in the Uffizi. Further north of here is the tall, traceried **Orsanmichele** (*map p. 177, 11*), built as a market and later turned into a church. The famous statues on the exterior were commissioned by the city guilds from the best artists of the age. They have all now been replaced by copies. The finest are Ghiberti's *John the Baptist*, patron saint of Florence, made for the guild of wholesale cloth importers, the wealthy Calimala (the drapery is a *tour de force*); Donatello's *St George*, the clean-shaven young soldier, made for the guild of armourers (marble original in the Bargello); and Verrocchio's *Christ and St Thomas*, where the Risen Christ allows the doubting disciple to touch the wound in his side. It was made for the merchants' tribunal.

The **Museo del Bargello** (*map p. 177, 11; open 8.30–1.50; closed first, third and fifth Sun and second and fourth Mon of month*), housed in a former seat of the popular government, gives an essential introduction to Florentine Renaissance sculpture, with works by Donatello, Verrocchio, Michelangelo, Cellini, Giambologna and the della Robbia. Here also we see how heavily—perhaps heavy-handedly—allegory was used to make the points required of it by the propagandists of the Florentine state, be they republican or grand ducal. Michelangelo's bust of Brutus stands for resistance to tyranny, in the shape of the champion of the Roman Republic who rose up against the demagogue Caesar. From the early days of the grand dukes we have Cosimo I in the guise of the emperor Augustus. Here also is Giambologna's *Virtue Repressing Vice* (alias Florence conquering Pisa) and Vincenzo Danti's *Honour Overcoming Deceit*. Again and again across the Medici world one encounters such treatments: Cosimo I is made to stand for bountiful Neptune or victorious Perseus. His unhappy, congenitally deformed Habsburg

Famed as the first free-standing nude since Antiquity, Donatello's *David* has also excited controversy: for its androgyny and as to whether it in fact represents David or Mercury.

daughter-in-law appears, preposterously, as Abundance in the Boboli Gardens. The Bargello contains two renderings of *David*, one by Donatello and the other by Verrocchio. Donatello's famous bronze of the boy victor standing on the Head of Goliath (c. 1440) is technically brilliant, but contains no noble emotion. Donatello went much further in his appeal to the human spirit in his *Mary Magdalen* or *Habakkuk* in the Museo dell'Opera del Duomo (*see overleaf*). It was a lesson he perhaps learned from Brunelleschi, who roundly abused his Crucifix in Santa Croce for possessing no finer feeling for its subject. That Crucifix and the one that Brunelleschi produced to show Donatello how such a subject should be tackled can still be seen *in situ* today (*see pp. 188 and 190–91*).

The duomo and campanile

The duomo of Florence (*map p. 177, 7; open 10–5, Sun and holidays 1.30–5*) was begun in the late 13th century on the site of a much older church. In 1331 Giotto was put in charge of construction. The dome (1420–36), the greatest of all Brunelleschi's works, is an extraordinary feat of engineering. The main west façade dates from the 19th century.

The wide, spacious **interior** contains, in the south aisle, a bust of Brunelleschi (1446), who is buried here. The bust of Giotto (1490), similar to Brunelleschi's, is by Benedetto da Maiano and has an inscription by the Humanist scholar Politian. Two famous frescoes in the north aisle commemorate the *condottieri* Sir John Hawkwood (by Paolo Uccello; 1436) and Niccolò da Tolentino (by Andrea del Castagno; 1456). They are painted to resemble equestrian statues such as those erected to commemorate Gattamelata (*see p. 106*) and Colleoni (*see p. 91*). The fresco in the dome, by Vasari and Federico Zuccari, shows the *Last Judgement* (1572–79).

The **dome** can be climbed (*open 8.30–6.20, first Sat of the month 8.30–3, other Sats 8.30–5; closed Sun and holidays*) up the very steps and spiral stairways used by the builders themselves. The views are superb, both of the duomo interior and of the city.

The cathedral **bell-tower** (*open 8.30–7.30*), begun by Giotto in 1334, is clad in coloured marbles that match the duomo's own exterior. The lower storeys have bas-reliefs illustrating the Creation of Man and the Arts and Industries. Above are niches with statues of prophets and sibyls (1415–36) by Donatello and his contemporaries. All are copies of originals moved to the Museo dell'Opera del Duomo (*see overleaf*).

The baptistery

The ancient baptistery (*open 12–6.30, Sun and holidays 8.30–1.30*) is, like so many early baptisteries, octagonal in design because the number eight was taken as the sign of infinity and hence of resurrection and the life everlasting. Its gilded bronze doors are one of the most famous sights of Florence. The north door (1403–24) was carried out by Lorenzo Ghiberti, after he won an open competition for their design. Two trial reliefs for that competition, one by Brunelleschi and the other, the winning entry by Ghiberti, are preserved in the Bargello. The reliefs depict scenes from the life of Christ and include Ghiberti's own portrait head (fifth from the top of the left door, in the central band). The east door (1425–52), also by Ghiberti, is the door that Michelangelo is said to have dubbed the 'Gate of Heaven'. The ten panels in low relief (replaced by copies; originals in the Museo dell'Opera del Duomo) have scenes receding into the background in a way that demonstrates a superb grasp of perspective. The subjects (left to right from the top) are: 1. The Creation and Fall; 2. Cain and Abel; 3. Noah's Sacrifice and Drunkenness; 4. Abraham and Isaac; 5. Jacob and Esau; 6. Joseph Sold and Recognised by his Brothers; 7. Moses Receiving the Tablets of the Law; 8. Joshua and the Fall of Jericho; 9. David and the Battle with the Philistines; 10. Solomon and the Queen of Sheba.

In the interior, the vault is covered with shimmering gold mosaics of the *Last Judgement* (13th–early 14th centuries), organised in bands, with a large *Risen Christ* in a roundel, shown displaying His wounds. It is clear that Vasari and Zuccari took inspiration from here for their own vault decoration of the duomo. The tomb of the antipope John XXIII (d. 1419) is by Donatello and Michelozzo.

Museo dell'Opera del Duomo

The museum, at no. 9 Piazza del Duomo (*open 9.30–6.50, Sun and holidays 9–1*), contains original sculpture from the baptistery, duomo and campanile. Highlights include Ghiberti's baptistery door panels and Michelangelo's beautiful *Pietà* (according to Vasari, the head of Nicodemus is a self-portrait). On the first floor are statues from the campanile, the most important being those by Donatello: *Jeremiah*, *Habakkuk*, *Abraham and Isaac* (a two-figure group). Donatello was proud of the bald Habakkuk and, so Vasari tells us, would from time to time enjoin it to speak. Donatello's famous wooden statue of *Mary Magdalen* (c. 1454), strikingly depicted not as a voluptuous wanton but as a dishevelled penitent with whom age has caught up, stood formerly in the baptistery.

Palazzo Medici-Riccardi

This fine town palace (*map p. 177, 7; chapel and gallery open 9–7 except Wed*) was built for Cosimo il Vecchio by his favourite architect, Michelozzo, after 1444. It remained the Medici family residence until 1540, when Cosimo I moved into Palazzo Vecchio. It is now the seat of the prefecture. The walls of the famous Chapel of the Magi are frescoed with Benozzo Gozzoli's *Procession of the Magi to Bethlehem*, begun in 1459. The scheme is busy and decorative: the main cavalcade winds its way through a rocky landscape, where a deer hunt acts as a sub-plot. The overall effect is reminiscent of Flemish tapestries, a typical feature of Benozzo's work. Some of the figures are clearly portraits, though their identities are uncertain. The man looking out of the fresco towards the back is certainly a self-portrait of Benozzo (his signature appears on the red hat). The man in a red cap behind the black archer is thought to be Cosimo il Vecchio.

The church of San Lorenzo

The harmonious Renaissance interior of San Lorenzo (*map p. 177, 7; open Mon–Sat 10–5.30, Sun and holidays from 1.30 except in Nov–Feb*) is the work of Brunelleschi, who received a commission from the Medici in 1425 to remodel this, the burial place of all the principal members of the family. Immediately below the dome lies the grave of Cosimo il Vecchio. The Old Sacristy, left of the nave, is also by Brunelleschi (1428), and is an important first example of the central plan in Florence (*see p. 191*). It is the burial

Michelangelo's tomb of Giuliano, Duke of Nemours. This is pure Mannerism. The anatomy makes no sense (if the male figure attempted to stand up he would fall over; his feet are too small) and neither does the architecture. The side niches serve no purpose, and the twinned pilasters support no weight.

place of Giovanni di Bicci de' Medici (d. 1429), founder of the dynasty and father of Cosimo il Vecchio. His sarcophagus is by Brunelleschi's adopted son Buggiano. The decorative details are mainly by Donatello (who is also buried in the church).

The **Laurentian Library** (*open 9–1 except Sun and holidays*) was begun by Michelangelo c. 1524 to house the Medici collection of manuscripts. In the vestibule all the elements combine to provide a vertical emphasis and the columns retreat into the wall, producing eerie shadow effects. The space is filled with a large free-standing staircase, a strange and idiosyncratic work.

The **Cappella dei Principi** (*entrance in Piazza Madonna degli Aldobrandini; open 8.15–1.50; closed second and fourth Sun and first, third and fifth Mon*) is the mausoleum of the Medici grand dukes. It is decorated in *pietre dure*, the technique of stone inlay that was developed in Florence in the late 16th century. In the sarcophagi around the walls are buried Cosimo I, his sons Francesco I and Ferdinando I, as well as later grand dukes.

The **New Sacristy** contains some celebrated works by Michelangelo, left unfinished when he went to Rome in 1534. They were commissioned by the Medici pope Clement VII. His aim was to restore lustre to the Medici name at a difficult point in the family fortunes. He himself had just presided over the humiliating Sack of Rome by the troops of the emperor Charles V in 1527, and his family risked another period of exile as a dissatisfied Florence once again looked to republican models. Michelangelo had supported the republican faction against Pope Clement, and it was to secure immunity from arrest that he accepted this commission. The two main tombs here are the resting places of men who ruled in the unstable time between the end of the republic in 1512 and the rise to power of Cosimo I in 1530. To the left of the entrance is the tomb of Lorenzo,

Enamelled terracotta by Andrea della Robbia (1487) on the façade of the Spedale degli Innocenti. The della Robbia workshop, founded by Andrea's uncle Luca in the 1440s, was famous for such works, made durable by a special lead glaze. The secret of how to make this glaze was subsequently lost, though della Robbian imitations were popular in the 19th century.

Duke of Urbino (1492–1519), grandson of Lorenzo the Magnificent, who conquered Urbino in 1516–17. On the sarcophagus below are *Dawn* (female) and *Dusk* (male). Opposite is the tomb of the third son of Lorenzo the Magnificent, Giuliano, Duke of Nemours (1479–1516; *illustrated above*). On his sarcophagus are *Night* (female) and *Day* (male; seemingly influenced by the *Belvedere Torso* in the Vatican; *see p. 272*).

San Marco

'If a girl's mind is filled with dreams of angels and saints, and she pauses before an Angelico because she thinks it must surely be like heaven, that is the right way for her to begin the study of religious art.' So wrote John Ruskin in his *Elements of Drawing* (1858). By far the best place to pause before the works of Fra' Angelico is the Dominican friary of San Marco (*map p. 177, 3; open 8.15–1.50, Sat–Sun 8.15–7; closed first, third and fifth Sun and second and fourth Mon of the month*), one of the loveliest and most peaceful museums in Florence. The apparently naïve works of this humble friar still speak to us today with an extraordinary moving eloquence, particularly those in the upstairs dormitory, where the famous *Annunciation* greets you at the top of the stairs. Numerous small cells open off the dormitory corridors, each with a beautiful fresco by Fra' Angelico and his assistants. Each fresco is different and each one repays at least a few moments' attention. It is impossible not to imagine the friars who occupied these cells, each contemplating day after day the image allotted to him. Three rooms in the corridor furthest from the entrance were occupied by Savonarola (*see p. 175*), who was prior here. His arrest took place outside the library (built by Michelozzo) in 1498. Two cells to the far right of the entrance corridor were used by Cosimo il Vecchio when he came here on spiritual retreat.

Galleria dell'Accademia

Map p. 177, 3–7. Open Tues–Sun 8.15–6.50, usually later on summer weekends. Queues can be long, and it is best to book a visit (see p. 195). The least crowded time is late afternoon. Most visitors to the Accademia come to see Michelangelo's *David*, the work which established his reputation, and which was commissioned by the city of Florence to stand outside Palazzo Vecchio. Like Donatello's David, this representation shows the hero nude, not, as was usual, at the moment of victory, but bracing himself before battle, nervously fingering his catapult. The gallery also has Michelangelo's four *Slaves* (1521–23 or c. 1530), intended for the tomb of Pope Julius II in Rome (*see p. 257*), but which were never finished. In fact, in two cases they seem barely begun, and are excellent examples of Michelangelo's famous *non-finito*, evoking his idea that the sculpture already exists within the stone, and it is the sculptor's job merely to help it to the surface.

Piazza Santissima Annunziata

Piazza Santissima Annunziata (*map p. 177, 7*) is the finest square in Florence, and the graceful **Spedale degli Innocenti** (foundling hospital) on the eastern side is one of the city's great works of architecture. It was designed in 1421 by Brunelleschi, who uses Corinthian columns to support wide round arches with a classical entablature above. The Gothic has been completely abandoned. In the spandrels of the colonnade are charming enamelled terracotta medallions of babies in swaddling clothes by Andrea della Robbia (*illustrated opposite*). In the centre of the square is an equestrian statue of Grand Duke Ferdinando I, by Giambologna (*see caption on p. 136*).

Santa Maria Novella

The Dominican church of **Santa Maria Novella** (*map p. 176, 6; open 9–5; Fri, Sun and holidays 1–5*) is famed for its magnificent façade. The lower part, dating from the 14th century, has a geometric design in green and white marble reminiscent of the baptistery. The upper part is superficially similar, but on closer inspection reveals a different underlying aesthetic. Completed c. 1470, it is the work of the great Renaissance theorist and architect Leon Battista Alberti. It takes the form of a temple front and is flanked by beautiful volutes, placed there to create a fluid transition between the narrow top and wide bottom.

The interior has Gothic vaulting, though many of the other Gothic features were removed by Vasari, who inveighed against the 'German'

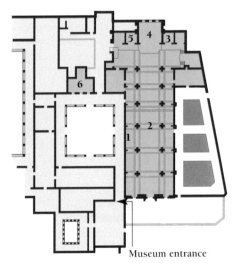

SANTA MARIA NOVELLA

1 Masaccio's *Trinity*
2 Crucifix by Giotto
3 Strozzi Chapel (frescoes by Filippino Lippi)
4 Sanctuary (frescoes by Ghirlandaio)
5 Gondi Chapel (Crucifix by Brunelleschi)
6 Spanish Chapel

style in his *Lives*. 'Such deformity compared with the beauty of our monuments,' he mutters, by which he meant the beauty of the works of ancient Rome and of the Florentine Renaissance. An example of the latter is Masaccio's **Trinity (1)**, painted in 1427 and one of the earliest works successfully to depict three dimensions on a flat surface using the system of linear perspective developed by Brunelleschi. The much older painted **Crucifix (2)** hanging above the nave is by Giotto (1290).

The **Chapel of Filippo Strozzi (3)**, the banker who built Palazzo Strozzi (*see below*), has frescoes by Filippino Lippi (1487–1502). Their design marks a departure from other Florentine fresco cycles of this period, being full of allusions to Antiquity. It is certain that Lippi was inspired by his experiences in Rome, where he had gone to work on Santa Maria sopra Minerva at the same time as he was working on this chapel. The Domus Aurea of Nero, with its painted grotesques, was discovered at precisely this time, and many Renaissance artists who went to see it left their signatures scratched in the wall: Filippino Lippi's is one of them. These classicising frescoes are an early example of a trend that soon spread across Italy.

The frescoes in the **sanctuary (4)** of scenes from the lives of the Virgin and John the Baptist are the masterpiece of Domenico Ghirlandaio (1486–90). Once again we can detect a Roman influence. Ghirlandaio was recently back from working on the Sistine Chapel walls. In these frescoes he uses Classically-inspired architectural settings, though the interiors are Florentine, and many of the figures are portraits of the Tornabuoni family (related by marriage to the Medici), for whom the frescoes were painted.

The Crucifix in the **Gondi Chapel (5)** was made by Brunelleschi, it is said after criticising a Crucifix by Donatello (now in Santa Croce; *see p. 191*), in order to show his friend how the crucified Christ should be portrayed.

The **Spanish Chapel** (*open 9–5, Sun and holidays 9–5; closed Fri*) **(6)**, so named because it was used by members of Eleanor of Toledo's retinue, is covered with splendid frescoes by the little-known Andrea di Bonaiuto (c. 1365). The subject of the frescoes is the Mission and Triumph of the Dominicans. Particularly striking are the black and white dogs, a symbol used by the Order because of the play on the name in Latin (*domini canes*; dogs of the Lord). The colours of the dogs reflect the colour of the Dominican habit. They are shown chasing away heretics and herding the faithful flock.

Palazzo Strozzi and Palazzo Rucellai

Via Tornabuoni is Florence's most elegant shopping street. Few of the original shops survive today, but **Procacci** at no. 64 is still going strong, and you can still pop in for a glass of *prosecco* and a tiny truffle sandwich. The huge **Palazzo Strozzi** (*map p. 176, 6*), built for the banker Filippo Strozzi, is a typical 15th-century town mansion—half-fortress, half-palace—austerely constructed with large, rusticated blocks. The nearby **Palazzo Rucellai** (Via della Vigna Nuova) was the town house of Giovanni Rucellai (1403–81), a wealthy cloth merchant and patron of Leon Battista Alberti. Rucellai commissioned Alberti to redesign the façade of Santa Maria Novella (*see above*), and it is now agreed that this palace was also built to a plan of Alberti's, by Bernardo Rossellino (c. 1446–51), who went on to use the design for his masterpiece in Pienza, Palazzo Piccolomini (*see p. 225*).

The church of Santa Croce

Santa Croce (*map p. 177, 12; open 9.30–5.30, Sun 1–5.30*) is the Franciscan church of Florence, consecrated in 1442. The marble façade dates from the 19th century, an age when the Gothic was once more in vogue (many of the original Gothic features of the interior were purged by Vasari's remodelling of 1560). The church is the burial place of Michelangelo, Machiavelli and Galileo, but it is famous above all for its works by Giotto and his school.

Of the works by Giotto himself, those in the **Peruzzi Chapel (1)**, showing scenes from the lives of St John the Baptist (left) and St John the Evangelist (right), are badly damaged, but nevertheless enough survives for us to recognise some Giottesque hallmarks: the early understanding of perspective in his treatment of three-dimensional buildings; the typical gabled canopies supported on long slender columns at the four corners; and the human figures, carefully posed to tell a story, as in a *tableau vivant*. Those in the **Bardi Chapel (2)**, of scenes from the life of St Francis, may have been partly carried out by his pupils.

SANTA CROCE

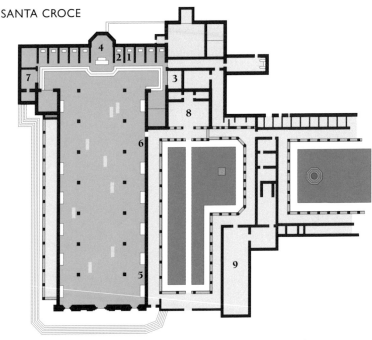

1	Peruzzi Chapel	6	Cavalcanti Tabernacle
2	Bardi Chapel	7	Donatello's Crucifix
3	Baroncelli Chapel	8	Pazzi Chapel
4	Sanctuary (True Cross frescoes)	9	Refectory
5	Tomb of Michelangelo		

Scene from Agnolo Gaddi's True Cross cycle (1388–93). Chosroes, King of Persia, is shown adored by his people. The Byzantine emperor Heraclius is in his tent dreaming, guarded by attendants. Above him appears a Cross, and an angel descending, arm outstretched. The angel and the conical tent (*praetorium*) echo Piero della Francesca's famous True Cross cycle in Arezzo (see p. 231), where he uses the same motifs not for the dream of Heraclius but for his *Dream of Constantine*. Over 70 years separate the two works, but it is surely impossible that Piero had not seen these Florentine frescoes.

In the **Baroncelli Chapel (3)** are frescoes of the life of the Virgin (1332–38) by Giotto's pupil Taddeo Gaddi. His son Agnolo painted the frescoes in the **sanctuary (4)** in 1388–93. Part of the scheme shows the Legend of the True Cross (*see pp. 231–32*), appropriate for the central fresco cycle of the church of the Franciscans: St Francis (*see p. 298*) was devoted to the image of the Cross, and one of the principal scenes in the sanctuary shows him receiving the stigmata, the wounds inflicted on Christ at His crucifixion.

The rest of the church

(5) Tomb of Michelangelo: The monument was designed by Giorgio Vasari, who knew Michelangelo well. Many would say it doesn't do him justice.

(6) Cavalcanti Tabernacle: The relief of the *Annunciation* in gilded limestone is one of Donatello's most moving works (c.

1434). The beautiful Virgin is shown taken by surprise by the angel, who fixes her with a deep and speaking gaze. The figures are portrayed with marked realism, without any crudity or coarseness.

(7) Donatello's Crucifix: When Donatello's friend Brunelleschi saw this

Crucifix (1425), he abused it for its lack of refinement, calling the man portrayed here a 'peasant on the Cross'. He then vowed to show Donatello how the cruci- fied Saviour should look: fine-featured, intelligent, graceful; a son of God, not of a labourer. Brunelleschi's version is pre- served in Santa Maria Novella (*see p. 188*).

The Pazzi Chapel

The **Pazzi Chapel (8)**, so named because it was commissioned by Andrea de' Pazzi, is a famous work by Brunelleschi, who worked on it from 1442 until his death in 1446. Soon after its final completion, in 1478, the Pazzi family brought ignominy on itself with a plot to murder Lorenzo the Magnificent while he was attending Mass in the duomo. Lorenzo escaped but his brother Giuliano was killed. The ringleaders were all hanged. The so-called 'Pazzi Conspiracy' is not an edifying tale, but it does illustrate how, even at the height of their magnificence, the Medici's position in Florence was always precar- ious. The chapel interior is one of the masterpieces of the early Renaissance, centrally planned with *pietra serena* used to pick out the Corinthian pilasters, entablature and other architectural features. The central plan (by which is meant a circular, octagonal or square space surmounted by a dome) was a feature of many ancient Roman buildings, particularly shrines or mausolea. It entered the Christian tradition in the form of bap- tisteries and pilgrimage chapels and was popular in Byzantine church architecture. The Latin tradition favoured the rectangular basilica form, and the introduction of the cen- trally-planned church to Florence was Brunelleschi's doing, in the Old Sacristy of San Lorenzo. The blue and white roundels of the Twelve Apostles (c. 1442–52) are by Luca della Robbia. In the pendentives are polychrome roundels of the Evangelists (c. 1460; by Donatello or Brunelleschi) glazed by the della Robbia. The lovely umbrella vault is completely plain, in striking contrast to the opulence of the vault in the portico, again with enamelled terracotta decoration by Luca della Robbia.

The **Museo dell'Opera di Santa Croce** is arranged in the cloisters. In the refecto- ry **(9)** is the famous painted Crucifix by Cimabue (1280), very badly damaged in the Arno flood of 1966 but restored since. Enough survives to make possible an interest- ing comparison between this old-style Tuscan Christ, heavily stylised, and that of Giotto in Santa Maria Novella, painted just ten years later.

Casa Buonarroti

The property on this site (*map p. 177, 12; open 9.30–1.30 except Tues*) was purchased in 1508 by Michelangelo. It is now a museum preserving three of his sculptures and a number of drawings. The *Madonna of the Steps*, a marble bas-relief, is his earliest known work, carved when he was 15 or 16. The wooden model for the façade of San Lorenzo was designed in 1516 but never carried out; San Lorenzo still lacks a façade today.

THE OLTRARNO

The Oltrarno is the name given to the part of Florence on the south bank of the river. Two fine bridges lead there. The more famous is the **Ponte Vecchio** (*map p. 177, 11*), reconstructed in its present form in 1345. It is lined with shops, as it has been since the Middle Ages. The premises were tenanted by butchers and grocers until 1593, when Grand Duke Ferdinando I decreed that gold and silversmiths should take their place. They remain here still. From the centre of the bridge there is a superb view of **Ponte Santa Trinita**, an exact replica (1957) of the graceful bridge commissioned from Ammannati by Cosimo I and built in 1567. It was destroyed by German mines in 1944.

Santa Felicita

The church of Santa Felicita (*map p. 176, 10*) contains some masterpieces of 16th-century Mannerist painting by Pontormo. His remarkable altarpiece of the *Deposition* (1528) is a triumph of the style, both in its use of colour, in its arrangement of the figures so that they seem to defy the laws of gravity, and in its composition, where the individual figures are subordinate to the overall scheme, except for the brilliantly executed body of the dead Christ, whose very pallor makes Him stand out from the whole.

Santo Spirito

The church of Santo Spirito (*map p. 176, 10; open 9.30–12.30 & 4–6; closed Wed*) has a beautiful Renaissance interior by Brunelleschi, designed in 1434–35. With its lateral colonnades and flat ceiling, it is the most perfect example of his return to the basilica form. There is no entablature running above and between the columns, yet the idea does exist segmentally, in the form of a stone block between each capital and the arch above.

This was the parish church of Luca Pitti, the wealthy cloth merchant who built Palazzo Pitti (*see p. 179*). In his family chapel at the far east end is an altarpiece of *Martyred Saints*, commissioned by a descendant from the best-known artist of the day, Alessandro Allori, in 1574. It incorporates a portrait of another of the artist's patrons, Cosimo I, in the centre (with moustache and beard). Luca Pitti features in the predella, standing outside his palace, which before it was enlarged was similar in proportion to the Strozzi and Rucellai palaces (*see p. 188*). By the time of this painting, the palace had been sold to the Medici. In the south transept is an altarpiece of the *Madonna and Child with the Young St John, Saints and Donors*, a fine work by Filippino Lippi (after 1494), with an early view of Florence in the background. The octagonal sacristy off the north aisle was not built by Brunelleschi, though its design clearly owes much to him. Here is displayed a Crucifix in painted poplar wood, attributed to Michelangelo.

Santa Maria del Carmine (Brancacci Chapel)

Map p. 176, 10. Open 10–4.30, Sun 1–4.30; closed Tues. Visitors must book (T: 055 276 8224 or 055 276 8558 daily 9–6) but in low season you can often go straight in. You must collect your ticket 10mins before the designated visiting time, and you may stay 15mins in the chapel.

Mannerism is the style which followed the High Renaissance and prefigured the Baroque. It is characterised by intense stylisation, contorted, elongated forms, illogical poses and a vivid, surprising palette. The finest Florentine exponents were Rosso Fiorentino (*see p. 222*) and Pontormo, whose *Deposition* of 1528 is illustrated here.

The frescoes here of the life of St Peter, with the *Temptation of Adam and Eve* and the unforgettable *Expulsion from Paradise*, were commissioned c. 1424 by Felice Brancacci, a rich Florentine silk merchant. Masolino at first worked on the cycle with his pupil Masaccio. Both artists died before the cycle was completed. Masaccio was only 27, and despite his youth, his achievement is extraordinary. He successfully bridges the world of Giotto and that of Brunelleschi, completely ignoring the courtly interlude of the International Gothic between the two. Here we see human figures as the protagonists, devoid of incidental detail. We also see a perfect realism in the way the figures and their settings are rendered. Masolino, on the other hand, had a more decorative instinct, and his art is closer to that of the International Gothic. This is well seen in his masterpiece at Castiglione Olona (*see p. 52*) The cycle was only completed c. 1480–85 by Filippino Lippi, who carefully matched his style to that of his predecessors.

San Miniato al Monte

San Miniato (*map p. 177, 16; open winter 8–12 & 3–6, Sun and holidays 3–6; summer daily 8–7*) is the finest of all Tuscan Romanesque basilicas. It is dedicated to Minias, a member of the early Christian community from the East, martyred c. 250 and buried on this hillside. The lovely geometric white and green marble façade was begun c. 1090. The superb interior, built in 1018–63, survives practically in its original state. It has a splendid mosaic floor, works by numerous Florentine masters, and a numinous, Eastern atmosphere quite unlike anything else in the city.

VISITING FLORENCE

GETTING AROUND

• **By air:** Florence airport is a few kilometres west of the city. Shuttle buses run every 30mins to the bus station next to Santa Maria Novella railway station from 6am–11.30pm. The service from the bus station to the airport runs from 5.30am–11pm. Journey time 20–30mins; tickets can be bought on board.

Trains connect Pisa airport to Florence (Santa Maria Novella station) roughly every 30mins. Trains leave from just outside the terminal; tickets must be bought at the office on the right as you exit the baggage claim area. The journey takes c. 90mins, and several stops are made on the way. There is also an express coach service between the airport and Florence, which takes about 1hr 10mins.

• **By car:** Cars are severely restricted in central Florence. Access is allowed to hotels and for the disabled. There are several underground car parks, for example at Santa Maria Novella railway station (*map p. 176, 2*) and in Piazza della Libertà (*map p. 177, 3–4*).

• **By public transport:** Buses run by ATAF and LI-NEA are a quick way of travelling around. Routes are displayed at bus stops. Most stops are request stops (*fermata a richiesta*), and each is indicated by its name on the stop itself. Tickets should be bought at newsstands, tobacconists or cafés displaying the ATAF logo and stamped on board, though you may purchase a ticket from the driver for an additional fee. Multiple tickets and an electronic pass (*Carta Agile*) are also available. See www.ataf.net.

Useful routes include: 7 (Stazione–San Marco–San Domenico–Fiesole); 11 (Porta

Romana–Stazione–Duomo–San Marco); 12/13 (Stazione–Piazzale Michelangelo-San Miniato a Monte–Porta Romana–Stazione).

• **By train:** Florence has good links to the major cities in Italy. Most trains use the main railway station, Santa Maria Novella (*map p. 176, 2*). Journey times to the main towns in Tuscany are: Lucca (90mins), Pisa (1hr), Siena (90mins) Arezzo (1hr), Chiusi (2hrs). Change at Siena or Chiusi for Montepulciano.

• **By bus:** Several companies run coaches to outlying towns; most leave from around Santa Maria Novella station. The most important operator is SITA (www.sitabus.it), which has a terminus on the south side of the station. For details, see the entries on the towns themselves in the following chapters.

• **By taxi:** T: 055 4390, 055 4499, 055 4798, 055 4242.

BOOKING SERVICE

There is a telephone booking service for the state museums in Florence (*T: 055 294883; Mon–Fri 8.30–6.30, Sat 8.30–12.30*). A booking fee is charged, but for the Uffizi, where queues can be very long, it is worth it. You are a given a time for your visit; pick up your ticket 5–10mins beforehand. You can also book online: www.polomuseale.firenze.it.

WHERE TO STAY IN FLORENCE

€€€€ **Helvetia & Bristol.** ■ Small, elegant, intimate and beautifully appointed. *Via de' Pescioni 2, T: 055 26651, www.royaldemeure.com. Map p. 176, 6.*

€€€€ **JK Place.** Attractive, comfortable boutique hotel in a fine central location. *Piazza Santa Maria Novella 7, T: 055 264 5181, www.jkplace.com. Map p. 176, 6.*

€€€ **Loggiato dei Serviti.** In a lovely old palace with stone floors and simple furnish-

ings. *Piazza SS. Annunziata 3, T: 055 289592, www.loggiatodeiservitihotel.it. Map p. 177, 7.*

€€ **Antica Dimora Johlea.** Charming and comfortable 19th-century palace close to Piazza San Marco. *Via San Gallo 80, T: 055 463 3292, www.johanna.it. Map p. 177, 3.*

€€ **Beacci Tornabuoni.** Old-fashioned, old-established hotel on Florence's smartest street. *Via dei Tornabuoni 3, T: 055 212645, www.hoteltornabuoni.it. Map p. 176, 10.*

€€ **Residenza Santo Spirito.** Small hotel, nicely furnished, in an old palace in the Oltrarno. *Piazza Santo Spirito 9, T: 055 265 8376, www.residenzaspirito.com. Map p. 176, 10.*

WHERE TO EAT IN FLORENCE

€€€ **Cavallino.** Old-established place in the very heart of old Florence. Closed Wed. *Piazza della Signoria 28, T: 055 215818. Map p. 177, 11.*

€€€ **Enoteca Pinchiorri.** One of the most famous restaurants in Italy. Elegant, ceremonious, serving fine cuisine. Closed Sun and Mon. *Via Ghibellina 87, T: 055 242777. Map p. 177, 12.*

€€€ **Taverna del Bronzino.** One of the best restaurants in the city, superb for fish. *Via delle Ruote 25–27, T: 055 495220. Map p. 177, 3.*

€€ **Borgo Antico.** A fine old Tuscan *trattoria* with tables outside in summer. *Piazza Santo Spirito 6, T: 055 210437. Map p. 176, 10.*

€€ **Del Carmine.** Well-known traditional *trattoria* ideally placed for the Brancacci Chapel. Closed Sun and two weeks in Aug. *Piazza del Carmine 18/r, T: 055 218601. Map p. 176, 10.*

€€ **Enoteca Boccadama.** A classic *enoteca* serving good simple food and wine. Good for lunch after seeing Santa Croce. *Piazza Santa Croce 25–26/r, T: 055 243640. Map p. 177, 11.*

€ **Coquinarius.** Lovely little place in the back streets near the duomo, with good wine and acclaimed food. Closed Sun. *Via delle Oche 15/r, T: 055 230 2153. Map p. 177, 7.*

FIESOLE

Fiesole (*map p. 420, B1*) is the most renowned and interesting of the towns in the environs of Florence, set in a wonderful position on a hill. The Medici family built summer villas and gardens in the environs, and Lorenzo the Magnificent and his Platonic Academy would discourse here on life, love and the human predicament. Fiesole's appeal to writers is perennial: Boccaccio chose it as the setting for his *Decameron* (1353); E.M. Forster for *A Room with a View* (1908). Fra' Angelico, the lyrical painter of the early Florentine Renaissance, took the Dominican habit in the friary here.

The archaeological area

Fiesole was an important Etruscan city, with an important **temple to Minerva Medica** (4th century BC; *archaeological area behind the cathedral apse; open April–Sept 10–7 except Tues, Oct–March 10–6 except Tues and Wed*). The temple, which has yielded numerous bronze votive offerings (now in the museum), was destroyed at the time of the Roman conquest (3rd century BC) and later rebuilt on a larger scale on the same site. The **Roman theatre**, built at the close of the 1st century BC, is exceptionally well preserved (it has been restored and is used for performances in summer). The **baths**, of which there are extensive remains, date from the same period.

The **Museo Bandini** across the street (*Via Dupré 1; open as ruins*) has exceptional works by Giotto's followers Taddeo and Agnolo Gaddi, and by Lorenzo Monaco. If you continue down Via Dupré and bear right, you will come to an imposing stretch of **Etruscan walls**, built of huge blocks of *pietra serena*, the fine-grained grey sandstone that was so prized in the Renaissance. In the past it was quarried here in Fiesole.

Via Panoramica

From the southeast corner of Piazza Mino, by the little church of Santa Maria Primerana, Via Verdi and its continuations form a sequence of scenic lanes that ascend gently along the south flank of the hill to the little park at **Monte Ceceri**, where Leonardo da Vinci conducted experiments in flight. The views over Florence and the Chianti hills are justly famous. You can return to Piazza Mino by a loop walk that takes you back along the picturesque lanes of the village's interior.

Via Vecchia Fiesolana leads west from Piazza Mino to **San Domenico di Fiesole**, where the church preserves an altarpiece by Fra' Angelico of the *Virgin Enthroned with Saints*. Two other works by Angelico, an *Annunciation* and a *Coronation of the Virgin*, were removed by Napoleon. One is now in the Louvre, the other in the Prado.

VISITING FIESOLE

GETTING AROUND

Pay parking is available on the main Via Garibaldi and the parallel Via Portigiani, and there is a free car park behind the duomo.

Bus no. 7 to and from Santa Maria Novella in Florence runs every 20mins. Journey time c. 35mins. The bus also stops at San Domenico.

€€€ **Villa San Michele**. Magnificent luxury hotel surrounded by gardens and woodland, on the sunny side of the hill. Restaurant and swimming pool. Superb views over Florence. *Via Doccia 4, T: 055 567 8200, www.villasanmichele.com.*

€€ **Bencistà**. ■ Charming family-run hotel romantically situated in the foothills between Florence and Fiesole. *Via Benedetto da Maiano 4, T: 055 59163, www.bencista.com.*

Basic rooms are also available at the **friary of San Domenico** (washbasin only; shared bathrooms). *Piazza San Domenico 4, T: 055 59230 (reception open 9–2 & 5–8), sandomenicodifiesole.op.org (click on foresteria).*

€ **Pizzeria Etrusca**. Simple place serving, as the name would lead you to expect, pizzas. They are good, too. Closed Thur in winter. *Piazza Mino 2, T: 055 599484.*

LUCCA

Lucca (*map p. 420, A1*) is one of the most appealing small towns in Italy. Its historic centre is enclosed by perfectly preserved brick ramparts, and a wide grassy glacis in turn divides the old walled town from its suburbs. The top of the ramparts has been laid out as a public promenade, and walking or cycling round the circuit (over 4km) provides a superb introduction to the city, its main sights and its layout.

History and sights of Lucca

Lucca became a Roman colony in the 2nd century BC, and the plan of the old Roman town is still clearly discernible in the streets and squares of the centre. The most famous and striking example is the **Piazza del Anfiteatro** (*map p. 198, 4*) an elliptical space surrounded by medieval buildings all built on the foundations of the amphitheatre walls.

In the early Middle Ages the counts of Lucca became margraves of Tuscia (the ancestor of modern Tuscany) and had their capital here. Although Florence replaced Lucca as capital in the 10th century, Lucca did not come under Florentine dominion, either then or later. This long tradition of independence is still palpable: Lucca is a city *sui generis*, and unlike so many other towns in Tuscany, it has never had to pay homage to the Medici: their emblem of six balls is nowhere to be seen here. In fact there is a statue on Piazza San Michele (*map p. 198, 3*) commemorating Francesco Burlamacchi, who planned a revolt in 1546 against Cosimo I, aimed at overthrowing his rule in Florence and other Tuscan towns.

Lucca's autonomy came to an end in 1799, when it was occupied by the French and Napoleon installed his sister, Elisa Baciocchi, as its ruler. Her palace stands on the broad, tree-surrounded **Piazza Napoleone** (*map p. 198, 3*). Assigned by the Congress of Vienna (1815) to the Bourbons of Parma, Lucca passed to the grand duchy of Tuscany in 1847 and was united to the kingdom of Italy in 1860.

Chief of all the heroes of Lucca is Puccini, who was born here in 1858. His childhood home (now the **Museo Puccini**) is in the centre of town, off Via di Poggio (*map* *p. 198, 4*). Of the noble families, those whose names a visitor will encounter most often are the Mansi (*see p. 200*) and the Guinigi. The Guinigi rose to prominence in the 14th century through their involvement in the lucrative silk trade. The **Guinigi Tower** on Via Sant'Andrea can be climbed (*map below, 3–4; open 9–7.30, winter*

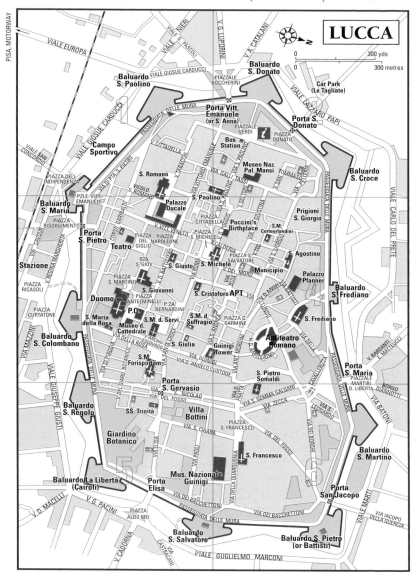

10–4.30), and there are superb views from the top. Lucca also has a fine tradition of masonry and stonecarving. Its most celebrated sculptor is Matteo Civitali (1436–1501), whose work is best seen in the town's principal churches.

Churches of Lucca

The church of **San Michele in Foro** (*map opposite, 4; closed 12–3*), standing on the site of the old Roman forum, has one of the finest and most memorable façades in Italy. It is an excellent example of the style known as the Pisan Romanesque, particularly as it manifested itself in Lucca. Above the lower part of the main elevation rise four tiers of arcades, each with intricately carved columns, all different. Between each tier is an inlaid marble frieze of animals. The loveliest painting in the church is the *Madonna and Child with Saints* by Filippino Lippi (south transept). In a corner of the west end is the original of the *Madonna and Child* statue by Matteo Civitali. A copy now adorns the exterior.

The work of Civitali can be appreciated better in Lucca's two other main churches. The first of these is the **duomo** (*map opposite, 3; open 9.30–5.45 or 4.45*). The façade is another magnificent example of the Pisan Romanesque, the work of a master mason from Como. Carved into the right-hand pier of the portico is a circular labyrinth, a symbol of the narrow and winding path that a Christian must follow to reach salvation. The dedication of the duomo is to St Martin, famous for slicing his cloak in half and giving one part of it to a beggar, and also, in his capacity as bishop, for his work to root out Arian heresy (*see p. 152*). Over the right-hand doorway is a relief showing St Martin meeting the Arians. The most famous work by Matteo Civitali in the church is the little octagonal temple-shrine which houses the *Volto Santo* (Holy Countenance), a cedarwood figure of the crucified Christ held by tradition to have been carved by Nicodemus and brought to Lucca in the 8th century. At the back of the shrine is a statue of St Sebastian, also by Civitali. In the sacristy (*entrance fee*) is the beautiful and serene tomb effigy (1407) of Ilaria del Carretto Guinigi, wife of the wealthy Paolo Guinigi. She was his second wife, and died in childbirth at the age of 26. Her tomb is the masterpiece of the Sienese sculptor Jacopo della Quercia.

At the north end of the old town, built up against the walls, is the church of **San Frediano** (*map opposite, 4*), its west front crowned by a tympanum filled with a 13th-century mosaic of the Ascension. Inside, to the right of the main west entrance, is the Chapel of St Zita, dedicated to the town's patron saint. Zita, who was housekeeper to a wealthy local merchant, was known for her piety and was canonised for her dedication to the city's poor. In the north aisle is a memorable polychrome wood figure of the *Virgin Annunciate*, her hands thrown up in alarmed surprise at the news she has just received. It is the work of Matteo Civitali, and the sharp features of the face are typical of his work. Also in this aisle are frescoes of the *Volto Santo* arriving in Lucca by the Bolognese artist Amico Aspertini. Vasari calls these his best works in fresco (though on the whole he was unimpressed by the art of Bologna; for him Florence was all in all).

Museums of Lucca

Two museums in Lucca stand out, both of them as interesting for their collections as for the remarkable buildings they occupy. **The Museo Nazionale Guinigi** (*map p. 198, 6; open Tues–Sat 9–7, Sun and holidays 9–2*) is housed in the brick-built castellated suburban villa of the Guinigi family, built in 1418. It contains Bronze Age, Etruscan, Roman and Lombard antiquities, medieval sculpture (including works by Matteo Civitali) and 16th- and 17th-century paintings.

The **Museo Nazionale di Palazzo Mansi** (*map p. 198, 2; open Tues–Sat 9–7, Sun and holidays 9–1*) occupies a formidable mansion which preserves several 17th- and 18th-century period rooms, among them the extraordinary *Alcova*, a bedchamber with a monochrome ceiling fresco of Cupid and Psyche and an elaborate gilt wood screen. The collection of paintings contains a number of Medici portraits, including works by the Pontormo and his contemporary Bronzino.

VISITING LUCCA

GETTING AROUND

• **By air:** Lucca is 36km from Pisa airport. Buses operated by Lazzi (www.lazzi.it) run hourly c. 6am–9pm; journey time 1hr. The train terminus at Pisa airport has frequent services to Pisa Centrale, from which there are trains to Lucca; journey time 40mins–1hr.
• **By car:** Parking is restricted inside the walls to less than 90mins. The free car park of Le Tagliate is outside Porta San Donato.
• **By train:** Lucca is easy to reach from either Florence or Pisa by rail. Services go to and from Florence in c. 90mins, and to and from Pisa in 20–30mins.
• **By taxi:** T: 0583 333434 or 0583 955200.

WHERE TO STAY IN LUCCA

€€€€ **Noblesse**. Quietly elegant boutique hotel inside the city walls. Garden restaurant. *Via Sant'Anastasio 23 (with entrance also on Via Santa Croce), T: 0583 440275, www.hotelnoblesse.it. Map p. 198, 3.*
€€ **Alla Corte degli Angeli**. Tiny, pink-washed central hotel. Bright, well-decorated rooms. *Via degli Angeli 23, T: 0583 469204, www.allacortedegliangeli.com. Map p. 198, 4.*
€ **Ai Cipressi**. Small, modern, motel-style

B&B. Very basic, clean rooms, comfortable beds, adequate bathrooms. *Via del Tiglio 126, T: 0583 496571, www.aicipressi.it. Map p. 198, 5.*
€ **Piccolo Hotel Puccini**. Welcoming, family-run hotel close to San Michele in Foro. *Via di Poggio 9, T: 0583 55421, www.hotelpuccini.com. Map p. 198, 4.*

WHERE TO EAT IN LUCCA

€€€ **Antico Caffè delle Mura**. Well-known restaurant on the city walls. Lovely in summer. *Piazzale Vittorio Emanuele 4, T: 0583 47962. Map p. 198, 1–3.*
€€ **Gli Orti di Via Elisa**. Popular restaurant, a nice blend of elegance and informality, just outside Porta San Gervasio. Closed Wed evening and Sun. Booking advised. *Via Elisa 17, T: 0583 491241. Map p. 198, 5.*
€ **Baralla**. Popular *osteria* just outside Piazza dell'Anfiteatro. Good local cuisine includes *insalata di farro*, spelt wheat mixed with chopped vegetables, and *tordelli lucchesi* (pasta pockets filled with spiced meat). *Via Anfiteatro 5, T: 0583 440240. Map p. 198, 4.*
€ **Trattoria da Leo**. Lively place serving simple but excellent Tuscan fare. Booking advised. No credit cards. *Via Tegrimi 1, T: 0583 492236. Map p. 198, 4 (V. Teg.).*

PISA

The spectacular flowering of medieval Pisa, together with its subsequent decline, are due entirely to the sea, the coast and its shifting sands. The city today (*map p. 420, A1*) lies a full 12km from the mouth of the Arno, but in the Middle Ages the shore was much closer. The harbour that was the key to Pisa's greatness lay just to the west of the city centre. The modern ensign of the Italian navy bears the coats of arms of Pisa together with the other former maritime republics of Venice, Genoa and Amalfi.

The growth of Pisa's power began after its participation in the first Crusade (1090s), when it established commercial outposts in the eastern Mediterranean, as well as in Sardinia, Corsica and the Balearic Islands. These were also the years of its maximum artistic splendour, during which the cathedral, baptistery and campanile (the famous Leaning Tower) were begun. The growth of its influence in the western Mediterranean brought it into conflict with Amalfi, which it defeated and then sacked in the 1130s. It disputed territory with Genoa, too, gaining possession of Sardinia and Corsica after defeating the Genoese in 1258. It was to enjoy its triumph for a mere quarter century, however, for in 1284 it was soundly and conclusively defeated by the Genoese in the naval battle of Meloria, just off the coast of present-day Livorno. From that time on, Pisa began to lose its colonial bases and was forced to cede Corsica to Genoa and Sardinia to the Aragonese. Sold in 1399 to Gian Galeazzo Visconti, duke of Milan, in 1406 it was conquered by Florence, who at last realised her ambition of gaining an outlet to the sea. The Medici were bountiful overlords to the former republic, investing heavily in its university (which had been founded in the 14th century). By this time, however, the great harbour had filled with silt and its surroundings had become marshy and malaria-ridden. Pisa shrank to a mere 8,000 souls, and when Florence took control of neighbouring Livorno in 1421, the latter city became Tuscany's most important port.

Piazza del Duomo

The famous monuments of the Piazza del Duomo (also called Campo dei Miracoli) are serenely isolated in both location and atmosphere from the modern reality of Pisa, which today is a busy, workaday, slightly scruffy university town. The square is always crowded with visitors, and cruise ships send great groups to view the monuments: do not expect to experience tranquillity when you visit, but do, nevertheless, rest assured that you will not be disappointed. Pisa's cathedral, its baptistery, bell-tower and walled cemetery form one of the most marvellous architectural ensembles in Europe.

The earliest of the buildings is the duomo (begun in 1063), followed by the baptistery (begun 1152) and the Leaning Tower (begun 1173). All three are supreme examples of the Pisan Romanesque style of architecture, though the baptistery was given a Gothic overlay in the 13th and 14th centuries.

Admission to the monuments

There are combined tickets for 5, 3 or 2 of the monuments and museums; you choose your combination. Tickets are sold at the Museo dell'Opera del Duomo, the Museo delle Sinopie or at the offices of the Opera Primaziale Pisana, just north of the Leaning Tower; T: 050 387 2210.

The duomo is open Nov–Feb 10–1 & 2–5, March 10–6, April–Sept 10–8, Oct 10–7. The Leaning Tower, baptistery, Camposanto, Museo delle Sinopie and Museo dell'Opera del Duomo are open Nov–Feb 10–5, March 9–6, April–Sept 8–8 (Leaning Tower 8.30am–11pm mid-June–early Sept), Oct 9–7. Admission times can change at short notice; it is advisable to check online (www.opapisa.it) before you visit. There is a separate admission charge for the Leaning Tower (limited to about 40 people, with entry about every half hour) and the time of the visit has to be booked. You can usually do this on the same day, but in summer there can sometimes be a delay of 2–3hrs. To avoid a wait, there is a booking service at www.opapisa.it (but you have to book at least 15 days in advance).

The baptistery

The baptistery and duomo both have exceptionally fine pulpits. The earlier is that of the baptistery (1260), by one of the most influential sculptors of the late Middle Ages in Italy: Nicola Pisano. He is thought to have been a native of Puglia, though his appellative, Pisano, comes from the town where he lived most of his life. The narrative quality of Nicola's work breaks away from medieval norms and looks forward to the Renaissance. The five reliefs on this pulpit, showing the *Nativity* (and in the background, the *Annunciation* and *Annunciation to the Shepherds*), *Adoration of the Magi*, *Presentation in the Temple*, *Crucifixion* and *Last Judgement* are extraordinarily animated, the figures densely packed in a way that is reminiscent of the carving on Roman sarcophagi (of which there are a number in Pisa). The Virgin has been likened to a Roman Juno.

The features of the Pisan Romanesque are well seen here: arcaded loggias rising in tiers, lozenge-shaped coffering, blind arcades, alternating bands of lighter and darker stone. In Pisa, too, because of its maritime contacts with the Muslim world, Islamic elements are also common: note the six-pointed star at the bottom of this picture.

The duomo

Light filtering through the clerestory illuminates a veritable forest of columns in the interior, creating an almost mosque-like effect. The pulpit (1302–11) is by Giovanni Pisano, son of Nicola, and though it broadly follows the design of the baptistery pulpit (*see above*), it is less delicate and at times over-dramatic, though still a masterpiece of Gothic sculpture. The reliefs represent scenes from the New Testament. The fine mosaic in the apse dates from the 13th century.

The Leaning Tower

Pisa's cathedral bell-tower is not the only cylindrical campanile in Italy (there is one at Sant'Apollinare in Classe), nor is it the only one to lean (Venice has several). The incline of the Pisa tower is spectacular, however (4m out of the perpendicular)—and most visitors today are so busy composing a photograph with a friend's arm positioned to 'prop it up', that they overlook just how beautiful and original a building this is. Entirely faced with white marble, with six tiers of colonnaded loggia wrapped around it, it is designed to complement the design of the cathedral apse, next to which it stands, and to provide a counterweight to the circular baptistery on the duomo's other side. Its design has been attributed to Bonnano da Pisa, who made the bronze entrance doors for the duomo (exterior south transept) as well as for the duomo of Monreale in Sicily.

The Camposanto

Pisa's cemetery stretches along the north side of Piazza del Duomo, its outer walls, adorned with simple blind arcades, the interior designed cloister-style around a central lawn; the arches were given their Gothic tracery in the 14th century. Numerous Roman sarcophagi are displayed in the four walks, and a large room off the north walk preserves one of the finest and most powerful fresco cycles of the Middle Ages, the *Triumph of Death, Last Judgement* and *Stories of the Anchorites*, attributed to Buffalmacco. The paintings are dated 1360–80 and may represent a response to the horrors of the Black Death of 1348, which claimed the lives of well over half the population of Pisa and its territory. Restored sinopie detached from the Camposanto are displayed in the separate Museo delle Sinopie.

Museo dell'Opera del Duomo

The cathedral museum holds architectural fragments, sculptures, paintings and liturgical objects from the duomo, baptistery and Camposanto. Highlights are Giovanni Pisano's *Madonna* from the main doorway of the baptistery and other works by him and his father Nicola.

VISITING PISA

GETTING AROUND

• **By air:** Pisa airport is just 1km south of

the city centre. Bus no. 7 (every 10–15mins) connects to the central railway station. The fast LAM Rossa runs to the Ospedale Santa

Chiara, a 5-min walk from Piazza del Duomo. Trains also link the airport with Pisa Centrale and Florence.

• **By car:** The town centre is closed to cars, but there are numerous paid parking areas just outside the limited traffic zone. Free park and ride in Via Pietrasantina, northwest of Piazza del Duomo.

• **By train:** Pisa Centrale station is used by trains to and from Rome, Florence, Genoa, Turin and Milan. To reach Piazza del Duomo from there takes c. 30mins on foot. Otherwise take bus 3 to Via Cammeo/Piazza Manin (*see map p. 201*), bus 4 to Via Cammeo, or Navetta A to Piazza Manin. All leave from the stop in front of the station. From Lucca trains run in 25mins to Pisa San Rossore station, which is 5mins walk from Piazza del Duomo.

WHERE TO STAY IN PISA

€€€ **Relais dell'Orologio**. One of the small luxury hotels of the world, created from a complex of houses dating back to the 14th century. Very close to the duomo and Leaning Tower, just two blocks east of Via Santa Maria. *Via della Faggiola 12/14, T: 050 830361, www.hotelrelaisorologio.com.*

€€ **Villa Kinzica**. Good plain rooms in a friendly, straightforward little hotel just a stone's throw from Piazza Duomo. *Piazza Arcivescovado 2, T: 050 560419, www.hotelvillakinzica.it.*

WHERE TO EAT IN PISA

€€ **L'Artilafo**. ■ Excellent food at a very reasonable price. Fish is a feature here (the name commemorates a Pisan fisherman famed for his Arno catches). On the southern bank of the Arno, well away from the crowds. *Via San Martino 33, T: 050 27010.*

€ **Osteria dei Cavalieri**. Good, simple and informal *osteria* in the university quarter. Closed midday Sat, Sun and in Aug. *Via San Frediano 16, T: 050 580858.*

THE CHIANTI

The Chianti (*map p. 420, B1*), the lovely region of low hills, cultivated fields, vineyards and olive groves that stretches between Florence and Siena, was once a buffer zone of fortified settlements between the two merchant republics. Today it is a peaceable land, the home of Chianti Classico, the famous wine denoted by the symbol of the black rooster.

Not so many decades ago, this was still a landscape of smallholdings. Now, partly because of changed systems of land ownership and partly because of the growth of the wine industry, it is becoming more and more a vine monoculture. This is not to suggest that the agricultural revolution in Tuscany is a 20th-century phenomenon: in fact it began under the Medici aegis, with reforms implemented by Cosimo I in the 16th century. It was then that landowners first engaged architects to design a farm type that could optimise agrarian life by anticipating needs instead of simply responding to them as they arose. These planned farms were both larger and more elegant than what had existed before. The so-called *casa colonica toscana*, many fine examples of which still exist in the region, is a fine example of early planning. Typically rectangular in outline, they had a kitchen, stables and workrooms on the ground floor surrounding an arched entryway where wagons could be housed out of the rain. Bedrooms were arranged

The small-scale mixture of field, woodland, vineyard and isolated farmhouse give the landscape of the Chianti its immense appeal.

around a central hall on the floor above. Above the arched entrance there was often a loggia for drying produce or laundry. Windows were arranged on all four sides to provide cross ventilation, and the thickness of the walls was such that the house retained warmth in winter and remained cool in summer. The hipped roof was tiled, and could be equipped with gutters to capture rainwater; in some cases a tower-like dovecote was erected at the top. Near the house was the bread oven and the hay barn. Many of latter still survive, with brick lattice- or louvre-work in the unglazed window apertures—a way of allowing air in but keeping rainwater out. The *casa colonica* design was codified as part of the land reform programme of the late 18th century.

Along the Via Chiantigiana

Some of the nicest places to visit in the Chianti are along the lovely Via Chiantigiana, which traverses the whole region. The tiny 13th-century village of **Radda**, once a formidable castle, is now an important wine centre. From the village a road is signposted north to **Volpaia**, a fortified hamlet on an estate that has been producing wine since the 11th century (the castle keep is now a wine shop).

The **Badia a Coltibuono**, a former Vallombrosan abbey east of Radda, is now a well-known winery with a celebrated restaurant (*see p. 208*).

At the crossroads between the Chianti district and the upper Arno valley stands the former market town of **Gaiole in Chianti**, with a medieval castle on one side and the village of Barbischio on the other. It makes a good base if you plan to stay and explore the region.

CHIANTI WINE

Grapevines have been cultivated in this region since the Middle Ages, but a wine district as such has only existed since the early 18th century. The Chianti Classico area, stretching between Siena and Florence, is now precisely delimited, and only producers within this area may use the emblem of the *Gallo Nero* (black cockerel). The original 'recipe' for the Chianti blend was written down by Baron Bettino Ricasoli, at his estate of Castello di Brolio, in 1874. Although the backbone of Chianti has always been the Sangiovese grape, the blend has changed over the years, and different growers use different grapes in different proportions. In 2006 the use of white grapes was outlawed altogether.

Old-fashioned Chianti is pale in colour, with a strong nose, but this is becoming rarer as producers, following market trends, shift their focus towards darker, more tannic or softer, fruitier wines. All Chiantis, regardless of vinification style, should be drunk relatively young. Tignanello, one of the 'Supertuscan' wines, is produced in the Chianti region but, because of its composition, may not label itself a Chianti. It is a blend of Sangiovese, Cabernet Sauvignon and Cabernet Franc.

VISITING THE CHIANTI

GETTING AROUND

• **By car:** The Chianti region is traversed by two principal roads: the old Roman Via Cassia (SR2), and the exceptionally beautiful Via Chiantigiana (SR222). The latter is the best route to Radda and the eastern Chianti. The historic centres of most villages are closed to cars, and cars must be parked on the outskirts.
• **By bus:** Country buses run by SITA (www.sitabus.it) run from Florence (outside Santa Maria Novella station) to Greve in 50mins (services c. every hour).

WHERE TO STAY IN THE CHIANTI

There is no shortage of places to stay in the region, both in the centre of the villages and in the country among the vines. Below are a very few suggestions.

Gaiole in Chianti

€€ **Castello di Spaltenna**. Superb accommodation in a 1,000-year-old fortified monastery-cum-country manor surrounded by vineyards and forest. Open March–Dec. *Località Spaltenna 13, T: 0577 749483, www.spaltenna.it.*

Radda in Chianti

€€€ **Relais Vignale**. Former manor house at the edge of the village offering refined interiors, verdant gardens and a pool. *Via Pianigiani 9, T: 0577 738300 www.vignale.it.*
€€€ **Palazzo Leopoldo**. Converted palace in the old centre. Closed Jan and Feb. *Via Roma 33, T: 0577 735605, www.palazzoleopoldo.it.*

WHERE TO EAT IN THE CHIANTI

Once again, the choice is ample—but one or two places stand out.

Castello di Volpaia

There are two good places here, both run by the same family. €€ **La Bottega** has a shady summer terrace with superb views over the vineyards and serves good country cooking (*Piazza della Torre 1, T: 0577 738001; closed Tues*). € **Bar-ucci** is a wine bar serving excellent simple lunches. The *Torta medioevale* is flavoured with aniseed and rosemary (*Piazza della Torre 9, T: 0577 738042; closed Mon*).

Gaiole in Chianti

€€ **Badia a Coltibuono** (with rooms), north of Gaiole, is a famous estate in a former monastery. The restaurant serves excellent Tuscan food and wine (including their own Coltibuono Riserva). Tours of the cellars and lovely garden can also be arranged (*Località Coltibuono, T: 0577 749424, www.coltibuono.com; closed Jan–Feb and on Mon except in May–Oct*).

SIENA

It is easy to be charmed by Siena (*map p. 420, B1*). It possesses one of the best preserved old centres in Italy—which, in a country of stunningly preserved old centres, is saying quite a lot. Its atmosphere is self-sufficient and independent; it is not a show town or a museum piece; and though there is much to see and do, you will more or less be left alone to see and do it, without being made to feel like a coin in the municipal coffer.

The city grew up beside the easiest pass over the hills separating the valley of the River Elsa from that of the Arbia. The walled centre extends over a Y-shaped formation of hilltops, its winding streets and brick-built houses still enclosed by 13th-century walls. Though the Sienese republic lost its autonomy to conquering Florence in 1555, it has clung tenaciously to its own ways and traditions, of which the best known is the Palio, possibly the only medieval festival in Italy that has survived rather than being revived. Siena is divided into 17 administrative wards or *contrade*, whose banners and emblems you will see displayed all over town. Membership of a *contrada* is restricted to those born within its boundaries; baptisms take place at an open-air font. The *contrade* and their loyalties have an all-pervading influence on the character of the town.

Siena in history

Just as Rome has a foundation myth, so too does Siena, and the two myths are, in fact, related. The Roman name for Siena was *Saena Julia*, and in the same way that Roma was named after its founder Romulus, so Saena was named after Saenus, twin son with his brother Aschius of the murdered Remus. These two boys, by an extraordinary quirk of fate, had been abandoned at birth and suckled by a she-wolf, just like their father and uncle. The she-wolves that you see in Sienese art refer to this, and not the Roman wolf.

But to move on from legend to history: medieval Siena saw the rise of a busy mercantile and banking community, led by families such as the Piccolomini and the Chigi, who together contributed three popes (Pius II, Pius III and Alexander VII). Private dwellings, shops and banks were constructed along the Via Francigena, the pilgrim route through Tuscany to Rome, which inside the city gates took the name of Banchi di Sopra (on the north side of the Campo) and Banchi di Sotto (south).

Siena: roofscape with Palazzo Pubblico and the Torre del Mangia.

Politically loyal to the Ghibellines, Siena enjoyed imperial privileges that enabled it to expand its trade and banking activities throughout Europe. It fought bitterly with its rival, Florence, and her Guelph allies, and in 1260 defeated them, only to be conquered in turn in 1269 by Florence assisted by Charles of Anjou, the new King of Naples, who had vanquished the last of the Hohenstaufen heirs of the emperor Frederick II the year before. Siena pragmatically changed allegiance, and for the next half century enjoyed peaceful relations with Florence, as well as growing prosperity at home. Siena at this time was governed by a middle-class oligarchy, ruled by the Council of Nine. It was during this period that the city's major monuments were erected.

Siena was devastated by the Black Death in 1348. Seven years later the Guelph oligarchy was overthrown by the Holy Roman Emperor. Instability, including a period of rule by the Milanese Visconti, followed, until a nobleman named Pandolfo Petrucci seized power in 1487. His regime did not long survive his death. By that time Italy was being fought over by the French and Spanish, and many Italian towns could do little more than choose the lesser of two evils. Siena chose first Spain and then France. In pique at this switch of allegiance, the Holy Roman Emperor Charles V joined forces with Cosimo I de' Medici, and Siena fell to Florence in 1555.

SIENESE ART & ARCHITECTURE

During Siena's early 14th-century apogee as an independent republic, a school of painting emerged that included Duccio di Buoninsegna, Simone Martini and the Lorenzetti brothers. These artists remained aloof from the developments that were being made in Florence by Giotto: while Giotto with his naturalism seeks to bring the divine down to earth and interpret it in human terms, Duccio and his followers persevere in their tradition, inherited from Byzantium, of taking man's gaze upward to the other-worldly. While Giotto is concerned first and foremost with the human protagonists of his scenes, the Sienese painters reserve their finest efforts for the minute details: the sub-plots acted out in the background, or small side-observations of the natural world. The main panels of Sienese altarpieces are very fine, though heavily stylised. It is in the lower scenes of the predella that the artists seem to come into their own. Bernard Berenson praised Giotto for his 'tactile values', and Giotto stood far higher in his estimation than Duccio. For admirers of the Sienese school, however, it is the very absence of the tactile that is so attractive, particularly in our 'hands on' world, where it is increasingly rare to find things which are intangibly, spiritually and more numinously beautiful, not merely physically perfect or experientially relevant.

Siena's greatest medieval sculptor was Tino di Camaino. Jacopo della Quercia is the foremost master of the early Renaissance. Sienese art remained idiosyncratic well after the Middle Ages. The Mannerist painter and sculptor Domenico Beccafumi, with his vivid pastel colours and suggestive use of shadow, is one of the most interesting and original figures of the 16th century.

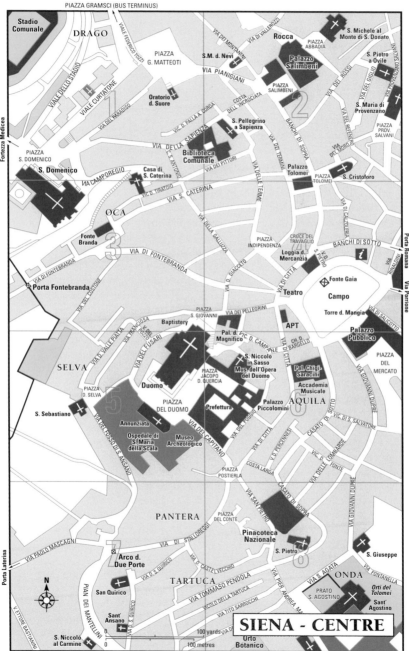

SIENA - CENTRE

The Campo and Palazzo Pubblico

The **Campo** (*map p. 211, 4*) Siena's famous, shell-shaped piazza, was used as the central market, public assembly space, military parade ground, theatre and sports arena. The other important area of the city was the hill of Santa Maria, where the duomo, Spedale di Santa Maria della Scala (originally a pilgrims' hospice) and bishop's palace were built. The churches of the mendicant orders of Franciscans and Dominicans are situated, as is traditional, at the outer limits of the old town. The basilica of San Domenico is noted for its relics of St Catherine of Siena (*see pp. 216–17*).

The Campo is built over the semicircular head of the Montone valley between the hill of Santa Maria and the ridge that descends toward Porta Romana. It was the market-place of the oldest settlement, at the point between the ancient town centre and the two main suburbs along the Via Francigena. The fountain in the Campo, the **Fonte Gaia**, was commissioned from Jacopo della Quercia (though what you see *in situ* is a copy) to channel the waters of the Montone for public use.

The focal point of the square is the **Palazzo Pubblico** (*open daily March–Oct 10–7, Nov–March 10–6; tickets available for the bell-tower only, or tower and museum*), one of the finest Italian civic buildings of the Gothic age. Half fortress, half palace, it was begun in the late 13th century to house the chambers of the Council of Nine. The central elevation bears a large copper disc with the monogram of Christ (IHS), the emblem of St Bernardino of Siena, who preached many sermons in the Campo. The Medici arms (six balls) on the first storey were added in 1560.

The tall bell-tower, the **Torre del Mangia**, was begun in 1325; it rises from stones carved with Greek, Hebrew and Latin letters, a charm conceived 'so that it would not be shaken by thunder or storm'. The little chapel at the base of the tower was built as a votive offering during the Black Death of 1348. The tower can be climbed and the views from the top are superb.

The **Museo Civico**, on the first floor of the *palazzo*, is known above all for its spectacular frescoes. These include, in the large main hall (the Sala del Mappamondo), Simone Martini's magnificent *Maestà* of 1315. This was the painter's first major commission and possibly his most ambitious painting. Simone portrays the Virgin seated upon a superb throne, holding the Christ Child in her arms and surrounded by an array of apostles, angels and saints. A vast canopy extends above the figures, unifying the whole. The haloes are made of embossed gold leaf and real gems sparkle here and there—you can see them clearly if you walk up under the painting. Opposite the *Maestà* is the famous fresco of Guidoricco da Fogliano, captain of the Sienese army, on a superbly caparisoned horse. From here a door leads to the Sala della Pace, the former chamber of the Council of Nine. Here Ambrogio Lorenzetti created the largest surviving secular cycle of the Middle Ages (1337–39).

The *Allegory of Good Government* occupies the wall opposite the window. An elderly sage representing the common weal sits flanked by Magnanimity, Temperance and Justice (on the right), and Prudence, Strength and Peace (left). Above his head flutter the Christian virtues, Faith, Hope and Charity; at his feet are the emblems of the Sienese Republic, the She-wolf with the twins Senus and Aschius. On the right we see

Justice, holding scales suspended by Wisdom, from which hang two cords in turn held by Concord, who nurses the plane for smoothing disputes in her lap.

On the entrance wall are *The Effects of Good Government*, where we see a city (evidently modelled on Siena) where all is peace, industry, prosperity and merriment. Beyond the walls lies a fertile countryside inhabited by hard-working peasants and elegant nobles riding out for a day's falconry. On the opposite wall is the badly damaged fresco of *The Effects of Bad Government* with Tyranny seated between Cruelty, Treason, Fraud, Fury, Discord and War. Justice appears chained and crushed, while Avarice, Pride and Conceit dominate the composition from above. Both town and country are ravaged by neglect, rapine and fire.

The duomo

Map p. 211, 5. Open 10.30–6.30 (7.30 in summer until Oct), Sun and holidays 1.30–5.30. The combined ticket to the duomo, Museo dell'Opera and baptistery allows you to go to the head of the queue at crowded times.

Siena's cathedral is one of the most exquisite examples of Gothic architecture in Italy. The splendid façade, made of white marble inlaid with red and green was begun in 1285 by Giovanni Pisano. Giovanni completed the lower part, up to the cornice above the doors, in 1299, using a scheme that combined the severe and simple Romanesque style with the more elaborate and ornamental Gothic. The upper part was added after 1376. It does not flow particularly logically from the lower part, but the exceptional richness of the sculpture—statues of prophets, patriarchs and philosophers by Giovanni Pisano and his school—largely distracts attention from this problem. The statues are copies; the originals are in the Museo dell'Opera.

In 1339 a scheme was drawn up for a new, even bigger cathedral. Designs were made for a colossal new nave south of the existing church, which was to become the transept of the new building. The *duomo nuovo* was begun, but plague and political turmoil put paid to it, and today only the shell of the new apse stands.

The interior of the cathedral, its walls consisting of bands of black and white marble, is magnificent. The inlaid marble pavement is wonderful in its intricacy, with over 50 designs showing the sibyls, biblical scenes and references to Sienese history. At the beginning of the nave is a tondo showing the **she-wolf of Siena (1)** surrounded by her allies. The allegory of the **Hill of Knowledge** further up **(2)** (the design is by Pinturicchio) shows Fortune leading a group of philosophers up a hillside, populated with beautifully rendered plants and small creatures. At the top sits a female figure representing Knowledge. One of the most charming pavement details (in the panel representing the **Hellespontic Sibyl (3)** in the north aisle) is the image of the Sienese wolf shaking paws with the Florentine lion.

Transepts and pulpit

In each transept is a small, circular chapel. That on the south side is the **Chigi Chapel (4)**, built in 1659–62 by Fabio Chigi (later Pope Alexander VII) to house the venerated image of the *Madonna del Voto*, painted in the late 13th century. The chapel was designed by Bernini, who also made the bronze angels who hold the painting and the statues of *St Jerome* and *St Mary Magdalen* on either side of the entrance. The north transept chapel, used as the **baptistery (5)**, is dedicated to St John the Baptist. The statue of the saint is by Donatello (1457). Also by Donatello is the bronze tomb slab at the other end of the transept, in front of the splendid Gothic tomb of Cardinal Riccardo Petroni by Tino di Camaino (1317–18).

Near the crossing stands the famous marble **pulpit (6)** designed by Nicola Pisano and executed (1268) with the aid of his son Giovanni. A little later than the equally famous pulpit in the baptistery of Pisa (completed

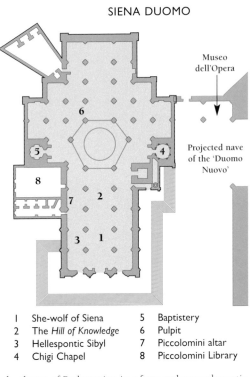

SIENA DUOMO

Museo dell'Opera

Projected nave of the 'Duomo Nuovo'

1	She-wolf of Siena	5	Baptistery
2	The *Hill of Knowledge*	6	Pulpit
3	Hellespontic Sibyl	7	Piccolomini altar
4	Chigi Chapel	8	Piccolomini Library

1260), the Siena pulpit develops the theme of Redemption in a freer and more dramatic style and with more ornamental details. The most spectacular of the busy relief scenes is the *Last Judgement*, shown in two panels divided by a sculpture of Christ in Judgement.

North aisle

Andrea Bregno's magnificent **Piccolomini altar (7)** (1485) has statues by Michelangelo in the lower niches (*St Peter, St Pius, St Gregory* and *St Paul*; 1501–04).

The beautiful **Piccolomini Library (8)** was built in 1495 by Francesco Piccolomini Todeschini (later Pope Pius III) to honour the memory of his maternal uncle, Aeneas Sylvius Piccolomini (Pius II; *see opposite and p. 225*), and to house his precious library. The interior is covered with beautiful decorative frescoes by Pinturicchio and his pupils (1502–07), each one alive with incident and detail, the colours all astonishingly vivid. The ceiling is painted with grotesques that surround mythological and allegorical scenes, with the Piccolomini coat of arms of crescent moons at the centre (the floor tiles also make use of this emblem). Pinturicchio had been to see the newly-discovered remains of Nero's Domus Aurea in Rome, and his use of grotesques derives from what he saw there. The ten frescoes on the walls show scenes from the life of Pius II. In the first scene, to the right of the window, we see him on his way to the Council of Basel, which was convoked in response to the Protestant Hussite threat. In 1435 he was sent on a mission to the king of Scotland (scene 2), aimed at attacking England and putting a final end to the Hundred Years War. In 1442, at the diet of Frankfurt, he met Frederick III of Habsburg, the future Holy Roman Emperor, who named him poet laureate (Pius wrote copiously before he entered the Church) and made him his private secretary (scene 3). In the name of Frederick, he made peace with Pope Eugene IV in 1445 (scene 4). The following year he took Holy Orders. As bishop of Siena he presided over the meeting of Frederick and his betrothed, Eleanor of Portugal (scene 5). In 1456 he was made a cardinal (scene 6). Aeneas was elected pope in 1458 (scene 7), taking the name Pius from the 'pius Aeneas' of Virgil. During the six years of his pontificate he reaffirmed papal authority and preached a crusade to free Constantinople, which had fallen to the Turks in 1453 (scene 8). Scene 9 shows him canonising St Catherine of Siena. In 1464 he took the Cross, but his Crusade was underfunded and under-supported. He died of fever in the Adriatic port of Ancona (scene 10).

The marble statue representing the Three Graces, in the middle of the room, is a 3rd-century Roman copy of the Greek original by Praxiteles. The group served as a model for Canova's famous sculpture of the same subject, now in the Hermitage.

Museo dell'Opera del Duomo

This museum (*open daily 10.30–6.30, 7.30 in summer, Sun and holidays 1.30–5.30*), occupying what would have been the south aisle of the enlarged cathedral, houses paintings and sculpture from the duomo and other churches. Its most famous possession is the **Maestà** (Madonna and Child in Majesty) by Duccio di Buoninsegna, in a small room on the first floor. It was unveiled to great public rejoicing in 1311, and until 1505 it formed the high altarpiece of the duomo. In the late 18th century it was dismantled and the panels dispersed. Some are now lost; still others are outside Italy. The current arrangement is an attempted reconstruction of the altar, though it is not known exactly how the work was fitted together. The other work by Duccio shown here, the *Madonna di Crevole*, forms a useful contrast with the *Maestà* panels. The earlier Madonna is static and archaic while the *Maestà* is much more individualised—though still far from being a real woman. It was many years before Italian art went back to the habits of the ancient Greeks and Romans in fashioning their gods in man's own image. The *Maestà* scenes, nevertheless, are only superficially Byzantine: in fact the realities of this world are fully present, in a number of very human details. Another work with fascinating everyday details is Pietro Lorenzetti's *Birth of the Virgin* (1342), displayed in the same room. Around the walls of the ground-floor **Sala delle Statue** are arranged the original statues of prophets carved for the duomo façade by Giovanni Pisano after 1285.

Other sights in Siena

The **Pinacoteca Nazionale** (*Via San Pietro 29; map p. 211, 8; open Mon 8.30–1.30, Tues–Sat 8.15–7.15*) preserves examples of Sienese painting from the 13th–17th centuries. Although the gallery is rather shabby (there are plans to move the collection to Santa Maria della Scala opposite the duomo), this is still a very fine place to study the

Duccio's *Last Supper*, from the *Maestà* altarpiece (1308–11). Last Suppers were a popular subject in art, frequently used to decorate monks' refectories, and depicting the moment when Christ announces that one of the Twelve will betray Him. Early examples tend to show the disciples sitting around the table. Leonardo da Vinci places them all on one side (*see p. 40*). The Florentine Andrea del Castagno placed only Judas on the near side of the table. Other artists, notably Tintoretto, have enjoyed the game of hinting at Judas' identity without being explicit. Tintoretto also made much of the disciples' consternation at Jesus' words and, along with other later artists, included elaborate background detail. He often presents the Last Supper almost as a scene in a busy tavern; Veronese liked to show it as a banquet in a rich palace, and included contemporary portrait faces.

work of Sienese masters, including some masterpieces by Domenico Beccafumi. A superb work by the artist still *in situ* in Siena is his *St Michael* in the church of **San Niccolò al Carmine** (*map p. 211, 7*).

The great brick basilica of San Domenico rises on a hill in the *contrada* of the goose, formerly the tanners' and dyers' quarter. It is near here that St Catherine of Siena was born, the daughter of a dyer, in 1347. Her house, the **Casa di Santa Caterina**, can be visited (*map p. 211, 1–3; open 9.30–7, winter 10–6*), and visitors are shown the former kitchen, now an oratory, and the Crucifix before which St Catherine received the stigmata in 1375 (at that time the Crucifix was in a church in Pisa). The nearby **Fonte**

Branda, the largest fountain in Siena, was formerly used as a public laundry. In the basilica of **San Domenico** (*map p. 211, 1–2; open 9–6*) there is a contemporary fresco portrait of St Catherine by Andrea Vanni (in the raised chapel at the far west end). The Cappella di Santa Caterina on the south side, frescoed by Sodoma, contains the reliquary of the saint's head. The chains that she used to mortify her flesh are displayed close by. St Catherine died in Rome at the early age of 33. Her greatest triumph had been, by means of eloquently chivvying letters, to persuade Pope Gregory XI to return to Rome from Avignon. Sadly the return of the Holy Fathers to the Holy City did not bring calm and concord to the Papal States: the Western Schism resulted, with France, Spain and Naples recognising Avignonese claimants as the true pope, and Rome, the Holy Roman Empire and northern Europe recognising the Roman claimant. The Schism continued until 1417.

VISITING SIENA

GETTING AROUND

• **By car:** Siena's centre is closed to cars. The most convenient places to park are the Duomo, an underground car park, and the Fortezza (except on Wed, which is market day, and Sun in football season). Metred parking can be found outside the major city gates.

• **By bus:** Buses operated by SITA (www.sitabus.it) and TRA-IN (www.trainspa.it) connect Siena to Florence Santa Maria Novella station and other points in Tuscany. Journey time by express bus is under 2hrs.

• **By train:** There are regular trains to Siena from Florence, journey time c. 90mins. From Siena there are hourly services to Castellina in Chianti (journey time 15mins). Siena station is 1.5km north of the centre. Buses run to the central Piazza Gramsci in c. 10mins.

SPECIAL TICKETS

The **Renaissance Trail Card**, available at museums and at the tourist information office in the Campo, gives free admission to Siena's major museums.

WHERE TO STAY IN SIENA

€€€€ **Grand Hotel Continental.** ■ Beautiful hotel in a 17th-century palace. Rooms have frescoed ceilings and are sumptuously appointed. The street is noisy at night; ask for a room on the other side if you like quiet. Excellent restaurant in the glass-roofed courtyard. *Via Banchi di Sopra 85, T: 0577 56011, www.royaldemeure.com. Map p. 211, 2.*

€€ **Palazzo Ravizza.** ■ Converted *palazzo* offering a lovely mix of simplicity and elegance. The hotel is near one of the town gates, and many of the rooms enjoy stunning views of the countryside. Garden and restaurant. *Pian de' Mantellini 34, T: 0577 280462, www.palazzoravizza.it. Map p. 211, 7.*

€ **Alle Due Porte.** ■ Tiny, simple B&B in an old house in the street where Duccio had his studio. *Via Stalloreggi 52, T: 0577 287670, soldatini@interfree.it. Map p. 211, 7.*

WHERE TO EAT IN SIENA

€€ **Osteria Le Logge.** ■ In a narrow lane leading from Piazza del Campo, just a stone's throw from the Palazzo Pubblico, this fine *osteria* offers good traditional dishes and old-

fashioned atmosphere. Closed Sun and holidays, and in Jan–Feb. *Via del Porrione 33, T: 0577 48013. Beyond map p. 211, 6.*
€ **Osteria Il Ghibellino**. This fine, genuine *trattoria* nestled in a narrow lane behind the duomo is known for delicious regional cuisine at very reasonable prices, attentive service and local colour. *Via Pellegrini 6, T: 0577 288079. Map p. 211, 4.*

€€ **Da Divo**. Good food in an unusual little place very near the duomo. *Via Franciosa 25, T: 0577 286054. Map p. 211, 5.*

FESTIVALS & EVENTS

The Palio, Siena's famous bareback horse race, is run in the Campo on July 2 and Aug 16; see www.ilpalio.org.

SAN GIMIGNANO

High on a hilltop overlooking the valley of the Elsa river and surrounded by olive groves and vineyards, **San Gimignano** (*map p. 420, A1*) has preserved its medieval appearance better than any town in Tuscany. Most of what you see here dates from the 13th and 14th centuries, including the ramparts, pierced by gates on the south and north. The most distinctive feature of the town are its tower-houses, which today number 13, a tiny proportion of the original 72.

THE TOWERS OF MEDIEVAL ITALY

From the 11th century onwards, the affluent families of many Italian *comuni* began to build tall residential towers. The principal motive was defence: early medieval Italy was torn by feuds between rival families and between the supporters of the popes (Guelphs) and the Holy Roman Emperors (Ghibellines). Very often a tower was sited next to a family's house. In times of trouble or revolt, a bridge could be thrown across from an upper-floor window (the towers did not have street-level entrances), and the family could flee to the tower for safety or take part in the mêlée below by throwing missiles from the top. Many families erected more than one tower. In San Gimignano, for example, early medieval life was coloured by the perpetual feuding of the Salvucci and Ardinghelli families. On the north side of Piazza del Duomo the twin Salvucci towers still rise, flanking the former family palace. The two Ardinghelli towers rise on Piazza della Cisterna. By the 13th century a tower had also become a status symbol, and families would vie with each other to build ever taller towers, the highest reaching to over 90m (Asinelli tower, Bologna). Many *comuni* passed laws restricting the height of towers; some even ordered that towers be demolished as punishment to families for insubordination or other misconduct. Many towns of northern and central Italy still possess towers, in most cases reduced to the lower stump. It is only at San Gimignano that so many survive to their original height, clustered together in the very heart of town.

The Collegiata

The Collegiata di Santa Maria Assunta (*open summer 9.30–7, winter 9.30–4.30*) on Piazza del Duomo is (apart from the view of the towers) the chief reason for most people's visit to San Gimignano. Its interior is almost overwhelming in its abundance of frescoes, with Old Testament scenes on the north wall and New Testament scenes on the south. The **Old Testament cycle**, 26 episodes from the Book of Genesis, was executed in the 1360s by the Sienese artist Bartolo di Fredi. The **New Testament cycle**, 22 scenes of the life and Passion of Christ, was executed somewhat earlier (probably 1330s) by another Sienese, from the school of Simone Martini. The **Cappella di Santa Fina** at the end of the south aisle is a 15th-century Tuscan Renaissance chapel of unusual beauty. The frescoes by Domenico Ghirlandaio tell the story of the Blessed Fina, a local girl struck down by paralysis at the age of ten, who bore her affliction with saintly fortitude and died five years later, on the same hard wooden board that had been her bed since she first fell ill. A few days before her death she had a vision of St Gregory, who told her that she would die on his feast day, March 12th. We see this scene on the right, together with the miraculous flowering of violets, which are reported to have sprung from her pallet. On the left we see Fina's funeral and the three miracles of her legend: the healing of her nurse's crippled hand, the blind choirboy regaining his sight, and the church bells rung by angels to announce her death.

At the top of the hill behind the Collegiata and the Palazzo del Popolo is the **Rocca di Montestaffoli**, a fortress built by the Florentines in the 14th century on the site of the town's earliest market-place. It preserves most of its walls and several towers, one of which offers sweeping views over the surrounding countryside. The long steel girder balanced on a sphere, entitled *Compressed Equilibrium*, is by the contemporary sculptor Eliseo Mattiacci.

Sant'Agostino

At the northernmost tip of the town are the church and convent of **Sant'Agostino** (*open 7–12 & 3–6*), on a quiet square usually overlooked by the crowds. The plain brick church (its flank bears a sundial by the Arte Povera artist Giulio Paolini) contains frescoes by Benozzo Gozzoli. In the nave St Sebastian, whose arrows have been removed and collected by angels, is shown interceding for the people of San Gimignano following the plague outbreak of 1464. The most famous works are in the choir, a cycle of 21 scenes (painted 1464–65) telling the story of St Augustine, from his first day at school to his vision of St Jerome, death and funeral. In the school scene (*illustrated below*) we see the slightly reluctant new boy, in his school uniform of green and red, being urged forward by his parents (his mother, Monica, has a halo) to greet his teacher. On the right hand side another teacher castigates a small child with a switch. The observations made by the saint himself, in his *Confessions*, are interesting for anyone who sees this fresco: 'As a boy I did not care for lessons, and I disliked being forced to study. […] We learn better in a free spirit of curiosity than under fear and compulsion. But your law, O God, permits the free flow of curiosity to be stemmed by force. From the schoolmaster's cane to the ordeals of martyrdom, your law prescribes better medicine to retrieve us from the noxious pleasures which cause

Scene from Benozzo Gozzoli's fresco cycle in Sant'Agostino, showing St Augustine's first day at school (1464–65).

us to desert you.' (Tr. R.S. Pine-Coffin). Benozzo was not an artist of great psychological subtlety. He loved pageantry and had a taste for rich tapestries, as is well seen in his *Procession of the Magi* in Florence (*see p. 184*). He has left behind him here a very enjoyable series of images, but we do not see St Augustine growing in stature over the course of them. The cycle conveys none of the great theologian's rigour of mind or austerity of spirit.

Rather overlooked in this church is the fine tomb of the Blessed Bartolo, by Benedetto da Maiano. Bartolo (d. 1300) devoted his entire life to the succour of lepers until himself carried off by the disease.

VISITING SAN GIMIGNANO

GETTING AROUND

Many thousands of people visit San Gimignano every year, and the little town can be uncomfortably crowded, especially during the summer months. Most visitors come only for the day, and as dusk approaches, the crowds thin. In the evening you can have the town virtually to yourself (apart from the inhabitants, of course).

• **By car:** There are several large pay car parks near the main Porta San Giovanni, on the south side of the town; if these are full you can continue around the ramparts and past the Porta San Matteo, on the north, to another large carpark outside the walls to the northwest. All are well marked.

• **By bus:** First, get yourself to Poggibonsi (trains from Florence in c. 60mins; from Siena in 30mins). From there, buses run by TRA-IN (www.trainspa.it) go to San Gimignano in 20mins.

WHERE TO STAY IN SAN GIMIGNANO

€€ **L'Antico Pozzo**. Quiet elegance with frescoed rooms and terracotta floors. Ignore the nonsense in the brochures about the eponymous well (*pozzo*) being used to duck maidens who refused to allow the local lords their *droit de seigneur*; this is a lovely small hotel. Open March–Dec. *Via San Matteo 87, T: 0577 942014, www.anticopozzo.com.*

€–€€ **Leon Bianco**. Old house on San Gimignano's lively central square. More rustic than the Antico Pozzo, and full of character. *Piazza della Cisterna, T: 0577 941294, www.leonbianco.com.*

WHERE TO EAT IN SAN GIMIGNANO

€€ **Il Pino** (with rooms). A real village restaurant, good food and genuine atmosphere. Closed Thur and in Jan–Feb. *Via Cellolese 6, T: 0577 942225.*

VOLTERRA

Volterra (*map p. 420, A1*) is dramatically situated in a position dominating the white clay highlands that separate the valleys of the rivers Era and Cecina. Called the 'Città del vento' (windy city) by its inhabitants, it is surrounded by the *balze*, striking cliffs created by the erosion of the sand-and-clay soil of its hill. It is an impressive ensemble of simple, monochrome stone architecture, and its historic atmosphere is exceptionally well preserved. As the ancient *Velathri* it was one of the 12 principal cities of the Etruscans. It is also known for its tradition of working alabaster and onyx.

The town's oldest monument is the **Porta all'Arco**, or Etruscan Arch, which pierces the ancient walls on the south. The gate originally belonged to the fortifications of the 4th–3rd centuries BC, but was transformed in the Roman period and again in the Middle Ages; it incorporates some large blocks of Etruscan stone, and very worn sculptures of Etruscan deities.

Piazza dei Priori, Volterra's beautiful medieval square, was the town's main market-place. Still the centre of city life, it is surrounded by sober palaces—some original, others built in a medieval revival style in the 19th century—made of the local brown sandstone. If you look closely at the stones you will see that they contain tiny, fossilised seashells, an indication that the hills in this part of Tuscany were once under water. **Palazzo dei Priori** (1208–57) is the oldest town hall in Tuscany.

Pinacoteca e Museo Civico

The museum (*Via dei Sarti 3; open daily March–Nov 9–7 & 3–6, Nov–March 9–1.30*) contains a fine collection of works by Tuscan masters. One painting stands out from all the rest: the *Deposition* by Rosso Fiorentino (1521), not only a masterpiece of Mannerism, but one of the most extraordinary versions of this subject ever painted. In this large altarpiece, originally painted for Volterra cathedral, form, colour and composition are used to create a most bizarre effect. Those who are involved in the business of taking the dead Saviour down communicate a sense of grief and haste through their poses and expressions. The billowing folds of the drapery suggest a gale-force wind, far from ideal conditions for such an undertaking. The ladders that neither stand firmly on the ground nor rest securely against the Cross heighten the atmosphere of hurry and discomfort. Rising serenely above it all is the figure of Christ, who seems to be smiling at death. It is interesting to compare this work with the slightly later version of same subject by Pontormo (*illustrated on p. 193*).

The Roman theatre

The little lanes beside and behind of the Pinacoteca lead to a belvedere overlooking the important remains of Volterra's Roman theatre, dating from the late 1st century BC. Parts of the cavea and stage (which would have presented a beautiful porticoed backdrop with Corinthian columns) are well preserved. Significant traces have been found, also, of the bath complex that occupied the area beyond the portico.

Museo Guarnacci

This is one of the most important Etruscan museums in Italy (*Via Don Minzoni 15; open daily March–Nov 9–7 & 3–6, Nov–March 9–1.30*). Its collections are noted for the immense number of cinerary urns, which take the form of small sarcophagi. In the earliest examples the chest is quite plain; later the sides are elaborately carved and the lid was adorned with a naturalistic portrait of the deceased, recumbent at a banquet, and holding an inverted libation dish, symbol of the cup of life overturned. The most famous

View of the cavea of the Roman theatre of Volterra, with its segment of preserved seats, and the section of the stage building behind (1st century BC).

such lid is the **Urna degli Sposi**, showing an elderly couple reclining on a banqueting couch, pygmy-sized to fit the lid, but their faces portrayed with astonishing realism.

The other outstanding treasure of the museum is the elongated bronze statuette of a young man, which was named *Ombra della Sera* ('Evening Shadow') by the poet Gabriele d'Annunzio. The stylised shape is strikingly reminiscent of the works of the Swiss sculptor Alberto Giacometti, and its 'modernity' makes it one of the master-pieces of Etruscan sculpture of the 3rd century BC.

VISITING VOLTERRA

GETTING AROUND

• **By car:** There is free parking outside the walls, and a large underground pay car park at the entrance to town, before Piazza Martiri della Libertà.

• **By bus:** Buses run by SITA (www.sitabus.it) run from Florence in just over 2¹/₂ hrs. Buses also run from San Gimignano and Pisa.

• **By train:** There are trains from Pisa and Florence to Pontedera (home of the Vespa museum), from where buses run to Volterra.

WHERE TO STAY & EAT IN VOLTERRA

Hotels include €€ **La Locanda**, well situated right in the old centre (*Via Guarnacci 24, T: 0588 81547, www.hotel-lalocanda.com*) and € **San Lino** (named after St Linus, a native of Volterra who is said to have succeeded St Peter as bishop of Rome), in a very pretty street in the western tip of the old town (*Via San Lino 26, T: 0588 85250, www.hotelsanlino.com*). A good place to eat is

€€ **Etruria**, a popular place on the main square and one of the best in town. *Piazza dei Priori 8, T: 0588 86064.*

THE CRETE SENESI, VAL D'ORCIA & CHIUSI

South of Siena, the landscape changes abruptly. The hills and narrow valleys of the Chianti give way to long, low ridges; vineyards and olive groves yield to vast cultivations of cereal crops—in the main, wheat, but also alfalfa, broad beans and sunflowers. As well as cultivation, there is barrenness. The natural phenomena of water and wind, together with centuries of use by humans, have in some places led to erosion on a grand scale: these are the so-called *biancane* (badlands, to give them their geological name), naked clay escarpments, their slopes striated with deep fissures (*calanchi*). These hillsides, with their wide horizons and sinuous contours, are known as Le Crete. You can see some excellent examples along the beautiful, winding road from Siena to Asciano, or around the Benedictine abbey of Monte Oliveto Maggiore. To some eyes this wild landscape is far finer than the safe, tame, hospitable Chianti. The most intensely beautiful and historically significant part of the region, the valley of the River Orcia and its surrounding hills, is now a UNESCO site.

Asciano and Monte Oliveto Maggiore

The old-fashioned, rural town of **Asciano** (*map p. 420, B1*) is home to a great treasure of Sienese art: the *Birth of the Virgin* by the 15th-century painter known as the Master of the Osservanza. For this work alone, it is worth making the detour to the Museo d'Arte Sacra, which also holds splendid works by Ambrogio Lorenzetti and others. Four kilometres further south, along the road to Buonconvento, is the monastery of **Monte Oliveto Maggiore**, the mother-house of the Olivetan Order (a branch of the Benedictines), which was founded here in 1319 by a Sienese lawyer-turned-monk, Giovanni Tolomei (known as the Blessed Bernardo). The abbey's great glory are its frescoes, in the main cloister, of the life of St Benedict, painted between 1497 and 1508 by Luca Signorelli and Sodoma. Sodoma was an eccentric artist, one of the great figures in Sienese art of the early 16th century. He was by all accounts unoffended by his nickname (his real name was Giovanni Antonio Bazzi), and even enjoyed using it. His art betrays the influence of the great men whose work he admired, Perugino and Leonardo da Vinci, and of the master under whom he worked in Rome, Raphael. Sodoma's self-portrait appears in the third scene on the east wall: a young man with heavy features, richly dressed, and with two badgers at his feet. Sodoma did indeed keep badgers; according to Vasari, his house was a veritable menagerie.

While the east, south and north walls are entirely frescoed by Sodoma, most of the (earlier) scenes on the west wall are by Luca Signorelli, and are very different in atmosphere. Signorelli was a less courtly painter; more thoughtful and less superficial, and his scenes do more than simply assemble the characters in a decorative cavalcade.

He was much admired by Michelangelo; in fact, Vasari claims that Michelangelo's *Last Judgement* in the Sistine Chapel owes a debt to Luca Signorelli's treatments of the human form. Luca was famous for his nudes, exceptional examples of which can be found in his *Day of Judgement* frescoes in the cathedral of Orvieto (*map p. 420, B2*).

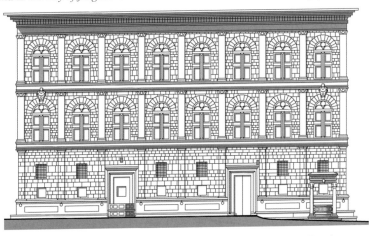

Palazzo Piccolomini in Pienza, the masterpiece of Bernardo Rossellino (1459) and a superb example of Renaissance architecture. The design of the front elevation is largely taken from Leon Battista Alberti's Palazzo Rucellai in Florence, which Rossellino built.

Pienza

Pienza (*map p. 420, B1*) is magnificently sited on a hilltop above the Orcia valley. It began life as the village of Corsignano, acquired in the 13th century by the Piccolomini of Siena. It was a son of this noble family, Aeneas Sylvius Piccolomini, born here in 1405, who transformed the small village into the astonishing Renaissance town you see today. Aeneas Sylvius became Pope Pius II in 1458, and his ultimate aim was to make his birthplace a permanent seat of the Vatican court.

Pienza, the new city built to a Renaissance ideal, was laid out by the Florentine Bernardo Rossellino, the pupil of the great Renaissance architectural theorist Leon Battista Alberti. The project remained unfinished due to the death in 1464 of both Pope Pius and Rossellino, but the part that was completed gives sufficient idea of the grandeur and elegance of the concept.

The most important buildings rise around the central **Piazza Pio II**. The square itself is a masterpiece of proportion and perspective. Rossellino had to make it fit into a relatively small space, right on the edge of the hillside. He responded to the challenge by retaining the existing trapezoidal shape, with the cathedral as its base on the site of an earlier church. Along the flanks he arranged two palaces in such a way that they open away from the cathedral, as a result making its elegant travertine façade and enormous papal coat of arms the focus of the square. The **cathedral** façade is clearly derived from Alberti's *Ten Books on Architecture*, being built in imitation of a Roman triumphal arch, as is the church of Sant'Andrea at Mantua (*see p. 60*). The architecture of the interior, with nave and aisles of the same height, borrows its form from German Gothic *Hallenkirchen*, which Pius had seen and admired on his travels. Subsidence problems as a result of the clifftop site are evident from the way the floor slopes noticeably downward towards the apse. The church holds several fine altarpieces, all of which were commissioned by Pius II from prominent Sienese masters.

The magnificent **Palazzo Piccolomini**, on the right side of the square, was the palace that Pius intended as the permanent residence of the popes. The elegant interior courtyard can be seen from the main entrance. Guided tours of the interior are given every half hour (*Tues–Sun 10–12.30 & 2–4, until 6pm in summer*).

Pope Pius's vision of a papal home away from Rome was not shared by many prelates, who were reluctant to forsake the Vatican for a remote corner of Tuscany. The only one who did so was the ambitious Valencian cardinal Rodrigo Borgia, who took up residence here and altered and enlarged the **bishop's palace** on the left of the piazza (his coat of arms appears on the corner). Borgia's ambition was rewarded when he became Pope Alexander VI in 1492. The Museo Diocesano on the top floor of this palace (*open April–Oct Wed–Mon 10–1 & 3–7; Nov–March Sat, Sun 10–1 & 3–6*) has a lovely *Madonna and Child* by Pietro Lorenzetti (1310–20) and Pius II's crozier, a Florentine work of 1460.

Just below the town walls, a lane winds its way down (*10mins walk*) to the Romanesque **Pieve di Corsignano**, a 10th–11th-century church with an unusual stout cylindrical bell-tower and beautifully carved doors and windows. It is here that Pope Pius was baptised. The church is rarely open, but its setting is very beautiful, in a coppice of mature trees with a little fountain close by.

THE VAL D'ORCIA

The beautiful Val d'Orcia is home to picturesque villages and hilltop castles. Its most important village is **San Quirico d'Orcia** (*map p. 420, B1*), a major halting place on the Via Francigena pilgrim route from northern Europe to Rome. Its Romanesque church has a fine Lombard portal. **Bagno Vignoni** is a spa town, famous for its main piazza, which is not a piazza at all but a hot pool, built by the Medici, and extremely atmospheric in cold weather, when the thermal water condenses into billowing steam.

Further to the north, high on a hilltop between the valleys of the Ombrone and the Asso, stands **Montalcino** (*map p. 420, B1*). It was to this fastness that the Sienese retreated in 1555 after the fall of their city to Florence, and here that they attempted to keep their republic alive, until 1559, when the treaty of Cateau-Cambrésis, concluded between France and Spain, assigned control of most of the Italian peninsula to the Spanish and their allies (who included the Florentine Medici). Montalcino gives its name to one of Italy's finest wines: Brunello di Montalcino. The visitor is made intensely aware of this, especially in summer, when the town has the air of an extended *enoteca*. Nevertheless, it is a picturesque and amiable place, enclosed by perfectly

The abbey church of Sant'Antimo.

preserved walls and provided with good restaurants. From the walls there are views of the sombre cone of **Monte Amiata**, an extinct volcano and the best-known landmark in this corner of Tuscany. The iron oxide pigments known as raw and burnt sienna were traditionally quarried from this mountain.

Just a few kilometres southeast of Montalcino (there is a beautiful waymarked walking trail) is the spectacularly-sited abbey of **Sant'Antimo**, founded, according to tradition, by Charlemagne but rebuilt in the 12th century. It was home to an important Benedictine community until the late 15th century, when it was suppressed by Pius II. Restoration began in the late 19th century and continued intermittently for over a hundred years until 1980, when a small group of French Augustinians brought monastic life back to Sant'Antimo.

The church, magnificently positioned amidst forests, olive groves and vineyards, echoes the Cistercian Romanesque aesthetic (though the bell-tower is not typical). It is faced with travertine inside and out, and the detailing is locally quarried onyx and alabaster, which gives the building a light golden glow. The interior (*open weekdays 10.15–12.30 & 3–6.30, Sun and holidays 9.15–10.45 & 3–6*) is wonderfully tranquil, best in early morning when flooded with sunlight from the windows at the east end. Many visitors prefer to come in the afternoon, however, and stay for Vespers in Gregorian chant (*weekdays at 7, Sun at 6.30*).

Montepulciano

This prominent town (*map p. 420, B1*), strategically set on a high hill commanding the

Val d'Orcia and Val di Chiana, has been a military outpost since Etruscan times, dominating as it does the region's major north–south and east–west highways. The first written mention of the town, as *Mons Politianus*, dates from the 8th century; throughout the Middle Ages it was bitterly disputed by Siena and Florence, becoming a permanent possession of the latter in 1511.

Montepulciano today is synonymous with fine wine. Vino Nobile di Montepulciano is made from a local variant of the Sangiovese grape. In the past the town was also a cultural centre of great brilliance. It was the birthplace of the Humanist scholar and poet Agnolo Ambrogini, known in English as Politian (in Italian Poliziano). He was personal secretary to Lorenzo the Magnificent and tutor to his sons Piero and Giovanni (later Pope Leo X). His *Stanze*, a collection of poems in the vernacular, were written in honour of Lorenzo's brother Giuliano de' Medici (murdered in the Pazzi conspiracy; *see p. 191*). It has been suggested that his poems provided the inspiration for Botticelli's *Birth of Venus* and *Primavera*.

The old centre of Montepulciano is beautifully preserved, its streets lined with patrician palaces, most still in private hands. At the top of the town is the magnificent Piazza Grande, surrounded by Montepulciano's most monumental buildings: Palazzo Cantucci and Palazzo Nobili Tarughi, attributed to the Florentine military engineer and architect Antonio Sangallo the Elder; the 14th-century brick Palazzo del Capitano del Popolo; and the crenellated Palazzo Comunale, begun in the 13th century and reworked in the 15th by Michelozzo, the favourite architect of Cosimo il Vecchio de' Medici, to resemble Florence's Palazzo Vecchio. The tower can be climbed in the morning (*open 8–1*), and the views stretch far across the immediate rooftops to Siena and Monte Amiata on one side, and to Assisi and Monte Subasio in Umbria on the other.

The duomo preserves a very fine high altarpiece by the Sienese artist Taddeo di Bartolo of the *Assumption of the Virgin* (1401). The most rewarding sacred building in Montepulciano, however, is on the southwestern outskirts: the church of the **Madonna di San Biagio**, reached by a beautiful cypress-lined lane (*open 9–1 & 3–7*). This pilgrimage church, built to commemorate a miracle that took place on this hillside, is one of the great buildings of the High Renaissance. It was designed by Antonio da Sangallo the Elder, who worked on it from 1518 until his death in 1534. Its Greek-cross, centralised plan is typical of churches of this kind (votive churches, shrines or martyria built over a saint's burial place), where the centralisation reflects the idea of pilgrimage to a holy spot. Had Bramante's plans for St Peter's in Rome been fully executed, we would have seen something remarkably similar there.

CHIUSI

On a tufa hill on the southern edge of the Valdichiana, Chiusi (*map p. 420, B1–2*), the ancient *Clevsin*, was the most important of the twelve cities of Etruria, the residence of Lars Porsena, the Etruscan king who is said to have conquered Rome in the 6th century BC. That Porsena is buried at Chiusi is known from ancient sources (his magnificent tomb is described by Pliny the Elder in his *Natural History*); but the Roman general Sulla is supposed to have wrecked the royal sepulchre so completely that all trace of it has been lost. What is now called the **Labyrinth of Porsena**, entered from the cathedral square, is an ingenious network of underground tunnels and cisterns that allowed the inhabitants of ancient Clevsin to use the streets of their city as impluvia and to conserve precious rainwater for times of drought or siege. Over 100m of low, narrow passageway have been been dug out and restored. Visits (*in small groups at 10.10, 10.50, 11.30, 12.10, 4.10, 4.50, 5.30 and 6.10*) begin in the bishop's garden.

Chiusi's **Museo Archeologico Nazionale** (*Via Porsenna 93; open daily 9–8*) preserves an important collection of Etruscan, Greek and Roman finds, largely from excavations in the town and its environs.

VISITING THE CRETE SENESI & VAL D'ORCIA

GETTING AROUND

• **By car:** In Chiusi you can park behind the museum. In busy Montepulciano there is pay parking at the north end of town. Cars can be parked outside the walls of Pienza, San Quirico d'Orcia and Montalcino.

• **By bus:** TRA-IN (www.trainspa.it) runs buses from Siena to Montalcino, Sant'Antimo, Pienza, San Quirico and Montepulciano (except Sun). Buses also run between Montepulciano and Chiusi. Buses from Florence go to Sinalunga-Bettolle (90mins) and from there to Montepulciano (c. 30mins).

• **By train:** Although the Crete Senesi and Val d'Orcia can be reached from Florence (with a change of trains at Siena or Chiusi) or Rome (changing at Chiusi), the bus is usually quicker and more convenient. Chiusi is on the main line from Florence and Rome. The station is 3km south of town; buses connect c. every 30mins.

WHERE TO STAY

Bagno Vignoni
€€ **Albergo Le Terme**. Pleasant, slightly old-fashioned place overlooking the thermal pool of the 'piazza'. *Piazza delle Sorgenti 13, T: 0577 887150, www.albergoleterme.it.*

Montalcino
€ **Le Camere di Bacco**. Charming B&B on the first floor of an old house. Central and nicely furnished. *Via Mazzini 65, T: 0577 849356, www.lecameredibacco.com.*

Montepulciano
€ **Meublè Il Riccio** is a good place in the centre of town, with simple rooms on the first floor of a small cloister (*Via di Talosa 21, T: 0578 757713, www.ilriccio.net*). Just below the town is the very pleasant €€ **Agriturismo Ardene** ■ (*Via di Valardegna 7, T: 0578 758648, www.agriturismoardene.it*).

Pienza
€€€ **Hotel Relais Il Chiostro di Pienza**. Lovely old monastery converted into a comfortable hotel. Swimming pool and restaurant. Closed Jan–March. *Corso Rossellino 26, T: 0578 748400, www.relaisilchiostrodipienza.com.*

San Quirico d'Orcia
€€ **Relais Palazzo del Capitano**. Rustic elegance of décor, a small private garden and a good restaurant. A charming place to stay. *Via Poliziano 18, T: 0577 899028, www.palazzodelcapitano.com.*

WHERE TO EAT

Chiusi
Just a few kilometres below the town is the

pretty Lago di Chiusi, where two simple little restaurants serve good lake fish and the famous wild beans (*fagioline*): €€ **Da Gino** (*Via Cabina Lago 43, T: 0578 21408; closed Wed*) and €€ **Pesce d'Oro** (*Via Sbarchino 36, T: 0578 21403; closed Tues*).

Montepulciano

€€€ **La Grotta** is an acclaimed place beside the church of San Biagio (*T: 0578 757607; closed Wed*). In town there is the charming, old-established €€ **Caffè Poliziano**, which

serves full meals or just snacks (*Via di Voltai nel Corso 27, T: 0578 758615*).

Pienza

€€ **Latte di Luna**. Popular, friendly *trattoria* serving good traditional fare. Closed Tues and July. *Via San Carlo 2, T: 0578 748606.*

San Quirico d'Orcia

€€ **Al Vecchio Forno**. Excellent Tuscan food and wine, served in the garden in summer. *Via della Piazzola 8, T: 0577 897380.*

AREZZO & EASTERN TUSCANY

Arezzo (*map p. 420, B1*) lies at the southern edge of the broad, fertile basin between the Valdarno and Valdichiana. It has a modern part on the plain and a historic centre on a low hill. The latter, the ancient *Arretium*, was an Etruscan and later a Roman town, known for its red clay vases, particularly common between the 1st century BC and the 1st century AD. In the early Middle Ages Arezzo supported the Ghibelline party, which brought it into conflict with Florence. It was defeated and came under Florentine control in 1384. The walls and fortress were built by the Medici. Arezzo is the birthplace of Petrarch and Vasari, whose houses can both be visited.

Major sights of Arezzo

The main monuments of Arezzo are close together in the old centre. Near the northern tip of the old town is the **house of Giorgio Vasari** (*open Mon–Sat 8.30–7.30, Sun 8.30–12.30*). Some of the decorations in the interior are by Vasari himself, and there is a collection of paintings by his contemporaries. Vasari was a prolific artist, both a painter and an architect, but his chief claim to fame lies in his *Lives of the Artists*, which he published in 1550, and which has guided the tastes and prejudices of art historians ever since. The long, porticoed Palazzo delle Logge on Piazza Grande was designed by him (1573). On the same square rises the beautiful, 12th-century **Pieve di Santa Maria**, with its superb colonnaded main façade and arcaded apse. The polyptych of the *Madonna and Child* in the presbytery is a masterpiece by Pietro Lorenzetti (1320).

The **duomo** of Arezzo (*open daily 7–12 & 3–6.30*) contains superb early 16th-century stained glass by one of the finest artists in that medium in Italy at that date. Guillaume de Marcillat, originally from Marseilles, carried out most of his best work in Arezzo. In a cramped corner of the north aisle there is also an extremely beautiful fresco of Mary Magdalen holding a little lantern-shaped oil jar, by Piero della Francesca. Piero was not a Florentine: he was born in rural Sansepolcro on the Umbrian border (*see overleaf*). His art had little influence on his contemporaries but he came to be recognised in the 20th century as a major figure of the Italian Renaissance. His finest works are here in Arezzo, in the church of San Francesco (*open April–Oct Mon–Fri 9–6.30, Sat 9–5.30, Sun 1–5.30; Nov–March Mon–Fri 9–5.30, Sat 9–5, Sun 1–5*). These frescoes (1453–66), showing the legend of the True Cross and its discovery by St Helen, mother of Constantine, are not only Piero's masterpiece, they are one of the most important achievements of all Italian painting.

Piero della Francesca's Dream of Constantine *from the True Cross fresco cycle (1453–66). Vasari praises this work, marvelling at the invention of the artist. Agnolo Gaddi, on the other hand, who produced a similar idea many decades before (*pictured on p. 190*), receives short shrift: 'Being born and brought up in ease, which is often a hindrance to application, he was more devoted to trading and commerce than to the art of painting'.*

The True Cross frescoes

As has happened with so many of Italy's most famous sights and works of art, pressure of visitor numbers here has led to restrictions on access. While you can see the frescoes in a general way, and gain an impression of them, from the head of the nave, to enter the sanctuary and view them more closely you need a special ticket and a time slot. You can get this in advance online (www.apt.arezzo.it) or from the office to the right of the church. Visitors are permitted to remain in the sanctuary for 30mins.

One of the greatest qualities of Piero's sacred art, as well as the marvellous use of colour, the lucidity of composition and mastery of perspective, which are present in all his works, is the way he gives a sense of the mystery of divine contact with the human and the familiar. In his *Flagellation* in Urbino, for example, the three rich merchants in the foreground pay no attention at all to the important event that is unfolding behind them. Christ and his persecutors are presented as almost incidental to the insistent thrust of the everyday. This sense of detachment is present in the True Cross cycle too.

The story of the frescoes (starting in the lunette on the right wall) is as follows: The final illness and death of Adam; Seth plants a tree on his grave, which takes root and flourishes; A plank from the tree is used as a bridge across the Siloam river; The Queen of Sheba, about to cross the bridge on a journey to King Solomon's court, foresees its future sacred purpose and kneels before it; Solomon orders the sacred plank to be buried; The emperor Constantine, asleep in his tent on the eve of the Battle of Milvian Bridge, dreams that an angel comes down from heaven announcing that victory will be his under the banner of the Cross (*see illustration on previous page*); Constantine, bearing a tiny little Cross, puts his rival, the emperor Maxentius, to flight; Helen, Constantine's mother, desires to find the True Cross, which has been buried after the Crucifixion, in a place known only to a Jew named Judas; Judas is made to reveal the location by being lowered into a dry well; Judas digs up the Cross and that of the two thieves in the presence of Helen and her retinue; The identity of the True Cross is revealed when it raises a man from the dead; The Byzantine emperor Heraclius goes into battle against Chosroes, King of the Persians, who had stolen the Cross; Victorious, Heraclius restores the Cross to Jerusalem, in a flurry of spectacular stovepipe hats.

SANSEPOLCRO, MONTERCHI & CORTONA

Sansepolcro (*map p. 420, B1*), the birthplace of Piero della Francesca, is a pleasant town, visited mainly for Piero's famous fresco of the *Resurrection*. The painting, probably dating from the late 1450s, is preserved in the Museo Civico (*Via Aggiunti 65, open June–Sept 9.30–1.30 & 2.30–7, Oct–May 9.30 1 & 2.30–6*). Piero reduces the scene to its essentials, representing the Resurrection not as a historical event but as a cornerstone of faith and a subject for meditation. Not coincidentally, the scene is bathed in the first light of the new day; it is set against a landscape background whose trees mark the transition from winter (on the left, where they are leafless) to spring (right). The most remarkable feature of the painting is the penetrating gaze of the Redeemer, who directly engages the eye of the observer, while the four guards sleep soundly in the foreground—again, Piero's divine world exists in parallel but with no tangible point of junction with the human. Christ's left foot, placed on the edge of the tomb, is a *tour de force* of foreshortening and perspective.

In nearby **Monterchi** is Piero's extraordinary *Madonna del Parto* (c. 1460), probably intended by the artist as a memorial to his mother, the eponymous Francesca, who was widowed before her son was born. The work is housed in a former school (*open Tues–Sun 9–1 & 2–6*) and shows the pregnant Madonna revealed by two angels.

South of Arezzo is **Cortona** (*map p. 420, B1*), the birthplace of Luca Signorelli and Pietro da Cortona, neither of whom worked chiefly in their home town, but who are both represented in the town's main museum (Museo dell'Accademia Etrusca e della Città di Cortona), which is famed also for its superb Etruscan holdings. The Futurist artist Gino Severini was another native, and the same museum has a good collection of his works. The duomo preserves an *Adoration of the Shepherds* by Pietro da Cortona. Fine works by the Sienese school and a beautiful *Deposition* by Luca Signorelli are shown in the Museo Diocesano next door. Apart from its art, Cortona is simply a delightful place to visit, with steep stepped streets, some good restaurants, and magnificent views of the open countryside.

VISITING AREZZO & EASTERN TUSCANY

GETTING AROUND

By train: Arezzo is easily reached from Florence in 45mins–1hr. Sansepolcro is on a direct line from Perugia (1hr 40mins). Cortona station (trains from Rome and Florence) is at Camucia, 5km from the centre. Buses go every 30mins to Piazza Garibaldi by the walls of the old town. Buses also link Piazza Garibaldi with Terontola station (trains from Florence and Perugia) every 25mins.

By bus: Buses run by LFI (www.lfi.it) link Arezzo with Cortona in 1hr, and with Siena in 90mins. The bus station in Arezzo is next to the railway station. SITA (www.sita.it) runs buses from the stop outside Santa Maria Novella station in Florence to Arezzo in c. 2hrs and also to Sansepolcro (1hr more from Arezzo).

WHERE TO STAY

Arezzo

Most hotels in Arezzo itself are aimed at business travellers. If you have your own transport, €€ **Villa I Bossi** makes a good base, a lovely old villa in the verdant hills a few kilometres south of town. Dinner is served three nights a week from May–Oct (*Località Gragnone 44/46, T: 0575 365642, www.villaibossi.com*). €€ **Il Falconiere** (*see below*) also has rooms and a swimming pool (*www.ilfalconiere.it*).

Cortona

€€ **San Michele**. Comfortable place in the lower part of the old town, in a restored palace on one of the streets leading down from the museum square. *Via Guelfa 15, T: 0575 630660, www.hotelsanmichele.net.*

Sansepolcro

€€€ **Palazzo Magi**. A good, central place to stay in a handsome old palace. *Via XX Settembre 160, T: 0575 733505, www.relaispalazzomagi.it.*

WHERE TO EAT

Arezzo

There is no problem with finding a good place to eat in Arezzo. The best-sited of all the restaurants is the €€ **Lancia d'Oro**, overlooked by the Pieve and under the long loggia built by Vasari (*Piazza Grande, T: 0575 21033*).

Cortona

Fans of Frances Mayes' *Under the Tuscan Sun* might like to know that her favourite restaurants include €€ **Il Falconiere**, 3km northwest of town at S. Martino a Bocena, off the main road to Arezzo. Known for its pecorino crème brûlée. Closed Mon and Tues lunch and Nov–March. *T: 0575 612679.*

Sansepolcro

€ **Da Ventura**. A simple place serving good local food, right in the centre of town (on the same street as the entrance to the museum). Closed Sun evening and Mon. *Via Niccolò Aggiunti 30, T: 0575 742560.*

CENTRAL ITALY

The influence which is felt most clearly in the central regions of Italy is, without question, that of the city of Rome, the settlement on the banks of the Tiber that rose to become the capital of perhaps the greatest empire the world has ever seen, and which later reinvented itself as the seat of the Roman Catholic Church.

The landscape is filled with reminders of how adept the Romans were at centralisation. Their manners and their usages spread everywhere. All across the Roman *campagna* are the remains of their great aqueducts, extraordinary feats of engineering, which ran for miles across the empty countryside, conveying water to the fountains, fulleries and bath houses of the capital. By the early Middle Ages, after the aqueducts had been cut by invading barbarians and the drainage channels left to fill up, the land had returned to its pristine state, as malarial swamp.

In the year 754 the leader of one of those tribes of 'barbarians', Pepin the Short, King of the Franks, captured Ravenna and presented his spoils to the pope, in his capacity as vicar of Christ on earth and the spiritual successor to St Peter. That land was the foundation block for the territory later to be known as the Papal States, which with Rome as their capital and the pope as their ruler, eventually stretched all the way across central Italy from the Tyrrhenian to the Adriatic coasts.

The pope's role as both spiritual leader of the Church and temporal sovereign of its territory was always problematic. The popes tended to be inept generals, and were constantly in conflict with the Holy Roman Emperor, a creation of initially symbolic significance whose existence dated back to the year 800, when Pope Leo III had crowned Charlemagne. The power-share between Emperor and Pope was never clear. The Pope was the acknowledged head of the Church, but the Emperor was its defender—against pagan barbarians, the Arab infidel and Byzantium. Not only that, but the Emperor, having received his imperial title, wanted to see it translated into tangible power, with real estates to govern. Frequent quarrels broke out over whether Pope or Emperor held sway, and these quarrels echo clamorously through the history not just of central Italy but of the whole peninsula, as successive emperors, notably Frederick Barbarossa, Frederick II and the Habsburg Charles V, and later the ambitious Napoleon, battled for control of Italy's towns and people and strove to humiliate the popes.

The spiritual legacy of central Italy is very great. Appalled at the veniality of the papal court, holy men went out into the wilderness to return to a contemplative ideal. The greatest of these was St Benedict, born in rural Umbria, whose first monastic community was at Subiaco, near Rome, from where he went on to found the great pilgrimage site of Monte Cassino. Monasteries following his rule sprang up like beacon lights across the western Christian world.

Central Italy today is visited for all these things: for remains left by the ancient Romans and their predecessors the Etruscans; for the legacy of the popes in terms of architecture, art and atmosphere; for its holy sites, notably St Peter's and the basilica of St Francis at Assisi, and for the enduring charm and interest of its smaller towns.

LAZIO

The region of Lazio (*map p. 420*) lies right at the centre of the Italian peninsula, between the Apennines and the sea. 'So sad, so quiet, so sullen; so secret in its covering up of great masses of ruin,' wrote Charles Dickens in his *Pictures from Italy* (1846). It is in fact a sombre place. Shelley called it 'the capital of the vanished world', though it is less the absence of that world than its secret, perpetuated presence that gives Lazio its atmosphere. The history of Lazio is, to all intents and purposes, either the history of Rome (*see below*) or the history of Etruria (*see p. 286*).

Food and wine of Lazio

The food of Lazio is simple, made with few ingredients and little refinement, but tasty for all that. Despite Rome's long tradition of aristocracy tied to the clergy and to the world of diplomacy, the origins of its cuisine are in the kitchens of the humble.

Many *trattorie* serve the famous *abbacchio*, suckling lamb roasted with garlic, rosemary, anchovies, hot pepper and white wine. There is a wide variety of tasty cheeses, and dishes that make use of them are the antipasto *crostini di provatura*, skewers of bread alternating with cheese and anchovies; *gnocchi alla romana*, served *au gratin*; and the simple but delicious *spaghetti a cacio e pepe*, with a sauce made of pecorino cheese and freshly grated black pepper.

The king of vegetables is the artichoke, prepared in a variety of ways: *alla giudea*, steamed and then baked with olive oil or else just fried in butter, and *alla romana*, stuffed with its own stem chopped up with mint. *Puntarelle*, chicory tips in a sauce of olive oil, garlic and anchovies, are to be found almost exclusively in Rome.

Saltimbocca alla romana, thin slices of veal stuffed with prosciutto and sage, and *coda alla vaccinara*, oxtail in ragout, are special meat dishes.

The vine has been an important part of agricultural life in Lazio since the time of the Roman Empire, and even today much of the region is given over to vineyards. The volcanic hills around Rome produce the best wines, for instance, the famous Colli Albani and Frascati, both dry whites.

ROME

The history of Rome, a city founded on seven hills—the Palatine, Capitoline, Esquiline, Viminal, Quirinal, Aventine and Caelian—on the left bank of the River Tiber, has informed the cultural history of Europe to a greater extent than many of us even realise. In the sphere of politics and statehood, the example of Rome inspired both the Holy Roman Empire of the Middle Ages and the European conquests of Napoleon. In the legal realm, Roman law became the basis of medieval and modern law throughout the Mediterranean, a heritage which remains one of the principal features distinguishing civil-law countries such as France and Italy from common-law countries such as Britain and the United States. In linguistics Latin—the official language wherever the empire was established—forms the foundation of the modern Romance languages. And in culture and the arts Rome has inspired artists and scholars of all epochs, giving rise to the Renaissance and Neoclassicism, but also underlying conventions of speech and writing. In religion the Roman Church, notwithstanding the numerous persecutions it suffered under Roman imperial institutions, used the breadth of the empire to spread its message when Christianity became the official religion of the state.

Civilisation in Rome began with pastoral groups of farmers and shepherds settled on the left bank of the Tiber; traces of an Iron Age village from the mid-8th century BC have been found on the Palatine Hill. The Sabines, another ancient people, whose heartland was in the mountains further east, are believed to have settled on the Esquiline.

It is not clear when Roman history began. All we have to go on are myths, set down in writing by early historians (Livy is the best known), but which are in fact just Roman recastings of stories from Greece or the Greek world. Among these legends is the story that a band of Trojans, led by Aeneas, abandoned their burning city for the shores of Latium, where they intermarried with the Latin populations to form a new people, the early ancestors of the Romans. Ascanius, Aeneas' son, founded the city of Alba Longa (present-day Castel Gandolfo; *see p. 285*). The last of his line had a daughter, Rhea Sylvia, who was forced to take vows as a vestal though she had been loved by the god Mars and secretly gave birth to two twins: Romulus and Remus. Romulus was to be the founder of Rome (*see p. 248*). As unreliable as they are historically, these tales do conceal a grain of truth. The legend of the capture of the Sabine women may only be a legend, but it is a useful metaphor to describe the subsequent merging of the Romans and Sabines. Earliest Rome is known to have been a kingdom with two classes, the patricians (nobles) and the plebeians (commoners): the Senate, or Council of Elders, elected the monarchs and limited their power. Even if it seems improbable that the kings of Rome were only seven in number—the monarchy lasted roughly three centuries—it is nevertheless thought that each sovereign named in early histories may represent a different phase in the evolution of the city. The passage from monarchy to republic, for example, conventionally made to coincide with the expulsion of Tarquinius Superbus, the last of three Etruscan kings in 509 BC, was in reality gradual, not sudden.

Republican Rome extended its control over Latium, and penetrated south into the Italic peninsula. For approximately four centuries the city not only consolidated its position but deployed its remarkable, disciplined army in a sequence of conquests, first of the Italic Samnites and the Greeks of Taras (modern Taranto), then of Syracuse in Sicily. With the Punic Wars (246–146 BC) that ended in the capture of Carthage in North Africa, Rome became master of the Mediterranean. The Republic was a canny conqueror. Its aim was not simply to crush, but to assimilate. Those who came over willingly to Rome were made citizens, and Rome asborbed much from the cultures of those it vanquished.

The last of the great republican Romans was Julius Caesar, who conquered Gaul, but whose career foundered on his leadership disputes with his former ally Pompey. It was

Caesar's adopted son Octavian who formally established the Roman Empire, with himself as emperor (reigned 27 BC–AD 14). Taking the title Augustus, 'revered one', he restored peace to a realm torn by civil strife after the murder of Julius Caesar. In the first two centuries of its existence, the Roman empire reached the height of its territorial, economic and cultural greatness, particularly during the reigns of the so-called 'Five Good Emperors' (Nerva, Trajan, Hadrian, Antoninus Pius and Marcus Aurelius; AD 96–180). These emperors are called 'good' because of their intelligence, culture, humanity and moderation—at least in comparison with their predecessors Caligula and Nero, and with their successors, who found themselves constrained, in part because of the sheer size of the territory to be controlled, to introduce more oppressive policies. The empire reached its greatest extent under Trajan, after whose conquest of Dacia (present-day Romania) the empire stretched for over six million square kilometres.

It was not only the size of the empire that called for a tough stance. It was also the rise of the 'barbarians', Vandals, Goths and Slavs, who threatened the empire's fringes. Many of the later emperors were little more than soldiers, raised to rule by the whim of their men, and just as easily murdered. Even today coins are still being discovered with the names of hitherto unrecorded rulers, whose names were on people's lips so briefly that they never entered the history books. There was a third factor too: the emperor Constantine. Constantine's famous Edict of Milan of 313 officially outlawed the persecution of Christians. This was a bold and visionary step. But his transfer of the capital of the empire to Constantinople, though aimed at bringing religious unity, in fact undermined the empire's political integrity and made inevitable a final, lasting division of the empire between East and West.

The last emperor of the West, Romulus Augustulus, was deposed in 476. For two centuries Rome was plunged into the Dark Ages. But at the beginning of the 7th century it passed under the temporal protection of the popes. The splendour of the Eastern empire at last began to be counterbalanced by Rome, in the shape of its Church. The popes allied themselves with the Franks against the Byzantines, ousting the Constantinopolitan exarchs from Ravenna and securing territory which was to grow into the Papal States, over which the popes ruled until 1870. In AD 800 the Frankish king Charlemagne took the crown of Holy Roman Emperor from Pope Leo III in St Peter's basilica—an act intended to establish the sacred character of the new medieval empire and to seal the most strategic of all possible alliances, that between emperor and pope. From that date until the 14th century, when the Holy See was transferred to Avignon, the history of the city was written by the Church. The papacy returned to Rome under Gregory XI in 1377. Four more decades of conflict were to ensue, with popes and antipopes disputing the pontificate, before the election of a Roman, Oddone Colonna, in 1417, who took the regnal name of Martin V. His pontificate marked the end of the Great Western Schism and established the absolute supremacy of a single pope in Rome.

Massive patronage by the popes and cardinals of the late 15th and 16th centuries made Rome the centre of European artistic life, overtaking Florence (which during the years of papal dispute had seen a great flowering of culture). The city was embellished and improved, and its appearance was greatly changed: palaces, villas and *piazze* were built, churches were erected and roads were laid out, and construction proceeded on a grander and more splendid St Peter's basilica. Particularly memorable as patrons of the arts are Julius II and Leo X, who called to Rome the greatest artists of their day, among them Michelangelo and Raphael.

An admonishment to these papacies, which so forcefully advanced their own worldly interests, came with the sack of Rome by mercenary troops of the Holy Roman Emperor Charles V in 1527, in retaliation for Pope Clement VII's pro-French policies. Rome survived, however. Charles and Clement were reconciled (the last coronation of a Holy Roman Emperor by a pope was Clement's of Charles at Bologna in 1530). Clement's wily successor Paul III was even more conciliatory, and called artists and architects to Rome to embellish and enrich it.

The passion for building and embellishment continued into the 17th century, which is distinguished by the work of two remarkable architects, Gian Lorenzo Bernini and Francesco Borromini. Their patrons' scarce interest in international affairs kept Rome out of the way of foreign invaders, although there was no lack of strife between the common people and the ever more numerous and idle aristocracy.

In the 18th century Rome enjoyed a period of relative calm. The destiny of the papacy tottered, however, during the Napoleonic period, when the French entered Rome and proclaimed a republic, carrying the pope as a prisoner to France and annexing the Papal States to the French Empire. The papacy was restored after the fall of Napoleon, but though Napoleon fell, his legacy lived on, and sprouted wings during the years of the Risorgimento. Dissatisfied with Austrian rule, more and more cities in the north of the peninsula were espousing the exciting idea of a united Italy, subject only to itself. Disaffection with Spanish rule in the south had similar results. In Rome and the centre of the peninsula, papal rule was found wanting. More and more Italians rallied to the cause of the great Piedmontese statesman Camillo Cavour, the nationalist reformer Giuseppe Mazzini and the charismatic guerrilla leader Garibaldi.

On 20th September 1870 the Italian army entered the city. The pope withdrew to the Vatican and Rome was declared the capital of the Kingdom of Italy, supplanting Florence, which had held that title since 1865. Massive immigration followed, bringing with it disorderly new building—a trend that continued under the Fascists, who added their own rhetorical ambitions to the architecture of the capital. Rome was not affected by the First World War, but the Second hit it hard, first with Allied bombing, and later with German occupation, which lasted until the war's end. The last king of Italy, Vittorio Emanuele III, abdicated in 1946, and the Republic of Italy was proclaimed.

THE CAPITOLINE & PALATINE HILLS

The Capitoline (Campidoglio in Italian; *map p. 240, C3*) was the religious centre of the ancient city. On its southern summit (the *Capitolium*) stood the **Temple of Capitoline Jupiter**, said to have been dedicated in 509 BC, the year that Rome traditionally thrust off monarchical rule and declared itself a republic. It was to this temple that victorious generals processed in triumph, and here that they would make a votive offering and sacrifice. On the northern summit of the hill stood the *Arx*, the citadel of Rome, famous in legend for its geese, sacred to Juno, whose cackling saved the city from a night raid by Gauls in 390 BC. A temple to Juno was subsequently built nearby; its foundations now lie under the church of Santa Maria in Aracoeli (*see p. 244*). On the site of the citadel today is the so-called 'Altar of the Fatherland', the vast white **monument to Vittorio Emanuele II**, first king of united Italy, erected in 1911 in a monumental, academic style.

After the fall of the Western Empire in 476, the Capitoline was abandoned, and was not returned to civic use until the Middle Ages. Its present configuration is due in large part to Pope Paul III (Alessandro Farnese; reigned 1534–49). It was he who commissioned Michelangelo to lay out the central piazza, and he who sited the equestrian monument of Marcus Aurelius here (the statue in the square is a copy: the original is inside the Capitoline Museums). The new square was given an important new orientation: no longer looking towards the ancient Forum, but towards St Peter's, whence flowed the life blood of modern, Catholic Rome.

On the south side of the square is Michelangelo's **Palazzo dei Conservatori** (completed after his death in 1564 by Giacomo della Porta). The tall pilasters uniting the two storeys are an example of the 'giant order' (Michelangelo probably took the idea from Leon Battista Alberti; *see p. 60*). The balustrade topped with statues was enthusiastically imitated by Palladio. Opposite is the **Palazzo Nuovo**, completed in 1655. The star-shaped pavement was laid in 1940 but follows Michelangelo's design.

The Capitoline Museums

Map p. 240, C3. Open Tues–Sun 9–8, last entry 1hr before closing. NB: Entrance to the museums at the time of writing was through Palazzo dei Conservatori (though this may change). However, the two palazzi are linked by a tunnel beneath the square, so if you wish to visit the Palazzo Nuovo collections first, you may easily do so. Once you have bought your ticket, you must cross between the two places below ground, not across the square. With your ticket you get a leaflet which includes a floorplan.

The history of these museums dates back to 1471, when Pope Sixtus IV (the pope after whom the Sistine Chapel is named) presented the people of Rome with a group of bronzes, including the *Spinario* and the *She-wolf*. Almost a century later, in 1566, Pope Pius V (the pope to whom Rome owes so many of its fountains) resolved to expel pagan statuary from the Vatican: many fine pieces found their way here as a result. Both museums have superb collections of Classical sculpture, and the Capitoline Picture Gallery in Palazzo dei Conservatori contains some well-known masterpieces.

Palazzo dei Conservatori

Famous pieces of a **colossal statue of Constantine** are arrayed against the courtyard walls. The statue was an acrolith: the exposed parts were of marble, while the body would have been of wood covered with bronze. The surviving pieces were found in the Basilica of Maxentius (*see p. 248*).

The stairs up to the the main collections lead past a landing where three splendid **reliefs from a monument to Marcus Aurelius** are displayed. Eight other reliefs from

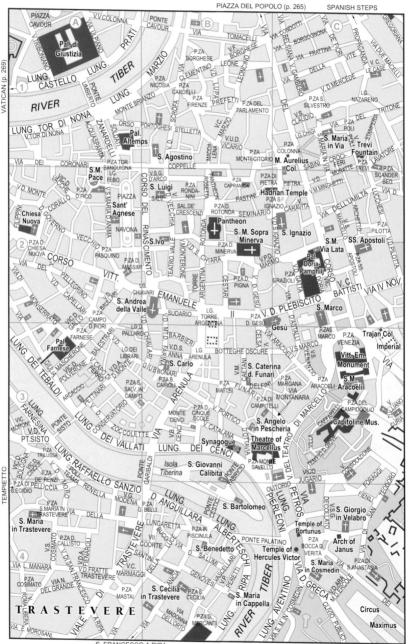

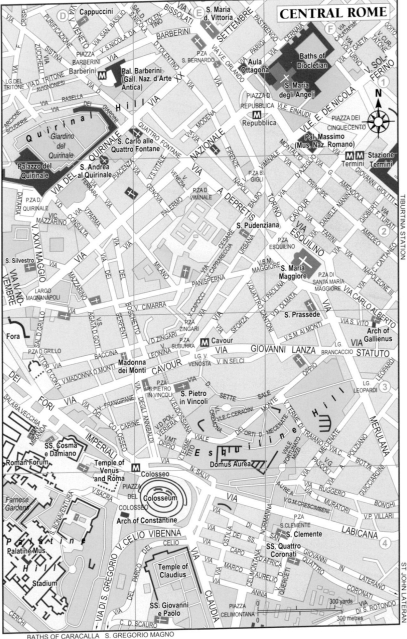

CENTRAL ROME

The bronze equestrian statue of Marcus Aurelius (2nd century AD) presented a challenge to the sculptors of the Renaissance, who strove to replicate the feat of balancing a heavy object on three slender legs (*see p. 106*).

this monument were incorporated into the arch of Constantine (*see p. 250*). The reliefs show Marcus Aurelius extending clemency to prisoners; riding in triumph in a quadriga; and burning incense preparatory to sacrificing a bull in front of the Temple of Capitoline Jupiter on this hill.

The rooms to the right of the stairs lead to and surround the **Exedra of Marcus Aurelius**, a spacious, airy hall designed specifically to display the 2nd-century AD equestrian statue of the emperor Marcus Aurelius (*illustrated left*). The statue is shown to certain advantage here, though the setting is not entirely successful. The equestrian monument, nevertheless, is superb in its majesty. When confronted with the original, you realise the inadequacy of the copy outside. This is indeed a masterpiece of Roman art, the only equestrian statue of an emperor to have survived from Antiquity (it was believed to represent Constantine, the first Christian emperor, and thus was not melted down in the Middle Ages). In the Renaissance, sculptors strove to match its technical brilliance (*see pp. 91 and 106*). Below floor level lie the great stone **foundations of the Temple of Capitoline Jupiter**, the city's earliest and most sacred temple. The podium has been restored and now stands to its full height.

Retracing your steps back from here to the stairway, you pass rooms with a number of important masterpieces, including the exquisite **Esquiline Venus** (1st century BC). Unlike so many other antique representations of the naked goddess, where the body is ungainly and the face lacks sweetness, this young girl is extremely lovely and graceful, shown in the act of pinning up her hair before taking a bath.

On the other side of the staircase is the so-called **Appartamento dei Conservatori**, the state rooms of the city magistrates. The first room (Room I; the treaty establishing the foundation of the European Union was signed here in 1957) contains two statues of popes: Urban VIII by Bernini (in marble) and Innocent X by Alessandro Algardi (in bronze). The two sculptors were contemporaries, and it has often been said that had it not been for Bernini's success, Algardi would have been considered the greatest sculptor of his age. His art has more Classical restraint than that of his rival, a quality which the Pamphilj pope Innocent X appreciated—unlike his predecessor Urban VIII, who enjoyed the Baroque in all its floridity and effusion.

The famous **Spinario**, a late Hellenistic work of the 1st century BC showing a boy pulling a thorn from his foot, is in Room VI, as is the memorable bronze portrait bust known as the **Capitoline Brutus**. This is a very early work, of the 3rd century BC, and its identification with Junius Brutus, first Roman consul and ancestor of the Brutus who murdered Julius Caesar, is entirely an exercise in propaganda, part of the myth-making which followed Rome throughout her ancient history.

More myth-making can be seen in Room VII. The famous bronze **She-wolf** (5th century BC) is in fact Etruscan not Roman. The figures of the twins were added in the 15th century to link the sculpture to the city's foundation legend.

Pinacoteca Capitolina

The second-floor picture gallery contains paintings by a number of important masters, including Titian, Veronese and Caravaggio. Caravaggio's *Fortune Teller* dates from his early, secular period. The *St John the Baptist* is a later work (1602) and its iconography is extremely unconventional. Normally St John, dressed in shaggy garments from his time in the wilderness, is shown pointing towards Christ; here we see a wild, naked boy embracing a ram, symbol of the sacrificial victim. The self-portrait by Velázquez was executed on his second visit to Rome (1649–51), when he also painted his famous portrait of Pope Innocent X (*see p. 253*).

Palazzo Nuovo

Palazzo Nuovo has been a museum of Classical sculpture since the early 18th century. The stairs leading to the first floor open into a long gallery lined with statues, busts and inscriptions. Many of the works are Roman copies of Greek originals—Greek art was much admired and emulated in the Roman Empire, and copying was regarded as an art in itself. Many of the Greek originals would have been in bronze rather than marble: because marble is a less tensile material, more liable to snap, a copyist would often insert a prop, in the form of an urn or tree stump, to support the work. Many of the pieces here are replicas of works by the most celebrated Greek sculptors, including Praxiteles, Lysippus, Pheidias and Polyclitus. The first room opening off the gallery on the right (Room II) is named **Room of the Doves** after the charming statue in the centre, showing a little girl cradling a pigeon (a copy of a Greek original of the 2nd century BC), and also after the exceptionally fine mosaic on the right wall, made of tiny tesserae, showing doves around a basin of water. It is a copy of a work by the famous 2nd-century BC mosaicist Sosius of Pergamon (in modern Turkey) and was discovered in a pavement of Hadrian's villa at Tivoli (*see p. 283*). The next room

(Room III), the **Cabinet of Venus**, displays the famous *Capitoline Venus*, a Roman replica of a Hellenistic original, of the so-called 'Cnidian' type. Venus was depicted in a number of stock ways: the famous *Aphrodite of Cnidos*, by Praxiteles, showed the goddess taken by surprise while bathing, and attempting to cover her nakedness. The *Medici Venus* in Florence (*see p. 181*) is another Cnidian representation. In the 18th century the *Capitoline Venus* was one of the most famous statues in Rome, visited by every Grand Tourist. Today one can only marvel at how our canons of beauty have changed. Rooms IV and V contain **portrait busts** of emperors, philosophers and poets. The imperial portraits are superb: as one wanders around Rome one becomes familiar with these faces and learns to recognise them. The earliest portraits are of Augustus and his wife Livia; the latest is a portrait of Helen, mother of Constantine, alleged discoverer of the True Cross (*see pp. 231–32*). Julia Domna, wife of Septimius Severus, is notable for her hairstyle, which was much imitated in Victorian Europe.

The last room (Room VIII) contains the famous **Dying Gaul**, a Roman marble copy of a 3rd-century BC Greek bronze, commissioned to celebrate a victory over the Galatians, a Celtic tribe. The stricken warrior is notable for his nudity (barbarians did not wear armour in battle) and for his moustache (Romans were either clean-shaven, or, from the age of Hadrian onwards, wore full beards). In front of the window is *Eros and Psyche*, showing physical and spiritual love locked in an embrace. It has been much copied, both in ancient times and in our own age.

Santa Maria in Aracoeli

This church, austere from the outside but beautiful within, stands on the foundations of the ancient Temple of Juno. The first chapel in the south aisle contains very fine late 15th-century frescoes by Pinturicchio (*see p. 293*), illustrating episodes in the life of St Bernardino of Siena. The church looks down on the busy, bus-filled Via del Teatro di Marcello (*map p. 240, C3*), named from the conspicuous remains of the **Theatre of Marcellus** (13 BC), named after a nephew of Augustus. Beside it are the ruins of a temple of Apollo, and beyond it lies the old Jewish ghetto (*see p. 261*). Further south of the theatre is the Piazza della Bocca della Verità (*map p. 240, C4*), site of the ancient cattle market, with the little circular **Temple of Hercules Victor**, the oldest parts of which date from the 2nd century BC. Under the portico of the church of Santa Maria in Cosmedin is the famous **Bocca della Verità**, an ancient drain-cover reconstituted as a sort of occult lie-detector (the mouth is supposed to snap shut on the hand of any perjurer).

THE ROMAN FORUM

Map p. 241, D3. Open daily 9–dusk. Entrance from Via dei Fori Imperiali or Via di San Gregorio, from where it is a short walk through the Palatine. Exit at Arch of Titus (Colosseum) or the Capitoline (by the Arch of Septimius Severus). The ticket covers three sites: the Roman Forum, Palatine Hill (including the House of Augustus) and the Colosseum. The low lying area at the foot of the Capitoline and Palatine hills was originally marsh-

View across the Roman Forum. The three columns of the Temple of Castor are very clear on the left. Those in the centre belong to the Temple of Saturn. On the right is the portico of the Temple of Antoninus and Faustina. The colossal monument to Vittorio Emanuele, with its crowning chariot and winged Victory, contrives to dominate the whole.

land, drained by the Etruscans and laid out as a market-place in the 7th century BC. After the market was moved closer to the Tiber, where ships could land with their goods, the area became the political centre of the city. Important temples stood here too, but with the suppression of pagan cults and the ultimate collapse of the Empire, the Forum was abandoned. Neglected and overgrown, its ruins inspired the artists of the Renaissance and the Romantic age.

The entrance to the Forum from Via dei Fori Imperiali brings you out onto the Sacra Via, the main street that ran across the entire area from the west to east, climbing to the Capitoline Hill. It was along this road that generals, and in the Imperial age emperors, would process in triumph, before making a sacrifice at the Temple of Jupiter at the top of the hill. The main sights of the Forum are marked on the map overleaf.

(1) Curia: This conspicuous square building, the Curia Julia, was the Roman Senate house (its brick would originally have been clad in marble and plaster). It was begun in the 1st century BC and restored several times, the last time by Diocletian in the 3rd century AD. That it survives so well is due to the fact that it was turned into a church in the 7th century. Its bronze doors are replicas of the Roman originals (which still survive, at the basilica of St John Lateran; *see p.* 258). The pavement inside is a remarkable survival from the age of Diocletian. At the back is a headless porphyry statue of Trajan or Hadrian.

THE ROMAN FORUM

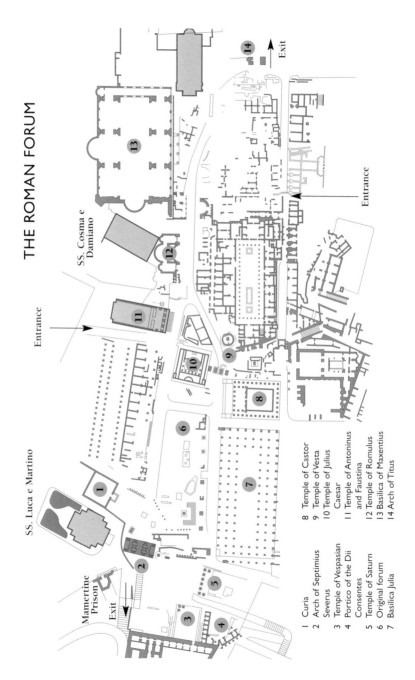

SS. Luca e Martino

SS. Cosma e Damiano

Entrance

Entrance

Exit

Exit

Mamertine Prison

1 Curia
2 Arch of Septimius Severus
3 Temple of Vespasian
4 Portico of the Dii Consentes
5 Temple of Saturn
6 Original forum
7 Basilica Julia
8 Temple of Castor
9 Temple of Vesta
10 Temple of Julius Caesar
11 Temple of Antoninus and Faustina
12 Temple of Romulus
13 Basilica of Maxentius
14 Arch of Titus

(2) Arch of Septimius Severus: This superb triumphal arch was erected in AD 203 and dedicated to the emperor and his sons Caracalla and Geta to commemorate their victories in Parthia (Iran). The name of Geta was erased after he was murdered by his brother Caracalla (AD 212). The two campaigns are illustrated in the large reliefs. The small friezes depict Eastern figures paying homage to Rome. On the bases of the columns are captive Parthians (distinguished by their caps and beards) and in the spandrels of the arches, river-gods and winged Victories.

(3) Temple of Vespasian: Three columns forming an angle are all that remain of this temple, dedicated to the emperor Vespasian by his sons Titus and Domitian after his death in AD 79.

(4) Portico of the Dii Consentes: This structure, the last pagan monument to be erected in the Forum, was once decorated with the statues of the twelve principal deities of the state cult.

(5) Temple of Saturn: This was one of the most ancient sanctuaries in the Forum, founded in 498 BC. The eight surviving columns are from a rebuilding of 42 BC (the capitals are from the 5th century). The festivities of the Saturnalia, when temporary freedom was granted to slaves and presents were exchanged, were celebrated here at the end of the Roman year (17th December).

(6) Area of the original forum: This open space was the original market-place, where all important ceremonies and meetings were held, including religious festivities, public executions and funerals. At the east end stood the rostra, the ora-tor's tribune, where magistrates' edicts, legal verdicts and official notices were published. It takes its name from the *ros-tra* once decorating its front. These were the iron prows of the ships captured in battle in 342 BC when Rome defeated the Volsci, a people who had formerly con-trolled southern Latium. Later this area became an official space, with a number of commemorative monuments and columns erected to illustrious citizens.

(7) Basilica Julia: This immense hall, surrounded by a deep portico contain-ing shops, was begun in 54 BC by Julius Caesar and completed by Augustus in AD 12. It was used by a civil magistrates' court.

(8) Temple of Castor: Built in 484 BC and dedicated to the Dioscuri (Castor and Pollux), the twin sons of Jupiter. According to legend, they led the Romans to victory over the Etruscans in 496 BC, at the same time miraculously appearing here to announce the victory.

(9) Temple of Vesta: The circular shape of this temple recalls the shape of the thatched huts used by the Latin peoples (traces of which have been found on the Palatine Hill). Inside the temple was kept the sacred fire, which the Vestal Virgins kept perpetually alight. It was believed that if it went out, the Roman state was in jeopardy.

(10) Temple of Julius Caesar: Very lit-tle remains of this temple; nevertheless, it is one of the most famous monuments of the Forum. After Caesar's assassina-tion in the Theatre of Pompey (Largo Argentina; *map p. 240, B2*) in 44 BC, his body was brought here. An altar (cov-ered by a roof) marks the spot where he was cremated. Caesar was deified by his adopted son Augustus and a temple was erected in his name here in 29 BC.

(11) Temple of Antoninus and Faustina: The appearance of this temple, dedicated to Antoninus Pius and his empress (2nd century AD) is quite extraordinary, with its soaring portico of ten monolithic Corinthian columns crowned by a Baroque coiffure of 1602.

(12) Temple of Romulus: What is remarkable about this 4th-century brick building is its doorway: two porphyry columns flank the door frame, within which hang the original ancient bronze doors. In the 6th century the temple was turned into the church of **SS. Cosma e Damiano** (*entrance on Via dei Fori Imperiali;* it contains superb early Christian mosaics). The dedication to Romulus refers not to the founder of Rome but to a son of Maxentius (d. AD 309).

(13) **Basilica of Maxentius**: This vast basilica was the last to be built in the Forum. It was begun by the emperor Maxentius and completed by his rival Constantine, after he defeated Maxentius at the Battle of the Milvian Bridge, on the Tiber north of the city, in 312. It was here that the famous fragments of the statue of Constantine (now in the Capitoline Museums; *see p. 239*) were found.

(14) Arch of Titus: The arch was erected by Domitian to commemorate the victories of his father Vespasian and his brother Titus in the Judaean War. In the interior of the arch are well-preserved reliefs showing, on one side, the goddess Roma guiding the emperor's triumphal quadriga with a winged figure of Victory, and, on the other side, the triumphal procession with war booty from Jerusalem (including the Menorah, or seven-branched candlestick). The frieze on the exterior shows another procession with the vanquished Jordan being carried on a stretcher.

THE PALATINE HILL

Map p. 241, D4–C4. Open daily 9–dusk. Ticket valid also for the Colosseum. Entrance from the Roman Forum or Via di San Gregorio.

The story of the Palatine stretches further back than history or even archaeology can penetrate, into the realms of legend. Traces of settlements going back to the 9th century BC have been found here, but those early inhabitants stir the imagination far less than the mythical Romulus and Remus, twin sons of Mars and the errant Vestal Virgin Rhea Sylvia. Abandoned as infants, they were nursed by a she-wolf until a shepherd from the Palatine found them and took them in. When they grew up they quarrelled over where to found a new city; Romulus killed Remus, and founded his city on the Palatine, naming it after himself. He became the first king of Rome on 21st April 753.

In the days of the Roman Republic, the Palatine was a prestigious residential district, home to prominent citizens (including Cicero) and even emperors, beginning with the first ruler to bear the title, Augustus. The central summit, the *Palatium*, was occupied by the residence now known as the Palace of Domitian, and the word Palatium gave us our word palace. After the fall of the Western Empire in 476 AD, the victorious Odoacer took up residence on the Palatine, as did his successor Theodoric, before his removal to Ravenna (*see p. 152*). During the Middle Ages, a few churches were built here, and some noble families chose to build their castles over the ruins. In the 16th century the northwest part of the hill was laid out for the Farnese with a villa and formal gardens.

The area at the southwestern edge of the hill is the most ancient. Here are traces of the first defensive wall (supposedly built by Romulus). The bases of three huts from the early Iron Age (8th century BC) were found here in the 1940s (they are now protected by iron roofs). A reconstruction of the settlement is exhibited in the Palatine Museum (*see below*). Also in this part of the hill is the **House of Augustus** (*visitors are admitted in small groups, and there can be a long wait*), which was used by the emperor as a private residence after 30 BC. Visitors are shown an upper-floor room with extremely fine paintings on the walls and ceiling, and a suite of lower-floor rooms, also with vivid wall paintings.

The eastern half of the hill is covered by the ruins of the vast **Palace of Domitian**, laid out in AD 81–96 over a number of earlier constructions. Among these was Nero's first palace, the Domus Transitoria, from which a long, narrow underground corridor survives. The part of the complex known as the **Domus Flavia**, was, if we are to believe the ancient poets, splendid in the extreme. Little enough remains today, though the fragments of stonework stacked around the perimeters of the ruins give some clue to its former opulence. The central courtyard with its fountain in the form of an octagonal maze can still be recognised. To the north of this was the **Aula Regia**, or imperial throne room, where the emperor presided over meetings and received embassies.

The **Palatine Museum** houses finds from excavations on the hill, including material from the earliest settlements to fine terracotta panels, fragments of statuary, wall paintings and pavements from Roman days. The 1st-century AD graffito of a man worshipping a crucified donkey is a famous early sneer at Christianity.

The eastern part of the palace, at a lower level, is the so-called **Stadium**, an enclosed area 160m long, with a curved wall at the south. It is thought that it was used as a hippodrome, and that the high exedra in the middle of the east wall functioned as a sort of royal box. The oval outline in stone is from a construction of the Middle Ages.

THE COLOSSEUM

Map p. 241, E4. Open daily 9–dusk. Ticket valid also for the Palatine. If you want to visit the Colosseum first, it is nevertheless a good idea to buy your ticket at the Forum or Palatine, where queues are much shorter. With your ticket, you can go straight into the Colosseum.

The Colosseum takes its familiar name from a towering statue of Nero as Apollo that once stood on this site. Nevertheless, the theatre's own dimensions are colossal: the largest amphitheatre ever built by the Romans, it was begun by Vespasian in AD 70 and completed by his son Titus in AD 80. The opening ceremony famously lasted for 100 days, during which time 5,000 beasts were killed. The toll of human lives is unrecorded. Gladiatorial combats were prohibited only in AD 483 and wild animal hunts in AD 523. The Roman appetite for animal slaughter knew few if any bounds. The extinction of the north African elephant, it is said, was due entirely to the games.

During the Middle Ages the Colosseum fell into disrepair as its stone was pillaged for other buildings; some of its travertine (used for the outer wall and load-bearing pillars) was even employed in the construction of St Peter's. The travertine blocks were originally held together with iron clamps that were torn out and melted down in the Middle

Ages for the production of arms and tools. The conspicuous holes in the exterior today mark the places where the clamps once were. The building rises four storeys tall, with three consecutive orders of engaged columns—Tuscan Doric at the bottom, Ionic in the middle and Corinthian at the top. This progression was subsequently taken as a rule by Renaissance architects. The topmost storey has composite pilasters. The corbels projecting from this upper level supported wooden poles that held the awning (*velarium*) to shade the audience from the sun. The ground-floor arches (there are 80 in total) were all numbered, and were used as entrances (the number would be indicated on the spectators' tickets, much as in a modern opera house). The wider, northeast entrance was used by the emperor, who shared a podium with senators, priests and Vestals—whom chastity must have made hardy: they were compelled to attend these spectacles of gore.

The interior of the Colosseum is of brick-faced concrete and tufa. You ascend shallow, steep steps (typical of ancient Roman theatre construction) to the cavea, divided into three tiers. In the lowest tier sat the knights (*equites*); in the middle, Roman citizens; at the top, plebeians, women and slaves. It is difficult to stand in this space without a thought for the lives that ended in agony here, or without wondering from how far away the roar of the crowd could be heard when the games were in full spate. The *arena* has been partially reconstructed. It takes its name from the sand ('arena') that covered the wooden floor to keep the gladiators from slipping and to soak up the blood. Beneath are underground passages and substructures for animals and scenery, which were hoisted up through trap doors.

THE ARCH OF CONSTANTINE

This famous and beautiful triumphal arch (*map p. 241, D4*) commemorates Constantine's victory over his rival, the emperor Maxentius, at the historic Battle of the Milvian Bridge in AD 312. The arch is decorated in part with splendid reliefs and sculptures taken from earlier monuments, and partly with sculpture of the age of Constantine. The latter examples are noticeably more stylised, and for this reason some critics have seen the monument as exemplifying the decline of the arts in late Antiquity. To dismiss it so sweepingly, however, is to miss its grandeur as well as to miss the point.

The battle scenes decorating the top of the short sides come from the Forum of Trajan (*see below*) and are thought to be by the same artist who carved Trajan's column. The eight medallions of the two long façades belong to the time of Hadrian and illustrate hunting scenes and sacrifices. At the very top, on both of the long sides, are four rectangular reliefs, taken (like the three in Palazzo dei Conservatori; *see p. 239*) from a monument to Marcus Aurelius. They represent a sacrifice, speeches to the army and the people, the departure of the emperor, and his triumphal entry into Rome. The narrow friezes above the lateral arches, the two roundels on the short sides with the personifications of the sun (the god Sol driving the solar chariot) and the moon (the goddess Luna, likewise with a chariot), the spandrel figures flanking the arches as well as the victories and captives at the base of the columns, were carried out at the time of Constantine. They are more stylised, certainly, and to modern tastes less masterful (hence the criticism of the arch). But the reasons for the use of earlier sculpture have less to do with the decline of the arts that with Constantine's desire to impress. By juxtaposing the various reliefs he likened himself to his most illustrious predecessors, under whose rule the empire had reached its greatest extent and stability. The likeness is not only implicit, but explicit too. In the relief where the emperor is shown addressing his troops (top of the south side), the face of what was Marcus Aurelius has been resculpted and given the familiar beaky nose of Constantine. The hieratic figures surrounding the emperor in the two friezes of the north façade reflect the new court etiquette with its ceremonial gestures and codified behaviour, and seem to anticipate early medieval art. The aim, in other words, was to convey a symbol rather than a convincing representation of reality, and the style of the sculpture belongs entirely to the artistic tradition as it was developing around this time. One need only look at the portrait bust of Constantine's mother, Helen, in the Palazzo Nuovo (*see p. 244*) to appreciate its Byzantinesque quality. Representations of the emperor and his family were no longer concerned with being realistic or heroic as they had been in the Republican and Imperial eras. Instead they were moving towards a representation of the emperor as a kind of higher being.

THE IMPERIAL FORA

Under Julius Caesar, the Roman Forum became less a market-place and more a civic centre, with large public buildings and a basilica bearing Caesar's name. His building projects also spilled northwards, beyond the Curia, where he constructed another forum, once again bearing his name, and containing a **temple dedicated to Venus**, from whom he claimed descent (and hence legitimacy). His successor Augustus, the first Roman emperor, continued the expansion into what is now known as the Imperial Fora. He was an astute propagandist. Not only did he hang a golden shield in the Curia celebrating his valour, probity, clemency and piety, but he also erected monuments that explicitly celebrated his achievements: his **Temple of Mars Ultor** (the 'Avenger') was built after Caesar's assassins, Brutus and Cassius, were defeated at the Battle of Philippi.

The fora built by the succeeding emperors, Vespasian, Nerva and Trajan, extend along the north side of Via dei Fori Imperiali, a processional avenue laid out by Mussolini in 1933. The **Forum of Trajan** stretches around the base of his famous column (*map p. 240, C3*). The column is a masterpiece of Roman art, commemorating Trajan's conquest of Dacia (modern Romania). The shaft is decorated by a spiral frieze, 200m long, depicting episodes in his campaigns (AD 101–02 and 105–06). After his death in AD 117, his ashes were kept in the column base. The statue of the emperor that originally crowned the column was replaced in 1587 by a statue of St Peter, just as two years later the statue of Marcus Aurelius on top of his, very similar column (*map p. 240, C1*) was replaced by a statue of St Paul.

Conspicuous also are the **Markets of Trajan**, an arcaded brick hemicycle of 150 rooms. This was the administrative centre of the fora, with shops on the ground floor. It is now a museum of ancient architecture (*open daily 9–7, last entry 1hr before closing*).

THE CAELIAN & AVENTINE

South of the Palatine Hill rise the Caelian and the Aventine, which together form the southernmost range of the original 'Seven Hills' of Rome. They are both mainly residential districts today, the Aventine particularly leafy and peaceful after the helter skelter of the streets below. It was on the Caelian Hill that Gregory the Great founded his monastery, on the site of his family house, and his church (**San Gregorio Magno**; *just beyond map p. 241, D4*) still stands there today. It was Pope Gregory who sent Augustine on his mission to evangelise the English.

The Aventine Hill is separated from the Palatine by the wide expanse of the **Circus Maximus** (*map p. 240, C4*). Little or nothing remains of the stonework, but the shape of the stadium is perfectly preserved. It was the largest ever built by the Romans, and was used for chariot races, gladiatorial combats, imperial ceremonies and as a hippodrome. Some way beyond the Circus Maximus, reached along Viale delle Terme di Caracalla, are the superbly preserved **Baths of Caracalla** (*beyond map p. 241, D4; Viale delle Terme di Caracalla 52; open daily 9–dusk, Mon 9–2; last entry 1hr before closing. To get there, Metro Line B to Circo Massimo and then walk, or bus 628 'Baronio' from the Theatre of Marcellus; map p. 240, B3*). These, the most luxurious of the many bath complexes of ancient Rome, were begun by the emperor Caracalla in AD 212, and fed by a purpose-built aqueduct. The extant ruins consist of a large rectangular central hall surrounded by a swimming pool, gymnasia, changing rooms and the vast, vaulted calidarium and tepidarium. We know from literary sources that the baths were exceptionally fine: writers speak of enormous marble columns, coloured marble pavements, glass and marble mosaics, frescoes, stuccoes and hundreds of statues set in niches or standing freely in the large halls and gardens. Excavations have yielded some extremely fine works of art now dispersed among public and private collections the world over. Some of the best are in the archaeological museum in Naples (*see p. 318*). Fragmentary mosaics—some figurative, others purely geometric, but all astonishingly beautiful—can still be seen *in situ* amidst the ruins. The baths fell into disuse in the 6th century, but their hold on the imagination has never slackened. Shelley composed *Prometheus Unbound* amid the ruins. Numerous architects have drawn inspiration from them, from Bramante and Palladio in the 16th century, to McKim, Mead & White (Pennsylvania Station, New York, 1910), and Philip Johnson and John Burgee (former AT&T Building, New York, 1986) in the 20th. Today they provide a magnificent setting for the summer season of the Rome opera.

THE PANTHEON & WEST OF THE CORSO

The long, busy **Via del Corso** (*map p. 240, C2–B1*) is always thick with traffic and thronged with pedestrians, jostling to get past each other on the narrow pavements, or dawdling to look in the shop windows. It runs northwards to Piazza del Popolo (*described on p. 264*), and is lined by grand but grimy *palazzi*. The finest of all these is the Palazzo Doria Pamphilj.

Galleria Doria Pamphilj

A visit to this gallery (*map p. 240, C2; open Fri–Wed 10–5; good tearoom*) is highly recommended. Not only because it contains some exceptionally fine artworks, but also
because of the building itself, which is still the family home, and which has a number of grandly decorated rooms. The collection was begun in 1651 by the Pamphilj
pope Innocent X (1644–55) and inherited by his nephew Camillo, a great lover of art
in his own right, who added to his family's holdings by marriage into the wealthy
Aldobrandini clan.

*NB: The audio guide, narrated by a member of the family, is idiosyncratic and enjoyable. The
works of art that are hung in the four wings around the central courtyard, in crowded 18th-
century style, are not captioned (though they do carry inventory numbers). If you wish to
identify them, ask for a list at the ticket office.*

There are some outstanding works of both painting and sculpture in the collection.
The sculptures include a bust (1646–47) by Alessandro Algardi of the formidable
Olimpia Maidalchini, the mother of Camillo Pamphilj. Not only is the character of
this redoutable dame amply rendered, but the handling of the material is astonishing.
The peaked, billowing widow's veil is rendered with exceptional virtuosity. The same
is true of the ruff worn by Benedetto Pamphilj (son of Camillo), another bust by the
same sculptor, also displayed in the gallery. Algardi was eclipsed in his own day (probably unfairly) by Bernini, whose bust of Pope Innocent X is displayed in the small cabinet off the Gallery of Mirrors, together with Velázquez's famous portrait of 1650. The
character of this stern but strangely weak man, morally irreproachable but unable to
trust others, hag-ridden by his sister-in-law Olimpia, his side repeatedly punctured by
the thorn of Cardinal Mazarin, has been admirably captured by the artist. When Pope
Innocent saw the likeness he is said to have exclaimed 'Alas, it is all too true!'

Most famous—and rightly so—among the paintings (apart from the Velázquez portrait) are two works by Caravaggio, hung side by side in the 'Room of the 600s'. The
Rest on the Flight into Egypt (c. 1595) is an extraordinary work, its iconography completely original. All the focus is on the figure of an angel, positioned with his back to
us, playing a tune on the fiddle while St Joseph holds his score. On the other side the
exhausted mother and Child sit tenderly locked in sleep. The work was much criticised at the time, because its content was deemed unsuitable to its theme. Most commentators today are charmed by it. The music has even been identified as a real motet,
a Flemish setting of a passage from the *Song of Songs*. The same model who sat for the
Virgin has been used for the *Penitent Magdalen* (c. 1597). The composition of this
work is masterly: the girl sits desolate in the corner of a cheerless room, one shaft of
light far above her head, her jewels and unguent jar discarded by her side. The four
rooms that make up this wing of the gallery, with works from the 15th–18th centuries
(largely by Italian, with some Flemish, artists), contain many other equally excellent
works, and one can happily linger here for some time.

Between the Corso and the Pantheon

Immediately behind the Doria Pamphilj palace is the Collegio Romano, a Jesuit training college. Attached to it is the church of **Sant'Ignazio** (*map p. 240, C2*), facing what must be one of the most exquisite Rococo squares ever built. The curve and sweep of the buildings is so theatrical that you might almost believe you had stumbled onto a stage set. The church (*open daily 7.30–12.30 & 4–7*) was begun in 1626 to celebrate the canonisation of Ignatius Loyola, founder of the Jesuit Order. The façade, the work of a Jesuit mathematician, takes its inspiration from that of the Gesù (*see p. 261*). Another Jesuit, Andrea Pozzo, produced the magnificent *trompe l'oeil* frescoes in the interior, the chief glory of the church. Adorning the nave ceiling are allegories of the Jesuits' missionary work, with the *Triumph of St Ignatius* in the centre. A yellow disc in the floor of the nave marks the spot from where the 'dome' is best viewed. Funds ran out and there is no dome, but to the casual eye Pozzo's impression of one is pretty convincing.

Immediately north of Piazza Sant'Ignazio is Piazza di Pietra. An outside table at the café and tearoom here (excellent freshly-brewed tea and good pastries) makes the perfect spot from which to admire the worn fluted columns of the Chamber of Commerce building, formerly a **temple of Hadrian** (AD 145). From here walk west along Via Pastini to reach the Pantheon.

The Pantheon

The incomparable Pantheon (*map p. 240, B2; open Mon–Sat 8.30–7.30, Sun 9–6, holidays 9–1*) should surely be considered one of the extant wonders of the world. No matter how many times one visits it, one never fails to be astounded. The building's superb state of preservation is due to the fact that it was converted into a church in the early 7th century, the first Roman temple to be accorded the distinction.

What you see when you view the Pantheon from the piazza in front of it is a massive, circular building in brick fronted by a tall pedimented temple front, with three rows of granite columns topped by marble capitals. One barely notices the dome; certainly the exterior view gives you no idea of what you will see inside. On the pediment is an inscription: M. AGRIPPA L.F. COS. TERTIUM FECIT (Marcus Agrippa, son of Lucius, consul for the third time, had this made). This was set up by Hadrian, who finished the existing temple in AD 128, in honour of Agrippa, whose original pantheon, a shrine to all the gods, had been built in 27 BC to commemorate the victory over Antony and Cleopatra at the Battle of Actium (where Agrippa had been commander of the Roman fleet). Hadrian retained the name, but not the design, of that first temple. Indeed it is probable that the current Pantheon was built to plans drawn up by Hadrian himself, who was a keen amateur architect.

The vast, lofty interior cannot fail to make an impact. Light streams into the building from the great central (unglazed) oculus, picking out the yellow of the *giallo antico* marble and the reds of the *pavonazzetto* and the porphyry. Part of the marble cladding

The coffered dome of the Pantheon, 43.3m in both height and diameter, with its central oculus (almost 9m across). This is the largest vault ever built in unreinforced concrete.

of the walls is the original. The pavement was relaid in the 19th century, but the design is also original. The height and diameter of the interior are the same (43.3m): if the dome were rotated on its horizontal axis, it would exactly touch the floor. The coffered vault is made of what a modern mason would call hydraulic concrete, a material that the Romans invented by mixing lime and gravel with *pozzolana*, a volcanic ash from Pozzuoli near Naples. This hardened into a substance that was at once extremely light, extremely strong, and completely water-resistant. The dome of the Pantheon was the largest ever constructed, and retained that title until the late 19th century—though to this day it remains the largest dome in unreinforced concrete.

The original function of the Pantheon as a national shrine has been to a large extent retained. The aedicules around the walls have been turned into chapels with the royal tombs of Vittorio Emanuele II (d. 1878) and Umberto I (d. 1900); and, most famously, the tomb of Raphael (d. 1520).

Santa Maria sopra Minerva

The Dominican church of Santa Maria sopra Minerva (*map p. 240, B2; open 8–7*) stands, as its name suggests, on the site of a temple to Minerva. In front of it is the famous elephant, designed by Bernini to support an obelisk taken from a nearby temple of Isis. The interior of the church is Gothic, a rarity in Rome. It was built (according to Vasari) by two friars, Sisto and Ristoro, who were also the architects of Santa Maria Novella in Florence. The Florentine connection continues with the frescoes by Filippino Lippi in the south transept (Carafa Chapel; 1489) of scenes from the life of the Dominican saint Thomas Aquinas; with the tombs of the two great Medici popes, Leo X and Clement VII in the chancel; and with the tomb of another Dominican, Fra' Angelico, who died in the friary here in 1455. By the chancel steps is Michelangelo's *Risen Christ* (1514–21). The body of St Catherine of Siena (*see pp. 216–17*) lies beneath the high altar.

THE ESQUILINE HILL

The Esquiline Hill (*map p. 241, E3–F3*), together with the Palatine, is one of the oldest-inhabited places in Rome. In Republican and Imperial days Pompey had a house here, which was later taken over by Mark Antony. The poet Virgil also lived here, as did the great patron of the arts Maecenas. Where Maecenas' villa had once stood Nero built his famous **Domus Aurea**, his 'Golden House', a vast and luxurious palace and pleasure dome extending over 50 hectares. When its remains were first discovered underground in the 1490s, they caused an instant sensation, and the style of decoration of the walls and vaults, known as *grottesche* (*see p. 395*), was much imitated. (*Restorations are periodically underway at the site; for information and to book a visit, T: 06 3996 7700; closed Mon*).

San Pietro in Vincoli

The famous basilican church of St Peter ad Vincula (*map p. 241, E3; open daily 8–12.30 & 3–6 or 7*) is famed for two great possessions: the chains with which St Peter is said to have been shackled in the Mamertine Prison (*map p. 246*), and Michelangelo's

Moses. The chains are displayed in the confessio beneath the high altar. The *Moses* (part of the unfinished monument to Pope Julius II at the end of the south aisle) is massive in its proportions and highly Mannerist in its rendering of the human form. It was carved c. 1515. The unfinished *Slaves* in Florence (*see p. 187*) were also to have formed part of this monument, of which no complete plan survives so it has been impossible to reconstruct it. Vasari praised the *Moses* for its awe-inspiring appearance (the two horns represent beams of light). Pope Julius is not buried here; he lies beneath the pavement of St Peter's.

Santa Maria Maggiore

There is something to be said for arriving at Santa Maria Maggiore (*map p. 241, F2; open daily 7–8*) early in the morning, as it is popular with coach parties and thus best enjoyed before their arrival. This is one of the four great patriarchal basilicas of Rome, and it retains far better than any of the others its ancient magnificence and atmosphere of spiritual mystery. Founded in the mid-4th century, the basilica was rebuilt and dedicated to the Virgin after the Council of Ephesus declared her to be the Mother of God (Theotokos) in 431. The chief glory of the interior are the **mosaics in the nave**, contemporary with this rebuilding, which show scenes from the lives of Abraham and Moses to left and right, and scenes from the life of Christ over the triumphal arch. Though the mosaic in the apse, showing the Virgin and Christ enthroned, is the logical culmination of the cycle, it is in fact much later (late 13th century).

Betraying a completely different aesthetic from the mosaics are the lavish **chapels of Sixtus V and Paul V**. That of the former (Cappella Sistina; end of right-hand aisle) dates from 1585, the work of Domenico Fontana, Pope Sixtus's favourite architect. It is to this pope that we owe the strategic resiting of Rome's Egyptian obelisks, including the one outside this church, which he brought from the mausoleum of Augustus (Augustus had, in turn, brought it from Egypt). At the end of the left aisle is the burial chapel of pope Paul V (Camillo Borghese), created in 1611. Just to the right of the high altar steps is the simple **tomb slab of Gian Lorenzo Bernini**.

Santa Pudenziana and Santa Prassede

Close to Santa Maria Maggiore are two other churches with exceptionally fine early Christian mosaics. **Santa Pudenziana** (*map p. 241, E2; open 8.30–12 & 3–6, Sun and holidays 9–12 & 3–6*) is dedicated to Pudentiana, a daughter of the Roman senator Pudens, who is thought to have offered lodging to St Peter in his house on this site. The apse mosaic of c. 390 is a fascinating illustration of how pagan iconography evolved to embrace the new religion: here we see a regal Christ presiding over a gathering of the Apostles in the same way as an emperor would have presided over the senate. The larger church of **Santa Prassede** (*map p. 241, F2; Via di Santa Prassede 9/a; open Mon–Sat 7–12.30 & 4–6.30, Sun 7.30–12.30*) is dedicated to Pudentiana's sister Praxedes. It is especially remarkable for the third south chapel (Chapel of St Zeno; on the left as you enter), the most important work of its date still surviving in the city. It was built by Pope Paschal I in the early 9th century as a mausoleum for his mother,

Theodora, and is covered inside and out with superb mosaics. The entrance is adorned with mosaic busts—Christ and the Apostles in the outer row; the Virgin and Child and female saints, including possibly Praxedes and Pudentiana, in the inner. Inside, the golden vault bears a roundel with Christ the Victor borne aloft by four angels, another example of pagan iconography—the triumphant general carried on his shield by winged Victories—being adopted for Christian purposes. Among the other saints depicted in the interior, you can recognise St Theodora by her square halo, indicating that she was still alive at the time the mosaics were made.

San Clemente

San Clemente is a beautiful and ancient small basilica (*map p. 241, F4; open 9–12.30 & 3–6 or 6.30, Sun 10–12.30 & 3–6 or 6.30*) preserving three clear strata of history. It consists of two superimposed churches, in turn built over the remains of a house of the 1st century AD. The upper church was begun in 1108, and has a magnificent apse mosaic of that time. The **Chapel of St Catherine** at the head of the north aisle contains important frescoes of the lives of St Catherine and St Ambrose, painted in 1428–31 by Masolino for Cardinal Branda Castiglione, who was titular cardinal of this church, and who also employed Masolino in his home town in Lombardy. The detail of the executioner sheathing his sword is similar in both cycles (*see p. 52*).

In the lower church are remains of frescoes from the 9th–11th centuries. Below this again are the remains of the ancient house. The most fascinating remains are not those of the house itself, but of the later **temple to Mithras** (2nd–3rd century). The cave-triclinium with its altar relief of Mithras slaying the bull is extremely well preserved (*for the cult of Mithras, see p. 280*).

St John Lateran

Beyond map p. 241, F4. Open daily 7–6 or 7. Baptistery open 7–12.30 & 4–7.30. Walk up Via di S. Giovanni in Laterano or take bus 117 which goes up Via Labicana to the basilica. The great church of St John Lateran, the cathedral of Rome and mother church of the whole Christian world, stands in a busy, unattractive part of the city, but deserves to be visited nonetheless. Constantine gave the land here to the pope, the bishop of Rome, very shortly after his edict officially condemning the persecution of Christians, and instructed that a church be built here. This was the first Christian basilica in the city, and until their move to Avignon in 1305, the Lateran Palace was the residence of the popes. Upon the popes' return in 1377, the Holy See was transferred to the Vatican.

The building has been remodelled many times. Its **main doors** are particularly special, being the original ancient Roman bronze doors from the Curia Julia in the Forum (*see p. 245*), transferred here in the 17th century. The present interior aspect is due in part to Borromini, who reconstructed the nave and aisles between 1646 and 1657. At the end of the nave is the confessio, with the tomb slab of Martin V, the pope who ended the Great Schism (*see p. 237*), and a Gothic baldacchino, above which are silver reliquaries said to contain the heads of St Peter and St Paul. On the first pier of the inner south aisle is a fresco fragment attributed to Giotto, showing Pope Boniface VIII proclaiming the first Holy Year (1300). The Holy Years had an enormous impact on pilgrimage in the medieval world: all those who made the journey to Rome during a Holy Year were promised temporal forgiveness of their crimes and transgressions. The opportunity to avoid a fine, a jail sentence or even the noose prompted many to make the trek.

The **cloister** (*entered from the north aisle; entry fee*) is very fine, a masterpiece of Cosmatesque art by Jacopo and Pietro Vassalletto (1222–32). This decorative technique, whereby fragments of ancient stone are arranged in geometric patterns to adorn floors, walls or other surfaces, is particularly widespread in Rome, and this is one of the best examples. It is named after the Cosmati family, who were its finest practitioners.

The **baptistery** (*entered from outside*) was built by Constantine on the site of a Roman villa and bath house. These were not, however, the baths where he infamously had his wife Fausta suffocated to death, nor was this the site of his baptism. It was, however, the only baptistery in Rome until the 4th century. Its octagonal form comes from a later remodelling.

On the east side of Piazza San Giovanni is an important survival from the old Lateran palace: the **Scala Santa** (now housed in a late 16th-century building by Domenico Fontana). In the 15th century the marble staircase of the old palace was declared to be the very staircase of the palace of Pontius Pilate which Christ descended after his condemnation, and which had allegedly been brought to Rome from Jerusalem by St Helen, mother of Constantine. The steps are now protected by boards, and worshippers are only permitted to ascend them on their knees. At the top is the Sancta Sanctorum, the private chapel of the popes.

THE CAMPUS MARTIUS OR RENAISSANCE QUARTER

This part of Rome, the land that juts out into a steep bend of the Tiber, was used in ancient times for naval arsenals and military drills (hence the name, 'field of Mars', an idea that Napoleon was to borrow for his new imperial Paris). It was not built up in any density until the 15th–16th centuries, which explains its other name: the 'Renaissance quarter'. The age of the Counter-Reformation witnessed the construction of important churches (notably the Gesù).

Piazza Navona

The dimensions of this famous 'square' (*map p. 240, A2*) reflect its origins as the Stadium of Domitian, inaugurated in AD 86. Haphazard building took place around the periphery, and it was not until the pontificate of Innocent X (1644–55) that today's piazza took on any ordered form. Pope Innocent oversaw the construction of an imposing palace (today the Brazilian Embassy) and set about transforming the square into a suitably stately milieu. Of all the popes whose reigns were spanned by Bernini's active life, Innocent X is the one who least admired his style. It is said, though, that when he saw the sculptor's designs for the **Fountain of the Four Rivers** in 1648, he was instantly smitten and ordered that work begin forthwith. The fountain is, after the Trevi, the most famous in Rome. The design is Bernini's, though most of the carving was carried out by his assistants. Seated on a massive travertine rock are four marble figures personifying the greatest rivers of the four continents then known. The Ganges (pictured with an oar) represents Asia; the Nile (with his head covered, as its source was as yet undiscovered) stands for Africa; the Rio de la Plata (with a heap of coins symbolising the wealth of the New World) represents America; and the Danube (with a horse) symbolises Europe. The rock is surmounted by an obelisk, made in Egypt but with hieroglyphs cut on the orders of Domitian, referring to himself as 'eternal pharaoh'. The bronze dove that surmounts it is the Pamphilj family emblem.

Bernini's rival Borromini provided the church of Sant'Agnese with its distinctive façade in 1653. A little further to the east is the church of **Sant'Ivo**, entered through a courtyard (*map p. 240, B2*). The spiral tower is another, much better, example of Borromini's extraordinary originality.

San Luigi, Sant'Agostino and Palazzo Altemps

The churches of Rome still exist, first and foremost, as places of worship (unlike those of Florence and, increasingly, Venice, which behave more like museums), and there is an awkwardness about going into one just to look at the art. The number of visitors doing precisely that, each clutching their guidebook, is increasing, and it is important to be respectful and circumspect. Two churches near Piazza Navona contain master-pieces by Caravaggio. **San Luigi dei Francesi** (*map p. 240, B2; open 10–12.30 & 2.30–7 except Thur pm*) is the church of the French community in Rome. In a chapel in the north aisle are three paintings which many consider to be Caravaggio's masterpiece: the *Calling of Matthew*, *Martyrdom of Matthew* and *Matthew and the Angel*, painted in 1597–1603 for the situation they occupy today. The church of **Sant'Agostino** (*map p. 240, B1; open Mon–Sat 7–1 & 4.30–7.30, Sun and holidays 7–1 & 3.30–7.30*), dedicated to St Augustine and containing the tomb of his mother, St Monica, has Caravaggio's lovely *Madonna di Loreto* in the first north chapel. The dirty bare feet of the two kneel-ing pilgrims caused some offence when the work was first unveiled in 1604.

The 15th–16th-century **Palazzo Altemps** (*map p. 240, A1; open Tues–Sun 9–7.45*), part of the Museo Nazionale Romano, displays the Ludovisi collection of Classical sculp-ture. Cardinal Ludovico Ludovisi began the collection in 1621, and commissioned Bernini and Algardi to restore many of the pieces. Restoration in many cases meant com-pleting them: adding missing limbs and heads to ancient fragments, often in attitudes that are purely the restorer's conjecture. One of the best examples of this is the *Torch-bearer* (*Dadoforo*), created by Algardi from an antique torso. The three greatest master-pieces of the collection are on the first floor. The famous *Ludovisi Ares* (2nd century BC), for centuries believed to show the god of war (Ares/Mars), is now placed beside a female statue as some scholars believe that the two belong together and are in fact the very sculptural group of Achilles with his mother Thetis described by Pliny as adorning the Temple of Neptune in the Campus Martius. The restorations to the statue in Italian Carrara marble (the statue itself is of Greek Pentelic marble) were carried out by Bernini. They include the little figure of Eros, added when the statue was believed to depict Mars, because the god of war, when at rest, would naturally turn to amatory pleasures. The

Galatian Committing Suicide, a 1st-century BC Roman copy of a Greek bronze, is a companion piece to the *Dying Gaul* in the Capitoline Museums (*see p. 244*). The *Ludovisi Throne*, a Greek work from the 5th century BC (its function is unknown, but it is unlikely to have been a throne), bears a beautiful stylised relief of the Birth of Aphrodite.

Campo de' Fiori, Piazza Farnese and the Gesù

The famous market-place of **Campo de' Fiori** (*map p. 240, A2–A3*), the liveliest and most accessible in Rome, stands on the site of a temple of Venus, which was part of a huge complex that made up the Theatre of Pompey, the site of Julius Caesar's murder in 44 BC. The line of the theatre's cavea can clearly be traced in Piazza Biscione; the site of the fatal stabbing was further to the east, near the ruins of temples in Largo Torre Argentina, which formed a sacred area that was also part of the theatre complex. The statue in the centre of Campo dei Fiori commemorates the Neoplatonist philosopher Giordano Bruno, who was burned as a heretic here in 1600.

Southwest of Campo dei Fiori, towards the Tiber, is **Piazza Farnese** (*map p. 240, A3*), laid out by the Farnese family in front of their palace, the finest Renaissance *palazzo* in Rome (now the French Embassy). It was designed by Antonio da Sangallo the Younger, and the upper part was completed after his death in 1546 by Michelangelo. When the palace passed by marriage to the Bourbon rulers of Naples in the 18th century, the famous Farnese collection of antique sculpture was removed to that city (*see p. 318*).

A short walk from Campo dei Fiori in the opposite direction, beyond Largo Torre Argentina, is one of the most important Baroque monuments in Rome, the church of the **Gesù** (*map p. 240, B2–C2; open 7–12.30 & 4–7.45*). It was built in 1568–75 at the expense of Cardinal Alessandro Farnese, grandson of Pope Paul III (who built Palazzo Farnese), and its design—both the façade by Giacomo della Porta and the interior by Vignola—became the prototype for all future Baroque churches. The architecture of the interior is adapted to the ideas of the Counter-Reformation, which sought to give greater prominence to the celebration of the Eucharist, almost as a theatrical spectacle. The church has no aisles: all the attention is focused on the high altar, which is clearly visible by all. The finest work of art in the church is the fresco in the vault, *The Triumph of the Name of Jesus*, a masterpiece of foreshortening by Baciccia (1672–83), showing the monogram of Christ in an upward-tending eddy of divine light. St Ignatius Loyola, the founder of the Jesuit Order, is buried in the north transept, in a sepulchre of extraordinary magnificence by the Jesuit artist and architect Andrea Pozzo.

THE GHETTO & TRASTEVERE

The area occupied by the old **Jewish ghetto**, where the synagogue stands today (*map p. 240, B3*) is still characterised by Kosher bakeries and restaurants serving Roman-Jewish specialities. The ghetto was enclosed between 1556 and 1848. From here one of the most charming footbridges in Italy leads across an arm of the Tiber. This is the **Ponte Fabricio**, a Roman survival of 62 BC, known also as the Ponte dei Quattro Capi from the twin herms of the double-headed Janus. Remains of another Roman bridge, the *Pons Aemilius*, the first stone bridge across the river, dating from the 2nd century BC, can be glimpsed downstream. Only a single arch remains, and it is known today as the Ponte Rotto (Broken Bridge).

The Tiber Island (Isola Tiberina), an easy crossing-place on the river, was settled early in Rome's history. On its further side is Trastevere, *Trans Tiberim*, the district beyond the Tiber. It is mainly a residential district today, full of ordinary Romans going about their daily business, and filled also with the cafés and *trattorie* that cater to them (as well as to tourists). Trastevere is visited by the latter mainly for its churches, which include **Santa Maria in Trastevere** (*map p. 240, A1*), with a superb early apse mosaic of 1140; **San Francesco a Ripa** (*beyond map p. 240, A4*), with Bernini's powerful funerary monument to the Blessed Lodovica Albertoni; and the lovely, tranquil church of **Santa Cecilia** (*map p. 240, B4*), with the famous, exquisite marble statue of the beheaded saint by Stefano Maderno (1600), showing her body lying as it was found when her tomb was opened in 1599. Cecilia, a Roman patrician and Christian convert, was martyred in her house on this site in 230. She was beheaded after an unsuccessful attempt had been made to suffocate her in her own calidarium. A corridor off the south transept of the church leads to the remains of the bath complex, where the old steam ducts can still be seen.

Also in this district is the circular **Tempietto** by Bramante (1502), in the courtyard of San Pietro in Montorio (*beyond map p. 240, A4*). It is an important Renaissance work, simple and harmonious and Clasically-inspired. In the words of Vasari, Bramante 'followed in the footsteps of Brunelleschi and paved the way for those that followed'.

THE QUIRINAL HILL & BAROQUE DISTRICT

The Quirinal Hill (*map p. 240, B1–C1*), site of the summer palace of the popes from the 16th–19th centuries and now occupied by the residence of the President of Italy, is busy and traffic-filled like the district that surrounds it, but leavened by the presence of important churches and the art collection of Palazzo Barberini. The area that stretches more or less from the foot of the hill to Piazza del Popolo is known as the 'Baroque district': its development began in the 16th century. Favoured by artists and visitors in the age of the Grand Tour, the area soon acquired international repute and started filling with hotels, fashionable cafés, art galleries and elegant shops. The **Caffè Greco** at Via Condotti 86 (*map p. 240, C1*) is the example *par excellence* of this. Founded in 1760, and host in its day to Goethe, Berlioz, Stendhal, Baudelaire and Wagner, its little marble-topped tables still purvey refreshment to culture vultures and shop hounds. Via Condotti takes its name from the conduits which channel the waters of the Acqua Vergine, a subterranean aqueduct which feeds the most famous of all the Baroque monuments in Rome, the **Trevi Fountain** (*map p. 240, C1*). This theatrical masterpiece, its stage-set effect enhanced all the more by the small dimensions of the square in which it stands, is by a little-known sculptor, Nicola Salvi, and was completed (after his death) in 1762. The theme of the sculptural ensemble is a marine one, with Neptune flanked by Health and Abundance. The fountain famously features in the films *Roman Holiday* (1953) and *La Dolce Vita* (1959). The custom of tossing a coin into the water is said to ensure a return to Rome.

Piazza di Spagna

Piazza di Spagna (*map p. 240, B3*) has become so famous over the centuries that no matter how crowded, one must see it at least once. It is named after the Spanish embassy to the Vatican, which has occupied a site at the south end of the square since 1622. At the centre of the square, always thronged, is the Fontana della Barcaccia, probably by Bernini (though attributed also to his father). The pink house at the right-hand foot of the Spanish Steps contains the apartment where the poet John Keats died, of tuberculosis, in 1821. It is now the **Keats museum** (*open Mon–Fri 10–1 & 2–6, Sat 11–12 & 3–6*). To the left of the steps are Babington's Tea Rooms. The **Spanish Steps** themselves, which rise from the square like an ascending catwalk, were built in 1723–26 by Francesco de Sanctis to replace steep ramps connecting the piazza with the church of Trinità dei Monti above. This masterpiece of theatrical design, curving along a series of terraces, will be appreciated best by early risers who get here before the crowds.

Sant'Andrea al Quirinale and San Carlo alle Quattro Fontane

These two little churches, situated within a few hundred metres of each other, provide an interesting comparison between the architectural styles of Gian Lorenzo Bernini, whom history remembers as one of the greatest exponents of the Baroque, and his rival Francesco Borromini, whom history remembers as an introverted eccentric and a suicide. If Algardi was eclipsed as a sculptor by Bernini, the same might be said of Borromini as an architect. Bernini's church of **Sant'Andrea** (*map p. 241, D2; open 8–12 & 4–7; closed Tues*) is a very interesting building, its façade an enormous single aedicule, almost masking the curved body of the church behind. This body is not circular; it is elliptical, and the side chapels are not arranged four-square; they depart radially from the nave, thus symbolically echoing the form of the cross of St Andrew, to whom the church is dedicated. The interior is gorgeous with gilding, stucco and pink marble. **San Carlo alle Quattro Fontane** (*map p. 241, E1; usually open 10–1 & 4–6, Sat 10–1, Sun 12–1*), on a cramped corner site, has an undulating façade of alternating concave and convex surfaces echoing the interplay of concave and convex in the interior. The church was commissioned by the order of discalced Trinitarians, and the dome, with its unusual pattern of coffers, bears a dedication to the Holy Trinity and to the titular saint, Charles Borromeo, Archbishop of Milan. The tiny cloister is seen by many as a miniature masterpiece. The supports of the upper balustrade are alternately turned upside down, and the corners of the lower level are not supported by pillars but are left open, thus softening the effect. Borromini makes use of the same technique in the nave, which is rhomboid in shape but given rounded ends.

Palazzo Barberini and its art collection

This palace, built for the Barberini pope Urban VIII, houses part of the Galleria Nazionale d'Arte Antica (*map p. 241, D1; open Tues–Sun 8.30–7.30*). Among its many masterpieces is the ceiling fresco in the first-floor *salone*, the *Triumph of Divine Providence* (1633–39), painted for Pope Urban by Pietro da Cortona. Pietro was also an architect; the façade of the church of SS. Luca e Martino, which overlooks the

Roman Forum (*map p. 246*) is his. But it is for his ceiling frescoes that he is most renowned. Divine providence here refers to the extraordinary good fortune of the Barberini family in having one of their number elected to the pontificate. The emblem of the family, three bees, together with the papal insignia, are shown in the act of being crowned with laurel. Masterpieces of the painting collection include Raphael's *La Fornarina* (1518–19), popularly supposed to be a portrait of his mistress; two important pieces by Caravaggio: *Judith and Holofernes* and *Narcissus*; and Quentin Massys's famous portrait of Erasmus.

Piazza del Popolo

This large, oval-shaped space (*map p. 265, A2*) took shape in the 16th century as part of the planning projects of Pope Sixtus V. On the south side of the piazza he sited the obelisk of Ramesses II, which had been brought to Rome by Augustus from Heliopolis. It was moved to the centre of the square in the 19th century, when the piazza received its fountains. The church of **Santa Maria del Popolo** (*open 7–12 & 4–7, Sun and holidays 8–1.30 & 4.30–7*), of ancient foundation, contains a number of important works of art. The first south chapel (Della Rovere) contains a lovely *Nativity* by Pinturicchio (c. 1484). In the north transept are two masterpieces by Caravaggio (1600–01), the *Conversion of St Paul* and the *Crucifixion of St Peter*. The naturalism and immediacy of Caravaggio's style could hardly be more different from the High Renaissance, idealised approach of Annibale Carracci, whose altarpiece of the *Assumption* is of the same date (1601). In the north aisle is the **Chigi Chapel**, begun by Raphael in 1513 for the Sienese banker Agostino Chigi. Raphael's early death in 1520 brought work to a halt; only the *Birth of the Virgin* over the altar was added (1530s), by Sebastiano del Piombo, a pupil of Bellini, who, it is said, was blocked from important commissions during Raphael's lifetime by the latter artist's jealousy. It was not until over a century later (1652) that another member of the family, Cardinal Fabio Chigi (the future Alexander VII), employed Bernini to complete the chapel. The result is a peculiar mixture of styles: the Classically-inspired, Renaissance designs of Raphael and the demonstrative Baroque of Bernini. The striking pyramidal design of the tombs is Raphael's (though the medallions are additions by Bernini). The design is derived from ancient Roman prototypes, and was famously echoed by Canova in his planned monument to Titian in Venice (*see p. 94*). In the four corners (the near ones are difficult to see) are statues of prophets. *Jonah* (left of the altar) and *Elijah* (by the entrance) were made to Raphael's design by his pupil Lorenzetto. *Habakkuk* (right of the altar) and *Daniel* (by the entrance; with the lion) are by Bernini.

The Mausoleum of Augustus and Ara Pacis

Close to the banks of the Tiber, in Piazza Augusto Imperatore (*map p. 265, A3*), stands the **huge circular tomb** built by Augustus in 28 BC to serve as the burial place of himself and his family. Surrounded now by architecture of the discredited Fascist age, the mausoleum is a sorry memorial to the great emperor. The **Ara Pacis** stands on the banks of the Tiber further north (*open Tues–Sun 9–7; excellent book and gift shop*), pro-

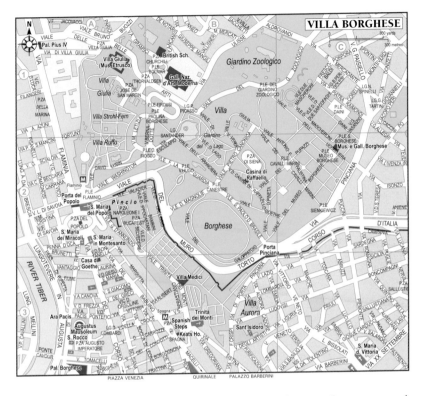

tected by a glass-and-travertine casing designed by Richard Meier. This monumental altar, erected in 13 BC and dedicated to the peace brought to the empire by Augustus, was reconstructed in the 1930s from retrieved fragments and reproductions. The area where the altar stood was once open ground, as is well shown by the model in the museum. Nearby stood an obelisk, brought by Augustus from Heliopolis to commemorate his victory over Cleopatra, and used as the gnomon for a solar calendar (that obelisk now stands in front of the Italian parliament in Piazza di Montecitorio; *map p. 240, B1*). The altar enclosure is a superb example of art of the early Imperial period, and the influence of Greek sculpture is clearly seen. The sacrificial slab itself is screened on four sides by tall stone walls, decorated with fine reliefs. On the entrance wall are a well-preserved scene of sacrifice and a very ruined *Lupercalia*, the Roman festival of purification, celebrated to banish evil spirits and to ensure fertility and health. On the opposite entrance is *Tellus, Goddess of the Earth* (surrounded by animals and children, possibly symbolising peace), and *Rome* (again much damaged). The side panels show the processions at the altar's dedication: on the west flank we see Augustus and members of his family. The family tree and replica busts at the entrance are helpful here, and behind the altar is a well labelled plan of the frieze showing exactly who is who.

GALLERIA BORGHESE

Map p. 265, C2. Open Tues–Sun 8.30–7.30. Advance booking required: T: 06 32810 or www.ticketeria.it. From Piazzale Flaminio, outside Porta del Popolo, take bus 490, 491, 495, 95 or 88 to the S. Paolo del Brasile stop, from where it is a short walk up Viale del Museo Borghese.

Cardinal Scipione Borghese, who built this beautiful suburban villa, was the first important patron of Bernini. He also had a fine collection of works by Caravaggio. His taste is reflected amply in the collection of this, one of the best museums in Rome, home to Bernini's famous *David* (its face a self-portrait), his *Apollo and Daphne* (1622–25; the face of the Apollo is modelled on the *Apollo Belvedere* in the Vatican; *see p. 272*), and his *Rape of Europa*, all three *tours de force* of carving. Six of the cardinal's original twelve Caravaggios still hang here, among them the *Boy with a Basket of Fruit* (the face of the boy, so familiar from Caravaggio's works, may be based on the artist's own, though it is not a self-portrait as such), and the *Madonna dei Palafrenieri*, painted for St Peter's in 1605 but rejected on the grounds of unsuitability (St Anne is portrayed as a rough peasant, and the Christ Child is totally naked). Another well-known work here is Canova's portrait of Pauline Borghese, the beautiful, shameless and dissolute sister of Napoleon, who married into the family in 1803. She is shown in the guise of Venus Victrix, reclining on a couch and holding an apple. Concealed in the base was a mechanism for rotating the sculpture so that the lovely Pauline might be admired from all angles.

The gallery of paintings on the upper floor contains other celebrated and important works: Raphael's *Entombment* (1507) and his *Lady with a Unicorn* (c. 1506). Correggio's titillating *Danaë* is one of a series of such scenes painted for Federico Gonzaga, first Duke of Mantua. Federico was known for his fleshly appetites (it was he who commissioned the Palazzo Te; *see p. 60*). It is said, however, that he intended this work as a gift for the Holy Roman Emperor Charles V, from whom he had received the title of duke in 1530, the year before this work was painted. Titian's *Sacred and Profane Love*, a masterpiece of his early career (1514), is also displayed here.

Galleria Nazionale d'Arte Moderna

This museum, also in the Villa Borghese park (*map p. 265, B1; Viale delle Belle Arti 131; open Tues–Sun 8.30–7.30*), houses an exceptional collection of 19th- and 20th-century Italian art, strong on all the important art movements including the Macchiaioli School, the Novecento, Futurism, Divisionism and Metaphysical painting.

THE VATICAN & ST PETER'S

Rome joined the kingdom of united Italy in 1870. Until that date, it had been the realm of the papacy, not just in spiritual terms but temporally as well. The popes had ruled Rome and its territories as monarchs; Pius IX was the last pope to do so. In exchange for relinquishing his governance, the Vatican State was created, a tiny papal fiefdom including the Vatican palace and gardens and the basilica of St Peter. By the

With Bernini, Classical restraint gives way to emotion and effusion: he is one of the most accomplished masters of Baroque sculpture. Here the nymph Daphne is shown turning into a laurel tree to escape the pursuit of Apollo. Bernini was very fond of depicting people with parted lips: he believed that the exact moment when a person stops speaking, before their mouth fully closes, was the best time to take a likeness.

terms of the separate Vatican Treaty of 1929, the privilege of 'extraterritoriality' was also granted to St John Lateran, Santa Maria Maggiore and the great pilgrimage basilica of San Paolo fuori le Mura, as well as to the papal chancellery in Palazzo della Cancelleria. The Vatican is the smallest independent state in the world, with its own currency, postal service, newspaper, radio station and internet suffix (.va).

Approaches: Ponte Sant'Angelo and St Peter's Square

The route across the Tiber to the Vatican City takes you over **Ponte Sant'Angelo** (*map p. 269, C2*), a wide pedestrian bridge decorated with ten famous wind-tossed angel sculptures, designed by Bernini and executed by his pupils in 1688. Each angel holds one of the Instruments of the Passion (the Cross, scourge, vinegar sponge, crown of thorns, garments and dice, to name but five). Before crossing the bridge, it is worth walking for a short way along the river front until you get a good view of it; for it is in fact extremely fine, a Roman construction of AD 134, built by Hadrian as a grand approach to his vast mausoleum, which still stands on the other side, and is known today as **Castel Sant'Angelo**. The lower part of the mausoleum, up to the first string course, is ancient. The upper section and the battlements date from the Middle Ages, when it became a fortress. It saw service in 1527 during the Sack of Rome by the troops of the emperor Charles V. Pope Clement VII and his cardinals and bishops took refuge here.

From here it is a short (though not terribly pleasant) walk to the head of the long, broad, ceremonious Via della Conciliazione, completed in 1937 and named in honour of the 'conciliatory' treaty of 1929, by which the papacy acknowledged that its territorial losses were irrevocable and the Italian state recognised that the Vatican was independent and exempt from Fascist law. At the end of the street you cross the busy Piazza Pio XII to enter St Peter's Square, contained within the wide white ribcage of Bernini's famous travertine colonnade.

The square is Bernini's architectural masterpiece, built in 1656–67, its semicircular roofed colonnades topped by statues of saints and martyrs. To the right of the basilica is the papal palace. The Pope appears at his study window on Sundays at midday, to deliver a short address and a public blessing.

St Peter's

Map opposite. Basilica open daily 7–7, Oct–March 7–6. The dome can be climbed 8–5 or 6. The Vatican Grottoes (with the tombs of the popes) can be visited 7–6, Oct–March 7–5. Mass is held on Sun at 9, 10.30, 11.30, 12.15, 1, 4, 5, 5.45. Visits are not permitted on Wed mornings. The dome is closed 1 Jan, 1 May, 25 Dec and Easter Sun and Mon. T: 06 6982.

St Peter was martyred under Nero on this spot in AD 65. In 324 the emperor Constantine ordered that a basilica be raised above his burial place. A long process of rebuilding and remodelling began in the 15th century, culminating in the nomination of Michelangelo as master of works in 1546. Michelangelo's church was conceived on a huge scale; he worked here until his death in 1564, at which point he had completed the dome as far as the drum. The dome was finished in 1590 by Giacomo della Porta. The façade is the work of Carlo Maderno. The basilica was finally consecrated in 1626, by Pope Urban VIII, who employed Bernini to supervise the decoration of the interior.

The impact of the interior, vast in its scale and resplendent in coloured marble and mosaic, is overwhelming. On the pavement in front of the central door is the **porphyry disc** on which Charlemagne was crowned in 800 (*see pp. 234 and 237*). Against the last nave pillar on the right, its foot worn shiny by centuries of worshippers, is a **bronze statue of St Peter**, also from the old basilica, attributed to Arnolfo di Cambio (13th century). Apart from these, there is little else from the Middle Ages or the Renaissance. Most things here are grandiose and grandiloquent, Mannerist or Baroque. In the first south chapel is **Michelangelo's *Pietà*** (1499; protected by glass since it was vandalised in 1972). The beautiful young face of the Madonna, gazing with tender pathos at the supine body of her dead son, makes this Michelangelo's most moving work.

The **dome** is supported by four pentagonal piers, each adorned with a statue: St Longinus, the Roman soldier who pierced the side of Christ (by Bernini); St Helen, mother of Constantine, who found the True Cross in Jerusalem; St Veronica, who mopped Christ's brow with her handkerchief on His way to Calvary; and St Andrew. The relics of these saints (the lance of St Longinus, a piece of the True Cross, and the cloth of St Veronica) are preserved in the pier of St Veronica and displayed in Holy

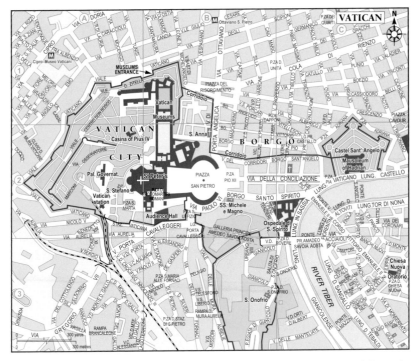

Week. The head of St Andrew was returned to Patras, Greece, at the end of the 20th century. The frieze below the drum bears a Latin inscription of the words pronounced by Jesus to St Peter ('Thou art Peter, and upon this rock I will build my church…. And I will give unto thee the keys of the kingdom of heaven').

Directly under the dome, the **location of St Peter's tomb** is marked by the confessio and surrounded by perpetually burning lamps. Behind this is Bernini's monumental **baldacchino**, completed for Urban VIII in 1633 and cast from bronze taken from the underside of the Pantheon's portico. The canopy is decorated with Pope Urban's heraldic bees.

In the apse is the **Cathedra of St Peter**, executed by Bernini in 1665. It consists of a gilt-bronze throne supported by the statues of Sts Augustine and Ambrose, Fathers of the Latin Church (wearing mitres), and Sts Athanasius and John Chrysostom, Fathers of the Greek Church. The throne encloses an ancient chair of wood with ivory inlay said to have been the episcopal seat of St Peter.

Papal monuments include two by Bernini: that of Urban VIII, clearly influenced by Michelangelo's Medici tombs in Florence; and that of Alexander VII, with its memorable death's head. It was Bernini's last work for St Peter's.

The tombs of the popes, in the **Vatican Grottoes**, are entered from a door in one of the four dome piers. The entrance to the **dome** is on the left side of the portico.

The Vatican Museums

The route to the museums on foot from St Peter's follows the line of the city wall, above which is the **Corridoio**, the raised walkway that links the Vatican with Castel Sant'Angelo. It was used as an escape route by Pope Clement VII during the sack of 1527.

Map p. 269, B1. Viale Vaticano. Access by public transport includes bus 913 from Piazza Augusto Imperatore (map p. 265, A3) to Piazza Cavour (map p. 269, C1), from where bus 49 goes along Via Cola di Rienzo to just outside the museums entrance. Metro line A goes to Ottaviano. The walk from St Peter's Square takes c. 15mins.

Open 8.30–6, last entry 4. Last Sun of the month (free admission) 8.30–2, last entry 12.30. Closed other Sundays and Vatican holidays: 1 Jan, 6 Jan, 11 Feb, 19 March, Easter Sun and Mon, 1 May, Ascension Day, Corpus Christi, 29 June, 14–15 Aug, 1 Nov, 8 Dec, 25–26 Dec. Opening times can be erratic: to check, see www.vatican.va.

The admission ticket is valid for one entry only, not for a full day as at other museums. Many galleries are open on a rotating basis, but the most important ones are rarely closed. The museums are always crowded, and a long queue forms outside the entrance long before the doors open. It is much better to go toward the end of the day, entering just before 4. This leaves c. 2hrs to see the collections. You can also book online in advance; a fee is charged (www.vatican.va).

The flow of visitors through the Raphael Rooms and Sistine Chapel is strictly one-way. If you wish to see the Picture Gallery, you must do so before entering the 'Sistine Route', which begins at the top of the entrance ramp.

The museum has several bookstalls, a cafeteria, a currency exchange office and a post office.

The long entrance ramp brings you up to the Cortile delle Corazze, where the museums begin. Here you have a choice: you can turn right to the Picture Gallery, and then return here to start the Sistine Route, or turn left into the hall known as Quattro Cancelli and start the Sistine Route straight away.

Vatican Picture Gallery

This collection of mainly Italian paintings (**1**), arranged chronologically and by schools, contains some superb masterpieces and has the additional advantage of almost never being crowded. The early works include the Stefaneschi altarpiece, a polyptych by Giotto; two beautiful panels by Fra' Angelico; and a representative collection of works by Melozzo da Forlì, a follower of Piero della Francesca whose style had a formative influence on Roman art of the late 15th century. An entire room is devoted to Raphael; Leonardo's little-known *St Jerome* is also here. There is a *Pietà* by Bellini and a dramatic *Descent from the Cross* by Caravaggio.

The Sistine Route

From the hall called Quattro Cancelli you come to a grand Neoclassical stairway, the Simonetti Staircase, beyond which is the spacious Cortile della Pigna. This takes its name from the huge bronze pine cone (*pigna*) displayed in a large niche. It is a Roman work of the 1st–2nd century AD, made of bronze. It once served as a fountain (holes

VATICAN MUSEUMS

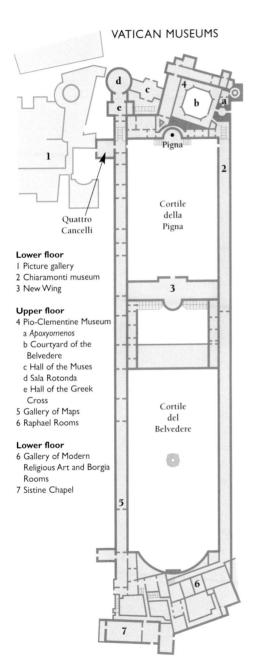

Quattro
Cancelli

Lower floor
1 Picture gallery
2 Chiaramonti museum
3 New Wing

Upper floor
4 Pio-Clementine Museum
  a *Apoxyomenos*
  b Courtyard of the
    Belvedere
  c Hall of the Muses
  d Sala Rotonda
  e Hall of the Greek
    Cross
5 Gallery of Maps
6 Raphael Rooms

Lower floor
6 Gallery of Modern
  Religious Art and Borgia
  Rooms
7 Sistine Chapel

under its scales functioned as water spouts). The large sculpture in the centre of the courtyard is Arnaldo Pomodoro's *Sphere within Sphere* (1990). There are several of them across the world, from New York to Iran.

From the point where you came in, cross the courtyard in a straight line. This brings you into the **Chiaramonti Museum (2)**, a long corridor filled with ancient sculpture and lapidary fragments, arranged in serried ranks. The pieces were organised like this by Canova, and have remained thus ever since. Portrait heads include Cicero, Pompey, Tiberius and Trajan. Exceptional among the works is a colossal head of Athena. The coloured eyes are restorations, but faithfully follow the manner of Greek statuary. This is a Roman copy of a 5th-century BC original, probably of the *Athena Promachos* by Pheidias, which stood on the Athens acropolis.

Beyond the Chiaramonti Museum, the **New Wing (3)** leads off to the right. Chief among its treasures is the *Augustus of Prima Porta*, showing the emperor as a general addressing his troops. The graceful pose, a studied blend of tension and relaxation (one leg supporting the body's weight, the other bent and at ease; one arm 'in use', the other at rest) clearly betrays a debt to Greek sculpture, evident particularly by

The *Apollo Belvedere*, a Roman marble copy of a famous Greek bronze. The forearms are 16th-century additions.

comparison with the famous 5th-century BC *Doryphorus*, which Polyclitus is said to have designed as an illustration of his canon of human proportion, a Roman copy of which also stands here.

Pio-Clementine Museum

Retrace your steps now to the beginning of the Chiaramonti Museum. A stairway decorated with grotesques leads up to the Pio-Clementine Museum (**4**). Beyond the circular vestibule at the top of the stairs is the **Cabinet of the *Apoxyomenos* (a)**. Here stands another Roman copy of another celebrated Greek bronze, this one by Lysippus, of the 4th century BC. It shows an athlete scraping himself down with a strigil. From the circular vestibule you enter the octagonal **Courtyard of the Belvedere (b)**, the former summer pavilion of Pope Julius II. The cabinets at the four short corners all contain world-famous masterpieces. Most famous of the famous is the *Apollo Belvedere*, named after this courtyard, where it has stood since the days of Pope Julius. The original 4th-century BC Greek bronze, of which this is, once again, a Roman copy, stood in the Agora in Athens. The copy was greatly admired in the 17th–19th centuries. Bernini reproduced its features in those of his own Apollo, in the Borghese Gallery (*see p. 267*); Byron writes of it ecstatically in *Childe Harold*, and even—or so said his friend Thomas Moore—began to model his own appearance on the statue. In the opposite corner is the *Laocoön* group, identified as the very statue that Pliny the Elder describes, by a trio of sculptors from Rhodes (1st century BC). Laocoön was a Trojan priest who warned his people that the Wooden Horse was a ruse. In anger, the gods who favoured Greece sent serpents to crush him and his sons. The other two cabinets contain a *Hermes Psychopompos*, conductor of spirits to the Underworld, a Roman copy of a bronze original by Praxiteles; and three works by Canova, produced to replace Classical works purloined by Napoleon. The Perseus clearly owes a debt to the *Apollo Belvedere*.

From here you pass through the 'Animal Room', with a large miscellany of sculptures, some of them restored and 'completed', some of them Roman originals, into the **Hall of the Muses (c)**, which has one of the most famous of all Classical fragments: the *Belvedere Torso*. It is signed by Apollonius, an Athenian sculptor of the 1st century BC. It was studied by many painters and sculptors, including Michelangelo and Raphael. The next room is the **Sala Rotonda (d)**, with a dome modelled on that of the Pantheon. In its centre is a magnificent porphyry dish, beautifully polished and vast in its dimensions (though it was made from a single block). It was found in the Domus Aurea (*see p. 256*). Porphyry is again the material for the two colossal sarcophagi in the next room (**Hall of the Greek Cross; e**), the tomb chests of St Helen, mother of Constantine, and Constantia, Constantine's daughter. The latter tomb is decorated with early Christian symbols of grapes and wine.

The Simonetti Staircase now takes you up a floor. If you go up two floors, you come to the **Etruscan collection** (a fine one, with some splendid jewellery, and the exceptionally well-preserved 4th-century BC bronze statue of a warrior known as the *Mars of Todi*). The Sistine Route takes you along three very long galleries, the **Gallery of Candelabra**, **Gallery of Tapestries** and **Gallery of Maps (5)**. This last is interesting for its early views of 16th-century Italy. They are the work of Egnazio Danti, a Dominican cosmographer and mathematician, and a member of the papal commission to reform the calendar. Rome abandoned the Julian calendar in 1582, naming the new reckoning system after the pope who had called the commission: Gregory XIII.

The Raphael Rooms

The so-called Raphael Rooms **(6; upper floor)** are a series of papal audience chambers begun in the mid-15th century. Julius II (1503–13) continued the work, employing a galaxy of artists, including Perugino and Lorenzo Lotto. When, at the suggestion of Bramante, Pope Julius employed Perugino's pupil Raphael, he was immediately so struck by the young man's talent that he dismissed the other artists, ordered that all earlier frescoes be destroyed, and entrusted the entire programme to Raphael (though the subject matter would not have been of Raphael's devising). The young artist from Urbino worked on the rooms until his death in 1520. The results are what you see today, though unfortunately not very well lit, and because of the strict one-way itinerary, one must visit the rooms in reverse chronological order. Nevertheless, if you want to see an epitome of the ideals of High Renaissance painting, with its harmony of line and idealised Classicism of form and subject matter, look no further than here.

The overall theme of the works is the triumph of the Church. In the first room, the **Sala di Costantino**, we see the Church victorious over paganism: Constantine, fighting under the banner of the Cross, defeats Maxentius at the Battle of the Milvian Bridge. In the **Stanza di Eliodoro** the Church is shown triumphant over its adversaries, be they thieves (Heliodorus), would-be conquerors (Attila the Hun), doubters (the Bohemian priest who doubted the miracle of Transubstantiation until the Host dripped blood at Bolsena in 1263) or secular lawgivers (the Romans who imprisoned St Peter). In each scene we also see a portrait of Julius II or his successor Leo X acting as symbols linking the important triumphs of the Church with contemporary papal successes.

The next room the **Stanza della Segnatura**, where the pope signed bulls and briefs, illustrates the intellectual and philosophical truth and wisdom of the Church. The

Raphael's *School of Athens*, a typical Renaissance piece in its mingling of Classical and Christian know-ledge and virtue (there is nothing Athenian about the vaulted roof, the barrel vault was a later invention). Many of the philosophers depicted are contemporary portraits: Plato's features are modelled on those of Leonardo da Vinci. He stands in the centre pointing upwards to the world of forms. Aristotle holds his plam flat, towards the ground, to indicate his system of logic and empirical enquiry. On the left, wearing armour, is Alexander the Great, with Socrates to his right, balding and in brown. Epicurus is on the far left, crowned with vine leaves. Diogenes sprawls on the steps. In the foreground are Heraclitus (a portrait of Michelangelo) and Pythagoras, both busily writing. On the right, making calculations on a slate, is Euclid (a fitting portrait of Bramante, since Vasari claims that he was 'always doing the abacus'). The young man peeping out on the far right is a self-portrait of Raphael. He portrays himself as Apelles, the famed Greek portraitist of Alexander the Great.

famous scenes are as follows: on the right as you come in is *Parnassus*, with Apollo, the Muses and poets. Opposite the entrance is the *Disputa* or *Triumph of Theology*, where the Church Triumphant above (saints, Evangelists and prophets) and the Church Militant below (theologians and Doctors of the Church) discuss the Holy Sacrament. Opposite that is the *School of Athens*, or *Triumph of Philosophy* (*illustrated above*), with savants and philosophers of all ages grouped around the figures of Plato and Aristotle.

In the last room, the **Sala dell'Incendio**, triumphs from the lives of earlier popes are used as allegories for the successes of the regnant Leo X. The *Victory of Leo IV over the Saracens*, for example, is made to allude to the crusade against the Turks proclaimed by Leo X. The *Coronation of Charlemagne by Leo III* is a reference to the diplomatic adroitness by which Leo X concluded an alliance with France in 1515.

LOWER FLOOR

The Borgia Rooms and Gallery of Modern Religious Art

Immediately below the Raphael Rooms is the gallery of modern religious art **(6; lower floor)**. The first six rooms are a suite formerly used by Rodrigo Borgia, Pope Alexander VI (1492–1503), who summoned Pinturicchio (already active in the Sistine Chapel) to decorate it. The grotesques (*see p. 395*) that form part of the scheme were inspired by the recently discovered Domus Aurea. The rooms continue into a long gallery filled with modern sacred art, which contains a study by Francis Bacon for his famous series of popes, based on Velázquez's portrait of Innocent X (*see p. 253*).

The Sistine Chapel

There are two things one can easily forget when visiting the Sistine Chapel **(7)**. The first is that it was designed as a chapel, that it remains a chapel, and that it is used regularly as a place of worship by some of the devoutest men in Christendom. The second is that the 15th-century works along the lateral walls are of the highest interest and beauty. Not only Michelangelo's bravura merits attention.

Despite the fact that the chapel's proportions mirror those of the Temple of Solomon, it is an unsatisfactory and rather undistinguished space: long and high and unarticulated. This makes its decorative scheme all the more important. It takes its name from Pope Sixtus IV, who had it decorated in 1481–83. What remains of those decorations are the **frescoes on the side walls**, by Perugino, Botticelli, Ghirlandaio, Cosimo Rosselli and perhaps Luca Signorelli, assisted by their pupils Pinturicchio and Piero di Cosimo. The scenes on the right wall as you enter are Old Testament scenes of the life of Moses; those on the left wall are New Testament scenes of the life of Christ. Each scene is somehow linked thematically with the one opposite it: *The Sermon on the Mount*, for example (fourth from the altar wall), where Christ gives expression to New Testament law, is shown opposite *Moses Receiving the Tablets of the Law*.

Michelangelo's great **ceiling** was created for Pope Julius II between 1508 and 1512, almost under duress: he famously hated painting it. The scheme illustrates the biblical history of mankind and of Israel, from the Creation to the witness by the prophets that a Messiah will come. Across the centre of the ceiling stretch nine rectangular panels telling the story of Genesis (*see plan overleaf*). The famous *Creation of Adam* is one of these. Surrounding the scenes is a painted architectural framework, on which sit the famous *ignudi*, nude figures thought to derive from Michelangelo's studies of the *Belvedere Torso*. On either side of the Genesis scenes are the pagan sibyls and Old Testament prophets, who foretold the redemption of mankind through a saviour.

The culmination of all of these scenes is the dramatic and emotional **Last Judgement**, painted on the altar wall by Michelangelo in 1536–41. It takes the form of a cyclone-like cyclical sweep, with Christ insurgent like a vengeful Apollo, his hand raised as if to smite the wicked, his mother the Virgin cowering by his side. On the left the blessed rise up to Heaven, and on the right the damned sink to everlasting tor-

SISTINE CHAPEL CEILING

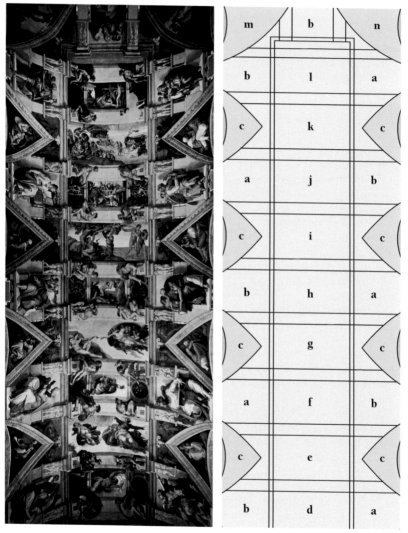

a Sibyls
b Prophets
c Ancestors of Christ
d *Separation of Light from Darkness*
e *Creation of Sun and Moon*

f *Separation of Land from Water*
g *Creation of Adam*
h *Creation of Eve*
i *Expulsion from Paradise*
j *Sacrifice of Noah*

k *The Flood*
l *Drunkenness of Noah*
m *David and Goliath*
n *Judith and Holofernes*

ment. Directly below Christ stands St Bartholomew holding his flayed skin; the ghoulish, slack face is thought to be Michelangelo's own self-portrait. The most memorable figure of all, perhaps, is that of the guilty soul, who clutches his face in anguished realisation that he has sinned and must be punished for all eternity. Immediately above the altar wall is Jonah, whose miraculous survival from his ordeal in the belly of a whale was taken as a prefiguration of Christ's—an ultimately all mankind's—resurrection from the dead.

VISITING ROME

GETTING AROUND

• **By air:** Rome is served by two airports. Fiumicino (Leonardo da Vinci), 26km west of the city, and Ciampino (www.adr.it), 13km southeast, used mainly by domestic and low-cost carriers.

To and from Fiumicino: The Leonardo Express train runs from the airport to Termini railway station (*map p. 241, F2*) every 30mins, c. 6am–11.30pm (6am–11pm from the city to the airport). Journey time is c. 30mins. Metro FR1 runs to Tiburtina station (*beyond map p. 241, F2*) at 25-min intervals 6.30am–9.30pm, and less frequently before and after. An airport shuttle operated by Terravision connects the airport with Termini station and other stops in central Rome 8.30am–8.30pm.

To and from Ciampino: Terravision and Sitbus (www.sitbus.com) operate shuttles between Ciampino airport and Termini station (*map p. 241, F2*) c. 4.30am–11.30pm. There is also a shuttle (operated by Atral) to the Anagnina stop on Metro Line A.

• **By train:** Most trains use Termini railway station (*map p. 241, F2*), although a few trains stop at the suburban Tiburtina station (*beyond map p. 241, F2*), from which there are frequent connections to Termini (in 8–10mins). Fast trains connect with Naples in 90mins and Florence in 1hr 40mins. To travel to Rome from Milan by Eurostar takes 4$^1/_2$ hrs, although faster trains are due to be introduced.

• **By public transport:** Most of the historic centre is closed to cars Mon–Sat. Pay parking is permitted in blue-marked spaces throughout the city. Walking is the best way to get around Rome; most of the major sights are easily accessible on foot and distances are not great. Rome's transport system, operated by ATAC (www.atac.roma.it) is efficient (though buses and trams can get very crowded, and the Metro is a bit seedy). Where relevant, bus, tram and Metro routes have been included in the text. Metro line A runs from Termini railway station to Piazza di Spagna and the Vatican (Ottaviano stop); Line B from Termini to the Colosseum and Circus Maximus. ATAC has a kiosk at Piazza dei Cinquecento, in front of Termini station (open Mon–Sat 8–8), with free maps of the main bus and tram routes.

• **By taxi:** T: 06 3570, 06 4994, 06 6645, 06 8822.

SPECIAL TICKETS

Tourist cards abound in Rome. The **Roma Pass** is a 3-day ticket valid for public transport and 40 museums and sights. The **Archeologia Card**, valid for 7 days, gives free entrance to the Colosseum, Palatine Museum, Palazzo Altemps, Baths of Caracalla and Colosseum. Cards are available at tourist information points, participating museums, monuments and sites, or online at www.romapass.it.

WHERE TO STAY IN ROME

€€€€ **Hotel d'Inghilterra**. ■ Discreetly elegant old hotel with a loyal following: many guests return year after year. A former favourite of Gregory Peck during the filming of *Roman Holiday*. Comfortable rooms and bathrooms. The small English-style bar is renowned for its Bloody Marys. *Via Bocca di Leone 14, T: 06 699811, www.hoteldinghilterraroma.it. Map p. 265, A3.*

€€€€ **Raphael**. ■ Charming old hotel in an 18th-century *palazzo* behind Piazza Navona. *Largo Febo 2 (Piazza Navona), T: 06 682831, www.raphaelhotel.com. Map p. 240, A2.*

€€€ **Arco dei Tolomei**. ■ Lovely, tranquil B&B in an old house in a quiet part of Trastevere. Delicious breakfasts. *Via Arco dei Tolomei 27 (off Piazza Piscinula), T: 06 5832 0819, www.inrome.info. Map p. 240, B4.*

€€ **Albergo Cesari**. Simple rooms in a good location just off Via del Corso, right in the heart of old Rome. *Via di Pietra 89/a, T: 06 674 9701, www.albergocesari.it. Map p. 240, C2.*

WHERE TO EAT IN ROME

€€ **Fortunato al Pantheon**. Traditional Roman restaurant serving very good food, all of it seasonal. Closed Sun. *Via del Pantheon 55, T: 06 679 2788. Map p. 240, B2.*

€€ **Piperno**. ■ Small place in the old ghetto. The Jewish-style artichokes are excellent, as is the light, refreshing house Frascati. Closed Sun evening and Mon. *Monte dei Cenci 9, T: 06 6880 6629. Map p. 240, B3.*

€€ **Settimio**. A simple restaurant with traditional Roman cuisine, near Campo de' Fiori. Closed Wed. *Via del Pellegrino 117, T: 06 6880 1978. Map p. 240, A2.*

€€ **Sora Lella**. Small *trattoria* on Isola Tiberina. Good home cooking, mostly traditional Roman. Closed Sun. *Via Ponte dei Quattro Capi 16, T: 06 686 1601. Map p. 240, B3.*

€ **Le Colline Emiliane**. Good, old-fashioned Roman restaurant conveniently placed for Palazzo Barberini. Closed Sun evening and all day Mon. *Via degli Avignonesi 22, T: 06 4817538. Map p. 241, D1.*

OSTIA ANTICA

The remains of the Roman port town of Ostia (*map p. 420, B3*) are well preserved and extensive, and a visit to this atmospheric site is one of the most rewarding day trips you can make from Rome.

Excavations open daily except Mon April–Oct 8.30–7.30 (last entry 6), Jan–Feb and Nov–Dec 8.30–5 (last entry 4), March 8.30–6 (last entry 5). Museum open Tues–Sat, summer 8.30–6.30, winter 8.30–5.30, Sun and holidays 8.30–1. NB: the museum takes a break for lunch. Ask for a plan of the site with your ticket. Self-service restaurant and café behind the museum, with a good bookshop opposite.

The excavations at Ostia tell us as much about life in a Roman town as do the more famous sites of Pompeii and Herculaneum. The town grew up at the mouth of the Tiber in the early 4th century, and was a centre for salt extraction. Later it developed

Ostia Antica: view of the decumanus maximus, looking towards the forum from the Marine Gate.

into a naval base and the port of Rome, providing the capital with goods and commodities from across the far-flung empire. The most important of those commodities was grain: the *procuratores annonae*, officials in charge of grain distribution (an important and unpopular position) always lived at Ostia. The town's commercial decline began under Constantine, who favoured a different seaport, closer to where the airport is today. Nevertheless, Ostia still lived on as a resort, and some fine houses of the villa type date from this time.

The site

The principal ruins can be grouped into three. Those around the upper decumanus maximus; those around the lower decumanus maximus, which led to the Porta Marina, the gate on the seaward side; and those around Via della Foce, which led to the river port.

Around the upper decumanus are the substantial remains of the **Baths of Neptune**, with large monochrome mosaics. The fine **theatre** is also here, behind which stretches the **Square of the Corporations**, which still preserves the outlines and floor mosaics of the offices of the different guilds and trade associations. Shipwrights and ivory traders (symbolised by the elephant) had their offices here, as did merchants trading grain. Some of the streets, lined with horrea, great storehouses for grain and other produce, and with brick dwelling houses with shops and taverns below and steep stairways leading to the flats above, are astonishingly well preserved. In **Via di Diana** is a thermopolium, a bar which served drinks and hot food, with the marble counter still intact, the rear courtyard where guests could sit in warm weather, the remains of a large clay storage jar sunk into the floor, and wall paintings of the food. The **museum** is near here too. Its displays are rather ramshackle, but one piece stands out: a sculptural group of the 1st century BC of Mithras slaying the bull. Ostia, like any port town, was home to a multitude of peoples from around the world, and many traces have been found of their cults. Serapis, a grain deity with Egyptian origins, was worshipped here, for example, as was Cybele, the Anatolian mother goddess or *Magna Mater*. Ostia was also home to at least 15 Mithraea, shrines of the popular cult of Mithras, a saviour god originating in Perisa, who brought initiates from darkness to light. He is often depicted in statuary astride a bull, which he is stabbing in the neck. The bull's spirit was believed to be released by this act, and the blood that it shed to cause a renewal of life.

The decumanus maximus crosses the wide, grassy area of the **forum**, with the massive base of the Capitolium, the city's most important temple, dedicated Juno, Jupiter and Minerva. At the other end of the forum, off to the left, are the remains of large **baths** and some of the best preserved *foricae* (latrines) in the Roman world.

The lower decumanus maximus leads past a **fishmonger's shop**, still with its large marble counter and fish tanks. In an isolated position outside the Porta Marina and only a few metres from the old coastline lie the ruins of the **synagogue**, possibly the oldest in western Europe (1st–4th centuries).

Via della Foce leads past the remains of grander houses, some with the remains of polychrome marble revetments, fine mosaics and traces of wall paintings.

VISITING OSTIA ANTICA

If you are driving, Ostia Antica is most easily reached from Rome by the SS8 (25km in 40mins). There is a pay car park at the entrance to the site. Trains to Ostia Antica leave every 15mins from the station on Piazzale Ostiense (*map p. 241, D4*), which shares a building with the Piramide Metro stop. Journey time 25mins. Ordinary ATAC bus or metro tickets valid for the train. When you arrive at Ostia, walk across the footbridge, cross the main road, and walk straight on then left to the ruins. There is a large cafeteria behind the museum, and a good bookshop.

TIVOLI

The town of Tivoli (*map p. 420, C3*) stands on a hilltop above the valley of the Aniene, at a point where the river narrows into a gorge forming dramatic waterfalls. Its refreshing air was much appreciated by the Romans (who knew it as *Tibur*). The poets Catullus and Horace visited often; the emperor Hadrian chose it as the site for one of the most extraordinary villa complexes from the ancient world (*see below*). The neighbouring hills were also quarried for their travertine, the white, striated calcareous stone of which so much of ancient Rome was built.

If you arrive in Tivoli by bus, you will be deposited in Largo Garibaldi (*map p. 282, 7*). Above it looms the Rocca Pia, a 15th-century fortress built by Pope Pius II. In the broad Piazzale there is an information kiosk. Below you across Largo Garibaldi is the Villa d'Este. If you arrive by train, it is a short walk into town across the Ponte di Legno, the wooden footbridge across the Aniene (*map p. 282, 8*).

Villa d'Este

Map p. 282, 5. Open daily 8.30–dusk. The water organ plays every two hours (at the time of writing at 10.30, 12.30, 2.30, 4.30, and also at 6.30 in summer). Pleasant café with tables outside overlooking the Fontana di Roma.

Cardinal Ippolito d'Este, son of the duke of Ferrara and Lucrezia Borgia, was governor of Tivoli from 1550 to 1572. At his villa here he created beautiful formal gardens, arranged on a succession of terraces and filled with elaborate fountains, water staircases and pools. Examples of most of the features of a Renaissance water garden can be found here: the **Fontana di Roma** is an elaborate water theatre, a combination of numerous water jets with statue groupings all turning around a single theme. Here we see a model of the Tiber (the boat represents the Tiber island), the she-wolf, some of the ruins of the ancient city, and the goddess Roma. The **Fontana dell'Ovato**, positioned at the end of a conduit from the Aniene, pours the river water over a steep drop. The **Fontana della Civetta** (sadly no longer working) used water to mimic the sound of songbirds chirruping until interrupted by the screech of an owl. The **Fontana dell'Organo** has as its centrepiece a water-operated organ (first constructed in 1568). There is also a lovely, long, weed-encrusted stone trough filled with water from myriad spouts.

Villa Gregoriana

The circular **Temple of Vesta** of the 1st century BC (*map below, 4*), superbly situated above the river, was a favourite subject for artists in the 18th and 19th centuries, and

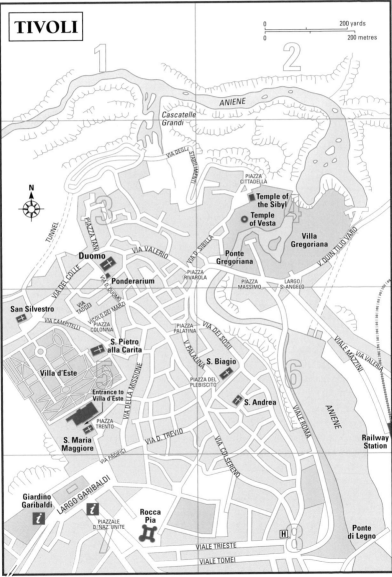

Hadrian's Villa

inspired many a folly in English landscaped gardens of that time. Close by is the rectangular **Temple of the Sibyl**, so named after the prophetess Albunea, whose cult developed here, although the original dedication of the temple is not known. The Antico Ristorante Sibilla (*see p. 285*) is a popular place to sit and admire the view. The park of the Villa Gregoriana (*open 10–2.30, until 6.30 in April–mid-Oct; closed Mon and open only by appointment in Dec–Feb; T: 06 399 67701*) provides spectacular views of the waterfalls from the other side of the valley (*exit from the park by Piazza Massimo*).

Hadrian's villa below Tivoli

Sprawled on the plain of the River Aniene, at the foot of the hill on which Tivoli stands, are the extensive remains of the largest Roman villa complex ever discovered (*Via di Villa Adriana 21; open daily 9–8*), the villa created by the emperor Hadrian (AD 117–138). It is probable that Hadrian himself was responsible for the design of many of the buildings: to borrow a comparison from another age, this was his own personal Las Vegas, a place that blended both a hedonistic and a cultural instinct, a place to give lavish and much-whispered-about supper parties, and a place where the most iconic structures of a vast and beautiful empire were recreated in miniature, so that he could 'visit' them or show them off whenever he chose. Here he recreated the famous Stoa Poikile of Athens, the Vale of Tempe in distant Thessaly, the Canopus at Alexandria.

The complex occupies 120 hectares. Living quarters, meeting halls, dining rooms, libraries and a theatre, as well as functional rooms (baths, storage rooms and lodgings for the praetorian guards and servants) are interspersed with gardens, open vistas and shaded walkways. The villa, however, was constantly a 'work in progress'; when Hadrian came here it must always have been a building site, for construction lasted throughout his reign. Nevertheless, there was much that was completed for him to enjoy. After luncheon he could ramble thrice around the colonnaded **Pecile**—quite enough exercise, according to his doctors, to aid the digestion and fend off heart trouble.

The design of the villa is unique. The interplay of concave and convex curves in the summer triclinium or the **Maritime Theatre** as well as the segmented domes so criticised by the architect Apollodorus of Damascus (who compared them to pumpkins) testify to Hadrian's eclectic taste. The domes are often described as 'baroque'. Apollodorus, who had been a favourite architect of Hadrian's predecessor Trajan, was put to death by Hadrian, it is said for detecting a fault in one of his designs.

Much of the villa was decorated with magnificent artworks. Many have vanished. Others are dispersed in museum collections around the globe, though several are in Rome, in the Vatican or Capitoline museums, for example. There were also statues of the deified Antinous, the beautiful Bithynian boy who drowned in the Nile while still only 20 (or, according to Cassius Dio, who had been offered for ritual sacrifice), and who had, it is surmised, been Hadrian's lover. His body was placed to rest in the villa and his cult disseminated across the empire. Museums all over Italy and beyond hold examples of his likeness: the mop of hair, full lips, Grecian nose and slightly downcast eyes soon become as familiar as a family photograph. The combination of so

HADRIAN'S VILLA

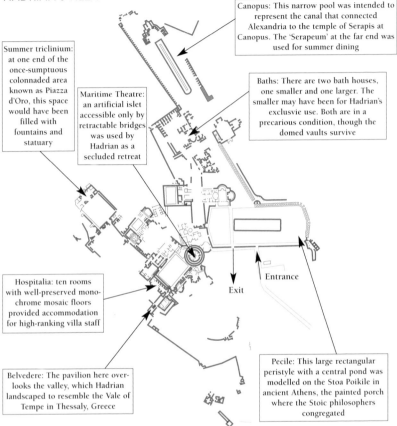

Canopus: This narrow pool was intended to represent the canal that connected Alexandria to the temple of Serapis at Canopus. The 'Serapeum' at the far end was used for summer dining

Summer triclinium: at one end of the once-sumptuous colonnaded area known as Piazza d'Oro, this space would have been filled with fountains and statuary

Maritime Theatre: an artificial islet accessible only by retractable bridges was used by Hadrian as a secluded retreat

Baths: There are two bath houses, one smaller and one larger. The smaller may have been for Hadrian's exclusvie use. Both are in a precarious condition, though the domed vaults survive

Hospitalia: ten rooms with well-preserved mono-chrome mosaic floors provided accommodation for high-ranking villa staff

Entrance

Exit

Belvedere: The pavilion here over-looks the valley, which Hadrian landscaped to resemble the Vale of Tempe in Thessaly, Greece

Pecile: This large rectangular peristyle with a central pond was modelled on the Stoa Poikile in ancient Athens, the painted porch where the Stoic philosophers congregated

much that was personal with the bold designs and sumptuous materials must have created an overall effect that was quite fitting for this most aesthetically-minded and secretive of Roman emperors.

VISITING TIVOLI & HADRIAN'S VILLA

The Aniene was navigable in Hadrian's day. Sadly in our times it is not, which means that for those who do not have a car, the journey to Tivoli from Rome is rather otiose—but per-fectly manageable. If you want to see Hadrian's Villa first, you need to go by bus.

Take Metro line B to Ponte Mammola (penul-timate stop). From there you take the bus marked Tivoli (run by COTRAL; ticket office one level down from where the bus leaves, or from the bar, also on the lower level). Ask the driver to let you off at Villa Adriana (c.

50mins from Rome, depending on the traffic), a request stop about 15mins' walk from the villa entrance: follow the brown signs. Bus no. 4 (c. every 20mins; run by CAT) runs from the villa into Tivoli. Taxis into Tivoli can be called. They can usually get to you in about 10mins (*T: 0774 317071 or 0774 334233*).

Trains to Tivoli leave from Rome's Tiburtina station c. every hour, and take about an hour. From Tivoli station, walk across the wooden bridge over the river to the centre of town (Largo Garibaldi), from where buses run by CAT (no. 4) go to Hadrian's Villa c. every 20mins. Tickets from kiosks and tobacconists.

WHERE TO STAY IN TIVOLI

€€ **Torre Sant'Angelo**. This castle rises over the ruins of a villa of the Latin poet Catullus, and enjoys spectacular views over Tivoli and its valley. The décor tries a bit too hard to be elegant, but the overall impression is one of great comfort and the staff is friendly and professional. *Via Quintilio Varo, T: 0774 332533, www.hoteltorresangelo.it. Map p. 282, 4.*

WHERE TO EAT IN TIVOLI

The €–€€ **Hotel Adriano**, just beside the entrance to the Hadrian's Villa, does a reasonable lunch. In Tivoli itself, the most famous place is the €€€ **Antico Ristorante Sibilla**, perched above the Aniene valley. It has been serving lunches with the same sublime view for 200 years (*Via della Sibilla 50, T: 0774 335281; closed Mon; map p. 282, 4*).

THE ALBAN HILLS

The Alban Hills (Colli Albani, the *Mons Albanus* of the ancient Romans) are an isolated group of old volcanoes lying just southeast of Rome. Their verdant landscape represents the last remnants of a huge caldera, 10km in diameter, and of a series of minor craters, two of which have filled with water to form small lakes, the Lago Albano and Lago di Nemi. The district is very fertile thanks to the volcanic nature of the soil, and the wines produced here are the best in Lazio.

The region is famous today for its picturesque towns—the Castelli Romani. Many were originally ancient Roman centres, but their collective name reflects the past custom of popes and patricians to build castles and villas here as summer retreats. **Castel Gandolfo** is still the summer residence of the pope, and its history is a venerable one. Here stood the city of *Alba Longa*, founded, so the Roman myth-makers and historiographers said, by Ascanius, son of Aeneas, who had fled with his father from Troy. Alba was the chief town of the Latin league, and the mother city of Rome itself.

Frascati

Frascati (*map p. 420, B3*) is the most elegant of the Alban hill towns and is famous for its villas and parks as well as its white wine. Its fame grew in the Renaissance, when cardinals and aristocrats, attracted by the cooler air of the hills, built magnificent villas here. Among the largest and finest is **Villa Aldobrandini** (*gardens open Mon–Fri 9–dusk*), located above the main square and immediately visible as one reaches the town. The impressive gardens, completed in 1621, are laid out along a series of terraces embellished with statues and fountains and include the elaborate Water Theatre, whose central figure of Atlas holding the world is said to be a portrait of Pope Clement VIII, uncle of Pietro Aldobrandini who built the villa.

The centre of Frascati was much damaged in the Second World War. Its cathedral contains the cenotaph of Prince Charles Edward, the Young Pretender ('Bonnie Prince Charlie'; d. 1788), whose body was buried here before being moved to the Vatican Grottoes. The **Church of the Gesù**, attributed to Pietro da Cortona, contains a *trompe l'oeil* dome by Andrea Pozzo, a replica of the one he painted in the church of Sant'Ignazio in Rome (*see p. 254*).

VISITING THE ALBAN HILLS

GETTING AROUND

• **By train and bus:** Frequent trains run from Rome Termini station to Castel Gandolfo and Frascati (journey time 30mins). Metro Line A runs to Anagnina station, from where buses (operated by COTRAL) run to all towns.

WHERE TO STAY IN THE ALBAN HILLS

Two gracious places to stay in this traditional stronghold of Roman patricians are the €€€ **Villa Tuscolana**, on a hill overlooking Frascati (*Via del Tuscolo, T: 06 942900, www.villatus-* *colana.it; shuttle into town*) and the €€€€ **Villa Grazioli** at Grottaferrata, part of the Relais & Chateaux group (*Via Umberto Pavoni 19, T: 06 945400, www.villagrazioli.com*).

WHERE TO EAT IN THE ALBAN HILLS

Frascati
€ **Zarazà**. Traditional *osteria* at the northern edge of town, with an outdoor terrace from which you can watch the lights of Rome twinkle on summer evenings. One of the best places to eat in the area. Closed Mon and in Aug. *Via Regina Margherita 45, T: 06 942 2053.*

ETRURIA

If the dominant culture in southern Italy before the rise of Rome was Greek, in the centre of the peninsula it was Etruscan. The Etruscans are one of the most sophisticated but least understood peoples of the ancient world. Their culture was highly developed, their burial customs elaborate and their metalworking second to none. Although we can read the letters of their alphabet, however, and can understand their funerary inscriptions, their language in its entirety is still unknown.

Etruria is not one of the official regions of Italy. The main centres of the Etruscan civilisation are spread between Lazio, Umbria and Tuscany (though at its greatest extent, Etruscan dominion spread far further). The influence of this mysterious people is still much felt.

Etruria in history

The Etruscans were the first people to build an urban civilisation in Italy. Their earliest cities precede the rise of Rome by half a millennium, and their civilisation reached its greatest splendour between the 7th and 5th centuries BC.

The origin of the Etruscans has been a matter of dispute since Antiquity. The Greek historian Herodotus claims they came from Lydia, in western Asia Minor, and this is accepted by the Roman historians Livy and Polybius. Dionysius of Halicarnassus, however, argues that the Etruscans were an indigenous people of Italy. Recent genetic studies (University of Turin, 2007) seem to confirm an eastern Mediterranean origin.

The formation of Etruria is perhaps easier. Archaeological evidence indicates that the first stable settlements (9th century BC) were on the Tyrrhenian coast. Tarquinia, in northern Lazio, is one of these. From here the Etruscans undertook a series of conquests that extended their control northwards to the River Arno and beyond, reaching the Po valley in the mid-6th century. On the site of modern Bologna rose the city of *Felsina*; on the Adriatic coast to the east they established Ravenna and Rimini (ancient *Ariminum*), from which they traded unworked raw materials, particularly iron from central Tuscany and Elba, with Illyrians and Greeks in the eastern Adriatic. From their conquests in the northeast—what are now the cities of Modena, Parma, Piacenza and Mantua—contacts were established with central European cultures.

Etruscan expansion to the south and east of the Tiber was hindered by resistance from the Umbri, who lived beyond the river to the south, and the Piceni or Picenes to the east, in the lands now known as Le Marche. Nevertheless, the Etruscans extended their reach into Latium (Lazio) and Campania towards the end of the 7th century, and in the 6th century they exerted a strong influence over Rome, where an Etruscan dynasty, the Tarquins, is said to have ruled until 509 BC.

The Etruscans never established an empire. Their confederation, as it is called, consisted of a number of autonomous city states, each under its own warrior prince. Numerous sources refer to a league of the 'Twelve Peoples' of Etruria, formed for religious purposes but evidently having some political functions. No firm list of the Twelve Peoples has survived (some scholars think 'membership' may have varied over the years), but they are likely to have come from *Caere* (Cerveteri), *Tarxuna* (Tarquinia), *Velathri* (Volterra) and *Clevsin* (Chiusi), along with Arezzo, Cortona, Perugia and Fiesole.

In response to the threat the Etruscans came to represent, the other Mediterranean powers—Greeks, Carthaginians and eventually Romans—joined forces more than once to thwart their expansion. In the 5th century BC Etruscan sea power was shattered when the Syracusans defeated them in a famous naval battle (474 BC). In 396 BC an emergent Rome conquered the Etruscan city of Veio, which was chafing at its northern borders.

By the mid-3rd century all Etruria appears to have come firmly under Roman control. In 90 BC Rome granted citizenship to all Italic peoples, an act that effectively unified the Italic-Roman state and eliminated the last vestiges of Etruscan autonomy. Romanisation was complete by the reign of Augustus (31 BC–AD 14). By this time the Etruscan language had been superseded by Latin. Many aspects of Etruscan culture were adopted by the Romans, however. The temple form came to them from Etruscan models, as did many elements of the religious observance. The triumphal procession of a victorious general was an Etruscan custom. The art of divination and the reading of entrails was also an Etruscan speciality enthusiastically embraced by Roman priests.

Few Etruscan buildings have come down to us. They were apparently built of wood, with the exception of fortifications and tombs, and only the terracotta decorations of some temples have survived. Excavations suggest that Etruscan homes were small and relatively humble. It is not known whether the images that survive in Etruscan tombs faithfully represent the forms of domestic architecture or indeed the habits of daily life. What is certain is that the Etruscan cult of death and the afterlife was, like that of ancient Egypt, of supreme importance.

D.H. Lawrence (in *Etruscan Places*) remarked that 'Italy today is far more Etruscan in its pulse than Roman: and will always be so. The Etruscan element is like the grass of the field and the sprouting of corn, in Italy'. Lawrence admired what he saw in Etruscan tombs, and liked to fancy that the Etruscans were a refined and pleasure-loving race, a world apart from the muscular, down-to-earth, military Romans.

We may never know what the Etruscans were really like. To explore Etruria today is to explore the cities of the dead: the great and small necropoleis sprinkled over the Italian countryside, as well as the wonderful treasures that they have yielded up: the mural paintings and sculptural decorations, the black bucchero ware pots, the jewellery and historiated bronze mirrors. Etruria does not have a centre, a single place that gives an idea of the whole. Do not look for a forum, a Capitol. The Romans were great unifiers: every Roman town had its cardo and decumanus, its theatre and baths, its mosaics of Neptune and its statues of Venus, its temples and its latrines. We today live more like they did, with our standardised high streets, our chains of shops, our universal road signs and our global brands. The cities of ancient Etruria developed each in its own way, and each had its own character. Contrary to what happens in Roman geography, where all roads lead to the *Caput mundi*, the Etruscans must be rooted out in little towns and down narrow dirt roads.

MAJOR SITES OF ETRURIA IN LAZIO

Cerveteri

Cerveteri (*map p. 420, B3*) lies near the Tyrrhenian coast, on the top of a tufa bluff on the southeastern rim of an extinct volcano. It developed gradually, becoming a major Etruscan centre between the 7th and 5th centuries BC, thanks largely to the strength of its fleet and the volume of trade that passed through its ports. Long allied with Carthage, it sided latterly with Rome, by which it was eventually absorbed and given the Latin name *Caere*. Much of the Etruscan city still awaits excavation, but several necropoleis have been brought to light, most famously at **La Banditaccia**, with exceptionally beautiful monumental tombs.

This immense necropolis (*open Tues–Sun 8.30–dusk; last entry 1hr before sunset*) extends over a hill a little north of the town, close enough to be reached on foot. The burial ground includes thousands of tombs ranging in date from the 9th to the 1st centuries BC and organised in a city-like plan, with streets, small squares—even districts. The site contains trench tombs cut in the rock and dating mostly from the 7th–6th centuries BC; tumulus tombs where a burial mound covers a suite of subterranean rooms, largely from the 6th–5th centuries BC; and the so-called dado tombs, carved in the rock in the shape of houses, with a wealth of structural detail.

Many of the tombs are beautifully sculpted; others have wall paintings of outstanding quality. The most remarkable are arranged along the ancient Via Sepolcrale Principale, and the Via delle Serpi, which diverges from the latter to give the site a Y-shape. The Tomba dei Dolii, Tomba dei Vasi Greci and Tomba dei Rilievi are among the dado tombs that some scholars see as surviving evidence of Etruscan residential architecture. In fact, these are dwellings for eternity, and are likely to be more sumptuous than ordinary homes, just as the treasures found within them are believed to be richer and more refined than ordinary possessions.

In the town of Cerveteri itself, the handsome halls of the 13th-century castle hold the **Museo Nazionale Archeologico Cerite** (*open Tues–Sun 8.30–7.30*), which displays antiquities dating from the 9th–1st centuries BC, all from tombs in the area.

Tarquinia

The ancient *Tarxuna* or *Tarxna*, modern Tarquinia (*map p. 420, B2*), was one of the most prominent cities of Etruria. It appears in the earliest history of Rome as the birthplace of two of its kings, Tarquinius Priscus and Tarquinius Superbus. By the 7th century BC it had become one of the great commercial and political centres of central Italy—a primacy it was to retain for well over 300 years until finally absorbed by Rome. The present town occupies a site first colonised after the Lombard invasions of the 7th century AD. The ancient city stood a few kilometres to the east, on a broad highland protected on three sides by high cliffs. Excavations have brought only a part of it to light; the most noteworthy find so far is a large temple called the Ara della Regina, built in the 4th century BC over a smaller and earlier sanctuary. It yielded the beautiful terracotta group of winged horses in the Hellenistic style, displayed in the museum (*see below*).

The Monterozzi necropolis

The necropolis is a short walk east from the town centre. The site (*open daily except Mon June–Sept 8.30–7.30, Oct and May 8.30–6.30, Nov–April 8.30–4; last entry 1hr before closing*) covers much of the hill immediately south of the ancient city, from which it is separated by the little San Savino creek. Over 6,000 tombs have been brought to light, nearly 200 of them decorated with wall paintings. These works are exceptional both for their form and for their content, which seems to speak eloquently of Etruscan attitudes to life and death.

Only a handful of the tombs (all with painted decoration) are accessible at any given time; for this reason they may appear to be isolated or grouped in clusters. In reality, the whole area between one tomb and another is occupied by other tombs that have been excavated, inventoried and resealed. The tombs can no longer be fully entered: a perspex screen protects the inner chamber from the viewing point at the foot of the stairs. Nevertheless, the experience is unforgettable.

The oldest paintings are essentially decorative in character (**Tomba delle Pantere**). They differ noticeably from the more narrative compositions that became fashionable

Girl in a diaphanous underskirt dancing to flute music while balancing an incense-burner on her head. She is watched by a seated man holding a staff, taken to be an image of the deceased. This painting, from the Tomba dei Giocolieri ('Tomb of the Jugglers'; 6th century BC) is, like many in Tarquinia, in a markedly Greek style.

in the 6th century BC, and which were drawn from Greek mythology or daily life (**Tomba dei Tori** with *Achilles and Troilus*; **Tomba degli Auguri** with battle scenes; **Tomba del Barone** with ritual scenes featuring musicians and horsemen; **Tomba della Caccia e Pesca** with hunting and fishing scenes; **Tomba Cardarelli** and **Tomba delle Leonesse** with dancers; **Tomba dei Giocolieri**, where the deceased is present at the ceremonies and games being held in his honour; *illustrated above*). The stylisation of these scenes is reminiscent of the images on Greek vases. On the other hand, there is a realism here too, which has more in common with traditions from further east, especially those of Egypt, where funerary paintings show the deceased behaving either as he would have behaved in life or as he hoped to behave in the afterlife.

In the 4th–3rd centuries BC, possibly as a consequence of the decline of Etruscan civilisation, the bright colours and serene motifs that had somehow cheered the contemplation of death give way to gloomier subjects, including scenes of suffering and grief (**Tomba dell'Orco**, with demons). These have rightly been considered the last vestiges of a disappearing world.

The Museo Nazionale Tarquiniense
The 15th-century Palazzo Vitelleschi (*Piazza Cavour 1; open Tues–Sun 8.30–7.30*) is now the seat of one of the largest museums of Etruscan antiquities in Italy, presenting a vast collection of material from excavations. Here are superb **Etruscan sarcophagi** carved with the reclining effigy of the deceased on the lid—particularly fine are the

sarcophagus of the Magnate (late 4th century BC), the Magistrate and the *Obesus* (early 3rd century). Other outstanding holdings include a magnificent collection of **Greek black- and red-figure vases** (with a fine bell-shaped vessel attributed to the Berlin painter). Also fascinating is an example of Etruscan dentistry: a **set of false teeth** attached to a gold wire. On the top floor are two special highlights of the museum: the exquisitely crafted polychrome **winged horses** from the Ara della Regina, dating from the late 4th or early 3rd century BC (they probably pulled a chariot, now lost); and a set of **reconstructed tombs** from the Monterozzi necropolis, with the original wall paintings detached and reassembled here. Those from the Tomba del Triclinio are the most famous in Tarquinia.

VISITING CERVETERI & TARQUINIA

GETTING AROUND

• **By train:** Cerveteri is best approached from Rome. Trains from Rome leave c. every 30mins from Termini station (journey time 45mins). Trains run from Rome Termini to Tarquinia in 1hr 20mins.
• **By bus:** Buses run by COTRAL link Rome with Cerveteri, departing from Via Lepanto, several blocks north of Castel Sant'Angelo. The bus stop is by the Lepanto metro stop (line A), with the ticket office on the lower level. The journey takes c. 1hr. From the bus stop in the centre of Cerveteri, it is a pleasant walk of c. 30mins to the Banditaccia necropolis.

WHERE TO STAY

Accommodation is quite basic in much of Lazio, and Tarquinia and Cerveteri are best visited as day trips from Rome. A number of simple B&B places exist, if you need to stay

the night, for example € **Al Corso** in central Tarquinia (*Via Giordano Bruno 1, T: 0766 856218, www.alcorsobedandbreakfast.com*). The € **Isola di Rosa** is a spa hotel near the beach at Cerveteri (*Via del Grano 20, T: 06 9955 2819, www.isoladirosa.com*).

WHERE TO EAT

Cerveteri
The nicest thing to do is to picnic at the site. If the weather isn't clement or you are unprovisioned, there are plenty of places to eat in town, all of them adequate.
Tarquinia
€ **Arcadia**. This little restaurant is the pride and joy of a young couple who are dedicated to good, wholesome cooking, with a strong emphasis on fish dishes. Centrally located by the museum. Closed Mon (except in July–Aug and in Jan). *Via Mazzini 6, T: 0766 855501.*

UMBRIA

Umbria (*map p. 420*) is peninsular Italy's only landlocked region, green and rural, with a population density of half the national average. Umbria's contribution to the sum of Italy's parts has been historic (the Battle of Lake Trasimene), spiritual (St Francis of Assisi), artistic (Perugino and the Umbrian school) and culinary (the sausages and black truffles of Norcia and the lentils of the Sibylline foothills).

Umbria in history

Umbria takes its name from the Umbri, who came to the region around the beginning of the 1st millennium BC. They derived their artistic and material culture from the Etruscans, with whom they fought bitterly for the territories east of the Tiber while maintaining a tenuous peace with the Romans, by whom they were eventually absorbed. The emperor Augustus made Umbria one of his administrative regions of Italy. In the 6th century AD, the Lombards incorporated most of Umbria into a duchy which had its chief town at Spoleto. Umbria then fell to the Franks, and ultimately was absorbed by the Papal States. Except for a brief Napoleonic interlude (1789–1814), it remained under the Holy See until its annexation, by plebiscite, to the kingdom of Italy in 1860.

Agriculture in Umbria

It was only in the 1960s that Italian agriculture entered the 'modern' world, after land reforms were passed that brought to an end the centuries old system of sharecropping (*mezzadria*), whereby the farmer gave half of what was produced to the landowner. *Mezzadria* tended to encourage the development of mixed farms on which cereals, vegetables, wine grapes and olives were grown to meet the nutritional needs of the farmer and his family. It was an economy geared to subsistence, and the results were the hundreds of picturesque smallholdings that still remain in the popular imagination of Italy. Although the large monoculture farms of the late 20th century have now become the norm here too, in Umbria much of the land has yet to be converted to single-crop intensive farming. This is an essential part of Umbria's charm, and the reason why it still seems so 'medieval' and historic.

Food and wine of Umbria

The art of *norcineria*, a traditional method of butchering pork, has made Umbria famous. It takes its name from Norcia, in the far southeast, where oak forests are plentiful and pigs would historically forage for acorns. Cured pork products from the region are widely available. Umbria's other great contribution to the world's kitchens is the black truffle (not to be confused with the white truffle, which is found mainly in Piedmont; *see p. 24*). Menus in Umbria often feature spaghetti or risotto *al tartufo nero* (with black truffle sauce). They grow wild in the area east of Spoleto, and truffle-hunting in season (Nov–March) is big business.

Most meat in Umbria is grilled or spit-roasted; specialities are *palombacci* (squab) and *mazzafegati*, pig's liver sausage with pine nuts, sugar and raisins. Freshwater fish is found on the shores of Lake Trasimene. The small lentils of Castelluccio are considered the tastiest in Italy; they appear in various dishes.

The best Umbrian red wines come from Montefalco, near Assisi. The DOC Rosso di Montefalco is a full-bodied blend of Sangiovese and Sagrantino, an indigenous variety; the DOCG Montefalco Sagrantino is made exclusively with Sagrantino.

THE ART OF UMBRIA

An independent Umbrian school of painting began to form as early as the 12th century, but did not break away entirely from Florentine and Sienese models until the 15th century, when it produced the famous trio of Perugino, Pinturicchio and Raphael (born in Urbino, now in the Marche), who exported the values of Umbrian painting to Florence, Rome and other centres.

Pietro Vannucci (1446–1523), known as Perugino, is the key figure of the Umbrian school. It was he who brought Umbria and particularly Perugia out of artistic obscurity and, as the teacher of Raphael, he may be said to have had a hand in shaping the High Renaissance. His style may seem Florentine at first glance (he worked in Florence in his youth, possibly under Verrocchio), but there is a soft sweetness to it which is entirely his own. His figures are recognisable for their flexuous *contrapposto*, Classical in a sense—the weight is generally placed on one foot, the other knee is bent and the head is tilted so that the figure seems to develop upward and outward—but there is a willowiness to the figures which is completely unsculptural. Raphael took this figure principle from Perugino and used it so extensively that it is sometimes difficult to separate Perugino's mature work from that of his young pupil.

Perugino's other famous pupil, Bernardino di Betto (c. 1454–1513), is known by the nickname of Pinturicchio, which translates roughly as 'the light-weight painter'. This may be so: there is no depth of philosophy in his art, and his instincts are more decorative than didactic. But he has been served ill by the critics. Vasari more or less dismisses him, and art historians ever since have been happy to follow Vasari's lead, perhaps afraid that if they admit to admiring Pinturicchio they will be seen as superficial. For a lay audience, however, Pinturicchio is one of the most appealing painters of the Quattrocento, precisely because of his decorative charm, his narrative skill, and his sheer delight in incidental detail. Pinturicchio made his début in Rome as Perugino's assistant on the Sistine Chapel wall frescoes (*see p. 275*), and returned to Rome to decorate the Vatican apartments of the Borgia pope Alexander VI. His masterpiece is his fresco cycle in the Piccolomini Library in Siena cathedral (*see p. 214*). But lovers of his work, while in Umbria, should certainly also go to Spello, to see the Baglioni Chapel (*see p. 301*).

PERUGIA

Perugia (*map p. 420, B1*) is not a beautiful city, but it is the best place to see the art of the Umbrian school and of its most famous painter, Perugino. The old town, which occupies a system of ridgetops, is reached from its sprawling modern suburbs by an escalator that penetrates the ruins of the **Rocca Paolina**, a massive fortress built by Antonio da Sangallo the Younger to enforce the authority of Paul III over a populace that was always restive under papal rule and which destroyed this stronghold after throwing off that rule in 1859–60. To support the fortress, the architect vaulted over an entire medieval neighbourhood, and the journey through this shadowy netherworld is strange in the extreme.

The light of day returns with a dazzle in Perugia's main street, Corso Vannucci, at the top of which is Piazza IV Novembre. The centrepiece of the square is the **Fontana Maggiore**, the terminus of an aqueduct that brought water to the city from the mountains 5km away to the north. The 13th-century reliefs and statues on the fountain are by Nicola Pisano and his son Giovanni.

Also on Piazza IV Novembre is **Palazzo dei Priori**, a magnificent example of a medieval town hall containing the former guildhall of the money-changers, the Collegio del Cambio (*open Mon–Sat 9–12.30 & 2.30–5.30, Sun 9–1*). The wonderfully decorated audience chamber (Sala di Udienza), where financial disputes were given a hearing, is covered with frescoes by Perugino, assisted by numerous others, perhaps including Raphael. It is perhaps appropriate that Perugino's masterpiece should be in this guildhall: if Vasari is to be believed he had no fear of God and an immoderate interest in money. His self-portrait appears on a pilaster on the left wall. The frescoes are typical of their time (1498–1500) in their portrayal of Christian virtues in Classical dress. Cato is made to stand for Wisdom. The Cardinal Virtues share wall space with

Perugino: *Cato*. The *contrapposto* posture with the body bent in an inverted S-shape, the weight on one leg and the head inclined, are typical of the artist.

Classical heroes. On the end wall are the *Transfiguration* and *Nativity*, and on the right wall the Eternal Father, above six prophets on the left and six sibyls on the right.

Galleria Nazionale dell'Umbria

The gallery, in Palazzo dei Priori (*open daily 8.30–7.30*) contains a good representative collection. Raphael is regrettably absent, but there is a fresco by him in the church of San Severo (*see below*), and the gallery does possess a copy of his famous *Deposition*, now in the Galleria Borghese in Rome. Perugino and Pinturicchio are both represented by significant works. One of the *chefs d'oeuvre* of the latter is the Santa Maria dei Fossi altarpiece (1496–98), its frame shaped like a church façade, with a triumphal arch below and an aedicule above flanked by volutes. At the top is a moving *Pietà* with the Holy Spirit in the gable. Below is the *Annunciation*, with the central figure of the Madonna and Child. St Augustine stands on the left, St Jerome on the right.

San Severo

Northeast of Piazza IV Novembre, Via del Sole leads up to the church of San Severo, thought to have been built over the remains of a temple to the sun (hence the name of the street, Sole). In a chapel here (*open March–Oct 10–1.30 & 3–6, Nov–Feb 11–1.30 & 2.30–4.30; closed Mon*) is preserved the earliest known fresco by Raphael (c. 1505), showing the Holy Trinity and saints. It remains as he left it, unfinished, for he abandoned work on it when summoned to Rome to work on the decoration of the Vatican. The saints underneath are the work of Perugino (1521). Though the fresco is damaged, its colours are still vivid. Raphael is universally recognised as the greatest painter of the Umbrian school. Although he was by no means a revolutionary artist in the manner of Michelangelo (who is known to have complained that Raphael received his commissions by virtue of his good looks), he took the Quattrocento aesthetic of Perugino and Pinturicchio to new heights, contributing significantly to the proliferation of High Renaissance classicism in both Florence and Rome.

VISITING PERUGIA

GETTING AROUND

• **By car:** Perugia's car parks are connected to the city centre by walkways or escalators. The large car park at Porta Nuova/Piazzale Umbria Jazz is connected by Minimetrò to the Pincetto terminal (Piazza Matteotti).
• **By train:** Perugia is c. 2hrs from Florence and 3hrs from Rome. A change (at Arezzo, Terontola or Foligno) is usually necessary. The station is connected by bus to Piazza Italia or by Minimetrò to Piazza Matteotti.

WHERE TO STAY IN PERUGIA

Perugia's finest hotel is the €€€ **Brufani Palace**, now one of the Leading Small Hotels of the World, near the Rocca Paolina, at the beginning of Corso Vannucci (*Piazza Italia 12, T: 075 573 2541, www.brufanipalace.com*). On the Corso itself is the €€ **Locanda della Posta**, an elegant and gracious town house (*Corso Vannucci 97, T: 075 572 8925, www.umbriatravel.com/locandadellaposta*).

€ **Bocca Mia** is a nice little restaurant just north of the duomo serving typically Umbrian dishes (*Via Rocchi 36, T: 075 572 3873; closed Sun and midday Mon*). In a fine old building on the street leading off Corso Vannucci from the corner of Palazzo dei Priori is € **Giancarlo**, which serves good traditional food in a warm, informal atmosphere (*Via dei Priori 36, T: 075 572 4314; closed Fri and a few days in Aug–Sept*).

LAKE TRASIMENE

The 'Umbrian Sea' (*map p. 420, B1*), though the fourth largest body of water in Italy, is shallow, reaching a maximum depth of just over 5m. Bounded by hills on three sides, with a broad plain to the west, it is notorious for sudden, severe storms, in which high winds from the north and west whip its waters into foamy crests. Historically it was subject to flooding, which made the surrounding area marshy and hard to cultivate. Fishing was always the principal activity here, and today the lake still furnishes Italy with about a third of its freshwater fish.

Works to control water levels began under the Romans, who built a subterranean outlet through which excess water could be drained. This extraordinary achievement of hydraulic engineering remained in use until the fall of the Empire. In recent times the chief concern became a shortage, not a surfeit, of water. To keep the lake from shrinking, two streams, the Tresa and Rigo Maggiore, were redirected to feed it.

The lake has always been an important nesting ground for aquatic birds and is inhabited by several fish species. It is now a protected nature reserve, and nothing is more pleasant than to wander its shores, stopping off at the villages and castles that rise on the gentle hills, or to take a boat ride to the islands.

Yet it is not the still small voice of calm that brings most visitors to Trasimene, but the clash and clamour of war. For it was on the plain near Tuoro, on the northern shore, that the Carthaginian general Hannibal defeated the Roman army under consul Gaius Flaminius in the spring of 217 BC—an event immortalised by Livy and commemorated today by a marked itinerary, with viewing platforms overlooking what is thought to be the battlefield (the exact location is still debated). In an early-morning ambush on a foggy midsummer day, Hannibal's troops attacked the Roman army as it marched close to the lakeshore, massacring 15,000 Romans, including Flaminius, and capturing some 6,000. The memory of the defeat lives on in placenames such as Sanguineto (from the Latin *sangue*, 'blood') and Ossaia ('boneyard'). For the Romans, however, this defeat was only a temporary reverse. The people of Umbria remained loyal to Rome, and in his progress southwards, Hannibal was unable to capture Spoleto.

The islands

Isola Polvese is the largest of three small islands in the lake. Broad, easy walking paths connect the boat landing to the main points of interest—the remains of the monastery of San Secondo, of three churches, and of the 14th-century castle. A visitors' centre near the landing stage serves refreshments.

The tiny **Isola Minore**, once inhabited by fishermen famed for their skill, is now uninhabited and not accessible to the public. **Isola Maggiore** still has a few inhabitants, is closed to cars, has a scattering of simple restaurants, a museum of lace-making, and a pretty path that skirts the waterfront.

VISITING LAKE TRASIMENE

GETTING AROUND

• **By train:** Trains from Perugia go to Terontola, from where there are connections to Tuoro and Passignano in 5–10mins.
• **By boat:** There is year-round daily service from Passignano via Tuoro to Isola Maggiore (and vice versa; journey time 30mins, 10mins from Tuoro). Boats run between San Feliciano and Isola Polvese daily May–Sept, and from Isola Polvese and Isola Maggiore July–Sept.

WHERE TO STAY & EAT

Between the lake (north of Tuoro) and Cortona is €€ **Villa di Piazzano**, a historic building in extensive grounds now restored as a comfortable hotel and restaurant (*T: 075 826226, www.villadipiazzano.com*). For complete seclusion there is the charming € **Da Sauro** on Isola Maggiore, with restaurant (*Via Guglielmi 1, T: 075 826168*). All the lakeside towns have fish restaurants, many serving the fish stew known as *tegamaccio*.

ASSISI

The approach to Assisi is wonderful. Olives, vines and cultivated fields grow right up to the walls of this little medieval town (*map p. 420, B1*), made of pink and white stone from the surrounding hills. The view of the famous basilica, stretching out on its spur of hill, with the great vaulted substructures that support it massed against the hillside, is one of the greatest sights in all Italy. The town is dominated on the north by a great fortress, the Rocca Maggiore, built in 1356 by Gil Álvarez Carrillo de Albornoz, the Spanish cardinal whom Pope Innocent VI made vicar-general of Italy with orders to subdue the feudal lords of the townships of the Papal States, and prevent their allying with the Holy Roman Emperor. There is a magnificent view from the fortress over the Rocca Minore, also erected by Cardinal Albornoz (1360), and beyond across the broad Valle Umbra, formed by affluents of the Tiber.

San Francesco

No one comes to see Assisi without visiting the basilica of St Francis, and a good many visitors take the time to see nothing else. Situated at the western edge of the town, this is the spiritual home of the Franciscan Order. The first stone was laid the day after St Francis was canonised in 1228 (which in turn was only two years after his death). The saint's body was brought to the new building for entombment in 1230. Just two years later it was decided to erect a second church over the first; this was consecrated in 1253, although it was not completed until 1367. Earthquakes in 1997 seriously damaged the

The basilica of St Francis at Assisi.

complex, bringing down several vaulted ceilings of the upper church and shattering frescoes by Cimabue and others. Restoration is still in progress.

Lower church

The lower church (*open dawn–dusk all year round*) is approached through a lovely porticoed square or by a double staircase from the green lawn of the Piazza Superiore di San Francesco. As soon as you step inside, you will be struck by the way the gloom is pierced by a profusion of glimmering frescoes. In the nave are stories of the Passion of Christ (right wall) and the life of St Francis (left), executed by the Master of St Francis. These are the oldest frescoes at San Francesco (1253), and are important not only as works of art but for what they tell us about the Franciscan approach to men's hearts and minds. St Francis himself was particularly devoted to the image of the crucified Christ. He was the first saint to receive the stigmata, the wounds of Christ, which appeared psychosomatically on his body. The lower church is even in the shape of a Tau cross (the letter T), which St Francis used as his emblem and as a symbol of his devotion to Christ's Passion. When this church was built and the frescoes begun, Francis was only recently dead, and his life's work and mission were still present in people's memories. In juxtaposing a mythologising cycle of the saint's own life with another of the life of Christ, the Franciscan fathers sought to bring people to faith in Christ through the immediate relevance of the lately deceased saint.

The high altar stands directly above the tomb of St Francis in the crypt. The vault above the high altar is divided into four compartments (the Quattro Vele) with frescoed allegories of the Franciscan virtues of Poverty, Chastity and Obedience, and the *Triumph of St Francis*, attributed to a Giottesque master. The south transept also has frescoes by followers of Giotto, and a *Madonna and Child Enthroned with Angels and St Francis* by Cimabue (1280), the only surviving part of the original decoration. The five saints on the end wall (including *St Francis*) are the work of Simone Martini; the *Crucifixion* is attributed by some to Giotto himself. Essentially, though, debate over authorship is unimportant. The official website of the basilica declines to be drawn on the subject, concentrating instead on what the works represent: the cornerstones of Franciscan doctrine. Official descriptions are at pains to point out that the entire iconographic scheme was under the supervision of a Franciscan theologian, whose strictures all artists at work here would have had to obey. Whether any of the works are by the hand of the most admired master of the Italian proto-Renaissance or by a humble pupil whose name we may never know is irrelevant to our response to them and what they stand for.

Upper church
The upper church of Assisi is tall and luminous, its entire wall surface covered with frescoes, all following a pictorial scheme which presents the importance of St Francis as intermediary between man and God. The nave frescoes are presented in three registers. The upper two show stories from the Old Testament on the south wall and from the New Testament on the north. They are probably the work of pupils of Cimabue and of painters of the Roman school, though many scholars believe that Giotto played at least a supervisory role in their execution. The two scenes from the story of Isaac in the second bay in particular have been identified with him, as have the four Doctors of the Church in the vault of the first bay.

The lower register shows episodes from the life of St Francis, and includes famous scenes such as the saint preaching to the birds (west wall; *illustrated overleaf*) and the saint receiving the stigmata (north wall). Once again, scholars debate the authorship of the works. Some clearly recognise the hand of Giotto, others do not. The lay visitor can be content to enjoy the works for their beauty and narrative power.

At the east end are the earliest works in the church, begun in 1272 by Cimabue and his pupils. The south transept has a large, very worn *Crucifixion*, with St Francis kneeling in adoration before the Cross.

The centre of town
Assisi's main square is Piazza del Comune, dominated by the **Palazzo del Capitano del Popolo**, dating back to the 13th century. Beside it is the perfectly preserved Corinthian portico of the **Temple of Minerva**, erected between the 1st century BC and the 1st century AD and transformed into a church in 1539. Corso Mazzini leads out of the square to the other important basilica of Assisi, that of **Santa Chiara** (*open 9–12 & 2–6*). This is the principal church of the Poor Clares, the order of Franciscan nuns founded at Assisi in 1212 by St Clare (1194–1253), St Francis' principal female follower. She lies buried in the crypt. In the chapel on the south side of the church is preserved the 12th-century painted Crucifix that St Francis heard speaking to him at San Damiano (*see below*).

St Francis Preaching to the Birds. Some scholars see this as the work of Giotto, others object that the human figures are too small in proportion to the frame as a whole.

Environs of Assisi

The **Convento di San Damiano**, lying 2km south of Assisi (*open winter 10–12 & 2–4.30 or 6*), is where St Francis renounced the world in 1205, and where St Clare died in 1253. The 14th-century frescoes in the nave show related scenes from the saint's life, such as his renunciation of worldly wealth and his angry father threatening to beat him back to common sense. The Crucifix is a copy of one said to have spoken to St Francis, addressing him with the command 'Rebuild my Church!' (now in Santa Chiara in Assisi).

Two other sites associated with St Francis are within easy reach of Assisi. The large domed church of **Santa Maria degli Angeli**, 5km southwest of town, stands on the site of the little chapel of the Portiuncula, where St Francis founded his Order based on vows of poverty, chastity and obedience. Much more rewarding is the **Eremo delle Carceri** (*open 6.15am–7.30pm*). Nestling on the lower slopes of Monte Subasio, east of Assisi, this woodland hermitage occupies a spot as peaceful and secluded now as it would have been in the early 13th century when St Francis and his companions retreated here. Visitors are shown the grotto where St Francis slept on the bare rock and the tree where the birds perched to listen to his preaching. Near the hermitage are three rather appealing bronze statues of friars (St Francis and two companions), shown gazing up at the night sky. St Francis lies flat on his back, his sandals cast aside. One of his companions draws the constellations of Ursa Major and Ursa Minor in the ground. The other points at the pole star.

VISITING ASSISI

GETTING AROUND

• **By car:** There are three metred car parks at the edge of the centre: Piazza Unità d'Italia (signposted A), Porta Nuova (B) and Piazza Matteotti (C). 'A' is the most convenient for San Francesco, but it is also the most crowded.

• **By bus:** Bus C from Piazza Matteotti passes

Santa Maria degli Angeli (Via Los Angeles), stopping at Assisi station first. The Eremo is a 4km uphill walk (no bus, it's a pilgrim route). San Damiano is less than a mile walk from the centre. To call a taxi, T: 075 813100.

• **By train:** Frequent trains link Perugia to Assisi in c. 25mins. Bus C links Assisi station with the central Piazza Matteotti (3km).

WHERE TO STAY IN & AROUND ASSISI

€ **Pallotta**. Very popular: central, friendly, clean, unpretentious and excellent value. It also has a good restaurant (*see below*). *Via San Rufino 6, T: 075 812307, www.pallottaassisi.it.*
€ **Umbra**. A small, quiet hotel tucked away behind the Temple of Minerva. Another popular choice. *Via degli Archi 6, T: 075 812240, www.hotelumbra.it.*
Two lovely places just outside Assisi are €€

Le Silve, a cluster of stone farmhouses (with restaurant) on the slopes of Monte Subasio 10km from town (*Località Armenzano, T: 075 801 9000, www.lesilve.it; closed Dec–Feb*) and € **Castello di Petrata**, a 14th-century castle in the hills 6km north (*Via Petrata, T: 075 815 451, www.castellopetrata.com*).

WHERE TO EAT IN ASSISI

€ **Pallotta**. One of Assisi's oldest restaurants. Family-run with local cooking. Closed Tues. *Vicolo della Volta Pinta 3, off Piazza del Comune, T: 075 812649.*
€ **La Stalla**. Atmospheric former cowshed, with smoke-blackened walls and a huge grill taking centre stage. Very popular; reservations recommended. 2km along the road to the Eremo delle Carceri. Closed Mon. *Via Eremo delle Carceri 8, T: 075 812317.*

SPELLO & SPOLETO

Spello (*map p. 420, B2–C1*), a splendid village of pink and white Subasio limestone, 14km south of Assisi, is a wonderful warren of narrow lanes and sudden, striking views. The main entrance from the south is by the **Porta Consolare**, a Roman gate where part of the paving of the original Roman consular road is preserved: this is the Via Flaminia, named after the consul who built it, Gaius Flaminius, killed at Lake Trasimene (*see p. 296*). From here Via Consolare leads up to the main north–south road through town (Via Cavour, becoming Via Garibaldi). A short way up on the right is the collegiate church of **Santa Maria Maggiore**. It was to this church that Pinturicchio came in 1500, to decorate a chapel for the church prior, a member of the prominent Baglioni family of Perugia. The paintings take the form of three large lunettes and show the *Annunciation, Adoration of the Shepherds* and *Christ Among the Doctors*, with four sibyls in the vault. Troilo Baglioni, the prior, appears as the figure in black in the scene of *Christ Among the Doctors*, and Pinturicchio's self-portrait hangs beneath a shelf in the *Annunciation*. Finished in 1501, the frescoes are among the artist's greatest achievements.

The Temple of Clitumnus and Spoleto

The **Temple of Clitumnus** (*open 8.45–5.45 or 7.45*) lies on the Via Flaminia, the main road between Spello and Spoleto (near Pissignano), but must be approached from the old road, which runs parallel. It is in fact an early Christian oratory, but because it was built using the remains of the pagan structures which once lined the river here, it has

Detail of Pinturicchio's *Annunciation* in Spello. Pinturicchio enjoyed painting minute background landscapes, and this is a superb example, full of activity and with a lovely use of colour. The designs at the sides and over the arch are inspired by the decoration of Nero's Domus Aurea (see p. 256).

always borne the name of the oracle Clitumnus. Fragments of wall paintings still survive inside. Further south are the **Fonti del Clitunno** (*open 9 or 10–dusk*), a lovely spot where the river swells into a limpid pool fringed with overhanging willow. The beauty of this sacred place, where white sacrificial oxen were bred in Antiquity, was celebrated by Propertius, Virgil and Pliny the Younger.

Spoleto (*map p. 420, C2*) is a beautiful, ancient hilltop town with some very interesting Roman and medieval monuments. It was colonised by the Romans as *Spoletium* in 241 BC, and survived an attack by Hannibal in 217. Relics of Roman days include the theatre (much restored); the Arch of Drusus (1st century AD), beside which lie the foundations of a Roman temple and Roman shops; and the Casa Romana (*entrance on Via Visiale; open daily 10–6 or 8*), which may have belonged to the mother of Vespasian. It has fine monochrome mosaic pavements.

In 570–76 the Lombards chose the site of Spoleto as the centre of a duchy which controlled a large area of Umbria and the Marche, until their holdings were taken over by the conquering Franks, and ultimately by the papacy. Centuries later Spoleto was again to be strategically important, when in 1353 a castle was built here for Cardinal Albornoz (*see p. 297*). It still dominates the town. Below it is the spectacular Ponte delle Torri, an aqueduct-bridge spanning a wooded ravine. This is reached by the peaceful Via del Ponte, which leads from the Porta Rocca, the eastern gate in the walls. The bridge was built at the same time as the castle, possibly on Roman foundations. It can be crossed on foot and is one of the most remarkable sights in Italy.

Spoleto's greatest medieval monument, also in the eastern part of town, is the duomo (*open 8.30–12.30 & 3.30–6 or 7*). The interior was partly transformed in 1634–44 for Urban VIII whose bust, by Bernini, is above the main door. The apse fortunately escaped the attentions of the Baroque modernisers, for here are some superb frescoes of the life of the Virgin (1467–69), by Fra' Filippo Lippi. He has included his self-portrait (looking straight at us from the foot of the bed) and a portrait of his son Filippino (the angel in front) in the central scene of the *Dormition of the Virgin*. The *Annunciation* is marvellously done, with a narrow path snaking suggestively off into the forest beyond. Fra' Filippo died in Spoleto and was buried in the south transept, in a tomb erected by order of Lorenzo the Magnificent, with a fine bust, and an inscription by Politian.

VISITING SPELLO & SPOLETO

GETTING AROUND

• **By train:** There are trains to Spello and Spoleto from Perugia and between Spello and Spoleto (make sure you get a direct service; some require a change at Foligno). From Florence the journey to Spello is c. 2$^1/_2$ hrs and from Rome c. 3hrs.

WHERE TO STAY IN SPELLO & SPOLETO

Spello
€€ **Palazzo Bocci**. Lovely, gracious place in an old *palazzo* in the heart of Spello. *Via Cavour 17, T: 0742 301021, www.palazzobocci.com.*
€€ **La Bastiglia**. Comfortable hotel in a converted mill at the northeast edge of the old town. Pool and restaurant. *Via Salnitraria 15, T: 0742 651277, www.labastiglia.com.*
Spoleto
€€ **Hotel dei Duchi**. Modern hotel opposite

the Roman theatre and the former monastery of Sant'Agata. *Viale Matteotti 4, T: 0743 44541, www.hoteldeiduchi.com.*
€€ **Hotel San Luca**. Charming hotel in the west of the old town, decorated like a comfortable private home. Restaurant, pretty courtyard, and garden with roses and jasmine. *Via Interna delle Mura 21, T: 0743 223399, www.hotelsanluca.com.*

WHERE TO EAT IN SPOLETO & SPELLO

Spello
€ **La Cantina**. Well-loved *trattoria* serving local, seasonal specialities and good wine. Closed Wed. *Via Cavour 2, T: 0742 651775.*
Spoleto
€€€ **Il Panciolle**. Well-regarded restaurant close to the duomo, known for its grilled meat. Reservations recommended. Closed Wed. *Via Duomo 3 (Vicolo degli Eroli), T: 0743 221241.*

View of the 'ideal city' of Urbino

THE MARCHE

Le Marche (*map p. 420*) is the region known as the Marches in English, the frontier land between Umbria, Emilia-Romagna and the Abruzzo. There are no big cities: tiny townships dot the countryside, usually built on hilltops and clustering around the keeps of their medieval castles.

The Marche in history

Early settlers of the region were the Umbri and the Piceni, the latter a fierce people who worshipped Mars, but who nevertheless traded with the Etruscans and the Greeks. With the rise of Rome both cultures came under Roman sway, and the territory of the Marche was divided into two administrative parts: the north became part of Roman Umbria while the south was known as *Picenum*. As Roman power declined, much of the south of the region was incorporated into the Lombard Duchy of Spoleto (*see p. 303*). The north followed the fortunes Ravenna, coming under the wing of Byzantium (*see p. 152*). Five cities strung out along the Adriatic coast formed an alliance known as the Maritime Pentapolis. These cities were Rimini, Pesaro, Fano, Senigallia and Ancona.

After the death of Charlemagne in 814, rivalry between Pope and Holy Roman Emperor was to become the norm, and the towns of the Marche found their overlords rallying behind one or the other. The Malatesta family, established at Rimini, became overlords of a number of towns in the Marche, including Gradara and Ancona. In 1356 the Avignon papacy sent Cardinal Albornoz to regain papal control; he built fortresses which can still be seen in many towns, here as in Umbria. From 1559, following the peace treaty signed between France and Spain at Cateau-Cambrésis (*see p. 6*), the Marche's history follows that of the Papal States.

While it was a Marche-born painter, Gentile da Fabriano, who in the 14th century became the foremost exponent of the International Gothic school of art, so it was a Marche-born painter who became one of the greatest masters of the High Renaissance: Raphael. His birthplace, Urbino, is the most important town in the Marche in terms of the impact it was to have on the life of the rest of the country.

Food and wine of the Marche

Cold meats are excellent in the Marche. *Ciausculo*, a kind of potted pork, is spread deliciously over *crescia*, a soft bread with pieces of cheese, lard or salami pressed into it. Another speciality are *olive all'ascolana*, olives stuffed with minced beef, egg and parmesan, then breaded and fried. Equally delicious is *pizza al formaggio*, a tall, dome-like savoury cake made with various cheeses.

The mountain towns of Acqualagna and Sant'Angelo in Vado, close to the Umbrian border, have markets where white truffles are sold. A special delicacy of the coastal region is *brodetto di pesce*, the fish stew that varies from one town to the next. Fish appears in pasta dishes too—for instance, *ravioli ai filetti di sogliola*, filled with sole,

The famous *View of an Ideal City*, probably by Francesco Laurana (after 1470), in the ducal palace of Urbino. The plan of the city is in perfect perspective, with streets running away from a wide central square with public fountains, dominated by a circular sacred building. The Renaissance admiration for the harmony and proportion of Classical Roman architecture is made manifest.

ricotta cheese, egg and nutmeg. *Vincisgrassi* are the typical lasagne of this part of Italy; they feature a robust meat filling.

Among the many wines of the region, the best known is the dry white Verdicchio; delicious, dry red wines include the full-bodied Conero Rosso, Rosso Piceno and Lacrima di Morro d'Alba.

URBINO

One of the loveliest of all Renaissance cities, Urbino (*map p. 420, B1*) is the scene of Castiglione's *The Courtier*, the famous handbook of Italian Renaissance manners and ideals. Under the auspices of Federico da Montefeltro, Urbino became the ideal city, and his palace was a meeting place of artists, architects, writers, poets and musicians.

Federico spent his youth as a soldier, serving as *condottiere* to the Visconti of Milan. He became lord of Urbino in 1444, and after the death of his first wife 16 years later, married Battista Sforza. It was she who convinced him to turn Urbino into an 'ideal city'. Battista died aged only 26. Their double portrait by Piero della Francesca hangs in the Uffizi, and Francesco appears as donor in the same artist's Montefeltro altarpiece in the Brera in Milan, painted just after his wife's death. In 1472 one of the daughters of Federico was given in marriage to Giovanni della Rovere, a nephew of

Pope Sixtus IV from the Ligurian town of Savona. Their son, Francesco Maria I della Rovere (1490–1538), inherited the duchy of Urbino when the Montefeltro family died out in 1508. The della Rovere were great patrons of the arts. Pope Julius II was the patron of Michelangelo. Guidubaldo II, son of Francesco Maria, commissioned from Titian the famous painting known as the *Venus of Urbino* (now in the Uffizi; *see p. 181*). The last of the della Rovere dukes died in 1631. His granddaughter Vittoria, the last of the family line, married Ferdinando II de' Medici, Grand Duke of Tuscany, in 1634. Her fabled dowry, which included works of art by Raphael, came with her to the Tuscan capital, where much of it is still on view in Palazzo Pitti.

Palazzo Ducale

The former residence of the Urbino dukes (*open Mon 8.30–2, last entry 12.30; Tues–Sun 8.30–7.15, last entry 6*) is the quintessential Italian Renaissance palace. Its sheer walls and tall towers dominate the town from every point of view. No expense was spared in its building and decoration, and when complete it housed a court that threw its doors wide to the leading Humanists and artists of the age: Leon Battista Alberti, Pisanello, Paolo Uccello, Francesco di Giorgio Martini, Piero della Francesca and Botticelli.

The palace as it appears today is largely the work of the Dalmatian architect Luciano Laurana, summoned by Federico in 1465 to enlarge the earlier palace, built some 20 years before. This older building, with its mullioned windows, overlooks Piazza del Rinascimento. Laurana's magnificent extensions include the harmonious, porticoed *cour d'honneur* and the famous valley front, with its tiered balconies and tall turrets. The versatile Sienese artist Francesco di Giorgio Martini, who was at once sculptor, engineer and architect, designed the two wings on Piazza Duca Federico.

Today the Palazzo Ducale holds the foremost museum in the region, the **Galleria Nazionale delle Marche**, arranged in the public and private apartments of Federico and his court—rooms that are themselves finely decorated with exquisitely detailed doors, windows, fireplaces and ceilings. The best works are in the Appartamento del Duca Federico. The highlights are two magnificent paintings by Piero della Francesca, the *Senigallia Madonna* and the *Flagellation* (c. 1460; *see p. 231*). The famous *View of an Ideal City*, attributed to Francesco Laurana (a relative of Luciano), is also here. In the duchess's apartment is Raphael's solemn portrait of a lady, known as *La Muta* (1507).

House of Raphael

Raphael (1483–1520) is the greatest figure of the Italian High Renaissance. His roots are in the Umbrian style of Perugino, from whom he borrowed the sweet, demure expressions, the dainty *contrapposto* and the stylised backgrounds. His career took him to Rome, where he reached his full maturity under the enthusiastic patronage of two popes, the Medici Leo X and the della Rovere Julius II. Here he was influenced by the work of Michelangelo (who disliked him and flew into paroxysms of jealous rage at his success), and his style acquired a monumentality to accompany the sweetness which many found an ideal combination. In the 19th century his compositions were taken as models by academicians. To the British Pre-Raphaelites he represented the beginning of standardisation in art: his technique, execution and use of colour being so perfect and harmonious that everyone sought to imitate them, instead of listening to the voice of their own, inner inspiration.

The house where Raphael is said to have been born in 1483 is north of Palazzo Ducale on Via Raffaello (*open Mon–Sat 9–2, Sun 10–1*). The display includes early works, copies of his most famous pieces, and paintings by his father, Giovanni Santi. The nearby Caffè Cartolari (*Via Raffaello 52*) is a good place for a coffee.

GRADARA

If you enter the Marche from Rimini and the north, you might consider taking a detour to Gradara (*map p. 420, C1*), which lies just off the Autostrada Adriatica and is famed for its Malatesta connections. Tradition sets the tragedy of Paolo and Francesca, a story of love, jealousy and bloodshed narrated by Dante in the *Inferno*, in the rooms of the castle. Francesca da Polenta, daughter of the lord of Ravenna, had married the uncouth Gianciotto Malatesta of Gradara, but fell in love with his handsome brother Paolo. When the cuckolded husband discovered the love affair, he murdered both his brother and his wife. The castle (*open Mon 8.30–1, Tues–Sun 8.30–6.30*) is a stout crenellated fortress, superbly restored in the early 20th century, with broad lawns enclosed in a battlemented enceinte, with views of cultivated fields. Visitors are shown a number of rooms with remains of 15th-century frescoes, including a rather revolting scene of 'hunting' putti (children torturing an otter), and a portrait of Lucrezia Borgia: her hair is as fair as Byron said (*see p. 43*). Lucrezia Borgia's first marriage to Giovanni Sforza had made her mistress of Pesaro and Gradara in 1494.

VISITING THE MARCHE

• **By car:** Urbino is just under 80km from Sansepolcro; admirers of Piero della Francesca can combine the two towns without difficulty (the mountain passes are very scenic, but require careful driving). The main road to Urbino from the west is the SS73/E43 from Arezzo.

Car parks in Urbino fill up quickly: there is one at Borgo Mercatale, with a ramp to the castle. There is also parking within blue lines on the streets. For this, either use the parking meters, or get a pre-paid Europark card, available from the tourist office in Borgo Mercatale. It saves having to rummage for coins.

• **By bus:** The bus station in Urbino is at Borgo Mercatale. AMI (www.amibus.it) operates services to other towns in the region including Pesaro, 35km away, from where there are trains up and down the coast and buses to Gradara (journey time c. 40mins, two buses a day).

WHERE TO STAY IN THE MARCHE

Urbino

€€–€€€ **San Domenico.** ▬ Comfortable hotel in a converted monastery, finely positioned in front of Palazzo Ducale. *Piazza Rinascimento 3, T: 0722 2626, www.viphotels.it.* The same group manages a number of other hotels, both in Urbino and elsewhere in the Marche. See the website for details.

WHERE TO EAT IN THE MARCHE

Gradara

€€ **La Botte.** Both a restaurant and an osteria: choose which you prefer. The *osteria* offers good value set menus including a selection of regional cold meats. The restaurant has classic cuisine. In the old centre. Closed Wed in winter. *Piazza V Novembre 11, T: 0541 964404.*

Urbino

€€–€€€ **Vecchia Urbino.** One of the best restaurants in town, serving local specialities. Here you can try *vincisgrassi*, the lasagne of the Marche, and the typical veal dish *Braciola all'Urbinate.* Good variety of cheeses and fine wines. In the northeast of the old town. Closed Tues. *Via Vasari 3/5, T: 0722 4447.*

€€ **L'Angolo Divino.** A very good little *osteria*, which works for either lunch or dinner. Good soups and other dishes that make use of local ingredients such as truffles and forest mushrooms. In the north of the old centre, on a street that runs alongside the botanic garden. Closed Sun evening and Mon. *Via Sant'Andrea 14, T: 0722 327559.*

€ **Il Girarrosto.** Typical *rosticceria* on the square used as a vegetable market in the morning, just south of Raphael's house. Eat outside in summer, snacks to take away in winter. The offering includes roast meat, sausages, sautéed vegetables and salads. Closed Mon midday in winter. *Piazza San Francesco 3.*

SOUTHERN ITALY

'Mantua bore me, Calabria stole me, Parthenope holds me.' Virgil's famous line, composed as the epitaph for his own tomb in Naples, goes some way to explain how a land which was Greek, colonised from the 8th century BC, became Roman and thus joined its history to that of Italy as a whole; and how the Romans, so stolid and manly and unsentimental, were swept off their feet by the siren singing of the South.

It was the emperor Augustus who brought Virgil to Naples, to a shore that echoed to the songs of Homer and the adventures of Odysseus as he passed down this coast on his protracted journey home. Augustus commissioned from Virgil a different poem: one that would celebrate the foundation of his empire's mother city by telling the story of Aeneas, the refugee from Troy who forged a new life in a new land. Tyrrhenian place-names began to be connected with the Aeneas myth: Misenum commemorates Aeneas' trumpeter; Palinuro his helmsman Palinurus.

The Romans were greatly drawn to the beautiful bay of Naples, partly shocked but mainly admiring of the cultured, leisured, indulgent lifestyle of its Greek inhabitants. The area became a famous resort, with luxurious villas strung out along the littoral. Veterans of Rome's wars were given land here too, and cities grew up to house them. Far removed from the capital, this part of the world must have seemed wonderfully *laissez faire*. Much more recent visitors in the 19th and 20th centuries felt something of the same, escaping from the constraints of their well-to-do bourgeois backgrounds to a wild and unbridled place where no one knew who they were or cared what they did.

This history is palpably preserved in southern Italy today, a place where homogeneity is hard to find. Around Naples and along the Amalfi coast the faded playground atmosphere is strong. In more out-of-the-way places, one might still be in Greece. In fact all the peoples who have inhabited this land have left indelible traces: the Normans in Sicily and around Bari, the Arabs in Sicily, the Swabians in Basilicata, the Byzantines in Calabria, and the Spanish, whose legacy is keenly felt in the art and the architecture everywhere.

Even the centralising Romans, despite their efforts to co-opt the land and its people with the grand and unifying myths of the *Aeneid*, were ultimately defeated by this refusal to conform to type. The Roman state religion was particularly reluctant to take root, certainly not in the later empire, with its enormous population of slaves. Several foreign cults were officially incorporated by Rome, and it was in the south more than anywhere (apart from Rome itself) that they took hold, particularly the mystic, mystery cults of the East. The god Mithras, of Persian origin, was worshipped at Capua, and Isis from Egypt had a great shrine at Pompeii. These deities offered their followers something more than the gods and goddesses of the traditional Roman pantheon: they offered the hope of an afterlife. The Greek goddess Demeter and her daughter Persephone, redeemed from the Underworld, are excellent examples, and they were widely worshipped, particularly on Sicily and at Locri in Calabria. And ultimately, of course it was a cult from the East, a merciful, peace-preaching prophet from the land of Judah, who was to overtake Italy completely and demonstrate that the old, pagan Roman hegemony could never be total. No hegemony has ever successfully obtained in these southern climes. The land is a law unto itself.

CAMPANIA

There is much to see in Campania (*map p. 421*). The beautiful Tyrrhenian coast from the Bay of Naples to Amalfi has been a place of resort since the days of ancient Rome. The name of the entire region in fact derives from the Romans, who called it *Campania felix* (the 'happy land') on account of its beauty and fertility. Important places to visit are Naples itself, with its teeming streets and superb museums; the remains of Pompeii and Herculaneum; the Amalfi coast with its precipitously built towns and villages; the island of Capri; and the magnificently preserved Greek temples at Paestum.

Campania in history

The history of Campania is essentially the history of Naples, which as the capital of a powerful kingdom influenced the whole course of history in this part of Italy. All the European powers—from the Greeks and Romans to the French, Spanish and Austrians—have left their mark here.

The Greeks began establishing colonies in Italy in the 8th century BC: soon the Bay of Naples marked the outer edge of what came to be called Magna Graecia (Greater Greece). Sybaris, Croton, Taranto and Naples on the mainland, and Messina and Syracuse on the island of Sicily, became the chief centres of a flourishing Hellenic civilisation. Greek power was weakened by conflict at home, in the form of the Peloponnesian Wars. Into the vacuum stepped the Samnites, a primitive hill people from the region north and east of Naples, whose federation of city-states was gradually conquered by the Romans in the 4th–3rd centuries BC. Not all the Greek cities capitulated easily. Some sought the help of Pyrrhus, king of Epirus, whose famous war elephants were a feature of his campaigns. His victories were won at so great a loss of life on his own side that the term Pyrrhic victory was coined—and Roman dominion spread inexorably through the south, bringing with it its power struggle against Carthage. Many bloody battles of the Punic Wars were fought on southern Italian soil.

The Romans finally defeated Carthage in 146 BC, and afterwards began to consolidate their presence in the south. They felt very at home in the area around Naples. By the 1st century AD it had become the riviera of its day, with the villas of emperors, senators and victorious generals strung out along the littoral. With the decline of the Roman empire and the invasions of barbarian tribes, Campania fell prey to the Goths and the Byzantines and, in the 6th century, to the Lombards, who established a duchy in the centre of the region, with its capital at Benevento. Cohesion did not return for many centuries, and when it did, it was once again to be the result of a foreign invasion.

The Norman conquest was a gradual process. Over the course of a century (1030–1130) these tall, rangy, red-haired knights, led by the descendants of Tancred de Hauteville, gradually gained control. By the mid-12th century, their dominion extended over the entire south, a vast territory which became the Norman Kingdom of Sicily, with its capital at Palermo (*see p. 368*).

In 1194 the Holy Roman Emperor Henry VI of Hohenstaufen inherited the crown of Sicily. He was succeeded, both as Holy Roman Emperor and as king of Sicily, by his son Frederick II (1197–1250), who, like many brilliant and charismatic rulers, left a troubled succession behind him. His legitimate son, Conrad, died young, and his bastard son Manfred, though brilliant, was not accepted by the pope (Urban IV), who chose Charles of Anjou, the younger brother of St Louis of France, to occupy the Sicilian throne. Charles slew Manfred in battle in 1266, and two years later disposed similarly of Frederick's grandson, the 16-year-old Conradin. On establishing himself as the first Angevin king of Sicily, he transferred his capital from Palermo to Naples.

Charles initially enjoyed the favour of his subjects, but his policy of oppressive taxation led to resentment. Revolt broke out in Palermo in 1282, in the uprising known as the Sicilian Vespers. The French were either expelled or massacred, and the Sicilian nobles summoned a Catalan, Peter of Aragon, to be their king. Two 'Kingdoms of Sicily' now existed: the island itself, ruled by the Aragonese; and Naples and the south of Italy, still ruled by the Angevins and still referred to as the Kingdom of Sicily. The peninsular 'Sicily' enjoyed a brief period of prosperity and importance under Charles' grandson, Robert (the Wise), who proved both a capable ruler and a discerning patron of the arts. His death was followed by long years of turmoil, brought to an end only when Alfonso of Aragon seized Naples and took sovereignty over both Sicily and the mainland, assuming the title Alfonso I of the Two Sicilies in 1443.

The kingdom then entered a period of renewed splendour, for Alfonso, called 'the Magnanimous', had a taste for art and learning to match his political and military acumen. His son Ferrante (Ferdinand I), who inherited Naples (Sicily once more was governed separately), was similarly inclined. But French claims were not forgotten. In 1495 Charles VIII of France seized Naples, and France and Spain were soon locked in a bloody fight for control. Spain gained the upper hand, though the Aragonese monarchs did not return. Instead they governed through a succession of viceroys, accountable to the sovereigns of imperial Spain. They retained their hold on Naples for two centuries, and the hallmarks of their rule can still be felt in the region today, notably in its art and architecture.

The Spanish viceroys were not beloved, nor did they deserve to be. Taxation was high, pirates roamed the seas, dukes and marquises were too numerous, so were priests, and so were beggars. All these ills roused the Neapolitans to insurrection (1647) under Masaniello, an Amalfi fisherman. The Parthenopean Republic (Parthenope being the name of the first Greek colony) that was proclaimed lasted only a few months. After the War of the Spanish Succession, Naples passed to Austria. In 1734, however, Charles of Bourbon, crown prince of Spain, seized Sicily and subsequently Naples. He founded the Neapolitan Bourbon dynasty, and once again ruled as king of the Two Sicilies.

The Bourbon dynasty ruled Naples until the Unification of Italy in 1860. Charles's successor Ferdinand IV was a bluff, vulgar man, popular with the people but disliked by the intellectual classes, whose republican hopes were stirred by the outbreak of revolution in France in 1789. The royalists rallied behind their king and his consort, Maria Carolina, a sister of Marie Antoinette, but when the French attacked Naples in 1798, the city was taken so much by surprise that the entire court had to be evacuated to Sicily. A second Parthenopean Republic was proclaimed, governing with the blessing of the French. Ferdinand attempted to retake Naples, aided by Nelson and the British, but Napoleon would not permit it. He awarded Naples first to his brother Joseph, and then, when Joseph was needed to rule Spain, to his brother-in-law Joachim Murat. It was not until Napoleon's final defeat at Waterloo in 1815 that Ferdinand returned to his throne, as Ferdinand I of the Two Sicilies. He reigned for another ten years.

His successors, Francis I (1825–30) and Ferdinand II (1830–59), were weak and irresolute rulers. It was only a matter of time before southern Italy joined the north in its ousting of foreign rule. In 1860 the Neapolitan army collapsed before the advance of Garibaldi, and when Francis II, the last of the Bourbons, capitulated in October of the same year, Naples voted overwhelmingly for unification with northern Italy. From that time onward, the south, including Campania, has shared the fate of the nation.

Food and wine of Campania

The Neapolitans are credited with the invention of *pasta asciutta*, simple flour-and-water pasta (in other words made without egg). *Fusilli alla napoletana* are served in a rich sauce of tomatoes, ricotta, salami, garlic and pecorino cheese. *Pasta alla sorrentina* adds diced scamorza cheese to the tomato sauce, to make it thick and stringy. Just as famous as pasta is pizza, also invented in Naples and originally just a flat piece of bread, baked in the oven with cheese and herbs; tomatoes were added after the discovery of America.

Sfogliatelle are perhaps the most famous of Neapolitan pastries, filled with fresh ricotta, chopped candied fruit, cinnamon, vanilla, and other ingredients. *Sproccolati*, sun-dried figs filled with fennel seeds and preserved on wooden sticks, are a speciality of Ravello and the Amalfi coast.

Produced around Taurasi, in the region's hilly interior, Taurasi is the great red wine of Campania and one of the premier wines of southern Italy, made from the Aglianico grape. In the hills southeast of Naples the Fiano grape is used to make Fiano d'Avellino, a lovely dry white. The slopes of Vesuvius produce the light, drinkable Lacryma Christi.

NAPLES

Naples (*map p. 421, A2*) is a complicated place, with a reputation for being crowded, dirty, chaotic, poor and lawless. It is certainly the first of these: with a population of over eight thousand people per square kilometre, it is one of the most densely inhabited cities in Europe. The second of the two charges can also be said to be justified, at least intermittently. The failure of Naples to deal with its own rubbish made world headlines in 2008. The chaos and lawlessness have, in the past few years, diminished greatly, and Naples today, if you take due care, is a safe and, in parts, a pleasant place to visit. It, together with the whole of southern Italy, remains poor compared to the regions of the north. If you arrive in Naples from Milan, Tuscany, or even Rome, take time to recalibrate. Naples is another country.

Castel Nuovo and Piazza del Plebiscito

Above the main sweep of Naples harbour rises the royal residence of the Angevin kings, the Castel Nuovo (*map p. 317, 11*), unmistakable with its fat, battlemented towers. It was originally built (by French architects) for Charles I in the late 13th century, and largely reconstructed under Alfonso of Aragon. Today it houses the meeting rooms of the Naples City Council and the Regional Council of Campania, as well as a fine museum (*open Mon–Sat 9–7*). You enter the castle between two of the towers, under the famous **triumphal arch**, erected in the mid-15th century to commemorate the entry into Naples of Alfonso of Aragon. Above two lions bearing the Aragonese coat of arms is a splendid panel carved in relief, showing Alfonso entering the city in triumph in a tall, canopied chariot.

From the courtyard, you enter the **Cappella Palatina** or church of Santa Barbara, the only building interior to survive intact from the Angevin period, long and narrow, with a single tall lancet at the east end. It was once covered with Florentine frescoes, and the splays still contain fragments, attributed to the school of Giotto. Florentine artists were attracted to the cultured atmosphere of the Neapolitan court, particularly under Robert the Wise (reigned 1309–43). The poet Boccaccio spent much time in Campania, both in Naples and at Baia. Also shown as part of the museum is the **Sala dei Baroni**, a large hall with a fine vaulted ceiling. It takes its name from the barons who were tricked into a meeting here by Ferrante I and summarily arrested for treason.

West of Castel Nuovo is Piazza del Plebiscito, whose east flank is entirely filled by the façade of the **Palazzo Reale** (*closed Wed*), built by Domenico Fontana in 1600–02 in anticipation of a visit by Philip II of Spain. It was the palace of the rulers of Naples during the viceregal period. The highlight of the exhibits inside are a pair of 15th-century bronze doors from Castel Nuovo, on which six reliefs depict Ferrante's struggle with the barons. The cannonball lodged in the lower left-hand relief is a relic from a naval battle between the French and the Genoese.

The other side of the square takes the form of a wide hemicycle with a Doric colonnade and equestrian statues of the first two Bourbon rulers, Charles III and Ferdinand IV, in the guise of Roman emperors. They are the work of Antonio Canova, completed by a follower after Canova's death. The church of **San Francesco di Paola** was founded by Ferdinand IV to celebrate the restoration of the Bourbon dynasty after the fall of Napoleon. It was clearly modelled on the Pantheon in Rome.

The Spaccanapoli

Via Benedetto Croce (*map p. 317, 7*) is the beginning of the 'Spaccanapoli', the thoroughfare that 'splits Naples', a characteristic street of dilapidated old palaces. At the western end stands the church of the **Gesù Nuovo**, with severe diamond rustication and three Baroque doorways. It was formerly a palace of the Sanseverino family, exiled by the viceroy Pedro da Toledo (father of Eleanor of Toledo; *see p. 179*) for opposition to the Spanish Inquisition. The palace and its garden were acquired by the Society of Jesus, who built this church. On the other side of the street is the church and Franciscan convent of **Santa Chiara**, built in the early 14th century for queen Sancha, second wife of Robert the Wise, who died here a nun. The church was damaged in the Second World War by incendiary bombs, which completely destroyed the Baroque fittings. The restoration has returned the church to its original Gothic form. A number of Angevin royal monuments survive, notably that of Robert the Wise himself (behind the high altar). The monument to his son Charles, Duke of Calabria is the work of the Sienese sculptor Tino di Camaino.

Further up the street, past the church of San Domenico Maggiore, you come to a district dominated by palaces of the Sangro family, princes of Sansevero. Their funerary chapel, the **Cappella Sansevero** (*map p. 317, 7; Via de Sanctis 19; open Mon–Sat 10–5.40, Sun and holidays 10–1.10*) is remarkable for three extraordinary sculptures: *Modesty* (completely veiled) by Antonio Corradini (1751); *Liberation from Illusion* (a man struggling to free himself from a net) by Francesco Queirolo (1752); and the *Dead Christ*, an alabaster statue by Giuseppe Sammartino (1753) of Christ covered by a winding sheet. All are virtuoso examples of technique, and all, particularly the last, are macabrely memorable.

San Lorenzo Maggiore and the cathedral

The Franciscan church of **San Lorenzo Maggiore** (*map p. 317, 3; open Mon–Sat 8–12, Sun and holidays 7.45–1 & 5–7.15*), built over a Roman basilica, was begun by Charles I of Anjou to commemorate his victory over Manfred of Hohenstaufen at Benevento in 1266, and completed by his son, Charles II. None of this is immediately obvious from the façade, though the modern statue of Augustus outside gives some clue. The interior is very fine, with a slender, soaring Gothic apse, ancient fresco fragments and large Baroque canvases. The excavations of the Roman city beneath the church (*admission fee*) are extremely interesting.

The **cathedral of San Gennaro** (*map p. 317, 3; open Mon–Sat 8–12 & 4.30–7, Sun and holidays 8–1.30 & 5–7*) also stands on ancient foundations: it was founded in the 4th century on the site of a Greek sanctuary of Apollo. The present building was begun in the French Gothic style by Charles I in the late 13th century; his tomb is inside, over the main west doorway. On the walls of the nave are saints, painted by Luca Giordano and his pupils. The Chapel of St Januarius (San Gennaro) opens off the south aisle. It provides a good introduction to the Baroque art of Naples and its main protagonists (*for more on art in Naples, see p. 320*). The chapel is closed by an immense grille of gilded bronze, based on a design by Cosimo Fanzago, a native of Bergamo whose exuberant Baroque imagination found fertile soil here. Four of the altars in the interior have paintings by Domenichino, completed after his death (*see p. 321*) by his fellow Bolognese Lanfranco. Above the altar on the right side is a large painting by Jusepe Ribera of St Januarius emerging unharmed from the furnace, which had also been part of Domenichino's unfinished commission. The balustrade of the main altar is by Cosimo Fanzago. The sumptuous silver altar-front is by Francesco Solimena, the most important Neapolitan artist of the 18th century. In a tabernacle behind the altar are preserved the head of St Januarius (martyred at Pozzuoli) and two phials of his congealed blood, which miraculously liquefies three times a year: on the first Sat in May at Santa Chiara, and here on 19 Sept and 16 Dec. The event attracts an enormous crowd.

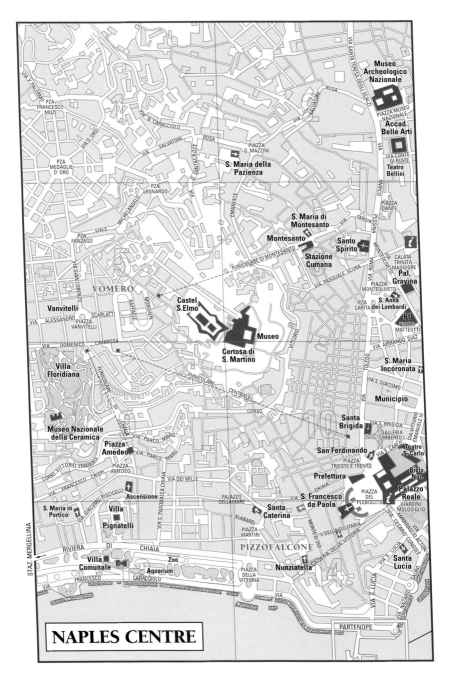

NAPLES CENTRE

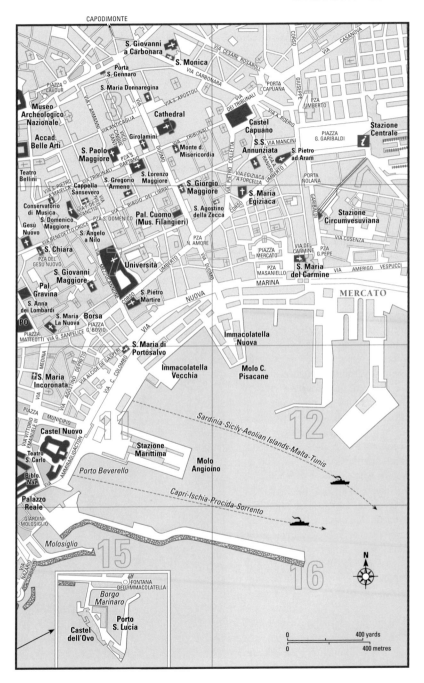

The **Pio Monte della Misericordia**, a charitable institution first founded to give succour to the needy, has a church (*map p. 317, 3; open 9–2.30 except Wed*) with Caravaggio's huge painting of the *Seven Acts of Mercy* (1607). The acts are the burial of the dead, visiting the incarcerated, feeding the hungry, clothing the naked, sheltering pilgrims, giving drink to the thirsty and tending the sick.

National Archaeological Museum

Map p. 316, 2. Open Wed–Mon 9–7.30. Metro 1 to Museo, Metro 2 to Piazza Cavour.
This museum is home to magnificent exhibits from Pompeii and Herculaneum, and if possible it should be visited after seeing the sites themselves, which provide a context for the exhibits. It was Charles III of Bourbon who began the excavations at the Vesuvian cities; he also inherited some magnificent pieces of ancient Roman sculpture from his mother, who was a Farnese (*see below*).

Greek and Roman sculpture collections

Most of the greatest works here belonged to the Farnese Collection, begun by Alessandro Farnese (Pope Paul III), who built the magnificent Palazzo Farnese in Rome (*see p. 261*) and adorned it and his other residences with a number of recently excavated sculptures. Some were found in the Baths of Caracalla, others in Nero's Domus Aurea, still others at the site of Hadrian's magnificent villa at Tivoli. The most celebrated pieces are the *Farnese Bull*, sculpted, according to Pliny the Elder, by two Rhodian sculptors in the 2nd century BC. It illustrates the story of two Theban youths who tied their stepmother to the horns of a bull to punish her for mistreating their real mother. The *Farnese Hercules* is a 2nd-century AD copy of a lost bronze attributed to the Greek sculptor Lysippus. Hercules is shown having completed the last of his labours, stealing the Golden Apples of the Hesperides (he holds

The *Farnese Hercules*, a Roman marble copy of a Greek bronze, found in the Baths of Caracalla in Rome.

one of them behind his back). The **Tyrannicides** is an example of a Greek statue copied by Hadrian for his villa at Tivoli (*see p. 283*). It shows two young Athenians who were hailed as champions of democracy for their murder of the tyrant Hipparchus, although they were sentenced to death for the deed. The Greek original (6th century BC) was one of the first statues to represent real people rather than gods or mythical heroes. The **cult image of the goddess Artemis** shows her as an icon of generative power, her chest covered with the scrota of bulls (not breasts, as is sometimes thought). Many copies of the original statue were made. This one dates from the 2nd century AD.

Campanian sculpture

The **Doryphorus** from Pompeii is the most complete copy of the famous spear-bearer of Polyclitus (c. 440 BC), which was considered the perfect model of manly proportions (*see pp. 271–72*). The **Aphrodite of Capua**, which once stood in the Capua amphitheatre, is a 2nd-century AD copy of a Classical Greek original. It showed the goddess of love gazing at herself reflected in the burnished shield of Ares, the god of war. The stern and memorable **Aphrodite Sosandra** shows the goddess not as an embodiment of erotic love but as the personification of aloof virtue. A bronze original existed in Athens in the 5th century BC. This version was found in the ruins of a copyist's studio at Baiae.

Art from Vesuvian sites

The mosaics, wall paintings, glassware and everyday objects in this superb collection are familiar, in many cases, through pictures and reproductions. Nothing, however, comes close to the experience of seeing them in real life: the very ordinariness of some of the things is their most memorable and moving quality. This is not to say that there are no great works of art here: though Pompeii and Herculaneum were essentially provincial towns, some of their inhabitants possessed both great wealth and impeccable taste, and there are pieces here of exceptional workmanship.

STYLES OF POMPEIAN WALL PAINTING

Pompeian painting is traditionally divided into four styles. In the **first style** (2nd century BC) plaster is simply painted to resemble coloured marble. In the **second style** (c. 80 BC to the end of the 1st century BC) the wall is covered with illusionistic architecture, landscapes or figure scenes. The **third style** (c. 20 BC–AD 45) was more decorative: monochrome panels are adorned with delicate patterns of garlands, swags, small-scale architectural features and wispy figures. It was this style that inspired the craze for 'Pompeian interiors' in 18th- and 19th-century Europe. The **fourth style** (after AD 62) is the most commonly found in the Vesuvian area. It blends the *trompe l'oeil* of the second style with the flatter elegance of the third. It is contemporary with the decorations of Nero's Domus Aurea in Rome and has much in common with them.

Museo e Gallerie Nazionali di Capodimonte

Beyond map p. 317, 3 (Via Miano 2). Open daily except Wed 8.30–7.30. Entrance through the most northerly of the building's three courtyards. The palace is 4km from Piazza del Municipio and 3.5km from Piazza Garibaldi (Stazione Centrale). To get there, take Metro 2 to Cavour (map p. 317, 3) then bus 178, M2 or 201 from Piazza Museo Nazionale, also buses C63 or R4 from Piazza Dante (map p. 316, 6).

The former palace of Capodimonte, the royal residence of the Bourbon monarchs, is magnificently situated in a fine park, enjoying a wide view of Naples. Its collections are divided into four sections. On the first floor are the Farnese Collections and the Royal Apartments. On the second floor is a representative collection of Neapolitan painting from the 13th–18th centuries. The third floor houses modern and contemporary art.

The Farnese Collections

The rectangular gallery at the top of the staircase (Room 2) is devoted to works celebrating Pope Paul III, to whom the fame and fortune of the Farnese family are largely due. He created the duchies of Parma and Piacenza and gave them to his son. His grandson made an advantageous alliance with the daughter of Charles V, the Holy Roman Emperor. Three famous portraits by Titian show Paul III, both alone and with two of his grandsons, Ottavio (who married Charles V's daughter) and Alessandro (who became a cardinal at the age of 14). Both young men are portrayed as obsequious in the extreme. After this room the collection is arranged chronologically and by schools.

The Royal Apartments

The Royal Apartments (Rooms 30–60) are a rich showcase of European decorative arts from the 18th and early 19th centuries. The rooms also hold some major paintings, including portraits of Charles III and the famous court portrait by Goya of his son, Charles IV of Spain, with his wife and family. Porcelain is also well represented here, including some fine pieces from the Capodimonte manufactory, founded by Charles III. His interest in porcelain came from his wife, Maria Amalia of Saxony, whose grandfather, Augustus the Strong, had founded the manufactory at Meissen. The **Museo Nazionale della Ceramica** in Villa Floridiana (*map p. 316, 9; open 8–2 except Tues*) has a much more extensive collection.

Painting in Naples from 1200–1700

The finest Neapolitan works date from the 13th century, with the artists called to Naples by the Angevin kings. While these rulers generally employed architects from France, they chose their artists from among the masters of the major Italian schools: Pietro Cavallini from Rome, Giotto from Florence, Simone Martini and Tino di Camaino from Siena. No works certainly by Giotto survive in Naples, but his follower, Roberto d'Oderisio, is represented here with a *Crucifixion* and a *Madonna of Humility*. Simone Martini's famous *St Louis of Toulouse Crowning Robert of Anjou* is also here. St Louis was the elder brother of King Robert the Wise, but he renounced the throne in favour of life as a Franciscan friar. He was canonised in 1317, and this painting was commissioned to celebrate that event.

The best Renaissance painting in Naples is typically by Florentine masters, summoned by the Aragonese viceroys. The major Neapolitan painter of the 15th century is Colantonio, who was in turn the master of Antonello da Messina (*see p. 371*), and whose style shows a debt to Flemish painting. A representative selection of his works is in Room 67. Andrea da Salerno, too, has left many fine works throughout Campania. His *St Nicholas of Bari Enthroned* is an example of his 'Raphaelism *alla neapolitana*': the pure colours and sweet-featured women are somehow given a southern cast.

The proliferation of churches and convents in Naples led to a great artistic flowering in the 17th century. This was Naples' artistic golden age, and the fame of its artists—Jusepe Ribera, Battistello Caracciolo, Salvator Rosa, Mattia Preti, Luca Giordano—spread throughout Europe. Perhaps the dominant name on this list is the first. Jusepe Ribera was a Spaniard, and his dark, dramatic style epitomises the mood of the Church in Naples in his day (his *St Jerome and the Angel of Judgement* is in Room 87). He was matched in darkness and drama by Caravaggio, exiled from Rome for murder and from Malta for insulting the Grand Master of the Order of St John. He took refuge in Naples until his involvement in a brawl in a waterfront tavern got him expelled from this city too. Ribera and another foreigner, Belisario Corenzio, born to a Greek family near Lecce, joined forces with the native Caracciolo in the 'Cabal of Naples' to prevent competition from the north. Using intimidation and death threats, they hounded the Bolognese artists Annibale Carracci and Guido Reni from Naples, and it is suspected that they poisoned Domenichino, who had come to Naples to work on the Chapel of St Januarius in the cathedral (*see p. 315*). Caravaggio's *Flagellation* is in Room 78; works by Caracciolo are in Room 79. After Caracciolo's death in 1641 and Ribera's in 1652, the soul of Naples found its most perfect expression in the compositions of the last name on the list: Luca Giordano. Luca had trained with Ribera, but his instincts were much lighter and more exuberant and his work combines Neapolitan drama with an attractive lightness of touch. Works by his hand are in Room 103.

Certosa di San Martino

Map p. 316, 10–6. Piazza San Martino 5. Open daily except Wed 8.30–7.30. Montesanto funicular to Via Morghen; Centrale funicular to Piazza Fuga; Metro 1 to Piazza Vanvitelli.
The Carthusian monastery of San Martino was founded in the 14th century but transformed into a splendid example of the Neapolitan Baroque by Cosimo Fanzago (director of works 1623–56). The church is a repository of Neapolitan art of the 17th century. Flanking the entrance are statues of *St John the Baptist* and *St Jerome* by Fanzago, and two paintings of *Moses* and *Elijah* by Jusepe Ribera. More prophets, also by Ribera, are in the spandrels above the chapels. The ceiling fresco of the *Ascension* is the work of the Bolognese artist Giovanni Lanfranco. The fourth chapel on the left has magnificent frescoes with stories of Mary by Battistello Caracciolo (the frescoes in the second chapel on the same side are also by his hand). Above the altar in the treasury (*entered through the sacristy*) is Ribera's masterpiece, the *Deposition* (*illustrated overleaf*). The early 18th-century fresco on the vault showing the *Triumph of Judith* is Luca Giordano's last work.

VISITING NAPLES

• **By air:** Naples airport is just north of the city. Two airport buses connect to the city centre: ANM *Alibus* to Piazza Garibaldi (Naples Central Station; *map p. 317, 4*) departs c. every 25mins; CLP to Piazza Municipio/Beverello (*map p. 317, 11*) departs c. every 40mins. Taxis charge fixed fares to principal destinations within city limits.

• **By car:** Paid parking is available throughout the city. The most useful car park is on Piazza Municipio (*map p. 317, 11*).

• **By train:** There are four main stations in Naples: Centrale (*map p. 317, 4*); Piazza Garibaldi (in the same complex but at a lower level); Mergellina (Piazza Mergellina, *beyond map p. 316, 13*); and Campi Flegrei (in the suburb of Fuorigrotta). Naples is c. 90mins by Eurostar from Rome, 4hrs from Bari, 4¹/₂ hrs from Reggio Calabria and 6hrs from Milan.

Two commuter railways serve the Bay of Naples. The Circumvesuviana line (www.vesuviana.it) runs to Pompeii and Sorrento from Stazione Circumvesuviana on Corso Garibaldi (*map p. 317, 8*). The Cumana and Circumflegrea lines (www.sepsa.it) run west to Pozzuoli, Baia and Cuma from Stazione Montesanto (*map p. 316, 6*).

• **Public transport in Naples:** There is no easy way to get around Naples except on foot. Traffic is so heavy that it is practically at a standstill all day. Where helpful, bus, tram and metro routes are given in the text. There are information offices (with a map of the system) at the central railway station. *Uniconapoli tickets* (which can be used on buses, funiculars or the underground) are sold at newsstands and tobacconists, and must be stamped on board. There are two types, one lasting 90mins and the other all day. Detailed information on routes and schedules at www.anm.it.

• **By taxi:** There are taxi stands in all the main squares. Keep watch on the meter. There are fixed supplements for holiday or night (11pm–6am) service, for luggage, and for radio calls (T: 081 570 7070, 081 556 4444 and 081 556 0202). A return fee must be paid for taxis sent beyond the city limits.

• **By sea:** Ferries depart from the Beverello pier (*map p. 317, 11*) to Capri (1hr 20mins), Pozzuoli (30mins) and Sorrento (1hr). Fast boats (hydrofoils and catamarans) run from Beverello and from Mergellina (*beyond map p. 316, 13*) to Capri (40–50mins) and Sorrento (30mins), daily. Fast boats are generally significantly more expensive than ferries. Tickets are available at the dock and from selected travel agents; schedules and other information at www.campaniatrasporti.it.

SPECIAL TICKETS

The **Campania Arte Card** offers admission to many of the region's museums and archaeological sites, free travel on local transport, and discounts on selected services. Cards may be purchased for 3 or 7 days at www.artecard.it, participating museums and monuments, major railway stations and many hotels. In Naples the card covers the museums at Santa Chiara and the Certosa di San Martino.

Deposition, Jusepe Ribera's masterpiece in the Certosa di San Martino. The sombre atmosphere of Spanish religious painting of the period is present here, together with a Caravaggesque depth of shadow and a bold use of pitch black. The contrast between the haggard flesh tints and the blood-red drapery is also typical.

The most luxurious hotels in Naples are on the waterfront overlooking the Santa Lucia yacht basin. The €€€ **Excelsior** ■ is a venerable establishment, famous among Neapolitans for its rooftop terrace, a favourite place to gather for an aperitif on warm evenings (*Via Partenope 48, T: 081 764 0111, www.excelsior.it; map p. 316, 14*). €€€ **Vesuvio** ■ offers elegant public spaces, including a *trompe-l'oeil* frescoed staircase, and a bounteous breakfast buffet (*Via Partenope 45, T: 081 764 0044, www.vesuvio.it; map p. 316, 14*).

Charming, small, central hotels include the €€ **Chiaia Hotel de Charme** ■, in a former patrician palace just a few steps away from Piazza del Plebiscito (*Via Chiaia 216, T: 081 415555, www.hotelchiaia.it; map p. 316, 10*) and €€ **Palazzo Alabardieri** ■, with elegant rooms and a cosy wood-panelled bar (*Via Alabardieri 38, T: 081 415278, www.palazzoalabardieri.it; map p. 316, 14, Alabard.*).

It is not difficult to eat well in Naples. All over town there are small, welcoming places serving good, traditional food and excellent pizza. €€ **Bersagliera** on the waterfront (down a ramp of steps across the street from Naples' luxury hotels) is an authentic *trattoria* where you can watch the boats come and go while enjoying delicious fish (*Borgo Marinaro, Banchina Santa Lucia, T: 081 764 6016; closed Tues and in Jan; map p. 317, 15 inset*). € **Caffè Gambrinus** ■ is a historic, popular café near Palazzo Reale, with excellent coffee and pastries (*Via Chiaia; map p. 316, 14*). €–€€ **Amici Miei** is an attractive, wood-panelled place specialising in meat dishes (*Via Monte di Dio 78, T: 081 764 4981, 081 764 6063; map p. 316, 14*).

THE PHLEGRAEAN FIELDS

Naples is surrounded by volcanoes. The most famous is Vesuvius, to the east. To the west stretch the Phlegraean Fields (*Campi Flegrei*), a broad region of craters and fumaroles encircling the bay of Pozzuoli. Activity below the surface is quiescent; there has been no eruption since the 12th century, though in 1538 a new cone did appear. The area was colonised first by the Greeks, and under the Romans became a favoured resort, with a host of luxurious summer villas. Little remains of these, though there are some scattered ruins. The landscape, however, is remarkable, and the area is easily accessible from Naples (*see p. 327*).

Pozzuoli and the Solfatara

The main town of the Phlegraean Fields is Pozzuoli (*map p. 421, A2*), today a cluster of colourful houses clinging to a craggy headland. It was colonised by the Greeks, who called it *Dikaearchia*. Its present name derives from the Latin *Puteoli* (from *puteus*, a well), a reference to the abundant hot springs. *Pozzolana*, the volcanic ash used by the ancient Romans to make waterproof concrete, came from here. Geological activity is still registered: in 1970 part of the town was damaged by bradyseism, a 'slow earthquake' that raised the ground more than 75cm in six months.

The spectacle (and odour) of naturally occurring sulphur amid dense clouds of steam make it easy to understand why the ancients placed the entrance to Hades in the Phlegraean Fields. Near Pozzuoli there is a cave named the 'Grotta del Cane', where foreign visitors in the 18th and 19th centuries would be treated to the spectacle of a dog being 'killed' by the noxious vapours and then miraculously revived.

The best-preserved remains of the ancient city are the so-called **Serapeum** on the waterfront (Via Roma), the ruins of a large enclosed complex with a central circular building. It was in fact a market, and not a temple to Serapis, as its name suggests, although the dedication would not have been inappropriate. Serapis was a grain deity of Egyptian origin, and his cult was widespread in port cities across the empire. Puteoli was the chief trading port of Italy, and grain ships from Alexandria would dock here. In the **Rione Terra archaeological area** on the old Roman acropolis (*open at weekends 9–6 or 7*) an industrial-scale bakery with flour mills has been found. Between the two railway lines which traverse the town is the **amphitheatre** (*open Wed–Mon 9–dusk*). Smaller than that of Capua, it was still very large (20,000 spectators), and dates from the same time as the Colosseum in Rome. The substructures below the arena (dens for wild beasts and rooms for stage machinery), added under Trajan or Hadrian, are in a remarkably good state. St Januarius (*see p. 315*) and his companions were imprisoned here under Diocletian before their executions near the **Solfatara**, the large crater that extends behind Pozzuoli. For long quarried for its sulphur (which still occurs naturally there), it takes the form of a great bubbling cauldron of vapour jets and puffs of smoke.

Lake Avernus and Cumae

Four kilometres to the northwest of Pozzuoli is another crater, this one filled with water to form the perfect caldera lake known as **Avernus** (Lago d'Averno). It was considered by the ancient Romans to be the entrance to Hades: Virgil describes it in his Book VI of the *Aeneid*, when Aeneas descends to the Underworld after consultation with the Cumaean Sibyl. Virgil would certainly have seen the lake. Though born near Mantua, he wrote his *Georgics* in Naples (a tomb alleged to be his can be seen at Piazza Piedigrotta on the outskirts of the city, at the foot of the Roman tunnel built to link Neapolis with Puteoli). Another such tunnel, built by the same engineer, exists at Avernus: the Grotta di Cocceio, which linked the lake to Cumae. It was built on the orders of Agrippa, who was naval commander under Octavian, the future Augustus (the Roman fleet was stationed here, at Misenum, today's Capo Miseno). The ruins on Lake Avernus' eastern shore, known as the Temple of Apollo, are in fact the scant remains of a bath house.

Cumae, perhaps the oldest Greek colony in Italy, appears today as nothing more than a mass of scattered ruins. Beyond the entrance to the excavations (*open daily 9–dusk, refreshments, Cuma bus stop*), a tunnel in the rock leads to the **Cave of the Cumaean Sibyl**, one of the most famous of ancient sanctuaries. The cave consists of a long, broad *dromos*, or passageway, ending in a rectangular rock-hewn chamber. The *dromos* is lit by six tunnels opening to the west (so it is best visited in the afternoon). At a lower level (reached by a path to the left) a huge Roman crypt c. 180m long burrows through the hill. This may be part of Agrippa's tunnel connecting Cumae to Lake Avernus (*see above*). Wide enough for chariots to pass, it is lighted at intervals by vertical openings, and could be travelled through with ease until it was damaged by fighting in 1943.

Baia

Baia, the ancient *Baiae*, is a large village standing on the bay of the same name, with splendid views across the Gulf of Pozzuoli. In was the fashionable bathing resort of Roman society, and successive emperors rivalled each other in the construction of magnificent seaside palaces. Large sections of the **ruins** now lie under the sea. Those that remain on dry land (*open Tues–Sun 9–dusk*) are beautiful and evocative. Their importance lies in their vaulted halls, which mark an important architectural development. The three large, domed thermal chambers (referred to as temples but now known to have been baths) presage later developments in Roman building, culminating in Hadrian's magnificent Pantheon in Rome. Particularly fine (and particularly like the Pantheon, though half the size) is the circular hall of the so-called Temple of Mercury.

The **museum** in the Aragonese castle at Bacoli (*Via Castello 39; closed Mon*) has finds from excavations all over the Phlegraean Fields.

The geological continuation of the Phlegraean Fields is the island of **Ischia**, famed for its thermal springs and now a sophisticated spa resort. Ferries from Pozzuoli take approximately 1hr.

VISITING THE PHLEGRAEAN FIELDS

GETTING AROUND

• **By car:** There is pay parking in Pozzuoli by the harbour, and in blue-marked spaces around town; in Baia by the castle/museum, and in Cuma at the archaeological park.
• **By metro and bus:** Country buses are infrequent. Metro line no. 2 from Naples goes to Pozzuoli. Once there, you can take city bus no. P9 from the harbour (Via Roma) to Cuma.
• **By rail:** Frequent trains to the Phlegraean Fields are operated by the Cumana and Circumflegrea railways from Naples Montesanto station (*map p. 316, 6*); trains run every 20mins to Pozzuoli (20mins), Baia (30mins), Fusaro and Licola (for Cumae, 40mins by rail + 2km on foot).

SPECIAL TICKETS

The Campania Arte Card (*see p. 322*) covers the amphitheatre and Serapeum in Pozzuoli, the museum in Baia (Bacoli) and the archaeological parks in Baia and Cumae.

WHERE TO STAY IN THE PHLEGRAEAN FIELDS

Bacoli
€–€€ **Villa Oteri.** ■ Elegant rooms and a good restaurant in an attractive villa. An excellent base for exploring the area. *Via Lungolago 174, T: 081 523 4985, www.villaoteri.it.*
Baia
€ **Batis**. Simple, handy guesthouse with restaurant and bar, very close to the ruins. *Via Lucullo 101, T: 081 868 8783, www.batis.it.*
Cuma
€€ **Villa Giulia.** ■ Small B&B in a lovely old farmhouse near the Sibyl's cave. Garden and pool. *Via Cuma Licola 178, T: 081 854 0163, www.villagiulia.info.*

WHERE TO EAT IN THE PHLEGRAEAN FIELDS

In Baia there are cafés and restaurants near the ruins, and Pozzuoli also has simple and adequate places to eat. The best place to be based, if you plan to spend any time in the area, is Bacoli, south of Baia, which has a clutch of popular restaurants. Among the best are €€ **A Ridosso**, on the road from Cuma to Capo Miseno, which serves good local fish (*Via Mercato di Sabato 320, T: 081 868 9233; closed Sun evening and Mon, late Aug and late Dec–early Jan*); €€ **Al Pontile** (*Via Spiaggia Torregaveta, T: 081 868 9180*) and € **Abraxas** (*Via Scalandrone 15, T: 081 854 9347; closed Tues, www.abraxasosteria.it*).

CAPUA & CASERTA

Santa Maria Capua Vetere (*map p. 421, A1–A2*) famously opened its gates to Hannibal in 216 BC and it is said that the Carthaginians were so dissipated by the *luxuria* of the Capuans that they never achieved another victory. On the northwest outskirts are the ruins of the famous amphitheatre (*open daily 9–dusk*), second in size only to the Colosseum in Rome, though it is several decades earlier and has survived less well. Of the original four tiers, only the lowest remains, and parts of the second. As at Pozzuoli, the most rewarding parts are the tunnels under the arena. Several of the statues that once adorned the seating area (including the famous *Aphrodite*) are now in the archaeological museum in Naples. Capua was a centre of the cult of Mithras (a small Mithraeum can be visited; *for the cult see p. 280*), and is famous for its links with the slave named Spartacus, who was sent to the renowned gladiator training school here. In 73 BC he and a band of followers escaped, using the crater of Vesuvius as a hideout while they gathered allies and found weapons. His resulting army, said to have been over 100,000 strong, won several victories against Roman battalions sent to crush them. They fought their way towards the Alps, and were about to cross them into safety when for reasons unknown they turned back. The decision was to prove a fatal mistake. Spartacus was defeated, and though he himself died a hero's death on the field, six thousand of his followers were crucified along the Via Appia between Capua and Rome. There is now a Museum of the Gladiators at Piazza I Ottobre (*combined ticket with amphitheatre*).

Caserta: the royal palace

Caserta is home to the most sumptuous royal palace in Italy, the vast Reggia. It was commissioned by Charles III of Bourbon, avowedly to rival the palaces of Versailles in France and Madrid in Spain: in its interior decoration and design it carries strong flavours of both. Charles laid the first stone in 1752. His architect was Luigi Vanvitelli. Born in Naples to a Dutch landscape painter, he had trained and enjoyed his early successes in Rome. The palace was completed under Charles' successor, Ferdinand IV, to a simpler design than originally intended. Nevertheless, the work remains Vanvitellian in spirit, a clear transitional piece between the late Baroque and the Neoclassical. Ferdinand used the palace for lavish receptions, balls and hunting parties. It passed to the state in 1921, and in 1945 was the scene of the surrender of the German forces in Italy.

The **royal apartments** (*open Wed–Mon 8.30–7.30, last entry 1hr before closing*), all with superb tapestries and period furniture, include the private rooms of Ferdinand IV, the bedrooms of his successors Ferdinand II and Francis II, and the Throne Room, where the ceiling painting shows Charles III laying the foundation stone. Around the walls are portrait medallions of the kings of Naples from the Norman Roger de Hauteville to the penultimate Bourbon ruler, Ferdinand II. Joseph Bonaparte and Joachim Murat are not included in the line-up. The charming **Palatine Theatre** on the ground floor was inaugurated by Ferdinand IV in 1769.

The **gardens** (*open Wed–Mon 8.30–dusk*) were laid out under Vanvitelli. They are vast, with lawns and walks stretching away into the far distance. Their crowning glory is the great cascade, a waterfall some 75m high that can be seen clearly from the palace 3km away (a shuttle bus will convey you there or back, if the distance defeats your stamina).

VISITING CAPUA & CASERTA

GETTING AROUND

• **By car:** Driving from Naples to Caserta and Santa Maria Capua Vetere takes 30–40mins. There is underground parking at the Reggia of Caserta, and pay parking by the amphitheatre in Santa Maria Capua Vetere.

• **By bus:** Country bus services (operated by ACMS) are quite good on weekdays. Buses from Caserta railway station go c. every hour to

and from Santa Maria Capua Vetere (15mins).
• **By train:** Frequent trains link Naples
(Centrale) with Caserta in 30–50mins. Trains
to Santa Maria Capua Vetere (on the Rome
line) take an extra 10–20mins. Eurostar trains
from Rome stop at Caserta (1hr 40mins).

SPECIAL TICKETS

The Campania Arte Card (*see p. 322*) covers
the royal palace and gardens of Caserta and
the Roman amphitheatre and museums in
Santa Maria Capua Vetere.

WHERE TO EAT IN CAPUA & CASERTA

Caserta
€€ **Le Colonne**. This is a curious place—a
quiet, comfortable restaurant specialising in
organic foods and fresh buffalo mozzarella:
one dish features mozzarella served at three
different temperatures. Dinner by reservation
only. Closed Tues and two weeks in Aug. *Via
Nazionale Appia 7–13, T: 0823 467494.*
€€ **Massa**. This simple *osteria* is at once rustic and sober, and the same can be said of its
cuisine; in a historic palace with garden seating in fair weather. Closed Mon and two
weeks in Aug. *Via Mazzini 55, T: 0823 456527.*
Santa Maria Capua Vetere
€ **Ninfeo**. Simple and straightforward, this
restaurant draws a good local following
thanks mainly to its delicious homemade
pastas and grilled meats. Closed Mon, two
weeks in Aug and one week in Dec. *Via
Cappabianca, T: 0823 846700.*

MOUNT VESUVIUS & ITS CITIES

The landscape east of Naples is dominated by the broken cone of one of the most
famous mountains in the world: Vesuvius (1277m). It is still an active volcano, prone
to what are known as effusive eruptions, characterised by the emission of thin lava.
The most recent of these was in 1944. There is no suggestion that violent eruptions
have ceased: the last was in 1631, and vulcanologists warn that another could be
imminent, posing grave danger to the lives of over two million people.

POMPEII

The ruins of Pompeii (*map p. 421, B2*) are one of the most popular sights in Italy,
attracting over two million visitors a year. The tragedy and pathos of the fateful eruption of AD 79 are brought home with extraordinary force: here we see real lives
exposed, people's homes and furnishings, their personal belongings, even the casts of
their bodies, still sprawled where they died, some trying to save their valuables, others their children, still others, like the chained gladiators or the famous guard dog,
unable to flee. We see human lives not as those who lived them would have wished
them to be portrayed to posterity, but as they really were. We see the town as it really was, too, with its luxurious villas, its hustling graffiti and its squalid brothels.

Pompeii in history

Pompeii was not founded by the Romans: it is much older, and by the 6th century BC

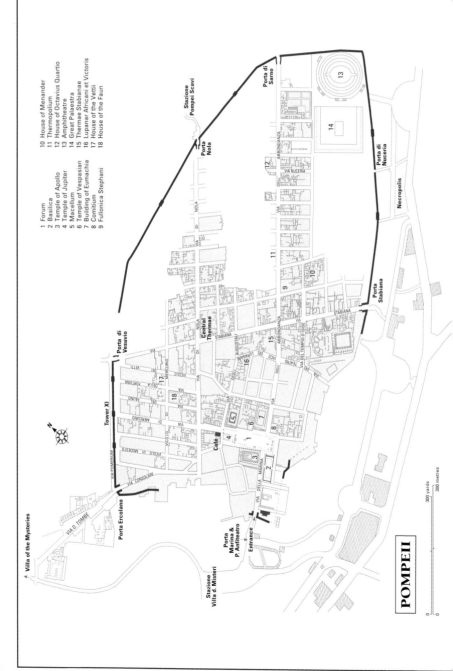

1 Forum
2 Basilica
3 Temple of Apollo
4 Temple of Jupiter
5 Macellum
6 Temple of Vespasian
7 Building of Eumachia
8 Comitium
9 Fullonica Stephani

10 House of Menander
11 Thermopolium
12 House of Octavius Quartio
13 Amphitheatre
14 Great Palaestra
15 Thermae Stabianae
16 Lupanar Africani et Victoris
17 House of the Vettii
18 House of the Faun

POMPEII

Villa of the Mysteries

Stazione
Villa d. Misteri

Porta Ercolano

Tower XI

Porta di
Vesuvio

Porta Nola

Stazione
Pompei Scavi

Porta di
Sarno

Porta di
Nuceria

Necropolis

Porta
Stabiana

Porta
Marina &
P. Anfiteatro

Entrance

Café

300 yards
300 metres

was already a flourishing commercial centre and one of the chief ports on the Campanian coast. Roman veterans were given property here, and Latin gradually eclipsed the native Oscan. Under the Romans it was a populous provincial centre. Seventeen years before the fatal eruption, in AD 62, a severe earthquake damaged Pompeii. At the time of the final disaster it seems that repairs were still being carried out to major buildings. Pompeii was preserved because it was covered with a layer of tiny fragments of pumice (*lapilli*) and afterwards by a similar layer of ash. All who had not left the city in the first hours died. It is estimated that of an approximate population of 20,000, two thousand perished.

No serious attempt was made to excavate at Pompeii until the mid-18th century. It has been a long and arduous process, and is still not complete. The greatest problem now faced by archaeologists, having unearthed the city and exposed it to the elements, is how shall it be preserved? The attempt to leave as much as possible *in situ* is a laudable one, and one from which scholars and casual visitors alike sincerely benefit.

Visiting the site

Reports of thefts from Pompeii, a shortage of custodians, a shortage of money to restore crumbling buildings, the sheer pressure of visitor numbers, and the lack of an effective strategy to keep the site open while at the same time coping with the inevitable deterioration of its fabric and the loss of wall paintings to atmospheric damage have led the Italian government to declare a state of emergency. Over the coming years closures are likely to many parts of the site. It is impossible to predict what will be closed, when, or for how long. The description below outlines the features of major importance.

The site is open daily April–Oct 8.30–7.30, last entry 6; Nov–Mar 8.30–5, last entry 3.30. The official custodians, stationed in different quarters of the ancient town, will open some of the closed houses and give information. They are not supposed to accept gratuities or accompany visitors. A brief visit can be made in about two hours. In hot weather the absence of shade is noticeable and some sort of hat is a must. Be sure, also, to wear comfortable shoes: the paving-stones are notoriously uneven.

The ancient city

The Roman city of Pompeii was surrounded by a rampart reinforced by towers and pierced by eight gates. The streets were paved with large blocks of Vesuvian lava and bordered by kerbed pavements. Stepping-stones for pedestrians are set at regular intervals in nearly all the roadways. The clean, dry avenues of today's site, with vistas of the volcano beyond, give little idea of the narrow, dark, malodorous reality that would have obtained in the 1st century AD. Fountains in Pompeii are numerous, and water in them was perpetually flowing and overflowing. The stepping stones would have been very necessary to cross streets which functioned, in effect, as arterial drains. Many of the exterior walls of the houses and shops bear graffiti, usually in red. These include campaign recommendations of candidates for city government, snatches of poetry, records of events, and the usual quota of personal remarks, declarations of love, and ribaldry. Little existed in the way of zoning as we understand it today: private homes rubbed shoulders with shops, taverns, brothels, bath houses, bakeries and laundries. The noise and the clatter, as well as the stench, must have been prodigious. Many establishments exhibit a phallus at the entrance (either carved, painted, or in mosaic). This is not an indication that the place was a brothel, but is the symbol of Priapus, the guardian-god, and was used as a talisman to ward off intruders.

The Pompeian house

The older dwelling houses at Pompeii consist of an interior courtyard (atrium) surrounded by a roofed arcade. Opposite the entrance was the tablinum or chief living room, where the family dined and received their guests. To right and left were the *cubicula* (bedrooms). In the days of the Roman Empire, many houses developed along more commercial or luxurious lines. Behind the tablinum came the peristyle (a porticoed courtyard, often laid out as a garden). The tablinum ceased to be the general living room and was occupied by the family archives. Its former role was taken by the triclinium, distinguishable by its larger size, its mosaic floor and the recesses in the lower part of the walls. In some houses, the rooms adjoining the main façade and at the sides might be converted into shops opening onto the street. Even in the most commercial districts, however, when the life of the householder was greatly encroached on by shop and factory, the residential part of the house remained a self-contained unit. Nowhere in Pompeii is there an example of the blocks of flats so typical of Ostia, the port of Rome.

The interior rooms had no windows, but were decorated with highly polished wall-paintings. Air and light came into the house through openings in the roof. The roof of the atrium sloped inwards leaving a space in the middle (compluvium). Below this was the impluvium, a basin that received the rainwater from the gutters of the compluvium and passed it on to the *puteus* or cistern.

Nearly every house had a second floor and some had a third; these were used by slaves or let out as lodgings. Each house had a *lararium*, a shrine for the household gods.

The principal ruins

The **forum** at Pompeii **(1)** is the best surviving example of a Roman town square. Along its two long sides ran a colonnade, above which was a gallery from which spectators could watch the games and events held here before the construction of the amphitheatre. The area enclosed by the colonnade was adorned with honorific statues, many pedestals of which survive. The larger base halfway down the west side is the orator's tribune. In a niche at no. 31 is a *tabula ponderaria* (table of weights and measures) showing the standard measures of capacity.

At the southwest corner of the forum was the **Basilica (2)**, the law court, with a raised tribune for the judges at the far end. To the north of it, on the other side of Via della Marina, is the **Temple of Apollo (3)**. At the north end of the forum stands the **Temple of Jupiter (4)**, the *capitolium* of the Roman town, believed to have contained cult images of the Capitoline Triad (Jupiter, Juno and Minerva). Beneath the temple was the treasury. The east side mixes commercial and religious spaces: the **macellum**, or general market **(5)**; the **Temple of Vespasian (6)**, begun after the earthquake and never completed; and the **Building of Eumachia (7)**, an imposing building erected by a priestess and benefactress of the cloth-workers and perhaps used by them as a salesroom. Symbols of empire were potent presences even in the far-flung provinces, and in the front vestibule of this building are niches which held statues of the founders of Rome and the architects of Roman greatness: Aeneas, Romulus, Julius Caesar and Augustus.

The building at the southeast corner of the forum, on the other side of Via dell'Abbondanza, was the **Comitium (8)** or polling booth.

Via dell'Abbondanza

The name Via dell'Abbondanza comes from a misinterpretation of a bust on a fountain at the back of the Building of Eumachia. It does not show a personification of Abundance, as was once thought, but is a figure of Concordia Augusta, the goddess of harmony within the imperial family and the deity to whom the Building of Eumachia was dedicated. The street leads east past the **Fullonica Stephani** at no. 7 **(9)**, a laundry where clothes were washed, bleached with urine and pressed in the *pressorium* (by the wall to the left on entering). The **House of Menander (10)**, a fine dwelling belonging to a kinsman of the empress Poppaea (a native of Pompeii, first the mistress, then second wife, then victim of Nero), where silver plate—now in the Naples museum—was found in 1930. During the eruption the family and their slaves took refuge in the room with the strongest roof, but they were trapped by the collapse of part of the peristyle and eventually killed when the roof came down on their heads. Among the wall paintings is a seated figure of the poet Menander, from which the house takes its name. The calidarium (warm room) of the private baths is well preserved.

Returning to Via dell'Abbondanza, you pass a **thermopolium** on the left **(11)**, a tavern where wine and hot meals were served. The rooms on the upper floor seem to have served as a brothel. Further along on the right, between two other taverns, is the **House of Octavius Quartio (12)**, a dwelling which perfectly evokes well-to-do Pompeian life. A wide portal, closed by a bronze door and flanked by benches, opens into the atrium with its impluvium. The rooms around it are small, but beyond lies the most famous feature of the house: its garden, with vine-clad pergolas and an elaborate water feature with a series of communicating basins and, at the east end, a summer dining area where the water ran between two couches surmounted by paintings of Narcissus and Pyramus and Thisbe.

Beyond, at the end of the street, rises the **amphitheatre (13)**. Begun in 80 BC, it is the oldest such structure known. To the west of it stretch the ruins of the **Great Palaestra (14)**, the city's gymnasium. In the latrine in the southeast corner the bodies of many youths were found, who had fled here for protection from the blast.

West of Via Stabiana

The **Thermae Stabianae (15)** were the largest baths in Pompeii. The entrance leads to the palaestra, where people would have exercised before bathing. The men's baths are to the right. These include the *apodyterium* (changing-room), complete with

Wall painting from the House of the Vettii. The amorini shown here are making perfume from fresh flowers. The wealthy Vettii brothers were freedmen who made their fortune from perfumery and the the cut-flower business.

recesses for clothes; the circular frigidarium (cold bath); the tepidarium with a plunge-bath; and (at the back) the calidarium (hot bath). Hot air circulated below floor level. The women's baths are adjacent.

On Vico del Lupanare is one of the most visited houses in all Pompeii: the notorious **Lupanar Africani et Victoris (16)**, a brothel where the lewd paintings on the walls fully depict the services on offer. Opposite is the Inn of Sittius, the sign of which was an elephant. Sadly a victim of the elements, he no longer trumpets the hostelry's wares.

On Vicolo di Mercurio stands one of the most famous of all the houses at Pompeii, the **House of the Vettii (17)**. It belonged to Aulus Vettius Restitutus and Aulus Vettius Conviva, two wealthy freedmen. Its lavish paintings are still in their original positions, but sadly the house has been closed for restoration for some time. Nevertheless, you can still see the famous Priapus in the entranceway, his huge penis more of an encumbrance than an asset. The **House of the Faun (18)**, the residence of the Casii family, occupies the whole of its insula. It was an old-fashioned house, comfortable but venerable. On the pavement in front is the salutation *have* ('welcome'). The name of the house comes from the bronze statuette of the *Dancing Faun* found near the impluvium. The one *in situ* is a copy; the original is in the archeological museum in Naples, as are most of the other treasures found here, including the mosaic floors of the four triclinia (one for each season), and the great mosaic of Alexander the Great in battle against Darius of Persia.

The Villa of the Mysteries

To reach the villa, walk along Via delle Tombe, or take the road that leads north from Villa dei Misteri station on the Circumvesuviana line.

The **Villa of the Mysteries** takes its name from a hall with vivid wall-paintings of life-size figures, dating from the 1st century BC. The paintings form a cycle, thought to represent a sexual initiation rite connected with the cult of the god Dionysus. The scenes have been interpreted as follows, starting on the wall to the left of the door: (a) A child reads the rite before a young bride and a seated matron; (b) a priestess and three female assistants make a sacrifice; (c) *sileni* play musical instruments in a pastoral setting; (d) the frightened initiate takes flight; (e) the marriage of Dionysus and Ariadne; (f) a kneeling woman unveils the sacred phallus while a winged demon raises a flagellum to strike the young initiate, who seeks refuge in the lap of a companion; (g) the orgiastic dance of Dionysus; (h) the dressing of a bride for initiation, and a seated woman who has undergone the initiation rite.

HERCULANEUM

Herculaneum (Ercolano; *map p. 421, B2*), destroyed with Pompeii in AD 79 and rediscovered in 1709, was a residential town, neither as large nor as commercially important as Pompeii, but surrounded by the villas of wealthy Romans. The site is small compared with Pompeii and less immediately striking. The domestic buildings, especially their upper storeys and wooden parts, are better preserved, however, for Herculaneum was not pummelled by ash and pumice but was buried in a river of soft mud. Though Pompeii is the more important and more famous site, those who are pressed for time and can only visit one of the two would do well to visit Herculaneum. The whole site can easily be seen in half a day, and you will be spared the nagging fear of having missed something, which is a persistent companion at Pompeii.

Overview of the ancient city

Roman Herculaneum was probably only about a third the size of Pompeii. It had something of the character of a coastal resort (the sea was much closer then than it is now), and on the seaward side it ended in a terraced promontory, lined with costly villas. The harbour itself lay outside the town walls.

While Pompeii was dominated by the commercial classes, Herculaneum was a town of genteel citizens, artisans and fishermen. In the richer houses, the Hellenistic plan of a building around a peristyle is often found, though the peristyle is often less of a colonnade and more of a closed loggia with windows overlooking a central garden court. The poorer classes lived in tenements.

The site

Open daily April–Oct 8.30–7.30, last entry 6; Nov–March 8.30–5, last entry 3.30; T: 081 732 4311, www.pompeiisites.org.

Some of the best-preserved buildings of middle- and working-class Herculaneum are

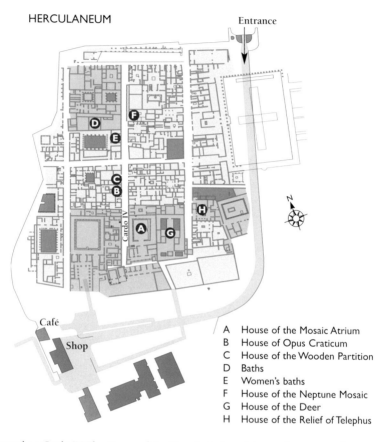

HERCULANEUM   Entrance

Café
Shop

A   House of the Mosaic Atrium
B   House of Opus Craticum
C   House of the Wooden Partition
D   Baths
E   Women's baths
F   House of the Neptune Mosaic
G   House of the Deer
H   House of the Relief of Telephus

located on Cardo IV. The **House of the Mosaic Atrium** (A) must have enjoyed a superb view from its *diaeta*, or siesta room, deliberately designed with low windows. The **House of Opus Craticum** (B) is a splendid example of the cheap wood-and-plaster construction of workers' housing. The structure consists of a shop with a workroom behind, and preserves its upper floor with a balcony overhanging the street. Next door is the **House of the Wooden Partition** (C), whose façade offers a striking picture of the external appearance of a Roman private house. The wooden partition that closes the tablinum has been reconstructed *in situ* with its ancient hinges and lamp brackets.

In the upper part of the Cardo IV are the well-preserved **baths** (D), erected c. 20 BC. In the centre is the palaestra, the main entrance of which was at no. 7 Cardo IV Superiore. The entrance to the **women's baths** (E) is next door. You enter a waiting-room and pass through a small linen-room to the changing-room, whose mosaic shows a triton surrounded by dolphins and cuttlefish. The small tepidarium and calidarium are virtually complete. Note the pretty marble bench with human feet.

On the lower floor of the **House of the Neptune Mosaic (F)** is the best-preserved shop in the town, with its specially constructed shelves for holding storage jars. A wooden partition separates the shop from the living quarters behind, where a little court has a nymphaeum with green and blue mosaic (to the left as you look in), and the famous *Neptune and Amphitrite* mosaic, which gives the house its name.

Two grand houses

The **House of the Deer (G)** is the grandest dwelling yet discovered at Herculaneum, with a frontage of 43m. The entrance leads into a covered atrium, from which an enclosed corridor leads to the spacious triclinium, painted with architectural motifs on black and red panels and paved in marble intarsia. The kitchen, latrine, and *apotheca* (store room) form a compact block to the right. The garden is surrounded by an enclosed corridor, lit by windows. The far walk leads to an arbour flanked by flower beds and siesta rooms, overlooking a sun terrace which would originally have opened directly onto the sea.

The **House of the Relief of Telephus (H)**, the most extensive of Herculanean mansions, is built around two sides of the neighbouring house and at two levels on the hillside. The peristyle, on the lower level, surrounds a garden with an azure basin at the centre. Off the south walk are the ruins of a once grand room with a polychrome marble floor and the reconstructed marble dado on one wall. In an adjacent room is a well-preserved relief of the myth of Telephus, showing Telephus, the son of Hercules, consulting the Delphic oracle, who tells him that a wound he received at the hands of Achilles will only heal if he shows Achilles the way to Troy.

VISITING MOUNT VESUVIUS & ITS CITIES

GETTING AROUND

• **By car:** There is ample paid parking at the entrance to the ruins of Pompeii. There is no car park at the site at Herculaneum, though pay parking is available in the surrounding streets.

• **By train:** The Circumvesuviana Railway (www.vesuviana.it) runs from Naples or Sorrento to Pompei Villa dei Misteri and Ercolano Scavi. Journey time is 20mins from Naples to Herculaneum and 35mins to Pompeii. Sorrento–Pompeii takes 30mins. From Ercolano station to the ruins it is a 10-min walk along the wide road descending seaward.

SPECIAL TICKETS

The Campania Arte Card (*see p. 322*) gives free entry to the excavations at Pompeii and Herculaneum.

WHERE TO EAT

There are snack bars at both sites. That at Herculaneum is pretty basic. For a proper meal, the € **Casa Rossa 1888 al Vesuvio** in the town is a reliable restaurant-pizzeria (*Via Vesuvio 30, T: 081 777 9763; closed Tues*). The Posto di Ristoro at Pompeii, behind the forum (*open as the ruins*) is more than adequate. A tavern stood on this site in the 1st century AD.

CAPRI

With its dazzling sunlight, its pure air, and its luxuriant vegetation, Capri (*map p. 421, A2*) has been famed as a resort for as long as mankind has been going on holiday. The emperor Tiberius built a villa on the island: towards the end of his reign he was increasingly in search of solitude, and he found it here, on this steep rock, which rises high and sheer out of the water. Swimmers and sunbathers will find the lack of beaches a deterrent. If you like walking, you will enjoy Capri more. For the crowds, there is designer shopping—bizarrely, on this crag in the middle of the wide blue sea, the best-known labels in the fashion industry have found it worth their while to open retail outlets.

Capri in history

Capri has been inhabited since ancient times. It was colonised by the Greeks, and subsequently passed to the Romans. It was the emperor Tiberius who really brought the island to the world's attention, when he retired here in AD 27. During the Middle Ages Capri was occupied by the Saracens, whose influence can be seen in the architecture, notably the plain barrel-vaulted roofs of many houses and churches. In 1806, during the Napoleonic wars, the island was taken and fortified by the British; in 1808 it was captured by the French, and in 1813 it was returned to the Bourbon rulers of Naples.

In the late 19th and early 20th centuries Capri gained a reputation as a home for expatriate artists and eccentrics. Axel Munthe, the Swedish physician, lived here and wrote the famous *Story of San Michele*; Maxim Gorky lived here in 1907–13 and ran a school for revolutionaries visited by Lenin and Stalin, and the writer Norman Douglas here enjoyed the kind of pederastic dalliance that was a punishable offence at home.

Capri town

Capri is a small, quaint town, lying 142m above sea level. Its main square is the broad Piazza Umberto Primo, the upper station of the funicular, which overlooks the Marina Grande. Leading off it is the smaller, enclosed 'piazzetta', filled with shops and cafés and flanked on one side by the church of **Santo Stefano**. The interior contains, in the chapel left of the high altar, a fragment of inlaid pavement from the Villa Jovis (*see opposite*). The main street of the town is the Via Camerelle, on which stands the famous Hotel Quisisana. The *camerelle* in question are the arched substructures of an ancient road, now transformed into expensive boutiques. Via Federico Serena leads down from here to the **Certosa di San Giacomo**, a venerable, dilapidated old charterhouse (*open Tues–Sun 9–2*) founded in 1371. In the lunette above the entrance to the church (deconsecrated) is a *Madonna and Child* with a kneeling queen with Angevin *fleurs de lys* on her gown. This is Joan I, Queen of Naples, and is possibly a portrait by the Sienese painter Andrea Vanni, who acted as ambassador to the popes in Avignon. He also painted the portrait of St Catherine of Siena in the Dominican church in that city (*see p. 217*). In 1553 the monastery was sacked by the corsair Dragut, after the defeat of his great adversary Andrea Doria (*see p. 165*). The death knell of San Giacomo was sounded by the Napoleonic administration, which dissolved it in 1807.

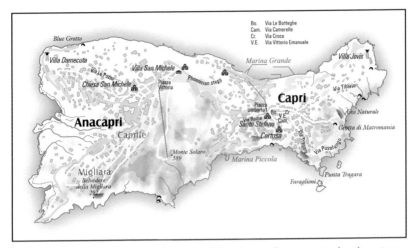

From the Piazzetta you can walk to two of Capri's most famous natural and semi-natural sights, the **Arco Naturale** (20mins) and the **Grotta di Matromania** (10mins more). From the northeast corner of the piazza follow the narrow Via Botteghe and Via Croce. Where the latter divides take Via Matromania (right), from which steps lead down to the Arco Naturale, a natural archway in the rock. Returning to the path continue to descend (10mins) to the Grotta di Matromania, a cave probably once used as a sanctuary of Cybele, the mother goddess. Via Pizzolungo continues back to town, hugging the coast, and offering splendid views of the water and the Faraglioni rocks that lie offshore.

Villa Jovis

It is easily possible to walk to the ruins of Tiberius' Villa Jovis (*open daily 9–dusk*). From the centre of town take Via Le Botteghe, then Via Croce, and where it forks, turn left to take the rising Via Tiberio. Gruesome legends surround this villa. Most can be traced to the writings of Tacitus and Suetonius, and have a distinct tabloid flavour to them: a reclusive emperor must surely have been peculiar, and most likely depraved as well. Hence the tales of him pushing victims off the cliff into the sea. Later commentators have not wanted to rehabilitate him: the emperor under whom Christ was crucified fits nicely into the mould of monster. The villa was once a residence of palatial proportions, but little real sense of this can be gained from the ruins, which have been too much plundered and offer too little of splendour to the lay imagination. The most evocative and atmospheric part is the Imperial Loggia, reached by a corridor and steps from the area where the imperial apartments once stood, below the flat terrace with the modern chapel and statue. This loggia takes the form of a long, straight belvedere, almost a kilometre in length and heavy today with the scent of pines, where it is thought the emperor would take a daily constitutional walk, much as Hadrian would walk around his Pecile, on the advice of his doctor, to aid digestion (*see p. 283*). Alcoves with the remains of benches on the landward side provided places to sit and admire the view. The view from the eastern end, down to the water far below, makes it easy to understand how legends of victims being tossed to their deaths could grow up. From the loggia paths lead to the dank remains of what might have been an observatory. In his last years Tiberius became obsessed about his own death, and employed augurs and astrologers to reassure him that it wasn't imminent.

Anacapri

The only way to reach Anacapri in past centuries was to climb the **Phoenician Steps**, a steep stairway built either by the Greeks or the Romans (not the Phoenicians). They are still in use today, but buses from Capri town make the journey less arduous. From the main square in Anacapri, Piazza Vittoria, a lane lined with souvenir shops (Via San Michele) leads to the **Villa San Michele** (*open daily Nov–Feb 9–3.30, March 9–4.30, April 9–5, May–Sept 9–6, Oct 9–5*), a house with a lovely garden and loggia created by the doctor, writer and antiquary Axel Munthe (1857–1949) on the site of one of Tiberius' villas. It houses a small collection of antiquities and copies of well-known pieces from Pompeii and other Campanian sites.

In Anacapri village itself is the church of **San Michele** (*on Piazza San Nicola; take Via Orlandi from Piazza della Vittoria; open from 9.30 or 10 to at least 5*), which has a majolica floor of the Garden of Eden (1761) thought to have been made to a design by the Neapolitan artist Francesco Solimena.

The Blue Grotto

Since its 'discovery' and publication to the wider world in the early 19th century, this cave on the north coast of the island, with its wonderful azure light effects, has been a popular destination for visitors. The approach is made by sea (*daily 9–dusk, except when strong north or east winds blow, making entrance to the cave impossible*), from the Marina Grande or from the landing at the base of the footpath from Anacapri (Via Lo Pozzo). The light effects are best between 11am and 1pm. The cave was used by Tiberius as a nymphaeum (above it are the scant remains of a villa, named Damecuta).

VISITING CAPRI

GETTING AROUND

• **By sea:** Ferries run daily from Naples (80mins), Sorrento (45mins), and seasonally from Amalfi and Positano (April–Oct). There are also fast hydrofoils and catamarans from Naples (50mins), Sorrento (20mins–1hr), Positano (50mins) and Amalfi (70mins). See www.capri.net/it/orari-traghetti. All services dock at Marina Grande. From here Capri town is reached by bus, by funicular railway, or on foot (Via Truglio and Via San Francesco).

• **On land:** Frequent buses go from Via Roma in Capri town to Marina Grande and Anacapri; and Capri is famous for its convertible-limousine taxis, though most of the antique models are now gone. A funicular railway connects the town and harbour (services every 15mins). Porters with electric trolleys can take your luggage around; hire them from beside the bus terminus on Via Roma.

Tinted photograph (c. 1900–10) of people boating in the Blue Grotto. The azure colour effects are obviously not shown, but one can fully appreciate how light enters and illuminates the cave.

WHERE TO STAY ON CAPRI

There are two grand luxury hotels on the island. One is at Anacapri (€€€ **Capri Palace**, *Via Capodimonte 2, T: 081 978 0111, www.capri-palace.com*), and the other is in Capri town, the €€€ **Grand Hotel Quisisana**, with sumptuous rooms, two restaurants, two pools, tennis courts, a sauna, Turkish bath, and a famous bar with panoramic terrace (*Via Camerelle 2, T: 081 837 0788, www.quisi.com; open April–Oct*). In keeping with the expatriate artist theme of the island is the €€€ **Punta Tragara**, designed by Le Corbusier, a curvaceous concrete hulk magnificently set on a clifftop amid lush gardens with two salt-water pools (*Via Tragara 57, T: 081 837 0844, www.hoteltragara.com; open Easter–Nov*). Those who remain unconvinced about the merits of concrete as a building

material might prefer the €€ **Villa Brunella** ■, a renovated villa with stepped terraces leading down to pool and sea. It also has a good restaurant (*Via Tragara 24, T: 081 837 0122; open Easter–Oct*). €€ **Villa Sarah**, a family-run establishment with rooms facing the sea or the garden, is a good, unpretentious place to stay (*Via Tiberio 3/a, T: 081 837 7817, www.villasarah.it; open Easter–Oct*).

WHERE TO EAT ON CAPRI

It is perfectly possible to eat adequately on Capri, but understandably, a place which does not produce its own food and relies on the delivery of supplies is not in the culinary vanguard. The most famous restaurant on the island is the €€€ **Quisi** at the Hotel Quisisana, which has its ups and downs, but is always elegant and ceremonious (*Via Camerelle*

2, T: 081 837 0788; closed Nov–March). €€ **Le Grottelle** is a good place, a secluded restaurant serving excellent seafood, in a grotto with a terrace overlooking the sea. It's a bit of a hike from the Piazzetta, but well worth it (*Via Arco Naturale 13, T: 081 837 5719; closed Thur except July–Sept).* The hotel restaurant at €€ **Villa Brunella** seves good food in a cordial atmosphere (*Via Tragara 24, T: 081 837 0122; closed Nov–March).* In **Anacapri** there are several places within easy distance of the Villa San Michele, on the main road from Piazza Vittoria.

THE AMALFI COAST

In the 19th and early 20th centuries, Sorrento and the stretch of precipitous shoreline on the south side of its peninsula, with the resort village of Positano, were some of the most famous destinations in Italy, their very names enough to conjure up scented visions of lemon and orange blossom, wide sea views, summer breezes and Neapolitan song. Things are somewhat different today. Beach tourism has stolen much traffic from these places, though the associations of their names linger on, and the coach tours do good business, clogging the winding coast road (which is slow and hair-raising to drive at the best of times), and making you wonder, perhaps, why on earth you came. There are a number of reasons. The landscape is as sublime as it ever was, the oranges and lemons are still there (and grapefruit trees as well), the climate is benign, and the architecture extremely interesting. The best art in the region is medieval. The best architecture is Saracenic, and fine examples are to be found in Amalfi and Ravello.

Sorrento and Positano

Sorrento (*map p. 421, B2*) is a busy, easy-going slightly scruffy little town, with the air of a resort whose finest hour has been and gone. It was the birthplace of the poet Torquato Tasso (1544–95), who returned here as a fugitive in 1577, on the run from the court of Ferrara after drawing his dagger on a pageboy. The town today is known for its limoncello liqueur and for its wood intarsia work. A museum on the latter subject (Museobottega della Tarsialignea; *Via San Nicola 28; open Tues–Sat 10–1 & 4–7*) preserves exquisite examples from the 15th century to the present day. In some of the old shops in town you can still see the marquetry workers at their jigsaws. Another museum on the east edge of town (Museo Correale di Terranova; *Via Correale 48; open daily except Tues 9–2*) contains more of the same, as well as a collection of landscape paintings by the Posillipo School, a group of artists who took their inspiration from the scenery of the Bay of Naples. Their best-known exponent is Giacinto Gigante.

   Positano, on the north coast, is remarkable for the way its characteristic square, white houses tumble down the steep slopes. Its wealth came from trade in the days when the Mediterranean was at its commercial height. The most direct way from the top of the town to the sea is down the narrow, bougainvillea-shaded Via dei Mulini, past the grand Palazzo Murat, once the summer retreat of Joachim Murat (whom Napoleon made king of Naples; *see p. 313*) and now a hotel. The church on the seafront has an ancient icon of the *Virgin and Child*. According to legend, it was stolen in a Saracen raid but spoke to its despoilers in a vision and persuaded them to return it. The raid is re-enacted every year on 14th August, the eve of the feast of the Assumption.

At Conca dei Marini, between Positano and Amalfi, the road passes close above the **Grotta di Smeraldo**. The cavern may be reached by steps or by lift, or by boat from Amalfi; a visit takes c. 1hr (*open March–May 9–5, June–Sept 8.30–6, Oct–Feb 9–4, seas permitting*). Its name derives from the colour of the interior, which glows with a remarkable emerald green light.

Amalfi

Amalfi (*map p. 421, B2*) is much more than a resort town. It was once a powerful maritime republic, one of the four greatest in Italy (with Pisa, Genoa and Venice). The town today has a venerable history, a magnificent cathedral, charm and bustle, superb views of sea and mountain, and a wide stretch of beach. It is not surprising to learn, therefore, that it is the most interesting and rewarding place to visit on this famous coast.

Amalfi in history

Amalfi's rise to prominence began in the mid-6th century, under the Byzantine Empire. During the early Middle Ages it became commercially important for its trade with Asia. It established itself as a maritime republic in the 9th century and remained independent until 1135. Its wealth and strength made it the object of rivalry and suspicion. It was subdued by the Norman king of Naples, Roger, in 1131 and twice captured by its rival Pisa (1135 and 1137). Though it lost its independence, its maritime laws, the *Tavole Amalfitane* (now on display in the Museo Civico), remained effective until 1570.

The duomo

Piazza del Duomo is dominated by the great 9th-century cathedral of St Andrew (*open daily July–Sept 9–7, Oct–June 10–5*), with a richly coloured façade in the Lombard-Norman style (restored in the late 19th century). The magnificent bronze main doors, with cross and saints in inlaid silver, were commissioned by the head of the Amalfitan colony in Constantinople and made there before 1066. The frescoes on either side of the entrance date from 1929.

One of the loveliest features of the duomo is its small 13th-century cloister, known as the 'Chiostro del Paradiso'. It has narrow interlaced arches in the Saracenic style. Once the burial-place of illustrious citizens, it is now a museum of architectural fragments and contains exquisite 12th-century mosaics of flowers, exotic birds and geometric designs. There is also an interesting, though damaged, fresco of the *Crucifixion* by a Campanian painter of the school of Giotto (possibly Roberto d'Oderisio). Giotto was in Naples in the 1330s, and influenced the work of many local artists.

The old cathedral, entered from the cloister, is deconsecrated and functions as an exhibition hall. Particularly beautiful are a 14th-century Sienese-school fresco of the *Madonna and Child*, and an exquisite 14th-century marble relief of the *Madonna della Neve*, attributed to the great Dalmatian-born master Francesco Laurana. Relics of St Andrew the Apostle are preserved in the crypt below, beneath an elaborate altar. From the crypt you ascend to the duomo itself. Highlights of the restored interior include the fine nave ceiling, a 16th-century silver-gilt reliquary of St Andrew holding fish (south aisle) and a lovely mother-of-pearl Crucifix from Jerusalem (west end).

Other sights of Amalfi

Seaward of the duomo is the town hall, where the *Tavole Amalfitane* (*see above*) are displayed in the **Museo Civico** (*hours subject to change, but usually open 8–2 except Sun*). From the main road west of the town you can climb the long flight of steps to the former **Convento dei Cappuccini**, now a hotel, with beautiful views.

The main street of Amalfi is Via Genova, which leads uphill to become a pleasant walk through the cool Valle dei Mulini, with its water-operated paper mills (now ruined). On the outskirts of town the small **Museo della Carta** (*open March–Oct daily 10–6.30, Nov–Feb 10–5.30 except Mon*) occupies a restored mill. Amalfi paper was highly sought-after in the Middle Ages, both by the papal curia and by the court of Naples.

Ravello

Ravello (*map p. 421, B2*) is an extraordinary phenomenon: an isolated village, cut off from the coast by narrow ravines and beetling rocks, set in a land of hardship and toil, where grain does not grow and where men still work with mules, yet filled with palaces and hotels in the highest luxury class—how on earth did it happen, and why?

The origins of Ravello are not known, though stories persist of patrician Roman founders, driven to these hilly fastnesses by barbarian incursions. By the 9th century it was under the rule of Amalfi; in 1086 it became independent, maintaining its liberty until 1813. It enjoyed great prosperity in the 13th century, deriving its wealth not from wool, as did the communities of Scala on the opposite side of the Dragone valley, but from maritime trade. Its merchants formed relations with Sicily and the East, and introduced the Norman-Saracenic style of architecture. That is all very well, but it does not explain the hotels. Responsibility for these must lie at the feet of all the artists and writers of the early 20th century, who abjured the rigidity of northern Europe for the freedom they found, or perceived to find, here. D.H. Lawrence was one: he wrote part of *Lady Chatterley's Lover* at Ravello. André Gide was another: he wrote *L'Immoraliste* here. A theme seems to be emerging.

The duomo

The duomo of San Pantaleone (*open 9–12 & 5.30–7*) dates from the days of Ravello's independence and commercial prosperity. It was built in 1086, with fine bronze doors by Barisano da Trani (1179), and contains, in the nave, two remarkable pulpits. The one on the left (c. 1131) has a mosaic of Jonah and the Whale. That on the right is a magnificent structure in marble, borne by six spiral columns resting on lions, three male and three female, and adorned with mosaics. It was commissioned in 1272 by Niccolò Rufolo, a member of one of Ravello's foremost families, who claimed descent from a Roman consul. The museum in the crypt preserves a beautiful bust of a woman, said to be Niccolò's wife Sigilgaita. Fresco fragments at the west end of the nave and in the south aisle are thought to owe debts of inspiration to Simone Martini and to Giotto. Martini was at the court of Robert of Anjou, and Giotto worked in Naples in the early 14th century.

Villa Rufolo and Villa Cimbrone

The tower gateway of the **Villa Rufolo** (*open daily: summer 9–8, winter 9–6*) stands to the south of the duomo. The building was begun in the 11th century, and exists today as an ensemble of Norman-Saracenic buildings, partly in ruins, famed above all for their gardens. It was here that Wagner found his inspiration for the magic garden of Klingsor in *Parsifal*. The quasi-Moorish arcading of the tiny cloister-like court is striking. The villa hosts the Ravello Festival in summer, a series of music and dance events stretching over four months between late June and October. The focus was originally on Wagner, but today you are just as likely—if not more likely—to find contemporary works on the programme.

From the cathedral square, Via San Francesco leads to **Villa Cimbrone** (now

Mosaic fragment of an exotic bird, displayed in the cloister of Amalfi cathedral. The Oriental influence on Campanian art is clearly seen in the geometric star patterns and in the two-dimensional, almost carpet-like nature of the design as a whole.

a hotel), with a famous garden (*open summer 9–8, winter 9–dusk*). Both villa and garden were created by an Englishman, Lord Grimthorpe, who fell in love with the spot and acquired it in 1904, forcing wild nature into formal parterres and walks, and turning the ramshackle farmhouse on the site into a fanciful palace with a tiny mock cloister. There are superb views from the Belvedere Cimbrone at the extreme edge of the gardens. Elsewhere one is assailed by plaques bearing snatches of sentimental verse or spooked by *déjà vu* visions of statuary: there are copies of Verrocchio's *David* from Florence and of the *Hermes Resting* from the archaeological museum in Naples (or Axel Munthe's villa at Capri, where there is another copy).

VISITING THE AMALFI COAST

GETTING AROUND

• **By car:** The 50km journey from Naples to Sorrento takes about 1hr; Positano is just

10km further, but it will take an additional 20mins to get there by the mountain road. Roads are winding and slow, and crowded in summer.

• **By bus:** Frequent buses run between Naples (Piazza Municipio) and towns on the peninsula. (SITA, www.sitabus.it).

• **By train:** The Circumvesuviana railway (www.vesuviana.it) runs about every 20mins from Piazza Garibaldi in Naples to Sorrento in 1hr 10mins. Trains also stop at Herculaneum and Pompeii.

• **By sea:** Fast boats (hydrofoils and catamarans) run several times daily, in 30mins, from Naples (Beverello pier) to Sorrento, from where there are daily boat and ferry connections to Capri.

WHERE TO STAY ON THE AMALFI COAST

Amalfi

€€€€ **Santa Caterina**, one of the Leading Small Hotels of the World, is an elegant, luxurious place famous for its terraced gardens, spacious rooms and enchanting views (*Strada Statale Amalfitana 9, T: 089 871012, www.hotelsantacaterina.it*). Right above the old harbour is the €€ **Luna Convento**, an unusual place in a 700-year-old monastery, with sea views from most rooms and breakfast in a Byzantine cloister (*Via P. Comite 33, T: 089 871002, www.lunahotel.it*). The lovely €€ **Villa Lara**, in a former private villa, is a tiny (7 rooms) *hotel de charme* set among lemon groves and bougainvillea and overlooking Amalfi and the sea (*Via delle Cartiere 1, T: 0898 736358, www.villalara.it*).

Positano

Positano takes its reputation as a glamorous resort seriously, and there are some senior hotels here. €€€€ **San Pietro**, a member of the Relais & Châteaux group, is 2km from the town, towards Amalfi. It is famous for its glass-walled rooms descending in flowering terraces to the sea (*Via Laurito 2, T: 089 875455, www.ilsanpietro.it; open April–Oct*). Two fine hotels in town are €€€ **Le**

Sirenuse ■ (*Via Cristoforo Colombo 30, T: 089 875066, www.sirenuse.it*) and €€€ **Palazzo Murat** (*Via dei Mulini 23, T: 089 875177, www.palazzomurat.it*). €€ **Villa Rosa** ■ is a simpler B&B. All rooms have private terraces and breakfast in bed is free (*Via C. Colombo 127, T: 089 811955, www.villarosapositano.it; open March–Nov*).

Ravello

€€€€ **Palazzo Sasso**. Simply one of Europe's top hotels: quiet luxury, unforgettable views and impeccable service come wrapped in the trappings of a medieval patrician palace. Open March–Nov. *Via San Giovanni del Toro 28, T: 089 818181, www.palazzosasso.com*.

€€€ **Villa Cimbrone**. Quirky fauxmedieval palace set in famous gardens. Open April–Oct. *Via Santa Chiara 26, T: 089 857459, www.villacimbrone.com*.

Sorrento

€€€ **Bellevue Syrene**. Fine old hotel on a quiet street overlooking the sea. *Piazza della Vittoria 5, T: 081 878 1024, www.bellevuesyrene.it*.

WHERE TO EAT ON THE AMALFI COAST

Amalfi

For fish and seafood there are €€ **Da Gemma**, an old-fashioned *trattoria* overlooking the duomo (*Via Fra' Gerardo Sasso 9, T: 089 871345; closed Wed and mid-Jan–mid-Feb, Aug open evenings only*) and €€ **La Caravella**, a well-known restaurant built into what used to be the old ship arsenal (*Via Matteo Camera 12, T: 089 871029; closed Tues except July–Aug, and in Nov–Dec*).

Positano

€€ **Buca di Bacco** is a traditional fish restaurant by the sea (*Via Rampa Teglia 8, T: 089 875699; closed Tues and Nov*). €€ **Le Tre Sorelle** is another, on the beach. Both are good

value, if such a thing is to be had in Positano (*Via Marina 5, T: 089 811922; closed Nov–Dec*).
Sorrento
€€ **Vela Bianca**. Once a sailors' tavern, the restaurant at Hotel Il Faro fills up with locals at lunchtime. The fish is good, so is the wine, and there is pavement seating in summer. *Marina Piccola 5, T: 081 878 1144.*

PAESTUM

South of the Sorrentine peninsula, between Salerno and Agropoli, is the wide alluvial plain of the River Sele (*map p. 421, B2*). This was a favoured area of Greek colonisation in Antiquity, and it is here, at the southern end of the floodplain, that one of the greatest of all survivals of Greek civilisation is to be found: the ruins of Paestum, which have stood for a thousand years, in Ozymandian majesty in the midst of this solemn wilderness.

The site
Originally called *Poseidonia*, the city of Poseidon, Greek god of the sea (the Roman Neptune), Paestum was founded c. 600 BC. Its favourable position, with easy access to trade routes and with an ample supply of water and fertile land, caused the colony to expand and thrive. The three main Doric temples are of Greek construction. In 273 BC the Romans took the city. Under the Latinised name of Paestum they enriched it with a forum, an amphitheatre, baths and the so-called Temple of Peace. The ruins you see today comprise remains of numerous public buildings, four major temples, the forum, an extensive residential quarter, and half of the ellipse of the amphitheatre (the other half still lies under the modern road).

The sanctuary of Hera
The temples of Paestum (*open daily 9–7; last admission 6.30*) belong to two groups, that to the south (dedicated to Hera) includes the Temple of Hera (often called the Basilica) and Temple of Neptune; that to the north (dedicated to Athena) includes the Temple of Ceres. The **Temple of Hera (1)** is the earliest temple at the site (c. 530 BC), misinterpreted as a basilica in the 18th century. Its Doric colonnade of nine columns at either end and twice nine (i.e. 18) at each side, is still standing. Within the colonnade, where the remains of the temple proper stand, you can see how the cella was divided by a central line of columns, which suggests that it was sacred to two separate deities.

Slightly to the north stands the **Temple of Neptune (2)**, originally dedicated as a later temple to Hera or to Apollo. It dates from c. 450 BC and is superbly preserved, rivalled only by the Theseion at Athens and the Temple of Concord in Agrigento (*see p. 378*). Not only is the cella still miraculously intact, with its front porch (pronaos) and back porch (opisthodomos; with no opening in the wall), but the entablature survives too, as do the pediments. Only the roof is lacking. To the east are the remains of a large sacrificial altar. Greek temples were typically orientated towards the east, to face the rising sun.

The sanctuary of Athena

Running south to north and connecting the two halves of the site was the Via Sacra. West of it stretched the **residential area** of Paestum **(3)**; to the east, roughly at its mid-section, was the wide, rectangular forum, with the **Curia** (law courts) on one side **(4)** and the **Comitium** (place of assembly) on the other **(5)**. Just north of the forum are the ruins of the **Sanctuary of Fortuna Virilis** of the 3rd century BC **(7)**, used during the *Veneralia*, festivities in honour of Venus, whose statue was taken in procession, immersed in a central pool, then placed upon a platform (thereby re-enacting the birth of the goddess from the sea). This ritual was performed by married and pregnant women in order to ensure safe childbirth.

Further north along the Via Sacra stands the so-called **Temple of Ceres (8)**, in fact dedicated to the goddess Athena and dating from some time between the two southern temples. Once again there are the remains of a sacrificial altar in front of the temple.

The museum

The National Museum (*open daily 8.45–7.45, last admission 7; closed first and third Mon of the month*) is most notable for the truly extraordinary paintings from the so-called **Tomb of the Diver**, perhaps the only extant examples of Greek painting (c. 480 BC). The four panels forming the coffin are decorated with a banqueting scene. The lid shows the diver from whom the tomb takes its name, a naked youth who executes a perfect dive into a blue lake—a beautiful and moving allegory of death.

VISITING PAESTUM

GETTING AROUND

• **By car:** The drive from Naples (100km) takes about 90mins. Traffic can be slow during the summer, even on the motorway.

• **By train:** Frequent local trains make the run from Naples (Centrale) to Paestum in c. 90mins.

SPECIAL TICKETS

The **Campania Arte Card** (*see p. 322*) gives free entry to the excavations and museum at Paestum.

WHERE TO STAY AT PAESTUM

€ **Tenuta Seliano**. The village of Paestum is mainly a strip of shops and restaurants serving visitors to the ruins, so you're much better off in the country—especially on this estate just a few kilometres from the temples, with 12 guest rooms, a lovely garden with patio and pool, and excellent cuisine featuring home-grown olives and vegetables and fresh mozzarella. Open March–Oct. *Via Seliano at Borgo Antico, T: 0828 724544, www.agriturismoseliano.it.*

WHERE TO EAT AT PAESTUM

€€ **Nettuno.** ■ This is the restaurant of the Hotel Nettuno, adjoining the excavations near the south gate. The food is good, but the most amazing thing here is the location, offering incomparable views over the temples, especially from the summer terrace. Closed evenings and Mon from Sept–June. *Via Nettuno 2 (Zona Archeologica), T: 0828 811028.*

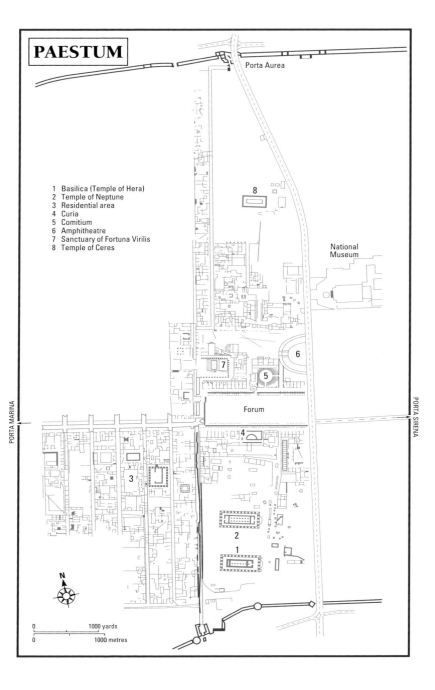

PAESTUM

Porta Aurea

1 Basilica (Temple of Hera)
2 Temple of Neptune
3 Residential area
4 Curia
5 Comitium
6 Amphitheatre
7 Sanctuary of Fortuna Virilis
8 Temple of Ceres

8

National
Museum

PORTA MARINA

PORTA SIRENA

7

6

5

Forum

4

3

2

1

N

0   1000 yards

0   1000 metres

BASILICATA, PUGLIA & CALABRIA

Sparsely-populated **Basilicata** (*map p. 421*) is a region of broad horizons. It was colonised from Greece in the 7th century BC and reached a high degree of prosperity, but was later drawn into the struggles between Rome and the Samnites and the campaign against Pyrrhus and Hannibal. Its ancient name was Lucania; the present name was assumed in honour of Emperor Basil II (976–1025), who overthrew Saracen power in Sicily and southern Italy.

The Norman conquest of the south was, one might say, completed in Basilicata, on the slopes of Mt Vulture, by Drago, grandson of Tancred de Hauteville, and by Humphrey and his half-brother Robert Guiscard. They were buried at Venosa, in the monastery church, but Melfi was their capital. It was at Melfi in 1231 that Frederick II set forth his new legal code, the *Constitutiones Augustales*. Frederick left a string of fine castles here, on the hills that overlook the great limestone plateau of central Puglia, on which stands his finest fortress of all, Castel del Monte.

Food and wine of Basilicata

Basilicata has particularly good cheeses. Most are fresh rather than mature—*mozzarella, burrino, provola, scamorza* and sweet or spicy *ricotta*. Equally interesting are Basilicata's sausages and salami. It seems that the art of preserving spiced meat in animals' entrails was invented here by the Lucani, the region's ancient inhabitants: from these ancient people the Romans derived the Latin name for sausage, *lucanica*. The modern Greek *loukaniko* must have the same origin. Basilicata is also known for a fine wine, Aglianico del Vulture, a magnificent red that has been cultivated on the volcanic slopes of Mt Vulture since ancient times. It comes as no surprise, perhaps, to be told that it was the favourite of Holy Roman Emperor Frederick II.

MATERA & ITS CAVE CITY

Matera (*map p. 421, C2*) is famous for the Sassi: two ridges (the Sasso Barisano and Sasso Caveoso) filled with a mixture of troglodytic habitations, churches and frescoed chapels, some of which are free-standing but most of which are carved out of the rock itself. The seemingly haphazard warren of buildings is indeed as arbitrary as it looks: this is 'spontaneous architecture', a manner of building that no longer exists in the developed West, and that elsewhere is characteristic of the shanty town or refugee camp. The dwellings really are piled one on top of another: the street that leads along one level of the ravine is in fact the roofs of the houses below. And although the dwellings can look cramped and mean from the outside, when you enter you will find that many are surprisingly spacious. Pressures of population in more recent times led to overcrowding and sanitation problems. The writer and artist Carlo Levi was a political prisoner in Basilicata from 1935; in his famous, unsparing portrait, *Christ Stopped*

Matera: detail of one of the Sassi.

at Eboli, he describes appalling hardship and squalor at Matera (Levi was also a painter, and there is a collection of his works in the Museo Nazionale dell'Arte Medievale e Moderna on the central Piazza Pascoli; *open Tues–Sun 9–1 & 3.30–7*). In the 1950s the Italian government cleared Matera, and moved its families away to new, sanitary housing. The troglodyte city, with its humble dwellings and simple painted churches, is now being restored, and is listed as a UNESCO site.

VISITING MATERA

GETTING AROUND

• **By car:** There is pay parking on most streets of the historic city.
• **By train:** Fast trains run from Naples to Ferrandina, where local trains connect to Matera. Travel time is roughly 3½ hrs, plus the wait between trains. Matera can be reached by trains (operated by FAL; www.fal-srl.it) from Bari in roughly 90mins.

WHERE TO STAY IN MATERA

€€ **La Casa di Lucio.** ■ Beautiful, romantic small hotel in the heart of the Sasso Caveoso. Rooms are former houses, some carved out of the rockface, some built into it. The décor makes the most of the limited natural light, and there is a good restaurant. *Via San Pietro Caveoso 66, T: 0835 312798, www.lacasadilucio.it.*
€ **Sassi.** ■ Central and comfortable, with views of the cathedral, this is another interesting hotel in the Sassi, with rooms half in and half out of the rock. *Via San Giovanni Vecchio 89, T: 0835 331009, www.hotelsassi.it.*

WHERE TO EAT IN MATERA

€€ **Basilico.** This is a local favourite, and with good reason. Everything is scrumptious, especially the oven-baked pasta dishes. *Via San Francesco 33, T: 0835 336540.*
€ **La Stalla.** *Trattoria* in a former stable carved out of the rock and overlooking the Sasso Barisano. Good local food at very reasonable prices. Closed Mon and one week in Aug. *Via Rosario 73, T: 0835 240455.*
€ **Le Botteghe.** Excellent little *trattoria* in the heart of the Sasso Barisano, with outdoor seating in summer. The cooking is traditional Materan, and they also rent rooms. Closed Wed. *Piazza San Pietro Barisano 22, T: 0835 344072.*

PUGLIA

There are many influences that have gone to make up Puglia (*map p. 421*). There are the ancient inhabitants—Pelasgians, Messapians, Daunians—who built their trulli and their dolmens. There were the Peloponnesian Greeks, who founded colonies at Taras (Taranto); the Saracens and Turks harassed the coasts; and the Spanish extended their rule here in the 16th century. The most impressive remains, however, were left by the Normans, who had a special relationship with Puglia. Prince of Taranto was the title given to the Norman ruler's second son. His eldest son and heir was Duke of Puglia. It is to Puglia, then, that we must go, to find out what it was that drew those adventurers here.

Puglia in history

Puglia flourished under the Roman rule that followed the defeat of Taras (modern Taranto), the splendid Spartan colony and focus of Greek culture in the region. After the fall of the Western Roman Empire, areas of Puglia came under Byzantine, Lombard and Arab rule before Byzantium finally brought the entire region under its sway in the 9th–10th centuries. Bari became the capital of a dominion that extended over much of present-day Basilicata as well as Puglia, and was administered by a *catapan* (governor). Long years of Byzantine rule lent a Greek character to the culture, religious worship and architecture of the region, traces of which are still evident today.

Puglia's rise to prominence came with the advent of the conquering Normans, who established the County of Puglia (1043), with its capital at Melfi, and later the Duchy of Puglia and Calabria. Prominence turned into prosperity under Frederick II of Hohenstaufen, whose Castel del Monte is one of the highlights of the region.

With Charles of Anjou's defeat of Frederick's heirs in the mid-13th century, Puglia followed the fortunes of Naples, becoming a province of that kingdom (*for the history of Naples, see p. 311*). Puglia joined the Kingdom of Italy by plebiscite in 1860. Today it is the richest and most dynamic region of southern Italy.

The geography of Puglia

The stones of Puglia, a mass of compact, crystalline limestone, figure prominently in the region's distinctive architecture. When the stone is quarried in blocks and is warm and creamy in colour, it is known (at least outside the region) as *pietra di Trani*: this is the basic material of the region's castles, churches and palaces. Also typical is the *pietra leccese*, a somewhat darker marl or sandstone, fine-grained and easy to work. More recently the tufa of northwestern Puglia has come into vogue. Its excellent insulating capacity makes it a valuable material for 'green', eco-friendly designs.

The Apennines protect Puglia from the west wind while leaving it open to influences from the Adriatic and from the south: it is partly because of this that the region receives much less rainfall than Italy's west coast. Surface water disappears into the porous limestone, so that Puglia is almost destitute of rivers, fully deserving its epithet of *seticulosa*, 'thirsty'. As is the case in so many Mediterranean lands, here too desertification is a risk. Nevertheless, the soil is well cultivated, and the land is well adapted for grain (Puglia is the only southern Italian region without mountains). Wheat is the chief crop in the almost treeless plain of the Tavoliere, or Capitanata, around Foggia. Further south, olives and vines predominate, interspersed with groves of almonds and figs.

Food and wine of Puglia

Like any other Mediterranean region, Puglia produces excellent olive oil, delicious fruit and vegetables, and good wine. But Puglia also produces wheat, and its bread is some of the finest in Italy. Puglia's history and position at the easternmost point of the Italian peninsula has also left it open to influences from the Levant and North Africa. The use of honey in sweets and the combination of sweet and savoury (chick peas with chocolate, for example, in the pancakes known as *cauciuni*) are examples of this.

Many Puglian dishes are found nowhere else in Italy. '*Ncapriata*, a very old Mediterranean dish (documented in ancient Egypt), is a simple purée of dried broad beans dressed with olive oil and chopped greens. *Orecchiette* are pasta 'ears' typically served with sautéed vegetables (rape, broccoli) or a rich horsemeat ragout. *Braciola alla barese* is veal wrapped around a filling of ham, parsley and pecorino, then sautéed slowly with tomatoes, olive oil and spices. Adriatic fish are also much on the menu here: sea bream (*dentice*) and gilthead bream (*orata*), usually grilled or oven-roasted.

Aleatico di Puglia is a historic wine, first developed for the table of Frederick II. It is made principally from the Aleatico grape, blended with much smaller quantities of Negroamaro, Malvasia Nera and Primitivo. Puglia's most famous white wines are Locorotondo and Martina Franca. Moscato di Trani is an exquisite dessert wine.

THE TERRA DI BARI

The area between Barletta and Bari, on Puglia's Adriatic coast, is famed for its splendid cathedrals. Though medieval Puglia first became truly prosperous under Frederick II, it was not he who instituted the great period of church building here. His attitude to the Church was ambivalent, and he famously included no chapel in any of his secular buildings. This is not to say that he was an atheist, as his detractors clamorously maintained. Nevertheless, the fact remains that castles, not churches, are his greatest architectural legacy. The great churches here were built by Frederick's predecessors, the Normans. These mercenaries-turned-conquerors combined diverse influences from France, Pisa, Lombardy and Byzantium into the style known loosely as the Apulian Romanesque, generally characterised by the massive solidity and rounded arches found in all Romanesque architecture as well as by a love of decorative moulding and carving, on door hoods and capitals, for example. But the style of decoration in this Apulian version is more obviously Oriental. Though the Normans were Latinisers, apostles of the Church of Rome and propagators of Benedictine monasticism in a land that had hitherto been subject to Eastern orthodoxy, the style of their church decoration is identifiably Byzantine or even Saracen.

Bari

Bari (*map p. 421, C1*) is the capital of Puglia and the second largest town in southern Italy after Naples. Its importance today reflects its history. Bari was the seat of the Byzantine governor during the days of the catapanate, and in the 11th century was a port of considerable importance, even rivalling Venice. The port is still very active today, and life in the old town revolves around it. The distinctive plan of maze-like, winding streets was designed to protect the inhabitants from the wind as well as from their enemies: it is said that Saracen invaders were lured into the blind alleys and attacked from the windows and rooftops above. In 1071, Bari fell to Robert Guiscard and his Norman knights. A few years later the remains of St Nicholas (the Nicholas who gave us Santa Claus) were brought here from Asia Minor. The Basilica di San Nicola, planned to house these relics, was begun in 1089.

San Nicola

Standing back to look at the main **west façade** of this church (*open 7.30–1 & 4–7.30, May–Oct 4–8*), you can see and appreciate some of the salient features of the Apulian Romanesque style, features which in varying ways are common to all these mighty buildings. The front is divided into three, with a tall, gabled central section. From the roofline descends a pattern of dwarf blind aracades. The apertures are quite numerous, but small. There is a central rose window. The **main entrance** is surrounded by a columned porch, richly carved with ornamental and symbolic motifs combining Arabian, Byzantine and Classical influences. There are two smaller, lateral doorways, also ornamented but less elaborately. There is a prevailing sobriety to the whole design.

The pure grey-whiteness of the interior is beautiful and dignified in the extreme. Even the anachronistic appearance of the 17th-century ceiling cannot really detract from it. An arched choir screen on tall columns with Romanesque capitals separates the nave from the transept. Beyond it is the high altar, preceded by three steps—the first decorated with palmettes, the second with birds, and the third with a Latin inscription commemorating two bishops—and surrounded by a 12th-century **ciborium**, the oldest in the region. The baldacchino, crowned by a double octagonal colonnaded dome, stands on four columns of crushed stone, the work of Como masters (*see p. 54*).

In the apse is the **tomb of Bona Sforza**, daughter of the duke of Milan (her Neapolitan-Aragonese mother is believed by some historians to have been the model for the *Mona Lisa*). Bona was duchess of Bari until her death in 1558. Also here is the **bishop's throne**, probably made for the Council of Bari of 1098 at which St Anselm defended the 'Filioque' clause in the Nicene Creed ('I believe in the Holy Ghost, the Lord, the giver of life, who proceedeth from the Father and the Son...'). The clause was added to the Creed by the Western Church, but the 'double procession' of the Holy Ghost was not accepted in the East.

The eastern, seaward-facing façade of San Nicola conceals the three apses of the interior and presents a stark front to the water, relieved by the fine main window, whose flanking columns are charmingly supported on elephants.

Trani

From Bari the coast road and railway run northwest through Molfetta, Bisceglie, Trani and Barletta, all of which have splendid cathedrals. That at **Molfetta** is particularly unusual, a geometric display of polygons, pyramids and rectangles, all relieved by intricate carving; the cathedral of **Barletta** was paid for in part by Richard Coeur de Lion. The finest of all, however, is without any doubt that at Trani.

Trani (*map p. 421, C1*) rewards the visitor with more than its cathedral. In a region that is often dishevelled and disorderly, Trani is a pleasing, whitewashed place with a pretty yacht harbour and a scattering of fish restaurants. Its cathedral is spectacular, rising high and narrow above the waterfront, its famous bell-tower pierced by an arch through which you can see the sea.

Under the Normans Trani was an important embarkation point for the Orient, and it became one of the busiest Crusader ports in Europe. The Templars, the religious

Two of the great architectural sights of Puglia: the Apulian Romanesque cathedral of Trani (11th–13th centuries), resplendent on the waterfront in the light of the evening sun (above), and (below right) the octagonal 'spy tower of Puglia', Frederick II's Castel del Monte (c. 1240), at once a fortress, a hunting lodge and a prison, which dominates the lonely landscape for miles around with its bright white geometric beauty.

military order of knighthood established to protect Christian pilgrims to the Holy Land, had their principal Italian hospital here. The cathedral at Trani (*open daily 9.30–12.30 & 5–8*), begun at the end of the 11th century and completed in the 13th, is dedicated to St Nicholas the Pilgrim, a young Greek much addicted to wandering the land with a cross and crying 'Kyrie eleison!'. He died here on his way to Rome.

There can be no doubt that the cathedral was built to impress. Set by the sea, at the entrance to the harbour, it gave new expression to the ancient Greek tradition of building temples where they could be used as aids to navigation. Such landmarks were essential for seamen making their way by dead reckoning. At Trani, however, the church played an additional role. As the last Christian edifice one saw before embarking for the Holy Land, and the first one encountered on one's return, it was of great consequence as a place of prayer.

The **façade**, reached by a flight of steps and preceded by an open terrace with a finely carved frieze, has a richly sculptured portal enclosing a plain wooden door, usually closed. The iconographic and decorative schemes of the portal's stone reliefs reflect Byzantine, Saracenic and Romanesque models. The beautiful, original 12th-century **bronze doors** by Barisano da Trani, who also cast the doors of the cathedrals of Ravello (*see p. 344*) and Monreale (*see p. 372*), have been moved inside for safekeeping. Now displayed at the west end, they are divided into 32 panels by bands of intertwining plants with figurative medallions. All but two of the panels are adorned with reliefs; the others held door-knockers, since removed.

Ruvo and Castel del Monte

Parallel to the coast, an inland road leads between Bitonto and Ruvo di Puglia, which also have fine cathedrals. That at **Ruvo** (*map p. 421, C1*), built in the 13th century, is richly ornamented in the late Apulian Romanesque style. The town is also home to the charming, small Museo Archeologico Nazionale Jatta (*Piazza Giovanni Bovio 35; open daily 8.30–1.30, Sat also 2.30–7.30*) with a good collection of local finds. Particularly abundant are the Apulian red-figure vases, of which Ruvo was the most important centre of production in the 4th–3rd centuries BC.

Twenty kilometres west of Ruvo, on a straight road across the plain (road no. S170), is **Castel del Monte**, the greatest architectural achievement of Frederick II (*map p. 421, C1; open daily March–Sept 10.15–7.45, Oct–Feb 9.15–6.45; last entry 30mins before closing*). Designed, so it is said, by the emperor himself and built c. 1240, it is an extraordinarily harmonious edifice, visible from afar in its gleaming whiteness among

the olive groves. The castle is octagonal in plan, with octagonal towers at each of the eight angles and an octagonal inner courtyard. Little survives in the interior, but the atmosphere is unparalleled. It is remarkable for its fusion of the geometric constructions of the Arab world with the Gothic style of northern Europe, while the fluted pilasters of the central doorway are Classical in inspiration. Frederick is said to have used one of the towers as a mews for his falcons.

VISITING THE TERRA DI BARI

GETTING AROUND

• **By air:** Bari airport at Palese, 8km west, is c. 30mins from the centre by shuttle, bus or taxi. AMTAB bus no. 16 runs at hourly intervals from 5am–11pm from Piazza Moro, in Bari, in 35–40mins. There is also a shuttle (Tempesta) which makes the run in 5–10mins less.
• **By car:** The best place to park in Bari is in Piazza della Libertà or Corso Vittorio Emanuele II. There are pay spaces all along the boulevard which divides the old town from the new, and in the side streets. Your car will be fairly safe here, thanks to the continuous passage of pedestrians. This may not be the case if you park in the old town. In Trani there is convenient pay parking at Piazza Re Manfredi and Piazza Duomo and free parking by the waterfront gardens of the Villa Comunale.
• **By train:** Bari and Trani are well connected to Rome: fast trains make the run in roughly 4¹/₂ hrs. However, there is no direct service from Naples. Bari and the other coastal towns are linked via the Bari–Ancona line down the coast. Journey time between Bari and Trani is 30–40mins. Trains run by Ferrovie del Nord Barese run from Bari to Ruvo in c. 40mins.

WHERE TO STAY IN THE TERRA DI BARI

Trani
€€ **San Paolo al Convento**. Trani is an excellent base for exploring the region. This new hotel offers elegant rooms in a 15th-century former monastery on the waterfront. *Via Statuti Marittimi 111, T: 0883 482949.*

WHERE TO EAT IN THE TERRA DI BARI

Bari
€€ **Ai 2 Ghiottoni**. One of the town's oldest and finest restaurants, known for its fresh fish and homemade pasta. Closed Sun. *Via Putignani 11/b, T: 080 523 2240.*
Trani
€€ **Corteinfiore**. Good food in a 16th-century *palazzo* by the yacht harbour. Eat either outside in the garden or in the minimalist dining room. Closed Jan. *Via Ognissanti 18, T: 0883 508402.*
€€ **Torrente Antico**. Excellent small restaurant just off the central Corso Vittorio Emanuele. Closed Sun evening, Mon, July and early Jan. *Via Fusco 3, T: 0883 487911.*

THE ALTOPIANO DELLE MURGE & TARANTO

The Altopiano delle Murge is a great limestone plateau rising to an elevation of 473m southeast of Bari. It is an agreeable, bucolic area, criss-crossed with drystone walls known as *parietoni*, today used as boundary markers, though their original function is unknown. **Locorotondo** (*map p. 421, D2*) is a strikingly beautiful town built on a hilltop on a circular plan (hence the name, 'round place'). From the Villa Comunale there are splendid views over the Itria Valley to **Martina Franca**, a graceful 18th-century town known for its many charming Baroque and Rococo town houses. The former Palazzo Ducale (now the town hall) has been attributed to Bernini.

The part of the Murge known as the Valle d'Itria is one of the most beautiful and exotic areas of southern Italy, famed for its neat *trulli*, the drystone dwellings with conical roofs that are such a distinctive feature here. One of the best and most famous places to see them is the town of **Alberobello** (*map p. 421, D2*) , which has a district made entirely of trulli. Although the town is now crowded with tourists from May to October, with shops selling trinkets that only vaguely recall the region's rural craft tradition, it remains a fascinating place to visit. Via Cavour, Corso Trieste e Trento, Via

Aerial view of Alberobello showing how trulli are agglomerated to make larger dwellings. The ancestral prototypes of modern modular buildings, they can be made up of a simple room, or multiple rooms, which are generally added by gemination (repeated doubling): a three-room trullo will appear from the outside as a cluster of three cones.

Battisti and Via Mazzoni form a sort of ring road separating the historic city centre on the south and west from the (pleasant but ordinary) new town on the north. Any of the narrow streets on the left if you arrive from Via Cavour, or on the right if you come from Via Mazzoni, will put you in the midst of the trulli. The best strategy is simply to wander: usually the further uphill you go, the less crowded it gets.

Trulli are built without mortar and are usually whitewashed. Their origin is remote (though their similarity to the tholos architecture of the ancient Mycenaeans is striking). The basic building unit is roughly circular in plan; usually the only aperture is the entrance door—though in rare cases there might also be a small window. The thickness of the walls preserves heat in winter and coolness in summer—at least until August, when the interior temperature finally exceeds the ambient temperature. The roof is self-supporting, made of concentric rings of flat-pitched limestone laid in steps (corbelled). Trullo-like buildings are found outside the Valle d'Itria too. Throughout Puglia there are similarly-constructed rural shelters, whose appearance differs so radically from that of farm architecture elsewhere in Europe that 18th-century visitors to the region thought the landscape was scattered with archaic funerary monuments.

Taranto

Taranto (*map p. 421, D2*) is an important commercial port and industrial centre and the second naval dockyard in Italy after La Spezia. It also gives its name to the tarantula, a spider whose bite was the reputed cause of a contagious melancholy madness (tarantism), curable only by music and violent dancing (the *tarantella*). Small reason, you might think, to recommend the city in a tourist guide: and that might be so were it not for Taranto's museum. The town began life as the Greek *Taras*, colonised from Sparta in the 8th century BC, and it rose to become the greatest city in Magna Graecia, famous for the purple dye it produced from the murex mollusc. The Città Vecchia stands on the site of the Greek acropolis. Across the swing bridge in the Città Nuova, in a former monastery overlooking the spacious Piazza Archita, just two blocks from the water, is the fine archaeological museum, **MARTA** (Museo Archeologico di Taranto; *Via Cavour 10; open daily 8.30–7.30, last entry 30mins before closing*), home to the largest collection of antiquities in southern Italy after that of the Museo Archeologico Nazionale in Naples. The museum's most renowned treasure is the so-called Taranto Gold, a collection of objects in precious metals and stones that paints a vivid picture of the standards of fashion and interior design in Greek Taras. One of the loveliest pieces is a bronze and gold nutcracker in the form of two delicate female hands.

VISITING THE MURGE & TARANTO

GETTING AROUND

• **By car:** The SS172 winds its way over the Murge to Locorotondo, Alberobello and Martina Franca, passing through the Valle d'Itria and ending at Taranto. The route is particularly scenic, as are many of the lesser roads that lead off among the fields. All these byways are well marked, and the hill towns provide good visual references. Pay parking can be found on the outskirts of the historic centres of most towns. At Alberobello there are car parks on the main approach roads, SS172 and SP239. In Taranto you can usually find a place to park in the old town by the castle.

• **By train:** The Ferrovie del Sud Est operate frequent train and/or bus services between Bari, Taranto and Alberobello, Locorotondo, Martina Franca, and most other towns on the Murge. Journey time from Bari to Alberobello is c. 80mins; to Taranto c. 2¹/₂ hrs. Timetables on www.fseonline.it. Trains run by the state railway (Trenitalia) offer a swifter service between Bari and Taranto.

WHERE TO STAY

Alberobello

€€ **Dei Trulli**. Like all small towns that have become popular tourist destinations, Alberobello is mobbed during the day but deserted after dark. This complex of trulli, with all modern comforts, in the historic centre of the village, offers a unique Puglian experience. *Via Cadore 32, T: 080 432 3555, www.hoteldeitrulli.it.*

Taranto

€€ **Akropolis**. By the duomo, in the heart of the old town, this fine establishment presents the history of Taranto in a single building: it was founded on the Greek acropolis and repeatedly rebuilt through the centuries, most notably in the 18th. There are antique majoli-

ca tiles and furniture, and a rooftop terrace with views over land and sea. *Vico I Seminario 3, T: 099 470 4110, www.hotelakropolis.it.*

In recent years a number of Puglian *masserie* (farmhouses) have been converted into luxurious, self-contained hotels and resorts. One of the nicest and most discreetly tasteful is the €€ **Masseria Marzalossa**, a few kilometres east of Alberobello, near the little town of Fasano (*Contrada Pezze Vicine 65, T: 080 441 3780, www.marzalossa.it; closed mid-Nov–mid-Dec*).

WHERE TO EAT

Alberobello

€€€ **Il Poeta Contadino**. ■ Alberobello's most famous restaurant really does merit its reputation, despite its location in the heart of one of the region's most popular tourist destinations. Outstanding Puglian cuisine is accompanied by the best regional wines. Closed Mon (except July–Sept) and mid-Jan. *Via Indipendenza 21, T: 080 432 1917.*

Taranto

€€ **Gesù Cristo**. Taranto is famous for its oysters (there are huge oyster beds just offshore), and this reliable *trattoria* is as good a place as any to try them, so long as there isn't an R in the month. In the Città Nuova, some way east of the museum. Closed Sun evening and Mon. *Via Cesare Battisti 8, T: 099 477 7253.*

LECCE & OTRANTO

Lecce (*map p. 421, D2*) is a sleepy place, every inch the small provincial capital, affluent and self-satisfied, where the rhythm of life is contentedly slow. Nowhere here do you feel the verve and dynamism of more frenetic places such as Bari. The old town owes its distinctive charm to the richly decorated Baroque architecture of its churches and houses, built in the local *pietra leccese*, a golden sandstone that is easy to work when first quarried, but hardens over time. The style of the decoration, known as *Barocco leccese*, flourished from the 16th–18th centuries and its leading exponents, whose names you will encounter all over town, were Gabriele Riccardi, Francesco Antonio Zimbalo, Giuseppe Zimbalo (Lo Zingarello), Giuseppe Cino and Cesare Penna.

Major sights of Lecce

Lecce was established long before the Baroque age. As the Roman *Lupiae*, it reached its greatest prosperity in the Imperial period, and preserves a theatre and amphitheatre (only partly visible) from that time. The church of **Santa Croce** (*open daily 8.30–12 & 5–7*), north of the central Piazza Sant'Oronzo (where one quarter of the amphitheatre has been excavated), is the most celebrated of the town's Baroque monuments. Begun in the mid-16th century by Gabriele Riccardi, and completed in 1679, it is a fine place to study the *Barocco leccese* at its most extravagant. The general plan of the façade is by Riccardi, who completed the lower part, with its columns, blind arcading and elegant frieze. Francesco Antonio Zimbalo added the main portal and the two lateral doorways. The upper portion (1646), which rests on a balcony supported by richly carved corbels, is the work Cesare Penna, who was working to a design by Giuseppe Zimbalo. Its centrepiece is an ornate rose window flanked by saints in niches and sculpted columns, and caricature portraits of the architects (the man with the enormous nose is Penna).

West of Piazza Sant'Oronzo, Via Vittorio Emanuele, a favourite street for the evening *passeggiata*, leads west past the church of Sant'Irene, whose façade prominently displays the Lecce coat of arms: a wolf and a holm oak. Beyond here opens the broad, spacious, traffic-free **Piazza del Duomo**, surrounded on three sides by grand buildings. This is the most monumental space in Lecce, its approach flanked by the so-called 'propylaia', curved buildings topped by a balustrade and statues. The duomo (*open daily 8.30–1 & 4.30–8*) was rebuilt by Giuseppe Zimbalo in 1569–70. On the right of the square stands the magnificent Seminario, built between 1694 and 1709 to a design by Giuseppe Cino.

On the northern outskirts of town, a short walk beyond the triumphal Porta Napoli (walk down Viale San Nicola), is the church of **Santi Nicola e Cataldo** (*open daily 8–11*), one of the finest Norman monuments in Italy. The Baroque façade is attributed to Giuseppe Cino and is no preparation for what lies within, where the confluence of Byzantine, Saracenic and Gothic styles is striking. The impression of height is similar, in miniature, to that of a Gothic cathedral. The Saracen arches on compound piers recall the cathedral of Monreale in Sicily.

Otranto

Otranto (*map p. 421, D2*) is a small resort and fishing centre standing on the site of a Greek city which became one of Republican Rome's leading ports for trade with Greece and Asia Minor. Under the Byzantines it was one of the most important centres of the Eastern Empire in Italy, and together with Taranto and Bari was one of the last Byzantine cities to fall to the Normans. At the time of the Crusades it became an embarkation point for the Orient and a leading centre of trade between Venice, Dalmatia and the Levant.

Anyone who has read Horace Walpole's *Castle of Otranto* will be surprised to learn that the fortress here has nothing to do with Gothick fantasy. It dates from the Aragonese period (late 15th century), and was reinforced by the Spanish a hundred years later.

Detail of the façade of Santa Croce in Lecce, the finest example of the crowded and exuberant *Barocco leccese* style.

Otranto has two main claims to a visitor's attention. The first is the **cathedral** of Santa Maria Annunziata (*open summer 9–12 & 4–7; winter 9–12 & 3.30–6.30*), founded by the Normans in the 11th century. The interior walls were once frescoed, but when the Turks sacked Otranto in 1480, they turned the church into a mosque and destroyed its images. At the end of the south aisle is an ossuary chapel, with the bones of those slaughtered preserved in cupboards around the walls. The great glory of the church is its 12th-century mosaic floor, roughly made but full of charming details. It shows the Tree of Life, the *axis mundi*, borne on the backs of two elephants, animals which were thought by the medieval mind to share the dual (spiritual and animal) nature of humanity. To right and left of the tree are allegories of Redemption (south transept) and Last Judgement (north transept). The boughs of the tree bear the entire cosmos, shown in images of the Months, each with its zodiac sign and appropriate agricultural or domestic activity. There are also biblical scenes (*Expulsion from the Garden, Cain and Abel, Noah's Ark*), scenes of chivalry (*Alexander the Great* and *King Arthur*) and mythological episodes.

Tucked away in a small square above and behind the cathedral is the little Byzantine church of **San Pietro** (*open mid-July–mid-Sept 10–12 & 3.30–8; at other times enquire at the cathedral*), said to have been the first cathedral of the city. The interior is covered with frescoes of various epochs. Most easily identifiable is the titular saint Peter himself, with the chains that fettered him in his prison in Rome, and St Catherine, who holds her wheel.

The rocky, picturesque coast south of Otranto is closely followed by a road (SP358) offering stunning views, on clear days, across the Adriatic to Albania and Corfu. Inland are some examples of dolmens, prehistoric structures that are quite common in Puglia and which have many affinities with the dolmens of Cornwall and Brittany. The best preserved is the **Dolmen di Scusi**, a large stone monolith propped on stone stilts, which stands in an olive grove outside Minervino di Lecce (on the road to Uggiano La Chiesa).

VISITING LECCE & OTRANTO

GETTING AROUND

• **By air:** The Aeroporto del Salento at Brindisi is c. 40mins from Lecce by car. Coach services (SITA) to Lecce 6 times daily.
• **By car:** The best place to park in Lecce is by the castle (pay parking), or along Viale dell'Università. In Otranto there is ample parking by the harbour.
• **By train:** Lecce is the last stop for fast trains on the main lines from Bologna (via Bari) and Rome. *Regionali* connect to Otranto in roughly 30mins.

WHERE TO STAY IN LECCE & OTRANTO

Lecce
€€€ **Patria Palace**. Very central, just across the square from Santa Croce and just a few steps away from Lecce's best restaurants and cafés. Regrettably, the renovation of this former town house has deprived it of atmosphere, but it is comfortable and still the best recommendation in town. *Piazzetta Gabriele Riccardi 13, T: 0832 245111, www.patriapalacelecce.com.*
Otranto
€€€ **Masseria Montelauro**. ■ A splendidly restored country house, historically authentic on the outside and tastefully modern within. There is a nice pool, and rooms have private garden entrances. 1km southwest of town. *Via Uggiano La Chiesa, T: 0836 806203, www.masseriamontelauro.it.*

WHERE TO EAT IN LECCE & OTRANTO

Lecce
€€ **Picton**. Vaulted ceilings in *pietra leccese*, lots of greenery, and a roaring fire in winter are the distinctive traits of this restaurant in a historic building near Porta Napoli. Traditional dishes and local wines. Closed Mon and late Sept, Jan and Nov. *Via Idomeneo 14, T: 0832 332383.*
€ **Cucina Casareccia**. Popular *trattoria* behind Santa Croce and north of Piazza Oronzo, affectionately known as 'Le Zie' (the aunts). Good home cooking in the best Lecce tradition. Closed Sun evening, Mon and early Sept. *Via Costadura 19, T: 0832 245178.*
Otranto
€€ **Da Sergio**. Fresh fish and shellfish are the hallmark of this historic restaurant, right in the town centre. Closed Wed (except in summer) and in Jan–Feb. *Corso Garibaldi 9, T: 0836 801408.*

CALABRIA

Calabria (*map pp. 421 and 419*) is the name given to the mountainous region between the Tyrrhenian and Ionian seas, which forms the toe of the Italian 'boot'. It is a severe land, a place of steep, harsh mountains, cactus and agave. Noisy and lively along the coast, inland it is silent and sometimes mournfully desolate. Yet it was not always thus. In the days of the Greek colonies of Magna Graecia, Calabria was a rich and favoured land. The colony of Croton was the chosen home of Pythagoras, who emigrated here from Samos. At the point where the Crati and Coscile rivers spill into the sea stood the town of Sybaris, a place of unparalleled luxury and dissipation, from which we take our term sybaritic. As little remains of that town now as remains of luxury anywhere in Calabria. But the land is not all harsh. On the Tyrrhenian side the moist west wind brings abundant rainfall and the vegetation is quite lush. This region gives its name to the variety of broccoli known as calabrese, a kind of wild cabbage first domesticated here; and the sweet red onions of Tropea (which is also known for its sandy beaches) are highly prized.

Food and wine of Calabria

Calabria has a fairly uniform culinary tradition, despite the relative isolation in which many towns have stood for centuries. Never a place of abundance, it has lately acquired a reputation for excellence—of its citrus fruits (especially bergamot oranges, used for scents and flavourings), its aubergines (reputedly the best in Italy) and its red onions. In the past both the conservatism and the poverty of the Calabrian farmer put chemical fertilisers out of reach—which means that the region today has become an ideal place to farm organic fruit, vegetables and livestock. Calabria is also known for its fish: much of the exquisite swordfish and tuna for which Italy is famous is fished, processed and packed by *calabresi*.

Calabrian wines reflect a very old oenological tradition, dating from before the Greek colonisation. The region's most famous wine is Cirò, made in the province of Catanzaro.

HIGHLIGHTS OF SOUTHERN CALABRIA

Stilo

Stilo (*map p. 419, D1*), beautifully situated on a mountainside above the Ionian sea, was the birthplace of Tommaso Campanella (1568–1639), a Dominican friar and Renaissance Humanist who used the 27 years spent as a prisoner of the Inquisition to write his masterpiece, *The City of the Sun*, describing an ideal commonwealth to be governed by men enlightened by reason, in which all labour would contribute to the good of the community and wealth and poverty would be non-existent. Campanella was not the first inhabitant of this arid, mountainous landscape to contemplate a better world: in the Middle Ages Stilo's environs had been a favourite resort of Basilian anchorites, hermit-monks who took their name from St Basil the Great, and who were responsible for the spread of Eastern monasticism in the lands of the far south still controlled by Byzantium, as opposed to the Benedictine (Latin) monasticism which spread from the abbey of Monte Cassino to the lands under Lombard rule. The tiny, brick church known as the **Cattolica**, which stands wedged into the hillside above the town, in a landscape of dry shrubs and prickly pear, is the best preserved relic of this Eastern tradition, in fact one of the best examples of Byzantine architecture in Italy. Built in the 10th century, the church follows the quincunx pattern: that is, it possesses a central dome flanked by four others at the corners. The interior (measuring only 6m by 6m) is divided into nine quadrants by four columns taken from antique buildings and placed upon upturned capitals to symbolise the defeat of paganism. The first column on the right bears the Greek inscription 'God is the Lord who appeared to us'.

Locri

The Greek colonies of Magna Graecia were numerous and flourishing, yet disappointingly little remains of any of them today. One of the most rewarding sites to visit is that of *Locri Epizephyrii*, founded in the late 8th or early 7th century BC, and located about 5km south of the modern town of Locri, on the Ionian coast (*map p. 419, D2*).

The Greek colony flourished, perhaps by virtue of its location on a major road (known as the *dromos*, it bisects the site, running parallel to the modern coast road) and by its contacts with Sicily and the Tyrrhenian colonies. It was an important cult centre of the goddess Persephone. After Locri's surrender to Rome in 205 BC, the town dwindled and was eventually destroyed by the Saracens. The **Antiquarium Statale di Locri** (*open Tues–Sun 9–8*) contains a fine collection of 5th-century BC *pinakes*, clay tablets with painted reliefs of Hades and Persephone, an item for which the craftsmen of Locri were famous; their handiwork was distributed throughout the Greek world, and they were used as grave offerings. The story of Persephone's abduction to the Underworld and her subsequent rescue by her mother Demeter (Ceres), goddess of the harvest, who was permitted to have her daughter back for six months of the year, is important not just as a myth to explain the changing seasons (earth was plunged in winter when Demeter and Persephone were apart) but also for its early formulation of a belief in an afterlife, in the person of the child redeemed from the dead. The **ruins** (*open as above*) include the remains of houses, temples, a theatre and the town walls. The Ionic temple has been suggested as the original location of the famous *Ludovisi Throne*, now in Rome (*see p. 261*).

Reggio Calabria

Reggio Calabria (*map p. 419, C2*) is the capital of Calabria and the last major city on the Italian peninsula before crossing to Sicily. It was here that Spartacus and his slave army found themselves trapped, unable to cross the water, in their flight from the Roman legions (*see p. 328*). Reggio has been repeatedly battered by earthquakes, most recently in 1908, when 5,000 people were killed and almost every building was damaged. Buildings are understandably low-rise, and are all now built of reinforced concrete. The poet Gabriele d'Annunzio described Reggio's *lungomare* as the most beautiful kilometre in Italy. One would need a generous conception of beauty to concur with him today, though the views commanded by the coast-side road are certainly fine ones. Reggio is known above all for its Museo Nazionale della Magna Grecia (*Piazza de Nava; open Tues–Sun 9–8*), home to an extensive collection from sites throughout Calabria, including *pinakes* from Locri (*see opposite*) Most famous of all the exhibits are the **Riace bronzes**, magnificent works of the 5th century BC, found in the sea off the Ionian coast. They are among the very few surviving examples of Classical Greek bronze statuary, standing over 2m tall and finished in ivory and glass (eyes), silver (teeth) and copper (lips and nipples). The pose of the hands and arms suggest that they each held a shield and lance.

VISITING STILO, LOCRI & REGGIO CALABRIA

GETTING AROUND

• **By car:** In Reggio Calabria there is pay parking by the museum and on the waterfront.

• **By train:** Calabria is not well served by rail. From Naples to Stilo and Locri trains run via Lamezia and/or Catanzaro Lido (where changes are necessary) in 5–6hrs; from Reggio Calabria to Locri and Stilo in 90mins–2hrs 10mins. Naples to Reggio Calabria takes 4hrs 20mins by Eurostar or Intercity. Reggio has three train stations: Centrale on Piazza Garibaldi at the south end of the town is used by all trains; Lido, more centrally placed near the hotels and the museum is served by most; Marittima is the terminus of trains from the east, but is not served from the north.

• **By sea:** Car ferries run throughout the year between Villa San Giovanni, just north of Reggio and Messina in Sicily. Journey time 40mins. Less frequent hydrofoils from Reggio.

WHERE TO STAY IN SOUTHERN CALABRIA

Locri
There is no shortage of basic B&Bs in Locri, but if you have transport, a much better option is the € **Casa di Gianna** ■, 9km inland in the pleasant town of Gerace (*Via Paolo Frascà 4, T: 0964 355024, www.lacasadigianna.it*).

Reggio Calabria
€€ **Excelsior**. Classic place, a bit business-touristy, but handily located across the street from the museum. Its rooftop Gala restaurant enjoys fine views of the waterfront, with Sicily across the straits. *Via Vittorio Veneto 66, T: 0965 812211, www.montesanohotels.it.*

Stilo
Accommodation in Stilo itself is limited. Better options lie in the surrounding countryside: € **Agriturismo Fassi**, a farmhouse 12km north of Stilo in Guardavalle, offers simple rooms but good facilities including a swimming pool (*Contrada Pietrarotta, Guardavalle, T: 0967 86431*). €€ **Villa Caristo** offers accommodation in a fine Baroque villa on an organic farm, just inland from Riace, where the famous bronzes were found (*Stignano, T: 339 823 2038, www.villacaristo.it*).

WHERE TO EAT IN SOUTHERN CALABRIA

Locri
€ **Il Delfino Blu**. Tasty dishes served on the seafront. The grilled aubergine is particularly good. *Corso Vittorio Emanuele 52, T: 0964 232807.*

Reggio Calabria
€€ **London Bistro** Simple, central place near the waterfront. Closed Mon, midday Sat and Aug. *Via Osanna 2/f, T: 0965 892908.*

Stilo
€ **La Vecchia Miniera**. A good place for lunch after visiting the Cattolica at Stilo. Situated in the village of Bivongi, 2km northwest. Country fare at reasonable prices. Closed Mon. *Contrada Perrocalli, T: 0964 731869.*

SICILY

'You must see Sicily, in order to understand Italy,' said Goethe, 'it is the key to the whole country'. He was referring to the long and extremely complex history of the island, a concentration of everything that has happened in nearby Italy, the nation of which it is now part. A triangular island of 26,000km square in the middle of the Mediterranean, 90 percent of which is hilly and mountainous, now with a population of five million and an economy based largely on agriculture, Sicily has always been the coveted possession of foreign powers; visited, exploited and sometimes dominated by Phoenicians, Greeks, Carthaginians, Romans, Byzantines, Arabs, Normans, Swabians, Angevins, Aragonese and Bourbons, each of whom added something of their character to the local traditions, language, gastronomy and economy.

Early Bronze Age inhabitants were the Sicels, probably of Celtic origin, who settled in the east; the Elymians, said to be refugees from Troy, who founded Segesta and Erice; and the Sicans, perhaps from Spain, who occupied the west, the south and the centre. In the mid-8th century BC, Greek colonists set up coastal settlements, some of which became great cities. By the late 3rd century BC, Rome had conquered the whole island. They planted it entirely with wheat, and it became the bread-basket of the empire.

Arab rule in the 9th century brought new agricultural techniques, such as terracing and irrigation, new crops, such as rice, citrus, cotton and sugar, and immense wealth. When the Normans took over in the late 11th century, they made no attempt to change the status quo. Showing a willingness to adapt to the Islamic, Greek and Latin traditions, they simply proceeded to place round pegs in round holes (Arabs were farmers, Greeks were employed in clerical posts and in the navy, Jews were doctors, dentists, lawyers and craftsmen, Normans were herdsmen), and to set up a parliament. A common language soon developed, based on Latin, Arabic, French and Greek.

When Roger II (d. 1154) was crowned king in 1130, he was the wealthiest ruler in Europe. In 1197 came the great Swabian king Frederick II of Hohenstaufen, an enlightened ruler, well prepared for his role. He was hampered by his long struggle with the papacy, or he would have achieved much more. His court in Palermo, which drew on Islamic and Jewish, as well as Christian cultures, was famous throughout Europe for its splendour and learning. The Sicilian vernacular was used for literature, paving the way for Dante's Tuscan. The Swabian era came to an end in 1268 when Sicily was handed over to Charles of Anjou, thanks to the connivance of the French pope Clement IV. The hated Angevin domination ended in 1282 with the famous rebellion known as the Sicilian Vespers (*see p. 312*), after which the Sicilians entrusted the crown to Peter of Aragon. Although he proved a just man and a firm ruler, when he died Sicily found herself a province of Aragon; she had lost her independence forever. In 1492, when Ferdinand and Isabella banished the Jews from Spain, Sicily's Muslims and Jews were also expelled, or forced to convert to Christianity, and their property was confiscated. Aragonese princes were followed by Spanish viceroys and Bourbon kings (*see the his-*

tory of Naples, pp. 312–13), who ruled foolishly or selfishly or both. In 1860 Garibaldi found the ideal terrain here for rallying people behind the dream of a unified Italy. Union, however, brought no solution to the problems of the Sicilians, quite the opposite; the economy collapsed completely at the end of the 19th century, when 1,400,000 people were obliged to emigrate. After the Second World War, Sicily was granted autonomy and a special statute, but this opportunity has been wasted by an inept political class. Today, in spite of her considerable resources, Sicily is the Italian region with the lowest per capita income, and the island is still wallowing in problems of the Mafia, petty crime, lack of investment, corruption and bad government—problems which the serious-minded majority are continually trying to address.

Food and wine of Sicily

Sicilian cuisine is as good-humoured as the people, as varied as the landscapes, and as complex as the history of the island. Fertile soil, an ideal climate and ample pastures ensure an endless supply of fruits and vegetables, excellent olive oil, honey, cheese, and the durum wheat used for pasta and bread, which is very good—72 different kinds are made. The sea provides all manner of fish, from swordfish and bluefin tuna to octopus, grouper, red mullet, sardines and anchovies. Confectionery is unique, and owes a lot to the introduction of sugar-cane by the Arabs. Using sugar, almonds, hazelnuts, pistachios, ricotta and citrus fruit to perfection, they laid the foundation for the infinite variety of sweets available today, which include marzipan, nougat and *paste di mandorla*, the original macaroons, prepared in glorious profusion for saint's days and especially for Easter. The finishing touch was probably the introduction of chocolate by the Spanish, which is still made to Aztec recipes in Modica.

Ice cream is thought to have been invented in Sicily. Its history can be traced from the Romans, who mixed carefully-stored snow with honey, wine and spices, to the Arabs, who perfected sherbet, by substituting sugar for honey and lemon juice for wine. Now known as *granita*, it is the favourite breakfast in summer. In the 18th century a young pastry-cook called Procopio de' Coltelli had the brilliant idea of adding cream to his frozen-fruit confections, and ice cream was born.

Legend has it that the first grapevine sprang from under the foot of Dionysus, whirling in a frenzied dance on the foothills of Etna. Wine production on Sicily has a very long tradition, and today 21 wines have the DOC appellation.

PALERMO & ITS PROVINCE

The beautiful capital of Sicily, **Palermo** (*map p. 419, B2*), stands on a wide bay dominated by the Monte Pellegrino headland. Although much spoiled in the 1970s, Palermo still shows ample traces of its past, when it was one of the greatest cities in the Mediterranean, and vied with Córdoba, Cairo and Constantinople as a centre of culture and learning, or when the Arabs called it 'the city of 1,000 minarets', famed for its gardens and fountains.

The cathedral and Norman palace

From the old harbour of La Cala, where the Phoenicians originally founded the city, Corso Vittorio Emanuele (usually known as the Cassero, from *qasr*, a castle) leads westwards past the Quattro Canti, the monumental crossroads of the two main streets, to the **cathedral** (*open 7–7*), which with its golden stone and eclectic contrasts, is a perfect example of the way the city blends diverse styles, materials and traditions to its own taste. Founded by the Normans in 1185 on the site of an Arab mosque, and much altered over the centuries, the interior is comparatively simple. The first two chapels of the south aisle house the royal tombs of kings and queens of Sicily, including those of Roger II, Frederick II of Hohenstaufen, his mother Constance de Hauteville and his father Henry VI, the Holy Roman Emperor.

Further west, in the highest part of the old city, stands the royal palace, **Palazzo dei Normanni**. It was built by the Arabs, enlarged by the Normans, and restored by the Spanish, who added the principal façade; it is now the seat of the Sicilian parliament. In the interior is the Palatine Chapel (*open Mon–Sat 8.30–12 & 2–5, Sun 8.30–2.30*), the royal oratory, a jewel of Arab-Norman art, built by Roger II in 1132. It is famous for the exquisite mosaics which cover the walls in the interior, and the carved and painted ceiling, with stalactite effects, the work of Arab craftsmen using cedarwood from Lebanon. The chapel, which much impressed Guy de Maupassant, is dominated by the image of Christ Pantocrator in the main apse. South of the royal palace is the charming church and garden of **San Giovanni degli Eremiti** (*open 9–7*), also built by Roger II in 1132, on the site of a mosque. The little church with its red domes is the symbol of Palermo, and the garden is a peaceful retreat on a hot day.

Palermo's museums

South of the Cassero at the harbour end, in a 15th-century palace, is the **Galleria Regionale Abatellis** (*Via Alloro 4; open 9–1.30; Tues, Wed and Thur also 2.30–7.30*) housing paintings and sculptures from the Middle Ages: three of them, at least, are worth the journey to Sicily to see. They are the *Triumph of Death* (Room 2), a large fresco painted c. 1449 showing Death on a spectral horse, mowing down the rich while allowing the poor and suffering to live, although they invoke his blows. The dramatic, unforgettable work inspired Picasso's *Guernica*. In Room 4 is a masterpiece by Francesco Laurana, the bust of Eleanor of Aragon (1475), daughter of the king of Naples, who married Ercole d'Este of Ferrara (*see p. 147*). In Room 10 is Antonello da Messina's greatest masterpiece, the *Virgin Annunciate* (1474–77). Compare this with his *Annunciation* from Palazzolo Acreide in the Bellomo Museum of Syracuse (*see p. 382*), which was painted perhaps at the same time. This painting, quite different, is essentially the portrait of a young girl from the streets of Palermo. Her exquisitely-rendered hands tell the story. The right hand is slightly raised in mild acquiescence ('be it unto me according to Thy word'); while her left hand secures her veil in a gesture of modesty.

In the modern centre, near the two great 19th-century theatres, is the **Museo Archeologico Regionale Salinas** (*Via Bara all'Olivella 24; open Tues–Fri 8.30–1.45 & 3–6.45; Sat, Sun, Mon and holidays 8.30–1.45*) with vast collections of antiquities from

Virgin Annunciate (1470s) by Antonello da Messina, probably the first Italian artist to perfect the use of working in oils, a technique that he may have learned from Netherlandish artists in Naples. He spent a year in Venice, where he had a profound influence on Giovanni Bellini. In his portraits he was one of the first masters of the art of revealing the personalities of his sitters.

all over Sicily; particularly worthy of note is the gallery dedicated to the metopes of Selinunte, vivid sculptures found in the 19th century among the temples of the ancient city, and the series of lovely black Etruscan vases from Chiusi, a private collection.

La Zisa and Mondello

West of the centre, in Piazza Zisa, the royal mansion called La Zisa (from *aziz*, 'splendid'), now houses the **Museo d'Arte Islamica** (*open 9–6.30*), the most important example of Arab-Norman secular architecture to survive in Sicily; explanatory panels explain the architectural techniques used to create the building and its fountains.

Near the summit of Monte Pellegrino is the **Santuario di Santa Rosalia**, a charming little church with a large collection of ex-votos, arranged in the cave where the saint lived as an anchorite. West of the headland is **Mondello**, a seaside resort with many beautiful Art Nouveau villas, developed by Donna Franca Florio in the 19th century, when she launched the fashion for sea-bathing. According to an American tourist, her husband Ignazio became rich because 'He was the dude who had the neat idea of putting tuna in cans'. He did—but he owned a huge merchant fleet as well.

Monreale

On the hillside behind Palermo, Monreale has one of the most superb churches in the world, and certainly the most important Norman building in Sicily. The duomo (*open 8–6*) was built as a political statement by William II, grandson of the great Roger II, in 1182, and he had to invent the discovery of a buried treasure to justify the expenditure. It is a supreme example of the diveristy of styles that made up Sicilian architecture of the time. From the Islamic tradition we have the interlaced arches and inlaid geometric decoration (particularly well seen on the outside of the apse); from further north in Italy come the bronze doors, the work of Barisano da Trani from Puglia (north door) and Bonnano da Pisa, the architect of the Leaning Tower (main door). The interior walls are entirely covered with a dazzling expanse of golden Byzantinesque mosaics. Christ Pantocrator is shown in the main apse: Byzantine strictures normally place Christ in the dome, as the part of a church symbolising the vault of heaven, and the Virgin in the womb-shaped apse. In Western basilicas, however (as here), there is no dome, and so Christ is placed in the apse instead, but above the Virgin, who appears in smaller scale below. Even in cases where there is a dome (Venice, Palermo), the habit of placing the Pantocrator in the apse still prevails.

The remarkable cloister (*open 9–7*) is a masterpiece of 12th-century art, its arches supported by 228 twin columns with carved capitals, of which very few are alike. In one corner is a Moorish fountain in the form of a palm tree.

Cefalù and Castelbuono

Under the great head-shaped rock which gives it its name, from the Greek *kephalos*, (head), and with its stunning cathedral, Cefalù (*map p. 419, B2*) is a picturesque town with a sandy beach. The old cobbled streets are still medieval in character, with many enticing shops, restaurants and cafés. The Norman **cathedral** (*open 8–12 & 3.30–5.30*), with its two artfully different bell-towers, built by King Roger II in 1131, dominates the whole town. The luminous interior, now stripped of its later Baroque additions, reveals the 16 stone columns from a nearby Roman temple, a wooden ceiling still bearing traces of painting, controversial modern stained glass windows, and

The Norman cathedral of Cefalù (1131), with its central arcade of interlaced Saracenic arches.

exquisite mosaics in the presbytery, the oldest and the best preserved in Sicily. They are perhaps the work of craftsmen from Constantinople, summoned here by Roger himself. The figure of Christ Pantocrator, once again, is found in the main apse. Near the cathedral is the **Museo Mandralisca** (*open 9–1 & 3–7*), the collections of a Sicilian aristocrat. Not to be missed is the enigmatic portrait by Antonello da Messina (*see above*) of the *Unknown Man* (?1470), perhaps a sailor.

In the Madonie mountains behind Cefalù lies **Castelbuono**, its little rose-coloured stone houses huddled under the protection of its castle (*open 9–1 & 3–7*). On the surrounding mountainsides the inhabitants collect sap from the manna-ash trees, used for medicinal purposes and confectionery, the only place in the world where this is still done.

VISITING PALERMO PROVINCE

GETTING AROUND

• **By air:** Palermo airport (Falcone Borsellino) has regular bus services to the railway station at Piazza Giulio Cesare, every 30mins or so, journey time c. 50mins. There are also regular express trains (Trinacria Express) into the city centre, journey time c. 45mins.

• **By car** Parking is difficult in Palermo. Pay car parks (with attendant) are near Piazza Castelnuovo, the station and Via Stabile. Elsewhere there are blue-line areas, for which tickets are purchased at tobacconists or newsagents and then displayed inside the windscreen. If you want to stay longer, you can leave two or three tickets at once.

• **Public transport in Palermo:** City buses run by AMAT, although crowded, infrequent and slow, run to all the major sights. Tickets must be purchased at tobacconists or newsagents and stamped on board. Buses 309 and 389 from Piazza Indipendenza (frequent service in 20–30mins) to Monreale.

• **By bus:** Direct daily buses from Via Balsamo, near the railway station, to Trapani (c. 2hrs, www. interbus.it); to Agrigento (operated by Cuffaro); to Cefalù, Piazza Armerina and Messina (operated by SAIS-Interbus, www.saisautolinee.it). From Cefalù buses run by SAIS leave from the railway station for the villages of the Madonie mountains.

• **By train:** Palermo has services to Agrigento, Messina, Trapani and Enna. Cefalù is on the main Palermo–Messina line.

WHERE TO STAY IN PALERMO PROVINCE

Castelbuono

€€€€ **Relais Sant'Anastasia.** ■ Beautiful old abbey with 29 lovely rooms, pool and restaurant, on an estate producing wine since Norman times. *Contrada Sant'Anastasia, T: 0921 672233, www.santa-anastasia-relais.it.*

Cefalù

€€ **Villa Gaia.** Tiny hotel on the seafront; 12 clean and very comfortable rooms with power showers and delicious breakfasts. *Via Pintorno, T: 0921 420992, www.villagaiahotel.it.*

Palermo

€€€€ **Villa Igiea Hilton.** Famous Art Nouveau masterpiece built for Donna Franca Florio (*see p. 372*) in a stunning setting under Mt Pellegrino. Many crowned heads of Europe have stayed here. At Acquasanta, north of the centre. *Salita Belmonte 43, T: 091 631 2111, www.villa-igiea-palermo.com.*

€€€ **Centrale Palace.** One of Palermo's oldest hotels, an 18th-century palace close to the cathedral. Good rooftop restaurant with won-

derful views over the city. Well-appointed rooms. Parking. *Corso Vittorio Emanuele 327, T: 091 336666, www.centralepalacehotel.it.*

€€ **Hotel Garibaldi.** Quietly elegant rooms in a restructured palace. *Via Emerico Amari 146, T: 091 601 7111, www.gshotels.it.*

WHERE TO EAT IN PALERMO PROVINCE

Castelbuono

€€€ **Nangalarruni.** ■ People come from afar to feast on home-made pasta, grilled and roasted meat, and especially on the wild mushrooms found by the owner, Giuseppe Carollo. Local wines. Closed Wed. *Via Alberghi delle Confraternite 5, T: 0921 671428.*

Cefalù

€€ **Otaria del Duomo.** Good Sicilian food and and wine, close to the cathedral. Closed Mon in winter. *Via Seminario 5, T: 0921 421838.*

Mondello

€€€ **Bye Bye Blues.** ■ Fish dishes a speciality, but the vegetable *antipasti* are magnificent, too. Superb desserts, good wine list. Closed Tues. *Via del Garofalo 23, T: 091 684 1415.*

Palermo

€€ **Antica Focacceria San Francesco.** ■ The place for traditional snacks, *panelle* (chick-pea fritters), *purpu* (boiled octopus), *stigghiole* (stuffed grilled lamb intestines). The owner has risked his life taking a stand against the Mafia. Closed Tues. *Via Alessandro Paternostro 58 (San Francesco), T: 091 320264.*

€€ **Antica Trattoria del Monsù.** Famous for delicious pizza. Great Sicilian atmosphere. Closed Mon evening. *Via Volturno 41 (Opera House), T: 091 327774.*

€€€ **Il Ristorantino.** Refined little restaurant offering many surprising starters and main dishes, followed by equally unusual desserts. Exceptional wine list. Closed Mon. *Piazza de Gasperi (Favorita), T: 091 512861.*

TRAPANI & ITS PROVINCE

Called *Drepanon*, scythe, in the past, for its perfectly-shaped harbour (said to have been dropped by the distraught Demeter, when searching for her kidnapped daughter Persephone; *see p. 366*), **Trapani** (*map p. 419, A2*) was the emporium of ancient Erice. It is now a large and busy city, the centre of the sea-salt industry, which dates back to the days of the Phoenicians. The old centre is largely unspoilt, and is little visited by tourists. In the modern part of town is the **Santuario dell'Annunziata** (*open 9–12 & 4–7*), once an isolated church outside the city limits, now an 18th-century building with some surviving medieval chapels. Here you will find the lovely, much venerated Madonna di Trapani, a 14th-century marble statue from Pisa, perhaps the work of Nino Pisano. During the days of Pisa's maritime republic (11th–13th centuries), she had extensive contact with the Muslim and Byzantine world. Close by, at 200 Via Conte Pepoli, is the **Museo Pepoli** (*open Mon–Sat 9–1.30, Sun and holidays 9–12.30*), with a superb collection of the work of local craftsmen from the 17th–19th centuries, in wax, alabaster, and especially the unique blood-red local coral.

Erice

Built entirely of grey limestone, Erice (*map p. 419, A2*) stands on the wind-blown, misty summit of Monte San Giuliano. It is a perfect example of a medieval walled city. Today it is a place of mossy churches, sequestered convents and surprising hidden courtyards with pots of basil and geraniums, its silent, cobbled streets filled with wafting aromas of vanilla, cinnamon and toasted almonds. In Antiquity it was the Elymian *Eryx*, founded by the legendary survivors of the Trojan War, who were led here by Aeneas. It was famous throughout the Mediterranean for its temple dedicated to Astarte, goddess of fertility, known to the Romans as Venus Erycina. The **Castello di Venere** (*open 9–1*), with views as far as Mt Etna, now stands on the site of what was once a centre of sanctified prostitution. Here girl slaves were dedicated as temple prostitutes, beginning their careers at the onset of puberty and retiring at 21, rich and plump (they were fed a special diet of milk and honey) and much in demand as wives.

Segesta

The view of the perfectly-proportioned Doric temple of Segesta (*map p. 419, A2; open 9–1hr before sunset*), amid the rolling hills with their vineyards and groves of olives, has been admired by travellers for centuries. It is thought that it was purpose-built in 426 BC to impress the Athenians, with whom the city was seeking an alliance, rather than as a place of worship; in fact it was never finished, and was probably never intended to be. The columns have no fluting, and there is no trace of a cella inside. Monte Barbaro, the hill to the east, was the site of the city; on the north slope is the ancient theatre, offering indescribably lovely views. The tyrant Agathocles of Syracuse sacked the town in 307 BC and catapulted thousands of the inhabitants to their deaths in the ravine behind the temple. Even today, in bright sunlight, it is an eerie place, with jackdaws cawing overhead. Although inhabited by the Arabs, Segesta was abandoned by the 13th century.

Marsala

Famous for its wine, first exploited on an industrial scale by British wine merchants and much appreciated by Nelson, **Marsala** (*map p. 419, A2*) was the landing-place of Garibaldi and his 'Thousand' (*I Mille*) on 11th May 1860, a crucial date in the history of the Unification of Italy. His subsequent victorious battles against the Bourbon troops, fought together with the enthusiastic Sicilians, were the first of the Unification move-ment. In the beautiful wide lagoon in front of the town, surrounded by salt-pans, is the island of **Mozia**, once the property of 'Pip' Whitaker, a wine merchant and amateur archaeologist. While excavating on the island he brought to light the remains of the Phoenician city of *Motya*, an identification confirmed by his house-guest Schliemann, fresh from his Trojan triumphs. In Villa Whitaker, now the **museum** (*open 9–6*), is one of the most important works of art ever found in Sicily, the *Motya Ephebus*, a superb Classical sculpture of a young man, perhaps an athlete, dressed in a finely-pleated tunic. Dated c. 440 BC, it has been attributed by some scholars to Pheidias.

Mazara del Vallo

A lively, colourful town with the largest fishing fleet in Italy, Mazara del Vallo was a Phoenician trading-post which became the emporium of Selinunte, and fell with it to Carthage in 409 BC. In AD 827 the Arabs, summoned by the governor Euphemius to help him in his quarrel with the Byzantine emperor, gained here their first foothold in Sicily. It became the capital of the Val di Mazara, one of the three administrative dis-tricts by which the Arabs governed the island. It was captured by the Norman Roger de Hauteville in 1075, and it was here in 1097 that the Sicilian parliament, one of the oldest in the world, was first convened. The church of Sant'Egidio in Piazza Plebiscito houses the **Museo del Satiro** (*open 9–6*), displaying the bronze statue of a *Dancing Satyr* found in 1998 by some fishermen when it caught in one of their nets. Miraculously, a few weeks later, they found one of the missing legs. Perhaps repre-senting Dionysus himself, and a little larger than life size, the satyr is shown with his body twisted in a dance of drunken ecstasy. Dated between 404 and 280 BC, some scholars believe it to be the work of Praxiteles.

Selinunte

In a superb position overlooking the sea on Sicily's south coast are the extensive ruins of the ancient city of Selinous (modern Selinunte; *map p. 419, A2; open 9–1hr before sun-set*). Founded in 651 BC as a colony of *Megara Hyblaea*, a Greek settlement north of Syracuse, the name derives from the wild celery, *Apium graveolens* (*selinon* in Greek), which grows here in abundance, and which appears on ancient coins. The ancient town with its acropolis occupied a raised terrace between the Modione river and a marshy depression called Gorgo di Cottone. It possessed a harbour at the mouth of each valley, a necropolis to the north, a sanctuary to Demeter to the west, and a group of large Doric temples to the east; it was very wealthy, and had a huge population. Attacked by Carthage in 409 BC, Selinous fell after only nine days' siege, in spite of the redoutable fortifications; the inhabitants were sold into slavery and the city destroyed. Forgotten for centuries, it was rediscovered in the 16th century, but serious excavations were begun only 300 years later. The temples are identified by letters of the alphabet because their dedication is still uncertain; they were found completely flattened, partly due to the Carthaginian destruction, partly to earthquakes. One of the eastern group has been reconstructed. A miniature train connects the most important areas in the park, or you can walk. Parking areas are available at the entrance and at the acropolis.

VISITING TRAPANI & ITS PROVINCE

GETTING AROUND

• **By train:** The central railway station in Trapani is in Piazza Umberto, with services to Palermo, Marsala (c. 40mins) and Mazara del Vallo (c. 1hr). Trains stop at Ragattisi, the nearest station for the boat to Mozia (c. 1km).

• **By bus:** AST buses from Trapani (www.aziendasicilianatrasporti.it) run to Trapani airport, also Erice, Castelvetrano (for Selinunte), Marsala, Mazara del Vallo and Segesta. SAU also has services to Erice in c. 40mins. Lumia connects Marsala to Mazara del Vallo and Agrigento. Salemi (www.autoservizisalemi.it) runs buses to/from Trapani, Mazara del Vallo and Palermo. Inter-city services from Piazza Malta in Trapani are run by Segesta (www.segesta.it) to/from Palermo and its airport.

WHERE TO STAY IN TRAPANI & ITS PROVINCE

Erice

€€ **Moderno.** ■ Fascinating old hotel ('*moderno*' is a misnomer) with an exceptionally good restaurant. Breakfast on the rooftop terrace is unforgettable. *Via Vittorio Emanuele 63, T: 0923 869300, www.hotelmodernoerice.it.*

Marinella di Selinunte

€€ **Alceste** in a quiet street, with 40 rooms (*Via Alceste 23, T: 0924 46184, www.hotelalceste.it*) and €€€ **Admeto**, overlooking the fishing harbour (*Via Palinuro 3, T: 0924 46796, www.hoteladmeto.it*), are two

modern, family-run hotels with restaurants serving memorable food; good value for money and a friendly welcome at both.

Trapani

€€ **Nuovo Albergo Russo**. A comfortable, traditional family-run hotel in an excellent location in the old town, just across from the cathedral. Parking. *Via Tintori 4, T: 0923 22166.*

WHERE TO EAT IN TRAPANI & ITS PROVINCE

Erice

€ **Pasticceria Grammatico.** ■ Maria Grammatico, immortalised by Mary Taylor Simeti in *Bitter Almonds* and *On Persephone's Island*, is Sicily's most accomplished pastrycook. Ask for *genovesi*, tiny shortcrust-pastry pies filled with confectioner's custard. *Via Vittorio Emanuele 14, near San Salvatore.*

Mazara del Vallo

€€ **La Bettola**. Tiny seafood restaurant in the heart of the old city. Try various kinds of raw fish, such as *aragosta agli agrumi*, lobster with citrus salad, and for a main course perhaps squid stuffed with the local cheese. Closed Wed. *Via Franco Maccagnone 32, T: 0923 946422 or 339 285 8541.*

Trapani

€€ **Cantina Siciliana**. Try the *bruschette con uova di tonno* (with tuna roe) as a starter, followed by fish couscous, then *cassatelle di ricotta*, an irresistible dessert. Next door there is a well-stocked wine shop run by the same management. *Via Giudecca 36, T: 0923 28673.*

AGRIGENTO

Founded as *Akragas* in 580 BC, Agrigento (*map p. 419, B3*) became the wealthiest city of Magna Graecia and boasted a series of Doric temples, defiantly built along a crest between the sea and the city as a demonstration of power and the protection afforded by the gods. It was the birthplace of the philosopher Empedocles (who famously leapt to his death in the crater of Etna) and, more recently, of the Nobel prizewinning writer Luigi Pirandello (1867–1936).

The town stands on a long narrow hill, perhaps the acropolis of ancient Akragas. The walk along the Valley of the Temples south of the town (*open 9–7, late closing in summer, combined ticket with museum*), where the golden sandstone columns emerge between the sea and the sky among olives and almonds, should begin at the **Temple of Hera**, or Juno Lacinia, on the highest point of the crest. Continue along the fortifications to the magnificently-preserved **Temple of Concord** (430 BC), which retains its complete entablature at both ends. Beyond here, past the Villa Aurea, which from 1921–33 was the home of Captain Alexander Hardcastle, an eccentric Englishman who provided the funds for much of the excavation, is the oldest temple of the group, the 6th-century BC **Temple of Heracles**, still showing the parallel ruts where the stones were dragged from the quarry to the site, after being fitted with wooden wheels. The catacombs to be seen here, with tunnels extending under the road, form part of a palaeochristian necropolis.

Across the road is the ticket office and the **Temple of Olympian Zeus**, the largest Doric temple in existence (110.1m by 52.7m), built to celebrate the victory over the Carthaginians in 480 BC. Abandoned still unfinished in 406 BC, its subsequent destruction is due to earthquakes and to 18th-century quarrying, when stones were taken from here to build the harbour structures at Porto Empedocle. Unique in design, the 14 columns along the sides were engaged in the walls, alternating with 38 colossal telamones and caryatids, almost 8m high, fragments of which can be seen in the museum. A cast of one of the giants can be seen in the middle of the temple. The U-shaped grooves on the stones were to accommodate the ropes used for shifting them into position.

West of the temple is the vast excavation of the **Sanctuary of the Chthonic Divinities** (gods of the earth; Dionysus, Demeter and Persephone), and the picturesque group of columns known as the **Temple of Castor and Pollux**, more probably the remains of the temple to Dionysus. Close by is the entrance to the **Garden of Kolymbetra** (*open May–Oct 9–7, Nov–Jan 10–5, Feb–Apr 9–6; closed Mon in Jan and during the almond blossom festival*), once an artificial lake dug by Carthaginian prisoners and used as a fishpond and reservoir. It was soon filled in, probably due to malaria, and later the Arabs turned it into a garden planted with oranges, dates and pomegranates. From the garden it is easy to cross the railway line in order to reach the two surviving columns of the **Temple of Hephaistos**.

The **museum**, on the main Via dei Templi (*open 9–7, Sun and Mon 9–1*), has a superb collection of painted vases, statues and sarcophagi found during the excavations. Not to be missed is the *Ephebus*, a 5th-century BC marble statue of a young man, representing perhaps a victor from Agrigento at the Olympic Games.

Temple remains in the Sanctuary of the Chthonic Divinites, which once held shrines to the gods of the earth: Dionysus, Demeter and Persephone.

VISITING AGRIGENTO

GETTING AROUND

• **By train:** Services link Agrigento with Palermo (2hrs) and Syracuse (over 5hrs).
• **By bus:** Town buses run by TUA (nos 1, 2 and 3) run from Piazza Marconi to the Valle dei Templi (request stops at the museum and, lower down, for the temples at the Posto di Ristoro). Autolinee Licata (www.autolineesal.it) run three buses a day from Agrigento to Palermo airport.

WHERE TO STAY IN AGRIGENTO

Agrigento
€€€€ **Villa Athena**. Beautiful 18th-century villa in an almond grove behind the temple of Concord. Good restaurant, garden, pool, and unbeatable views. *Via Passeggiata Archeologica 33, T: 0922 596288, www.athenahotels.com.*
€€ **Akropolis**. Comfortable B&B in the old city, run by two tour-guides. Air-conditioned rooms, panoramic views, delicious breakfasts. *Via San Girolamo 113, T: 0922 401003 or 330 363308, www.agrigentoakropolis.com.*
Montallegro
€€€ **Relais Briuccia**. ■ In the village of Montallegro, between Agrigento and Selinunte, an Art Nouveau villa with a wonderful garden restaurant, run by a prizewinning chef. *Via Trieste 1, T: 0922 845577 and 339 759 2176.*

WHERE TO EAT IN AGRIGENTO

Agrigento
€€ **Trattoria dei Templi**. Excellent local dishes served with Sicilian wines. *Via Panoramica dei Templi 15, T: 0922 403110.*

ENNA & ITS PROVINCE

At 931m, Enna (*map p. 419, B2*) is the highest provincial capital in Italy, surrounded by wheatfields. This was in fact the legendary home of the goddess Demeter, who gave wheat to humanity, and her daughter Persephone, who was snatched away by Hades and carried off to his underground kingdom through a doorway concealed under nearby Lake Pergusa. Her subsequent marriage to her kidnapper, and Zeus' decision to allow her to stay six months of each year with her husband and six months with her mother, is the origin of the seasons and an early formulation of the idea of resurrection (*see also p. 336*). The view from Enna to the adjacent medieval hill-town of Calascibetta is exceptional, while the vast Castello di Lombardia (*open 9–1*), visually dominating the whole island, was an almost impregnable stronghold for centuries. It takes its name from the Lombard troops who came with the Normans in the 11th century and to whom it was assigned. In the 13th century Frederick II rebuilt it, providing it with 20 towers, of which six remain, and a secret passage (*now closed*) connecting it to the mysterious Torre di Federico, an octagonal tower on the opposite side of the town, thought by some authorities to mark the exact centre of the island.

Piazza Armerina

From Enna a country road leads by Lake Pergusa and through dense woods to the old

hill town of Piazza Armerina (*map p. 419, B2–B3*), with its well-defined medieval districts and stone-paved streets, scented with freshly-baked bread and resonant with the sounds of the Lombard dialect still spoken by the people. In the valley 6km to the southwest is the extraordinary **Villa Romana del Casale** (*open 10–6 summer, 10–5 winter*), 3,500m square of splendid 4th-century AD Roman mosaic floors, the most extensive in the world, and protected for posterity by a providential mud-slide in the early Middle Ages. Perhaps the hunting lodge of an emperor, or the retreat of a wealthy merchant

Ostrich being embarked for the amphitheatre. Mosaic detail from the Roman villa at Casale.

dealing in the animal trade, the villa, now a UNESCO site, comprises c. 50 rooms. Some of the scenes portrayed on the floors are dedicated to the hunt, and to the capture abroad and transport to Rome of wild animals destined for the arena. Particularly notable among these are the richly-detailed Room of the Small Hunt, and the long corridor known as the Great Hunt. Well known is the triclinium, the banqueting hall with its masterful portrayals of the Labours of Hercules; and the Room of the Ten Girls, where female athletes are shown wearing prototype bikinis. A small room is entirely devoted to the moment when Ulysses offers wine to the cyclops Polyphemus, while close by is the famous 'Erotic Scene', in fact a fairly innocent embrace between a half-naked young lady and her lover, and nothing at all compared to the erotica at Pompeii. The colossal, expensive enterprise of creating these floors in what must have been a relatively short time (5–10 years) involved bringing hundreds of skilled craftsmen from various North African ateliers (although contemporary with each other, the floors are very different stylistically), and providing enormous quantities of material for them to work with—the rich chromatic effects were obtained by using cubes of coloured stone together with pieces of terracotta and glass. Some of the yellow and green marble, from quarries which were already exhausted at that time, must have been recuperated from earlier buildings elsewhere.

Morgantina

A short distance (14km) from Piazza Armerina, near the little farming community of Aidone, is Morgantina (*map p. 419, B2–C2; open 8–1hr before sunset*), the site of a city inhabited by both Greeks and Sicels, which reached its moment of greatest splendour in the 3rd century BC. It was sacked and totally destroyed by the Spanish mercenary soldiers of the Roman general Marcus Marcellus, as a reward for helping him take the recalcitrant city of Syracuse in 212 BC. The site is hauntingly beautiful, dominated by Mt Etna to the north, and you can explore the ruined town street by street, with its unusual stepped agora, fine houses, temples, industrial areas and theatre.

VISITING ENNA & ITS PROVINCE

GETTING AROUND

• **By bus:** From Enna buses run by SAIS (www.saistrasporti.it) and Interbus (www.interbus.it) go to Piazza Armerina in 45mins.

WHERE TO STAY & EAT IN PIAZZA ARMERINA

The €€€ **Villa Trigona**, a beautiful old country house close to town, offers good food and comfortable accommodation (*Contrada Bauccio, T: 0935 681896, www.villatrigona.it*). €€ **Gangi** is a comfortable hotel in a medieval palace near the public gardens (*Via Generale Ciancio 68, T: 0935 682737, www.hotelgangi.it*). Near the Roman villa, the €€ **La Ruota** serves simple, good local fare. Try the *coniglio alla stemperata* (rabbit with tomatoes, olives and capers) accompanied by the house wine (*Contrada Paratore Casale, T: 0935 680542*).

SYRACUSE & THE BAROQUE CITIES

Founded in 733 BC as a colony of Corinth in Greece, Syracuse (*map p. 419, C3*) soon eclipsed all the other settlements on Sicily thanks to several favourable circumstances: two harbours, one for the military and one for the merchant fleet, abundant fresh water, a position dominating the approach to the Straits of Messina, and a series of excellent governors (known as tyrants), including Gelon, who obtained the victory over the Carthaginians at Himera in 480 BC, and Dionysius, who came to power in 406 BC, a household name for despotism, but a great leader. Archimedes, the great scientist and mathematician, was born in Syracuse, where he died during the Roman attack in 212 BC. Under the Romans the city gradually lost all its former glory. In 1693 it was almost totally destroyed by earthquake, and was rebuilt in the Baroque style. Now a UNESCO World Heritage Site, this small provincial town is quite prosperous thanks to its much-maligned oil refineries and flourishing agriculture.

Ortygia

The small island of Ortygia (meaning quail, so called because of its bird-like shape), which separates the two harbours, is the heart of the city, where it was originally founded, and where you will find the ruins of the late 7th century BC **Temple of Apollo**, the first Doric temple to be built in Sicily. In the centre of the island is the **duomo**, still recognisably the Doric Temple of Athena, complete with most of its columns and the interior cella, still intact; the arches in its wall were cut by early Christians. It was built under the orders of Gelon by Carthaginian prisoners taken at the Battle of Himera (*see above*), and was renowned for its beauty and the richness of its fittings: the doors were made of gold and ivory, the cult statue of the goddess had a golden shield, while above the entrance another great golden shield acted as a landmark for shipping by reflecting the rays of the sun. The cathedral is dedicated to the Madonna, although the patroness of Syracuse is St Lucy, who suffered martyrdom here in 304.

Not far from the cathedral, at Via Capodieci 16, is the museum of medieval art, the **Galleria Regionale di Palazzo Bellomo** (*open 9–7, closed Mon*), housed in a 14th-century palace and a 15th-century convent. Among the precious works of art displayed here is a masterpiece by Antonello da Messina, the *Annunciation* (1474), strongly reminiscent of Piero della Francesca in its gentle mood and the arrangement of the figures.

Where Via Capodieci emerges onto the Great Harbour is a freshwater pool with papyrus, ducks and fish: the Fountain of Arethusa, said to be the spring into which Arthemis transformed the nymph Arethusa when she was being pursued by the river-god Alpheus. The nearby River Anapo is in fact the only place outside Africa where papyrus is found growing in the wild. Local craftsmen prepare the paper according to ancient Egyptian techniques, and local artists paint the pictures offered for sale. At the tip of the island is the **Castello Maniace** (*open 9–1, closed Sun*), built by Frederick II in 1234.

The mainland

In the archaeological park (*map opposite, 1; open 9–1hr before sunset*), beyond the ruins of the perfectly elliptical, 1st-century AD Roman amphitheatre, is the so-called **Altar of Hieron**, the great altar (198m long, it is the largest known) built by Hieron II c. 240 BC to accommodate the annual sacrifices to Zeus, said to consist of 450 bulls slaughtered in one day. Only the part carved into the rock is visible, the upper stones were removed

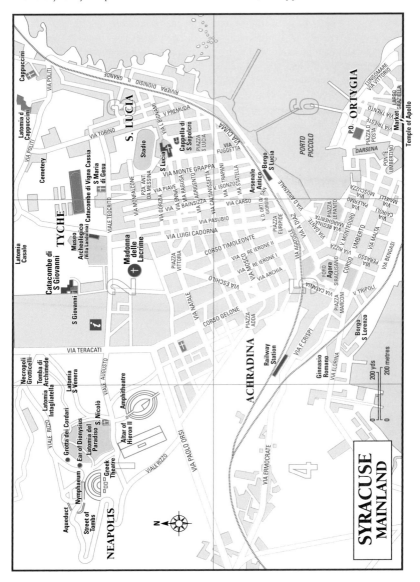

by the Spanish in 1528 to fortify the harbour. From here the path turns to reach the celebrated **Greek theatre**, begun by Gelon in 478 BC and inaugurated by Aeschylus two years later, with the first performance of his *Women of Aetna*. The immense cavea is carved into the limestone, and together with a superstructure which was successively dismantled, could accommodate 15,000 people. Close to the theatre, steps meander down into the **Latomia del Paradiso**, one of the many limestone quarries surrounding the city, now verdant with lemons, magnolias and pomegranates—hence the paradise of the name, although prisoners were flung here by the ancient tyrants. In the heart of the quarry is the 'Ear of Dionysius', a strange, man-made cave with surprising acoustics.

East of the archaeological park, opposite the horrible modern church dedicated to the Madonna delle Lagrime (Our Lady of the Tears; said to resemble a lemon-squeezer with an egg-beater on the top), is the **Museo Archeologico Regionale Paolo Orsi** (*map p. 383, 2; open Tues–Sat 9–7, Sun 9–2*), with magnificent collections of objects found during excavations in the surrounding area, but also from other sites in Sicily. The grinning terracotta relief of the running Medusa clutching the winged horse Pegasus, her child by Poseidon (7th century BC), is from the first temple of Athena on Ortygia. The *Venus Anadyomene*, a Roman copy of a Greek original, shows an Aphrodite of the Cnidian type (*see p. 244*).

Still further east, in Piazza Santa Lucia, is the church of **Santa Lucia** (*map p. 383, 3*) marking the spot where the saint was interred in the catacombs. In 1608 Caravaggio, who had arrived here from Malta after escaping from prison, painted the large canvas over the altar of the *Burial of St Lucy*, one of his most impressive works.

NOTO, RAGUSA & MODICA

Often called *il giardino di pietra*, the 'garden of stone', **Noto** (*map p. 419, C3*) is a World Heritage Site famed for the beauty of its Baroque architecture. The flourishing ancient city was destroyed by the earthquake of 1693, which wreaked havoc all over the eastern part of the island. Towns were rebuilt in a florid and characteristic Baroque style, intensely theatrical, making use of elaborately curling volutes and groups of columns arranged in tiers, creating a sense of upward motion. The new Noto, built 14km away from the original site (against the wishes of the majority of the inhabitants), was planned by some of the greatest engineers, architects and master masons of the time, and is filled with lovely limestone churches, palaces and monasteries. In the centre is the imposing cathedral, and close by is Palazzo Nicolaci Villadorata, with delightfully lavish Baroque balconies, each one telling a different story.

Ragusa Ibla and **Ragusa Superiore** (*map p. 419, C3*) stand on a limestone plateau, deeply scored by its waterways, which have formed canyons luxuriant with vegetation in their depths. Ibla is of ancient origin; it, like Noto, was devastated by the 1693 earthquake. The aristocracy decided to rebuild the city where it was, with a new cathedral dedicated to St George, while the middle classes preferred to build Ragusa Superiore, a new city close by, with a cathedral dedicated to St John the Baptist. The resulting cities, with their splendid late Baroque churches and palaces in creamy-gold limestone, represent in their quality and consistency a vivid final flowering of the style in Italy, and have been recognised by the UNESCO as World Heritage Sites. There was intense rivalry between the two Ragusas until 1926, when they were finally united as one city, with one bishop and one official cathedral, the solemnly elegant San Giovanni Battista in Ragusa Superiore. From here, a spectacular walk leads south to the town limit on the edge of the plateau, and thence down through Ibla, a seemingly interminable sequence of stepped streets, passing little churches and decrepit palaces, to the soaring grandeur of its former cathedral, San Giorgio.

Modica, too, is a World Heritage Site (*map p. 419, C3*), its 100 Baroque churches forming a series of theatrical backdrops in a maze of tiny streets. Sixteenth-century Modica was known as the Venice

Three-tiered façade of the church of San Giorgio in Ragusa Ibla (1744), a superb example of the theatrical Baroque style which developed in the years following the 1693 earthquake.

of Sicily for its position at the confluence of two rivers, which were used for the transport of people and goods. The rivers were covered after a flood in 1902, and are now the main streets. The town is in two parts: Modica Bassa, at the foot of the church of San Pietro, and Modica Alta, dominated by the church and monumental stairway of San Giorgio. The people are proud of their cuisine, based on the use of prime-quality local produce and fish. Modica is also famous for its grainy chocolate, hand-made according to the Aztec tradition. It can be found at the Antica Dolceria Bonaiuto (*Corso Umberto 159*).

VISITING SYRACUSE & THE BAROQUE CITIES

GETTING AROUND

• **By bus:** In Syracuse take city bus no 4 for the Archaeological Museum and no 2 for Santa Lucia. Inter-city buses run by AST and SAIS/Interbus offer services to Messina.

• **By train:** Ragusa is linked by rail with Modica (30mins) and Syracuse (2½ hrs).

Trains also link Syracuse and Noto (30mins).

WHERE TO STAY: SYRACUSE & THE BAROQUE CITIES

Modica

€€€€ **Palazzo Failla.** ■ Small hotel in a grand old town house in the centre of Modica Alta, recently voted Best in Sicily.

Two restaurants, one Michelin-starred, the other a friendly *trattoria. Via Blandini 5, T: 0932 941059, www.palazzofailla.it.*

Syracuse

€€€€ **Roma**. A venerable hotel (1880) on Ortygia, close to the cathedral, with 44 elegant rooms and a restaurant. *Via Roma 66, T: 0931 465626, www.hotelroma.sr.it.*

€€€ **Cavalieri**. Family-run hotel in a totally renovated building. Comfortable rooms, good breakfasts. *Via Malta 42, T: 0931 483635, www.cavalierisiracusa.it. Map p. 383, 5.*

€ **Approdo delle Sirene**. In a panoramic position on the Great Harbour, family-run establishment, very good breakfasts. *Riva Garibaldi 15 (just south of Ponte Umbertino), T: 0931 24857, www.apprododellesirene.com. Map p. 383, 6.*

Ragusa Ibla

€€€€ **Duomo**. Renowned throughout Italy, a restaurant with two Michelin stars, run by the culinary genius Ciccio Sultano. Very expensive, but worth the splurge. Closed Sun evening and Mon. *Via Bocchieri 31, T: 0932 651265, www.ristoranteduomo.it.*

Syracuse

€€ **Don Camillo.** ■ In the heart of Ortygia, superb pasta dishes, innovative *antipasto,* unusual preparations such as *zuppa di mucco,* whitebait soup, from the inventive genius of master chef Giovanni. Remarkable wine cellar. Closed Sun. *Via Maestranze 96, T: 0931 67133.*

MOUNT ETNA & TAORMINA

Mount Etna

At 3350m, Mt Etna is not only Europe's largest active volcano, but one of the major volcanoes of the world. Together with the four summit craters, which are all open and act as safety-valves by constantly releasing gases and steam, there are hundreds of side craters on the slopes, which never erupt twice. Thought to have formed about 500,000 years ago, it is almost three times the size of Mt Vesuvius, which is over a million years old. The frequent eruptions are usually more spectacular than damaging, but from time to time the slow-moving rivers of lava cover cultivated areas and sometimes even towns and villages. The inhabitants accept the situation philosophically, and passionately defend from criticism their volcano, which they call simply 'a muntagna', the mountain. Now a national park, created to protect flora, fauna and the characteristic lava flows, the best approaches are from the villages of Nicolosi, Linguaglossa or Zafferana.

Taormina

In a magnificent hilltop position, dominating the Straits of Messina, the Ionian Sea and Mt Etna, the little walled town of Taormina (*map p. 419, C2*) is thought by many to be the most beautiful place in the world. The rich colours, perfect climate, breathtaking panoramas, lush gardens, and the irresistible shop windows and pavement cafés along Corso Umberto, the ancient main street, make it the ideal retreat, but for this very reason it gets impossibly crowded in spring, just when it is at its best.

Piazza Duomo, with the 13th-century cathedral dedicated to St Nicholas and the Baroque fountain of the Centaur, symbol of the city, is near Porta Catania, at the southern end of the corso. The northern limit is defined by Porta Messina, close to the medieval Palazzo Corvaia, housing the tourist office. The street leads east to the 4th-century BC **Greek theatre** (*open 9–1hr before sunset*), later enlarged and rebuilt by the Romans. The impressive remains have inspired writers, artists and musicians. The luxuriant public gardens, with plants and trees from the five continents, were designed and planted in the late 19th century by Florence Trevelyan, once lady-in-waiting to Queen Victoria.

High above Taormina and its ancient castle (*closed*) is **Castelmola**, voted one of Italy's most beautiful villages, but with a dwindling population. It can be reached by a stepped footpath (785 steps) from Taormina's Corso Umberto, or, more comfortably, by road.

VISITING MOUNT ETNA & TAORMINA

GETTING AROUND

• **By train:** Trains link Messina and Taormina with Syracuse (just over 2hrs).
• **By bus:** Catania airport is well served by bus. There are frequent buses from Catania to the villages on the slopes of Etna. Buses run by Etna Trasporti run to Piazza Armerina (2¹/₂ hrs) and Taormina.

Inter-city bus services from Messina run by SAIS-Interbus (terminus by the railway station, in Piazza della Repubblica, www.saisautolinee.it) go to Catania in 90mins (continuing to Catania airport); to Taormina in 90mins. From Taormina there are buses to the Etna foothills, as well as services to Catania (and its airport).
• **By sea:** Frequent ferries (every 40mins) operated by Caronte (www.carontetourist.it) link Messina and the mainland. No need to book, but expect queues in summer. Less frequent hydrofoils go to Reggio Calabria.

WHERE TO STAY: MOUNT ETNA & TAORMINA

Etna
€€ **Bosco Ciancio**. At 1260m, among the woods on the western slopes of the volcano, 20 comfortable rooms in a newly-converted hamlet, with good restaurant/pizzeria, hors-es, quad- and mountain-bikes. *Vigne di Biancavilla, T: 328 413 5213, www.boscociancio.com.*

Taormina
€€€€ **Timeo**. Taormina's oldest, most exclusive hotel (1873), tucked under the Greek theatre. Good restaurant, pool, marvellous views and wonderful breakfasts. *Via Teatro Greco, T: 0942 23801, www.framon-hotels.it.*
€€ **Soleado**. Comfortable, central hotel with pool and garage. *Via Dietro Cappuccini 41/a, T: 0942 24138,www.hotelsoleado.com.*

WHERE TO EAT: MOUNT ETNA & TAORMINA

Messina
€€€ **Le Due Sorelle**. Tiny restaurant near the town hall, famous for fish dishes and for hearty fare from the Nebrodi mountains. Excellent cheese-board. Closed Sat, Sun and Mon evening. *Piazza Municipio 4, T: 090 44720.*

Taormina
€€ **Bougainville**. ■ Opposite the public gardens, this restaurant proudly offers dishes prepared only with local produce, accompanied by local wines. Try *spaghetti al limone*, delicately flavoured with lemon. *Via Bagnoli Croce 88, T: 0942 625218.*

PRACTICAL INFORMATION

Italy is an easy country to visit. Tourism is one of the mainstays of the economy and visitors are generally made extremely welcome. That is not to say that grumpy waiters, bad-tempered bus drivers and offhand museum custodians don't exist—they do, just as everywhere else in the world, but on the whole people are very friendly and willing to help and are completely used to dealing with foreigners in their midst. While more and more people, even outside the main centres, are able to speak good English, any attempt to communicate in Italian is always appreciated.

GETTING AROUND

Maps

The small Italy atlas in this book marks all the places visited in detail by this guide in black type. Other places, mentioned in passing or included to give context, are marked in grey. For full detail, the road maps published by the Touring Club Italiano are extremely good. Their *Carta Stradale d'Italia*, on a scale of 1:200,000, is divided into 15 maps covering all of Italy. They are also published as a three-volume road atlas.

Travelling by car

One of the joys of visiting Italian cities is their accessibility to pedestrians. Most old centres cover quite a small area, and many of them are closed to private cars, making them a delight to meander around on foot. A car is useful, though, if you plan to do a lot of touring. Not only does it make you the master of when you go where, but in some parts of the country, particularly those without a railway line, public transport can be sparse in the extreme, making a car a necessary evil. All airports and major towns have car hire offices.

If you are driving, remember that by law you must use your headlights on roads outside towns and cities. In most cases, cars entering a road from the right have right of way. If an oncoming driver flashes his headlights, it means he is proceeding and not giving you precedence. In towns, Italian drivers frequently change lanes without warning, pedestrians plunge into the street with serene confidence in the quality of your reflexes and your brakes, and few people respect zebra crossings.

Italy's motorways (*autostrade*) are indicated by green signs, and are toll roads. At the entrance, the two directions are indicated by the name of the most important town (not by the nearest town, nor, necessarily, the place you are aiming for), which can be momentarily confusing. Lorries are banned from motorways on Sundays, making that the best day to travel. Secondary roads are indicated by blue signs.

In the south, and in Sicily in particular, keep car doors locked when driving through busy city centres, place all bags and cameras under the seats, and beware of fake 'accidents', usually involving scooters, intended to make you get out of the car to check the damage, in order to snatch your handbag or wallet. Keep windows closed too, because bags and jewellery are often snatched from cars by fast-moving urchins on motorbikes. On the whole, driving in Italy requires a certain panache, but you will find other road-users good-humoured and patient. For parking in Italy, see p. 393.

Travelling by train

The Italian railway network is efficient and cheap—in fact, in some parts of the country, particularly in the north, you might find that you need no other form of transport. The Italian state railways have a good website (www.trenitalia.it) which gives timetables and journey times. You can usually buy tickets online: either collect your ticket from a machine on arrival at the station, or select the 'ticketless' system where you are given a customer code which you must show to the conductor on the train. Otherwise stations have automatic vending machines or manned ticket desks. The high-speed trains called Eurostar, which run only between the largest towns, require that you book a seat number as well. For all other trains except Eurostar (Intercity, Espressi, Regionali) you must validate your ticket in the machine near the head of the platform before you board. You can buy tickets on the train, but a fairly large supplement will be charged.

Some small private railway companies also exist, mainly serving outlying areas. Where relevant, details of these are included in the body of the guide.

Travelling by bus

Cities and provinces in Italy all have separate transport companies, usually known by their acronym (CAT, SITA, ACTV etc). These are given in the text, together with their websites, though these tend to be in Italian only. We have tried to give more ample information in each section of the guide, though all services are of course subject to change.

Tickets are not usually sold on board the bus. You can buy them from kiosks, tobacconists or other shops and bars displaying the relevant acronym and/or logo. At larger bus stations there will be a ticket office (*biglietteria*). In some cases you show your ticket to the driver when you board. Most city buses have machines where you validate or time-stamp them. Bus stops infuriatingly do not display timetables, and to find out when a bus might be due you need to ask a local or, if you are going to be using the service a lot, get a timetable from the tourist office. Drivers are almost always helpful about telling you which stop to get off at.

Many rural bus services are very infrequent, and are designed for commuters and schoolchildren, so only run on weekdays or in the early morning and evening.

Travelling by taxi

These are hired from ranks or by telephone; there are no cruising cabs. Always make sure that the meter is switched on, or agree the fare before you set out. Only a very small tip is expected. Supplements are charged for late-night journeys and for luggage and sometimes for airport routes. There is a surcharge when the destination is outside the town limits. There is a national number you can call to order a taxi: T: 892192. Otherwise numbers to call for taxis are given in the body of the guide.

ACCOMMODATION

Each chapter gives suggestions of places to stay. As well as hotels, there are also rooms available on farms in the countryside (*agriturismi*), which if you plan to spend any length of time in a region can be a more charming and authentic experience than a city-centre hotel. Lists of these can be found at www.agriturist.it, www.terranostra.it and www.turismoverde.it. Some Italian monasteries and convents also offer rooms. Most impose a curfew at 10 or 11pm and many require you to share bathroom facilities. All are very good value. See www.monasterystays.com.

Prices are as follows, for a double room per night in high season:

€€€€ (over €300)
€€€ (€200 or over)
€€ (100–200)
€ (under €100).

BLUE GUIDES RECOMMENDED

Hotels, restaurants and cafés that are particularly good choices in their category—in terms of excellence, location, charm, value for money or the quality of the experience they provide—carry the Blue Guides Recommended sign:■. All these establishments have been visited and selected by our authors, editors or contributors as places they have particularly enjoyed and would be happy to recommend to others. To keep our entries up-to-date reader feedback is essential: please do not hesitate to contact us (www.blueguides.com) with any views, corrections or suggestions, or join our online discussion forum.

FOOD & DRINK

Italian food and wine is famous, and rightly so. It is still strictly regional in character, and is always based on good-quality, seasonal ingredients simply prepared. Italians enjoy eating, and food is sensibly priced. Of course there are numerous superstar restaurants, which are an experience in themselves, but for good, honest country cooking, in most towns you will find yourself spoiled for choice. Each chapter includes a short summary of the most typical and famous specialities of the region.

Restaurants

In general an establishment terming itself an *osteria* is less smart than a *trattoria*, which in turn is less smart than a *ristorante*. If you are looking for an elegant dinner, choose a *ristorante*. If all you want is a good meal, you are just as likely to find it in an unpromising-looking *osteria* next to the bus station as in a beautifully decorated tavern in the town centre. The culture of eating out is still strong in Italy and the good food goes where the people are. Suggestions of places to eat are given in each chapter. Note that prices on the menu do not include a cover charge, which is added to the bill. A service charge is now almost always automatically added, so tipping is not strictly necessary, but a few euros are appreciated. You should be given a receipt.

For Blue Guides Recommended, see opposite. Prices are categorised as follows, for a full meal with wine:

€€€ (€80 or more per head)
€€ (€30–80)
€ (under €30).

An excellent source of information on traditional Italian restaurants is *Osterie & Locande d'Italia* (available in English), published by Slow Food.

Bars and cafés

Bars and cafés are open from early morning to late at night and serve numerous varieties of snacks which most Italians usually take standing up. As a rule, you must pay the cashier first, then present your receipt to the barman in order to get served. If you sit at a table the charge is usually higher, and you will be given waiter service (so don't pay first). However, some simple bars have a few tables that can be used with no extra charge, and it is always best to ask, before ordering, whether there is waiter service or not. Some bars also offer *tavola calda* (hot food).

Coffee

Italians are serious about their coffee and they drink a lot of it. The sounds of the espresso machine frothing the milk and of the barman banging the detachable arm against the side of the bin to get the coffee grounds out are familiar on every street corner. There are many ways to drink your coffee. The most common are:

Caffè or *espresso*, a small black coffee, which can be ordered *lungo* (diluted);
Macchiato, espresso with a dash of milk;
Latte macchiato, hot milk with a dash of coffee;
Cappuccino black coffee with a frothed milk top;
Caffè freddo, iced coffee.

OTHER INFORMATION

Banks

There are ATM machines widely available in all towns. If you need to change you can do so at banks, post offices, travel agencies and some hotels, resta shops, though exchange rates vary. Banks are open Mon–Fri 8.30–1.30 and for an hour in the afternoon, usually 2.30–3.30. A few banks are open on Saturday morning. They all close early (about 11) the day before a national holiday (*see below*).

Churches

Although cathedrals and some of the most important churches are often open all day (and some charge an entry fee), most smaller churches tend to close for an hour or two in the middle of the day. Opening times are usually given in the text. Where they do not appear, 9–12 & 4–6 is a safe estimate, though many open even earlier, and some do not reopen in the afternoon until around 5pm. The key for locked churches and oratories in villages can often be found by enquiring locally. Some churches ask that sightseers do not enter during a service, but if you are on your own, you may normally do so, especially in larger churches, provided you are silent and do not approach the altar in use or take blinding flash photographs. In some towns (for example Venice), where tourism is threatening to swamp churches and render them impossible to maintain as places of quiet contemplation, you are only allowed to visit at certain times, must pay to do so, and can expect to receive the sharp edge of the sacristan's tongue if you attempt to photograph the altarpieces. At all times you are expected to dress with decorum and you are often not allowed to enter churches wearing shorts or with bare shoulders. Paper ponchos are sometimes provided in summer. Churches are frequently unaligned: descriptions in the text always refer to liturgical, not compass, north, east, west and south: in other words, the high altar is always taken to be at the 'east' end.

Entrance fees

These vary according to age and nationality; EU citizens under 18 and over 65 are entitled to free admission to national museums, but you need to be able to prove your age. During the Settimana per i Beni Culturali e Ambientali (Cultural and Environmental Heritage Week; usually in March or April), entrance to national museums is free.

Crime and personal security

Pickpocketing is a widespread problem in towns all over Italy: it is always advisable not to carry valuables, and to be particularly careful on public transport. Women should keep their handbags on the side nearer the wall (never on the street side). Crime should be reported at once to the police or the local *carabinieri* office (found in every town and small village). A statement has to be given in order to get a document confirming loss or damage (essential for insurance claims). Interpreters are provided.

Emergency numbers

Police T: 113 (Polizia di Stato) or 112 (Carabinieri); **Medical assistance** T: 118.

Opening times and public holidays

Opening hours of museums, churches and monuments have, where possible, been given in the text, though they often change without warning so allow time for variations.

Up to date information should be available from tourist offices. National museums, monuments and sites are usually open daily 9am–dusk, and if they have a closing day it is usually Monday (the most important sites sometimes have longer hours in summer). Some museums are closed on the main public holidays, which are as follows:

1 January

Easter Sunday and Easter Monday

25 April (Liberation Day)

1 May (Labour Day)

15 August (Assumption)

1 November (All Saints' Day)

8 December (Immaculate Conception)

25 December (Christmas Day)

26 December (St Stephen)

Parking

Towns have pay car parks just outside their historic centres. On streets, white lines indicate free parking. Blue lines mean you have to pay: tickets are from nearby parking meters. Do use the meters; beware of fake parking attendants. Some parking spaces let you stay for a set amount of time and display a symbol of a parking disc (*disco orario*). You can buy these at petrol stations, tobacconists and newsagents. Set it to the time you arrived and place it in your windscreen.

Pharmacies

Pharmacies (*farmacie*), identified by their street sign, which shows a luminous green cross, are usually open Mon–Fri 9–1 & 4–7.30 or 8. A few are open also on Sat, Sun and holidays (listed on the door of every pharmacy). In all towns there is also at least one pharmacy open at night (also shown on the door of every pharmacy).

Public holidays

Each town keeps its patron saint's day as a holiday. There are a many traditional festivals in Italy. Towns become lively with parades and pageantry, often in medieval dress, and markets are usually held at the same time. Fireworks and bonfires are popular, local food and wine abounds, and the events are always extremely good fun.

Telephoning

The country code for Italy is 39. To dial the UK from Italy (00 44) + number; to dial the US from Italy (001) + number. Italian telephone numbers require the area code, even if you are dialling from within that area. With all numbers, including mobiles, you always need to dial all the digits (don't delete the initial 0). Italian telephone numbers vary greatly in length.

Tipping

Large gratuities are not expected in Italy. To convey appreciation, it is fine just to round up the price to the nearest euro or two. Even taxi-drivers rarely expect more, as the charge officially includes service. In hotels, porters who show you to your room and help with your luggage or find you a taxi usually expect a coin or two.

GLOSSARY

Acrolith, a statue with a wooden trunk and the head and extremities of stone or metal

Aedicule, small opening framed by two columns and a pediment, originally used in Classical architecture; a niche of this shape

Agora, public square or market place of an ancient Greek city

Ambo (pl. *ambones*), pulpit in a Christian basilica; two pulpits on either side of the nave from which the Gospel and Epistle are read

Ambulatory, typically the section of a church beside and around the high altar

Amorino (pl. *amorini*), a small cupid or putto

Amphitheatre, Roman arena, elliptical in shape, with seats all round a central 'stage'; used for public spectacles

Amphora (pl. *amphorae*), antique vase, usually large, for oil and other liquids

Angevin, pertaining to the house of Anjou, rulers of medieval Naples and Sicily

Annunciation, the appearance of the Angel Gabriel to Mary to tell her that she will bear the Son of God; an image of the 'Virgin Annunciate' shows her receiving the news

Apse, vaulted semi-circular end wall of the chancel of a church or chapel

Apulian, of or pertaining to the region of Puglia

Architrave, the horizontal beam placed above supporting columns; the lowest part of an entablature; the horizontal lintel above a door

Assumption, the ascension of the Virgin to Heaven, 'assumed' by the power of God

Baldacchino, canopy supported by columns, for example over an altar

Basilica, originally a Roman hall used for public administration; in Christian architecture an aisled church with a clerestory and apse and no transepts

Bas-relief, sculpture in low relief

Black-figure ware, ancient Greek pottery style where the figures appear black against a clay-coloured ground

Blind arch, an arch attached to a wall for purely decorative purposes, i.e. not framing an opening

Bucchero, Etruscan black pottery

Cabochon, an uncut, unfaceted gemstone in a fixed setting

Calidarium, room for hot or vapour baths in a Roman bath complex

Campanile, bell-tower, often detached from the building to which it belongs

Campionese, pertaining to a group of medieval masons and stone carvers from Campione on Lake Lugano

Capitolium, a temple dedicated to the main Roman (previously Etruscan) deities, the 'Capitoline Triad' (Jupiter, Juno and Minerva), worshipped on the Capitoline Hill in Rome

Cardo, principal street of a Roman town, at right-angles to the decumanus

Carthaginians, the inhabitants of the ancient city of Carthage on the north African coast

Cartoon, a full-size preparatory drawing for a painting or fresco

Caryatid, sculpted female figure used as a supporting column

Catapan, governor of a Byzantine province

Cavea, the part of a theatre or amphitheatre occupied by the rows of seats

Cella, sanctuary of a temple, usually in the centre of the building

Chi-Rho, Christian symbol formed by the superimposition of the first two letters of Christ's name in Greek, X and P

Chiaroscuro, distribution of light and shade in a painting

Christ Pantocrator, in Byzantine iconography the Almighty, the ruler of the Universe

Ciborium, casket or tabernacle containing the Host (Communion bread)

Classical, in ancient Greece, the period from 480–323 BC; in general, when spelled with a capital C, denoting art etc from the ancient world as opposed to classical ('classicising') modern or Renaissance works

Clerestory, upper part of the nave wall of a church, above the side aisles, with windows

Cloisonné, enamel decoration where areas of colour are partitioned by thin strips of metal

Codex (pl. *codices*), medieval manuscript book (i.e. hand-written, not printed)

Collegiata, a collegiate church where worship is led by a college of canons

Comune, city of medieval Italy ruled by a government of the people (*cf seigniory*)

Condottiere (pl. *condottieri*), soldier of fortune, employed in Italy by popes and emperors, republics and duchies, to lead armies to fight their cause

Confessio, area reserved for relics near an altar, often below floor level

Contrapposto, where the body is posed on an S-shaped axis. Used in Classical statuary and characteristic of Michelangelo's sculpture and Perugino's painting

Corbel, a projecting block, usually of stone

Corinthian, ancient Greek and Roman order of architecture with a capital decorated with acanthus leaves (*see illustration on p. 399*)

Cornice, topmost finishing rim of a temple entablature (*qv*); any projecting ornamental moulding at the top of a building beneath the roofline or ceiling

Cosmatesque (or Cosmati), medieval style of mosaic decoration or cladding consisting of geometric patterns made up of (often) ancient marble fragments

Crenellations, battlements, specifically the indented sections

Crocketed, of a spire or pinnacle, oranamented with carved foliage jutting out to the sides like icing-sugar peaks

Cryptoporticus, vaulted underground corridor

Decumanus, the main street of a Roman town running parallel to its longer axis, the cardo

Dioscuri, name given to Castor and Pollux, twin sons of Zeus

Diptych, painting or tablet in two sections

Dolmen, a prehistoric monument (possibly a tomb) made up of two or more upright stones supporting a horizontal stone slab

Doric, ancient Greek order of architecture characterised by fluted columns standing close together and with no moulded base (*see illustration on p. 399*)

Engaged column, a column (or pilaster) that is not free-standing but partially embedded in the wall

Entablature, the upper part of a temple above the columns, made up of an architrave (*qv*), frieze and cornice (*see illustration on p. 399*)

Etruscans, the people who occupied much of central Italy before the Romans (*see p. 286*)

Eucharist, Christian sacrament (Holy Communion) in which bread represents the body of Christ and wine His blood. The Eucharist is often symbolised in Christian art as baskets of fish, loaves of bread, manna, and garlands of grapes

Evangelists, the authors of the gospels, Matthew, Mark, Luke and John, in Christian art usually represented by their symbols: a man or angel (Matthew), a lion (Mark), a bull (Luke) and an eagle (John)

Exarch, in the Byzantine world, a viceroy

Exedra, semicircular recess or bay

Ex-voto, tablet or small painting expressing gratitude to a saint

Flavian, of the emperors Vespasian, Titus, Domitian, Nerva and Trajan; or the period of their rule

Fresco, painting executed on wet plaster (*intonaco*), beneath which the artist had usually made a working sketch (*sinopia*)

Frigidarium, rooms for cold baths in a Roman bath complex

Fumarole, volcanic spurt of vapour (usually sulphurous) emerging from the ground

Genre scene, in art, a scene from everyday life, often domestic or light-hearted

Ghibellines, in medieval Italian cities, supporters of the imperial faction in politics, largely drawn from the nobility; the problematic partisan rivalries between Ghibellines and Guelphs (*qv*) led to the breakdown of the communes (*comuni; qv*) in favour of rule by an overlord or *podestà* (*qv*)

Giant order, column or pilaster (*qv*) with a vertical span of two or more storeys on a façade

Greek cross, church plan based on a cross with arms of equal length

Grottesche (or grotesques), delicate ornamental decoration characterised by fantastical motifs, patterns of volutes, festoons and garlands, and borders of vegetation, flowers and animals or birds. This type of decoration, first discovered in Nero's Domus Aurea in the late

15th century, became very fashionable and was widely copied by late Renaissance artists

Guelph, supporters of the papal faction in medieval cities, largely drawn from the merchant classes. They were the rivals of the pro-imperial Ghibellines (*qv*)

Hellenistic, Greek culture of the period from the death of Alexander the Great to the victory of Rome over Antony and Cleopatra (323–30 BC). Art from this period often displays more sentiment than Classical works

Hemicycle, a semicircular structure or space

Heracles, the Greek name for Hercules

Herm, pillar surmounted by a head

Historiated, decorated with figures of humans, animals, birds etc, especially in narrative form

Humanism, *see p. 173*

Hypocaust, ancient Roman heating system in which hot air circulated under the floor and between double walls

Iconoclasm, Byzantine movement of the 8th century which forbade the literal, human depiction of God, Christ or the saints, believing such works to be graven images

Impluvium, a rainwater pool in the atrium of an ancient Roman house

Impost, a block placed above a capital from which an arch rises

Intarsia, a decorative inlay made from wood, marble or metal

International Gothic, painting style characterised by a poised elegance, static but without the rigidity of pure Gothic. There is also a mingling of strong design with loving attention to detail, such as birds, animals and flowers. The style is often called 'courtly', because the natural and the stylised come together in images redolent of medieval courtliness

Ionic, order of Classical architecture identified by its capitals with two volutes (*qv*). Columns are fluted, stand on a base, and have a slimmer shaft than in the Doric order (*see illustration overleaf*)

Istrian stone, hard-wearing limestone which can be polished to resemble marble, from Istria, a peninsula in modern Croatia

Lancet, tall, slim, early Gothic aperture with a pointed arched head

Lantern, a small circular or polygonal turret with windows all round, crowning a roof or dome

Latin, **Latins**, pertaining to the people of ancient Latium (Lazio)

Latin cross, a cross where the vertical arm is longer than the transverse arm

Liberty, the Italian version of Art Nouveau

Loggia (pl. *logge*), covered gallery or balcony

Lunette, semicircular space in a vault or ceiling or above a door or window, often decorated with a painting, mosaic or relief

Macellum, ancient Roman market hall

Maestà, representation of the Madonna and Child enthroned in majesty

Mannerist, a period of mainly Italian art between the High Renaissance and the Baroque (c. 1520–1600). Unnatural light, lurid colours and elongated forms are among the characteristics of this style (*see p. 193*)

Metope, panel carved with decorative relief between two triglyphs (three vertical bands) on the frieze of a Doric temple

Mithraeum, a shrine of Mithras, a Persian sun-god worshipped in Imperial Rome

Monolithic, made of a single block of stone

Narthex, vestibule of a church or basilica, before the west door

Novecento, 20th-century art movement; *see p. 32*

Nymphaeum, a summer house in the gardens of baths and palaces, originally a temple of the Nymphs, decorated with statues of those goddesses, and often containing a fountain

Oculus, round window or aperture

Oeil de boeuf, elliptical window or aperture

Ogee, of an arch or tracery, shaped in a double S-curve, when two are fitted together they form an onion shape

Orders of architecture, Doric, Ionic, Corinthian (*see illustration overleaf*)

Pala, large altarpiece

Palaeochristian, from the earliest Christian times up to the 6th century

Palaestra, a public place for exercise or athletic training in ancient Greece or Rome

Passion, the sufferings of Christ, ending with His death on the Cross. The Instruments of the Passion are symbols of these sufferings and include the crown of thorns and the column at which Jesus was flagellated

Paten, small plate, usually of precious metal, for holding the Eucharistic (*qv*) bread

Patera (pl. *paterae*), small circular carved ornament, often Byzantine; a ritual drinking dish

Pavonazzetto, streaked or blotched marble in colours ranging from white to deep red

Pediment, gable above a portico, door or window, usually triangular in shape or shallowly curved (segmental)

Pendentive, concave spandrel descending from the four 'corners' of a dome

Peristyle, court or garden surrounded by a columned portico

Phoenicians, ancient civilisation from the area of modern Lebanon who pioneered maritime trade routes in the western Mediterranean and founded cities, including Carthage

Piano nobile, main floor of a palace

Pietà, representation of the Virgin mourning the dead Christ

Pietre dure, hard or semi-precious stones, cut and inlaid in intricate patterns to decorate furniture such as cabinets and table-tops

Pietra forte, fine-grained limey sandstone used as a building material in Florence, often for the rustication (*qv*) of palace façades

Pietra serena, fine-grained dark grey sandstone, easy to carve. Although generally not sufficiently resistant for the exterior of buildings, it was used to decorate many Renaissance interiors in Florence

Pilaster, a shallow pier or rectangular column projecting only slightly from the wall

Piscina, Roman tank; a pool for ablutions; a basin for an officiating priest to wash his hands before Mass

Podestà, chief magistrate who ruled a medieval city with the help of a council and representatives from the corporations. He had to be someone who was not a native of the city, and was only a military leader

Polychrome, made up of multiple colours

Polyptych, painting or panel in more than three sections

Porphyry, dark blue, purple or red-coloured igneous rock, much prized in the ancient world and used almost exclusively for imperial commissions

Predella, small painting or panel, usually in sections, attached below a large altarpiece, illustrating scenes of a story such as the life of a saint

Presbytery, the eastern part of a church chancel, beyond the choir

Pronaos, porch in front of a temple cella

Punic Wars, conflict between Rome and the Carthaginians; three wars were fought between 264 and 146 BC. The second was led by Hannibal

Putto (pl. *putti*), sculpted or painted figure of a nude male child

Quadriga, a two-wheeled chariot drawn by four horses abreast

Quadriporticus, rectangular court or atrium arcaded on all four sides, derived from the atria in front of palaeochristian basilicas

Quatrefoil, where the points tending inward from a traceried arch or opening create a pattern of four lobes

Quattrocento, Italian term for the 'four hundreds', i.e. the 15th century. Important artists include Brunelleschi, Michelangelo, Bellini and Leonardo da Vinci

Red-figure ware, ancient Greek pottery style where the background was painted in black leaving the outlined figures in the natural reddish colour of the clay

Reredos, decorated screen behind the altar

Risorgimento, the period when the idea of a united Italy took root (mid-19th century)

Rocca, a castle, derived from the Persian *rukh* (hence a 'rook' in chess)

Rood-screen, a screen below the Rood or Crucifix dividing the nave from the chancel of a church

Rostra, orator's platform named from ships' prows captured in battle, often used to decorate such platforms by the ancient Romans

Rustication, the grooves or channels cut at the joints between huge blocks of facing masonry (ashlar) on the outer walls of buildings

Sabines, an ancient people whose territory lay in the northeast of modern-day Lazio

Samnites, an ancient people, an offshoot of the Sabines, in south-central Italy

Saracens, nomadic Arab people who conquered Sicily in the late 9th century, and continued to raid the Italian coasts in the Middle Ages

Scena, the stage building of an ancient theatre

Schiacciato, term used to describe very low relief in sculpture, where there is an emphasis on the delicate line rather than the depth of the panel. A technique perfected by Donatello, under whose influence it was also used by Michelangelo

Schola cantorum, enclosure for the choristers in the nave of an early Christian church, adjoining the sanctuary

Scuola (pl. *scuole*), Venetian lay confraternity, dedicated to charitable works

Seigniory, a city in medieval Italy ruled by one powerful leader or *signore*

Sibyls, the prophetesses of the pagan world; in Christian art they appear as precursors of the prophets of the Old Testament

Silenus (pl. *sileni*), a drunken companion of Dionysus, often shown riding a donkey

Sinopia (pl. *sinopie*), large sketch for a fresco made on the rough wall in a red earth pigment called sinopia (because it originally came from Sinope, a town on the Black Sea). When a fresco is detached for restoration, it is possible to see the sinopia beneath

Soffit, underside of an arch or beam

Solomonic column, twisted 'barley-sugar' column, so called from its supposed use in the biblical Temple of Solomon

Spandrel, the triangular surface between two arches in an arcade or on either side of a single arch

Stele (pl. *stelae*), upright stone bearing a monumental inscription

Stigmata, marks appearing on a saint's body in the same places as the wounds of Christ (nail-holes in the feet and hands, and the sword wound in the side)

Swabian, denoting the inhabitants of part of southern Germany (from the Suebi, ancient people of the region), more particularly used to refer to the Hohenstaufen dynasty in Italy

Tablinum, the reception or family room in a Roman house

Telamon (pl. *telamones*), supporting column in the form of a sculpted male figure

Tempera, a painting medium of powdered pigment bound together, in its simplest form, by a mixture of egg yolk and water

Tepidarium, room for warm baths in an ancient Roman bath complex

Tessera (pl. *tesserae*), small cube of marble, stone or glass used in mosaic work

Theatre, in the ancient Greek and Roman world, a semicircular auditorium, as opposed to an amphitheatre which is elliptical and has seats all the way round

Thermae, originally simple Roman baths, later elaborate buildings fitted with libraries, assembly rooms and gymnasia

Thermal window, large, semicircular window derived from those used in ancient Roman public baths (*thermae*)

Thermopolium, in an ancient Roman town, a bar or tavern serving hot and cold drinks and snacks

Tholos, circular building in the ancient world, sometimes with a beehive-shaped roof, used as a tomb or for ritual purposes

Tondo (pl. *tondi*), circular painting or relief

Travertine, rock quarried near Tivoli, used as a building material

Trefoil, where the tracery tending inwards from an arch or opening creates a pattern of three lobes

Tribune, the part of a basilica that contains the throne; the throne itself

Triclinium, dining- and reception-room of a Roman house

Triglyph, small panel of a Doric frieze carved with three vertical channels

Triptych, painting or tablet in three sections

Triton, sea god, a son of Poseidon/Neptune

Trompe l'oeil, literally, a deception of the eye; used to describe illusionist decoration and painted architectural perspectives

Tuscan Doric, similar to the Doric order, but with columns unfluted and resting on a base, and without triglyphs in the frieze

Tympanum, the area between the top of a doorway and the arch above it; also the triangular space enclosed by a pediment

Tyrant, the sole, autocratic ruler of an ancient or medieval city

Vedutisti, landscape painters whose works show a detailed, often romanticised, view (*veduta*) of the subject; Canaletto and Guardi are well-known exponents of the genre

Virtues, The Cardinal Virtues are Fortitude, Temperance, Justice and Prudence; the Theological Virtues are Faith, Hope and Charity

Volute, scroll-like decoration at the corners of an Ionic capital; also typically present console-style on the façades of Baroque churches

ORDERS OF ARCHITECTURE

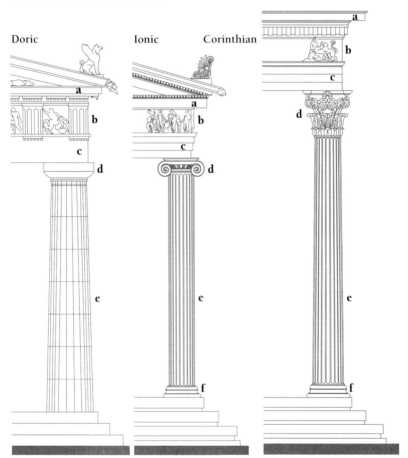

a cornice (the horizontal cornice and rising gable above it make up the pediment)
b frieze (in the Doric order, made up of figured panels called metopes separated by vertical grooves called triglyphs)

c architrave (the architrave, frieze and cornice together make up the entablature)
d capital
e column shaft (fluted, i.e. grooved)
f base (absent in the Doric order)

CHRONOLOGY

From earliest times to the fall of Rome

Of the many early peoples who inhabit the Italian peninsula, the most sophisticated are the Etruscans who, although they are eventually conquered by Rome, influence many aspects of Roman culture. The conquest of Etruria leads to the rise of the Roman Republic, which begins with lofty ideals in the 6th century BC, becomes increasingly strife- and faction-torn, and is finally reorganised along imperial lines by Augustus, adopted son of Julius Caesar. Imperial Rome conquers all of Italy and beyond, reaching far into western Europe and Asia, until it becomes overstretched and weakened. By the end the emperors choose to hold their courts at Milan, Ravenna or Constantinople. The city of Rome becomes a backwater, and falls prey to barbarian invaders.

9th century BC: The Etruscans establish themselves on Italy's west coast

8th century BC: Greek colonists found cities in Sicily and the south of Italy

753: Date of the legendary founding of Rome

509: Rome ousts its Etruscan king and ushers in republican rule

4th–3rd centuries BC: The Romans push southwards into the Italian peninusla

146 BC: Final victory of Rome against the Carthaginians. Inspired by success, Rome goes on to conquer the entire Italian peninsula, much of Gaul, Illyria and Greece

90 BC: A law proposed by Julius Caesar offers Roman citizenship to all Italic citizens who have not rebelled against Roman rule

88–86 BC: Strife between two military leaders, Marius and Sulla, fills the Roman world with conflict

49 BC: Leadership disputes between Pompey and Julius Caesar lead to civil war

44: Assassination of Julius Caesar

27: Octavian assumes the title Augustus and founds the Roman Empire. He brings peace to his realm, the *pax Romana*

67: St Peter martyred in Rome under Nero

79: Eruption of Vesuvius

88–117: Reign of Trajan, during which time the Roman Empire reaches its greatest extent

285 and 293: Diocletian divides the unwieldy empire into two and then four parts. This is to be the beginning of the split between the Eastern and Western empires, and leads to the ultimate decline of the city of Rome

313: The emperor Constantine ends the persecution of Christians. Shortly afterwards he orders a church to be raised over the burial place of St Peter on the Vatican Hill

330: Constantine moves his seat of government to Byzantium. He reunites the empires of East and West, but only briefly

401: Rome in decline and vulnerable to barbarian attack. Honorius, emperor of the West, moves the imperial capital to Ravenna

410: Rome sacked by the Goths

476: The last Roman emperor of the West is deposed and forced to abdicate by the Goth Odoacer

The Dark Ages

When the last Emperor of the West, Romulus Augustulus, loses his throne in 476, Italy enters the 'Dark Ages'. The Lombards invade the peninsula, and strife between them, the Goths and the Byzantines plagues the land. The Byzantines control the Adriatic coast around Ravenna. Later invaders, the Franks, defeat the Lombards. The bishop of Rome (the pope) obtains sovereignty of the city, and by this reasserts the status of the West vis à vis the Byzantine emperor. When the Frankish king Charlemagne becomes Holy Roman Emperor, however, he and his successors begin to challenge the pope's authority, and instead of the Byzantine emperor, the pope finds himself the rival of the Holy Roman Emperor. Venice begins trading with the Islamic East in the 8th century, though still recognises Byzantine suzerainty. The Saracens harass the south.

483: Gladiatorial combats are outlawed

493: Odoacer is defeated by Theodoric, who becomes ruler of the Western Empire

529: St Benedict founds the monastery at Monte Cassino

540: Byzantines under Justinian take Ravenna, which becomes the capital of an Eastern outpost in Italy, ruled by an exarch

549: Totila the Ostrogoth holds the last games in the Circus Maximus in Rome

568: The Lombards invade Italy and establish themselves at Pavia. Refugees fleeing from their advance found Venice. The Lombards set up duchies around Spoleto and Benevento

590: Accession to the pontificate of Gregory the Great, who settles power disputes between Goths and Byzantines by asserting control himself, and founding the temporal power of the papacy

609: The Pantheon is consecrated as a church, the first pagan temple to be Christianised

754: The Papal States are born after the Frankish king Pepin captures Ravenna and its territory, which had been seized by the Lombards, and instead of restoring it to the Byzantines, presents it to the papacy

774: Pepin's son Charlemagne defeats the Lombards outright. Charlemagne is crowned King of the Lombards and Franks

800: Charlemagne is crowned Holy Roman Emperor

812: The Byzantine emperor recognises Charlemagne as Emperor of the West

877: The Saracens complete their conquest of Sicily

The Middle Ages

Against a backdrop of power struggles between popes and Holy Roman Emperors, the first self-governing communes of Italy emerge, the earliest being merchant maritime states, where trade is allowed to develop to the common advantage. The maritime republic of Amalfi emerges in the 9th century, when Venetian wealth also blossoms. Genoa becomes a naval power in the 11th century; Pisa is at its height in the 12th. Florence develops as a centre of the wool trade in the 13th century, and greatly expands her territory over the course of the next two centuries, becoming a dominant inland power. Government of the cities is always faction-riven, however, and gradually the heads of powerful individual families begin to exert control as overlords. The south follows a different pattern. The Byzantines erode Saracen power and establish a province. The region is successively controlled by Byzantines, Normans, Swabians, Angevins and Aragonese.

1030: Arrival of the Normans. Over the course of the next century they will conquer the entire south of Italy, making Palermo their capital

1087: Genoa and Pisa oust the Arabs to gain control of the western Mediterranean

1138: Power struggles between Henry the Proud of Bavaria and the Swabian Hohenstaufen clan are the first stirrings of what will become known as Guelph and Ghibelline rivalry

1194: Beginning of the Hohenstaufen era in Sicily and the south

1204: Fourth Crusade. With the help of the Franks Venice defeats Constantinople, and takes much of its territory in the Mediterranean

1259: The Este come to power in Ferrara

1268: The last of the Hohenstaufen is defeated by Charles of Anjou, who moves his capital from Palermo to Naples

1277: The Visconti rise to power in Milan and are to be a force in northern Italy for 150 years, chivvying at Florence and Venice

1282: The uprising known as the Sicilian Vespers overthrows Angevin rule and gives Sicily to the Aragonese. The Kingdom of Sicily splits between Sicily itself and Naples

1284: Genoa defeats Pisa, whose maritime power is brought to an end

1300: The first Holy Year is proclaimed by Boniface VIII. Anyone making the pilgrimage to Rome in that year would obtain temporal absolution from their sins. Pilgrim numbers soar

c.1300: Giotto's *Maestà* (Uffizi). His art becomes the springboard for the Italian Renaissance

1302: The *Neri* (Black Guelphs) of Florence drive out the *Bianchi* (Whites). Dante goes into exile. Pope Boniface VIII publishes his bull *Unam Sanctam*, stating the superiority of spiritual over temporal power, and claiming that no one who is not subject to the pope can obtain salvation

1309: Clement V moves the seat of the papacy to Avignon

1343: Death of Robert the Wise of Anjou. Angevin rule in Naples totters

1348: Black death

1351: Giovanni Visconti of Milan tries to take Tuscany, provoking war with Florence

1353: Cardinal Albornoz is sent to Italy by the popes in Avignon to prevent the city states from forming alliances with the Holy Roman Empire. He builds fortresses all over central Italy

1378: The papacy under Gregory XI returns from Avignon to Rome and takes up residence in the Vatican. The Great Schism begins when dissident cardinals elect a so-called antipope. Popes and antipopes dispute claims to the papal chair for the next four decades

1406: Florence gains control of Pisa, and thus acquires access to the sea

The Renaissance

Rome is magnificently embellished when the Great Schism ends, and the Papal States increase in size and influence. Spearheaded by economic and territorial expansion, art and architecture flourish in Florence, with the Classically-inspired designs of Brunelleschi and the new use of perspective by its painters and sculptors. During the 15th century, Italy leads the world in science and letters from its universities of Bologna, Padua, Pisa and Parma. Venice expands its holdings on land and its art begins to rival that of Florence in sophistication. Aragonese rule in the south is contested in vain by the French. The Spanish destiny of Naples and Sicily is confirmed.

1417: The Great Schism ends with the accession of Pope Martin V

1420: Venice expands her territory on the mainland, incorporating Udine, Verona and Padua. The Serene Republic remains intact until dissolved by Napoleon

1434: Cosimo il Vecchio comes to power in Florence. His family, the Medici, is to shape the city's—and much of central Italy's—fortunes for centuries to come

1436: Brunelleschi's dome of Florence cathedral completed, the highest of its time (91m)

1443: Alfonso of Aragon briefly reunites the kingdoms of Naples and Sicily

1444: Federico da Montefeltro becomes Duke of Urbino and ushers in the city's golden age

1453: Fall of Constantinople to the Ottomans. Greek scholars are received as refugees in Florence

1471: The oldest public art collection in the world is inaugurated by Pope Sixtus IV (now part of the Capitoline Museums in Rome)

1475: Michelangelo born

1483: Raphael born at Urbino; Leonardo da Vinci goes to Milan, where he is to have a profound influence on its art

c. 1485: Birth of Titian, who is to revolutionise painting and bring Venice to the forefront of the artistic world with his use of oil on canvas

1490s: Discovery of Nero's Domus Aurea in Rome, with its painted walls and vaults, the design of which is to influence generations of Renaissance and Neoclassical artists and architects

1494: Charles VIII of France enters Italy. He seizes Naples in 1495 but is ousted, and Naples comes under the Spanish viceroys

1499: Charles VIII takes Milan

The 16th and 17th centuries

France and Spain begin expansion into Italy and spend the next 60 years fighting for territory in the peninsula, France under Charles VIII and Francis I, and Spain under Charles V and Philip II. This is also the age of the Counter-Reformation, in response to the perceived threat from Protestant northern Europe. Italy is no longer the cultural or economic leader of Europe. Trade routes expand outside the Mediterranean, and Venice begins its decline. In the face of the Franco-Spanish wars, many Italian cities come under papal control. Wars with the Ottoman Turks are a feature of this period, as they seek to oust Venice from the Mediterranean and to expand westwards into Christian territory.

1504: Michelangelo's *David*. The sculpture assumes importance for Florence as a symbol of the republican spirit prevailing against the Papal States

1506: Bologna annexed to the Papal States

1508–12: Michelangelo: Sistine ceiling

1513–21: Papacy of Leo X (Giovanni de' Medici of Florence), great patron of Raphael

1525: Battle of Pavia. Francis I of France is defeated by Charles V of Spain. France gives up its territorial claims in northern Italy

1527: Rome is sacked by the troops of Holy Roman Emperor Charles V, whose rival Francis I of France had been supported by the Medici pope Clement VII

1530: Charles V crowned at Bologna in a symbolic gesture of rapprochement made by Pope Clement

1531: Parma passes to the papacy

1545–63: The Council of Trent is convened to tackle the threat of Protestantism

1547: The viceroy Pedro de Toledo attempts to introduce the Spanish Inquisition to Naples. Fierce opposition from the nobility follows

1550: Giorgio Vasari: *Lives of the Artists*. Though Florence's greatest hour is behind her, his work does much to inform our view of Tuscan supremacy in painting, and of the Medici as great patrons

1555: Siena conquered by a joint force of Florentine and Spanish soldiers. It comes under the control of the Medici

1559: Treaty of Cateau-Cambrésis ends the wars between France and Spain, with the Spanish Habsburgs as the dominant power in Italy; the Papal States retain independence

1563: Turin becomes the capital of the Duchy of Savoy

1570: Cosimo I becomes Grand Duke of Tuscany, his title explicitly hereditary

1571: Battle of Lepanto. The combined forces of Venice, Spain, Genoa, Naples and the Papal States defeat Ottoman Turkish naval power

1582: Pope Gregory XIII completes the reform of the calendar at Frascati

1592: The 21-year-old Caravaggio arrives in Rome and establishes his reputation

1598: The Papal States gain Ferrara

1623–44: Papacy of Urban VIII. His Inquisition condemns Galileo for upholding the Copernican theory. He is also a great patron of Bernini

The 18th century and Napoleon

Spanish hegemony in Italy leads in general to economic decline. This is the age of the great shuffling of Italian territory, back and forth between the French, the Spanish and the Austrians. Romantic ideals inspired by the revolution in France kindle sparks of hope for independence and unity in an Italy grown weary of misrule or of rule by outsiders. When Napoleon proves to have imperial and dynastic ambitions, such illusions are shattered. The age of the Grand Tourist: young men from northern Europe travel through Italy hungry for first-hand experience of the world they have hitherto known only from their studies.

1713: The end of the War of the Spanish Succession (which for the last few years has been characterised by French skirmishes with Italian rulers) results in a French Bourbon taking the Spanish throne. To maintain a balance of power, Spanish holdings in Italy pass to the Austrian Habsburgs: Lombardy goes to Austria, as does Sicily. The Savoy prince Vittorio Amedeo, former king of Sicily, is made king of Piedmont-Sardinia instead

1734: The heir to the Spanish throne, Charles of Bourbon, takes Naples and Sicily from

Austria. He rules as king of the Two Sicilies

1737: The last of the Medici dies. Florence passes to the house of Lorraine under Franz Stephan, husband of Maria Theresa of Austria

1767: J.J. Winckelmann publishes his categories of ancient art, which influence all subsequent taste for the Antique

1776: Gibbon: *Decline and Fall of the Roman Empire*

1796: Napoleon's first Italy campaign

1797: Extinction of the Venetian Republic, which is annexed by Napoleon

1798–1814: Napoleon creates a series of shifting republics and kingdoms in Italy as he captures and reconfigures the territory to suit his aims. He crowns himself King of Italy in Milan in 1805. His placemen are often his siblings: he makes his sister Elisa Grand Duchess of Tuscany and his brother Joseph King of Naples

1815: Napoleon defeated. The Congress of Vienna reparcels Italy as follows: Tuscany is restored to the (Austrian) grand dukes of Lorraine; the Veneto, Lombardy and Trieste go to Austria; the Papal States are restored to the papacy; Parma and Piacenza go to Napoleon's widow, the Austrian archduchess Marie-Louise; the Bourbons return to Naples and Sicily; Liguria is transferred to Piedmont. Canova retrieves from France many Italian artworks purloined by Napoleon

Towards a republic

The mid-19th century is the age of the Risorgimento, a surge of nationalist fervour and armed rebellion against foreign rule and the rule of the popes, led on an intellectual level by Giuseppe Mazzini. Popular support is won by the guerrilla leader Giuseppe Garibaldi. A governable united Italy is made possible by the great statesman Camillo Cavour.

1848: Revolts against Austrian rule in Milan and Venice. Venice declares a short-lived republic

1859: The Austrian army is defeated at Magenta and Solferino by Italian troops allied with Napoleon III. Italy wins Lombardy but not the Veneto. Appalled by the carnage, Jean-Henri Dunant, an eye-witness at Solferino, begins a campaign that will lead to the foundation of the Red Cross. Florence throws off the house of Lorraine and joins the kingdom of Piedmont

1860: Papal forces suffer a defeat by the Italian army, which occupies Umbria and the Marche. Garibaldi, sensing that he will be able to mobilise public opinion in the south, which has been ill governed for so long, embarks from Genoa for Sicily with his thousand volunteers (the 'Mille' of Italian street names). He wins important victories

1861: Gaeta, last stronghold of the Kingdom of Naples, falls to the Italian army. The Piedmontese kingdom officially becomes the Kingdom of Italy under Vittorio Emanuele II

1865: Vittorio Emanuele moves his capital from Turin to Florence

1866: Prussian defeat of Austria at Königgrätz. The Veneto joins Italy

1870: The Italian army enters Rome on 20th September (hence the many Italian streets named Via XX Settembre). Pope Pius IX retreats to the Vatican, his temporal power at an end

1871: Rome becomes the capital of a united Italy

1915: Italy enters WWI on the side of the Entente (Britain, France and Russia) after receiving promises of territorial reward at the expense of Austria-Hungary in the event of an Entente victory

1918: Collapse of the Austro-Hungarian empire. Italy receives the South Tyrol

1922: Mussolini becomes prime minister

1929: The Lateran Treaty creates the Vatican State, regularising relations between the papacy and the Italian government

1940: Italy enters WWII on the Axis side; burial place of St Peter discovered beneath the Vatican Grottoes

1943: Mussolini sets up a Nazi-supported republic at Salò on Lake Garda

1945: Mussolini is killed by partisans

1946: Abdication of King Vittorio Emanuele III. Italy votes to become a republic

INDEX

More detailed or explanatory references (where there any many references listed), or references to an artist's masterpiece (in cases where it is not listed by name), are given in bold. Numbers in italics are picture references. Dates are given for all artists and sculptors. Saints' names for towns are written out in full (San Gimignano); churches are listed as S. Martino, S. Agata etc. Note that artists in medieval and Renaissance Italy are often named for their parentage, provenance or occupation (Piero della Francesca = son of Francesca; Pietro da Cortona = Pietro from Cortona and Paolo Veneziano = Paolo the Venetian; Lorenzo Monaco = Lorenzo the monk). They are indexed under ther first names.

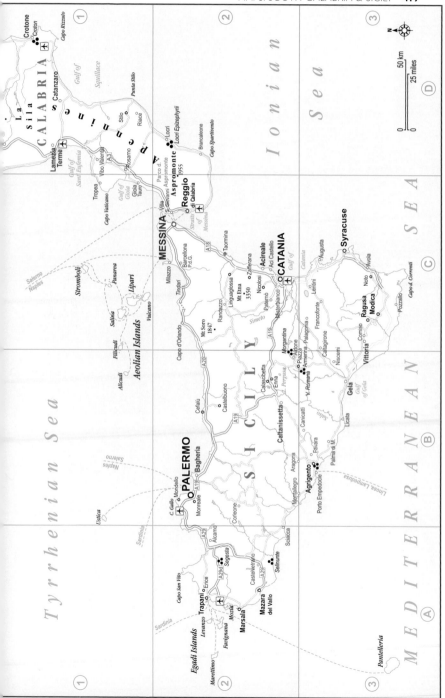

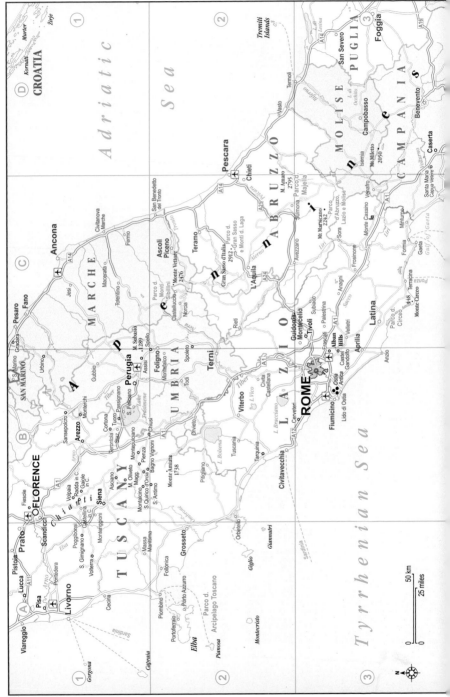

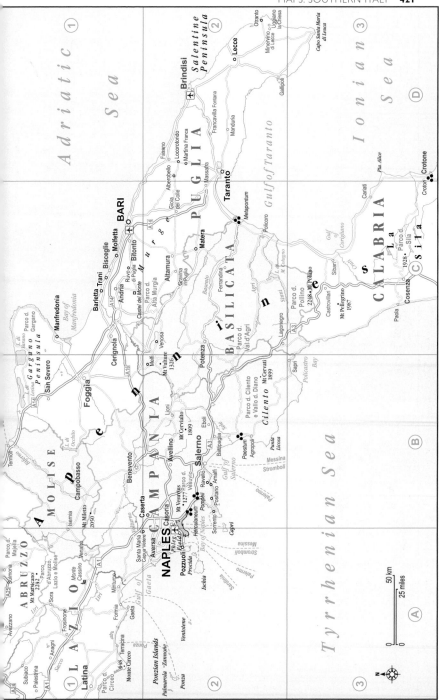

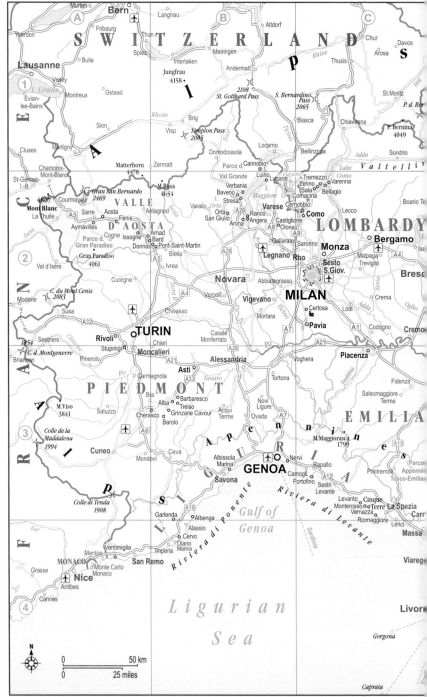

contd. from p. 2

Compiled and edited by Annabel Barber
Assistant editor Judy Tither; Editorial assistant Sophie Livall

Layout and design: Anikó Kuzmich
Regional maps and maps of Rome: Dimap Bt; City maps updated by Anikó Kuzmich;
Capri map by Imre Bába
Floor plans by Imre Bába
Architectural line drawings: Gabriella Juhász & Michael Mansell RIBA

Photo research, editing and pre-press: Hadley Kincade
Photographs by Phil Robinson: pp. 1, 91, 136, 223, 351; Bill Hocker: pp: 172, 202, 298, 356;
Andrea Federici: pp. 63, 111, 227; Giacomo Mazza: pp. 379, 380; Radoslav C. Merkiev: p. 325;
Annabel Barber: pp. 102, 186, 209, 242, 245, 255, 272, 279, 290, 345, 363; Franco Cosimo
Panini Editore ©Management Fratelli Alinari: pp. 61, 141; Folco Quilici ©Fratelli Alinari: pp. 55,
357, 359; Alinari Archives, Florence: pp. 52, 115, 119, 182, 193, 294, 306, 318, 341; Alinari
Archives, Florence, with the permission of the Ministero per i Beni e le Attività Culturali: pp. 31,
85, 95, 145, 231, 267, 334; Alinari/The Bridgeman Art Library: p. 138; Bencini/Alinari Archives,
Florence: p. 178; Bridgeman/Alinari Archives, Florence: pp. 40, 89, 155, 190, 216, 274, 276, 300,
323; Seat Archive/Alinari Archives: pp. 19, 107, 125, 129, 302; Ullstein Bild/Alinari Archives
ullstein bild-AKG Pressebild: p. 164; Red Dot/©Arco Images GmbH/Alamy: p. 23;
Red Dot/©isifa Image Service s.r.o./Alamy: p. 206; Red Dot/©MARKA/Alamy: p. 26;
Red Dot/©The Art Archive/Corbis: pp. 64, 90; Red Dot/©Christophe Boisvieux/Corbis: p. 71;
Red Dot/©Elio Ciol/Corbis: p. 128; Red Dot/©Owen Franken/Corbis: p. 158; Red Dot/©Goodlook
Pictures/Corbis: p. 79; Red Dot/©Summerfield Press/Corbis: pp. 181, 185; Red Dot/© Topcris:
p. 8; ©1990 Photo Scala, Florence: pp. 39, 150, 371; ©1990 Photo Scala, Florence–courtesy of the
Ministero Beni e Att. Culturali: p. 10; ©1992 Photo Scala, Florence–courtesy of the Ministero Beni
e Att. Culturali: p. 220; ©2007 Photo Scala, Florence/Mauro Ranzani Luciano Romano–courtesy of
the Ministero Beni e Att. Culturali: p. 47; Stockexpert: p. 219; Valeria Cantone/Stockexpert: p. 304.

Cover photograph by Monica Larner
Spine: Detail from Botticelli's *Birth of Venus* (photo: Red Dot/©Summerfield Press/Corbis)
Frontispiece: detail of Ghiberti's doors for the Florence baptistery (photo: Phil Robinson)
Back cover: Botticelli's *Birth of Venus* (photo: Red Dot/©Summerfield Press/Corbis)
and Temple of Castor and Pollux at Agrigento (photo: Giacomo Mazza)

Acknowledgements
The compiler of this guide is especially indebted to the Blue Guides to Rome, Central Italy,
Venice, Umbria, Tuscany and Florence, which have been an invaluable source. Also to Ellen
Grady. Paul Blanchard would like to thank local, provincial and regional tourist authorities
throughout the country, and many friends, colleagues and family members for their
knowledge and generosity. Thanks from Ellen Grady go to Laura Cassataro, Claudio
Castiglione, Michele Gallo, Giacomo Mazza, Margherita Perricone, the ever-helpful staff
at the tourist offices of Sicily, and the Touring Club Italiano.

Printed in Hungary by Dürer Nyomda Kft, Gyula

ISBN 978–1–905131–28–0